LEARNING STATISTICS
USING R

Earl L. McCallon
January 20, 1936, to August 31, 2012
A friend, colleague, mentor, and business partner
who enjoyed teaching statistics
to thousands of students.

LEARNING STATISTICS USING R

Randall E. Schumacker

The University of Alabama

Los Angeles | London | New Delhi
Singapore | Washington DC

Los Angeles | London | New Delhi
Singapore | Washington DC

FOR INFORMATION:

SAGE Publications, Inc.
2455 Teller Road
Thousand Oaks, California 91320
E-mail: order@sagepub.com

SAGE Publications Ltd.
1 Oliver's Yard
55 City Road
London EC1Y 1SP
United Kingdom

SAGE Publications India Pvt. Ltd.
B 1/I 1 Mohan Cooperative Industrial Area
Mathura Road, New Delhi 110 044
India

SAGE Publications Asia-Pacific Pte. Ltd.
3 Church Street
#10-04 Samsung Hub
Singapore 049483

Acquisitions Editor: Vicki Knight
Assistant Editor: Katie Guarino
Editorial Assistant: Jessica Miller
Production Editor: Brittany Bauhaus
Copy Editor: QuADS Prepress Pvt. Ltd.
Typesetter: C&M Digitals (P) Ltd.
Proofreader: Jeff Bryant
Indexer: Naomi Linzer
Cover Designer: Cristina Kubota
Marketing Manager: Nicole Elliott

Copyright © 2015 by SAGE Publications, Inc.

Printed in the United States of America

Library of Congress Cataloging-in-Publication Data

Schumacker, Randall E., author.
Learning statistics using R / Randall E. Schumacker, The University of Alabama.

pages cm
Includes bibliographical references and index.

ISBN 978-1-4522-8629-7 (pbk. : alk. paper) —
ISBN 978-1-4833-1332-0 (web pdf) —
ISBN 978-1-4833-2477-7 (epub)

1. R (Computer program language) 2. Statistics—Data processing. I. Title.

QA276.45.R3S38 2014
519.50285'5133—dc23   2013031343

This book is printed on acid-free paper.

14 15 16 17 18 10 9 8 7 6 5 4 3 2 1

BRIEF CONTENTS

DETAILED CONTENTS

ABOUT THE AUTHOR

Dr. Randall E. Schumacker is Professor of Educational Research at The University of Alabama. He has written and coedited several books, including *A Beginner's Guide to Structural Equation Modeling* (third edition), *Advanced Structural Equation Modeling: Issues and Techniques, Interaction and Non-Linear Effects in Structural Equation Modeling, New Developments and Techniques in Structural Equation Modeling*, and *Understanding Statistics Using R*. He was the founder and is now Emeritus Editor of *Structural Equation Modeling: A Multidisciplinary Journal*, and he established the Structural Equation Modeling Special Interest Group within the American Educational Research Association. He is also the Emeritus Editor of *Multiple Linear Regression Viewpoints*, the oldest journal sponsored by the American Educational Research Association MLR:GLM SIG (Multiple Linear Regression: General Linear Models Special Interest Group). He has conducted international and national workshops, has served on the editorial board of several journals, and currently pursues his research interests in measurement, statistics, and structural equation modeling. He was the 1996 recipient of the Outstanding Scholar Award and the 1998 recipient of the Charn Oswachoke International Award. In 2010, he launched the *DecisionKit* App for the iPhone, iPad, and iTouch, which can assist researchers in making decisions about which measurement, research design, or statistic to use in their research projects. In 2013, he received the McCrory Faculty Excellence in Research Award.

PREFACE

This book was written as a text for use with any introductory and/or intermediate statistics courses taught at the undergraduate level in the core curriculum or at the graduate level in psychology, business, nursing, education, and related academic areas. The chapters are ordered along the lines of topics covered in a statistics course. Each chapter covers specific content in statistics and builds on previous learning to enrich the student's use and application of statistics in research. The chapters provide discussion, explanations, and examples that include R functions. The chapter exercises reinforce the understanding of the content in the chapters. The author has provided historical references about the statistics covered in the chapters; a glossary of terms; a glossary of R packages, functions, and commands used in the book; answers to the chapter exercises; and answers to the true/false questions in each chapter.

The early chapters in the textbook offer a rich insight into how probability forms the basis for the statistical procedures in the behavioral sciences. This is followed by chapters that explain how random sampling and probability form sampling distributions of statistics, which are used in hypothesis testing. In the middle chapters, the chi-square, z, t, F, r, and R (coefficient of determination) statistics are described and explained. The final chapters cover replicability of statistical tests and synthesis of research findings. This includes cross-validation, jackknife, and bootstrap procedures, which are conducted when a researcher does not replicate his or her research study. The final chapter covers the basics of meta-analysis, which is a procedure used to synthesize or combine findings in several research studies. The final chapter also discusses statistical significance versus practical interpretation, which completes the book.

The chapters are designed to provide a clear understanding of statistics and related concepts. The content of each chapter is appropriate for any undergraduate- or graduate-level statistics course. Computational skills are kept to a minimum by including R functions in script files that run the examples provided in the chapters. Students are not required to master writing of R functions; rather, a brief explanation of how the functions work and the program output are included in each chapter. Using R in teaching statistics is great because students do not have to purchase the software and can install the software on their own computer, whether Mac or PC. R is a free statistical package that has an extensive library of functions, which offers flexibility in computing statistics and writing one's own functions. There are also many useful tips and websites that further explore and explain how to use R commands and functions.

● ORGANIZATION OF THE TEXT

The chapters of the book are organized in a logical progression of topics in an elementary statistics course (Part I), which then leads to topics in an intermediate statistics course (Part II). The first chapter covers R Basics, so students can install and become familiar with how the R software works. This includes the RStudio software, which is a Windows graphical user interface that makes navigating and using R easier. The next chapter introduces some basic concepts related to conducting research: levels of measurement, types of variables, and the hypothesis-testing steps. The next two chapters cover probability and sampling (random sampling), which form the basis of inferential statistics. Chapter 5 presents the central limit theorem, which is an important concept to understand in inferential statistics. The central limit theorem provides an understanding of how random samples from any population distribution will result in a normal sampling distribution of a statistic, especially as the sample size increases. The central limit theorem provides the basis for testing mean differences in hypotheses, which also forms the basis for later discussion on confidence intervals, Type I error, and Type II error. Chapter 6 explains the importance of understanding sampling distributions, while Chapter 7 presents the sampling distributions for different statistics. The sampling distribution of a statistic is the basis for the statistical formula and test of the null hypothesis. Chapters 5 to 7 are therefore central to understanding statistics and the family of distributions for different statistics. If a student fully understands how a sampling distribution of a statistic is created and interpreted, then interpreting a statistical outcome using the tabled values from a statistical distribution should be an easy concept to grasp. Chapters 5 to 7 are considered essential for a researcher to understand when conducting hypothesis testing, which is described in Chapter 10.

Part III (Chapters 8 and 9) covers the descriptive methods used in research. This includes graphing data, measures of central tendency and dispersion, and data transformation concerns. This section may seem basic, but from my research point of view, it is essential in understanding your data. This includes the effect of sample size, missing data, skewness, kurtosis, nonlinearity, and outliers on the statistical analysis covered in later chapters.

Chapters 11 to 19 (Part IV) cover the inferential statistics taught in a statistics course. The chapter content includes examples using the statistic and how results are interpreted in a hypothesis-testing situation. Chi-square and z tests involve categorical data, t and F tests involve mean differences, while r and R (coefficient of determination) involve correlation and regression methods. The chapter content also includes examples using the statistic and how to conduct a five-step test of a null and an alternative hypothesis. R functions created by the author are referenced in script files, and R commands are included throughout the chapters.

Since many research studies are not replicated due to lack of time, money, or resources, methods that provide an estimate of the stability of research findings are covered (Part V). Chapter 20 covers the cross-validation, jackknife, and bootstrap methods. Cross-validation randomly splits the data set into two parts. The regression equation is estimated on the first set of data, and this equation is applied to the second data set. R-squared shrinkage (lower value) is expected for the second data set because the regression weights were estimated using the first data set. The jackknife method is also called *leave-one-out* because the sample statistic is calculated multiple times, but each time, a different single observation is left out. The jackknife method helps determine the influence of a single observation on the sample statistic. The chapter also presents the basic nonparametric and parametric bootstrap methods. The bootstrap method takes a random sample from the population and treats this as a pseudopopulation; thus, the population parameters are known. When taking repeated random samples with replacement from the pseudopopulation, the average value from the sampling distribution can be compared with the pseudopopulation parameter. This provides a measure of how much bias exists in the random sample drawn from the population.

The final chapter, Chapter 21, covers synthesis of research findings, which is a quantitative method used to combine or synthesize findings from several research studies on a single topic. An easy method that takes the natural log of the p values from research studies is presented, as well as a discussion of the r and d effect size measures. A second R function includes an adjustment for sample sizes, which commonly vary from study to study. Several R packages are also presented and illustrated. The chapter concludes by discussing statistical significance versus practical interpretation. Basically, a researcher is in command of the criteria for determining statistical significance, so practical interpretation related to effect size needs to be considered when interpreting the importance of the research findings.

The chapter exercises are organized to enhance the basic knowledge and use of statistics acquired from the chapters. After mastering the statistical procedures in the chapters, researchers can either use the R functions in the book for hypothesis testing and data analysis or write their own user-defined functions. An additional text, *Understanding Statistics Using R* (2013), by Randall Schumacker and Sara Tomek runs simulation script programs for researchers to better understand the statistical concepts related to the statistical procedures in this book. It is recommended that the instructor use this as a supplemental text when teaching statistics.

Each chapter contains one or more R functions that are helpful in examining the various applications presented in the chapters. The R functions are explained in each chapter according to the basic input, process, and output operations. The R functions can be opened and run in the RGui Console window or in RStudio. The results will be the same as in the chapters, except where it is noted that the *set.seed()* command was not used. The R script files that contain the functions used in the chapters are available from the website http://www.sage.com/schumacker.

R software will need to be installed by students on their Mac or Windows PC computer; it is available at http://www.cran.r-project.org/ or http://lib.stat.cmu.edu/R/CRAN. After installing the R software, the RStudio software can be installed and used, which is available at http://www.rstudio.com/. RStudio makes accessing packages, locating files, and running functions easier. The instructor will need a computer, projector, and projection screen in the classroom. Many university classrooms come equipped with a computer on a roll cart connected to a projector. These instructor workstations are usually connected to a local area network for use in a computer-equipped classroom. The instructor workstation should permit easy download and installation of the R and RStudio software. If you have problems with the download and installation of the software, contact your computing center personnel for assistance.

—Randall E. Schumacker

ACKNOWLEDGMENTS

The students who I have taught statistics over the past 30 years contributed to this book in many different ways. Their questions helped me understand what I had missed in my lectures. Their desire to better understand statistical concepts led me to better examples. They have made me a better teacher by providing feedback on what made sense to them when learning statistics. There is no better testing ground for teaching and learning statistics than the classroom.

I wish to thank Drs. John Dantzler and Sara Tomek at The University of Alabama for providing edits and suggestions during the preparation of this book. Their experience in teaching statistics and their knowledge of the subject matter were very helpful in guiding my approach to writing the book. Their final review of the chapter contents provided several important corrections and additions to the book chapters.

Drs Kim Nimon, University of North Texas, and David Walker, Northern Illinois University, reviewed earlier drafts of the subject matter covered in an earlier book. They both have experience in teaching statistics and using it in research, so their independent review was valuable. Both of them helped with the review of the book *Understanding Statistics Using R*. It contains numerous R script files that simulate important concepts when learning statistics. It was written as a supplemental textbook for this book.

A special thanks to the reviewers who provided external reviews for the book proposal and draft of the book. Their edits, suggestions, and related comments helped clarify several important points in the book. They were

Thomas Cleland, Cornell University;

Keith F. Donohue, North Dakota State University;

Gregg Hartvigsen, State University of New York, College at Geneseo;

Michael Hollingsworth, Old Dominion University;

Paul E. Johnson, Center for Research Methods and Data Analysis, University of Kansas;

Murray Richardson, Carleton University;

Maureen Sartor, University of Michigan;

Jason Seawright, Department of Political Science, Northwestern University; and

Zhi Wei, New Jersey Institute of Technology.

A special thanks to Vicki Knight, editor at SAGE Publications, who understands the discipline and its authors, who play a key role in writing books. Her guidance and help were necessary in meeting the expectations of students and faculty who would use this statistics book. Finally, I wish to thank Jessica Miller, Editorial Assistant, Research Methods, Statistics, and Evaluation, SAGE Publications, Inc., who coordinated the book production efforts, making all this possible.

I would appreciate your citing this book when using the various R functions in the book chapters. The R script files were created to compute and understand the statistics presented in the book and therefore are my creation.

—Randall E. Schumacker

PART I

INTRODUCTION AND BACKGROUND

## CHAPTER 1

R BASICS

● INTRODUCTION TO R

R is a free open-shareware software that can run on Unix, Windows, or Mac OS X computer operating systems. Once the R software is installed, additional software packages or routines are available from an extensive library. You first select a Comprehensive R Archive Network (CRAN) site near you; then, using the main menu, select "Load Package." Knowing which R package to use will take some experience, but those you will need are covered in the book. Once an R package is loaded, you access it by simply issuing the command, *library(x)*, where x is the name of the package. This process will become clearer and easier to implement as you go through the chapters in the book. Let's get started by downloading and installing the R software on your computer or laptop.

Downloading and Installing R

The R software can be downloaded from the CRAN, which is located at http://cran.r-project.org/. There are several sites or servers around the world where the software can be downloaded. They are located at http://cran.r-project.org/mirrors.html, referred to as CRAN mirror sites. The R version for Windows will be used in this book, so if you are using Linux or Mac OS X operating systems, follow the instructions on the CRAN website.

After entering the CRAN website, you should see the following screen:

Download and Install R

Precompiled binary distributions of the base system and contributed packages, Windows and Mac users most likely want one of these versions of R:

- Download R for Linux
- Download R for MacOS X
- Download R for Windows

R is part of many Linux distributions, you should check with your Linux package management system in addition to the link above.

After clicking on "Download R for Windows," the following screen should appear, where you will click on Base to go to the next screen for further instructions.

R for Windows

Subdirectories:

Base	Binaries for base distribution (managed by Duncan Murdoch). This is what you want to install R for the first time.
contrib	Binaries of contributed packages (managed by Uwe Ligges). There is also information on third party software available for CRAN Windows services and corresponding environment and make variables.
Rtools	Tools to build R and R packages (managed by Duncan Murdoch). This is what you want to build your own packages on Windows, or to build R itself.

Please do not submit binaries to CRAN. Package developers might want to contact Duncan Murdoch or Uwe Ligges directly in case of questions/suggestions related to Windows binaries. You may also want to read the R FAQ and R for Windows FAQ.

NOTE: CRAN does some checks on these binaries for viruses, but cannot give guarantees. Use the normal precautions with downloaded executables.

After clicking on Base, the following screen should appear to download the Windows installer executable file, for example, R-3.0.1-win.exe. (The version of R available for download will change periodically as updates become available; this is version R 3.0.1 for Windows.)

Note: FAQs are available to answer questions about updating the package, and so on. Click on the underlined Download R 3.0.1 for Windows to begin the installation.

R-3.0.1 for Windows (32/64 bit)

Download R 3.0.1 for Windows (52 megabytes, 32/64 bit)

Installation and other instructions

New features in this version

You will be prompted to Run or Save the executable file, R-3.0.1-win .exe. Click on Run to install, or once the file has been downloaded, simply double-click on the file name, R-3.0.1-win.exe, which will open the R for Windows setup wizard below.

Note: The Download R 3.xx.x for Windows version will have changed to a newer version, so simply download the latest version offered.

You will be prompted with several dialog box choices. Simply follow the instructions to complete the installation. For example, the first dialog box will install Core files, 32-bit files, and 64-bit files (uncheck the 64-bit box if your computer is not 64-bit compatible).

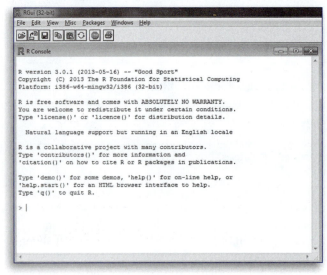

Getting Help

The R icon should appear on your desktop with the version number underneath. Click on this R icon to open the R software. The window to the left should appear.

You can access additional R manuals, references, and material by issuing the following command in the RGui window:

```
> help.start()
```

For example, click on the underlined Packages under the heading Reference. This will open a dialog box with a library directory of R packages.

If we select the *base* package, another dialog box with related R functions will open. Now we can select specific R functions that are listed from A to Z in the documentation.

For example, if we select "abs," the specific R function and argument (x) required are displayed for obtaining the absolute value of a number.

To illustrate using the RGui window, enter the R function for the number −10, and the absolute value, a positive 10, will be computed:

```
> abs(-10)
[1] 10
```

Online Documentation

A comprehensive "Introduction to R" is available online at http://cran.r-project .org/doc/manuals/R-intro.html.

The URL should open with the heading and table of contents (abbreviated here in the screenshot to the right). It covers everything from A to Z that you may want or need to know if you choose to become more involved in using R. It covers the basics (how to read data files, how to write functions), statistical models, graphical procedures, and packages.

And so on.

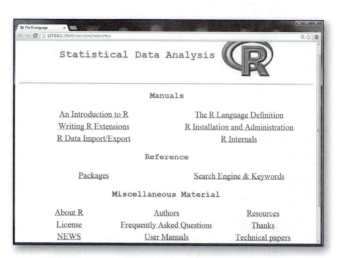

Updating the R Software Version

I have found it very easy to update or install the latest version of R for Windows from the CRAN website. You simply need to uninstall the older version of R. You do this by going to Start > Control Panel > Uninstall Programs; then, you find the older version of R and click on it to uninstall. Now go back to the URL http:// cran.r-project.org/, repeat the download instructions, and run the latest Windows executable file. I have found this to be the easiest and quickest way to update the R software version.

Note: Many of the R functions require a certain version of the R software, usually a newer version, and generally you will be notified when running an R function if it is not compatible.

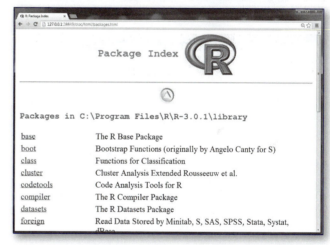

Loading, Installing, and Updating R Packages

Once R is installed and the RGui window appears, you can load, install, or

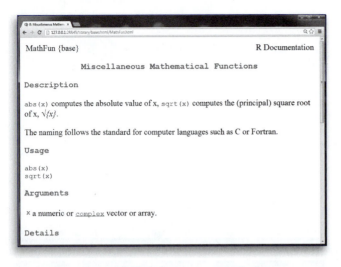

update packages and functions that are not in the base package by using the main menu. Simply click on Packages in the main menu of the RGui window, then make your selection, for example, Load packages.

A dialog box will appear that lists the base package along with an alphabetical list of other packages. I selected the *stats* package from the list, and clicked OK. This makes available all of the routines or commands in the stats package. Prior to running any R commands in the RGui Console window, you will need to load the package using the following command:

```
> library(stats)
```

To obtain information about the R stats package, issue the following command in the RGui Console window:

```
> library(help = "stats")
```

This will provide a list of the functions in the stats package. An index of the statistical functions available in the stats package will appear in a separate dialog box. The various functions are listed from A to Z, with a description of each. You will become more familiar with selecting a package and using certain functions as you navigate through the various chapters in the book.

Running R Functions

To run the R functions or commands that are presented in the book, you should click on File, then select Open script from the main menu in the RGui window. Locate the R script file, chap1.r, in your computer directory.

The file will open in a separate R Editor window.

The R script file is run by first clicking on Edit in the pull-down menu, then Select all, to select all of the command lines in the R script file. Next, click on the "run" icon (in the middle of the main menu), and the results will appear in the RGui Console window. Optionally, click on Edit, then Run All.

If syntax errors occur, they will appear in the RGui Console window with little or no output provided. You can correct your errors in the R script file, save the file, and then rerun. The variable *total* specifies the values that will be read into the *chap1()* function.

The *chap1.r* function computes basic summary statistics, combines them into a data frame, assigns names, and then prints the results. The input, process, and output steps form the basic understanding of the operations. A better understanding of this basic programming and process will become clearer as you navigate through the chapters.

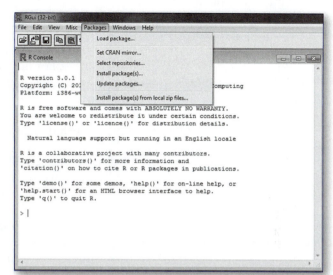

● INPUT, PROCESS, AND OUTPUT IN R SCRIPT FILES

R is similar to other software packages such as SAS, SPSS,[1] S-Plus, STATA, Maple, and so on, all of which have the same three basic operations that govern their usage: input, process, and output. These three operations can be described as follows:

- *Input:* Import data from other packages; read in a comma-delimited, tab-delimited, or ASCII raw data file; enter or create your own data.
- *Process:* Conduct mathematical or statistical operations on the data.
- *Output:* List or print results in a table, graph, or chart.

An R script file can be created that would read in the R commands for each operation. R software has built-in functions that assist in the data *input* operation; that is, they import data

from other software packages (e.g., SPSS, SAS). It also has commands to read in comma-delimited, tab-delimited, or ASCII data files. R commands can also generate or simulate data from different types of distributions. After data have been input, R commands *process* the data by either mathematical expressions or built-in statistical routines (located in packages). Many of the basic mathematical expressions are easy to compute when using a matrix format for the data or a vector of data values. Likewise statistical calculations can be performed when data reside in a matrix or vector. Many of the R functions have default values that are output. These can be simply listed or individual values selected to produce more elaborate output. R commands can therefore be used to *output* the results of the mathematical and statistical operations by listing the results or presenting results in a matrix- or table-style output format with rows and columns that have variable labels.

The approach taken in each chapter is to provide an author-written R script file that contains the input values for a function. You will provide certain variable values that are read into the function and processed with the accompanying output. The R commands are presented in three subsections: Input, Process, and Output. A presentation of each operation (input, process, and output) with basic R commands is given next.

Input

Calculator and Assignment

The first input operation that allows R to perform basic mathematical operations (addition, subtraction, multiplication, division, or square root) as a calculator is the assignment of data to a variable. This is accomplished using the R Console window and the "=" or "<-" assignment symbol ($x = 5$ and $x <-5$ are the same assignment command; ">" is the command line symbol in the R Console window). The example assigns the value 5 to the variable x and the value

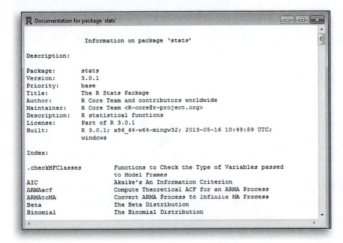

4 to the variable y, and then adds them together for variable z. Entering the variable name z displays its value along with an index number, [1].

```
> x = 5
> y = 4
> z = x + y
> z
[1]  9
```

You can build on these basic assignment operations to include other variables and other mathematical calculations. Please note that the operations are taken in order as specified and retained in the memory workspace for R. Also, variable names are case sensitive, so a lowercase variable name will not be recognized if misspelled or entered as uppercase. Additional commands can continue that show another variable calculation:

```
> t = z/3
> t
[1]  3
```

We can continue, for example, with basic subtraction as follows:

```
> j = z - 10
> j
[1]  -1
```

A variable can also be assigned a character string, which allows for naming conventions. All character strings must be between quotation marks, " ". For example,

```
> x = "new"
> x
[1]  "new"
> y = "old"
> y
[1]  "old"
```

Note 1: The author-written R script files use the assignment operator "=." The chapters also include applied examples using R functions. In this

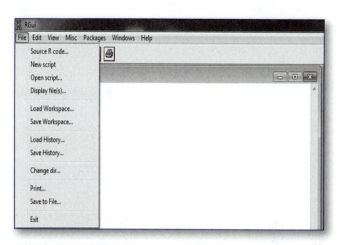

case, the assignment operator "<–" is shown, which is the original usage and typically used by R programmers. For example,

```
> y <- "old"
> y
[1] "old"
```

Note 2: R functions can use either "=" or "<–" as assignment operators, but they also use "= =" to represent "equals" in expressions found inside R functions.

Vectors

Data usually contain more than a single value or observation for a variable. We therefore create vectors for observations or data points using i (rows) and j (column) subscripts. In a vector, we generally create a single column of data with i (row) subscripts for a variable. Vectors must also be of the same data type, either all numeric or all character strings (*do not mix data types in vectors*). We can assign more than one value to a variable using the ":" expression with a beginning and ending number. For example, y can take on values from 1 to 5.

```
> y = 1:5
> y
[1] 1 2 3 4 5
```

To place several test scores in a data vector for a variable *score*, we would use the *c()* function:

```
> score = c(57,85,76,80,55,85,90)
> score
[1] 57 85 76 80 55 85 90
```

If we wanted to add a couple of new test scores, we could continue by creating another column vector with the new test scores (*new*) and then combining the two vectors (*score* and *new*) to obtain the complete set of scores in the vector *total*. For example,

```
> new = c(78,91)
> total = (score, new)
> total
[1] 57 85 76 80 55 85 90 78 91
```

A vector can also contain character strings, for example, the names of students. For example,

```
> student =
c("John","Paul","Steve","Bill","Juan","Suzy","Anita","Mary","Jill")
```

However, it is better to have the student names and the test scores printed together, so a much easier way of doing this is to use the *names()* function. This places each student's name above the respective test score. For example,

```
> names(total) =
c("John","Paul","Steve","Bill","Juan","Suzy","Anita","Mary","Jill")
> total
 John  Paul Steve  Bill  Juan  Suzy Anita  Mary  Jill
   57    85    76    80    55    85    90    78    91
```

The data vector *total* can be viewed in a separate R Editor window by using the Data Editor in the Edit pull-down menu and the *edit()* or the *data.entry()* function. The *data.entry()* function opens a spreadsheet in the R Data Editor window that allows you to add or delete data values. For example, *100* is added in the column for the variable *total*, and the value shows up in the data vector. Close this window, and enter the name of the vector, *total*, in the RGui window.

```
> data.entry(total)
> total
 [1] 57 85 76 80 55 85 90
78 91 100
```

The value *100* is now listed in the RGui window output.

Missing Values

When a label or data value is left out (missing) in R, the ""NA"" or "<NA>" expression is printed. For example, we added *100* to our data vector *total*, but this was not given a name, so it would be printed as follows:

```
> names(total)=
c("John","Paul","Steve","Bill","Juan","Suzy","Anita","Mary","Jill")
> total

 John  Paul Steve  Bill  Juan  Suzy Anita  Mary  Jill  <NA>
   57    85    76    80    55    85    90    78    91   100
```

You can add a name by simply entering it in the *names(total)* vector.

We can determine if a data vector contains missing values using the *is.na()* function. The data vector *total* indicates "FALSE" (no missing data values) because 10 numbers are indicated. For example,

```
> is.na(total)
 John   Paul  Steve Bill   Juan   Suzy  Anita Mary   Jill   <NA>
FALSE  FALSE  FALSE FALSE  FALSE  FALSE FALSE FALSE  FALSE  FALSE
```

However, the *names* vector would indicate a missing value ("TRUE") because no name was listed for the new data value. For example,

```
> is.na(names(total))
[1] FALSE FALSE FALSE FALSE FALSE FALSE FALSE FALSE FALSE TRUE
```

We would therefore have to supply the additional name in the *names()* function to replace the missing-value symbol:

```
> names(total)=
c("John","Paul","Steve","Bill","Juan","Suzy","Anita","Mary","Jill","Judy")
> total

John Paul Steve Bill Juan Suzy Anita Mary Jill Judy
  57   85    76   80   55   85    90   78   91  100
```

We can delete missing values from our statistical analysis using the *na.rm = TRUE* argument in most statistical functions. You also have the option of removing individuals from the data set by using the *na.omit()* function, which is run as follows:

```
> mydata = na.omit(newdata)
```

Matrices

Mathematical and statistical operations on data require the data to be in a vector or matrix format, that is, in rows (i) and columns (j). The *matrix()* function makes this operation easy to perform. You should specify whether the data should be read by row or by column. For example, a 2×3 matrix named y where data are read by row (Row 1 and Row 2 for Column 1; then Row 1 and Row 2 for Column 2, etc.) would be run as follows:

```
> y = matrix(c(1,2,3,4,5,6), nrow=2)
> y

     [,1] [,2] [,3]
[1,]  1    3    5
[2,]  2    4    6
```

You can contrast this with a y matrix that is read as two columns, which results in a very different set of matrix values:

```
> y = matrix(c(1,2,3,4,5,6), ncol=2)
> y

     [,1] [,2]
[1,]  1    4
[2,]  2    5
[3,]  3    6
```

Recall that use of the *edit()* function can open up a spreadsheet to view these data values, or you can use the *data.entry()* function to add data values. For example,

```
> edit(y)
```

	col1	col2	col3	var4	var5	var6	var7	var8
1	1	3	5					
2	2	4	6					
3								
4								
5								
6								

To add variable names to the rows and columns in the *y* matrix, we can use the *dimnames()* function along with the *c()* function. The row variable names are listed first, followed by the column names. The data now have meaning because they are represented by variable names. For example,

```
> dimnames(y)  =  list(c("subj1","subj2"),c("v1","v2","v3"))
       v1  v2  v3
subj1  1   3   5
subj2  2   4   6
```

The variable names will also appear in the spreadsheet. Simply enter the command

```
> edit(y)
```

Data Frame

We can work with individual data sets (data vector) or a matrix (rectangular or symmetric), but more than likely you will be working with a set of data that has multiple variables and corresponding names to provide meaning for the data. Data frames therefore provide a better structure for data than a vector or matrix. A data frame puts all the variables together, making it better organized, easier to save the work and perform functions on the data. The data frame would usually have each row correspond to a person or subject,

	row.names	v1	v2	v3	var5	var6	var7	var8
1	subj1	1	3	5				
2	subj2	2	4	6				
3								
4								
5								
6								
7								
8								
9								
10								
11								
12								
13								
14								
15								
16								
17								
18								
19								

while the column would correspond to variables, for example, gender, school, test scores, whether numeric or character data. Gender could be coded "male" and "female," rather than "1" and "2." Although a data frame is not necessarily a matrix, they do share similarity in performing mathematical and statistical calculations. A data frame, however, provides subject data by row, with each column indicating the data for each variable.

The *data.frame()* function is used to put separate data vectors together or provide a better structure than a matrix. We create the *x* vector with numbers from 1 to 5 and the *y* vector with numbers from 6 to 10. We then combine the two in a data frame named *z*, which has the variable names *x* and *y*. For example,

```
> x = 1:5
> y = 6:10
>z = data.frame(x,y)
> z
   x y
1  1  6
2  2  7
3  3  8
4  4  9
5  5 10
```

The *names()* function is used to replace the default variable names of *x* and *y*. You can therefore specify variable names by using the *names()* function. For example,

```
> names(z)=c("pre","post")
> z

  pre post
1   1   6
2   2   7
3   3   8
4   4   9
5   5   10
```

The *dim()* function will report the number of observations (rows) and variables (columns) in the data frame or matrix. For example, the data frame *z* has five observations (rows) and two variables (columns):

```
> dim(z)
[1] 5 2
```

The *describe()* function in the *psych* package will provide more information about each variable in the data frame:

```
> library(psych)
> describe(z)
```

```
          var n mean   sd median trimmed mad min max range skew kurtosis se
pre     1 5 3    1.58   3      3    1.48  1   5     4    0   -1.91   0.71
post    2 5 8    1.58   8      8    1.48  6  10     4    0   -1.91   0.71
```

The *str()* function will reveal the structure of the data frame, including the variable labels and type of data ("int" = interval):

```
> str(z)
'data.frame':  5 obs. of 2 variables:
 $ pre: int 1 2 3 4 5
 $ post: int 6 7 8 9 10
```

Importing Data Files

Usually, we input raw data files or import data from a file. To import data files, it is important to know where they are located. The *getwd()* function will indicate the working directory on your computer where the data file is located. To change the working directory, specify the new path using the *setwd()* function. The *data()* function will display the contents of a data set in the current working directory. For example,

```
> data(Nile)
> Nile      # Water flow in the Nile River from 1871 to 1970
Time Series:
Start = 1871
End = 1970
Frequency = 1
 [1] 1120 1160  963 1210 1160 1160  813 1230 1370 1140  995  935 1110  994 1020
[16]  960 1180  799  958 1140 1100 1210 1150 1250 1260 1220 1030 1100  774  840
[31]  874  694  940  833  701  916  692 1020 1050  969  831  726  456  824  702
[46] 1120 1100  832  764  821  768  845  864  862  698  845  744  796 1040  759
[61]  781  865  845  944  984  897  822 1010  771  676  649  846  812  742  801
[76] 1040  860  874  848  890  744  749  838 1050  918  986  797  923  975  815
[91] 1020  906  901 1170  912  746  919  718  714  740
```

The *read.table()* function inputs data that are already in a table format, for example, from an ASCII text file or a data-delimited file. The *file =* command can be used to specify the file location, the file name, and whether variable names are included. The separation values can be specified by using the *sep = " "* command (spaces, commas, tabs). The *header = TRUE* command indicates that variable names are in the data set.

There are three different ways to input a data file named sample.txt, depending on its location. This R function reads in the data file in the current work directory:

```
> read.table("sample.txt", header = TRUE)
```

This R function uses the *file =* command to specify the path where the data file is located:

```
> read.table(file = "C:/sample.txt", header = TRUE)
```

This R function uses the *file* = command to open a Windows dialog box where you can search for the data file:

```
> read.table(file = file.choose())
```

The *file.choose()* option is by far the best, rather than guessing where data files are located, but it does require personal action, unlike specifying a file location directly in an R script file or function.

An example will help illustrate these R functions for locating and inputting the two different data file types, ASCII (sample.txt) and comma separated (CSV, sample.csv), into an R data frame.

```
> getwd()
[1] "C/Users/Name"

> setwd("C:/Users/Documents")
> read.table(file = "sample.txt", header = TRUE)

# Alternative read.table(file = "C:/Users/Documents/sample.txt", header = TRUE)

# Alternative read.table(file = file.choose())

   student  score
1     1     16
2     2     14
3     3     24
4     4     23
5     5     25
6     6     22
```

If a CSV file type is located in a Desktop working directory with a comma-separated file structure,

```
student,score
1,16
2,14
3,24
4,23
5,25
6,22
```

then this file type can be located and read as follows:

```
> setwd("C:/Desktop")
> mydata = read.table(file = "sample.csv", header = TRUE, sep = ",")
> mydata
```

```
  student  score
1    1      16
2    2      14
3    3      24
4    4      23
5    5      25
6    6      22
```

The *setwd()* command defines the directory location. The *read.table()* function identifies the file with names (*header = TRUE*) and comma-separated data (*sep = ","*), which are assigned to the file name *mydata*.

Importing Other File Types

The R software has built-in functions designed to read in data from Excel, SPSS, SAS, and other software packages. This is a better way to obtain data than entering the data or placing them in a matrix. The other software packages also permit import and export features that help to easily convert data from one software package to another. Examples will further illustrate how R software can import files from these other software packages.

Excel

The best way to read an Excel file is to export the data to a comma-delimited file (sample .csv) and then import it into R. Otherwise, you will have to install the *gdata* package and Perl software to use the *read.xls()* function, or you can purchase the third-party program *xlsReadWrite*. In the future, someone may provide a free function in R.

SPSS

You must first export your SPSS data file into the transport format prior to inputting it into an R data frame. The SPSS option permits this special file type, for example, sample.por. Prior to reading the SPSS transport file, sample.por, you will activate the *Hmisc* package to obtain the *spss .get()* function. The *use.value.labels* command converts SPSS value labels to R factors. For example, these SPSS syntax commands will save the special file type:

```
# save SPSS dataset in transport format in SPSS software

get file = 'c:\sample.sav'
export outfile = 'c:\sample.por'
```

Next, these R commands will import the SPSS transport file:

```
# read SPSS transport file in R
> library(Hmisc)
> mydata = spss.get("c:/sample.por", use.value.labels = TRUE)
> mydata
```

SAS

You must first export your SAS data file into the transport format prior to inputting it into an R data frame. For example, the following SAS commands will save the transport file sample.xpt:

```
# save SAS dataset in transport format in SAS software

libname out xport 'c:/sample.xpt';
data out.sample;
set sasuser.sample;
run;
```

Next, these R commands will input the SAS transport file:

```
# Read SAS transport data file in R

> library(Hmisc)
> mydata = sasxport.get("c:/sample.xpt")
> mydata
```

STATA

The *library(foreign)* function is used for inputting data from the STATA software package. It uses the *read.dta()* function to input the data into an R file. For example,

```
> library(foreign)
> mydata = read.dta("c:/sample.dta")
> mydata
```

SYSTAT

The *library(foreign)* function is also used for inputting data from the SYSTAT software package. It uses the read.systat() function to input the data into an R file. For example,

```
> library(foreign)
> mydata = read.systat("c:/sample.dta")
> mydata
```

Note: Check the R manuals for how to input data files from other software packages. A unique feature of R is that programmers are continually providing useful packages and functions to accomplish the task of inputting data into R.

Summary

This section has demonstrated the many different ways to access and input data in R. You can input your own data from the terminal into variables, data vectors, or matrices. You can create data frames with variable names or read data into data frames. You can also input data from other software packages such as Excel, SPSS, SAS, STATA, SYSTAT, and so on. Overall, the input process is as varied as the R functions created to input the data. The most useful approach is to open the

RGui Windows dialog box, then read in a comma-separated data file with variable names using the *read.table()* function:

```
> read.table(file = file.choose(), header = TRUE, sep = ",")
```

The *file.choose()* function opens the directory on your computer where you can locate the file to input. The RStudio software makes this activity much easier because the directories and packages are provided in a GUI window.

> **TIP**
>
> ✓ Use *c()* to combine the observations into a vector.
>
> ✓ Use *names()* to add names for each observation.
>
> ✓ Use *edit()* to view the data set.
>
> ✓ Use *data.entry()* to edit/add the data set in a spreadsheet format.
>
> ✓ *is.na()* returns TRUE to indicate a missing value, else FALSE.
>
> ✓ Use *help.start()* to view the documentation and resources for R.
>
> ✓ Parentheses ( ) are used for functions in R.
>
> ✓ Brackets [ ] are used for data vectors in R.
>
> ✓ Use *file = (file.choose())* to open the Windows dialog box to locate the data file.
>
> ✓ Use *ls()* to list all the active variables in the work environment.
>
> ✓ Use *rm()* to remove one or more of the variables in the work environment.

Process

After inputting data, whether creating a data frame or reading in a data file, there are several ways to process the data. R software has an extensive number of packages and functions that can perform statistical analysis of data, graphing of data, and database operations. Several of the R packages and functions are used in the chapters of the book. Processing of data can range from the basic mathematical operations in a calculator to more advanced loops and functions, or even naming conventions. The statistics available for use are immense. The many ways to process data are presented next.

Calculator

R can work as a calculator to perform mathematical operations. For example,

```
> 1 + 1
[1] 2
```

or

```
> y = 5
> x = 6
> z = (x + y)/2
> z
[1] 5.5
```

Functions

We introduced two R functions in the input data section that made our work easier, *c()* and *names()*. There are other R built-in functions, many of which are used to process the input data file. I will illustrate a few of the functions here and use several later in the book. For example, given the data file *total*,

```
> total = c(57,85,76,80,55,85,90,78,91,100)

> total
[1] 57 85 76 80 55 85 90 78 91 100
```

We can run these R functions individually to process the data:

```
> length(total)  # total number of observations in vector, total
[1] 10

> min(total) # minimum value for observations in vector, total
[1] 55

> max(total) # maximum value for observations in vector, total
[1] 100

> mean(total) # mean of the observations in the vector, total
[1] 79.7

> sd(total)  # standard deviation of the observations in the vector, total
[1] 14.31433
```

A self-created function can also bundle the individual commands into a set of operations. So instead of running these command lines separately, we can create a function:

```
# Create data vector

total = c(57,85,76,80,55,85,90,78,91,100)

# Enter these commands in R Editor, then copy and paste in R Console

scores = function(total)
```

```
{
a = length(total)
b = min(total)
c = max(total)
d = mean(total)
e = sd(total)
f = data.frame(a,b,c,d,e)
names(f) = c("length","min","max","mean","sd")
return(f)
}
```

```
# This runs the scores() function and lists the results:
```

```
> scores(total)

    length min max mean    sd
1     10    55  100 79.7 14.31433
```

You can save this function in an R script file. Select File, then New Script from the main menu, and a dialog box will open. Enter the following commands, and save as an R script file (chap1.r). Once you have saved the R script file, it can easily be opened and run at a later date. This permits you to save a set of R commands as well as the R function that will input, process, and output the results. For example, the R script file included in the book, chap1.r, contains

```
# Input data vector
```

```
total = c(57,85,76,80,55,85,90,78,91,100)
```

The name *chap1* is assigned as a *function()* with the commands between braces, { }, as follows:

```
chap1 = function(total)
{
# Input - data vector name in brackets above

# Process
a = length(total)
b = min(total)
c = max(total)
d = mean(total)
e = sd(total)
f = data.frame(a,b,c,d,e)
names(f) = c("length","min","max","mean","sd")

# Output
print(f)
}
```

Once you copy and paste these lines from the R script file into the RGui Console window, the *chap1()* function can be run as follows:

```
# Running the chap1() function

> chap1(total)
  length min max mean    sd
1    10  55  100 79.7 14.31433
```

If we change the values in the data vector *total*, we simply rerun the *chap1()* function to obtain the new summary statistics. For example,

```
> total = c(50,70,90,100)
> chap1(total)
  length min max mean    sd
1     4  50  100 77.5 22.17356
```

The ability to use the different functions provided in the R packages makes our data analysis efforts much easier. We can open the R functions, modify them, and save them for our own use. This is a real advantage of the R open-share software, that is, being able to reuse the many R functions. You can see the contents of most R functions by simply typing the name of the function. For example, type in the name of the function we created to see the contents. This is helpful if you forget what the input values are for the function. Our function only required a data vector named *total*. So simply enter the name of the function.

```
> chap1
```

The contents of the function chap1() will be displayed:

```
function(total)
{

# Input - data vector name in brackets above

# Process

a = length(total)
b = min(total)
c = max(total)
d = mean(total)
e = sd(total)
f = data.frame(a,b,c,d,e)
names(f) = c("length","min","max","mean","sd")

# Output
print(f)
}
```

Loops

Loop operations permit repetitive calculations or select certain data values for calculations. The *for()* and *while()* functions permit the selection of data values under certain conditions. The *if* and *else* commands are often used in these two functions. Operations in functions begin and end with braces, { }. The generic form is

```
for(variable in sequence)
{
if()
{expression}
else
{expression}
print()
}
```

For example, we create the variable *x*, which ranges from 1 to 10, and a variable *z*, which has not been assigned any values (NULL).

```
> x = 1:10
> z = NULL
```

We next create a loop using the *for()* function, assigning values to the variable *z* based on values of the variable *x*:

```
> for(i in seq(x))
{
if(x[i] < 5)
{z = 5}
else
{z = 9}
print(z)
}

[1] 5
[1] 5
[1] 5
[1] 5
[1] 9
[1] 9
[1] 9
[1] 9
[1] 9
[1] 9
```

We could assign this *for()* function a name (*myloop*), save it, and use it repeatedly as desired.

```
myloop = function(x,z)
{
  for(i in seq(x))
  {
  if(x[i] < 5)
  { z = 5 }
  else
  { z = 9 }
  print (z)
  }
}
```

We create the *x* and *z* variables required in the *myloop()* function, then run it.

```
> x = 1:20
> z = NULL
> myloop(x,z)
```

Output

After inputting data and performing mathematical and statistical operations, you will most likely want to provide additional output, that is, tables, graphs, or charts. Please note that many of the functions you run while processing data have their own standard output, so no additional output is necessary. I will cover graphing, statistical analysis, and exporting of data files to provide a basic understanding of the output capabilities in R. Some of the output in the chapter script files is customized prior to printing.

Listing and Printing

Some commands provide the same basic output. For example,

```
> p = matrix(c(5,6,7,8,2,1))
```

And these commands give the same output:

```
> p
> list(p)
> print(p)
      [,1]
[1,]   5
[2,]   6
[3,]   7
[4,]   8
[5,]   2
[6,]   1
```

Graphs

There are functions that output data in charts or graphs. For example, a histogram can be graphed using

```
> hist(total)
```

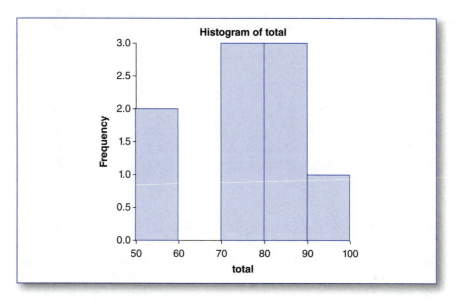

or

```
> dotchart(total, xlab = "scores")
```

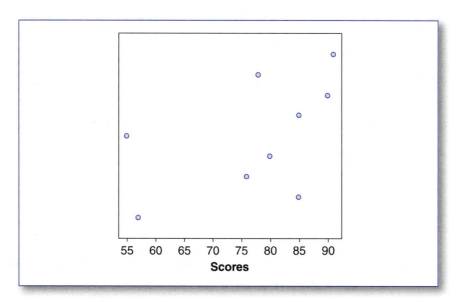

Line plots with *x*- and *y*-coordinate values are obtained using the *plot()* function. For example,

```
> x = 1:5
> y = 6:10
> z = data.frame(x,y)
> plot(z)
```

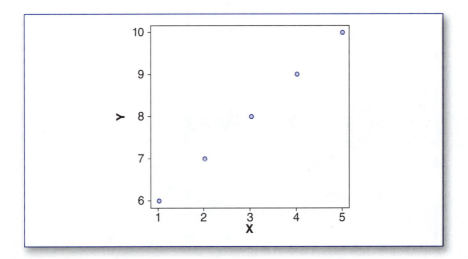

There are a few R packages that provide more features when graphing data (e.g., graphics, lattice, ggplot2). For example, load the *graphics* package (select Packages, then Load Package from the main menu). Next, enter the command

```
> library(help = "graphics")
```

This will provide a list of the numerous R functions that can be used, including the *plot()* function above.

Statistical Analysis

The statistical functions used to process data also have defined output built into them. For example, if *x* and *y* correlate, the *cor()* function can be used to obtain the **correlation** coefficient. The basic commands would be

```
> x = c(4,2,6,7,12)
> y = c(2,4,6,8,10)
> cor(x,y)                # correlation of x and y

[1] 0.8811404
```

If *x* predicts *y*, we use the *lm()* function for **linear regression** and *anova()* for **analysis of variance** output. These basic commands would be as follows:

```
> results = lm(y ~ x)                  # linear regression y = a + bx
> results

Call:
lm(formula = y ~ x)

Coefficients:
(Intercept)        x
    1.4155      0.7394

> anova(results)                       # analysis of variance

Analysis of Variance Table
Response: y
       Df Sum Sq Mean Sq F value Pr(>F)
x       1 31.0563 31.0563 10.417 0.0483 *
Residuals 3 8.9437 2.9812
---
Signif. codes: 0 '***' 0.001 '**' 0.01 '*' 0.05 '.' 0.1 ' ' 1
```

We will explore the use of these R functions in later chapters and demonstrate how the output can be improved, but for quick results, these will generally suffice.

Exporting R Data Files

R provides the ability to output or export its data files to the different file types discussed during the input data operations, using the *write.table()* function. Several examples, given the various file types, are shown next.

Tab Delimited

```
> write.table(students, "c:/students.txt", sep = "\T")
```

Comma Separated

```
> write.table(students, "c:/students.txt", sep = ",")
```

Excel

You must have xlsReadWrite installed on your computer.

```
> library(xlsReadWrite)
> write.xls(student, "c:/student.xls")
```

SPSS

```
# write out a text file with SPSS program to read it
> library(foreign)
> write.foreign(student, "c:/student.txt", "c:/student.
sps",package="SPSS")
```

SAS

```
# write out a text file with SAS program to read it
> library(foreign)
> write.foreign(student, "c:/student.txt", "c:/student.sas", package =
"SAS")
```

STATA

```
# export data frame to STATA binary format
> library(foreign)
> write.dta(student, "c:/student.dta")
```

It is helpful to fully understand the steps that are taken when analyzing data. The input, process, and output steps are outlined in the author-written R functions that are in the R script files of each chapter. This is intended to clearly outline each step. The applied data examples in the chapters will lay out the use of R functions run in the RGui Console window to accomplish similar data-analytic steps.

TIP

✓ Use *print()* to output results.

✓ Use *hist()* for a histogram.

✓ Use *plot()* for a line graph.

✓ Use *write.table()* to output results or files.

✓ Copy and paste any R source code in the RGui Console window.

✓ Copy and paste any R source code in the R Editor window, then save the file as (file name).r.

✓ Use the Edit menu with the Run All option to run the R script command lines.

✓ Type the function name to see the contents of an R function, for example, "chap1."

● RSTUDIO

The RStudio software must be installed after the R software program is installed. It requires R 2.11.1 version or higher. It is highly recommended that you install RStudio to make using the R software easier. You can download RStudio at the URL http://www.rstudio.com/. It will automatically prompt you when new versions of RStudio are available.

RStudio provides an easy to use GUI Windows interface. The following desktop icon can be placed on the desktop after installation:

The RStudio window provides an enhanced RGui Console window. It provides a Workspace/ History window with load/save/import data set features. Another window provides easy access to files and a list of packages available. A Plots tab shows a created plot and permits easy export to a GIF image or PDF file, or access to a copy to the clipboard feature to insert into a Word document.

✓ Check out these two recommended websites, which make running R functions easier:

1. http://www.rstudio.com/ (Windows interface, but first install R 2.11 or a higher version on PC, Linux, or Mac OS X 10.5 or a higher version before downloading and installing this software)

2. http://www.statmethods.net/ (R code and R function help)

SUMMARY

This chapter has presented the R basics to help you with the installation of the R software, the inputting of data, the processing of data, and the outputting of data. The R script files for this book can be downloaded from http://www.sagepub.com/schumacker. Each chapter will use the basic input, process, and output format in the author-written R script files to illustrate data analysis and important concepts in statistics. Some chapter examples will simulate data in the author-written R script files and/or in the functions with R commands, separated into the basic input, process, and output sections described in this chapter. For example,

```
# Input
> X <- {1:5}
# Process
mean(X)
# Output
3
```

The three operations above essentially input a vector of numbers from 1 to 5 for X, process these data by calculating the **mean** of X, and then output the result for X, which is a value of 3.

The input, process, and output operations can all be combined in an R function that provides a single name to execute all of these operations. The following function, *results*, has the input, process, and output operations between braces, { }. Issuing the function name, *results()*, executes the operations in the function. For example,

```
x = {1:5}
y = {5:9}

results = function(x,y)
  {
  # Input data x and y in function
  # Process
  output = matrix(1:2)
  output = c(mean(x),mean(y))
  names(output) = c("xmean","ymean")
  output
  # Output
  }
> results(x,y)

xmean  ymean
   3     7
```

The applied examples will input a data set, conduct a statistical analysis, and then show the outputted results from the function. These R functions created by the author will use an equal sign (=); however, the R functions you acquire from packages will use the assignment operator arrow (<-) and/or a special double equal sign (= =) embedded in a function to represent an equal expression. In some cases, a *Warning* or *Note* is posted to indicate unusual circumstances required to input data, process data, or print results. I use the equal sign, although it is not the preferred choice of traditional R programmers.

TIP

✓ It may be difficult to remember all of the functions in R, so use one of the following help command formats to either learn more about a function or find which routines use the function. A separate help page will open up on your computer—a separate terminal window or browser window.

✓ Information about the *mean()* function can be obtained by entering one of the following commands in the R Console window:

- > ?mean
- > help("mean")

✓ This command provides an example of the use of the function:

- > example(mean)

✓ These commands indicate which other routines use this function:

- > help.search("mean")
- > ??mean

✓ *Using Help menu options:* The Help menu has the function *R functions(text)*, where you can enter the name of a function, and it will give optional specifications and examples of its use. Click on the Edit menu and then R functions(text) for a Windows dialog box to open:

✓ Download the R Quick Reference Card, which summarizes most of the R commands: http://cran.r-project.org/doc/contrib/Short-refcard.pdf.

Warning

When running the R script files, the workspace keeps track of variable names, functions, data vectors, and so on. If you run several script files one after another, eventually R will crash or the results will be unstable or incorrect.

✓ Use *ls()* to view the active variables.

✓ Use *rm()* to remove the active variables (one or more variables).

```
> rm(a)
> rm(a,b,myloop)
```

Always run one R function at a time in RGui. It is good programming technique to use the *detach()* function to clear out the previous values created by R syntax; or close and then reopen RGui to run another R function. The *detach()* function is used to remove an attached data frame (e.g., *total*) or package (e.g., *lattice*, a previously loaded graphics package) from a library.

✓ `my = data.frame(total)`
✓ `detach(my)`

or

✓ `detach(package:lattice)`

EXERCISES

1. What command would you use to obtain R manuals and reference material?

2. What command would you use to obtain information about the stats package?

3. What R commands would yield z as the sum of $x = 5$ and $y = 6$?

4. What R command would yield *test* as a data vector with values 10, 20, 30, 40, and 50?

5. What R command would add the labels A, B, C, D, and E to the data values in *test*?

6. Create a matrix P with two columns from these data: 1, 2, 3, 4, 5, 6.

7. What R command would create a data frame J from matrix P?

8. What R command would provide pre and post labels for the columns in data frame J?

9. What R command would return TRUE or FALSE for the missing values in data frame J?

10. What R command lists all the active variables in the work environment?

TRUE OR FALSE QUESTIONS

T   F   a.   R software can only be run on an IBM PC.

T   F   b.   R software has extensive manuals, references, and documentation material available for the user.

T   F   c.   R functions can only analyze numerical data.

T   F   d.   R software can analyze data similarly to other statistical packages, for example, SPSS, SAS, or STATA.

T   F   e.   You should not mix data types in a data vector.

NOTE

1. SPSS was acquired by IBM in October 2009.

WEB RESOURCES

Chapter R script file: http://www.sagepub.com/schumacker/chap1.r

Introduction to R manual: http://cran.r-project.org/doc/manuals/R-intro.html

R Quick Reference card: http://cran.r-project.org/doc/contrib/Short-refcard.pdf

R Software: http://cran.r-project.org/

RStudio Software: http://www.rstudio.com/

## CHAPTER 2

RESEARCH METHODS

● WHAT ARE RESEARCH METHODS?

We conduct research using one of two predominant methods: quantitative and qualitative. This book explains research methods used in the quantitative approach—that is, numerical data, statistical estimation, and inference to population parameters. Quantitative research methods can be further broken down into experimental methods and correlation methods. The experimental method involves the manipulation of one or more **independent variables** in a controlled scientific study to determine the cause-and-effect outcome. The experimental method tests the *mean* differences between or among groups, for example, between a treatment group and a control group. The statistical tests commonly used are the *t* test, for mean differences between two groups, and the ***F* test**, for mean differences between three or more groups. In contrast, the correlation method involves measuring the association, or prediction or explanation, of the variation between two or more variables—commonly referred to as inferential statistics. The correlation method tests the significance of correlation coefficients and related measures of association. The statistical tests commonly used are the **Pearson correlation** and multiple regression general linear models.

The experimental and correlation methods differ in their basic approach to research. Experimental methods use small **samples**, controlled settings, and **random assignment** to treatment and control groups. Correlation methods use larger samples of data, taken at random from an infinitely large population, and then use measures of association to infer relations among variables. William Gosset Jr. created the *t* test, and Sir Ronald Fisher created the *F* test to determine if mean differences existed between experimental and control groups in basic agricultural crop studies. Francis Galton is credited with the concept of regression, while Karl Pearson created the correlation coefficient as a measure of association between two things. Their research into hereditary characteristics involved taking large samples of data, calculating measures of association and prediction, and then making inferences about the relations among variables.

The basic concepts of sample, population, **random sampling**, population distributions, and descriptive statistics are essential in conducting research (Trochim, 2006). Both experimental and correlation methods utilize random sampling from populations and descriptive statistics. Also, irrespective of whether a researcher uses an experimental method or a correlation method, the statistical tests covered in this book will be helpful to use and understand. The research steps included in the statistical chapters further an understanding of the quantitative research method. The basic research steps are (a) statement of the research hypothesis, (b) selection of the sample size and **sample statistic**, (c) selection of the **confidence level** and **region of rejection**, (d) collection and analysis of data, (e) statistical tests, and (f) interpretation of findings.

● LEVELS OF MEASUREMENT

Stevens (1946, 1951) published articles on the characteristics of scales of measurement in the social sciences. His scales of measurement have become known as nominal, ordinal, interval, and ratio. The characteristics of each scale were defined based on the mathematical properties permitted given the level of measurement of the data.

Nominal data have mutually exclusive categories, where a value can only be in one category—for example, your primary residency in a state. The data only permit a mathematical count or frequency of how many persons are in each state. A person can only have primary residency in one state in the United States, thus the designation of a mutually exclusive category.

Ordinal data have mutually exclusive categories, where a value can only be in one category; however, the additional characteristic is that the categories can be ordered—for example, the average income of residents in each state, where the states are ordered (ranked) based on their average income. This permits a mathematical ranking of the individual states based on the average income of residents.

Interval data have mutually exclusive categories, can be ordered, but also have the property or characteristic of a numerical scale—for example, test scores of residents in several states. This permits a mathematical calculation of mean and **standard deviation** for the residents of a state; each state is mutually exclusive, and the means could be ranked if so desired. Interval data permit the calculation of a test score mean and standard deviation. The interval data (test score) do not have a true zero point or equal distances between categories; that is, although a zero score could be obtained on a test, it is assumed that residents have some knowledge, not zero knowledge, and the scores on the scale 0 to 100 do not have equal distances. We interpret this lack of a true zero point to imply that a test score difference from 60 to 70 is not the same as a test score difference from 80 to 90.

Ratio data have all of the characteristics of nominal, ordinal, and interval scales of measurement, but they have the added characteristic of having a true zero point and equal distances on the scale. For example, the average Fahrenheit temperature of each state could be recorded (true zero point), and the Fahrenheit scale has equal temperature points. This permits a mathematical calculation of mean and standard deviation for the average temperature in each state; each state is mutually exclusive, and the means could be ranked. The ratio scale has a true zero point; that is, temperature on the Fahrenheit scale has a true zero point. We interpret this true zero point to allow for meaningful differences or ratio of scale. For example, if Dallas had a temperature of 60°F and Miami had a temperature of 80°F, then Miami is 20°F warmer than Dallas.

The researcher can notice three key points when considering the characteristics or properties of scales of measurement. First is the importance of a true zero point and equal scale point distances. Research that lacks this characteristic of ratio data must recognize that a starting point other than a true zero exists, for example, the lowest test score. In addition, the distance between scores of 50 and 60 is not the same as the distance between scores of 70 and 80. Raw test score differences do not match the percentile differences. These two characteristics or levels of measurement properties have important implications when interpreting data analysis results.

Second, only certain mathematical calculations can be performed based on the scales of measurement. Basically, nominal data permit counts or frequencies in each mutually exclusive category; ordinal data permit ranking mutually exclusive categories using frequency counts; interval data permit the calculation of means and standard deviations, but the interpretation must not disregard the lack of a true zero point and equal distances in scale points; and finally, ratio data permit the calculation of means and standard deviations with a valid interpretation using a true zero point and equal distances in scale points.

Third, there is a loss of information when using data with mathematical properties less than the ratio scale. The most we can ascertain from nominal data is how many are there in each mutually exclusive category. Ordinal data only permit ranking of mutually exclusive categories. The magnitude of difference between the ranked categories is not interpretable; that is, a rank of 1, 2, and 3 does not necessarily imply the same amount of difference between the ranks. Interval data provide much more information, that is, the mean and standard deviation. They permit the comparison of averages in each category and, more important, the measurement of how much the data vary. Variation in data is the cornerstone of statistics because it indicates whether individual differences exist. If test scores did not vary, then everyone would have the same test score. When variation in data exists, our research interest is in determining or explaining why the individual differences exist. This forms the basis of many important research questions.

● TYPES OF VARIABLES

Our use of quantitative variables in experimental or correlation research methods can be further described as *discrete* or *continuous*. A discrete variable is one that has data that are recorded as a whole number—for example, number of siblings or number of cars in a parking lot: It doesn't make sense to interpret someone having 2.5 siblings or 4.5 cars in a parking lot. In contrast, a continuous variable is one where the data recorded have any number of possible values—for example, height in feet and inches or weight in pounds and ounces. We routinely report a person's height or weight in more precise measurement—for example, 6 feet 2 inches tall or weighing 225 pounds and 6 ounces.

We also encounter the difference between a *true dichotomy* and an *artificial dichotomy*. A true dichotomy variable occurs when a researcher uses an existing variable with only two, mutually exclusive groups—for example, laptop versus desktop computer, boy versus girl, or American versus international student. An artificial dichotomy variable is formed when a researcher takes a continuous variable and creates a dichotomous variable. For example, age is coded into young versus old, trees are coded into hard wood versus soft wood, or height is coded into tall versus short. The key issue in creating artificial dichotomous variables is where you make the cut point when creating the two groups. Different cut points would create different groups, which can cause classification error when creating the dichotomous variable. *Classification error* is a term implying that some objects, events, or individuals were incorrectly placed in a group.

Dependent and *independent* variables are common terms in experimental and correlation research methods. The researcher decides which variables are given these names. A **dependent variable** is typically one a researcher measures and wishes to understand or predict. An independent variable is one a researcher manipulates or uses to explain the variation in the dependent variable scores. In the experimental research method, the independent variables are under the control of the researcher and are manipulated to determine a cause-and-effect outcome in the dependent variable measures. For example, the researcher controls the level of caffeine given to three groups of students at 0%, 10%, and 20% (independent variable) while measuring pupil dilation (dependent variable). If the students' pupils dilate more as caffeine dosage increases, then a cause-and-effect outcome is interpreted: That is, caffeine levels increase pupil dilation in students.

In the correlation research method, the independent variable is correlated with the dependent variable to determine if they covary or go together—that is, whether a relationship exist between them. For example, test scores and amount of time spent studying are correlated; therefore, a relationship exists. A researcher then makes an inference that as the amount of time spent studying (independent variable) increases, test scores (dependent variable) increase.

Experimental and correlation research methods differ in their interpretation of the independent variable and dependent variable relationship. Experimental research methods design studies where the independent variable values are selected and controlled to determine the cause and effect on a dependent variable that is being measured. In many studies, the independent variable is manipulated in a controlled laboratory setting to provide a strong causal interpretation. In contrast, the correlation method first establishes whether a relationship exists between an independent and a dependent variable. The independent variable values can increase or decrease in relation to the values of the dependent variable. An inference is made that a relationship exists, which can be used to explain the variation in the dependent variable values or predict the dependent variable values given knowledge of the independent variable values.

● THE RESEARCH PROCESS

The knowledge gained in this statistics book should help you better understand the required steps in the research process. The research process begins with reviewing the literature; continues through the research design, selection of participants and measurement instruments, and statement of the statistical hypothesis; and ends with the interpretation of the data analysis results and recommendations. Our interest in the research process stems from a desire to better understand the world around us, that is, the objects, events, and individuals who have an impact on the Earth, our society, our culture, and our well-being. Essentially, we are attempting to explain why individuals, objects, or events vary—that is, are different. We adopt the scientific method because it provides a common approach, or standard methods, to our scientific inquiry.

The initial area of inquiry for our research helps define whether an experimental or correlation research method is required. Afterward, we select the types of variables needed given prior research studies, cognizant of the levels of measurement and permissible mathematical operations. The research question and/or statistical hypothesis provide the framework for statistical analysis. They define the type of research method, the independent and dependent variables, and the statistical test required to analyze the data. We adhere to the publishing standards of the American Psychological Association (APA), so once the statistical analysis is completed, the results are placed in APA-style tables and graphs. Our primary goal in the research process is to answer the research questions—for example, do caffeine levels affect pupil dilation? It may seem obvious, but many published studies fail to answer their research questions. Once our research reaches one or more conclusions, we are excited to have added to the body of knowledge in a theoretical subject area of research. Your recommendations provide the basis for you or others to follow up even further to explore and better understand the topic of interest.

It is important to understand the flow of activity a researcher undertakes leading up to the statistical analysis of data, which is covered in this book. The steps a researcher follows are similar to those in a quantitative dissertation, which are outlined as follows:

1. Introduction
    a. Theoretical and conceptual basis of the research
    b. Purpose and aim of the research
    c. Rationale for the research
    d. Problem statement of why the research is important
    e. Definition of terms others may not be familiar with

2. Review of the literature
    a. What others have reported when researching the topic
    b. What other variables have been used
    c. What designs and statistical tests have been used

3. Methodology
    a. Define the sample and participants
    b. Instruments used to measure the variables
    c. Design of the study (experimental or correlation)
    d. Hypotheses (research questions to be tested)
    e. Statistical analysis

4. Results
    a. Research questions
    b. APA-style tables with statistical results
    c. Interpretation of statistical analysis results for each research question

5. Conclusions and recommendations
    a. Relate the review of the literature to your study results
    b. Recommend other variables or areas for future research

The choice of a statistical test is based on the study design and, more important, the research question. The research question should reveal the types of variables (independent, dependent), the study design, and the statistical analysis that should be used. A simple example will help clarify the importance of having a well-written research question.

Correct: Is there a statistically significant mean difference between fifth-grade boys and girls' math test scores as measured by a teacher-made Algebra 1 exam?

Incorrect: Boys and girls differ in math ability.

The correct phrasing of a research question permits clarification of the variables, design, and statistical test. For example, the research question indicates that gender (boy vs. girl) is the independent variable (group membership). The dependent variable is math test scores (what is measured). The design is based on the mean difference between two independent groups, which indicates that an **independent *t* test** should be used to statistically test whether their means differ on the math test. The content of this book should help you write better research questions that provide for a clearer understanding of what statistical test to use to answer them. Appendix B contains a "Guide to Selecting a Statistical Test."

SUMMARY

Research methods are used in every academic discipline. They provide a structured way to understand, share, and conduct scientific inquiry. There are different research methods ranging from experimental design to correlation, survey methods, evaluation methods, and longitudinal study designs. These different approaches to research are generally encapsulated in coursework offered at many universities. Regardless of the quantitative research method, the statistics covered in this book will help your understanding of data analysis.

The research methods that you choose require your understanding of how the different levels of measurement and types of variables affect your research design and statistical analysis of data. It would be uncommon to find a researcher calculating the mean and standard deviation on the variable *gender*. After all, if males were coded 1 and females coded 0, what would a mean = 0.5 imply? It is important therefore to clearly understand your data, the levels of measurement of variables, the types of variables, and what is permissible when conducting a statistical analysis of data. It is also important to have clearly written research questions that can be converted into statistical hypotheses to be tested.

EXERCISES

1. Define qualitative and quantitative research methods.

2. Give an example of a qualitative and a quantitative research method type.

3. Define the properties of nominal, ordinal, interval, and ratio scales of measurement.

4. Define dependent and independent variables.

TRUE OR FALSE QUESTIONS

T   F   a. Qualitative research methods frequently use the *t*-test, analysis of variance, or regression methods.

T   F   b. Levels of measurement for quantitative variables are important to consider when conducting a statistical analysis of data.

T   F   c. A nominal variable has mutually exclusive categories.

T   F   d. Gender is an ordinal variable.

T   F   e. An example of a discrete variable would be number of family members.

T   F   f. An example of a continuous variable would be age.

T   F   g. The research process provides the steps used for scientific inquiry.

## CHAPTER 3

PROBABILITY

Probability plays a key role in statistics. Knowledge of probability had its early beginnings with practical applications in gambling. A player knowing the odds of winning a hand in a poker game or obtaining a certain roll in a dice game helped beat the odds at the gambling table. This involved *finite* probability because all of the outcomes were known. Probability can also be estimated given an *infinite* number of outcomes. Calculating the probability of an outcome can involve **joint probability**, additive probability, multiplicative probability, and/or **conditional probability**. Early gamblers quickly learned that probability operated under certain fundamental rules, which are covered in this chapter.

One's ability to determine the probability of an event is based on whether the event occurs in a *finite* or **infinite population**. In a **finite population**, the number of objects or events is known. An exact probability or fraction can be determined. For example, given a forest with 1,000 trees—500 oak, 200 maple, 200 pine, and 100 spruce—the probability of selecting an oak tree is 1/2, or 50% (500/1,000); the probability of selecting a maple tree is 1/5, or 20% (200/1,000), the probability of selecting a pine tree is 1/5, or 20% (200/1,000); and the probability of selecting a spruce tree is 1/10, or 10% (100/1,000). When you have a finite number of persons, objects, or events, the individual probabilities will always add up to 100%.

● INFINITE PROBABILITY

In an *infinite population*, the numbers of objects or events are so numerous that the exact probabilities are not known. One approach to determine the probability of an event occurring in an infinite population is to use the relative frequency definition of probability. Using this approach, trials are repeated a large number of times, designated as N. The number of times the event occurs is counted, and the probability of the event is approximated as $P(A) \approx n(A)/N$, in which $n(A)$ is the number of times Event A occurred out of N trials. We therefore estimate the probability of an event based on what is observed after taking N counts.

For example, the probability of obtaining heads when a coin is tossed could be determined by tossing the coin 1,000 times, counting the number of heads, $n(\text{heads}) = 450$, and computing

P(heads) ≈ 450/1,000 = .45. The probability of getting heads in the population is therefore estimated to be approximately 45%. The probability of *not* getting heads is 55%, that is, 1 − *P*(heads), since the two probabilities of the event must sum to 100%. We know from past experience that the probability of obtaining heads when a coin is tossed should be approximately 50%, or 1/2, given an unbiased coin (a coin that is not weighted or is not a trick coin). The rationale follows that you have two choices, heads or tails, and at some point, the number of tosses will approximate 50% heads and 50% tails, we just don't know how many tosses it will take to have a count of heads and tails that will achieve this probability. It will be different each time—that is, for the number of times, *N*, that we toss the coin.

An important point needs to be emphasized. For an estimate to be reasonable (representative of the population), the relative frequency of the event (heads) must begin to stabilize or become a fixed number as the number of trials increase. If this does not occur, then very different estimates or approximations would be assigned to the same event as the number of trials increased. Typically, more trials (coin tosses) are required to potentially achieve the 50% probability of obtaining heads. Experience in the real world has shown that the relative frequency of obtaining heads when coins are tossed stabilizes or better approximates the expected probability of 50% as the number of trials increases. So we should see the probability more closely estimate 50% as we increase the number of tosses of the coin.

This approximation phenomenon (stabilization or representativeness) occurs in the relative frequencies of other events too. There is no actual proof of this because of the nature of an infinite population, but experience does support it. Using the relative frequency definition, the approximation, which the relative frequencies provide, is regarded as our best estimate of the actual probability of the event.

We can use some basic R commands to choose the probability of an event and simulate the number of tosses or trials. Schumacker and Tomek (2013) present numerous script files that simulate probability. As the number of trials increase, the relative frequency of the event is computed and plotted on a graph. The probability and size are input into the R script file, chap3a.r. The *infinite probability function* in the R script file (chap3a.r) starts with a sample size of 100 and increases the sample size in increments of 100 up to 1,000 with a probability of .50. You only need to provide the input values for *Probability* and *Size* (Recall that upper- and lowercase letters are recognized in R functions). All you need to do is run the function with the variable names *Probability* and *Size*, that is, > chap3a (Probability, Size). You would open this R script file in the RGui Console window, then select Edit, Run All. *Note:* The output will change each time because no *set.seed()* function is used.

The output shows a tendency for the probability to more closely approximate the true probability (*P* = .50) as the sample size increases—that is, stabilize or be more representative as an estimate. We can visually see this in the plot of the proportions by the sample size increments from 100 to 1,000. The *%Error* indicates how close the sample estimate was to the true population value. Notice that sometimes the sample estimate was higher and at other times lower than the true population value. You would enter the following values, then run the function.

```
> Probability = .50
> Size = seq(100,1000,100)
> chap3a(Probability, Size)
```

The results would be printed in the RGui Console window as follows:

```
PROGRAM OUTPUT

                        Sample  %Pop  %Error
sample size = 100       0.53    0.5   0.03
sample size = 200       0.525   0.5   0.025
sample size = 300       0.48    0.5  -0.02
sample size = 400       0.52    0.5   0.02
sample size = 500       0.484   0.5  -0.016
sample size = 600       0.538   0.5   0.038
sample size = 700       0.487   0.5  -0.013
sample size = 800       0.49    0.5  -0.01
sample size = 900       0.497   0.5  -0.003
sample size = 1000      0.511   0.5   0.011
```

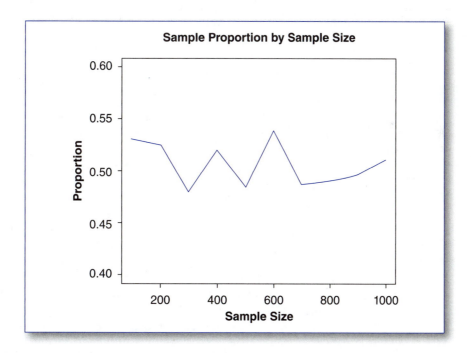

We can run this R function over and over again selecting different values for *Probability* (population proportion) and *Size* (sample size drawn from the population). This activity demonstrates how our estimates of a population proportion can be more or less accurate depending on the size of our sample. It also illustrates that sampling from an infinite population, N times, is an approximation of a population value, not an exact estimate (as from a finite population). The *%Error* indicates how much the sample approximation is in error of estimating the population proportion. The graph shows the sample proportion by sample size.

● JOINT PROBABILITY

A probability can be estimated for the joint occurrence of two independent events and reflected in the relative frequency of their joint occurrence (called *joint probability*). This uses the **multiplication law** or addition law of probability for two independent events. The theoretical probability for the union of two events is reflected in the relative frequency of the occurrence of either event. This will become clearer with an example.

If an unbiased coin is flipped two times, the possible joint outcomes form a finite sample space, S. S = {HH, HT, TH, TT}, where H stands for a head and T for a tail, with the pair of letters indicating the order of the outcomes. Therefore, with two separate flips of a coin, four possible joint outcomes can occur: (1) first a heads, then a heads; (2) first a heads, then a tails; (3) first a tails, then a heads; and, finally, (4) first a tails, then a tails. Probabilities for S are obtained by using the addition law of probability for mutually exclusive events. For example, $P(1) = P(HT) + P(TH)$.

The sample space that contains the number of heads in the two flips is S = {0, 1, 2}. If the sample space being used is S = {0, 1, 2}, with the integers representing the number of heads, then the frequency of 0 is the frequency of TT, the frequency of 1 is the frequency of HT plus the frequency of TH, and the frequency of 2 is the frequency of HH. If an unbiased coin is flipped two times, over N trials, the outcomes can be used to compute the frequencies for each of the categories in the sample space S. The frequencies can be used to approximate the joint probabilities of the joint outcomes in the sample space S.

Probabilities can also be assigned to the outcomes by using the multiplication law. Since a head and a tail are equally likely to occur on a single flip of an unbiased coin, we can use a definition of probability that is applicable to **equally likely events**. The probability of a head, $P(H)$, is because a head is one of the two equally likely outcomes. The probability of a tail, $P(T)$, is 1/2, since a tail represents the other equally likely outcome. Since the two flips of the coin are independent, the multiplication law of probability for independent events can be used to find the joint probability for the joint outcome pairs in the sample space. For example, the probability of flipping an unbiased coin and getting heads both times is $P(HH) = (1/2) * (1/2) = 1/4$; the probability of getting a head and then a tail would be $P(HT) = (1/2) * (1/2) = 1/4$; the probability of a tail and then a head would be $P(TH) = (1/2) * (1/2) = 1/4$; and, finally, the probability of getting tails both times is $P(TT) = (1/2) * (1/2) = 1/4$. The sum of these probabilities in the sample space, S, would be 1.0 or 100%—that is, $1/4 + 1/2 + 1/4$. If the coin is *biased*, which means that the chance of an outcome is not independent, then some other value will occur. For example, if $P(H)$ is some value other than .50, for example, .70, then $P(T) = 1 - P(H) = 1 - .70 = .30$. The independence of the coin flips, however, still permits an ability to find the joint probability for the pair. For example, $P(HT) = P(H) * P(T) = (.70) * (.30) = .21$. The *joint probability function* in the R script file (chap3b.r) simulates the joint probability outcomes. You would enter the following values, then run the function:

```
> pH = .5
> Coins = 2
> N = 100
> chap3b(pH,Coins,N)
```

PROGRAM OUTPUT

```
          Frequency   Probability
0 Heads     0.21          0.25
1 Heads     0.53          0.50
2 Heads     0.26          0.25


     Frequency   Probability
TT     0.21        0.25
HT     0.27        0.25
TH     0.26        0.25
HH     0.26        0.25
```

The output indicates that the population probabilities for S are $P(0) = .25$, $P(1) = .50$, and $P(2) = .25$. These probabilities add up to 100%. Our sampling probabilities are close, given pH = .5, Coins = 2, and $N = 100$, that is, sample $P(0) = .21$, $P(1) = .53$ (.27 + .26), and $P(2) = .26$. If we increase the value of N in the function, we should get a closer sample approximation to the population values. We can change the values for pH, Coins, and N to see what effect they have on joint outcome probability. Changing N, the number of trials, would be the most important value to change, since increasing the number of samples provides a closer approximation to the population values. This would be accomplished by entering $N = 1,000$, then run the function again, that is, *chap3b(pH, Coins, N)*. Recall that N would be reset in the workspace for R and entered into the function.

● ADDITIVE PROBABILITY

There are several examples to illustrate additive probability. Take, for example, the number of hearts, diamonds, spades, and clubs in a deck of 52 playing cards. Each category has 13 cards for a total of 52 cards (4 × 13 = 52). The probability of each category is 13/52 = .25, for example, 25% chance of drawing a diamond from the deck of cards. Adding the four category probabilities together equals 1.0 or 100%. We could also obtain other probabilities, for example, given four Kings in a deck of cards, the probability of selecting a King out of a deck of 52 cards would be 4/52 = .076923. We can compute the exact probabilities in these examples because we have a finite population, that is, a known number of objects.

Another example is the rolling of two dice. We can compare the relative frequencies of the sums of the numbers on the two dice with our expected probabilities or sample space. The sample space for the sum of the numbers on the two dice can be conceptualized as seen here:

		First Die					
Second die	+	1	2	3	4	5	6
	1	2	3	4	5	6	7
	2	3	4	5	6	7	8
	3	4	5	6	7	8	9
	4	5	6	7	8	9	10
	5	6	7	8	9	10	11
	6	7	8	9	10	11	12

If the dice are unbiased, 36 outcomes are possible (6 × 6 matrix). Each outcome (*S*) is a sum of the numbers on two dice. The probability of any sum, *S*, can be calculated by the formula: $P(S) = (S/36)$. For example, $P(3) = 3/36 = 1/12$; the number of times two dice sum to 3 divided by the total number of outcomes, 36, which has a probability of .0833.

The theory of additive probability relates to possible outcomes of events occurring in a finite population. The relative frequencies for the different sums are not all the same, but rather, certain sums occur more frequently (numbers six and seven). The theory of probability helps us understand the frequency of outcomes and apply this in practice. For example, if asked to bet on a number you would get when rolling two dice, your highest probability or best number choices would be a six or a seven. This doesn't always mean you will get a six or a seven when rolling two dice, but it gives you the best chance of winning the bet.

The *additive probability function* in the R script file (chap3c.r) simulates the tossing of two dice. It records the number of times that each of the possible sums of the two dice occurred and then changes these counts into relative frequencies. These relative frequencies are compared against the TRUE frequencies of the sum of two dice in the 6 × 6 matrix. For example, $P(12) = 1/36 = .0278$. You would enter the following values and then run the function.

```
> Size = c(100,500,1000,5000)
> Probs = c(.0556,.0833,.1111,.1389,.1667,.1667,.1389,.1111,.0833,
.0556,.0278)
> DiceFreq = NULL
> chap3c(Size, Probs, DiceFreq)
```

PROGRAM OUTPUT

	N= 100	N= 500	N= 1000	N= 5000	TRUE
2	0.02	0.040	0.021	0.0282	0.0556
3	0.05	0.050	0.054	0.0518	0.0833
4	0.04	0.074	0.091	0.0816	0.1111
5	0.13	0.120	0.114	0.1036	0.1389
6	0.17	0.130	0.156	0.1398	0.1667
7	0.15	0.170	0.168	0.1746	0.1667
8	0.16	0.146	0.144	0.1410	0.1389
9	0.12	0.102	0.113	0.1110	0.1111
10	0.10	0.088	0.075	0.0900	0.0833
11	0.03	0.050	0.039	0.0514	0.0556
12	0.03	0.030	0.025	0.0270	0.0278

Each time you run the chap3c.r function, you will get different sample estimates of the TRUE population values. This is because you are sampling or taking different rolls of two dice where different sums of numbers occur for the two dice, which range from 2 through 12. Try this by simply running the function again.

● MULTIPLICATION PROBABILITY

One of the basic properties of probability is the multiplication law for independent events. For example, if two dice are tossed, the probability of A and B are as follows:

A: An odd number on the first die

B: An odd number on the second die

Then the multiplication law for independent events permits us to estimate the probability that both dice would have odd numbers. The P(Event C) = Probability (Event A) × Probability (Event B). The first die has a probability of 1, 3, and 5 or 3/6 = .50, and the second die has a probability of 1, 3, and 5 or 3/6 = .50. P(Event C) = .5 × .5 = .25, or there is a 25% chance that both dice will have an odd number.

This multiplication law of probability reflects the properties of relative frequency in practice. If two dice are tossed a large number of times, the relative frequencies of events A, B, and C should approximate the probabilities of these events. Also, the product of the relative frequency of A times the relative frequency of B should approximate the relative frequency of C. This can be stated as follows: Frequency (Event C) ≈ Frequency (Event A) × Frequency (Event B). The *multiplication probability function* in the R script file (chap3d.r) demonstrates this multiplication probability.

The R script file (chap3d.r) simulates the tossing of two dice and records the frequency of an odd number on the first die, an odd number on the second die, and an odd number on both of the dice, which should approximate .25, or 25%. The frequencies are then changed to relative frequencies, and the results are rounded to three decimal places. The R function only needs to input the number of times the two dice are tossed, that is, *Size* or number of trials. The R function illustrates a comparison between relative frequency and the multiplication law for the probability of independent events. Since sample size can be changed, the effect of sample size on the relative frequency as it relates to the multiplication law can be observed. The *Error* indicates how close the *Both Odd* percentage is to the percentage for *F1 * F2*. You only need to enter a data vector for *Size* in the function.

```
> Size = c(100,500,1000)
> chap3d(Size)
```

```
PROGRAM OUTPUT
```

	Die1 Odd	Die2 Odd	Both Odd	F1 * F2	Error
N = 100	0.460	0.520	0.230	0.239200	-0.009200
N = 500	0.514	0.542	0.286	0.278588	0.007412
N = 1000	0.465	0.484	0.224	0.225060	-0.001060

We should notice that as N increases from 100 to 1,000, the *Error* value or difference becomes smaller. *Error* can be positive or negative, indicating under- or overestimation. In these results, the *Error* values did indicate a smaller difference between *Both Odd* and *F1 * F2* as the number of trials increased. This supports our understanding that increasing the number of trials yields a closer approximation or estimate to the true population value.

● CONDITIONAL PROBABILITY

Conditional probabilities are related to joint probabilities and marginal probabilities. For example, a child has a toy train that requires four "C" batteries to run. The child has accidentally mixed two good batteries with two bad batteries. If we were to randomly select one of the four batteries without replacement, the odds of getting a bad battery are conditionally determined. Let's assume that the first battery chosen was bad (Event A), and the second battery chosen was good (Event B). The two selections of the two batteries are dependent events (conditional). The probability of Event B has two different values depending on whether or not Event A occurs. If Event A occurs, then there are two good batteries among the three remaining batteries, and the probability of Event B is 2/3. If a second battery is chosen that is good, then Event A did not occur, so there is one good battery remaining among the two batteries, and the probability of Event B is 1/2.

In probability terms, this can be represented as follows: $P(B \mid A) = 2/3$ and $P(B \mid \text{not } A) = 1/2$. These terms are read as "the probability of B given A" and "the probability of B given not A," respectively. Probabilities of this type are called *conditional probabilities*, because the probability of B is conditional on the occurrence or nonoccurrence of A. This relationship can be illustrated by the following example. Consider a sample space that contains all pairs of batteries selected from the four batteries without replacement. The Xs in the table below indicate the possible outcomes or sample space.

		Second Battery			
		Bad 1	Bad 2	Good 1	Good 2
First battery	Bad 1	—	X	X	X
	Bad 2	X	—	X	X
	Good 1	X	X	—	X
	Good 2	X	X	X	—

Since the 12 outcomes are equally likely, the joint probabilities, $P(A \text{ and } B)$, can be summarized in the following Event table.

		Second Battery		
		Bad	Good	Marginal
First battery	Bad	.067 (2/12)	.267 (4/12)	6/12
	Good	.267 (4/12)	.40 (2/12)	6/12
	Total	6/12	6/12	12/12

The row totals are the *marginal probabilities* for the first battery:

$$P(\text{First is bad}) = 6/12$$

$$P(\text{First is good}) = 6/12.$$

The column totals are the marginal probabilities for the second battery:

$$P(\text{Second is bad}) = 6/12.$$

$$P(\text{Second is good}) = 6/12.$$

Conditional probabilities are related to the joint probabilities and marginal probabilities by the following formula:

$$P(B\,|\,A) = P(B \text{ and } A)/P(A).$$

If Event A results in a bad battery and Event B results in a good battery, then

$$P(B\,|\,A) = P(\text{Second is good}\,|\,\text{First is bad})$$

$$= P(\text{Second is good and First is bad})/P(\text{First is bad})$$

$$= (2/12)/(4/12).$$

$$= 6/12$$

$$= .50.$$

These conditional probabilities are theoretical probabilities assigned to the events by making use of the definition of probability for equally likely events (it is assumed that each of the batteries and each of the pairs are equally likely to be chosen). If these conditional probabilities are reasonable, they should reflect what happens in practice. Consequently, given a large number of replications in which two batteries are selected from a group of four batteries (in which two of the batteries are dead), the relative frequencies for the conditional events should approximate the expected conditional probabilities.

The *conditional probability function* in the R script file (chap3e.r) will simulate random selection without replacement of two batteries from a group of four in which two of the batteries are bad. The R function inputs the number of batteries, the number of bad batteries, and the number of replications in the function. So far, we have learned that the relative frequencies from a small number of replications will not provide good approximations of the true probabilities, so $N = 500$ for the number of trials. "Bad = 0" or "Both batteries are good" indicates a true frequency, .167 (2/12), while "Bad = 1" or combined good/bad and bad/good outcomes (8/12) indicates a true frequency, .666 (.333 + .333), and "Bad = 2" or "Both batteries are bad" indicates a true frequency, .167 (2/12). A large number of replications should provide relative frequencies that will be very close to these expected probabilities.

The values you would enter in the function are as follows:

```
> numBatteries = 4
> numBad = 2
> Size = 500
> chap3e(numBatteries, numBad, Size)
```

The results are printed as follows:

```
PROGRAM OUTPUT

nBattery     bad     Size
    4         2       500

                 Second Battery
                 Bad     Good
     First Bad   0.132   0.334
Battery Good     0.364   0.17

No. Bad Rel Freq   Probability
     0      0.17     0.167
     1      0.698    0.666
     2      0.132    0.167
```

The true frequency for both batteries being bad (Bad = 0) is .167 (2/12). Our sample estimate was .17, which is a good approximation. For the combined good/bad and bad/good outcomes (Bad = 1), the true frequency = .666 (.333 + .333). Our sample estimate was .698, which was an overestimate of .032 in error. For both batteries being bad (Bad = 2), the true frequency = .167 (2/12). Our sample estimate was .132 or an underestimate of −.035 in error. Overall, these sample estimates are close to the true population values. If we did not know the true population values, the sample estimates would be our best approximation, which is what occurs given an infinite population.

● PERMUTATIONS AND COMBINATIONS

There are seven basic rules of probability that come together when examining the probability of getting different **permutations** or **combinations** from events in a group. These have guided how probability is used in practice. These are as follows:

1. The probability of a single event occurring in a set of equally likely events is one divided by the number of events, that is, P(Single event) = 1/N. For example, a single marble from a set of 100 marbles has a 1/100 chance of being selected.

2. If there is more than one event in a group, then the probability of selecting an event from the group is equal to the group frequency divided by the number of events, that is, P(Group|Single event) = Group frequency/N. For example, a set of 1,000 marbles contains 200 red, 500 green, 200 yellow, and 100 black. The probability of picking a black marble is 100/1,000 or 1/10.

3. The probability of an event ranges between 0 and 1, that is, there are no negative probabilities and no probabilities greater than 1. Probability ranges between 0 and 1 in equally likely chance events, that is, $0 \leq P$(Event) ≤ 1.

4. The sum of the probabilities in a population equals 1, that is, the sum of all frequencies of occurrence equals 1.0, Σ(Probabilities) = 1.

5. The probability of an event occurring plus the probability of an event *not* occurring is equal to 1. If the probability of selecting a black marble is 1/10, then the probability of *not* selecting a black marble is 9/10, that is, $P + Q = 1$, where P = Probability of occurrence and $Q = 1 - P$.

6. The probability that any one event from a set of mutually exclusive events will occur is the sum of the probabilities (addition rule of probability). The probability of selecting a black marble (10/100) *or* a yellow marble (20/100) is the sum of their individual probabilities (30/100 or 3/10), that is, $P(B$ or $Y) = P(B) + P(Y)$.

7. The probability that a combination of independent events will occur is the product of their separate probabilities (multiplication rule of probability). Assuming sampling with replacement, the probability that a yellow marble will be selected the first time (2/10) and the probability that a yellow marble will be selected the second time (2/10) combine by multiplication to produce the probability of getting a yellow marble on both selections (2/10 * 2/10 = 4/100 or .04), that is, $P(Y$ and $Y) = P(Y) * P(Y)$.

Factorial Notation

Factorial notation is an important concept when computing combinations of events from a group or permutations for ordered events from a group. Factorial notation is useful for designating probability when samples are taken *without* replacement. For example, the owner of a car dealership must rank the top four salesmen according to the number of cars sold in a month. After ranking the first salesman, only three salesmen remain to choose from. After ranking the second salesman, only two salesmen remain, and after ranking the next, only one salesman remains. If the owner of the car dealership selects a salesman at random, then the probability of any order of salesman is 1/4 * 1/3 * 1/2 * 1/1, which is 1/24.

The probability is based on the total number of possible ways the four salesmen could be ranked by the owner of the car dealership. This is further based on the number of salesmen working at the car dealership available to select from, which changes each time. Consequently, the product yields the total number of choices available: 4 * 3 * 2 * 1 = 24. This product is referred to as **factoring** and uses factorial notation to reflect the product multiplication, $n!$. The factorial notation, 4! (read "4 factorial"), would imply 4 * 3 * 2 * 1, or 24, which indicates the number of different ways four things could be ordered. Imagine a restaurant that serves hamburgers with the following toppings: pickle, onion, and tomato. How many different ways could you order these ingredients on top of your hamburger?— pickle only (1), onion only (1), tomato only (1), pickle and onion (1), pickle and tomato (1), and onion and tomato (1). So in total you have six different ways to order toppings for your hamburger, 3! = 6.

Permutations

Permutations involve selecting objects, events, or individuals from a group and then determining the number of different ways they can be ordered. The number of permutations (different ways you can order something) is designated as n objects taken x at a time, or

$$P(n, x) = \frac{n!}{(n-x)!}.$$

For example, if a teacher needed to select three students from a group of five and order them according to mathematics ability, the number of *permutations* (or different ways three out of five students could be selected and ranked) would be

$$P(n, x) = \frac{n!}{(n-x)!} = \frac{5!}{(5-3)!} = \frac{5*4*3*2*1}{2*1} = 60.$$

Probability can also be based on the number of *combinations* possible when choosing a certain number of objects, events, or individuals from a group. The ordering of observations (permutations) is not important when determining the number of combinations. For example, a teacher must only choose the three best students with mathematics ability from a group of five (no ordering occurs). The number of possible combinations of three students out of a group of five is designated as follows:

$$P(n, x) = \frac{n!}{x!(n-x)!} \text{ or } \frac{5!}{3!(5-3)!} = 10.$$

The number of possible combinations can be further illustrated by determining the number of students in a classroom who have their birthday on the same day. This classic example can be used in a class to determine the probability that two students have the same birthday. The probability of two students having a common birthday, given six students in a class, can be estimated as follows (assuming 365 days per year and equally likely chance):

$$P(2 \mid 6) = 1 - \frac{365}{365} * \frac{364}{365} * \frac{363}{365} * \frac{362}{365} * \frac{361}{365} * \frac{360}{365} = 1 - .958 = .042.$$

The numerator in the formula decreases by 1 because as each student's birthday is selected, there is one less day available.

The probability of at least two students out of six *not* having the same birthday is $1 - P$ (Probability rule 5), which is .958 or 96%. This probability of *no* students having a birthday in common for a class of six students is computed as follows:

$$P(\text{No } 2 \mid 6) = \frac{365}{365} * \frac{364}{365} * \frac{363}{365} * \frac{362}{365} * \frac{361}{365} * \frac{360}{365} = .958.$$

Therefore, the probability of at least two students having the same birthday is the complement of *no* students having the same birthday, or $P(2 \mid 6) = 1 - .958 = .042$. The formula clearly indicates that this probability would increase quickly as the number of objects, events, or individuals in the group increases. Also, the two probabilities sum to 1.0, that is, $P(2 \mid 6) + P(\text{No } 2 \mid 6) = .042 + .958 = 1.0$ (Probability rule 5).

The *birthday function* in the R script file (chap3f.r) simulates the birthday example for N individuals by using a **random number generator** and checking for a common birthday. The relative frequency of at least one common birthday is reported. A higher frequency or chance of at least one birthday in the group increases as the group size increases. This relative frequency approximates the probability of occurrence in a group of N individuals. The size of the group and the number of replications can be changed, that is, *People* and *Size* values. The following data vector for *People* and value for *Size* are entered as follows:

```
> People = c(4,10,20,50)
> Size = 250
> chap3f(People,Size)
```

The function returns the following output:

```
PROGRAM OUTPUT

          Rel. Freq.      Dupl Prob.        Error
N = 4      0.012        0.01635591    -0.004355912
N = 10     0.168        0.11694818     0.051051822
N = 20     0.404        0.41143838    -0.007438384
N = 50     0.984        0.97037358     0.013626420
```

The results indicate that as the group size *N* increases from 4 to 50, the probability of having two students with a common birthday increases from .01 to .98. We can also see that the error is smaller with larger group sizes of people. In a class of 20 students, we would estimate a .40 or 40% chance of two students having the same birthday. Any number of group sizes can be run by changing the values in the *People* data vector.

SUMMARY

Probability theory helps us determine characteristics of a population from a **random sample**. A population is generally considered to be an *infinite* population where sampling *without replacement* occurs, that is, we do not know all of the objects, events, or individual in the population, and when we sample an object, it is not available to be sampled again. *Sampling with replacement* is when any object or event is put back in the population each time after taking a sample; thus, it could be drawn one or more times. A random sample is chosen so that every object, event, or individual in the population has an equal chance of being selected (unbiased selection). The probability that the object, event, or individual will be selected is based on the relative frequency of occurrence of the object, event, or individual in the population. For example, if a population consisted of 1,000 individuals with 700 men and 300 women, then the probability of selecting a male is 700/1,000, or .70. The probability of selecting a woman is 300/1,000, or .30. The important idea is that the selection of the individual is a chance event. We will explore sampling concepts in statistics more in Chapter 4.

EXERCISES

1. Define *finite* and *infinite* population in a few sentences.

2. Define random sample in a few sentences.

3. If the population of China had 2 billion men and 1 billion women, what is the probability of selecting a man for an interview?

4. What is the expected probability of obtaining a heads when tossing an unbiased coin 100 times?

5. What is the probability of rolling an odd number on both dice when tossing two dice?

6. Write out the value for the factorial notation 4!, given sampling without replacement.

7. What is the probability of drawing a playing card that is a *heart* from a deck of 52 cards?

8. If the probability of rain is 35%, what is the probability it will not rain?

9. A population has the following ethnic breakdown: 20% Greek; 30% Indian; and 50% Muslim. What is the probability of selecting a Muslim twice on two separate random samples with replacement?

10. Explain the difference between sampling with replacement and sampling without replacement in a few sentences.

TRUE OR FALSE QUESTIONS

T   F   a.   Relative frequencies from a small sample of replications provide a good approximation of probability.

T   F   b.   As the sample size increases, the relative frequency of an event more closely approximates the population or true value.

T   F   c.   The relative frequency of an event with probability of .65 is better estimated than an event with probability of .10.

T   F   d.   In understanding probability, it helps to know whether the population is finite or infinite.

T   F   e.   The relative frequency of an event in 100 trials is the probability of the event.

WEB RESOURCES

Chapter R script files are available at http://www.sagepub.com/schumacker

Additive Probability Function R script file: chap3c.r

Birthday Function R script file: chap3f.r

Conditional Probability Function R script file: chap3e.r

Infinite Probability Function R script file: chap3a.r

Joint Probability Function R script file: chap3b.r

Multiplication Probability Function R script file: chap3d.r

CHAPTER 4

SAMPLING AND POPULATIONS

● SAMPLE VERSUS POPULATION

We have learned that **populations** are finite or infinite. Exact probabilities can be computed from a finite population because all objects, events, or individuals are known. Sampling from a finite population permits a comparison of the sample results with the known true population values. However, in an infinite population, where all objects, events, or individuals are not known, we must estimate the population values by taking a random sample because we don't know the true population values. We use random sampling so that each selection has an equally likely chance of being picked. The random sample is considered unbiased because no selection bias occurs. We use random sampling in practice oftentimes, whether from an infinitely large population or to simply ensure no selection bias when picking names out of a hat. Historically, researchers have used tables of **random numbers** to select subjects, after assigning ID numbers to the subjects. Computer software is now available to conduct random selection and random assignment to groups (Ahrens & Dieter, 1972; Urbaniak & Plous, 2013).

Random sampling and stratified random sampling are considered probability sampling, which are a necessary first step before using the **parametric statistics** in this book. There are other different types of sampling approaches, but they are not based on probability. Nonprobability sampling methods include quota samples, purposive samples, convenience samples, and nth-selection methods. The nonprobability nature of these sampling methods makes them unsuitable for our parametric statistics. The nonprobability sampling methods contain one or more of the following sample bias types: accessibility bias, affinity bias, cluster bias, nonresponse bias, order bias, self-selection bias, termination bias, and visibility bias. Random sampling and random assignment to groups provide an unbiased approach to subject selection and subject assignment to groups that controls for threats to the internal validity of a research design: history, maturation, testing, instrumentation, statistical regression, subject selection, experimental mortality, and diffusion of treatments (Campbell & Stanley, 1963, 1966).

We have also learned that if the sample size or number of trials is increased, then a better approximation or estimate of the population value is given. This makes sense because the random sample has more information or data from the population. We have also learned that a sample estimate of the population value may underestimate or overestimate the true population value. To better understand random sampling from an infinite population, random numbers are generated and used to create simulated population distributions. R has several functions that permit the generation of random data; *rnorm()* is used in this chapter, while others are discussed in Chapter 5.

● GENERATING RANDOM NUMBERS

Random numbers are used in **statistics** to investigate the characteristics of different population distributions. For example, in the social sciences, the characteristics of the **normal distribution** are generally examined (**central tendency** and dispersion). This is because many of the variables that we measure in the social sciences are normally distributed. The statistics we use to test hypotheses about population **parameters** are based on random samples of data, which are based on certain assumptions and characteristics of the normal distribution. Other population distribution types are presented in Chapter 5.

Early tables of random numbers helped gamblers understand their odds of winning. In some instances, exact probabilities or odds of certain outcomes were generated for cards and dice. Today, high-speed computers using computer software with a numerical procedure (algorithm) produce tables of random numbers. The first mainframe computer, a UNIVAC, produced a set of 1 million random numbers, which was published in a book by the Rand McNally Corporation. Personal desktop computers today run software that can generate random numbers. A set of true random numbers would not repeat, that is, every number would be unique.

Although many computers have software (mathematical algorithms) to generate random numbers, the software algorithms are not all the same and do not produce the same set of random numbers. Basically, a set of computer-generated numbers is not truly random, so they are called **pseudorandom numbers.** This is because the numbers tend to repeat themselves after a while (repeatedness), correlate with other numbers generated (correlatedness), and don't produce a normal distribution (normality). Consequently, when using a random number generator, it is important to report the type of computer used, the type of random number generator software (algorithm), the start value (start number), repeatedness (when numbers repeat themselves in the algorithm), correlatedness (when numbers begin to correlate in a sequence), and normality (whether or not a normal distribution was produced). A sequence of random numbers is therefore not truly random (unique) when using a pseudorandom number generator software program, so a long sequence of random numbers will tend to repeat, correlate, and not appear normal when graphed.

A true random set of numbers has no pattern and, if graphed, would appear as scattered data points across the graph, similar to a shotgun blast on a target. Because true random numbers have no pattern, the next number generated would not be predicted and would appear with approximately the same frequency as any other number. The concept is simple but often requires visual confirmation (graph) or other statistical tests of randomness and/or normality. Software programs often include statistical tests for testing the randomness and normality of computer-generated pseudorandom sample data. Schumacker and Tomek (2013) demonstrated random sampling using R simulation programs.

Because all pseudorandom number generators are not the same, acceptable properties for random numbers should include the following:

1. Approximate, equal proportions of odd and even numbers should occur.

2. Each number between 0 and 9 is generated approximately 1/10 of the time.

3. For five consecutive sets of generated number combinations, the percentages should be approximately equal to the theoretical probabilities.

The *random numbers function* in the R script file (chap4a.r) contains a random number function that produces randomly sampled data and then calculates the relative frequencies of odd and even digits, and each individual digit. Random numbers are sampled from the integer values 0 through 9. The relative frequency of the odd numbers is determined using the modulus (or remainder function) in combination with the sum function and then divided by the sample size. The relative frequency of the even numbers is determined in the same manner, only using all values that were not determined to be odd. The relative frequency of each digit is determined by the familiar **factor** and table combination, and then all raw data are put into groups of five numbers. A seed number is introduced in the function so that the same results will occur each time the function is run. You can obtain different results each time you run the function by simply omitting the *set.seed()* value. The only value to be entered is for *SampleSize*:

```
> SampleSize = 60
> chap4a(SampleSize)

PROGRAM OUTPUT

Number groups:
17217 85232 15374 98818 31342 37582 03219 91904 87105 17230
96584 83506
```

	Rel. Freq.	Prob.
Odd	0.57	0.5
Even	0.43	0.5

	Rel. Freq.	Prob.
0	0.08	0.1
1	0.15	0.1
2	0.12	0.1
3	0.13	0.1
4	0.07	0.1
5	0.10	0.1
6	0.03	0.1
7	0.10	0.1
8	0.13	0.1
9	0.08	0.1

	Rel. Freq.	Prob.
No duplicates	0.5833	0.3024
One pair	0.2500	0.5040
One triple	0.0833	0.0720
Two pairs	0.0833	0.1080
Pair & triple	0.0000	0.0090
Four alike	0.0000	0.0045
All alike	0.0000	0.0001

The number groups indicate 12 sets of five groups of numbers = 60 numbers. We expected 0.50 odd numbers (1, 3, 5, 7, 9) but got 34/60 = 0.566 (~0.57). We expected 0.50 even numbers (0, 2, 4, 6, 8) but got 26/60 = 0.43. The frequency of numbers from 0 to 9 should be equal, that is, $P = .10$; however, from the **frequency distribution**, we see that some numbers were higher and others lower than expected ($p = .10$). Finally, the probability of having random numbers repeat is given, where $p = .3024$, or a 30% chance of having no duplicated numbers; $p = .5040$, or a 50% chance of having one pair of numbers repeated; and so on.

● RANDOM SAMPLING

The field of statistics uses numerical information obtained from samples to draw inferences about populations. A population is a well-defined set of individuals, events, or objects. A sample is a selection of individuals, events, or objects taken from a well-defined population. A sample is generally taken from a population in which each individual, event, or object is independent and has an equally likely chance of selection. The sample average is an example of a random sample estimate of a population value, that is, population mean, which is called a population parameter. Population characteristics or *parameters* are inferred from sample estimates, which are called sample statistics. Examples of population parameters are population percent, population mean, and population correlation.

The relation between a sample statistic and a population value can be further clarified with the following examples. A student wants to estimate the percentage of teachers in the state who are in favor of year-round school. The student might make the estimate on the basis of information received from a random sample of 500 teachers taken from the population composed of all teachers in the state. In another example, a biologist wants to estimate the percentage of tree seeds that will germinate. The biologist plants 1,000 tree seeds and uses the germination rate to establish the rate for all seeds. In marketing research, the proportion of 1,000 randomly sampled consumers who buy one product rather than another helps advertising executives determine product appeal. The Gallop Poll uses a random sample of 1,500 people nationwide to estimate the presidential election outcome within ±2% error.

Because a sample is only a part of the population, how can the sample statistic (estimate) accurately reflect the population parameter? There is an expectation that the sample estimate will be close to the population value if the sample is representative of the population. The difference between the sample estimate and the population parameter is called **sample error**. In a random sample, all objects have an equal chance of being selected from the population. If the sample is reasonably large, this equally likely chance of any individual, event, or object being selected makes it likely that the random sample estimate will represent the population parameter. Most statistics are based on this concept of random sampling from a well-defined population. **Sampling error**, or the error in using a sample statistic as an estimate of a population parameter, does occur. In future chapters, you will learn that several random sample estimates can be averaged to better approximate a population parameter, although sampling error will still present.

The *proportion function* in the R script file (chap4b.r) simulates the sampling of data from a population to estimate a population percent. The R function determines what percentage of a certain large population of people favor stricter penalties. A random number generator will determine the responses of the people in the sample. A random number generator uses an initial start value to begin data selection and then uses the computer to generate other numbers at random. We can use the results of these simulated random samples to draw conclusions about the population, that is, the difference between the *population parameter* and the *sample statistic*. The R function is run using a seed number. The R function uses a pseudorandom number generator to select a random number between 0 and 1 for the population percent. The probability of a 0 (1 minus the population percent) and the probability of a 1 are the same as the population percent. Random samples of various sizes input into the function are taken, and the sample percent and estimation errors are calculated. We expect the *sampling error* to be smaller as the sample size increases.

You will need to enter the values for the data vector *Samples*, then run the function.

```
> Samples = c(10,100,500,1000,1500)
> chap4b(Samples)
```

PROGRAM OUTPUT

	Size	No. in Favor	Pop Percent	Sample Percent	Sampling Error
Sample 1	10	3	0.1085	0.3000	-0.1915
Sample 2	100	9	0.1085	0.0900	0.0185
Sample 3	500	47	0.1085	0.0940	0.0145
Sample 4	1000	106	0.1085	0.1060	0.0025
Sample 5	1500	160	0.1085	0.1067	0.0018

Results indicate that the sampling error decreases as the sample size increases, which meets our expectations. Basically, our sample percent more closely approximates the population percent when our random sample size increases. These types of simulations help our understanding of when sample statistics become better estimates of population values.

The *random sampling function* in the R script file (chap4c.r) takes a random sample from a normal population using the *rnorm()* function. The *rnorm()* function takes a random sample from a normal distribution after specifying the sample size, population mean, and population standard deviation. The resulting sample distribution should appear as a nearly normal distribution as the sample size increases. Our sample distribution, given $n = 10,000$, should appear close to a normal distribution with mean = 30 and standard deviation = 5. We can use smaller sample sizes and rerun the function to examine how the histogram takes on a less than normal distribution shape. The output lists the population mean and sample mean along with an indication of sampling error or the difference between the population and sample means. The sampling error will be larger when sample sizes are smaller, which gives an indication that the sample distribution deviates from a normal distribution.

You will enter values for *n*, *popmean*, and *popsd*, then run the function.

```
> n = 10000
> popmean = 30
> popsd = 5
> chap4c(n, popmean, popsd)

PROGRAM OUTPUT

Sample Size  Pop Mean Sample Mean Sample Error
  1000.0000    30.0000    30.0104      -0.0104
```

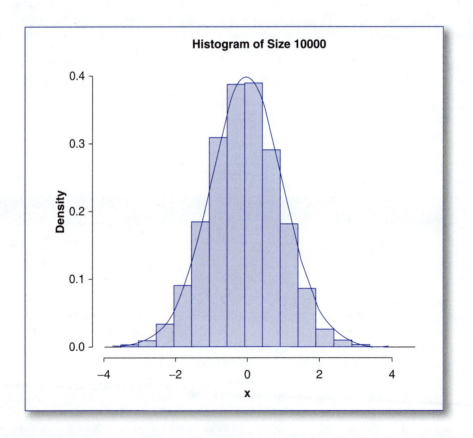

The population mean = 30, and the sample mean = 30.0104, with a sampling error of −0.0104. The sample mean slightly overestimated the known true population mean. In practice, the sample mean would be a very close approximation of the population mean. The histogram shows values of *x* that range from −4 to + 4 under a standardized normal distribution. A line is drawn over the histogram that visually indicates a normal frequency distribution. When specifying smaller sample sizes, the shape of the histogram will change, but the normal distribution line will remain the same, so you can see the difference.

We have learned that computer software uses a pseudorandom number generator, which indicates that the numbers are not truly random. We have also learned that a random sample is part of a population. Random samples are used to obtain data to calculate sample statistics, which are used to make inferences about population parameters. Different random samples lead to different sample estimates of the population parameter. The estimate from a sample is usually not equal to the population parameter value, thus some sampling error is present. However, if a large sample is taken, the sampling error is expected to be smaller. The R function uses a seed number that allows for exact replication of results, even when changing the sample size.

TIP

✓ Random number generators are computer algorithms that usually do not provide a true set of random numbers.

✓ A sample statistic estimates a population parameter and has some amount of sampling error.

✓ Random sampling yields an unbiased sample because of no selection bias.

✓ Generally, as the sample size increases, the sample statistic more closely approximates the population parameter.

SUMMARY

This chapter began by illustrating the nature of random sampling from a population. Two basic concepts were demonstrated. First, the sample statistic is an estimate of the population parameter. Second, the sample statistic more closely approximates the population parameter when the sample size increases. The normal distribution was assumed for the population data in this chapter, but other population distributions are presented in the next chapter. The **central limit theorem** (in the next chapter) plays a key role in our understanding of random sampling from a population distribution.

EXERCISES

1. Define *pseudo–random number* generation by computers in a few sentences.

2. What does the *set.seed()* function do if used in an R script file?

3. A *sample statistic* is an estimate of a population _____.

4. Define *sampling error* in a few sentences.

5. What command do you use to obtain the arguments needed for the *rnorm* function?

6. What is the R command to randomly sample 100 numbers from a normal distribution?

7. What is the R command to graph 100 randomly selected data values in a histogram?

8. For the following set of numbers, round the mean without any decimal places: $x = 1:30$.

9. For the following set of numbers, provide summary statistics: $x = 1:30$.

10. Use the normal distribution to generate 100 numbers in a data vector Q, then graph in a histogram.

TRUE OR FALSE QUESTIONS

T   F   a.   Sampling error becomes smaller as the sample size increases.

T   F   b.   The random number generator software produces random numbers.

T   F   c.   A normal distribution of data should appear bell-shaped when graphed.

T   F   d.   Sample statistics only come from normal population distributions.

T   F   e.   We expect a mean = 50 given a random sample of data from a normal distribution of 100 numbers between 0 and 100.

T   F   f.   The *summary()* function produces whole numbers without decimal places.

T   F   g.   The *hist()* function yields the mean and standard deviation in a set of scores.

T   F   h.   Sample statistics can be computed for normal distributions.

WEB RESOURCES

Chapter R script files are available at http://www.sagepub.com/schumacker

Proportion Function R script file: chap4b.r

Random Numbers Function R script file: chap4a.r

Random Sampling Function R script file: chap4c.r

Research Randomizer: http://www.randomizer.org/

PART II

STATISTICAL THEORY AND INFERENCE

## CHAPTER 5

POPULATION DISTRIBUTIONS

I t is common in the field of mathematics, for example, geometry, to have theorems or postulates that establish guiding principles for understanding analysis of data. The same is true in the field of statistics. An important theorem in statistics is the central limit theorem, which provides a better understanding of sampling from a population.

● CENTRAL LIMIT THEOREM

The central limit theorem is an important theorem in statistics when testing mean differences using *t* tests, *F* tests, or post hoc tests in analysis of **variance**, and these are explained in later chapters. It is a misunderstood theorem that many quote incorrectly. For example, the following statements are *wrong* when discussing the central limit theorem in statistics:

1. As the sample size increases, especially greater than 30 in the ***t* distribution**, the sample distribution becomes a **normal curve**.

2. Regardless of the shape of the population, a large sample size taken from the population will produce a normally distributed sample.

3. The more data you take from a population, the more normal the sample distribution becomes.

To the untrained person, these points seem correct when explaining the central limit theorem. Unfortunately, the descriptions do more harm than good when trying to teach the importance of the central limit theorem in statistics.

The correct understanding is the following: Let X_1 to X_n be a random sample of data from a population distribution with mean μ and standard deviation σ. Let $\bar{X}$ be the sample average or arithmetic mean of X_1 to X_n. Repeat the random sampling (with replacement) of size N, calculating a mean each time, to produce a frequency distribution of sample means. The distribution of the sample means is approximately normal with mean μ and standard deviation $\sigma / \sqrt{n}$, referred to as the *standard error of the mean*. This correctly describes the steps taken to produce the **sampling**

distribution of the means for a given sample size. The correct statements about the central limit theorem are as follows:

1. The sample distribution of means approaches a normal distribution as the sample size of each sample increases. (Sample means computed with $n = 5$ are not as normally distributed as sample means computed with $n = 25$.)

2. The sum of the random samples ΣX_i is also approximately normally distributed with mean $n\mu$ and standard deviation $\sqrt{n}\sigma$.

3. If the sample data, X_i, is normally distributed, then the mean, $\bar{X}$, and the sum, ΣX_i, are normally distributed, no matter the sample size.

The central limit theorem is based on the sampling distribution of the means—a distribution of an infinite number of samples of the same size randomly drawn from a population each time a sample mean is calculated. As the sample size for each sample mean increases, the sampling distribution of the means will have an average value closer to the population mean. Sampling error or the variability of the sample means around a population mean becomes less as the sample size for calculating the mean increases. Therefore, the mean of the sampling distribution of means becomes closer to the true population mean with a smaller standard deviation of the sample means. The important point is that a sampling distribution of the statistic, in this case the sample means, is created where the average indicates the population parameter.

The complexity of understanding the central limit theorem and its many forms can be found in Wikipedia (http://en.wikipedia.org/wiki/Central_limit_theorem), where the classical (central limit theorem) and other formalizations by different authors are discussed. Wikipedia also provides an explanation for the central limit theorem as follows:

The sample means are generated using a random number generator, which draws numbers between 1 and 100 from a uniform probability distribution. It illustrates that increasing sample sizes result in the 500 measured sample means being more closely distributed about the population mean (50 in this case). It also compares the observed distributions with the distributions that would be expected for a normalized Gaussian distribution, and shows the chi-squared values that quantify the goodness of the fit (the fit is good if the reduced chi-squared value is less than or approximately equal to one).

The chi-square test refers to the Pearson chi-square, which tests a **null hypothesis** that the frequency distribution of the sample means is consistent with a particular theoretical distribution, in this case the normal distribution. Fischer (2010) presented the history of the central limit theorem, which underscores its importance in the field of statistics, and the different variations of the central limit theorem.

In my search for definitions of the central limit theorem, I routinely see the explanation involving random number generators drawing numbers between 1 and 100 from a uniform probability distribution. Unfortunately, my work has shown that random number generators in statistical packages do not produce true random numbers unless the sample size is above $N = 10,000$ (Bang, Schumacker, & Schlieve, 1998). It was disturbing to discover that the numbers repeat, correlate, and distribute in nonrandom patterns when drawn from pseudorandom number generators used by statistical packages. This disruption in random sampling, however, does not deter our understanding of the central limit theorem; rather, it helps us understand the basis for **random sampling without replacement** and **random sampling with replacement**.

● WHY IS THE CENTRAL LIMIT THEOREM IMPORTANT IN STATISTICS?

The central limit theorem provides the basis for hypothesis testing of mean differences using the *t* test, *F* test, and post hoc tests. The central limit theorem provides the set of rules when determining the mean, **variance**, and shape of a distribution of sample means. Our statistical formulas are created based on this knowledge of the frequency distribution of sample means and used in tests of mean difference (mean μ and standard deviation $\sigma/\sqrt{N}$).

The central limit theorem is also important because the *sampling distribution of the means is approximately normally distributed, no matter what the original population distribution looks like* as long as the sample size is relatively large. Therefore, the sample mean provides a good estimate of the population mean (μ). Errors in our statistical estimation of the population mean decrease as the size of the samples we draw from the population increase. Sample statistics have sampling distributions, with the variance of the sampling distribution indicating the error variance of the statistic—that is, the error in estimating the population parameter. When the error variance is small, the statistic will vary less from sample to sample, thus providing us an assurance of a better estimate of the population parameter. The basic approach is taking a random sample from a population, computing a statistic, and using that statistic as an estimate of the population parameter. The importance of the sampling distribution in this basic approach is to determine if the sample statistic occurs beyond a chance level and how close it might be to the population parameter. Obviously, if the population parameter were known as in a finite population, then we would not be taking a sample of data and estimating the population parameter.

● TYPES OF POPULATION DISTRIBUTIONS

There are different types of population distributions that we sample to estimate their population parameters. The population distributions are used in the chapters of the book where different statistical tests are used in hypothesis testing (chi-square, **z test**, *t* test, *F* test, correlation, and regression). Random sampling, computation of a sample statistic, and inference to a population parameter are an integral part of research and hypothesis testing.

The different types of population distributions used in this book are binomial, uniform, exponential, and normal. Each type of population distribution can be derived using an R function (*binom, unif, exp, norm*). For each type of population distribution, there are different frequency distributions, namely, *d* = probability density function, *p* = central density function, *q* = quantiles of distribution, and *r* = random samples from population distribution. Each type of distribution has a number of parameters that characterize that distribution. The following sections of this chapter provide an understanding of these population distribution types and their associated frequency distributions with their parameter specifications.

Binomial Distribution

The family of **binomial distributions** with their parameter specifications can be found using the help menu, *help("rbinom")*. The R functions and parameter specifications are

```
dbinom(x, size, prob, log = FALSE)
pbinom(q, size, prob, lower.tail = TRUE, log.p = FALSE)
qbinom(p, size, prob, lower.tail = TRUE, log.p = FALSE)
rbinom(n, size, prob)
```

The parameters are defined as follows:

x, q	Vector of quantiles
p	Vector of probabilities
n	Number of observations; if length(n) > 1, the length is taken to be the number required
Size	Number of trials (zero or more)
Prob	Probability of success on each trial
log, log.p	Logical; if TRUE, probabilities p are given as $\log(p)$
lower.tail	Logical; if TRUE (default), probabilities are $P(X \leq x)$, otherwise $P(X > x)$

Each family type for the binomial distribution is run next with a brief explanation of the results.

Probability Density Function of Binomial Distribution (dbinom)

```
# dbinom(x, size, prob, log = FALSE)
# Compute P(45 < X < 55) for value x(46:54), size = 100, prob = .5
      > result = dbinom(46:54,100,0.5)
      > result

      [1] 0.05795840 0.06659050 0.07352701 0.07802866 0.07958924 0.07802866 0.07352701
      [8] 0.06659050 0.05795840

      > sum(result)

      [1] .6317984
```

The probability of x being greater than 45 and less than 55 is p = .63 or 63%, from summing the probability values in the interval of x. This is helpful if wanting to know what percentage of values fall between two numbers in a frequency distribution. The *dbinom* function provides the sum of the individual number probabilities in the interval for x.

Central Density Function of Binomial Distribution (pbinom)

```
# pbinom(q, size, prob, lower.tail = TRUE, log.p = FALSE)
> result = pbinom(46:54,100,.5)
> result

[1] 0.2420592 0.3086497 0.3821767 0.4602054 0.5397946
0.6178233 0.6913503
[8] 0.7579408 0.8158992
```

The increasing probability from one number to the next is given, that is, the cumulative probability across the interval 46 to 54 (nine numbers). For example, the increase from .2420592 to .3086497 is .06659050 or the probability increase from 46 to 47. The increase from .3086497 to .3821767 is .07352701 or the probability increase from 47 to 48. The *pbinom* function provides the cumulative probability across each of the number intervals from 46 to 54, which sums to the percentage given by the *dbinom* function.

The *summary()* function indicates the descriptive statistics, which show the minimum probability (.2421) and the maximum probability (.8159) with the first **quartile**, third quartile, **median**, and mean probability values for the score distribution.

```
> summary(result)

  Min.   1st Qu.   Median    Mean   3rd Qu.   Max.
0.2421   0.3822    0.5398   0.5351   0.6914   0.8159
```

Quantiles of Binomial Distribution (qbinom)

```
# qbinom(p, size, prob, lower.tail = TRUE, log.p = FALSE)
> result = qbinom(.5,100,.25)
> result
[1] 25
```

The *qbinom* function returns a number from a binomial frequency distribution, which represents the quantile breakdown. For example, a vector of probabilities (p) is created for size = 100, with probability indicating the score at the percentile. For p = .5, 100, and probability = .25, the score at the 25th quantile (percentile) is 25. This provides the raw score at a certain percentile in a frequency distribution of scores.

Random Samples From Binomial Distribution (rbinom)

```
# rbinom(n, size, prob)
> result = rbinom(100, 10, .5)
> result
[1] 3 6 5 4 7 4 6 5 3 6 5 5 7 6 3 6 4 7 3 4 7 5 2 7 6 5 3 6 7 5 5 5 5 4 7 6 5
[38] 8 7 5 5 4 5 5 6 4 8 3 7 3 7 3 5 5 5 6 6 4 8 5 5 4 4 4 4 5 4 4 3 4 4 4 6 4
[75] 6 5 5 6 7 5 7 6 6 7 7 7 3 3 7 5 5 7 7 5 6 5 4 6 6 4
```

```
> summary(result)
```

```
Min.  1st Qu. Median  Mean   3rd Qu.  Max.
2.00  4.00    5.00    5.19   6.00     8.00
```

The *rbinom* function returns 100 numbers (*n*) with 10 successive trials, and probability of success on each trial equal to .5. The *summary()* function provides descriptive statistics indicating the median (middle value) of the 10 successive trials (=5.00), while mean = 5.19 indicates some random variation from the expected value of 5.0. The first quartile (25%) had a score of 4, and the third quartile (75%) had a score of 6. Scores ranged from 2 (minimum) to 8 (maximum). Because the *rbinom()* function is using random numbers, these summary values will change each time you run the function.

The binominal distribution is created using dichotomous variable data. Many variables in education, psychology, and business are dichotomous. Examples of dichotomous variables are boy versus girl, correct versus incorrect answers, delinquent versus nondelinquent, young versus old, part-time versus full-time worker. These variables reflect mutually exclusive and exhaustive categories; that is, an individual, object, or event can only occur in one or the other category, but not both. Populations that are divided into two exclusive categories are called **dichotomous populations** or binomial populations, which can be represented by the binomial probability distribution. The derivation of the binomial probability is similar to the combination probability presented earlier.

The **binomial probability distribution** is computed by

$$P(x \text{ in } n) = \binom{n}{x} P^x Q^{n-x},$$

where the following values are used:

   n = size of the random sample.

   x = number of events, objects, or individuals in the first category.

   n − *x* = number of events, objects, or individuals in the second category.

   P = probability of event, object, or individual occurring in the first category.

   Q = probability of event, object, or individual occurring in the second category, (1 − *P*).

Since the binomial distribution is a theoretical probability distribution based on objects, events, or individuals belonging to one of only two groups, the values for *P* and *Q* probabilities associated with group membership must have some basis for selection. An example will illustrate how to use the formula and interpret the resulting binomial distribution.

Students are given 10 true/false items. The items are scored correct or incorrect with the probability of a correct guess equal to one half. What is the probability that a student will get five or more true/false items correct? For this example, *n* = 10, *P* and *Q* are both .50 (one half based on guessing the item correct), and *x* ranges from 0 (all wrong) to 10 (all correct) to produce the binomial probability combinations. The calculation of all binomial probability combinations is not necessary to solve the problem, but these are tabled for illustration and interpretation.

The following table gives the binomial outcomes for 10 questions:

X	$\begin{bmatrix} n \\ x \end{bmatrix}$	P_x	Q_{n-x}	Probability
10	1	$.5^{10}$	$.5^0$	1/1024 = .0001
9	10	$.5^9$	$.5^1$	10/1024 = .0097
8	45	$.5^8$	$.5^2$	45/1024 = .0439
7	120	$.5^7$	$.5^3$	120/1024 = .1172
6	210	$.5^6$	$.5^4$	210/1024 = .2051
5	252	$.5^5$	$.5^5$	252/1024 = .2460
4	210	$.5^4$	$.5^6$	210/1024 = .2051
3	120	$.5^3$	$.5^7$	120/1024 = .1172
2	45	$.5^2$	$.5^8$	45/1024 = .0439
1	10	$.5^1$	$.5^9$	10/1024 = .0097
0	1	$.5^0$	$.5^{10}$	1/1024 = .0001
Total = 1,024				1024/1024 = 1.00

NOTE: The $\begin{bmatrix} n \\ x \end{bmatrix}$ combinations can be found in a binomial coefficient table (Hinkle, Wiersma, & Jurs, 2003, p. 651).

Using the addition rule, the probability of a student getting 5 or more items correct is (.2460 + .2051 + .1172 + .0439 + .0097 + .0001) = .622. The answer is based on the sum of the probabilities for getting 5 items correct plus the probabilities for 6, 7, 8, 9, and 10 items correct.

The combination formula yields an individual coefficient for taking x events, objects, or individuals from a group size n. Notice that these individual coefficients sum to the total number of possible combinations and are symmetrical across the binomial distribution. The binomial distribution is symmetrical because $P = Q = .50$. When P does not equal Q, the binomial distribution will not be symmetrical. Determining the number of possible combinations and multiplying it by P and then by Q will yield the theoretical probability for a certain outcome. The individual outcome probabilities should add to 1.0. A binomial distribution can be used to compare sample probabilities with theoretical population probabilities if

a. there are only two outcomes, for example, success or failure;

b. the process is repeated a fixed number of times;

c. the replications are independent of each other;

d. the probability of success in a group is a fixed value, P; and/or

e. the number of successes x in group size n is of interest.

Knowledge of the binomial distribution is helpful in conducting research and useful in practice. The *binomial function* in the R script file (chap5a.r) simulates binomial probability outcomes, where the number of replications, number of trials, and probability value can be input to observe various binomial probability outcomes. The R function can be replicated any number of times, but extreme values are not necessary to observe the shape of the distribution. The relative frequencies of successes (*x*) will be used to obtain the approximations of the binomial probabilities. The theoretical probabilities—mean and variance of the relative frequency distribution—and error will be computed and printed. Trying different values should allow you to observe the properties of the binomial distribution.

You should observe that the binomial distributions are skewed except for those with a probability of success equal to .50. If $P > .50$, the binomial distribution is skewed left; if $P < .50$, the binomial distribution is skewed right. The mean of a binomial distribution is $n * P$, and the variance is $n * P * Q$. The binomial distribution given by $P(x$ in $n)$ uses the combination probability formula—multiplication and addition rules of probability. The *binomial function* outputs a comparison of sample probabilities with expected theoretical population probabilities given the binomial distribution. Start with the following variable values in the function:

```
> numTrials = 10
> numReplications = 500
> Probability = .50
```

The function should print out the following results:

```
> chap5a (numTrials, numReplications, Probability)

PROGRAM OUTPUT

Number of Replications = 500
Number of Trials = 10
Probability = 0.5
```

	Actual Prob.	Pop. Prob	Error
Successes = 10	0.000	0.001	-0.001
Successes = 9	0.014	0.010	0.004
Successes = 8	0.044	0.044	0.000
Successes = 7	0.144	0.117	0.027
Successes = 6	0.206	0.205	0.001
Successes = 5	0.250	0.246	0.004
Successes = 4	0.192	0.205	-0.013
Successes = 3	0.106	0.117	-0.011
Successes = 2	0.038	0.044	-0.006
Successes = 1	0.006	0.010	-0.004
Successes = 0	0.000	0.001	-0.001

```
Sample mean success = 4.86
Theoretical mean success = 5
```

```
Sample variance = 2.441
Theoretical variance = 2.5
```

These results indicate actual probabilities that closely approximate the true population probabilities, as noted by the small amount of difference (*Error*). The descriptive statistics, mean, and
variance also indicate that sample mean and variance values are close approximations to the theoretical population values. In later chapters, we will learn how knowledge of the binomial distribution is used in statistics and hypothesis testing.

Uniform Distribution

The **uniform distribution** is a set of numbers with equal frequency across the minimum and
maximum values. The family types for the uniform distribution can also be calculated. For example, given the uniform distribution, the different R functions for the family of uniform distributions
would be *dunif()*, *punif()*, *qunif()*, or *runif()*. The R functions and parameter specifications are
as follows:

```
dunif(x, min = 0, max = 1, log = FALSE)
punif(q, min = 0, max = 1, lower.tail = TRUE, log.p = FALSE)
qunif(p, min = 0, max = 1, lower.tail = TRUE, log.p = FALSE)
runif(n, min = 0, max = 1)
```

The parameters are defined as follows:

x, q	Vector of quantiles
P	Vector of probabilities
N	Number of observations; if length(n) > 1, the length is taken to be the number required
min, max	Lower and upper limits of the distribution; must be finite
log, log.p	Logical; if TRUE, probabilities p are given as $\log(p)$
lower.tail	Logical; if TRUE (default), probabilities are $P(X \leq x)$, otherwise, $P(X > x)$

Each family type for the uniform distribution is run next with a brief explanation of results.

Probability Density Function of Uniform Distribution (dunif)

```
# dunif(x, min = 0, max = 1, log = FALSE)
    > out = dunif(25, min = 0, max = 100)
    > out
    [1] 0.01
```

The results indicate that for *x* = 25 and numbers from 0 to 100, the density is .01, or 1%, which it is for any number listed between 0 and 100.

Central Density Function of Uniform Distribution (punif)

```
# punif(q, min = 0, max = 1, lower.tail = TRUE, log.p = FALSE)
    > out = punif(25, min = 0, max = 100)
    > out
    [1] .25
```

The central density function returns a value that indicates the percentile for the score in the spec-ified uniform range (minimum to maximum). Given scores from 0 to 100, a score of 25 is at the 25th percentile. Similarly, if you changed the score value to 50, then *p* = .50; if you changed the score to 75, *p* = .75; and so on.

Quantiles of Uniform Distribution (qunif)

```
# qunif(p, min = 0, max = 1, lower.tail = TRUE, log.p = FALSE)
    > out = qunif(.25, min = 0, max = 100)
    > out
    [1] 25
```

The quantile function provides the score at the percentile, so specifying the 25th percentile (.25) for the uniform score range, 0 to 100, returns the score value of 25. Similarly, changing to the 50th percentile (.50) would return the score of 50 and for the 75th percentile (.75) a score of 75.

This is obviously the opposite or reverse operation of the *punif* function.

Random Samples From Uniform Distribution (runif)

```
# runif(n, min = 0, max =1)
    > out = runif(100, min =0, max = 100)
    > out

 [1] 94.632655 68.492497  2.692937 98.358134 77.889332 24.893746 74.354932
 [8] 57.411356 90.285205 50.102461 63.353739 46.640251 62.644004 97.082284
[15] 93.135579 64.210914 59.927144  5.616103  2.663518 11.678644 23.276759
[22] 75.818421 73.052291 47.706978 65.428699 41.795180 49.852117 52.377169
[29] 65.572710 43.436643 33.300152 87.189956 91.112259 92.621849 11.144048
[36] 35.358118 24.617452 15.238183 68.673094 76.500651 99.894234  1.085388
[43]  4.731420 30.666119 63.273506 92.029171 14.394401 28.718632 93.116036
[50] 19.064123 35.976356 82.335034 67.944665 34.220174 78.324919 48.405500
[57] 60.662242 74.024813 88.946688 75.620636 31.651819 77.462229 75.286610
[64] 18.056070 19.750348 70.685768 10.277177 52.396420 47.876609 79.345406
```

```
[71] 22.632888 77.957625 59.774774 19.765961 52.908461 83.293337 29.119818
[78] 20.349387 16.253181 34.095846  6.697402 47.862945 60.338858 29.153045
[85]  3.070333 89.497876 32.761239 67.834647 77.408672 97.316590 55.387126
[92] 75.691257 24.723647 98.158398 61.029116 14.492436 30.917152  6.182239
[99] 77.982800 14.938247
```

The random uniform function returns a set of numbers (n) drawn randomly between the minimum and maximum interval (0–100). Since these numbers were drawn at random, they will be different each time the *runif()* function is executed. The *summary()* function returns the descriptive statistics. The minimum and maximum values are close to the ones specified, with the 25th and 75th quartiles close to the score values 25 and 75, respectively. The mean and median values are higher than the expected value of 50 due to random sampling error.

```
> summary(out)

  Min.   1st Qu.  Median    Mean    3rd Qu.   Max.
 1.085   24.850   54.150   51.840   75.990   99.890
```

These numbers could be output as whole numbers using the round() function, that is,

```
> out = round(runif(100, min = 0, max = 1))
> out
 [1]  51 38 55 21   58 17 18 65 40 94 41 43   3 42 87 15 61 62
[19]  96 81 22 59   88 46 54 25 30 14 90 87 33 95 47   9 76 78
[37]  59 59 54 12   62 52 25   1 39 89 97 90 53 93 67 31 68 61
[55]  89 65 58 13   61 69 53 64 47 29 46 36 44 72 46 86 90 21
[73]  77 22 10 97   78 28 65 12   2 14 35 44   9 99   9 63 82 57
[91]   2 32 13 18 100 50   2 39 31 58
```

Exponential Distribution

The exponential distribution is a skewed population distribution. In practice, it could represent how long a light bulb lasts, muscle strength over the length of a marathon, or other measures that decline over time. The family types for the exponential distribution have parameter specifications different from those for the binomial and uniform distributions. The rate specification parameter has an expected mean = 1/rate (Ahrens & Dieter, 1972). The family types have the same corresponding prefix letter, which would be *dexp()*, *pexp()*, *qexp()*, or *rexp()*. The R functions and default parameter specifications are

```
dexp(x, rate = 1, log = FALSE)
pexp(q, rate = 1, lower.tail = TRUE, log.p = FALSE)
qexp(p, rate = 1, lower.tail = TRUE, log.p = FALSE)
rexp(n, rate = 1)
```

The parameters are defined as follows:

x, q	Vector of quantiles
p	Vector of probabilities
n	Number of observations; if length(n) > 1, the length is taken to be the number required
rate	Vector of rates
log, log.p	Logical; if TRUE, probabilities *p* are given as log(*p*)
lower.tail	Logical; if TRUE (default), probabilities are *P*(*X* ≤ *x*), otherwise, *P*(*X* > *x*)

Probability Density Function of Exponential Distribution (dexp)

```
# dexp(x, rate = 1, log = FALSE)
    > out = dexp(10,1/5)
    > out
    [1] 0.02706706
```

Central Density Function of Exponential Distribution (pexp)

```
# pexp(q, rate = 1, lower.tail = TRUE, log.p = FALSE)
    > out = pexp(10,1/5)
    > out
    [1] .8646647
```

Quantiles of Exponential Distribution (qexp)

```
# qexp(p, rate = 1, lower.tail = TRUE, log.p = FALSE)

    > out = qexp(.5,1/4)
    s> out
    [1] 2.772589

    > out = qexp(.5,1/2)
    > out
    [1] 1.386294

    > out = qexp(.5,3/4)
    > out
    [1] .9241962

    > out = qexp(.5,1)
    > out
    [1] .6931472
```

The set of printed outputs above illustrate the nature of the exponential distribution, that is, a declining mean (rate) from 1/4 to 1.0 for probability = .5.

Random Samples From Exponential Distribution (rexp)

```
# rexp(n, rate = 1)
    > out = rexp(100,1/4)
    > out
```

```
     [1]  1.73219601 4.79446254   4.05993483   0.01993972 0.71048239  9.27332973
     [7]  0.09475147 0.30871046  18.67428167   4.54117962 0.20011834 12.10793260
    [13]  6.71499044 4.39452344   3.41575969   0.62199891 1.99674704  5.62720221
    [19]  7.68300392 2.54739105   0.01261893   0.83366385 0.64003242  2.77188435
    [25]  7.36239492 2.19021500  11.12823335   4.91269828 0.09457513  9.09668340
    [31]  8.68860153 4.08004465   0.01582165   0.99745539 6.22968806  4.65259742
    [37]  3.69919861 2.86701042   2.04004912   1.52114971 2.70196299  1.58343604
    [43]  1.43875399 4.62656192   0.85969632   8.56874815 0.03083349  4.23918701
    [49]  7.08692575 3.83158464   6.06974040  15.72454008 3.25873445  3.17955369
    [55]  2.96277823 0.27656749  18.88864346   2.17009741 2.89771483  0.19832493
    [61]  1.97309666 9.79389141   3.02614917   0.73000261 0.82187165  1.64273408
    [67]  1.60989941 1.48664650   5.97639396   6.61353025 4.73888451  5.78233026
    [73]  7.25732945 2.67668794   6.19065313   1.22899983 3.93594436  0.90478376
    [79]  1.37091390 2.15105686   1.64585406   3.11505961 0.16988907  1.61230988
    [85]  1.30485435 0.65339027   2.73573552   4.44513769 1.39099021  4.27877563
    [91]  3.93888001 2.52360336   2.85476127   2.54926806 3.23218544  1.13216361
    [97]  3.19003494 0.35972108   0.87244059   3.79803757
```

These exponential data will change each time you run the R function due to random sampling. The *hist()* function graphs the exponential data. The theoretical exponential curve for these values can be displayed using the *curve()* function.

```
> hist(out)
> curve (dexp(x,1/4))
```

Normal Distribution

The normal distribution is used by many researchers when computing statistics in the social and behavioral sciences. The family types for the normal distribution can also be calculated. For example, given the normal distribution, the different R functions for the family of normal distributions would be *dnorm()*, *pnorm()*, *qnorm()*, or *rnorm()*. The two key parameter specifications are for the mean and standard deviation. The default values are for the standard normal distribution (mean = 0 and *sd* = 1). The R functions and parameter specifications are

```
dnorm(x, mean = 0, sd = 1, log = FALSE)
pnorm(q, mean = 0, sd = 1, lower.tail = TRUE, log.p = FALSE)
qnorm(p, mean = 0, sd = 1, lower.tail = TRUE, log.p = FALSE)
rnorm(n, mean = 0, sd = 1)
```

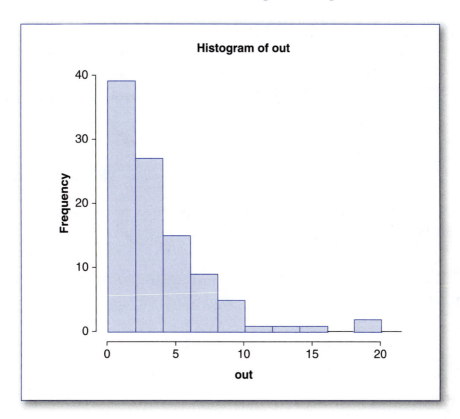

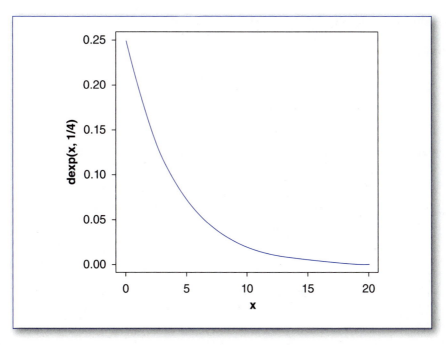

The parameters are defined as follows:

---

x, q	Vector of quantiles.
p	Vector of probabilities
n	Number of observations; if length(n) > 1, the length is taken to be the number required
Mean	Vector of means
sd	Vector of standard deviations
log, log.p	logical; if TRUE, probabilities *p* are given as log(*p*).
lower.tail	logical; if TRUE (default), probabilities are $P(X \leq x)$ otherwise, $P(X > x)$.

Probability Density Function of Normal Distribution (dnorm)

```
# dnorm(x, mean = 0, sd = 1, log = FALSE)

    > out = dnorm(100, mean = 0, sd = 1)
    > out

    [1] 0
```

The *dnorm* function yields 0 in a standardized normal distribution.

Central Density Function of Normal Distribution (pnorm)

```
# pnorm(q, mean = 0, sd = 1, lower.tail = TRUE, log.p = FALSE)
    > out = pnorm(100, mean = 0, sd = 1)
    > out
    [1] 1
```

The *pnorm* function yields 1 in a standardized normal distribution.

Quantiles of Normal Distribution (qnorm)

```
# qnorm(p, mean = 0, sd = 1, lower.tail = TRUE, log.p = FALSE)
    > out = qnorm (.25, mean = 0, sd = 1)
    > out
    [1] -.6744898

    > out = qnorm (.5, mean = 0, sd = 1)
    > out
    [1] 0
```

```
> out = qnorm (.75, mean = 0, sd = 1)
> out
[1] .6744898
```

The three *qnorm* functions illustrate that with $p = .25$, the one standard deviation below the mean is approximately −0.68, or 68%; with $p = .50$, mean = 0; and with $p = .75$, the one standard deviation above the mean is approximately +0 .68, or 68%. The 25th and 75th quantiles therefore approximate the normal distribution percentages.

Random Samples From Normal Distribution (rnorm)

```
# rnorm(n, mean = 0, sd = 1)
    > out = rnorm(1000, mean = 0, sd = 1)
    > summary(out)

      Min.    1st Qu.    Median      Mean     3rd Qu.    Max.
   -2.963000  -0.683600  -0.017690  -0.006792  0.689600  3.485000
    > sd(out)
```

The *rnorm* function outputs 1,000 scores that approximate a normal distribution, which has mean = 0 and standard deviation = 1. The *summary()* function provides the descriptive statistics. The mean = −0.006792, which for all practical purposes is zero. The median = −.017690, which again can be considered close to zero. A normal distribution has a mean and median equal to zero. The *sd()* function yields a value of 1.026045, which is close to the expected value of 1.0 for the normal distribution of scores. Increasing the sample size will yield an even closer estimation to the mean = 0 and standard deviation = 1 values in the standard normal distribution and should range from +3 to −3 (the minimum and maximum score values, respectively). Finally, the *hist()* function provides a frequency distribution display of the randomly sampled 1,000 score values that approximates a normal **bell-shaped curve**.

```
> hist(out)
```

The binomial and normal distributions are used most often by social science researchers because they cover most of the variable types used in conducting statistical tests. Also, for $P = .50$ and large sample sizes, the binomial distribution approximates the normal distribution. Consequently, the mean of a binomial distribution is equal to $n * P$, with variance equal to $n * P * Q$. A standardized score (**z score**), which forms the basis for the normal distribution, can be computed from dichotomous data in a binomial distribution as follows:

$$z = \frac{x - nP}{\sqrt{nPQ}},$$

where x is the score, nP the mean, and nPQ the variance.

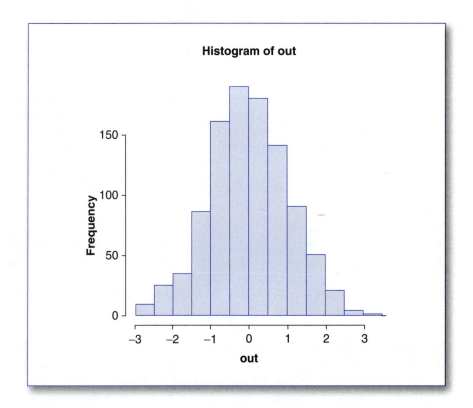

A frequency distribution of standard scores (*z* scores) has a mean of 0 and a standard deviation of 1. The *z* scores typically range in value from −3.0 to +3.0 in a symmetrical normal distribution. A graph of the binomial distribution, given *P* = *Q* and a large sample size, will be symmetrical and appear normally distributed.

TIP

✓ Use *q = rbinom(100, 10, .5)* to randomly sample binomial distribution (*n* = 100 numbers, size = 1 to 10, with probability = .5).

✓ Use *j = runif(100, min = 0, max = 100)* to sample from a uniform distributions numbers between 0 and 100.

✓ Use *h = rexp(100, 1)* to randomly sample 100 numbers from the exponential distribution.

✓ Use *x = rnorm(100, 20, 5)* to randomly sample 100 scores from a normal distribution with mean = 20 and standard deviation= 5.

✓ Use *hist()* to display results for any of the *q*, *j*, *h*, or *x* variables above.

✓ Use *curve()* to draw a smooth line in the graph.

✓ Use *summary()* to obtain basic summary statistics.

● POPULATION TYPE VERSUS SAMPLING DISTRIBUTION

The central limit theorem can be shown graphically, that is, by showing a nonnormal skewed distribution of sample data that becomes normally distributed when displaying the frequency distribution of sample means. Increasing the sample size when computing the sample means also illustrates how the frequency distribution of sample means becomes more normally distributed as sample size increases.

To illustrate, the *central limit theorem function* in the R script file (chap5b.r) creates population distributions of various shapes, takes random samples of a given size, calculates the sample means, and then graphs the frequency distribution of the sample means. It visually shows that regardless of the shape of the population, the sampling distribution of the means is approximately normally distributed. The random samples are taken from one of four different population types: uniform, normal, exponential, or bimodal (*distType = "Uniform" # Uniform, Normal, Exponential, Bimodal*). The sample size for each sample mean (*SampleSize = 50*) and the number of random samples to form the frequency distribution of the sample means (*NumReplications = 250*) are required as input values for the function. Change *distType = "Uniform"* to one of the other distribution types, for example, *distType = "Normal"*, to obtain the population distribution and the resulting sample distribution of means for that distribution.

You only need to specify the sample size, number of replications, and distribution type, then run the function.

```
> SampleSize = 50
> NumReplications = 250
> distType = "Uniform" # Uniform, Normal, Exponential, Bimodal
> chap5a(SampleSize, NumReplications, distType)
```

Note: The *distType* variable is a character string, hence the quotation marks.

```
PROGRAM OUTPUT

                        Inputvalues
Sample Size                  50
Number of Replications     250
Distribution Type       Uniform
```

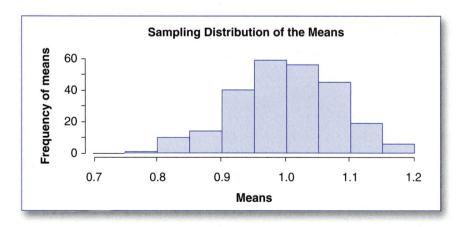

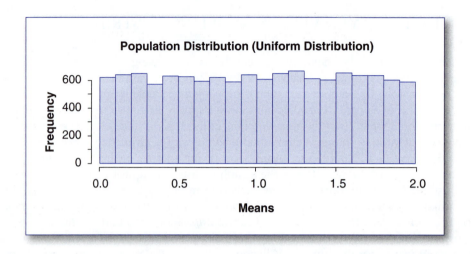

For the same sample size and number of replications but a normal distribution,

```
> SampleSize = 50
> NumReplications = 250
> distType = "Normal"  # Uniform, Normal, Exponential, Bimodal
```

```
PROGRAM OUTPUT
                        Inputvalues
Sample Size                  50
Number of Replications      250
Distribution Type        Normal
```

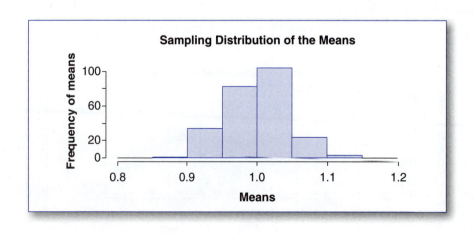

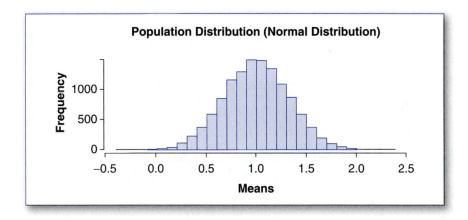

For the same sample size and number of replications but an exponential distribution,

```
> SampleSize = 50
> NumReplications = 250
> distType = "Exponential" # Uniform, Normal, Exponential, Bimodal
```

```
PROGRAM OUTPUT
                        Inputvalues
Sample Size                  50
Number of Replications    250
Distribution Type     Exponential
```

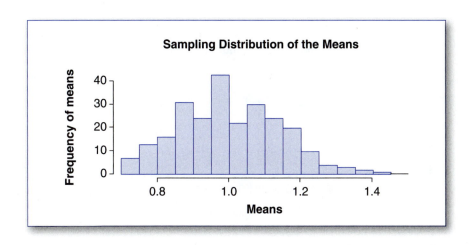

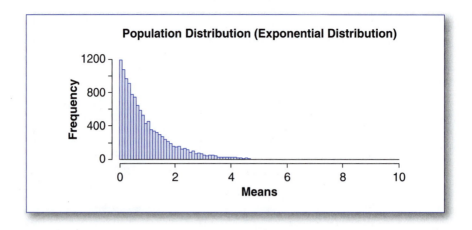

For the same sample size and number of replications but a bimodal distribution,

```
> SampleSize = 50
> NumReplications = 250
> distType = "Bimodal" # Uniform, Normal, Exponential, Bimodal
```

PROGRAM OUTPUT

```
                      Inputvalues
Sample Size                  50
Number of Replications    250
Distribution Type     Bimodal
```

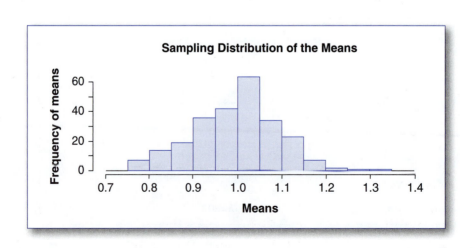

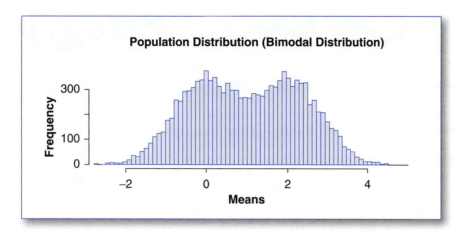

The uniform (rectangular), exponential (skewed), and bimodal (two distributions) are easily recognized as not being normally distributed. The *central limit theorem function* outputs a histogram of each population type along with the resulting sampling distribution of the means, which clearly shows the difference in the frequency distributions. The sampling distribution of the means for each population type is approximately normally distributed, which supports the central limit theorem.

To show even more clearly that the central limit theorem holds, one need only increase the number of replications from 250 to 1,000 or more for each of the distribution types. For example, the sampling distribution of the means for the exponential population distribution will become even more normally distributed as the number of replications (number of sample means drawn) is increased. Figure 5.1 shows the two frequency distributions that illustrate the effect of increasing the number of replications. We can also increase the sample size used to compute each sample mean. Figure 5.2 shows the two frequency distributions that illustrate the effect of increasing the sample size from 50 to 100 for each sample mean. The sampling distribution of the means with increased sample size is also more normally distributed, further supporting the central limit theorem.

```
PROGRAM OUTPUT

                        Inputvalues
Sample Size                  50
Number of Replications   1000
Distribution Type        Exponential


PROGRAM OUTPUT

                        Inputvalues
Sample Size                 100
Number of Replications   1000
Distribution Type        Exponential
```

Figure 5.1 Sampling Distribution of Means: Number of Replications (*n* = 1,000) and Sample Size (*n* = 50)

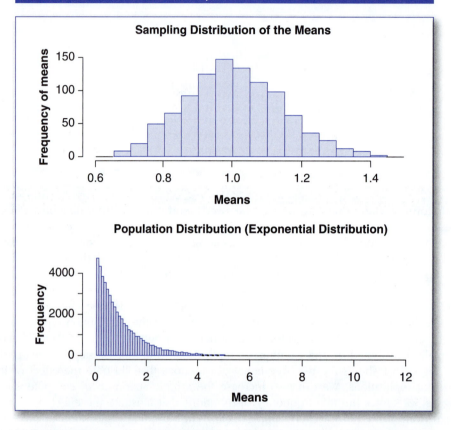

Figure 5.2 Sampling Distribution of Means: Number of Replications (*n* = 1,000) and Sample Size (*n* = 100)

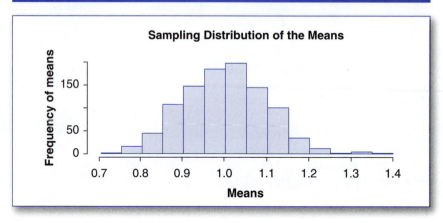

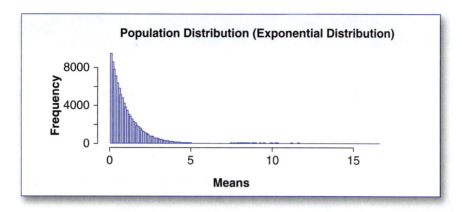

SUMMARY

The central limit theorem plays an important role in statistics because it gives us confidence that regardless of the shape of the population distribution of data, the sampling distribution of our statistic will be normally distributed. The sampling distributions are used with different types of statistics to determine the probability of obtaining the sample statistic. The hypothesis-testing steps covered in the later chapters of the book will illustrate this process of comparing a sample statistic with a value obtained from the sampling distribution, which appears in a statistics table for given levels of probability. This is how a researcher determines if the sample statistic is significant beyond a chance level of probability.

When the number of replications and the size of each sample increases, the sampling distribution becomes more normally distributed. The sampling distribution of a statistic provides the basis for creating our statistical formula used in hypothesis testing. We will explore in subsequent chapters how the central limit theorem and the sampling distribution of a statistic are used in creating a statistical formula and provide a basis for interpreting a probability outcome when hypothesis testing.

TIP

✓ Use *par()* to set the graphical display parameters, for example, two frequency distributions can be printed.

✓ Use *hist()* to display a histogram of the frequency distribution of data.

✓ Use *args()* to display arguments of functions.

✓ You can right-click the mouse on a graph, then select Save to Clipboard.

✓ The central limit theorem supports a normal distribution of sample means regardless of the shape of the population distribution.

✓ Four desirable properties of a sample statistic (sample estimate of a population parameter) are *unbias*, *efficient*, *consistent*, and *sufficient*.

EXERCISES

1. Define the central limit theorem.

2. Explain why the standard deviation is a better measure of dispersion than the range.

3. What percentage of scores fall within ±1 standard deviation from the mean in a normal distribution?

4. What theorem applies when data have a skewed or leptokurtic distribution?

5. Describe the shape of a uniform population distribution in a few words.

6. Describe the shape of an exponential distribution in a single word.

7. Describe the shape of a bimodal distribution in a few words.

8. What are the four desirable properties of a sample statistic used to estimate the population parameter?

TRUE OR FALSE QUESTIONS

T	F	a.	The range is calculated as the largest minus smallest data value.
T	F	b.	An estimate of the population standard deviation could be the sample range of data divided by 6.
T	F	c.	As the sample size increases, the sample distribution becomes normal.
T	F	d.	The sampling distribution of the mean is more normally distributed as the sample size increases, no matter what the original population distribution type.
T	F	e.	Populations with two exclusive categories are called dichotomous populations.
T	F	f.	We expect a mean of 50, given a random sample of data from a uniform distribution of 100 numbers between 0 and 100.
T	F	g.	Sample statistics can be computed for binomial and exponential distributions.

WEB RESOURCES

Chapter R script files are available at http://www.sagepub.com/schumacker

Binomial Function R script file: chap5a.r

Central Limit Theorem Function R script file: chap5b.r

## CHAPTER 6

SAMPLING DISTRIBUTIONS

● INTRODUCTION TO SAMPLING DISTRIBUTIONS

The statement "A statistic is to a sample as a parameter is to a population," is a very important concept in statistics. This basic statement reflects the idea behind taking a random sample from a population, computing a sample statistic, and using that sample statistic as an estimate of the population parameter. The sampling distribution of a statistic is a frequency distribution of the statistic created by taking repeated random samples of a given size from a population. These repeated random samples of a given sample size from a population can produce a sampling distribution of percents, means, correlation, and even standard deviations. *When the population values are known, the population parameter is known, and we would not need to take a sample of data and estimate the population parameter*. Regardless of the type of sampling distribution, the purpose is to determine if the sample statistic is a good estimate of the corresponding population parameter. The sampling distribution of a statistic permits the calculation of the **standard error of the statistic**, which is used in our tests of statistical significance and is necessary when forming a **confidence interval** around the sample statistic. We also find that the standard error of the mean is affected by the sample size; that is, larger sample sizes afford better approximations, resulting in a smaller standard error for the sample statistic.

All sample statistics have sampling distributions, with the variance of the sampling distribution indicating the error in the sample statistic, that is, the error in estimating the population parameter. When the error is small, the statistic will vary less from sample to sample, thus providing us an assurance of a better estimate of the population parameter. Basically, larger sample sizes yield a smaller error or variance in the sampling distribution, thus providing a more reliable or efficient statistical estimate of the population parameter. For example, the mean and median are both sample statistics that estimate the central tendency in population data, but the mean is the more consistent estimator of the population mean because the sampling distribution of the mean has a smaller variance than the sampling distribution of the median. The variance of the sampling distribution of the mean is called the *standard error of the mean*. It is designated in the population of data as

$$\frac{\sigma}{\sqrt{n}},$$

where σ is the population standard deviation and n, the sample size; and it is estimated in a sample of data as

$$S_{\bar{X}} = \frac{S}{\sqrt{n}},$$

where S is the sample standard deviation and $\bar{X}$ represents the sample mean. In the formula, it is easy to see that as the sample size, n, becomes larger, the denominator in the formula becomes larger and the standard error of the statistic becomes smaller; hence, the frequency distribution of the statistic or sampling distribution has less variance. This indicates that a more precise sample estimate is achieved with larger sample sizes. The standard error of a sampling distribution applies to any sample statistic that is used to estimate a corresponding population parameter.

● PROPERTIES OF SAMPLE STATISTICS AS ESTIMATORS OF POPULATION PARAMETERS

An important concern in using sample statistics as estimators of population parameters is whether the estimates possess certain properties. Sir Ronald Fisher (1922) in the early 20th century was the first to describe the **properties of estimators**. The four desirable properties of estimators are *unbiased*, *efficient*, *consistent*, and *sufficient*. If the mean of the sampling distribution of the statistic equals the corresponding population parameter, the statistic is *unbiased*; otherwise, it is a biased estimator. If the sampling distributions of two statistics have the same mean, then the statistic with the smaller variance in the sampling distribution is more *efficient* (more precise or less variable) while the other statistic is an inefficient estimator. A statistic is a *consistent* estimator of the population parameter if the statistic gets closer to the actual population parameter as the sample size increases. If several statistics compete as estimates of the population parameter, for example, mean, median, and **mode**, the statistic that has the most desirable properties is the *sufficient* statistic while the other statistics are insufficient. We are therefore interested in sample statistics that are unbiased, efficient, consistent, and sufficient as estimates of population parameters.

The sample mean (*statistic*) is considered an unbiased, efficient, sufficient, and consistent estimator of the population mean (*parameter*). All sample statistics, however, don't possess all these four properties. For example, the sample standard deviation is a biased but consistent estimator of the population standard deviation. The sample standard deviation therefore more closely approximates the population standard deviation as the sample size increases; that is, it is a consistent, but biased, estimate.

● UNIFORM SAMPLING DISTRIBUTION

The *uniform sampling distribution function* in the R script file (chap6a.r) generates a single sampling distribution for a given sample size from a known uniform population distribution; the R function is *uniform()*. A different sampling distribution exists for every sample of size N, given by *SampleSize* in the R function. Consequently, the function will need to be run several times, each time with a different sample size, in order to determine whether the mean of the sampling distribution more closely approximates the population parameter.

Note: The *set.seed()* function will need to be deleted, otherwise the same results will occur each time.

The uniform population distribution is defined as a random uniform set of numbers from 0 to 100 using the command line *mySample = runif(SampleSize, 0, 100)*, where *runif()* is the built-in R function for generating random numbers from the uniform distribution. The mean is the middle of the interval, $(a + b)/2$, where $a = 0$ and $b = 100$; thus, $(0 + 100)/2 = 50$. The standard deviation is the square root of $(b - a)^2/12$; thus, $\sqrt{(100 - 0)^2 / 12} = 28.8675$.

This basic approach can be used to determine whether any sample statistic is a consistent estimator of a corresponding population parameter, for example, population standard deviation. A sample statistic that estimates a population parameter is unbiased when the average value of the sampling distribution is equal to the parameter being estimated. The sample mean is an unbiased estimator of the population mean if the average of all the sample means in the sampling distribution equals the population mean. The difference between the average of all the sample means and the population mean is the amount of bias, or *sampling error*. This holds true when comparing any sample statistic in a sampling distribution with the population parameter.

The characteristics common to the sampling distribution based on different sample sizes are the most descriptive information we can obtain about theoretical population distributions. The sampling distribution of sample means is therefore a frequency distribution of sample means computed from samples of a given size taken from a population. The variance (*standard deviation*) of the sample means that form the sampling distribution will indicate how precise the sample statistic is as an estimator of the population parameter. The variance of a sampling distribution of a statistic becomes smaller as the sample size increases; that is, the *standard error of the statistic* becomes smaller. In this chapter, you will need to make a judgment about whether or not the sample statistic is a biased or an unbiased estimator of the population parameter.

The sample size and number of replications are the only two values you will need to specify prior to running the function.

```
> SampleSize = 10
> NumReps = 500
> chap6a(SampleSize, NumReps)
```

The function returns the following results:

```
PROGRAM OUTPUT
```

	Values
Sample Size	10
Number of Replications	500
Mean of Distribution	49.54
SD of Distribution	8.925
Square Root of N	3.162
Standard Error	2.822

The output lists the *Sample Size* (the number of scores used to compute each sample mean), the *Number of Replications* (how many sample means to compute), the *Mean of Distribution* (the mean of all the means in the sampling distribution), the *SD of Distribution* (the standard deviation of all the means in the sampling distribution), the *Square Root of N* (the square root of the sample size), and, finally, the *Standard Error* (the standard deviation of the sampling distribution divided by the square root of N). The standard error for this sampling distribution is called the standard error of the mean and indicates the precision of the sampling mean in estimating the population mean.

The mean of the 500 sample means taken at random, each having a sample size of 10, was 49.54. Our known population mean of 50 would suggest a *sampling error* of 50 − 49.54 = 0.46. The standard deviation indicates that 68% of the 500 sample means varied within 49.54 ± 8.925, an indication of how precise our sample statistic is as an estimate of the population mean. We would conclude that the sample mean is an unbiased estimate of the population mean.

The *hist()* function graphs the sampling distribution of the means for sample size = 10 and 500 sample means. The mean of these 500 sample means is 49.54. When compared with the known population mean of 50, the mean of the sampling distribution underestimates the population mean by 0.46 (50 − 49.54). The sampling distribution mean is 49.54 with a standard deviation of 8.925; therefore, ±1 standard deviation or 68% of the sample means fell within (40.615, 58.465) and ±2 standard deviations or 95% of the sample means fell within (31.69, 67.39). This indicates the range of sample mean values in the frequency distribution of the sampling distribution of means.

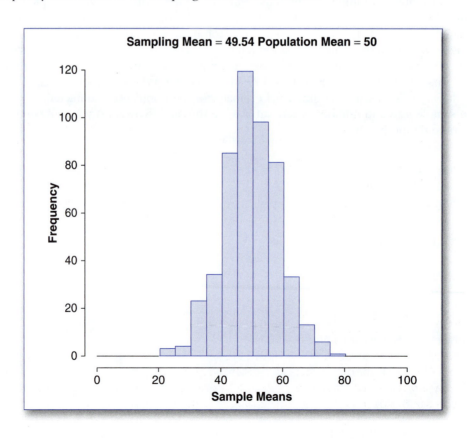

The standard error of the mean is 2.822 and indicates the precision of the sample mean in estimating the population mean. This precision is indicated by 49.54 ± 2.822 for the 68% confidence interval (46.718, 52.36). We interpret this by stating that we are 68% confident that the population mean falls between 46.718 and 52.36. The 95% confidence interval using $t_{.05}$ = 1.96 is (44.00, 55.07). We are more confident with a 95% confidence interval, but the upper and lower values indicate a wider range. A smaller standard error of the mean value would provide a narrower range of values, indicating better precision in the sample mean as an estimate of the population mean. In actual practice, we do not know the population mean, so it is important to calculate the standard error of the statistic and the confidence interval to indicate the range of values that capture the population mean.

To gain a better understanding of how the standard error of a statistic is affected by sample size, the following results are listed for different sample sizes. (*Note:* set.seed() has been deleted, so you will get different results every time you run the function!). Basically, as the sample size for computing the sample mean increases, the standard error decreases, providing a narrower range of lower and upper values in the confidence interval. This is interpreted as providing a more precise sample estimate of the population mean. For example, with sample size = 10, our sample mean = 49.53, and the population mean could be between 46.608 and 52.452. However, increasing the sample size to 50, our sample mean is 49.44, but the population mean is probably between 48.847 and 50.033—a much narrower range. Our interpretation, with sample size = 50, would be that our sample mean of 49.44 is a good estimate of the population mean, which only varies between 48.8 and 50.03.

Sample Size	Sample Mean	Standard Error of Mean	68% Confidence Interval
10	49.53	2.922	46.608, 52.452
20	49.47	1.41	48.052, 50.888
30	49.15	.954	48.196, 50.104
40	49.67	.725	48.945, 50.395
50	49.44	.593	48.847, 50.033

NOTE: These results will vary each time the R function is run.

● ROLE OF CONFIDENCE INTERVALS AND CONFIDENCE LEVELS IN STATISTICS

The *standard error of the mean* is used to establish a confidence interval around a sample statistic that should capture the population parameter. The sample size and the confidence level (68%, 95%) affect the width of the confidence interval. We can gain a better understanding by simulating a number of samples from a known population and determining the confidence intervals of these samples. Basically, the population mean should be within the confidence intervals around the sample statistic for a given sample size and confidence level.

Confidence intervals can be computed for many different population parameters by using the standard error of the statistic and the confidence level. The standard error of the statistic for the previous example was called the standard error of the mean because the sample statistic was the sample mean. We could just as easily investigate the sample standard deviation (S) as an estimate of the population standard deviation (σ). The variance of a sampling distribution indicates the amount of error in estimating the population parameter. Smaller sampling variance reflects less error in estimating the population parameter. The standard error of the statistic is computed as the standard deviation of the sampling distribution divided by the square root of the sample size. Consequently, as the sample size increases, the standard error of the statistic decreases. A confidence interval is computed using the sample statistic and the standard error of the statistic (standard deviation of the statistic in the sampling distribution). The confidence interval around the sample statistic is a range of values that should contain the population parameter. A confidence level is used that defines how confident we are that the interval around the sample statistic contains the parameter being estimated. The confidence interval is determined by picking an area in the tail of the sampling distribution in which the value of the statistic is improbable. Recall that a sampling distribution is a frequency distribution; therefore, we could pick a 5% probability area, leaving 95% of the sample statistics in the frequency distribution as plausible estimates of the population parameter.

The confidence interval around the sample statistic is computed by using the standard error of the statistic. The confidence interval indicates the precision of the sample statistic as an estimate of the population parameter. The confidence interval around the sample statistic is said to include the population parameter with a certain level of confidence. It should be common practice to report confidence intervals for various population parameters such as proportions, means, or correlations. The confidence interval contains a high and a low score, above and below the sample statistic, between which we feel confident the population parameter occurs. Confidence levels are used to determine the width of the confidence interval. Commonly used confidence levels are 90%, 95%, or 99%. These confidence levels for sample data are indicated by a critical t value of 1.65 (10% probability area), 1.96 (5% probability area), and 2.58 (1% probability area), respectively, which are given in Table 2 (Distribution of t for Given Probability Levels).

The 95% confidence interval for the population mean is computed as

$$\bar{X} \pm 1.96\left(\frac{S}{\sqrt{n}}\right),$$

where S is the sample standard deviation, n the sample size, and $\bar{X}$ the sample mean., which are used to compute the standard error of the mean. The value of 1.96 corresponds to the t value that indicates 5% of the sample means in the tail of the sampling distribution that are improbable. This implies that 5 times out of 100 replications, a confidence interval for a sample mean may not contain the population mean. In contrast, 95 times out of 100, the confidence interval around the sample mean will contain the population mean. Stated differently, 5% of the time the sample mean will not be a good estimate of the population mean, or conversely, 95% of the time we are confident that the sample mean will be a good estimate of the population mean. These are probability statements because we typically do not know the value of the population mean, as we are randomly sampling from an infinite population.

If the sample mean was 50, the sample standard deviation 10, and the sample size 100, and we wanted to be 90% confident that the confidence interval captured the population mean, then the confidence interval around the sample mean would range between 51.65 and 48.35. This range of values is computed as

$$CI_{.90} = \bar{X} \pm t\left(\frac{S}{\sqrt{n}}\right) = 50 \pm 1.65\left(\frac{10}{\sqrt{100}}\right) = 50 \pm 1.65$$

$$CI_{.90} = (51.65, 48.35).$$

If we replicated our sampling 10 times, we would expect the population mean to fall in the range of values approximately 90% of the time (i.e., 9 times out of 10 the confidence intervals would contain the population mean).

● SAMPLING DISTRIBUTION OF THE
    MEAN FROM A NORMAL POPULATION

The *sample mean function* in the R script file (chap6b.r) will simulate random samples from a normally distributed population and compute the confidence intervals around the sample mean (the process is the same for other population parameters because it would be based on the sampling distribution of the statistic). A population with a normal distribution ($\mu = 50$ and $\sigma = 10$; μ represents the population mean) will be sampled. Different sample sizes and confidence levels are entered to see the effect they have on estimating the confidence interval. The function uses the population standard deviation rather than the sample standard deviation in the confidence interval formula because it is assumed to be a known value. The 90% confidence interval would be computed as

$$\bar{X} \pm 1.65\left(\frac{\sigma}{\sqrt{N}}\right).$$

If the population standard deviation is known, one would use the population standard deviation with a z value for the confidence interval. If the population standard deviation is *not* known, one would use a sample standard deviation estimate with a critical t value for the confidence interval. The sampling distribution of the mean will be based on 20 replications. For each sample mean, the 90% confidence interval around the mean will be computed, and the function will check to see whether or not the population mean of 50 is contained in the confidence interval. Due to sampling error, one may not achieve the exact number of confidence intervals that contain the population mean as indicated by the confidence level, that is, 90%. The confidence level can be changed to 95% ($z = 1.96$) or 99% ($z = 2.58$) in the function.

You will need to specify the sample size, the number of replications, and a z value for the probability under the normal curve prior to running the function.

```
> SampleSize = 100
> NumReps = 20
```

```
   > Zvalue = 1.65   # Zvalue = 1.65 (90%), Zvalue = 1.96 (95%), or
Zvalue = 2.58 (99%)
   > chap6b(SampleSize, NumReps, Zvalue)
```

The results from the function are printed in the RGui Console window as follows:

```
PROGRAM OUTPUT

Confidence Intervals for Zvalue = 1.65

              Values
Pop. Mean       50
Pop. SD         10
Sample Size    100
Replications    20

Sample Mean CI (high-low) Pop. Mean Within CI
   50.4       52.05-48.75     50    Yes
   50.29      51.94-48.64     50    Yes
   49.33      50.98-47.68     50    Yes
   50.5       52.15-48.85     50    Yes
   50.48      52.13-48.83     50    Yes
   49.21      50.86-47.56     50    Yes
   49.03      50.68-47.38     50    Yes
   50.1       51.75-48.45     50    Yes
   49.44      51.09-47.79     50    Yes
   49.57      51.22-47.92     50    Yes
   49.9       51.55-48.25     50    Yes
   50.08      51.73-48.43     50    Yes
   50.84      52.49-49.19     50    Yes
   52.01      53.66-50.36     50    No
   49.14      50.79-47.49     50    Yes
   49.78      51.43-48.13     50    Yes
   48.52      50.17-46.87     50    Yes
   52         53.65-50.35     50    No
   50.04      51.69-48.39     50    Yes
   48.87      50.52-47.22     50    Yes

Confidence Intervals That Contain Population Mean = 18/20 = 90%
```

SUMMARY

The sampling distribution of a statistic is important in establishing how much the sample statistic varies around the mean of the sampling distribution. The mean of the sampling distribution is our best estimate of the population mean. The variation of the sample statistics in the sampling distribution is used to calculate the standard error of the statistic. The standard error of the statistic is used to create confidence intervals for different confidence levels. The confidence interval reflects a range of values (high, low) around the sample mean for different confidence levels, for example, 90%, 95%, and 99%. A confidence interval indicates the precision of a sample statistic as an estimate of a population parameter. If a confidence interval has a 95% level of confidence, this indicates that approximately 95 out of 100 confidence intervals around the sample statistic will contain the population parameter. If the confidence level remains the same but the sample size increases, the width of the confidence interval decreases, indicating a more precise estimate of the population parameter.

EXERCISES

1. Define each of the four desirable properties of an estimator in a sentence:

    a. unbiased

    b. efficient

    c. consistent

    d. sufficient

2. A sampling distribution is a frequency distribution of a statistic. Name three types of sampling distributions.

3. What is the sample formula for calculating the *standard error of the mean?*

4. Compute the standard error of the mean, given mean = 50, $S = 10$, and $n = 25$.

5. Compute the 95% confidence interval around the sample mean = 50, $S = 10$, $n = 25$ using $t_{.05} = 1.96$. Show your work.

6. Explain the 95% confidence interval obtained in #5.

7. Explain *sampling error* in a few sentences.

8. Explain the difference between confidence intervals and confidence levels in statistics.

TRUE OR FALSE QUESTIONS

T   F   a.   A statistic is a *consistent* estimator of the population parameter if the statistic gets closer to the actual population parameter as the sample size increases.

T   F   b.   If the population parameter is known, then we would not need to take a random sample of the data.

T   F   c.   The standard error of a statistic is not affected by sample size.

T   F   d.   As the sample size for computing the sample means in the sampling distribution increases, the standard error decreases.

T   F   e.   The 95% level of confidence indicates that 95 times out of 100 the sample statistic estimates the population parameter.

WEB RESOURCES

Chapter R script files are available at http://www.sagepub.com/schumacker

Sample Mean Function R script file: chap6b.r

Uniform Sampling Distribution Function R script file: chap6a.r

## CHAPTER 7

STATISTICAL DISTRIBUTIONS

The concept of sampling distributions in the previous chapter provides the basis to understand how several statistical distributions are formed. These statistical distributions are used to create a statistic and compute a statistical test. In addition, the statistical distribution serves to indicate whether the statistical value obtained from a random sample of data would occur beyond a reasonable chance or level of probability. A few popular statistical distributions used by researchers are the z (normal) distribution, used to create a z test for percent differences; the t distribution, used to create the t test for mean differences between two groups; the **F distribution**, used to create the F test for mean differences between three or more groups; and the chi-square (χ^2) distribution, used to create the chi-square test for independence of observations. Without these statistical distributions, we would not know if the sample statistic we calculated was beyond a chance occurrence or level of probability under the respective statistical distribution. These statistical distributions are further explained in this chapter.

● z DISTRIBUTION

The z distribution has certain properties and characteristics that have made it ideally suited to represent the frequency distribution of scores on many variables used by researchers. More important, it has distinct probability areas under a **normal curve** that have proved useful in statistics, that is, to determine the probability of obtaining a certain score. It has a long history of use, which dates back to its being referred to as an *error curve* or a *bell-shaped curve* by de Moivre (1756; Pearson, 1924).

In the 17th and 18th centuries, two mathematicians were asked by gamblers to help them improve their chances of winning at cards and dice. The two mathematicians, who first studied the area of probability under a normal curve, were James Bernoulli and Abraham de Moivre. Bernoulli developed the formula for combinations and permutations, and their binomial expansions, which led to the binomial distribution and approximation to the normal distribution. de Moivre, who first developed probability in games of chance, coined the phrase *law of errors*, from observing events such as archery matches. The basic idea was that negative errors occurred about as often as positive errors. de Moivre used this understanding to derive an equation for an error curve. de Moivre, in 1733, was credited with developing the mathematical equation for the *normal curve*, although some question whether he understood the concept of the probability density function. His work was more in the area of the binomial and multinominal distribution. In the 19th century, Carl Fredrick Gauss (1777–1855), working in the field of astronomy, further developed the concept of a mathematical bell-shaped curve and corresponding areas of probability, which he related to the method of least squares regression (Viklund, 2008). Today, his picture and his mathematical equation for the normal curve appear on the zehn deutsche mark currency of Germany.

The normal curve equation was defined by Gauss as

$$Y = \frac{1}{\sigma\sqrt{2\pi}} e^{-(x-\mu)^2/2\sigma^2},$$

where

Y = the height of the curve at a given score,

X = the score at a given height,

μ = the mean of the X variable,

σ = the standard deviation of the X variable,

π = a constant equal to 3.1416 (pi), and

e = a constant equal to 2.7183 (base of the natural logarithm).

When a set of X scores is transformed to have a mean of 0 and a standard deviation of 1, the scores are called standard scores or z scores, and the Gauss mathematical equation can be reduced to

$$Y = \frac{1}{\sqrt{2\pi}} e^{-z^2/2}.$$

This equation using standard scores (z scores) is referred to as the *standard normal curve*, with z-score values that range primarily from −4 to + 4 and correspond to the ordinates of Y (density or height of the curve).

The Carl Friedrich Gauss equation for the standard normal probability density function can be computed using the following R command for y, with x ranging from −4 to +4 for 200 data points:

```
> x = seq(-4,4, length = 200)
> y = 1/sqrt(2 * pi) * exp(-x^2/2)
> plot(x, y, type = "l", lwd=2)
```

The *plot()* function displays the bell-shaped curve derived from the equation, which today is referred to as the normal curve or normal distribution based on z scores.

The normal distribution or normal curve is a mathematical equation for random chance errors. The frequency distribution of scores from continuous variables used in research closely approximates the normal distribution. Consequently, the normal distribution is a useful mathematical

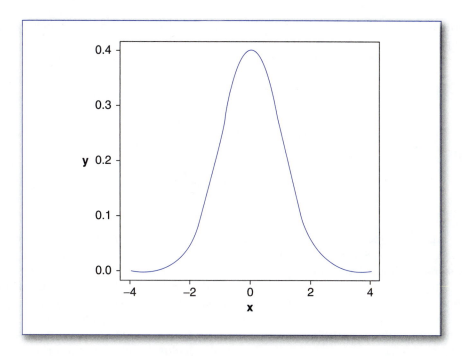

model in which to study variable relationships in the physical and social sciences. The mathematical equation for the normal distribution indicates a normal density that is an **exponential function** of a quadratic form. The normal curve equation defines an infinite number of curves, depending on the values of the mean and standard deviation used in computing z scores. A z score is calculated as

$$z = \frac{(X - \mu)}{\sigma},$$

where μ is the population mean and σ the population standard deviation. However, we seldom know the population mean or population standard deviation, so we substitute our sample statistic values. The sample z score is then calculated as

$$z = \frac{(X - \bar{X})}{S}.$$

The z score indicates the deviation of a score from the sample mean in standard deviation units.

Table 7.1 indicates the z-score values between −4 and +4 in 0.5 increments corresponding to each y-ordinate value (Hinkle et al., 2003). A graph of these values yields a normal distribution or bell-shaped curve that has an asymptote or y ordinate = 0.3989 for a z score of 0. These z scores and y ordinates can be plotted to obtain a *rough approximation* to what the normal curve would be if all z-score and y-ordinate values were plotted with a smooth curved line. For example,

```
> z = c(-4.0,-3.5,-3.0,-2.5,-2.0,-1.5,-1.0,-.5,0,.5,1.0,1.5,2.0,
2.5,3.0,3.5,4.0)
```

```
> y = c(.00003,.0002,.0044,.0175,.0540,.1295,.2420,.3984,.3989,
.3984,.2420,.1295,.0540,.0175,.0044,.0002,.00003)
```

```
> plot (z, y, type = "l", main = "Normal Distribution", xlab = "z
scores", ylab = "Y ordinates")
```

Note: The argument *type = l* (this is a lowercase *L*, not the number *1*) designates drawing a line rather than data points. See Help("plot") for other function arguments.

The standard normal distribution with a mean of 0 and a standard deviation of 1 has important characteristics used in statistics. The standard normal distribution is bell-shaped and symmetrical. The probability area under the standard normal curve is 1.0, corresponding to 100% of the area under the curve. The density function is reasonably complex enough that the usual method of finding the probability area between two specified values requires using integral calculus to calculate the probabilities. The standard normal table of z values in the appendix of textbooks has been derived by this method of integral calculus. It is not necessary, therefore, to use calculus to derive the exact probabilities because tables of probabilities under the normal curve are provided in statistical textbooks. They are also routinely output in statistical packages.

The family of distributions for the normal distribution can also be used to generate the normal bell-shaped curve after providing the function parameters. For example, recall that *dnorm()* gives the density, *pnorm()* gives the distribution function, *qnorm()* gives the quantile distribution, and *rnorm()* generates random sampled data points. So to obtain the standard normal distribution, enter the following commands to generate a random sample of 200 data points, then create a histogram of the data points, which will be more normally distributed as the sample size increases,

```
> y = rnorm(200, mean = 0, sd = 1)
> hist(y)
```

Table 7.1 z-Score and y-Ordinate Values

z Score	y Ordinates
−4.0	0.00003
−3.5	0.0002
−3.0	0.0044
−2.5	0.0175
−2.0	0.0540
−1.5	0.1295
−1.0	0.2420
−0.5	0.3984
0.0	0.3989
+0.5	0.3984
+1.0	0.2420
+1.5	0.1295
+2.0	0.0540
+2.5	0.0175
+3.0	0.0044
+3.5	0.0002
+4.0	0.00003

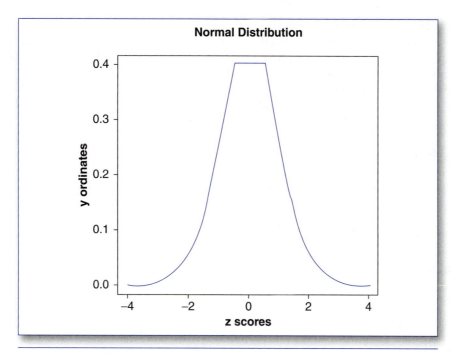

NOTE: Plot is an approximation to the normal curve using the data in Table 7.1.

or plot the values using the density function *dnorm()*:

```
> x = seq(-4,4, by = .1)
> y = dnorm(x)
> plot(x, y, type = "l", main = "Normal Distribution", xlab = "z
scores", ylab = "Y ordinates")
```

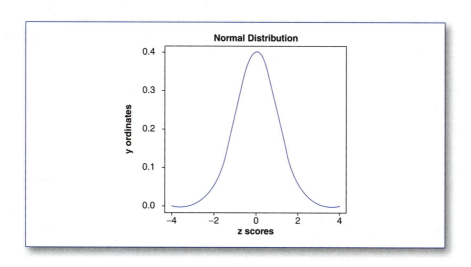

The *z distribution function* in the R script file (chap7a.r) can be run to compare the true population percent with the sample percent, where the difference is due to sampling error. The function approximates the standard normal probabilities—instead of our having to use calculus or values from a table in a statistic book, where the algorithm has a calculation error of less than 0.001.[1] Initial values are set for 1,000 random numbers between the *z*-score intervals 0 and 4 to correspond to ±4 standard deviations around the mean. The *DensityHeight* value is fixed at 0.3989, corresponding to the normal distribution *y*-ordinate asymptote value (normal curve height is calculated as $1 / \sqrt{(2*3.1416)} = 0.3989$). Changing the *IntervalMax* value to 3 can change the function to modify the range of *z*-score values to correspond to ±3 standard deviations around the mean.

You will enter values for the number of points, and the minimum and maximum range of values, then run the function.

```
> NumPoints = 1000
> IntervalMin = 0
> IntervalMax = 4
> chap7a (NumPoints, IntervalMin, IntervalMax)
```

The function will return the following values:

```
PROGRAM OUTPUT

Sample Size = 1000 Width +/- 4

      Result
Sample P = 0.507
True P   = 0.500
Error    = 0.007
```

The *Error* value will change each time you run the function because a *set.seed()* function value was not specified in the function. This output indicates that the sampling error was 0.007, or the difference between the true population percent (*True P*) and the sample percent (*Sample P*).

The *z*-score normal distribution also permits determination of the probability of selecting a number under the *z*-score normal distribution. For example, the area under the standard normal curve that is 1/2 standard deviations to the left of *x* (0.5) or 1/2 standard deviations to the right of the mean can be computed using the *pnorm()* function:

```
> pnorm (.5, mean = 0, sd = 1)
[1] 0.6914625
```

The results indicate that if we draw a number at random from the standard normal distribution, the probability that we will draw a number less than or equal to 0.5 is .69, or 69% of the total area under the normal curve (note that 31% of the area is left over). Also note that from −4 to 0, the normal curve represents 50% of the total area under the normal curve, while 19% of the area falls between 0 and 0.5 standard deviations. The remaining 31% of the total area is between +0.5 and +4 standard deviations.

To visually see the shaded 69% area under the standard normal distribution, the following R commands can be used:

```
> x = seq(-4,4, length = 200)
> y = dnorm(x)
> plot(x, y, type = "l", lwd = 2)
> x = seq(-4,.5, length = 200)
> y = dnorm(x)
> polygon(c(-4,x,.5), c(0,y,0), col = "gray")
```

The R commands can be placed in the File > New Script, R Editor window and then run using the Edit > Run All commands in the pull-down RGui menu.

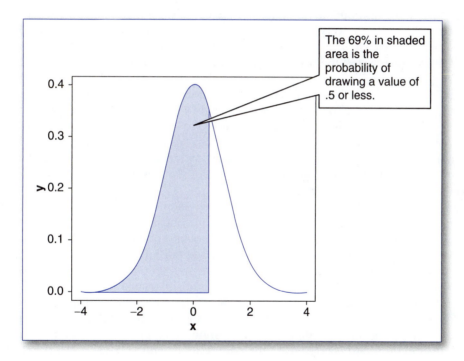

We can also do the opposite, that is, indicate the probability area under the normal distribution and obtain the corresponding z-score value. For example, what is the z score that corresponds to the probability area $p = .6914625$? The *qnorm()* function returns the z-score value of 0.50, which corresponds to the $p = .69$ or 69% probability area:

```
> qnorm(0.6914625, mean = 0, sd = 1)

[1] 0.500000
```

The normal distribution according to the Carl Friedrich Gauss equation was an exponential function that yielded a symmetrical curve with equal halves, but the bell-shaped curve never touches the x-axis. The normal distribution has an infinite number of different curves based on the values of the mean and standard deviation, with the normal probability density function based on z scores called the standard normal curve or standard normal distribution. We use the normal distribution with a sample of data to determine where a raw score converted to a z score falls under the normal distribution, thereby determining if the raw score has a probability of occurrence beyond a chance level.

● *t* DISTRIBUTION

The early history of statistics involved estimating probability and inference using large samples and the normal distribution. The standard normal curve provided a probability distribution that was bell-shaped for large samples but peaked for small samples, which resulted in larger probability areas in the tails of the distribution. At the turn of the century, a chemist named William S. Gossett, who was employed at a brewery in Dublin, Ireland, discovered the inadequacy of the normal curve for small samples. Gossett was concerned with the quality control of the brewing process and took small samples to test the beer, but he didn't obtain a normal bell-shaped curve when his results were graphed.

Gossett empirically established sampling distributions for smaller samples of various sizes using the body measurements of 3,000 British criminals. He started with an approximate normal distribution, drawing large samples and small samples, to compare the resulting sampling distributions. He quickly discovered that probability distributions for small samples differed markedly from the normal distribution. Gossett wrote a mathematical expression for these small sample distributions, and in 1908, he published the results under the pen name *Student*. *Student's t* distribution was a major breakthrough in the field of statistics.

The standard normal distribution is bell-shaped, symmetrical, and unimodal and has a mean of 0 and standard deviation of 1. The *t* distribution is unimodal and symmetrical and has a mean of 0 but not a standard deviation of 1. The standard deviation of the *t* distribution varies, so when small sample sizes are drawn at random and graphed, the *t* distribution is more peaked (leptokurtic). The probability areas in the tails of the *t* distribution are consequently higher than those found in the standard normal distribution. For example, the probability area = .046 ~ .05 in the standard normal distribution at 2 standard deviations from the mean, but the probability area = .140 in the *t* distribution at 2 standard deviations for a sample size of four. This indicates a greater probability of making an error using smaller samples when referring to the probability area under the normal distribution. As sample sizes become larger, the *t* distribution and standard normal distribution take on the same bell-shaped curve; that is, they become the same. In fact, the *t* values and the *z* values become identical around sample sizes of 10,000, which is within the 0.001 error of approximation, as indicated in the previous chapter. Researchers today often use the *t* distribution for both small-sample and large-sample estimation because the *t* values become identical to the *z* values in the normal distribution as the sample size increases.

In many disciplines, such as education, psychology, and business, variable data values are normally distributed. Achievement tests, psychological tests, the height or weight of individuals, and the time to complete a task are examples of variables commonly used in these disciplines. In many instances, the population mean and standard deviation for these variables are not known but rather are estimated from the sample data. This forms the basis for making an inference about the population parameters (e.g., mean and standard deviation) from the sample statistics (sample mean and standard deviation). Given small random samples, the *t* distribution would better estimate the probability under the frequency distribution curve. Given large random samples, the standard normal distribution and the *t* distribution would both yield similar probabilities under the frequency distribution curve.

The *z* values (and corresponding *t* values) are computed somewhat differently than the *z* value used previously to form the normal distribution. We are now interested in testing how far the sample mean (sample statistic) is from the population mean. The square root of *n* is included in the denominator of the formula to account for the change in the shape of the frequency distribution (and thus the area under the probability curve) due to varying sample sizes, which affects the probability area under the *t* distribution. If the population standard deviation is known, the *z* score can be computed as

$$z = \frac{\bar{X} - \mu}{\sigma / \sqrt{n}}.$$

Otherwise, the sample standard deviation can be used to compute a *t* value:

$$t = \frac{\bar{X} - \mu}{S / \sqrt{n}}.$$

We usually do not know the population mean, therefore the *t* statistic is calculated using the following equation, where the population mean is set to 0:

$$t = \frac{\bar{X} - 0}{S / \sqrt{n}}.$$

The sample standard deviation, *S*, as an estimate of the population standard deviation, σ, is typically in error (sample values do not always equal the population values), thus the sample means are not distributed as a standard normal distribution but rather as a *t* distribution. When sample sizes are larger, the sample standard deviation estimate becomes more similar to the population standard deviation; then, the shape of the *t* distribution becomes similar to that of the standard normal distribution.

This points out why the estimate of the population standard deviation is critical in the field of statistics. A researcher can estimate the unknown population standard deviation by one of the following methods:

1. Using test publisher norms when available (μ, σ)

2. Taking an average value from several research studies using the same variable

3. Taking large samples of data for better representation

4. Dividing the range of sample data by 6 (the approximate range of normal distribution)

We can quickly generate the *t* distribution similar to the *z* distribution by using one of the family of distribution functions (*dt()*, *pt()*, *qt()*, and *rt()*). For example, a random sample of 40 data points for *y* with 5 degrees of freedom (*df*) can be plotted across the ±4 range of scores with the *y*-ordinate set from 0 to 0.40 (recall that the density height of *y*-ordinate values is 0.3989).

```
> y = rt(40,5)
> plot(function(y) dt(y, df = 5), -4, 4, ylim = c(0,0.40), main =
"Central t - Density", yaxs = "i")
```

A plot of the sampling distributions of the *t* values will permit a visual display of the probability area underneath the curve and show that the curve is more peaked for the *t* distribution than for the *z* distribution with small sample sizes. If we increase the sample size and the **degrees of freedom**, then the *t* distribution equals the *z* distribution; that is, it becomes normally distributed.

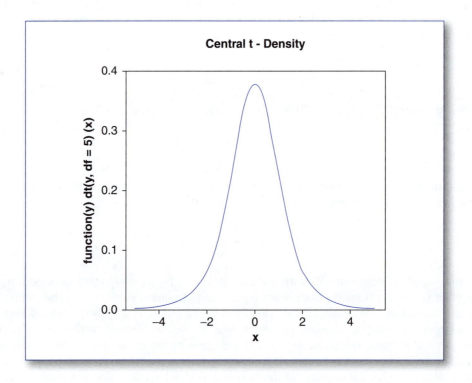

The *t distribution function* in the R script file (chap7b.r) will select a random sample (*N* = 10), compute the sample mean and sample standard deviation, and then calculate the *z* and *t* statistics. This will be repeated 500 times. The resulting 500 *z* and *t* statistics will be tabulated and printed in frequency tables. A comparison of the frequency tables will show higher probabilities in the heavier tails of the *t* distribution as compared with the *z* distribution for this small sample size. The histogram of the *z* statistic and *t* statistic will be displayed to illustrate their similarity as the sample size increases. By varying the sample size, the shape of the *t* distribution will change and more closely approximate the normal distribution—that is, become less peaked (leptokurtic).

You will enter values for the population mean, population standard deviation, sample size, and number of replications, then run the function.

```
> popMean = 0
> popSD = 1
```

```
> sampleSize = 10
> repSize = 500
> chap7b(popMean, popSD, sampleSize, repSize)
```

The function will return the following output:

```
PROGRAM OUTPUT

                          Result
Pop Mean =                  0
Pop SD =                    1
Sample Size =              10
Number of Replications = 500

Interval     Freq t Freq z
(-4.0,-3.5) 0.002   0.002
(-3.5,-3.0) 0.004   0.002
(-3.0,-2.5) 0.014   0.008
(-2.5,-2.0) 0.016   0.014
(-2.0,-1.5) 0.032   0.040
(-1.5,-1.0) 0.114   0.102
(-1.0,-0.5) 0.126   0.136
(-0.5, 0.0) 0.198   0.208
(0.0, 0.5)  0.188   0.186
(0.5, 1.0)  0.146   0.146
(1.0, 1.5)  0.070   0.092
(1.5, 2.0)  0.044   0.040
(2.0, 2.5)  0.024   0.016
(2.5, 3.0)  0.010   0.004
(3.0, 3.5)  0.004   0.004
(3.5, 4.0)  0.002   0.000
```

The following is a plot of z and t statistical values for $N = 10$:

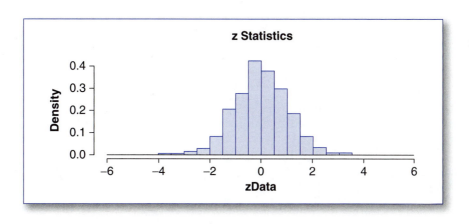

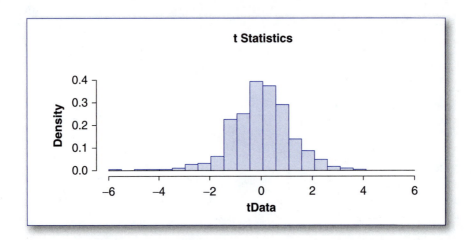

As a rule, the probability is higher for *t* values than for *z* values under the frequency distribution, given a small sample size.

If we increase the sample size to 1,000 in the function, then the probabilities become more similar, and the two frequency distributions look similar in the graph.

```
PROGRAM OUTPUT

Pop Mean  =      0
Pop SD  =        1
Sample Size = 1000
Number of Replications = 500

Interval       Freq t  Freq z
(-4.0,-3.5)    0.000   0.000
(-3.5,-3.0)    0.004   0.004
(-3.0,-2.5)    0.006   0.006
(-2.5,-2.0)    0.020   0.020
(-2.0,-1.5)    0.028   0.028
(-1.5,-1.0)    0.112   0.114
(-1.0,-0.5)    0.158   0.156
(-0.5,0.0)     0.180   0.180
(0.0,0.5)      0.186   0.182
(0.5,1.0)      0.168   0.170
(1.0,1.5)      0.092   0.090
(1.5,2.0)      0.030   0.032
(2.0,2.5)      0.008   0.012
(2.5,3.0)      0.008   0.006
(3.0,3.5)      0.000   0.000
(3.5,4.0)      0.000   0.000
```

The following is a plot of z and t statistical values for $N = 1,000$:

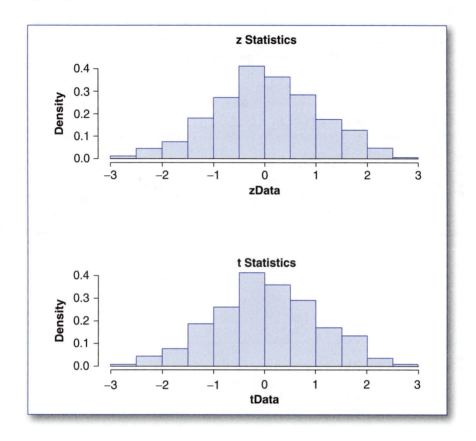

From the t-distribution intervals for $N = 10$, we can see the frequency of t values in the intervals of 1.5 and higher in both tails of the distribution. For $t > +1.5$, $p = .068$ (.032 + .016 + .014 + .004 + .002). For $t < -1.5$, $p = .084$ (.044 + .024 + .010 + .004 + .002). The combined probability for $t > +1.5$ and $t < -1.5$ is $p = .152$. From the same intervals in the t distribution with $N = 1,000$, we find for $t > +1.5$ that $p = .046$ (.030 + .008 + .008 + .000 + .000) and for $t < -1.5$ that $p = .058$ (.028 + .020 + .006 + .004 + .000). The combined probability for $t > +1.5$ and $t < -1.5$ is $p = .104$. The comparison of probabilities for $N = 10$ and $N = 1,000$ indicates a sample size effect for the frequency of t values ($p = .152$ for $N = 10$; $p = .104$ for $N = 1,000$). The frequencies of the t and z values for $N = 10$ are dissimilar, while the frequencies of the t and z values for $N = 1,000$ are similar. This is why the t table in Appendix A is used for determining the probability in the sample distribution, because it adjusts for the probability in the distribution given small sample sizes. When the sample size becomes large enough, $t = z$, so either will yield the same frequency of values or probability in the sample distribution.

A comparison of z and t probabilities when $N = 1,000$ points out that $z = t$ for larger samples sizes; thus, the probability area under the curve is more similar. When sample sizes are smaller, the t distribution should be used to determine the probability of obtaining a t value. When sample sizes are larger, the t or z distribution tables can be used because the probability areas under the distributions are similar. Researchers typically use the t values, knowing that they will eventually equal the z values when their sample sizes are large enough. The use of t values keeps researchers from making a mistake in the probability of obtaining a t statistic from a sample of data. The t distribution table in Appendix A only provides t values for certain probability levels (.20, .10, .05, .02, .01, .001). Computer programs use algorithms to compute and print out the sample t statistic, degrees of freedom, and corresponding p value, which is obtained from the specific statistical distribution generated for the degrees of freedom. Researchers are therefore given the exact p value for their sample t statistic on the computer printout.

Degrees of freedom in statistics are determined by $n - 1$ observations. This implies that one observation or statistical value is determined or known, while the others are free to vary. For example, suppose we had five numbers: 1, 2, 3, 4, and 5. The sum of the five numbers is 15, and the mean is 3. If we knew the sum (15) and the mean (3) but only had the numbers 2, 3, 4, and 5, the missing number is determined or fixed. It can only be 1, to obtain the sum and mean values. Therefore, we have 4 degrees of freedom, that is, four numbers can vary, but the fifth number is determined or fixed. This also applies to a statistical distribution. If we had a frequency distribution of 100 sample means, then $df = 99$; that is, one sample mean will always be determined or fixed given knowledge of the other 99 sample means and their sum and average.

● *F* DISTRIBUTION

The F distribution, named after Sir Ronald A. Fisher, was formed to determine the probability of obtaining an F value. The F value is generally computed as a ratio of variances. Fisher was interested in extending our knowledge of testing mean differences to analysis of the variability of scores, that is, variance of the sample scores. He was specifically interested in comparing the variance of two random samples of data. For example, if a random sample of data was drawn from one population and a second random sample of data was drawn from a second population, then the two sample variances could be compared by computing an F *ratio*, the ratio of the larger sample variance over the smaller sample variance: $F = S_1^2 / S_2^2$. The F ratio has an expected value equal to 1.0 if the variances of the two random samples are the same, otherwise it increases positively to infinity (∞). The F distribution in Appendix A reveals this for F values with $df = \infty, \infty$ in the numerator and denominator. (The F ratio could be less than 1.0 depending on which sample variances were in the numerator and the denominator, but F values less than 1.0 are not considered, so we always place the larger sample variance in the numerator.)

If several random samples of data were drawn from each population and the F ratio computed on the variances for each pair of samples, a sampling distribution of the F values would create the F distribution. Fisher determined that like the t distribution and **chi-square distribution**, the F distribution was a function of sample size, specifically the sizes of the two random samples. Consequently, a family of **F curves** can be formed based on the degrees of freedom in the numerator and the denominator. An F curve is positively skewed, with F-ratio values ranging from 0 to ∞. If the degrees of freedom for both samples are large, then the F distribution approaches symmetry (bell-shaped).

There exists a family of distributions for the F value (similar to the z and t distributions)—that is, $df()$, $pf()$, $qf()$, and $rf()$. These can be used to easily display the F distribution for varying pairs of degrees of freedom. For example, we can plot the density curve for the *F* distribution with 4 and 10 degrees of freedom using the *plot()* function with *type = l* (lowercase *L*, to draw lines):

```
> x = seq(0,4, length = 100)
> y = df(x, 4, 10)
> plot(x, y, type = "l")
```

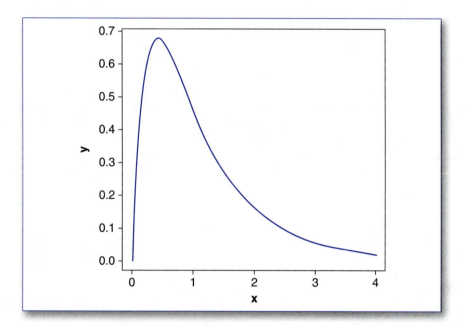

F curves for other degree-of-freedom pairs are also possible, as illustrated by the following graph:

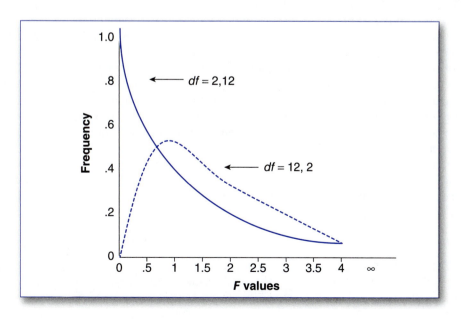

Because there are 2 degrees of freedom associated with an F ratio, F tables were constructed to list the F values expected by chance, with the degrees of freedom for the numerator across the top (column values) and the degrees of freedom for the denominator along the side (row values). The corresponding intersection of a column and row would indicate the tabled F value for a certain probability level. If the computed F value is greater than the tabled F value, we conclude that the two sample variances are statistically different at a specified level of probability, for example, the .05 level of probability.

Hartley F_{max} Test

The early work of Fisher was expanded to include a formal test of the equality of variances. The assumption of equal variances in groups became important when testing mean differences in an analysis of variance. We have previously learned that an extreme value can inflate the mean, which would inflate any mean difference. So having groups with similar variances indicates that no groups have inflated means, thus providing for a fair test of mean differences.

Test of Difference Between Two Independent Variances

The sampling distribution of the F ratio of two variances cannot be approximated by the normal, t, or chi-square sampling distributions because sample sizes seldom approach infinity and, unlike the normal and t distributions, F sampling distributions range from 0 to ∞ rather than from $-\infty$ to $+\infty$. Consequently, the F distribution will need to be used to test whether two independent sample variances are the same or different.

The ratio of the two sample variances is expressed as $F = S_1^2 / S_2^2$, with a numerator and a denominator degrees of freedom. For example, the distance *20 suburban* housewives traveled to the grocery store varied by 2 miles, and the distance *10 rural* housewives traveled to the grocery store varied by 10 miles. We want to test if the suburban and rural mileage variance is equal: $F = 10/2 = 5.0$, with $df_1 = 9$ and $df_2 = 19$. (*Note:* Degrees of freedom are 1 less than the respective sample sizes.) We compare this computed F ratio with the tabled F value in the Appendix A for a given level of significance, for example, the .01 level of significance. We find the 9 degrees of freedom (df_1) across the top of the F table and the 19 degrees of freedom (df_2) along the side of the table. The intersection of the column and row indicates an F value equal to 3.52. Since $F = 5.0$ is greater than the tabled $F = 3.52$, we conclude that the *rural* housewives vary more in their mileage to the grocery store than the *suburban* housewives. Another way of saying this is that the sample variances are not homogeneous (equal) across the two groups. Since we conducted this test for only the larger variance in the numerator of the F ratio, we must make a correction to the level of significance. This is accomplished for any tabled F value by simply doubling the level of significance, for example, .01 to .02 level of significance. Therefore, $F = 5.0$ is statistically different from the tabled $F = 0.52$ at the .02 level of significance (even though we looked up the F value in the .01 level of significance table).

Test of Difference Between Several Independent Variances

H. O. Hartley (1950) extended the F ratio test to the situation in which three or more sample variances were present, which was aptly named the **Hartley F_{max} test**. A separate F_{max} distribution table was therefore created (Appendix A). The Hartley F_{max} test is limited to using equal sample sizes and sample data randomly drawn from a normal population. Henry Winkler, in 1967 at Ohio University, compared the Hartley F_{max}, Bartlett, Cochran, and Levene tests for equal variances in his master's thesis and concluded that the Hartley F_{max} test was the most robust (best choice) when sample sizes were equal.

For example, the amount of variance in study hours for freshman, sophomore, junior, and seniors in high school for a sample size of 61 students is indicated below. The Hartley F_{max} test uses the largest variance over the smallest variance in the groups as follows:

Step 1. Calculate the sample variances:

Freshman $\quad S^2 = 5$

Sophomore $\quad S^2 = 4$

Junior $\quad S^2 = 10$

Senior $\quad S^2 = 2.$

Step 2. Calculate the F_{max} test by placing the largest variance over the smallest variance:

$F_{max} = 10/2 = 5.0.$

Step 3. Determine the two separate degree-of-freedom values for the F_{max} test (Table 7, Appendix A):

k = number of sample variances (column values in the table)

$k = 4$

df = sample size − 1 (row values in the table)

$df = 61 − 1 = 60.$

Step 4. Compare the computed F_{max} with the tabled F_{max} values at the .01 significance level (Table 7, Appendix A):

$F_{max} = 5.0$ is greater than the tabled $F_{max} = 2.3$ for 4 and 60 degrees of freedom at the .01 level of significance. We conclude that the sample variances are *not* homogeneous (not the same) across the four groups.

F Functions

The *F distribution function* in the R script file (chap7c.r) will compute *F* values that correspond to the number of observations (*numRep*) and the numerator (df_1) and denominator (df_2) degrees of freedom using the *df()* function. The function is initially set to replicate 100 times with $df_1 = 2$ and $df_2 = 9$, then plot the *F* values using the *plot()* function. Changing the number of observations and degrees of freedom for the numerator and denominator will create different *F*-distribution curves. You only need to enter the two degree-of-freedom values and the number of replications and then run the function.

```
> df1 = 2
> df2 = 9
> numRep = 100
> chap7c(df1, df2, numRep)

PROGRAM OUTPUT

                            Result
Df1 =                         2
Df2 =                         9
Number of Replications = 100
```

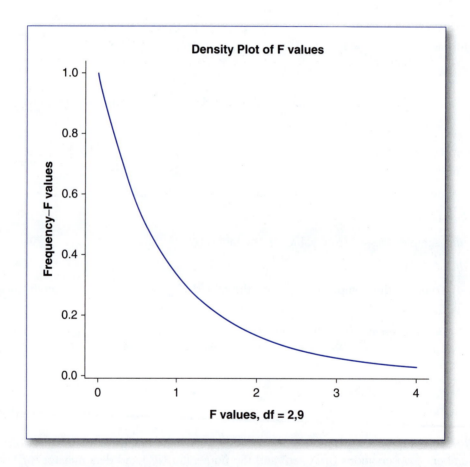

The *F ratio function* in the R script file (chap7d.r) provides a simple way to examine whether the variances from two independent samples of data are equal or different. The function requires the sample size and variance for each set of data plus the alpha or probability level. The *F ratio* computed is compared with the *F-critical value* found in the table in Appendix A for a given degree-of-freedom value and **alpha level**. If the *F*-ratio value is less than the *F*-critical value, then the *Decision* is to accept the assumption of equal variances between the two groups. If the *F*-ratio value is greater than the *F*-critical value, then the *Decision* is to reject. A good rule to follow is if the two sample variances have a ratio of 4:1, then reject. A couple of examples will illustrate the 3:1 ratio and 4:1 ratio concepts for testing whether sample variances are equal (accept) or different (reject).

We need to enter the sample size and variance for each along with an alpha probability level, then run the function.

F Ratio Function

```
> sampSize1 = 20
> variance1 = 30
> sampSize2 = 20
> variance2 = 10
> alpha = .01
> chap7d(sampSize1, variance1, sampSize2, variance2, alpha)
```

The results print out the sample size and variance values for the groups, plus the alpha level. The *F* ratio is reported with the critical *F* and the decision whether to accept or reject the assumption of equal variances between the two groups.

```
PROGRAM OUTPUT

                    Result
Sample Size 1 =  20.00
Variance =          30.00
Sample Size 2 =  20.00
Variance =          10.00
Alpha =              0.01


F ratio F Critical Decision
   3         3.03        accept
```

Changing the ratio of variances to 40:10 yields the following results:

```
PROGRAM OUTPUT

                    Result
Sample Size 1 =  20.00
Variance =          40.00
Sample Size 2 =  20.00
Variance =          10.00
Alpha =              0.01


F ratio F Critical Decision
   4         3.03        reject
```

In the first run, the F ratio = 30/10 = 3.0 (3:1), with the F-critical value = 3.03 at the .01 level of probability. The F ratio is less than the F-critical value, so our *Decision* is to accept, that is, that the two variances are equal. However, when the F ratio = 40/10 = 4.0 (4:1), with the F-critical value = 3.03 at the .01 level of probability, the F ratio is greater than the F-critical value, so our *Decision* is to reject the assumption of equal variances for the two samples.

● CHI-SQUARE DISTRIBUTION

It may seem surprising to learn that the chi-square distribution is based on the normal distribution. In fact, the chi-square values are computed as $\chi^2 = (N - 1)S^2/\sigma$ (where S^2 is the variance of a sample of size N from a normal distribution with variance σ^2). The chi-square distribution (χ^2), like the z, t, or F distribution, is a function of sample size. There are an infinite number of chi-square frequency curves based on sample size. In fact, as the sample size increases, the chi-square distribution becomes symmetrical and bell-shaped (normal), but with a mean equal to the degrees of freedom and mode equal to $df - 2$. The distribution of the chi-square values can also be graphed to visually see the effect of sample size on the shape of the chi-square distribution.

Karl Pearson first derived the chi-square distribution as a frequency distribution of squared z-score values. The **chi-square statistic** was computed as

$$\chi^2 = \Sigma\left(\frac{X_i - M}{\sigma}\right)^2,$$

with $df = N - 1$. A z score was calculated as $z = [(X - M)/\sigma]$, where X is a raw score, M the sample mean, and σ the population standard deviation. The z score transformed a raw score into a standard score based on standard deviation units. The population standard deviation (σ) is indicated in the formula, but as noted in earlier chapters, a sample standard deviation estimate was generally used because the population value was not typically known.

Chi-square is related to the variance of a sample. If we squared both the numerator and the denominator in the previous formula, we would get

$$\chi^2 = \frac{\Sigma(X - M)^2 / N - 1}{\sigma^2}.$$

The numerator of the formula can be expressed as the sample variance because $\Sigma(X - M)^2$ represents the **sum of squared deviations**, denoted as SS; so the sample variance in the numerator can be written as $S^2 = SS/(N - 1)$. With a little math, $SS = (N - 1)S^2$. Consequently, if samples of size N with variances S^2 are computed from a normal distribution with variance σ^2, the chi-square statistic could be written as

$$\chi^2 = \frac{(N - 1)S^2}{\sigma^2},$$

with $N - 1$ degrees of freedom. The chi-square statistic is therefore useful in testing whether a sample variance differs significantly from a population variance, because it forms a ratio of sample variance to population variance. Since the chi-square distribution reflects this ratio of variances, all chi-square values are positive and range continuously from 0 to +∞.

The chi-square distribution also has a family of distributions similar to the *z*, *t*, and *F* distributions (*dchisq()*, *pchisq()*, *qchisq()*, *rchisq()*). A few simple commands can generate a plot of the chi-square distribution for different degree-of-freedom values. For example, the chi-square distribution for *df* = 5 would be generated and graphed by the following R commands:

```
> x= seq(0,30)
> df = 5
> chisqvalues = dchisq(x, df)
> plot(x, chisqvalues, type = "l", main = "Density Plot of Chi-
square values",
    Xlab = paste("Chi-square values, df =", df), ylab = "Frequency -
Chi-square values")
```

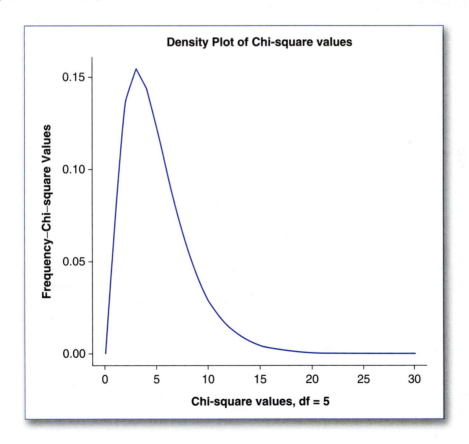

The *chi-square function* in the R script file (chap7e.r) can produce an unlimited number of chi-square distributions, one for each degree of freedom. For small degree-of-freedom values, the chi-square distribution should be skewed right. As the degrees of freedom increase, that is, the sample size increases, the mode of the chi-square distribution moves to the right. The chi-square values should be positive and range continuously from 0 to +∞. The function permits selection of different sample sizes from a normal distribution. The function will initially select 250 samples of the desired sample size. The chi-square statistic is calculated each time. The 250 sample results will simulate the theoretical chi-square distribution. The 250 chi-square statistics are graphed using the *hist()* function. Since you can vary the underlying normal distribution and the sample size, you will have an opportunity to observe the effect of the sample size (degree of freedom) on the chi-square distribution.

You will need to enter the population mean, population standard deviation, sample size, and number of replications, then run the function.

```
> popMean = 0
> popSD = 1
> sampleSize = 6
> repSize = 250
> chap7e(popMean, popSD, sampleSize, repSize)
```

The function results print out the values you entered plus a histogram of the chi-square values:

```
PROGRAM OUTPUT

                 Result
Pop Mean =          0
Pop SD =            1
Sample Size =       6
Replications =    250
```

A random sample of size $N = 6$ was drawn from a normal distribution (mean = 0, standard deviation = 1), and a chi-square value was computed each time for 250 replications. A visual graph of the chi-square frequencies indicates the expected skewed distribution for the given sample size. Chi-square values for different degrees of freedom are tabled in Appendix A for a select number of probability levels. Researchers use the table to determine if the sample chi-square value is greater than or less than the chi-square critical value from the theoretical distribution one would expect by chance alone. We can also obtain the critical chi-square value for a given probability level using the *pchisq()* function. For example, if we obtained a sample chi-square = 15 from the distribution above, what is the probability level under the curve?

```
> pchisq(15,5)
[1] 0.9896377
```

A chi-square = 15 with 5 degrees of freedom falls at the .9896 ~ .99 probability area under the chi-square distribution. This corresponds to approximately $p = .01$ of the probability area beyond

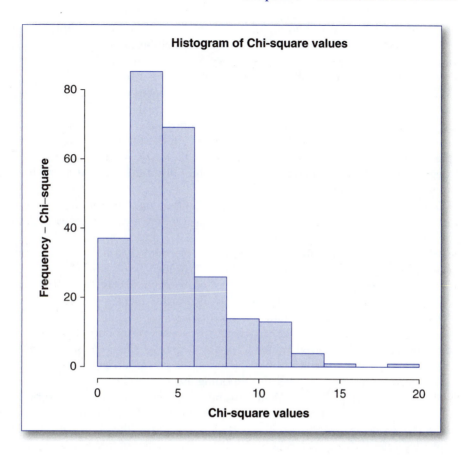

the chi-square value of 15. If we look at the table of critical chi-square values in Appendix A, we find that chi-square = 15.086 at $p = .01$ for 5 degrees of freedom.

● RELATIONSHIP BETWEEN z, t, F, AND CHI-SQUARE STATISTICAL DISTRIBUTIONS

In this chapter, sampling distributions of statistics were graphed based on various sample sizes. We learned that with large sample sizes, t values and z values were similar, as were their sampling distributions (frequency distributions). Like the t distribution, the chi-square distribution is also a function of sample size. In fact, as the sample size increases, the t, z, and chi-square sampling distributions will become more symmetrical and bell-shaped (normal). The sampling distribution of the F ratio also operates similar to the t, z, and chi-square families of statistical distributions based on sample size.

The t distribution with degrees of freedom equal to infinity is the normal distribution. Consequently, t values become equal to z values when sample sizes are large ($n > 10,000$ to ∞). Check this by referring to the last row of the tabled t values in Appendix A, where you will find that the

t values are the same as the z values in the normal distribution table. For example, $t = 1.96$ is equal to $z = 1.96$ at the .05 level of significance. The normal distribution can be considered a special case of the t distribution because as the sample size increases the shape of the t distribution becomes the same as that of the normal distribution, that is, t values $= z$ values.

The F distribution with 1 degree of freedom in the numerator and the same degree of freedom in the denominator is a t value that is equal to the square of the t-distribution value. To check this, refer to the first column of the tabled F values ($df_1 = 1$) in Appendix A, where you will find that the F values are the square of the t values in the t-test table ($df_2 =$ degrees of freedom for the t test). For example, if $F = 3.84$, then $t = 1.96$ for $df_1 = 1$ and $df_2 = \infty$. In fact, $t^2 = z^2 = F$ for 1 degree of freedom given large samples, so the t distribution and normal distribution are special cases of the F distribution.

The F-distribution values with degrees of freedom in the denominator equal to ∞ can be multiplied by the F-value numerator degrees of freedom to compute a chi-square value. To check this, refer to the last row of the tabled F values in Appendix A, where you will find that the F values multiplied by the corresponding numerator degrees of freedom (df_1) equal the chi-square values in the chi-square distribution table. For example, $F = 2.10$ for $df_1 = 6$ and $df_2 = \infty$ at the .05 level of significance; therefore, $\chi^2 = 12.60$ with 6 degrees of freedom, that is, $6 * 2.10 = 12.60$. Table 4 shows the chi-square value ($df = 6, p = .05$) to be 12.592. Consequently, the chi-square distribution is also a special case of the F distribution.

The statistical distributions are created based on a frequency distribution of the statistical values. An attempt to list all of the statistical values for every degree of freedom (sample size) would be overbearing. Therefore, what statistics books have done is create tables with degrees of freedom corresponding to certain probability levels for reporting the expected or critical statistic values. Typical probability levels are .10, .05, and .01 in most tables, which correspond to the probability area under the statistical distribution. For each of these probability levels and a given degree of freedom, the statistic in the frequency distribution is reported. For example, the chi-square distribution table in Appendix A indicates a chi-square value of 18.493 for 30 degrees of freedom and probability level $= .95$ ($p = .05$). This is the expected chi-square value from the chi-square statistical distribution. So if you obtain a random sample of data with 30 degrees of freedom and then compute a sample chi-square value, it can be compared with this tabled value. If your sample chi-square value is greater than this tabled value, you would conclude that your sample statistic is significant beyond a chance level, at the .95 level of probability, so it falls in the remaining .05 area under the curve.

TIP

✓ Statistical distributions comprise the family of distributions:

z Distribution: *dnorm()*, *pnorm()*, *qnorm()*, and *rnorm()* in library Normal{stats}

t Distribution: *dt()*, *pt()*, *qt()*, and *rt()* in library TDist{stats}

F distribution: *df()*, *pf()*, *qf()*, and *rf()* in library FDist{stats}

Chi-square distribution: *dchisq()*, *pchisq()*, *qchisq()*, and *rchisq()* in library Chisquare{stats}

✓ You can obtain a list of distributions in the stats package:

```
> help("distributions")
```

✓ You can obtain a full list of all functions in the stats package:

```
> library(help = "stats")
```

✓ Use the Help menu to obtain plot function arguments:

```
> Help("plot")
```

✓ The family of distributions with root names is as seen here:

Distribution	Root name
Beta	Beta
Cauchy	Cauchy
Chi-square	Chisq
Exponential	Exp
F	F
Gamma	Gamma
Normal	Norm
Student's t	T
Uniform	Unif
Weibull	Weibull

TIP

✓ Degrees of freedom is an important concept in statistics and statistical tests.

Degrees of freedom are related to sample size because they usually take on a value of $N - 1$. The degree-of-freedom concept relates to the number of values or parameters free to vary. If a set of five numbers is given, for example, {5 4 3 2 1}, and the sum of the numbers is known, that is, $\Sigma X = 15$, then the knowledge of four of the numbers implies that the fifth number is not free to vary. For example, suppose four out of five numbers are 10, 15, 25, and 45 and $\Sigma X = 100$. Since the four numbers sum to 95, the fifth number must be 5 for the sum of the five numbers to equal 100. This same principle applies to a set of numbers and the mean. If the mean = 20 and $\Sigma X = 100$, then the sample size must be $N = 5$, since $100/5 = 20$.

EXERCISES

1. What is the z score that corresponds to a raw score of 7 given mean = 10, $S = 2$, and $n = 30$?

2. Generate a random sample of 500 data points for y with mean = 0 and $S = 1$, then graph in a histogram. Show the R commands and histogram.

3. Explain the difference between the normal distribution and the t distribution.

4. What is the t value that corresponds to mean = 10, $S = 2$, and $n = 30$?

5. Define degrees of freedom in a few sentences.

6. Calculate the F test for comparing the wind temperature variance of 10 for a sample size of 41 with the heat temperature variance of 5 for a sample size of 61. Given a .01 level of probability, are the wind and heat temperature variances the same or different?

7. A researcher computed a $\chi^2 = 5$ with 3 degrees of freedom. What is the probability area beyond this chi-square value?

8. Briefly explain how the z, chi-square, t and F distributions are the same.

TRUE OR FALSE QUESTIONS

T   F   a.   Statistical distributions are used to create a statistic or a statistical test.

T   F   b.   The normal distribution or curve is a mathematical equation for random chance errors.

T   F   c.   The probability area under the normal curve is 100%.

T   F   d.   As sample sizes become larger, the t distribution and standard normal distribution become the same.

T   F   e.   Statistical distributions are a function of sample size.

NOTE

1. To avoid entering a standard normal probability table into the function, an approximation was used (Derenzo, 1977). For $A \geq 0$, the approximation is

$$P(Z < A) = 1 - \frac{1}{2}\exp\left[-\frac{((83A + 351)A + 562)A}{703 + 165A}\right],$$

in which 1/2 exp(x) means 1/2 e^x. This approximation has an error of no more than 0.001 for sample sizes of 10,000 or more, which you may recall was the minimum sample size from pseudorandom number generation to obtain a close approximation to true randomness.

WEB RESOURCES

Chapter R script files are available at http://www.sagepub.com/schumacker

Chi-Square Function R script file: chap7e.r

F Distribution Function R script file: chap7c.r

F Ratio Function R script file: chap7d.r

t Distribution Function R script file: chap7b.r

z Distribution Function R script file: chap7a.r

PART III

DESCRIPTIVE METHODS

## CHAPTER 8

GRAPHING DATA

● BASIC GRAPH FUNCTIONS

The graphical display of data is very important in understanding the type of variables in your study. The type of graph depends on the variable level of measurement, that is, are variable values nominal, ordinal, interval or ratio. Different types of graphs are therefore used depending on the data. We will explore some of the popular ways data are displayed using R functions.

Pie Chart

The **pie chart** is used to display frequency counts or percents in mutually exclusive categories. It is displayed as a circle that is partitioned into the different mutually exclusive categories. The set of mutually exclusive categories in the pie chart should be exhaustive so that the category values sum to 100%. The pie chart uses summary or aggregate data, so it is limited to nominal data. The R function is *pie()*, and the help command is *?pie*, which provides the arguments that can be used with the command.

The following data indicate the number of students attending 2-year community college, 4-year university, or trade schools in Alabama: Community College ($n = 60,000$; 10%), University ($n = 500,000$; 83%), and Trade School ($n = 40,000$; 7%). This represents all students attending some type of education, thus considered exhaustive mutually exclusive categories for our purpose. Notice that the *names* are placed outside the circle. Also notice that I have provided the N and percent for each category and given a title with the total number of students. All of this information is important to be able to show the number and percentage in each labeled category of the pie chart. Also, the density and angle arguments in the *pie()* function were used so that lines rather than colors are drawn in the pie chart. The pie chart was created using the following R commands:

```
> student = c(60000,500000,40000)
> names(student) = c("Community College(60k - 10%)","University
(500k - 83%)","Trade School (40k - 7%)")
> pie(student, main = "Number of Students Attending School
(N = 600,000)", density = 10, angle = 15 + 10 * 1:6)
```

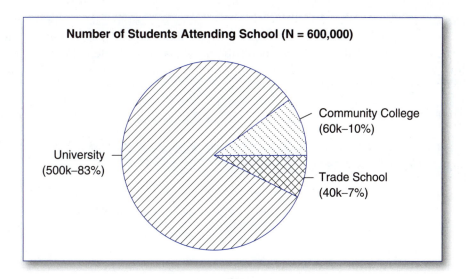

Note: The default pie chart selects one of six colors automatically (function arguments allow you to select different colors). However, unless you have a color printer or save output for a power point presentation, these will turn out solid black when making copies.

Bar Chart

The *bar chart* displays categorical data in a vertical or horizontal position. Each category is separated on the bar chart. The *y*-axis and *x*-axis are labeled. The bar chart is useful for displaying the frequency of each category in an ordinal manner—that is, ranked from least to most. The R function is *barplot()*, where *?barplot* help command displays the arguments. There are more arguments for this function, which indicates that you have more graphical control over how to display the bar chart. I have chosen to use additional arguments to label the *y*-axis, establish a range of values for the *y*-axis, and add the total number of students below the *x*-axis.

We will use the same data from the pie chart, but notice that the data vector, *student*, now has values entered in a specific order (least to most). Also notice that the labels, *names*, have been rearranged to correspond to the data and one of the titles has been shortened to fit on the *x* axis of the bar chart. We can use additional arguments to set the upper and lower values for the *y*-axis using the *ylim* argument, label the *y* and *x* axes, and place *N* below the *x*-axis.

```
> student = c(40,60,500)

> names(student) = c("Trade School(40k - 7%)","Community
(60k - 10%)","University(500k - 83%)")

> barplot(student, main = "Number of Students Attending School",
sub = "(N = 600,000)", xlab = "Type of School", ylab = "Frequency
(in thousands)", ylim = c(0,1000))
```

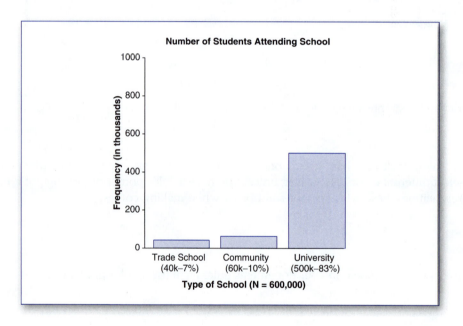

The bar chart could also be displayed in a horizontal rather than vertical position by adding or changing other arguments in the function. We would add *horiz = TRUE* to have the data displayed in a horizontal position. The data vector, *student*, now uses values in thousands. This makes it easier to display tick marks on the *y*-axis. We would need to change the *ylim* to an *xlim* range and change the *ylab* and *xlab* titles. Finally, shortening one of the category titles makes it easier to print on the *y*-axis. The *barplot()* function with these changes would produce the chart in a horizontal position as follows:

```
> student = c(40,60,500)

> names(student) = c("Trade School(40k - 7%)","College
(60k - 10%)","University(500k - 83%)")
```

```
> barplot(student, main = "Number of Students Attending School",
ylab = "Type of School (N = 600,000)", xlim = c(0,1000), xlab =
"Frequency (in thousands)", horiz = TRUE)
```

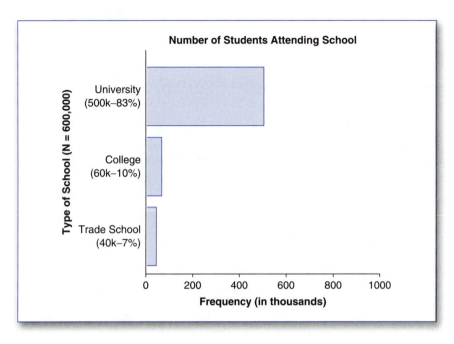

Note: The R barplot function wraps around to the next sentence, but in the R script window, these will need to be on the same line.

Histogram

A **histogram** is a graph that displays the frequency distribution of numerical data for different categories of events, individuals, or objects. Histograms are a popular way to graph data, often seen in newspapers and magazines. Histograms display data similar to a bar chart, but they are not the same. Data used with histograms indicate frequency or proportion for intervals, not categories. Visually, the bars are contiguous or connected, rather than displayed as separate bars, so it represents the distribution of data.

The R function to display data in a histogram is *hist()*, with associated arguments available using the *?hist* help command in the R script window. A simple example with no arguments is shown for a set of test scores. The data vector, *scores*, contains the test scores.

To display them in a histogram, simply use the data vector name in the *hist()* function as follows:

```
> scores = c(70,71,72,73,74,75,76,77,78,79,80,81,82,83,84,85,86,
87,88,89,90)
> hist(scores)
```

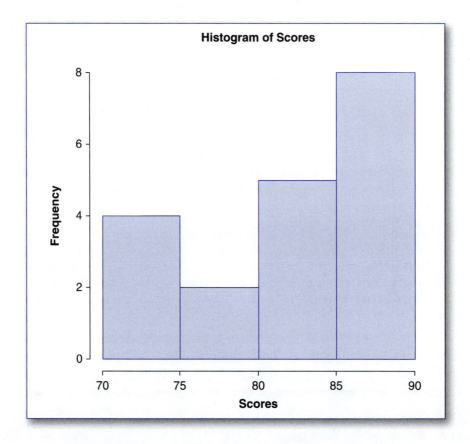

The histogram by default labels the *y*-axis and *x*-axis, inserts a title, and establishes a 5-point range for the data values on the *x*-axis and a 2-point range on the *y*-axis. If this is acceptable, no arguments need be included in the histogram function. Notice that the horizontal bars are connected indicating a distribution of data across the *score* intervals. The histogram has no argument permitting it to be printed in a vertical position similar to the bar chart.

Ogive

An **ogive** is a graph of the cumulative frequency distribution of numerical data from the histogram. A **cumulative frequency distribution** indicates the successive addition of the number of events, individuals, or objects in the different categories of the histogram, which always sums to 100. An ogive graph displays numerical data in an S-shaped curve, with increasing numbers or percentages that eventually reach 100%. An ogive always increases from 0% to 100% for the cumulative frequencies. Because cumulative frequency distributions are rarely used in newspapers and magazines, most people never see them. Frequency data from a histogram, however, can easily be displayed in a cumulative frequency ogive.

Histograms, and therefore ogives, have different shapes and vary depending on the frequency distribution of data. The shape of a histogram determines the shape of its related ogive.

When a uniform histogram is flat, its ogive is a straight line sloping upward. An increasing histogram has higher frequencies for successive categories—its ogive is concave shaped. A decreasing histogram has lower frequencies for successive categories—its ogive is convex shaped. A unimodal histogram contains a single mound—its ogive is S-shaped. A bimodal histogram contains two mounds—its ogive can be either reverse S shaped or double S shaped depending on the data distribution. A right-skewed histogram has a mound on the left and a long tail on the right—its ogive is S shaped with a large concave portion. A left-skewed histogram has a mound on the right and a long tail on the left—its ogive is S shaped with a large convex portion. Given the many shapes possible, it is no wonder that examining the frequency distribution of data for your variables is so important in statistics.

The *frequency function* in the script file (chap8a.r) displays the frequency distribution data in both a histogram and a corresponding ogive graph. These are both output in the same GUI window using the *par()* function. The *par()* function permits changing the size and content of the graphic output window; *?par* provides the arguments used for configuring the graphic window.

The *frequency function* uses 10 categories, and the frequency data for each category are not listed; rather the categories are numbered 1 to 10. The frequency data for each of the 10 categories must be entered into the function, and the frequencies must be integers greater than 0. The function will list the frequencies entered along with the relative frequencies and the less-than-or-equal cumulative relative frequencies. Some rounding error may occur in the calculations when summing the relative frequencies to obtain the cumulative relative frequencies. The *par(mfrow = c(2,1))* function indicates that two graphs can be output in a single column. The relative frequencies indicate the percentage in each category (histogram), while the relative cumulative frequency indicates the sum of these values across the categories (ogive). Notice that although the frequencies in the histogram categories are decreasing, the ogive will always increase from 0% to 100%.

You only need to input the values in a data vector, *Class*, then run the function.

```
> Class = c(50,45,40,35,30,25,20,15,10,5)

> chap8a(Class)
```

PROGRAM OUTPUT

	Freq.	Relative Freq.	Rel Cum Freq.
Class 1	50	0.18	0.18
Class 2	45	0.16	0.35
Class 3	40	0.15	0.49
Class 4	35	0.13	0.62
Class 5	30	0.11	0.73
Class 6	25	0.09	0.82
Class 7	20	0.07	0.89
Class 8	15	0.05	0.95
Class 9	10	0.04	0.98
Class 10	5	0.02	1.00

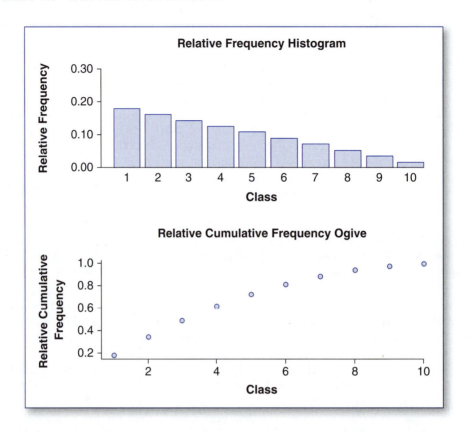

Stem-and-Leaf Plot

Another way to display frequency data is with a **stem-and-leaf plot**, which is a type of histogram. The *stem()* function is used to graph a stem-and-leaf plot, *?stem* provides the arguments used in the function. In graphing stem-and-leaf data, a decision must be made about the number of groups that will contain data. A few large groups may obscure information, and too many small groups may make summarization meaningless. Consider the following data set of weights (in pounds) for UPS (United Parcel Service) parcel post packages:

1.2	3.6	2.7	1.6	2.4
3.5	3.1	1.9	2.9	2.4

The **stem** would be the numbers in the ones position or 1, 2, and 3, while the **leaf** would be the numbers in the tenths or decimal place position that corresponds to each of the stem numbers. The numbers to the left not only form the stem but also indicate the number of groups. The numbers to the right in the tenths place are the leaf. For example, in the stem-and-leaf plot, the "1 | 269" represents the numbers 1.2, 1.6, and 1.9. Since there is only one number listed for the stem, there is only one group—that is, only a one for each digit in the stem. The stem-and-leaf plot for all the data with three groups would be as follows:

A finer subdivision could have been displayed in the stem-and-leaf plot. For example, see the bottom plot on the right.

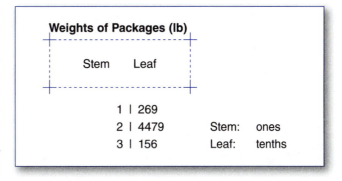

There are six groups in this stem-and-leaf plot. The first stem only has leaf values from 1.0 to 1.4, while the second stem has leaf values from 1.5 to 1.9, and so on. The choice of stems (or groups) will affect the look of the frequency distribution. A stem-and-leaf plot of adult heights in inches could have a stem in tens with the leaf in ones. A stem-and-leaf plot of family incomes might have a stem in ten thousands with the leaf in thousands. A stem-and-leaf plot is a convenient way to summarize data, but the number of stems greatly affects the shape of the frequency distribution. The number of stems can make the stem-and-leaf plot either unimodal or bimodal. However, for some data sets, a change in the stem causes very little change in the shape of the frequency distribution.

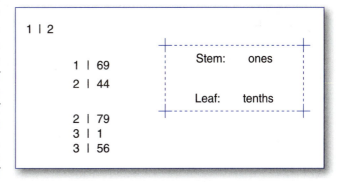

The *stem-leaf function* in the R script file (chap8b.r) inputs two data sets with 50 student grades each, which range between 0 and 100 inclusive. The function prints two versions of a stem-and-leaf plot for each set of student grades. The first set of student grades has a stem-and-leaf plot with 11 groups followed by 6 groups. The second set of student grades has a stem-and-leaf plot with 15 groups followed by 8 groups. It is a subjective decision as to which of the two plots provides a better display of the data. You will need to input values for the variables *Grades1* and *Grades2* in a data vector, then run the function.

```
> Grades1 = c(0,15,23,27,30,31,35,37,41,44,45,47,50,55,58,59,61,61,
64,64,66,68,69,70,71,71,72,72,73,74,74,85,85,85,87,88,88,88,88,90,9
1,92,92,92,94,94,96,98,99,100)

> Grades2 = c(30,31,36,38,42,44,45,47,50,53,53,54,56,58,58,59,61,
62,63,64,65,66,67,69,70,71,72,74,75,76,77,77,80,80,83,83,85,87,88,
89,91,92,93,94,95,97,97,99,100,100)

> chap8b(Grades1, Grades2)
```

The function will return the values for the first data set (*Grades1*) with the stem-and-leaf output for 11 groups and then 6 groups. Next, the second data set is listed (Grades2) with the stem-and-leaf output for 15 groups and then 8 groups.

```
PROGRAM OUTPUT

First Data Set

 [1]   0 15 23 27 30 31 35 37 41 44 45 47 50 55 58 59 61 61 64
[20]  64 66 68 69 70 71 71 72 72 73 74 74 85 85 85 87 88 88 88
[39]  88 90 91 92 92 92 94 94 96 98 99 100
```

11 Groups: First Data Set

The decimal point is 1 digit(s) to the right of the |

```
  0 | 0
  1 | 5
  2 | 37
  3 | 0157
  4 | 1457
  5 | 0589
  6 | 1144689
  7 | 01122344
  8 | 55578888
  9 | 0122244689
 10 | 0
```

6 Groups: First Data Set

The decimal point is 1 digit(s) to the right of the |

```
  0 | 05
  2 | 370157
  4 | 14570589
  6 | 114468901122344
  8 | 555788880122244689
 10 | 0
```

Second Data Set

```
 [1] 30 31 36 38 42 44 45 47 50 53 53 54 56 58 58 59 61 62 63
[20] 64 65 66 67 69 70 71 72 74 75 76 77 77 80 80 83 83 85 87
[39] 88 89 91 92 93 94 95 97 97 99 100 100
```

15 Groups: Second Data Set

The decimal point is 1 digit(s) to the right of the |

```
  3 | 01
  3 | 68
  4 | 24
  4 | 57
  5 | 0334
```

```
 5 | 6889
 6 | 1234
 6 | 5679
 7 | 0124
 7 | 5677
 8 | 0033
 8 | 5789
 9 | 1234
 9 | 5779
10 | 00
```

8 Groups: Second Data Set

The decimal point is 1 digit(s) to the right of the |

```
 3 | 0168
 4 | 2457
 5 | 03346889
 6 | 12345679
 7 | 01245677
 8 | 00335789
 9 | 12345779
10 | 00
```

Scatterplot

A **scatterplot** displays pairs of numbers for *y* and *x* variables, which are called coordinate points. This can be accomplished using either the *dotchart()* function or the *plot()* function. They both display pairs of numbers, but the *plot()* function is more versatile. The *plot()* function displays the pairs of numbers for two variables, *?plot* provides the arguments to use in the function. This function is useful for understanding the relationship between two variables. The variable values can increase, decrease, or simply look like a shot gun blast (circle of data points).

The following example illustrates the use of the *dotchart()* function. Given a set of students test scores (*y*) and their corresponding number of hours spent studying (*x*), a graph is displayed with the coordinate points indicated by a dot (circle). The first variable entered in the function appears on the *x*-axis and the second variable on the *y*-axis. I have created a graphics window with two-inch borders using the *par()* function, listed the *x*-axis from 60 to 100 using the *xlim* argument, and then labeled the *x*-axis and *y*-axis.

```
> scores = c(70,75,80,85,90,98)
> hours = c(5,7,8,10,15,20)
> par(mai = c(2,2,2,2))

> dotchart(scores, hours, xlab = "Study Time", ylab = "Test Scores",
xlim = c(60,100))
```

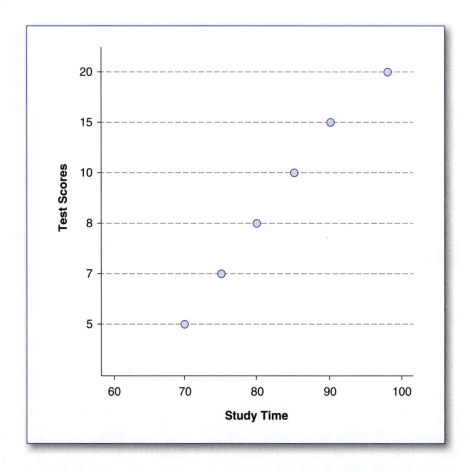

The graph shows that as the number of hours spent studying increases, the test scores increase. In other words, a positive linear relationship exists between hours spent studying and test scores.

The next example illustrates the use of the *plot()* function. Given the same set of students' test scores (*y*) and their corresponding number of hours spent studying (*x*), a scatterplot graph can be displayed. The function also inserts the *x* variable first followed by the *y* variable.

```
> scores = c(70,75,80,85,90,98)
> hours = c(5,7,8,10,15,20)
> plot(scores, hours)
```

The scatterplot graph shows a slightly different increase in the coordinate points because of the plot window configuration. The *plot()* function is more versatile because it prints the variable names for *x* and *y*, permits changes in the symbol used for displaying the coordinate points, and draws a line connecting data points, rather than a circle. The scatterplot displays the coordinate

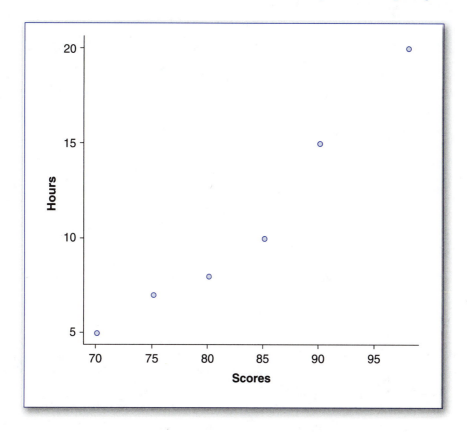

data points or pairs of scores. It visually reveals that as the number of hours spent studying increases, the test scores tend to increase accordingly, same as before.

An argument that can be used in the plot function is *type*, which permits displaying data points, lines, overlay plots, histogram like vertical lines, and stair steps across intervals. You can also label the *y*-axis and *x*-axis using *ylab* and *xlab*, respectively. For example, inserting *type* = *"l"* (lowercase letter *L*) in the plot function with labels for the axes, yields the following graph:

```
> plot(hours, scores, type = "l", ylab = "Test Scores", xlab =
"Hours Spent Studying")
```

The graph now contains lines across the intervals rather than coordinate data points and provides better labeling of the two axes. If you wanted both the data points and the lines, then use *type* = *"b"* in the plot function. Notice that the value for the *type*, *ylab*, and *xlab* arguments must be in quotation marks. It is common in computer programming that text be placed in quotes.

There are other functions, *abline()*, *lines()*, and *curves()*, which are used in conjunction with the plot function. These will be explained in the chapters on correlation and regression statistical methods. They provide the option of printing the statistical values along with either straight or curved lines in the scatterplot graph.

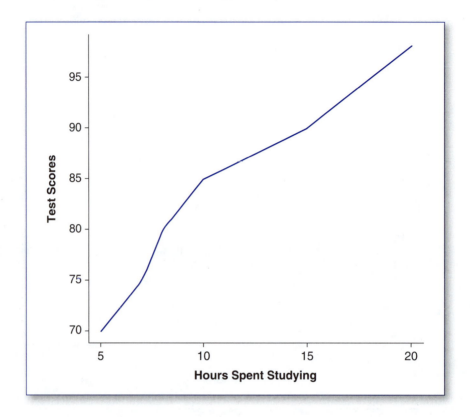

Box-Whisker Plot

A **box-whisker** plot displays the distribution of scores on a variable where the middle of the data distribution is indicated. A box is placed around this middle value to indicate the upper and lower range of values where 50% of the scores are distributed. Extending out the top and bottom of the box are two lines referred to as whiskers, hence the name "box-whisker plots."

The *boxplot()* function displays the data and *?boxplot* provides the arguments that can be used in the function. I used the test scores from the previous example with the basic box plot function to produce the box plot. The middle score is 82.5 and indicated by a dark line drawn in the box. The top and bottom lines drawn around this middle line in the box indicates where 50% of the scores fall—that is, between 75 and 90. The whiskers or lines extending up and down from the top and bottom of the box indicate the top 25% and bottom 25% of the score distribution, respectively.

```
> scores = c(70,75,80,85,90,98)
> boxplot(scores)
```

If we add more test scores to the data vector, *scores*, we can see the value of using a box plot function to display the data for our variables. I have added a label for the *y*-axis, *ylab*, and set the range of values using *ylim*. The *scores* data vector and box plot function are now run as follows:

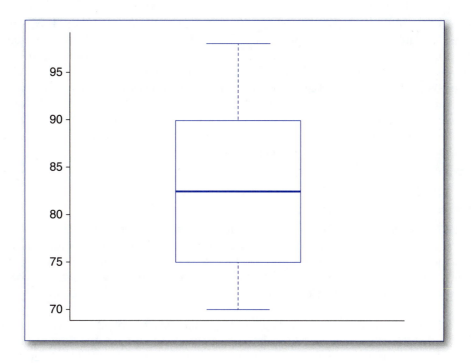

```
> scores = c(20,70,72,75,80,84,85,90,95,98)
> boxplot(scores, ylab = "Test Scores", ylim = c(0,100,10))
```

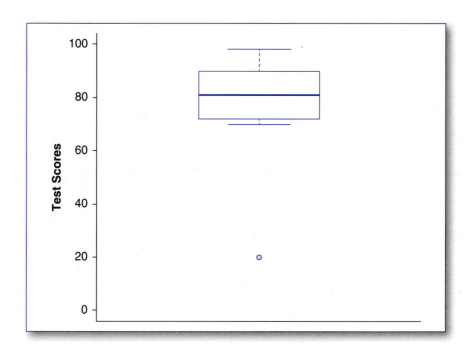

The middle value of 82 is indicated by the dark line in the center of the box, with 50% of the scores indicated by the box. Approximately 50% of the scores fall between test scores of 73 and 89. The whisker line extending from the top is around a test score of 99, and the whisker line extending from the bottom is around 70, which indicate the top 25% and bottom 25% of the test scores. The box-whisker plot also shows a data point value of 20, which falls well below the box-whisker plot (circle at bottom of plot). This indicates an extreme score that is not typical of the test score distribution. It is most likely a recording error but is easily detected given the box-whisker plot. How to obtain the middle score as well as the top and bottom scores in the box-whisker plot is covered in the next chapter.

● GGPLOT2 PACKAGE

The *ggplot2* package contains functions that permit making very sophisticated graphs (Wickham, 2009). The included *geoms()* function designates geometric objects to be placed on the graph. These include bars, points, lines, histograms, box plots, and text. The included *aes()* function designates aesthetic values for the graph, which control elements within the *geom* function. Aesthetics refers to the selection of variables, types of lines to draw, color, and shape of data values.

The official website for this R package is http://had.co.nz/ggplot2/, which uses the better functions of the *R base* package and *R lattice* package used in graphing data. The website also has additional documentation and provides a link to the code used in the Wickham (2009) book. In addition, other resources are listed, such as future workshops you can attend and sample code to produce stunning graphs.

The ggplot2 package when installed will prompt for setting up your own personal library, which is not a problem; it will also prompt you to select a CRAN site for downloading the package. The ggplot2 package is installed by issuing the following command in the RGui Console window (*Note:* Be patient because it will download a series of other packages):

```
> install.packages("ggplot2")
```

Next, issue the following command to load the package:

```
> library(ggplot2)
```

The *ggplot()* function is now ready to use, with *?ggplot* showing the arguments to be used in the function when graphing data. I used the data from the scatterplot example, but this time I had to create a data frame rather than use a data vector. The data frame is called *results* and created by the *data.frame()* function. This function combines the variable labels with the data in a column format. Type in the name of the data frame, and the contents will be printed.

```
> scores = c(70,75,80,85,90,98)

> hours = c(5,7,8,10,15,20)

> results = data.frame(hours, scores)
```

```
> results
```

	hours	scores
1	5	70
2	7	75
3	8	80
4	10	85
5	15	90
6	20	98

The *ggplot()* function includes the data frame name; the *aes()* function includes the variable names for *x* and *y*. This creates a general blank framework for the graph. What is required next is to add the type of geometric object, specified by *geom_point()*, which in this case specifies data points (color, size, and other aesthetics can be included in the parentheses) and aesthetics for variables specified in *aes()*. If you run *ggplot()* at this point, it would print out a scatterplot.

We can continue to add features to the graph by using the *labs()* function. This allows for printing a title and labels for the *x*-axis and *y*-axis. Many more features are available in the *ggplot()* function, so I recommend reading Wickham (2009) and exploring the ggplot2 website. Execute the following R commands to obtain a scatterplot:

```
> ggplot(results, aes(x = hours, y = scores)) + geom_point() + labs(title =
"Hours Spent Studying and Test Scores", x = "Hours Studying", y = "Test Scores")
```

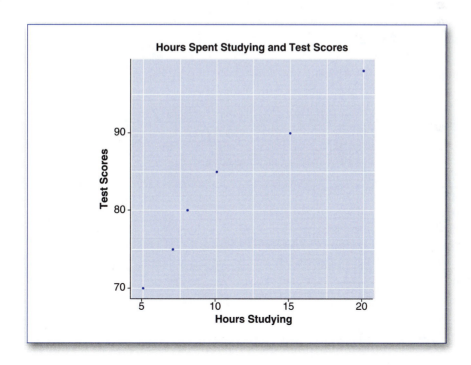

● DISPLAYING FREQUENCY DISTRIBUTIONS

A large sample of data from a population should provide a bell-shaped frequency distribution—that is, a normal distribution. Some frequency distributions of sample data, however, may have the appearance of a camel with two humps, which indicates two populations are present (bimodal), or tilted to the left or the right. It is important to view your data prior to conducting any statistical tests—that is, to examine the frequency distribution or plot of your data for each variable.

The heights of adult men have a bell-shaped frequency distribution in the population—that is, a **symmetrical distribution** with one mode (**unimodal**). Mode is a term used to describe the most frequent value in a frequency distribution—that is, the score that occurs most often in a frequency distribution of data. The heights of adult women have a similar bell-shaped frequency distribution in the population. However, because, on average, women are shorter than men, the combined population frequency distributions would appear to have two modes (**bimodal**).

The *population function* in the R script file (chap8c.r) creates a random sample of 250 male and 250 female adults and the height of each person is determined. The sample consists of both men and women who have height recorded in categories from 0 to 12 in 0.5 increments. In that way, the sample will reflect the fact that it was drawn from a combination of two different populations. The function provides the first population with a mean of 4.0, but you will need to provide the second population, which is initially set at a mean of 9.0. The histogram will show two different population frequency distributions—that is, a bimodal frequency distribution. If the mean of the second population is changed so that it equals the first population mean, then a unimodal or single population distribution will be displayed.

```
> PopTwo = 9

> Size = c(250,250)

> chap8c(PopTwo, Size)
```

PROGRAM OUTPUT

	Rel Freq
0.0-0.5	0
0.5-1.0	0
1.0-1.5	0
1.5-2.0	3
2.0-2.5	13
2.5-3.0	28
3.0-3.5	34
3.5-4.0	53
4.0-4.5	44
4.5-5.0	39

5.0–5.5	25
5.5–6.0	7
6.0–6.5	7
6.5–7.0	3
7.0–7.5	14
7.5–8.0	18
8.0–8.5	41
8.5–9.0	49
9.0–9.5	46
9.5–10.0	36
10.0–10.5	26
10.5–11.0	10
11.0–11.5	3
11.5–12.0	1

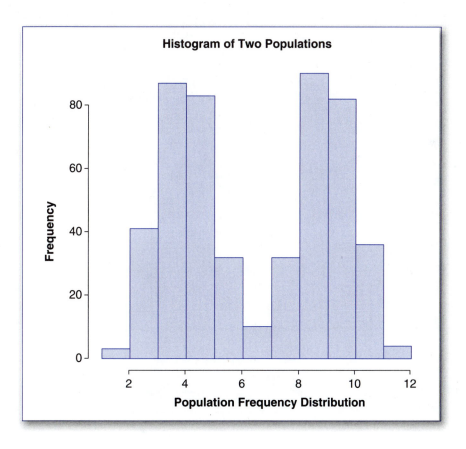

If you specify *PopTwo* = 4, then a histogram with a single unimodal population frequency distribution will be shown because it is equal to the first population mean.

PROGRAM OUTPUT

	Rel Freq
0.0-0.5	0
0.5-1.0	0
1.0-1.5	3
1.5-2.0	6
2.0-2.5	27
2.5-3.0	46
3.0-3.5	75
3.5-4.0	102
4.0-4.5	90
4.5-5.0	75
5.0-5.5	51
5.5-6.0	17
6.0-6.5	7
6.5-7.0	1

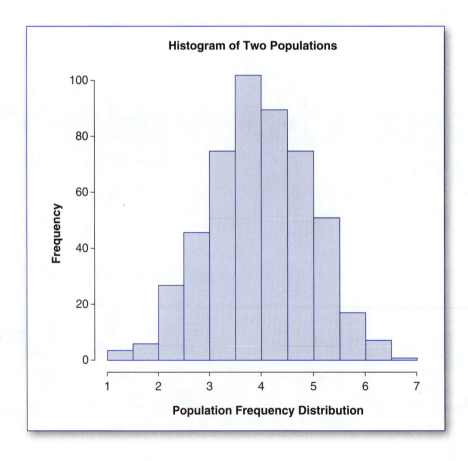

SUMMARY

In this chapter, we have learned that it is important to graph or plot your variable values to visually see the distribution of data. A frequency distribution, whether displayed in a histogram, ogive, stem-and-leaf plot, box-whisker plot, or scatterplot, provides meaningful information about the frequency distribution of your data. We typically take a sample of data, calculate a sample statistic, and then infer that it represents a population parameter, so our frequency distributions tell us something about the population data.

The next chapter will explore our sample data by summarizing the frequency distribution data using sample statistics. These descriptive statistics allow us to explain the sample data without having to report the individual data values. We use these sample statistics (mean, median, mode; standard deviation and variance) to estimate the corresponding population value or parameter. Population distributions are, therefore, defined as infinitely large requiring sampling and estimation of parameters using sample statistics.

TIP

- ✓ Histograms and ogives provide a visual display of frequency distributions.
- ✓ Stem-and-leaf plots can be manipulated using different number of groups.
- ✓ Box-whisker plots display any extreme data values.
- ✓ Population and sample frequency distributions can be unimodal or bimodal.
- ✓ The *barplot()* function produces a histogram plot of frequency data.
- ✓ The *plot()* function produces a scatterplot of data for two variables.
- ✓ The *rnorm()* function takes a random sample from a normal population.
- ✓ The *hist()* function produces the histogram plot of the two combined populations.
- ✓ The *par()* function permits printing more than one graph in the GUI window.

EXERCISES

1. Define *histogram* in a few sentences.
2. Define *ogive* in a few sentences.
3. What are the *stem* values for the following numbers: 5.6, 6.8, 9.2?
4. What are the *leaf* values for the following numbers: 5.6, 6.8, 9.2?
5. Define mode.
6. Define bimodal.

7. Run *barplot(rnorm(100))* and *hist(rnorm(100))*. Briefly explain the difference.

8. Run the R frequency function with Class = c(90,85,75,60,50,40,35,30,20,10). Display the output and graphs.

TRUE OR FALSE QUESTIONS

T   F   a.   A histogram graphs data based on exclusive categories.

T   F   b.   The stem in a stem-and-leaf graph indicates the number of groups.

T   F   c.   A bimodal distribution is the same as a normal distribution.

T   F   d.   A modal value is the most frequent data value in a frequency distribution.

T   F   e.   It is important to examine the frequency distribution of data.

WEB RESOURCES

Chapter R script files available at http://www.sagepub.com/schumacker

Frequency Function R script file: chap8a.r

Population Function R script file: chap8c.r

Stem-Leaf Function R script file: chap8b.r

ggplot2 Package: http://had.co.nz/ggplot2/

## CHAPTER 9

CENTRAL TENDENCY AND DISPERSION

CENTRAL TENDENCY ●

Central tendency is a term used in statistics that refers to certain sample statistics from a population of data. Central tendency is where most scores occur in the middle of a symmetrical distribution and then spread out (dispersion). The mode, mean, and median are central tendency values that would all be the same score in a normal distribution. The mean score is the arithmetic average of numbers in a data set. The mean is computed by taking the sum of the numbers and dividing by the total, or how many numbers were summed. The median score is the middle score found by arranging a set of numbers from the smallest to the largest (or from the largest to the smallest). If the data set contains an odd number of values, the median is the middle value in the ordered data set. If there are an even number of data values, the median is the average of the two middle values in the ordered data set. The median value is the score that divides the distribution into two equal halves. The mode is the value that occurs most often in the frequency distribution. (*R does not list more than one mode value, even if two or more are present in the data.*)

The sample statistics summarize the frequency distribution of sample data taken from a population. Three important sample statistics are the mean, median, and mode. In a bell-shaped unimodal frequency distribution, the mean, median, and mode will have the same score value. However, in bimodal or other shaped frequency distributions, these sample statistics have different values. These sample statistics help describe or estimate the population value, called a population parameter. A random sample of data should therefore indicate the population data, and sample statistics should be good estimates of the population parameters; that is, a *sample statistic is an estimate of a population parameter*.

There are a number of R functions designed to provide these summary statistics for a sample of data (Kabacoff, 2011). Several R packages with these functions are available: *Hmisc*, *pastecs*, or *psych*. You must first locate a CRAN mirror site and then install one of the packages. After installing the package(s), *Hmisc*, *pastecs*, or *psych*, you can issue the commands

```
> library(Hmisc)
> describe(mydata)
```

or the commands

```
> library(pastecs)
> stat.desc(mydata)
```

or the commands

```
> library(psych)
> describe(mydata)
```

You can also obtain central tendency statistics by group, that is, separately for males and females, by issuing the following commands:

```
> library(psych)
> library(help = "psych") # Shows all of the functions in the
psych library
> data(mydata)
> describe.by(mydata, mydata$gender)
```

TIP

✓ You can use Packages in the main menu to locate a CRAN site and install packages.

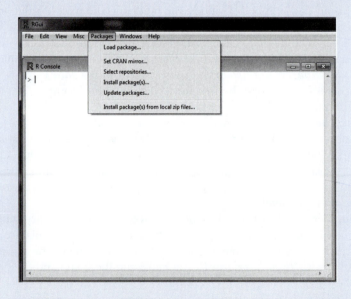

✓ You must first select a CRAN site (Set CRAN mirror).

✓ Next, select Install package(s) from the main menu.

CRAN mirror	Packages
Argentina (La Plata)	hier.part
Argentina (Mendoza)	hierfstat
Australia (Canberra)	highlight
Australia (Melbourne)	hints
Austria	hisemi
Belgium	HistData
Brazil (PR)	histogram
Brazil (RJ)	hitandrun
Brazil (SP 1)	hive
Brazil (SP 2)	HiveR
Canada (BC)	HLMdiag
Canada (NS)	hlr
Canada (ON)	Hmisc
Canada (QC 1)	HMM
Canada (QC 2)	hmm.discnp
Chile	HMMmix
China (Beijing 1)	HMP
China (Beijing 2)	HMPTrees
China (Beijing 3)	HMR
China (Guangzhou)	hof
China (Hefei)	holdem
China (Xiamen)	Holidays
Colombia (Bogota)	homals
Colombia (Cali)	homeR
[OK] [Cancel]	[OK] [Cancel]

Of course, the basic function, *summary()*, also works.

The *summary function* in the R script file (chap9a.r) provides the mean, the median, and the mode in a set of sample data. The individual commands, *mean()* and *median()*, or the function, *summary()*, will provide the mean and median values in a data set. The *summary()* function does not return the mode but returns the minimum and maximum values in the frequency distribution, along with the first quartile (25% score value) and third quartile (75% score value). The function with sample data (10,20,30,40,50,50,60,70,80,90,100) will return mean = 54.55, median = 50, and mode = 50 (with the number 50 also being indicated as the fifth position in the data array). The mode is obtained by using the *which.max()* function for data in a table format. You will only need to enter the data vector x, then run the function:

```
> x = c(10,20,30,40,50,50,60,70,80,90,100)
> chap9a(x)
```

The results report the mean, median, mode, and summary statistics, which show the minimum and maximum values along with the quartile values.

```
PROGRAM OUTPUT

Mean
[1] 54.54545

Median
[1] 50

Mode
50
 5

Summary Statistics
Min.   1st Qu.  Median  Mean    3rd Qu.  Max.
10.00  35.00    50.00   54.55   75.00    100.00
```

● FACTORS THAT AFFECT CENTRAL TENDENCY

The sample statistics are affected by missing values, **outliers** (extreme values), adding a constant, and multiplying by a constant. Missing values are indicated as "NA" in R data sets. (*It is important to handle missing data prior to statistical analysis.*) For example, sample data are sometimes modified or transformed to permit comparisons and aid in the interpretation of sample estimates. If the length of cars in inches was changed to meters, one could multiply 0.0254 times the car length to yield the value in meters. What effect does this multiplication have on the mean value representing car length? What if an instructor decides to adjust a set of test grades for an exceptionally long test by adding 10 points to each student's score? What effect does this addition have on the mean score? If the price of the most expensive house in a neighborhood increases, what happens to the median value of the houses in that neighborhood? What happens to the average value of houses in that neighborhood? We will now explore each of these factors to determine what effect they have on our sample statistic as an estimate of a population parameter.

The *central tendency function* in the R script file (chap9b.r) enters an initial data set with 11 data values from the smallest to the largest. The initial data set is then transformed in three different ways: (1) adding a constant to each data value, (2) multiplying each data value by a constant, and (3) replacing the last data value with a smaller data value. The function includes other individual functions (*mean, median,* and *which.max*) to illustrate how the central tendency sample statistics are affected.

When a constant is added to all of the values in the data set, the new mean is the mean of the initial data set plus the constant, the new median is the median of the initial data set plus the constant, and the new mode is increased by the constant. When data values are multiplied by a constant, the new mean is the mean of the initial data set times the constant, the new median is the median of the initial data set times the constant, and the mode is increased times the constant. When a larger value is replaced by an even larger value (outlier), the new mean is larger than the mean of the initial data set, but the new median is unchanged, and the mode is unchanged if not the most frequent data value. Extreme values or outliers affect the mean but do not affect the median or mode (unless the most frequent data value).

You will first enter the values in the data vector *InitialData*, select the *"Add"* argument to add a constant to each data value in the vector, and then specify the constant value to add, which is 20; then run the function:

```
> InitialData = c(10,20,30,40,50,50,60,70,80,90,100)

> Resp = "Add"

> adjValue = 20

> chap9b(InitialData, Resp, adjValue)
```

Addition, Multiplication, and Outliers

Adding a Constant of 20 (Resp = "Add")

```
PROGRAM OUTPUT

Initial Data = 10,20,30,40,50,50,60,70,80,90,100

Mean = 54.55 Median = 50
Mode = 50
 5


Added 20 to the original data

Modified Data = 30,40,50,60,70,70,80,90,100,110,120
Mean = 74.55 Median = 70
Mode = 70
 5
```

You can now simply replace the *Resp* argument value to see the impact of multiplying by a constant.

Multiplying by a Constant of 20 (Resp = "Multiply")

```
PROGRAM OUTPUT

Initial Data = 10,20,30,40,50,50,60,70,80,90,100

Mean = 54.55 Median = 50
Mode = 50
 5


Multiplied the original data by 20
```

```
Modified Data = 200,400,600,800,1000,1000,1200,1400,1600,1800,2000
Mean = 1090.91 Median = 1000
Mode = 1000
  5
```

The function also permits specifying an outlier or extreme data value to examine how the mean is affected by an extreme score, that is, a score not typical of the rest of the data set.

Adding Outlier (Resp = "Replace Last") With adjValue = 1,000

```
PROGRAM OUTPUT

Initial Data = 10,20,30,40,50,50,60,70,80,90,100

Mean = 54.55 Median = 50
Mode = 50
  5

Replaced largest value with 1000

Modified Data = 10,20,30,40,50,50,60,70,80,90,1000
Mean = 136.36 Median = 50
Mode = 50
  5
```

Missing Values (NA = Missing Value)

Missing values can dramatically affect the mean and median values. In R, the symbol NA is added for any data value that is missing. A simple option, *na.rm = TRUE*, is used to designate missing values in the data. If this option is omitted, no computations are done, and NA is returned, indicating that R could not compute a value. For example, x is a vector with 12 data values, but 1 is missing, that is, NA. The sum, mean, and median all show an NA value, while *length()* does not exclude the NA (missing) value.

```
> x = c(10,20,30,40,50,50,NA,60,70,80,90,100)
> sum(x)
> length(x)
> mean(x)
> median(x)

OUTPUT - Indicates NA

> sum(x)
[1] NA

> length(x)
[1] 12
```

```
> mean(x)
[1] NA
```

```
> median(x)
[1] NA
```

Adding the option *na.rm = TRUE* permits a calculation for mean and median using only the 11 data values. For example,

```
> x = c(10, 20, 30, 40, 50, 50, NA, 60, 70, 80, 90, 100)
```

```
> mean(x, na.rm = TRUE)
[1] 54.54545
```

```
> median(x, na.rm = TRUE)
[1] 50
```

● DISPERSION

Dispersion refers to the spread of the data values in a frequency distribution. Measures of dispersion in a sample data set are **range**, standard deviation, and variance. Range indicates the distance between the largest (maximum) and the smallest (minimum) data values in a data set. The range indicates the width of the frequency distribution. The standard deviation indicates the spread of the data in standard score units. Variance is the standard deviation value squared and possesses many important properties when conducting statistical analysis of data, which will be discussed in later chapters. In statistics, the variance reflects whether data vary around the mean, thus indicating whether individual differences exist that we wish to describe, explain, or predict.

The formula for the range is

$$\text{Range} = \text{Maximum data value} - \text{Smallest data value}.$$

The formula for standard deviation is

$$S = \frac{\sum(\text{Each data value} - \text{Mean data value})^2}{\text{Number of data values}} = \sqrt{\frac{SS}{n}}.$$

The formula for the variance is

$$\text{Variance} = S^2$$

or

$$\text{Variance} = \frac{\sum(\text{Each data value} - \text{Mean data value})^2}{\text{Number of data values}} = \frac{SS}{n}.$$

The numerator indicates that the sample mean is subtracted from each data value, squared, and summed. The summing of the squared values is denoted by the symbol Σ. The expression *SS* refers to the sum of squared deviations from the mean, or simply sum of squared deviations. The sum of squared deviations divided by the number of data values is another way to understand how variance is computed. It is the average of the squared deviations from the mean.

The standard deviation provides a measure in standard units of how far data values deviate from the sample mean. For example, in a normal distribution, 68% of the data values fall approximately 1 standard deviation (1 *SD*) on either side of the mean, 95% of the data values fall approximately 2 standard deviations (2 *SD*) on either side of the mean, and 99% of the data values fall approximately 3 standard deviations (3 *SD*) on either side of the mean.

The variance indicates how much the data vary around the sample mean; for example, if student scores did not vary (deviate from the mean), then variance = 0, and everyone would have the same score. As the variance increases, scores will deviate more around the mean, which indicates more individual differences in the scores. So the larger the sample variance, the more individual differences in the scores, and conversely, a smaller variance indicates less variation around the mean.

To fully understand measures of dispersion, the same operations will be conducted on the range, standard deviation, and variance that were conducted for the mean, median, and mode, namely, (1) adding a constant to each value in a data set, (2) multiplying each value in a data set, and (3) adding an extreme value (outlier) to the data set. When a constant is added to all the values in a data set, the range, standard deviation, and variance are unchanged. When all of the values in a data set are multiplied by a constant, the new range is the original range times the constant, the new standard deviation is the original standard deviation times the constant, and the new variance is the original variance times the constant squared. If the last data value is replaced by a smaller data value, then the range, standard deviation, and variance are all decreased. If the last data value is replaced by a larger value, then the range, standard deviation, and variance are all increased.

The *dispersion function* in the R script file (chap9c.r) enters an initial data set with 11 data values from the smallest to the largest. The initial data set is then transformed in three different ways: (1) adding a constant to each data value, (2) multiplying each data value by a constant, and (3) replacing the last data value with a smaller data value. The function uses other individual functions (*mean, median,* and *which.max*) to illustrate how the central tendency statistics are affected. You will enter a data vector, *InitialData*, a *Resp* argument, and a constant value to add, then run the function.

```
> InitialData = c(10,20,30,40,50,50,60,70,80,90,100)
> Resp = "Add"
> adjValue = 5
> chap9c(InitialData, Resp, adjValue)
```

The results show the initial data, range, standard deviation, and variance. This is followed by the modified data set where a constant value of 5 has been added to each of the initial data values. You should notice that the range, standard deviation, and variance do not change, unlike when modifying the data and calculating the mean.

```
PROGRAM OUTPUT

Initial Data = 10,20,30,40,50,50,60,70,80,90,100

Range = 90 Std Dev = 28.76 Variance = 827.27
```

```
Added 5 to the original data

Modified Data = 15,25,35,45,55,55,65,75,85,95,105

Range = 90 Std Dev = 28.76 Variance = 827.27
```

● FACTORS THAT AFFECT DISPERSION

We can continue to elaborate on how measures of dispersion are affected by adding a constant, multiplying by a constant, and adding an outlier (extreme data value).

Addition, Multiplication, and Outliers

Adding a Constant of 20 (Resp = "Add")

```
PROGRAM OUTPUT

Initial Data = 10,20,30,40,50,50,60,70,80,90,100

Range = 90 Std Dev = 28.76 Variance = 827.27

Added 5 to the original data

Modified Data = 15,25,35,45,55,55,65,75,85,95,105

Range = 90 Std Dev = 28.76 Variance = 827.27
```

Multiplying by a Constant of 20 (Resp = "Multiply")

```
PROGRAM OUTPUT

Initial Data = 10,20,30,40,50,50,60,70,80,90,100

Range = 90 Std Dev = 28.76 Variance = 827.27

Multiplied the original data by 5

Modified Data = 50,100,150,200,250,250,300,350,400,450,500

Range = 450 Std Dev = 143.81 Variance = 20681.82
```

Adding an Outlier of 5 (Resp = "Replace Last")

```
PROGRAM OUTPUT

Initial Data = 10,20,30,40,50,50,60,70,80,90,100
```

```
Range = 90 Std Dev = 28.76 Variance = 827.27

Replaced last value with 5

Modified Data = 10,20,30,40,50,50,60,70,80,90,5

Range = 85 Std Dev = 28 Variance = 784.09
```

Adding an Outlier of 1,000 (Resp = "Replace Last")

```
PROGRAM OUTPUT

Initial Data = 10,20,30,40,50,50,60,70,80,90,100

Range = 90 Std Dev = 28.76 Variance = 827.27

Replaced last value with 1000

Modified Data = 10,20,30,40,50,50,60,70,80,90,1000

Range = 990 Std Dev = 287.48 Variance = 82645.45
```

We see that adding a constant does not affect the range, standard deviation, and variance. Multiplying by a constant increases the range by 5 (5 × 90 = 450), the standard deviation by 5 (5 × 28.76 = 143.81), and the variance by 5^2 (25 × 827.27 = 20681.82). Adding a smaller outlier value (5 replaces 100) reduces the range, standard deviation, and variance, while adding a larger outlier value (100 replaced by 1,000) increases the range, standard deviation, and variance.

● SAMPLE SIZE EFFECTS

A **finite population** would not use sample statistics because one could directly calculate the population parameters, that is, mean, median, mode, range, standard deviation, and variance. However, in an infinite population, where all the data values are not known, we would need to use sample estimates of these population parameters. It should be obvious that more sample data could provide better estimates of the population parameters, that is, a sample of 3 data values would not provide as good a sample estimate as a sample of 100 data values.

Random sampling is used to acquire sample data values because it provides an equally likely chance of being selected from the population. Random sampling therefore controls for any bias in data selection or subject selection in research studies. Random sampling can occur in two different ways, sampling with replacement and sampling without replacement. Both are used in the field of statistics, with researchers predominantly using sampling without replacement when selecting participants for their research studies. Sampling without replacement assumes that data values are *not* returned to the population from which they were drawn. Sampling with replacement assumes that data values are returned to the population from which they were drawn, which is useful when studying population characteristics, such as when examining sample size effects. The probability of selection is affected depending on which sampling technique is used, which we learned in Chapter 3.

The *sample size function* in the R script file (chap9d.r) allows us to observe the sample size effect on the mean, median, range, standard deviation, and variance. When the size of the sample increases, better sample estimates of the mean should occur, the range of data values will generally increase, and the standard deviation should equally divide the frequency distribution of the sample data. As the sample size increases, the sample range usually increases because observations are chosen from the extreme data values in a population. As observations are added to a sample, the range of the sample cannot decrease. As observations are added to a sample, the standard deviation fluctuates in an unpredictable manner; however, when randomly sampling from a normal distribution using the function *rnorm()*, the standard deviation should indicate six divisions (range divided by 6), which approximates the standard deviation of the normal distribution. Given the uniform distribution used in the function, this would not be the case; rather, the standard deviation would indicate around four equal divisions. The mean and median should become more stable estimates of the population parameters as sample size increases.

The *sample size function* creates a uniform population of integers from 1 to 1,000 based on sampling with replacement. Various sample sizes are listed in the *Size* vector, ranging from 100 to 10,000, which is possible because the function continues to sample with replacement until it reaches the desired sample size. The random sampling will be repeated with a new set of observations for each sample size listed in the vector, if a seed number is not used. A summary table will be printed with the results to show the effect of sample size on the sample statistics. The function can be repeated many times since the sampling is random. The use of a seed number, *set.seed()*, will provide the same results every time the function is run, and removing the seed number will permit different results. Not using a seed number permits the testing of your understanding of random sampling fluctuations and conclusions about how various sample sizes affect sample statistics.

You will only need to enter a data vector, *Size*, then run the function

```
> Size = c(100,200,300,400,500,1000,5000,10000)
> chap9d(Size)
```

PROGRAM OUTPUT

N	Mean	Median	Range	SD	Variance
100	485.01	478.5	966	297.79	88676.92
200	490.70	500.0	979	292.63	85631.74
300	486.42	448.0	990	285.59	81562.06
400	500.54	496.0	996	288.57	83270.20
500	510.04	509.5	992	289.81	83988.09
1000	505.24	513.0	998	288.24	83082.90
5000	498.06	499.0	998	288.09	82993.65
10000	499.15	501.0	998	287.48	82646.61

The results for $N = 10,000$ indicate that the mean = 499.15 and median = 501.0, which is close to the uniform distribution of numbers from 1 to 1,000, which has a mean and median equal to 500. For sizes less than 10,000, the mean varies above and below the population mean of 500, which is expected due to random sampling.

● DATA TRANSFORMATIONS

Researcher will sometimes find themselves being asked to transform data because of violations of assumptions in computing a particular statistic. The assumptions include normality of the data distribution, **homogeneity** of variance between groups, and linearity. The related issues of missing data, outliers, and restriction of range in data affect the mean and variance of a variable, thus affecting the linearity, normality, and homogeneity of variance assumptions. Past research has shown that in most cases, our inferential statistics are robust to violations of assumptions. However, as presented in later chapters, they can have a serious impact on the statistical test and results. I will therefore explain these issues briefly and cover a few basic data transformation methods. Please note that the data transformations will change the data values, which affects interpretation of the results. These data transformations can be problematic, may not always yield the desired results, and can affect the interpretation of the descriptive statistics (mean and standard deviation). It is recommended that you select a data transformation method that makes your data conform to the required assumption for the statistical test you are conducting.

Missing Data

It is best not to have missing data when possible, so take care in your research design and data collection efforts. The first approach would be to eliminate subjects who have data that are missing. This is okay if your loss of subjects is low, thus not affecting your analysis results. A second approach is to substitute the mean value, which has been shown effective with 10% or fewer cases having missing data. A third approach is to replace the missing value(s) with a predicted value based on variables that have complete data. This is referred to as the regression method, which has been shown to be effective with 15% or fewer missing cases. For cases that have 20% to 30% missing data, the expectation maximum likelihood estimation method is recommended. When faced with more than 30% missing data, researchers are advised to examine their data collection methods. Many software programs have these options readily available, which are referred to as data imputation methods. There are many different definitions of missingness and treatment of data, but they are beyond the scope of this book, so consult Davey and Savla (2010) or Enders (2010) for a more in-depth treatment of the subject matter. I recommend running a statistical test with and without replacement of missing data to compare the impact on the estimates and the statistical test.

A simple example demonstrating mean substitution is given below. I generated 100 numbers between 1 and 100 and calculated the assumed population mean and variance.

```
> j = 1:100

> mean(j)
50.5

> var(j)
841.67
```

Now if we drop the value 100 as missing from our sample of data and compute the mean and variance, we obtain

```
> j = 1:99

> mean(j)
50

> var (j)
825
```

Now if we add the mean value (50.5) to our sample data for the missing value of 100, we obtain

```
> k = c(j, 50.5)

> mean(k)
50.005

> var (k)
816.67
```

These results show that a single missing value has an effect on the variance, which may or may not be important when running a statistical test. Obviously, more missing data values could have a greater or lesser impact on the descriptive statistics and statistical test you conduct. Mean substitution may or may not be effective in handling your missing data, so please learn about the other advanced methods of handling missing values.

Outliers

Outliers are defined as extreme values, which can drastically inflate our descriptive statistics and resulting statistical tests. In some cases, we would use **trimmed means** as an option in our statistical test. A trimmed mean essentially eliminates extreme data values at the top and bottom of a data distribution. This option may or may not be available when running a statistical test. Once again, we should compare the sample mean and variance with and without a trimmed mean value. It is easy to see how extreme values affect the descriptive statistics. Given our previous example, I added 1,000 to the data vector with the following results:

```
> j = c(1:100, 1000)

> mean (j)
59.90

> var(j)
9759.49
```

The extreme value of 1,000 inflated the mean and more dramatically inflated the variance. Both of the descriptive statistics would affect our statistical tests. The stem-and-leaf or box-whisker plots presented in Chapter 8 should be used to view whether any extreme data values are present.

Restriction of Range

The restriction of range in data will affect the mean and variance. A researcher may not be aware that variability (variance) indicates individual differences or that equal variance in groups is an assumption for many different statistical tests. When reducing the variance, the ability to examine individual differences is reduced. An extreme example highlights this point. A test is given where all students score the same; hence, there is no variance (no individual difference). The sample statistic for all students is therefore the same—the mean test score.

Using our previous example, the sample data will be reconfigured to demonstrate a restricted range. Comparing the results with the assumed population data (1–100) provides some insight into how this could affect our statistical tests. The population parameters are given as follows:

```
> j = 1:100

> mean(j)
[1]  50.5

> var(j)
[1]  841.6667
```

We now restrict the range of data in our sample to data values from 20 to 70, which results in the following descriptive statistics:

```
> J = 20:70

> mean(J)
[1]  45

> var(J)
[1]  221
```

The mean and variance for the sample data with a restricted range are lower than than the values for the population. Researchers should be sensitive to whether their sample data reflect the range of data in the population. If not, the sample mean may not be a good estimate of the population mean.

Transforming Data Values

A researcher will usually be faced with data transformation methods when variables are skewed or leptokurtic, with the goal in mind to create a more normal distribution of data values.

Transforming data values obviously changes the data values, which must be taken into consideration when conducting the statistical analysis and interpreting the results. Generally, data transformations will not change the ordering of the observations in a data set and thus are permissible scale transformations. A researcher should realize that data transformation should be the last attempt to work with data that violate the assumptions of the researcher's statistical test. Also, there may be no functional data transformation that works. However, in many disciplines such as biology and political science, logit and probit transformations, respectively, are commonly done when using logistic regression methods.

Types of Transformations

The square root transformation appears to work best with a mild positive-skewed distribution. This might be used in log-linear regression analysis where frequency count data are used. The data transformation is simply

$$Y = \sqrt{Y}.$$

An example of this type of data distribution is when the dependent variable measures frequency counts of attitude preference commonly found in Likert-type scale questions on survey questionnaires (SA, A, N, D, SD). A logarithmic transformation would be used when the **skewness** is more pronounced across the scale categories. Rating scale software would convert the ordinal measures into log-transformed linear measures, where the logarithmic scale ranges from $+\infty$ to $-\infty$ (Linacre, 2013). The log transformation can be executed on base e (Naperian value = 2.718) or log base 10; however, log base e is more commonly used. The log transformation is simply

$$Y = \log_E(Y).$$

When faced with more extreme skewness, the reciprocal transformation or probit transformation (useful with proportions or probabilities under the normal curve) is generally recommended. The reciprocal transformation (add 1 to the denominator to protect against zero values in data) is simply

$$Y = \frac{1}{Y} \quad \text{or} \quad Y = \frac{1}{Y+1}.$$

The probit transformation is computed by

$$Y = \Phi^{-1}(p),$$

where Y is the probit-transformed value, p is the proportion (data value/total), and the inverse function of p is the $100 * p$ percent quantile from the standard normal distribution.

It would be wise for researchers to compare these transformations on their data to determine which one provides the best results for their data and statistical test. Box and Cox (1964) provided one of the earliest presentations of data transformation methods, which showed that no one data transformation works for all data distribution types. This is easy to determine by simply conducting a histogram or plot of the sample data before and after using each data transformation method.

R Functions

Square Root: sqrt()

```
> Y = 1:100
> Ymod = sqrt(Y)
> Ymod
```

```
 [1]  1.000000  1.414214  1.732051  2.000000  2.236068  2.449490  2.645751
 [8]  2.828427  3.000000  3.162278  3.316625  3.464102  3.605551  3.741657
[15]  3.872983  4.000000  4.123106  4.242641  4.358899  4.472136  4.582576
[22]  4.690416  4.795832  4.898979  5.000000  5.099020  5.196152  5.291503
[29]  5.385165  5.477226  5.567764  5.656854  5.744563  5.830952  5.916080
[36]  6.000000  6.082763  6.164414  6.244998  6.324555  6.403124  6.480741
[43]  6.557439  6.633250  6.708204  6.782330  6.855655  6.928203  7.000000
[50]  7.071068  7.141428  7.211103  7.280110  7.348469  7.416198  7.483315
[57]  7.549834  7.615773  7.681146  7.745967  7.810250  7.874008  7.937254
[64]  8.000000  8.062258  8.124038  8.185353  8.246211  8.306624  8.366600
[71]  8.426150  8.485281  8.544004  8.602325  8.660254  8.717798  8.774964
[78]  8.831761  8.888194  8.944272  9.000000  9.055385  9.110434  9.165151
[85]  9.219544  9.273618  9.327379  9.380832  9.433981  9.486833  9.539392
[92]  9.591663  9.643651  9.695360  9.746794  9.797959  9.848858  9.899495
[99]  9.949874 10.000000
```

Logarithmic: $\log_{10}()$ or log()

```
> Y = 1:100
> Ylog10 = log10(Y)
> Ylog10
```

```
 [1]  0.0000000  0.3010300  0.4771213  0.6020600  0.6989700  0.7781513  0.8450980
 [8]  0.9030900  0.9542425  1.0000000  1.0413927  1.0791812  1.1139434  1.1461280
[15]  1.1760913  1.2041200  1.2304489  1.2552725  1.2787536  1.3010300  1.3222193
[22]  1.3424227  1.3617278  1.3802112  1.3979400  1.4149733  1.4313638  1.4471580
[29]  1.4623980  1.4771213  1.4913617  1.5051500  1.5185139  1.5314789  1.5440680
[36]  1.5563025  1.5682017  1.5797836  1.5910646  1.6020600  1.6127839  1.6232493
[43]  1.6334685  1.6434527  1.6532125  1.6627578  1.6720979  1.6812412  1.6901961
[50]  1.6989700  1.7075702  1.7160033  1.7242759  1.7323938  1.7403627  1.7481880
[57]  1.7558749  1.7634280  1.7708520  1.7781513  1.7853298  1.7923917  1.7993405
[64]  1.8061800  1.8129134  1.8195439  1.8260748  1.8325089  1.8388491  1.8450980
[71]  1.8512583  1.8573325  1.8633229  1.8692317  1.8750613  1.8808136  1.8864907
[78]  1.8920946  1.8976271  1.9030900  1.9084850  1.9138139  1.9190781  1.9242793
```

```
[85] 1.9294189 1.9344985 1.9395193 1.9444827 1.9493900 1.9542425 1.9590414
[92] 1.9637878 1.9684829 1.9731279 1.9777236 1.9822712 1.9867717 1.9912261
[99] 1.9956352 2.0000000

> Yloge = log(Y)
> Yloge

 [1] 0.0000000 0.6931472 1.0986123 1.3862944 1.6094379 1.7917595 1.9459101
 [8] 2.0794415 2.1972246 2.3025851 2.3978953 2.4849066 2.5649494 2.6390573
[15] 2.7080502 2.7725887 2.8332133 2.8903718 2.9444390 2.9957323 3.0445224
[22] 3.0910425 3.1354942 3.1780538 3.2188758 3.2580965 3.2958369 3.3322045
[29] 3.3672958 3.4011974 3.4339872 3.4657359 3.4965076 3.5263605 3.5553481
[36] 3.5835189 3.6109179 3.6375862 3.6635616 3.6888795 3.7135721 3.7376696
[43] 3.7612001 3.7841896 3.8066625 3.8286414 3.8501476 3.8712010 3.8918203
[50] 3.9120230 3.9318256 3.9512437 3.9702919 3.9889840 4.0073332 4.0253517
[57] 4.0430513 4.0604430 4.0775374 4.0943446 4.1108739 4.1271344 4.1431347
[64] 4.1588831 4.1743873 4.1896547 4.2046926 4.2195077 4.2341065 4.2484952
[71] 4.2626799 4.2766661 4.2904594 4.3040651 4.3174881 4.3307333 4.3438054
[78] 4.3567088 4.3694479 4.3820266 4.3944492 4.4067192 4.4188406 4.4308168
[85] 4.4426513 4.4543473 4.4659081 4.4773368 4.4886364 4.4998097 4.5108595
[92] 4.5217886 4.5325995 4.5432948 4.5538769 4.5643482 4.5747110 4.5849675
[99] 4.5951199 4.6051702
```

Reciprocal: 1/Y or 1/Y + 1

```
> Yrecp = 1/Y
> Yrecp

 [1] 1.00000000 0.50000000 0.33333333 0.25000000 0.20000000 0.16666667
 [7] 0.14285714 0.12500000 0.11111111 0.10000000 0.09090909 0.08333333
[13] 0.07692308 0.07142857 0.06666667 0.06250000 0.05882353 0.05555556
[19] 0.05263158 0.05000000 0.04761905 0.04545455 0.04347826 0.04166667
[25] 0.04000000 0.03846154 0.03703704 0.03571429 0.03448276 0.03333333
[31] 0.03225806 0.03125000 0.03030303 0.02941176 0.02857143 0.02777778
[37] 0.02702703 0.02631579 0.02564103 0.02500000 0.02439024 0.02380952
[43] 0.02325581 0.02272727 0.02222222 0.02173913 0.02127660 0.02083333
[49] 0.02040816 0.02000000 0.01960784 0.01923077 0.01886792 0.01851852
[55] 0.01818182 0.01785714 0.01754386 0.01724138 0.01694915 0.01666667
[61] 0.01639344 0.01612903 0.01587302 0.01562500 0.01538462 0.01515152
[67] 0.01492537 0.01470588 0.01449275 0.01428571 0.01408451 0.01388889
[73] 0.01369863 0.01351351 0.01333333 0.01315789 0.01298701 0.01282051
[79] 0.01265823 0.01250000 0.01234568 0.01219512 0.01204819 0.01190476
[85] 0.01176471 0.01162791 0.01149425 0.01136364 0.01123596 0.01111111
[91] 0.01098901 0.01086957 0.01075269 0.01063830 0.01052632 0.01041667
[97] 0.01030928 0.01020408 0.01010101 0.01000000
```

Probit: qnorm(p)

```
> Y = 1:100
> p = Y/100
> p
```

```
 [1]  0.01 0.02 0.03 0.04 0.05 0.06 0.07 0.08 0.09 0.10 0.11 0.12 0.13 0.14 0.15
[16]  0.16 0.17 0.18 0.19 0.20 0.21 0.22 0.23 0.24 0.25 0.26 0.27 0.28 0.29 0.30
[31]  0.31 0.32 0.33 0.34 0.35 0.36 0.37 0.38 0.39 0.40 0.41 0.42 0.43 0.44 0.45
[46]  0.46 0.47 0.48 0.49 0.50 0.51 0.52 0.53 0.54 0.55 0.56 0.57 0.58 0.59 0.60
[61]  0.61 0.62 0.63 0.64 0.65 0.66 0.67 0.68 0.69 0.70 0.71 0.72 0.73 0.74 0.75
[76]  0.76 0.77 0.78 0.79 0.80 0.81 0.82 0.83 0.84 0.85 0.86 0.87 0.88 0.89 0.90
[91]  0.91 0.92 0.93 0.94 0.95 0.96 0.97 0.98 0.99 1.00
```

```
> Yprobit = qnorm(p)
> Yprobit
```

```
 [1]  -2.32634787 -2.05374891 -1.88079361 -1.75068607 -1.64485363 -1.55477359
 [7]  -1.47579103 -1.40507156 -1.34075503 -1.28155157 -1.22652812 -1.17498679
[13]  -1.12639113 -1.08031934 -1.03643339 -0.99445788 -0.95416525 -0.91536509
[19]  -0.87789630 -0.84162123 -0.80642125 -0.77219321 -0.73884685 -0.70630256
[25]  -0.67448975 -0.64334541 -0.61281299 -0.58284151 -0.55338472 -0.52440051
[31]  -0.49585035 -0.46769880 -0.43991317 -0.41246313 -0.38532047 -0.35845879
[37]  -0.33185335 -0.30548079 -0.27931903 -0.25334710 -0.22754498 -0.20189348
[43]  -0.17637416 -0.15096922 -0.12566135 -0.10043372 -0.07526986 -0.05015358
[49]  -0.02506891  0.00000000  0.02506891  0.05015358  0.07526986  0.10043372
[55]   0.12566135  0.15096922  0.17637416  0.20189348  0.22754498  0.25334710
[61]   0.27931903  0.30548079  0.33185335  0.35845879  0.38532047  0.41246313
[67]   0.43991317  0.46769880  0.49585035  0.52440051  0.55338472  0.58284151
[73]   0.61281299  0.64334541  0.67448975  0.70630256  0.73884685  0.77219321
[79]   0.80642125  0.84162123  0.87789630  0.91536509  0.95416525  0.99445788
[85]   1.03643339  1.08031934  1.12639113  1.17498679  1.22652812  1.28155157
[91]   1.34075503  1.40507156  1.47579103  1.55477359  1.64485363  1.75068607
[97]   1.88079361  2.05374891  2.32634787  Inf
```

Probit data transformations first compute a proportion for each data value, then they assign the corresponding quantile value under the standard normal distribution, $Y = \Phi^{-1}(p)$. The quantile values range from .1 to .99, where values of 0 and 1 define infinity (*Inf*) end points. So prior to computing a mean and variance, any extreme infinity value (*Inf*) will require extrapolation or deletion. This can be accomplished by simply deleting the extreme value:

```
> newprobit = Yprobit[1:99]
```

The impact of these transformations can be seen in their descriptive statistics:

```
> mean(Ymod);var(Ymod)
[1] 6.714629
[1] 5.468435
```

```
> mean(Ylog10);var(Ylog10)
[1] 1.5797
[1] 0.162448

> mean(Yloge);var(Yloge)
[1] 3.637394
[1] 0.8612827

> mean(Yrecp);var(Yrecp)
[1] 0.05187378
[1] 0.01379692

> options (scipen = 999)   # removes scientific notation
> mean(newprobit);var(newprobit)

[1] -0.00000000000000000655778
[1]    0.931573
```

The probit transformation is used quite often by researchers because it returns a data distribution that is closer to the standard normal distribution, with mean = 0 and standard deviation = 1 (variance = 1). Researchers must decide which transformation would make sense for their data and statistical test.

Note: You could replace the value of 1.00 in the *Y* data vector with .99 as follows:

```
> Y[100] = .99
```

● GRAPHICAL DISPLAY OF DATA TRANSFORMATIONS

It is important to visually see the effect of any data transformation. I demonstrate a skewed distribution of data followed by each of the data transformations (square root, reciprocal, log, and probit). These are presented together to determine which one provides a more normal distribution of data. The R package *sn* is downloaded from the main menu. The functions in the *sn* package are described as follows:

```
Density function, distribution function, quantiles and random number
generation for the skew-normal (SN) distribution.
```

Usage

```
dsn(x, location = 0, scale = 1, shape = 0, dp = NULL, log = FALSE)
psn(x, location = 0, scale = 1, shape = 0, dp = NULL, engine, ...)
qsn(p, location = 0, scale = 1, shape = 0, dp = NULL, tol = 1e-8,
engine, ...)
rsn(n = 1, location = 0, scale = 1, shape = 0, dp = NULL)
```

The package is installed as follows:

```
# Install Package {sn} from main menu
> library(sn)
```

The original data with the square root data transformation yield the following graphical output:

```
> set.seed(13579)
> par(mfrow = c(2,1))
> Y = rsn(100,0,5,100)
> hist(Y)
> Y1 = sqrt(Y)
> hist(Y1)
```

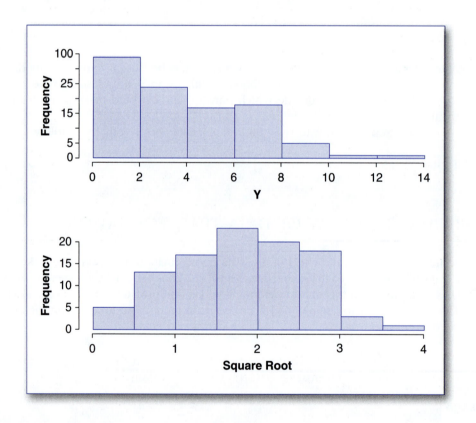

The reciprocal data transformation yields the following graphical output:

```
> Y2 = 1/(Y + 1)
> hist(Y2, xlab = "Reciprocal", main = "")
```

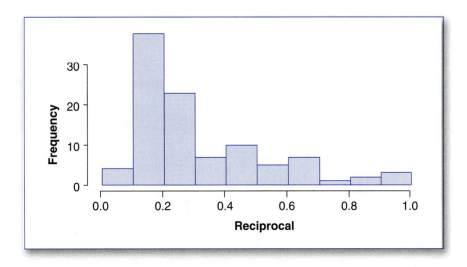

The log data transformation yields the following graphical output:

```
> Y3 = log(Y)
> hist(Y3, xlab = "Log", main = "")
```

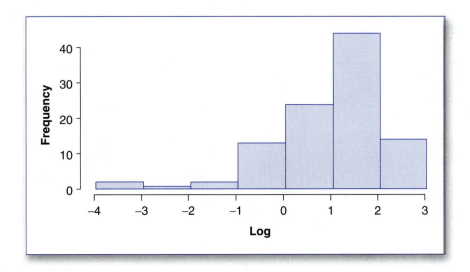

The probit data transformation yields the following graphical output:

```
> p = Y/100
> Y4 = qnorm(p)
> hist(Y4, xlab = "Probit", main = "")
```

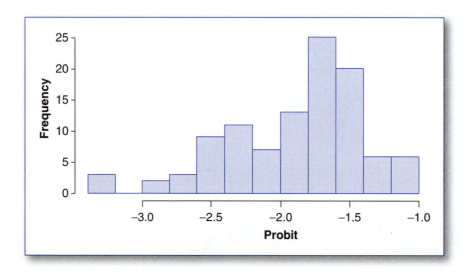

The right, positively skewed values for Y indicate that a square root data transformation is the choice to make. If the data were left, negatively skewed for Y, a different data transformation might work better. This is why it is important to visually look at the transformed data distribution to make your selection.

TIP

✓ Many statistical test procedures in software packages today provide options for different estimation methods and analysis of data that provide robust parameter estimates.

✓ Outliers, missing data, and restriction of range affect the linearity, variance, and normality of sample data.

✓ Data transformation methods change the data values, which can affect the interpretation of results.

✓ Graph the original variable data and the transformed data to view the impact of the data transformation method used.

SUMMARY

It is easy to see how central tendency and dispersion sample statistics are affected by missing values, outliers, adding a constant, multiplying a constant times the data values, sample size, and data transformations. These are important issues that should be remembered when analyzing data in statistics. For example, a sample mean could be inflated if a single extreme value is present in a data set; likewise the mean could be decreased if a smaller value is present, both being considered outliers. Missing values will also have an effect on the sample estimates for central tendency and dispersion. Sample size effects are also present, with more randomly sampled data providing better or more stable sample estimates. Although data transformations are easy to compute and sometimes useful in correcting skewness, they can be problematic when the time comes to interpret the results. Overall, our sample statistics will be good estimates of population parameters if the data are randomly sampled and representative of the population data. After all, our goal is to infer what the population parameters are, without actually knowing them, from these sample estimates.

TIP

✓ When using R libraries with built-in functions such as *summary()*, *describe()*, or *stat. desc()*, it is important to remember how they handle missing data.

✓ Use *na.rm = TRUE* if missing values are present.

✓ Sample statistics are affected by extreme scores, called outliers.

✓ Sample statistics are affected by missing values.

✓ Data transformations, especially probit, are useful if skewness affects normality assumptions.

✓ Sample statistics are estimates of population parameters.

✓ Sample estimates of population parameters are affected by the sample size.

EXERCISES

1. Define arithmetic mean in a distribution of scores.

2. Define median value in a distribution of scores.

3. What R command gives the mean, median, and minimum and maximum Y scores in a data set?

4. A sample is to a _____ as a statistic is to a _____.

5. Given $Y = c(1,2,3,4,,6,7,8,9,10)$, how is the missing value in the fifth position handled?

6. When computing the mean of Y above, what is the correct R command?

7. What is the mean and standard deviation of the following data: $x = c(10,20,30,40,50)$?

8. What is the mean and standard deviation of q, which adds 10 to each data value in x above?

TRUE OR FALSE QUESTIONS

T   F   a.   The mode, mean, and median would be the same value in a normal distribution.

T   F   b.   Missing values do not affect measures of central tendency.

T   F   c.   Sample statistic estimates are affected by sample size.

T   F   d. Ninety-five percent of scores fall approximately ±2 standard deviations from the mean.

T   F   e. When adding a constant to all data values, the standard deviation is the same.

WEB RESOURCES

Chapter R script files are available at http://www.sagepub.com/schumacker

Central Tendency Function R script file: chap9b.r

Dispersion Function R script file: chap9c.r

Sample Size Function R script file: chap9d.r

Summary Function R script file: chap9a.r

PART IV

STATISTICAL METHODS

## CHAPTER 10

HYPOTHESIS TESTING

S cience, as a way of understanding the world around us, has for centuries encompassed the classification, ordering, and measuring of plants, the characteristics of the earth, animals, and humans. Humans by their very nature have attempted to understand, explain, and predict the phenomena in the world around them. When individuals, objects, or events are described as a well-defined, infinite population, then random sampling and probability statistics play a role in drawing conclusions about the population. The problem when conducting research in the social sciences is essentially one of drawing conclusions about the characteristics of an infinitely large population.

Our understanding of sampling, probability, theorems, sampling distributions, and statistical distributions—specifically our ability to hypothesize and test whether a statistical outcome occurs beyond a chance level of probability—is important if we are to better understand scientific inquiry. This chapter introduces the basic idea behind hypothesis testing, including the issue of making a **Type I error** or **Type II error**, since probability determination is not 100%. In addition, our testing of a hypothesis should also include a discussion of the statistical significance of a point estimate (sample statistic), confidence interval, **power**, and **effect size**, which aid our interpretation of the research findings. These ideas and concepts will be further explained in this chapter.

● RESEARCH QUESTIONS AND STATISTICAL HYPOTHESES

The scientific community investigates numerous phenomena in the world. The areas for scientific inquiry are many and have led to the creation of numerous academic disciplines, for example, botany, biology, education, psychology, business, music, and so forth. A first step in any academic discipline that conducts scientific investigation is to ask a research question. Research questions can be expressed in many different ways—for example, "In the upcoming election, who will be elected president of the United States?" or "Which is better, margarine or butter, in lowering cholesterol?"

A research question is transformed into a statistical hypothesis, which can be tested using probability theory and the sampling distribution of the statistic. There are many different kinds of statistical hypotheses depending on the level of measurement (nominal, ordinal, interval, or ratio) and type of research design used in the study. In addition, our sample statistic can be tested for significance based on a directional (one-tailed) or nondirectional (two-tailed) test of the statistical hypothesis. The use of a directional or nondirectional test affects the **level of significance** (alpha) and the region of rejection, which are the probability areas under the sampling distribution of the sample statistic. In addition, the *p* value also designates the region of rejection, which is the area under the curve where a statistic is considered beyond a chance level of occurrence.

The next important steps are to design a study, gather data, and test the research question. This requires converting the research question into a statistical hypothesis. A statistical hypothesis is the cornerstone for testing two possible outcomes (null or alternative), which are always stated in terms of population parameters, given the kind of data collected (percents, ranks, means, or correlation coefficients). The two possible outcomes of a statistical hypothesis are stated in a null (H_0: no difference) and an alternative (H_A: difference exists) format, using symbols for the population parameter. The alternative statistical hypothesis is stated to reflect the outcome expected in the research question. This involves either a directional (a "greater than" difference) or a nondirectional (a difference exists) expression. The null hypothesis is the corresponding opposite expected outcome of a "less than" difference or no difference, respectively.

A research question and a statistical hypothesis for each type of data are listed in Table 10.1. The statistical hypotheses given in the table indicate percent (nominal data), rank (ordinal data), mean (interval/ratio data), and correlation (interval/ratio data) as the four types of sample statistics we express in a statistical hypothesis. Therefore, we are interested in whether one of these sample statistics differs from a population parameter or whether these sample statistics differ between groups, which implies a difference in the population parameters of each group. Although we take a sample of data and calculate a sample statistic, we are always representing (inferring) the population parameter; therefore, all statistical hypotheses use population parameter symbols.

Table 10.1   Research Question Types

Research Question	Data	Statistical Hypotheses
Is the percentage of people smoking in Texas greater than the national average?	Percents	$H_0: P_{Texas} \leq P_{National}$ $H_A: P_{Texas} > P_{National}$
Is there a difference in the ranking of a person's weight gain on two different diets?	Ranks	$H_0: R_{Diet\,A} = R_{Diet\,B}$ $H_A: R_{Diet\,A} \neq R_{Diet\,B}$
Does my ninth-grade class on average score higher than the national average in math?	Means	$H_0: m_{Class} \leq \mu_{National}$ $H_A: m_{Class} > \mu_{National}$
Is the relationship between math ability and science in my sample of students different from that for the population?	Correlations	$H_0: \rho_{Sample} = \rho_{Population}$ $H_A: \rho_{Sample} \neq \rho_{Population}$

● DIRECTIONAL AND
NONDIRECTIONAL STATISTICAL HYPOTHESES

The probability of an outcome is seldom 100%; therefore, two kinds of errors are associated with our decision to retain the null hypothesis based on the outcome of the statistical test (Type I error and Type II error). Type I error is specified by selecting a level of significance (probability area); if the sample statistic falls in this probability area, then we reject the null hypothesis in favor of our **alternative hypothesis**. Type II error corresponds to the probability of retaining the null hypothesis when it is false. When the statistical hypothesis states that the outcome is *greater than*, we designate only one tail of the sampling distribution of the statistic because of the directional nature of the research question. When the statistical hypothesis states that a *difference exists*, we designate both tails of the sampling distribution of the statistic because of the nondirectional nature of the research question. Consequently, the probability area corresponds to different critical tabled statistics (z, t, F, chi-square) found for certain probability levels of a statistic, given in Appendix A.

Once the probability area is determined for the statistical hypothesis, we can select a tabled statistical value to set our region of rejection. The tabled statistical values were generated using probability theory and were created from the sampling distribution of the statistic for different sample sizes (degrees of freedom) and levels of significance. Only the more popular levels of significance (.05, .01, and .001) are generally included in the tables due to page-length consideration. Consequently, it is common for researchers to select a region of rejection and test statistical hypotheses based on the .05, .01, or .001 level of significance. The relationship between the level of significance (alpha symbol) and the probability area for the region of rejection (vertical hash marks) can be depicted as follows:

Nondirectional (two-tailed) Research Question:

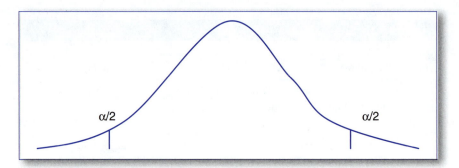

Directional (one-tailed) Research Question:

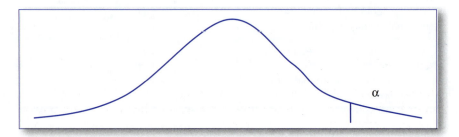

An example (a research question and a corresponding statistical hypothesis) will help illustrate the relationship between the nondirectional/directional thrust of the research question, the level of significance, and the region of rejection. The research question—"Is the ACT population mean in Texas greater than the ACT population mean for the United States?"—is converted into a null and an alternative statistical hypothesis:

$$H_0: \mu_{\text{TEXAS}} \leq \mu_{\text{U.S.}}$$

$$H_A: \mu_{\text{TEXAS}} > \mu_{\text{U.S.}}$$

This is a directional research question; hence, the alternative statistical hypothesis has a "greater than" expression for the population parameters, while the null statistical hypothesis has a "less than or equal to" expression. We test our hypothesis by random sampling 100 students in Texas, compute the sample mean, and conduct a statistical test at the .05 level of significance. Once we have selected a sample size and level of significance for the study, a tabled statistical value can be selected. Under the normal probability curve in Table 1 (Appendix A), a z value of 1.64 corresponds to a probability value (p value) that indicates an area approximately equal to .05 (the probability area beyond $z = 1.64$) for the one-tail test. This z value is used to set the region of rejection for testing our statistical hypothesis (Region of rejection$_{05}$: $z > 1.64$). When we conduct a z test for the difference between the means, a computed z value greater than 1.64 will imply that the population mean in Texas is greater than the population mean in the United States. In other words, the computed z value falls in the probability area of the sampling distribution of the statistic that we have designated to be a highly improbable outcome. The probability area for the null hypothesis and the alternative hypothesis is therefore depicted along with the tabled z value and level of significance for a directional research question as follows:

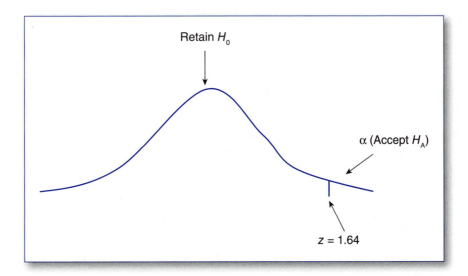

Given our selection of the .05 level of significance, only 5% of the time would we expect a mean difference to exceed $z = 1.64$ if the null hypothesis is true, that is, the population means are equal. Consequently, if the mean difference is large enough and we compute a z value greater than 1.64, we are 95% confident in our decision to reject the null hypothesis in favor of accepting the alternative hypothesis. The retain H_0 area represents 95% of the z values, whereas the accept H_A area represents the remaining 5% of the z values under the sampling distribution.

Assume that we computed a Texas ACT mean of 520 for the 100 randomly sampled students and the U.S. ACT population mean was 500 with a population standard deviation of 100. A one-sample z test to determine the statistical significance of this mean difference is computed as

$$z = \frac{\bar{X} - \mu}{\sigma / \sqrt{N}} = \frac{520 - 500}{100 / \sqrt{100}} = \frac{20}{10} = 2.0.$$

Since the computed $z = 2.0$ is greater than $z = 1.64$ at the .05 level for a one-tail test, and falls in the area designated as the region of rejection, we reject the null hypothesis of no difference in favor of accepting the alternative hypothesis that the population ACT mean in Texas is greater than the population ACT mean in the United States. We are 95% confident in our decision because 95% of the z values fall in the retain H_0 probability area. However, we also know that 5% of the time our decision might be wrong (Type I error), because although our sample z statistic is large enough to fall in the accept H_A probability area, the sample data may not have been representative of the population data. We would answer the research question by stating that the population ACT mean in Texas is statistically significantly higher than the population ACT mean in the United States, given our 95% confidence level.

This example used a z test because the population standard deviation for the ACT was known. In many research studies, the population standard deviation is not known, so we would use a t test. The t-test formula that uses the *sample standard deviation (S)* in place of the population standard deviation (σ) is

$$t = \frac{\bar{X} - \mu}{S / \sqrt{N}}.$$

● HYPOTHESIS TESTING

Research questions involving a test of differences in population means are commonplace in several academic disciplines. An engineer needs to know the average weight of vehicles that can safely travel across a bridge. A psychologist needs to test whether a group of clients have an average cognitive ability greater than the national average. A sociologist needs to determine the average family size for different ethnic groups. The auditor of a large oil company wants to know the average amount of error in the bills prepared for customers. A doctor studying the possible reduction in blood pressure caused by a new medicine is concerned about the average reduction in blood pressure for patients. These and many other research questions reflect a need for a statistical procedure to test whether population means are statistically different.

Tests of statistical hypotheses do not provide exact outcomes. Instead, the tests are based on sample data to reach a conclusion with some degree of uncertainty. In other words, it is possible to reject the null hypothesis when in fact the null hypothesis of no difference is true. We preset the probability of making this kind of error when selecting the level of significance and the corresponding tabled statistic, which is based on the sampling distribution of the statistic. We find that increasing the sample size, using a directional hypothesis, willingness to detect a larger mean difference, and the level of significance are factors that influence whether the statistical test is powerful enough to detect a difference in the population parameters when one exists.

In hypothesis testing, the null hypothesis is retained as true unless the research findings (sample statistic) are beyond the chance probability level (the area where the sample statistic is unlikely to have occurred by chance). A Type I error occurs when a true null hypothesis is rejected erroneously (falsely), which usually happens with an atypical research outcome. The region of rejection is specified by the level of significance (.05, .01, .001), which indicates the probability of making a Type I error. If the z value falls in the region of rejection probability area, then the null hypothesis is rejected in favor of accepting the alternative hypothesis. For different values of alpha (levels of significance) and sample size, the region of rejection will be indicated by a tabled statistic from the sampling distribution of the statistic. A Type II error occurs when a false null hypothesis is retained, that is, we conclude that there is no difference in the population parameters but a difference does exit. A Type II error generally occurs when we have insufficient data to reject the null hypothesis.

In testing whether the population SAT mean in Texas was significantly different from the population SAT mean in the United States, knowledge of the population standard deviation and sample size played a role. A larger random sample of students would dramatically reduce the standard error in the formula, which would result in a larger computed z value, for example, $z = 30$ if $N = 10,000$. A smaller sample size would result in a smaller z value. If the population standard deviation is not known, a sample standard deviation estimate might produce a very different result. A z statistic is generally reported if the population standard deviation is used, while a t statistic is reported when the sample standard deviation is used. The t statistic is usually computed and reported in the research.

The *hypothesis test function* in the R script file (chap10a.r) will specify a population mean and variance for the *rnorm()* function to randomly sample data from the population. In the output, a t test is computed for several null and alternative statistical hypotheses using the *t.test()* function, where you can manually check each individual calculation using the *t-test* formula. The function will select a random sample of size N from the population, compute the sample mean and standard deviation, compute the t statistic and the p value, and indicate the decision outcome. The decision to reject the null hypothesis is based on $p < .05$ for either a one-tailed or a two-tailed test. The function uses the sample mean and standard deviation when calculating the t statistic, which will vary for each randomly drawn sample of data. The number of times you wish to draw a random sample of data and calculate the t statistic is determined by the *numRep* value, which is initially set at 20, so 20 sample means, sample standard deviations, t statistics, decisions, and p values are printed.

You will need to enter the population mean, the population variance, the mean for the null hypothesis, whether a one- or two-tailed directional hypothesis, the sample size, the alpha level, and the number of replications, then run the function. You can begin with these values, but select others to examine how it affects the hypothesis-testing outcomes:

```
> popMean = 10.5
> popVar = 2
> nullMean = 10
```

```
> tails = 1 # 1 = Ha > Null one tail, 2 = Ha = Null two-tail
> sampleSize = 36
> alpha = .05
> numRep = 20
> chap10a(popMean, popVar, nullMean, tails, sampleSize, alpha, numRep)
```

The results will first show the values you input into the function; then a list of sample means, sample standard deviations, and *t*-test values; whether your decision was to retain the null hypothesis or reject the null hypothesis; and finally the *p* value for each *t* statistical value. The results listed are for the number of replications, which was 20:

PROGRAM OUTPUT

                      Result
Hypothesis test Ha > Null one tail
Null Mean =   10
Sample Size =   36
Alpha =   0.05
Replications =   20

Sample Mean	Sample SD	t statistic	Decision	p-value
9.9082	1.221563	-0.4508959	RETAIN NULL	0.674
9.964729	1.043981	-0.202712	RETAIN NULL	0.581
10.92201	1.270874	4.35298	REJECT NULL	0.001
10.47112	1.020314	2.770454	REJECT NULL	0.003
10.53156	1.367978	2.331439	REJECT NULL	0.01
10.6986	1.454529	2.881772	REJECT NULL	0.002
10.64063	1.258819	3.053461	REJECT NULL	0.002
10.5013	1.577593	1.906574	REJECT NULL	0.029
10.15093	1.647151	0.5497709	RETAIN NULL	0.292
10.27824	1.280999	1.303251	RETAIN NULL	0.097
10.33261	1.405113	1.420287	RETAIN NULL	0.078
10.39505	1.287069	1.841645	REJECT NULL	0.033
10.24464	1.512967	0.9701814	RETAIN NULL	0.166
10.64191	1.452036	2.652437	REJECT NULL	0.004
10.34056	1.534153	1.331903	RETAIN NULL	0.092
10.42234	1.380842	1.835126	REJECT NULL	0.034
10.11325	1.302805	0.5215463	RETAIN NULL	0.301
10.68266	1.438285	2.847794	REJECT NULL	0.003
10.52402	1.240335	2.534885	REJECT NULL	0.006
10.41935	1.560571	1.612292	RETAIN NULL	0.054

The output shows 20 individual *t* tests, with six decimal places to minimize rounding error in the *t*-test calculations. We can easily check the calculations by inserting the values into the *t*-test formula. For example, the first calculated *t*-test would indicate the following value:

$$t = \frac{\bar{X} - \mu}{S / \sqrt{N}}$$

$$t = \frac{9.9082 - 10}{1.221563 / \sqrt{36}} = \frac{-0.0918}{0.2035938} = -0.45089.$$

Since $t = -0.45089$ is less than $t = 1.645$ at the $p = .05$ level (critical tabled value for a one-tail test), we would *retain the null* because our sample mean is not greater than the null mean. Notice that the actual p value associated with the t value is printed in most computer printouts, which makes our comparison and decision much easier. Computer programs (SPSS, SAS, STATA, R) routinely output the t statistic and associated p value; however we still plan our research decision based on the t statistic being greater than the critical tabled t value for a given degree of freedom (sample size minus 1) and probability level. Researchers have become accustomed to using $t = 1.96$ with $p = .05$ as the critical tabled value for making their hypothesis-testing decisions.

The confidence level (.05, .01, .001) indicates the probability of making a Type I error, that is, rejecting the null hypothesis when it should have been retained. The sample statistics that fall in the Type I error region of rejection are affected by the degrees of freedom (sample size) and the confidence level. In previous chapters, we saw how the sampling distributions of the sample statistic and probability area changed based on the degrees of freedom (sample size). Given that the confidence level and sample size affect the region of rejection, the width of the confidence interval is also affected. We generally find that given a .05 confidence level for a specific degree-of-freedom value, the population mean will fall within the confidence interval 95% of the time and outside the confidence interval 5% of the time.

The use of a random sample to compute a sample statistic as an estimate of a corresponding population parameter involves some degree of uncertainty. In this chapter, we will discover that the sample mean doesn't always fall in the confidence interval and therefore isn't always accurate in the estimation of the population parameter. The number of times the sample mean falls in the confidence interval is called the confidence level (probability of occurrence), and the number of times it doesn't fall in the confidence interval is called the Type I error (probability of nonoccurrence). The Type I error therefore indicates the amount of uncertainty or probability of error, especially when making a decision about a population parameter. We generally make a decision about a population parameter in the context of a research question.

● RESEARCH STEPS

The research question could be whether or not to use a new experimental drug for the treatment of a disease. In other words, how confident are we that the drug will work? It could also be whether or not to spend money on an innovative math program for high school students. How confident are we that the innovative math program will be better than the traditional math program? In business, the research question of interest might be whether or not to implement a new strategic plan. We conduct research, formally or informally, to answer these types of questions. In simple terms, we ask a question, gather data, and then answer the question. This is the essence of the research process. However, in making our decision to release a drug for public use or spend thousands of dollars on an innovative math program, we can never be 100% certain it will work. There is always some uncertainty involved in our decision, just as sample means don't always fall within the confidence interval!

The research steps involve the formulation of a question that can be tested, the collection of relevant data, the analysis and presentation of the data, and the answering of the question. This formal process embodies the use of the following scientific research steps:

a. Statement of the research hypothesis

b. Selection of the sample size and sample statistic

c. Selection of the confidence level and region of rejection

d. Collection and analysis of data

e. Statistical test and interpretation of the findings

In conducting research using random samples from a population, our statistical hypothesis is related to the probability of whether an event occurs or not. The probability of an event occurring and the probability of an event not occurring are equal to 100%. As researchers, we accept some level of probability or uncertainty as to whether an event occurs or not. Our statistical test and interpretation of findings are linked to the Type I error in our decision.

The statistical hypothesis expresses the outcome expected in the research question. The outcomes are expressed as a null hypothesis and an alternative hypothesis. The null hypothesis is a statement of no difference between the sample mean and population mean or, in general terms, between a sample statistic and a population parameter. The alternative hypothesis is a statement that a difference exists between the sample mean and population mean, typically based on some intervention, treatment, or manipulation of participants, objects, or events. For example, the null hypothesis would state *no difference* in the average mathematics test scores of students in a traditional math program versus an innovative math program. The alternative hypothesis would state that the average mathematics test score of students in the innovative math program is greater (*statistically different*) than the average mathematics test score of students in the traditional math program.

The sample size and sample statistic chosen to make a comparison between the sample estimate and population parameter is our next research step. The sample size is an important consideration because as the sample size increases the sample statistic more closely approximates the population parameter. The sample statistic is computed by taking the difference between the sample estimate and the population parameter and divided by the standard error of the mean difference, which is based on the sampling distribution of the statistic. We will learn more about conducting several different types of statistical tests in the next several chapters.

The confidence level and region of rejection are now established, which set the amount of uncertainty we are willing to accept for the two possible outcomes of the research question, that is, null versus alternative. If we want to be 95% confident in our decision that the innovative math program produced higher average mathematics test scores, then we must also have a 5% level of uncertainty (Type I error) in our decision. This probability of making a mistake (uncertainty) is called the level of significance and is denoted by the symbol α (alpha). It is the chance we take of rejecting the null hypothesis statement when it is true and erroneously accepting the alternative hypothesis statement. If we *reject* the null hypothesis statement when it is true, and *accept* the alternative hypothesis statement, we commit a Type I error. If we *retain* the null hypothesis statement when it is false, and thus *don't accept* the alternative hypothesis statement, we commit a Type II error. In either instance, we do so with a level of confidence and a level of error in our decision, because the outcome is based on probability, which is not 100% in either decision.

The region of rejection refers to the selection of a statistical value from the sampling distribution that is at the cutoff point for the beginning of the probability area in which we would reject the null hypothesis in favor of accepting the alternative hypothesis. Statistical values for varying sample sizes and different types of sampling distributions for the 90%, 95%, and 99% confidence levels can be found in the appendix of most statistics books. We refer to these statistical values as the *tabled critical statistics*. If the sample statistic computed from the sample data falls in the 5% area, corresponding to a 95% confidence level, then we reject the null hypothesis and accept the alternative hypothesis. We make this decision knowing that 5% of the time it might not be the correct decision, which is the Type I error.

The next research step would involve randomly sampling students and randomly assigning them to either a traditional math program or an innovative math program. After a semester of study, each group would take the same mathematics test. The sample means and standard deviations for each group would be computed. A statistical test would determine if the means were statistically different for our level of confidence and corresponding level of significance. In this instance, an independent *t* test would be computed to test the mean difference.

The final step involves a comparison of the tabled critical statistic (based on the level of significance and region of rejection) and the sample statistic computed from the sample data. If the sample statistic is greater than the tabled statistic, a decision is made to reject the null hypothesis and accept the alternative hypothesis. If the sample statistic does not exceed the tabled statistic, then a decision is made to retain the null hypothesis and reject the alternative hypothesis. Our interpretation of the findings of the research is based on this decision to reject or accept the statistical hypothesis, which relates to the two possible outcomes of the study, Type I or Type II error.

● TYPE I ERROR

The *Type I error function* in the script file (chap10b.r) investigates the relationship between the confidence level and the width of the confidence interval in the context of making a Type I error. In addition, different sample sizes can be input to observe the effect of sample size on the confidence level, the width of the confidence interval, and the Type I error. A single sample of size *N* will be chosen from a normally distributed population with a mean of 50 and a standard deviation of 10. The function will then compute and graph the 95% confidence interval, which corresponds to the 5% level of uncertainty (level of significance). Since a population standard deviation will be used, *z* values are used to determine the width of the confidence interval, which is shown as dashed lines on both sides of the mean value. The *z* value of 1.96 corresponds to alpha = .05 and the 95% confidence level. The function also prints the location of the sample mean as a solid line so that it can be compared with the population mean of 50.

We wish for the population mean to fall within the confidence interval, which would indicate that the sample mean is a good estimate of the population mean,

You will need to enter the sample size, the population mean, the population standard deviation, the z value for the confidence interval, and the number of replications, then run the function. We can first use these values and then change them to view other outcome solutions:

```
> SampleSize = 10
> PopMean = 50
> PopSD = 10
> Zvalue = 1.96 # confidence interval
> numRep = 100
> chap10b(SampleSize, PopMean, PopSD, Zvalue, numRep)
```

The results will first list the values you entered for the function, then produce a plot that shows the sample mean and confidence interval (dashed lines):

```
PROGRAM OUTPUT

                          Results
Sample Size              = 10
Pop Mean                 = 50
Pop SD                   = 10
z value                  =  1.96
Confidence Interval      = 38 - 51
Interval Width           = 12
Sample Mean              = 44.75
Location of Sample Mean  = Inside CI
```

The sample mean = 44.75, and the population mean = 50; the sample mean (shown by a solid line) will change each time the *Type I error* function is run. The confidence interval is 38 to 51 (shown by the dashed lines), so the population mean is within the 95% confidence interval, established by selecting $z = 1.96$ ($p = .05$). When the level of confidence is increased, for example, $z = 2.58$ (99% confidence level; $p = .001$), the Type I error is decreased and the width of the confidence interval increases. However, as the sample size is increased, the width of the confidence interval is decreased. The sample mean is always within the confidence interval, but the population mean sometimes is outside the confidence interval, so the percentage of the intervals that contain the population mean is the confidence level, while the percentage of the intervals that do not contain the population mean is the Type I error probability. We normally expect that 95% of the time the confidence interval will capture the population mean and 5% of the time (Type I error), the population mean will fall outside the confidence interval. This outcome applies to our hypothesis-testing decision, that is, 5% of the time we will reject the null hypothesis when it is true, but 95% of the time we are confident that a correct decision was made.

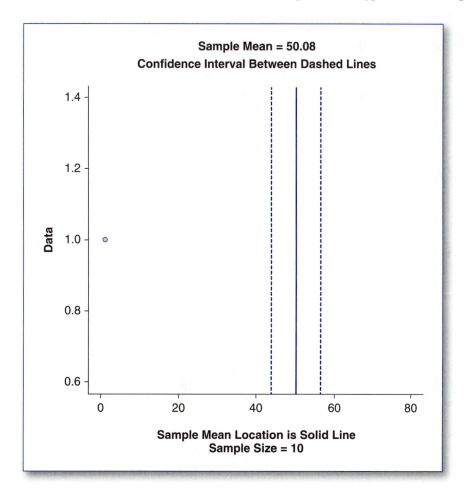

● TYPE II ERROR

Type II error is committed when we retain the null hypothesis when it should have been rejected. This usually occurs because we do not have enough information or data to reject the null hypothesis, which can be thought of as power to detect a difference when it exists. The confidence level (alpha, level of significance), the directionality of our research question (one-tailed/two-tailed), the population variance, and the sample size each affect the probability of Type II error. Two new concepts are introduced, power (the ability to detect a difference) and effect size (the difference between the population parameter and the sample statistic), that further help in our understanding of Type II error.

The research process, as stated before, begins with the formulation of a research question. The research question is then stated in the form of a statistical hypothesis that can be tested. The two possible outcomes of the statistical hypothesis are the null hypothesis and alternative hypothesis. These hypotheses can be stated in either a directional or a nondirectional format. A **directional**

hypothesis states that one population parameter is greater than the other population parameter. A **nondirectional hypothesis** states that the two population parameters "are different" but doesn't specify which is greater.

An example of both the nondirectional and the directional statistical hypothesis will help us visualize how they are presented using population parameters. The nondirectional hypothesis sets School A and School B *equal* in the null hypothesis (H_0), while School A and School B are *not equal* in the alternative hypothesis (H_A), which is indicated as

$$H_0 : \mu_{SchoolA} = \mu_{SchoolB}$$

$$H_A : \mu_{SchoolA} \neq \mu_{SchoolB}.$$

The directional hypothesis sets School A *less than or equal to* School B in the null hypothesis (H_0) and School A *greater than* School B in the alternative hypothesis (H_A), which is indicated as

$$H_0 : \mu_{SchoolA} \leq \mu_{SchoolB}$$

$$H_A : \mu_{SchoolA} > \mu_{SchoolB}.$$

The alternative hypothesis (H_A) indicates that the population mean for School A is greater than the population mean for School B, thereby only testing a specific directional difference in the population means of the two schools.

The probabilities related to the two possible outcomes, the null hypothesis and the alternative hypothesis, are given the name Type I error and Type II error. A Type I error occurs when the null hypothesis is rejected but is in fact true. This means that you gathered evidence (data) and concluded that the evidence was strong enough to reject the null hypothesis and accept the alternative hypothesis, but you did so erroneously. A Type II error occurs when the null hypothesis is retained (accepted), but in fact it is false. This means that you gathered evidence (data) and concluded that the evidence wasn't strong enough to reject the null hypothesis, so you retained the null hypothesis but did so erroneously. Not rejecting the null hypothesis was due to a lack of sufficient evidence (data). Neither decision, to reject or retain the null hypothesis, is 100% certain; therefore, we make our decision with some amount of uncertainty. Whether the Type I error or Type II error is more important depends on the research situation and the type of decision made. An example will help clarify the Type I and Type II errors and the possible outcomes.

A corporation is going to use data from a sample of people to test a research question of whether or not a new product design will increase the average sales above that of the current product design. Using the current product design, the company sold an average of 85 cars. The company, in planning the study, realizes that two types of error are possible in the study. If the new product design is used, the average sales of the product may not be greater than 85 cars but the analysis could incorrectly lead to the conclusion that the average sales were higher—a Type I error. If the new product design was used and the average sales did exceed 85 cars but the statistical analysis failed to indicate a statistically significant increase, then a Type II error has occurred, and our conclusion that sales did not exceed 85 cars would be erroneous.

When planning this study, the company can control the probability of a Type I error by setting the level of significance (alpha) to a stringent probability level. For example, setting the level of significance to .05 implies that 95 times out of 100 replications of the study a correct decision would be made and 5 times out of 100 an incorrect decision would be made. Setting the level of significance to .01 implies that 99 times out of 100 a correct decision would be made and only 1 time out of 100 an incorrect decision would be made. These probabilities for a correct decision and an incorrect decision are applicable only when the null hypothesis is true. Therefore, we set the Type I error to a probability level that instills confidence in our decision to reject the null hypothesis (no difference) and accept an alternative hypothesis (difference exists).

A Type II error requires a further concern for many other factors in the study. The probability of a Type II error depends on the level of significance (alpha), the direction or nondirection of the research question, the sample size, the population variance, and the difference between the population parameters we want to be able to detect (effect size). These concerns determine how powerful (power) our test will be to detect a difference when it actually exists in the population(s) we study. In planning the study, the company needs to be concerned about both Type I and Type II errors, as well as the consequences of the decision made based on the statistical outcome.

In testing hypotheses, four possible outcomes exist with regard to the Type I and Type II decisions made:

Actual Population Condition			
		Null Hypothesis Is True	Null Hypothesis Is False
Research Decision	Reject null hypothesis	Type I error (Probability = α)	Correct decision (Probability = $1 - \beta$)
	Retain null hypothesis	Correct decision (Probability = $1 - \alpha$)	Type II error (Probability = β)

The probability of making a Type I error in the null hypothesis is denoted by the symbol alpha, α, and is referred to as the level of significance, with the probability of a correct decision equal to $1 - \alpha$. The probability of making a Type II error in the alternative hypothesis is denoted by the symbol beta, β, with the power of the test for a correct decision given by $1 - \beta$, probability of

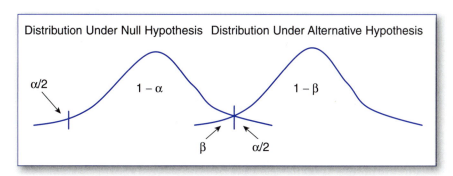

making a correct decision. The relationship between Type I error and Type II error is typically graphed using vertical hash marks to denote the area for the region of rejection in the sampling distribution of a statistic. The two overlapping graphs below indicate the probability areas for the four decision outcomes.

The probability in the tails of the distributions can change because the null and alternative hypotheses can be stated in directional or nondirectional formats. In this example, the hypotheses are in a nondirectional (two-tailed) form; for example, is there a statistically significant mean difference between boys and girls on the mathematics test? If the level of significance is .05, then one half of the area ($\alpha/2 = .025$) would be the probability area in the tails of the distribution. If we chose only the one tail ($p = .025$), then the alternative research question would be stated as directional; for example, will the girls on average score higher than the boys in mathematics achievement? The statistical tables in Appendix A adjust for the directional versus nondirectional nature when selecting a tabled critical statistic value.

The basic concern in selecting a Type II error is the value of power, which is $1 - \beta$. Power is the probability of *not* committing the error. In conducting research in education, psychology, business, and other disciplines, we are concerned about the power of our statistical test to detect a difference in the population parameters. Statistics books typically provide tables or graphs of power values for different population parameter values given different levels of significance and sample sizes. R can provide the power values of various statistical tests used in hypothesis testing through the *pwr* package.

The *Type II error function* in the script file (chap10c.r) demonstrates how the probability of a Type II error is affected by four criteria: alpha level, sample size, population variance, and effect size. The function chooses a sample of a size specified by you from a population and determines whether or not to reject the null hypothesis. The function is initially repeated 100 times. The relative frequency of occurrence with which a false null hypothesis is retained is an approximation of the probability of a Type II error, β. The power of the test is calculated as 1 minus this relative frequency. Power is equal to $1 - \beta$ when the null hypothesis is false. The theoretical values for the probability of retaining the null hypothesis and power are also given. If the true mean is equal to the mean in the null hypothesis, then the probability of retaining the null hypothesis is equal to $1 - \alpha$. In this case, power is equal to α, the level of significance. The hypothesis testing in the function is directional, to determine whether the mean of a population with a normal distribution is greater than a specified value; therefore, the level of significance is located in one tail of the distribution. The function specifies the mean in the null hypothesis, the population mean and variance, the sample size, and the level of significance, α. These values would be entered into the function for 100 replications:

```
> options(scipen = 999)
> nullMean = 0
> popMean = 0
> popVar = 1
> sampleSize = 100
> alpha = .05
> tails = 1 # 0 = one-tailed less than null, 1 = one-tailed greater than
null
> numRep = 100
> chap10c(nullMean, popMean, popVar, sampleSize, alpha, tails, numRep)
```

The results will first list the values you entered, then the obtained null percent (.97) and alpha (.03), which are compared with the true null percent (.95) and alpha (.05), respectively.

```
PROGRAM OUTPUT

                Results
Null Mean     =    0.00
Pop Mean      =    0.00
Pop Var       =    1.00
Sample Size = 100.00
Alpha         =    0.05


 % Accept Null Alpha % True Null True Alpha
    0.97          0.03    0.95        0.05
```

The true null and alpha (.95; .05) are compared with the obtained null and alpha (.97; .03) given the effect size (*Pop Mean − Null Mean*), sample size, and level of significance (alpha). The goal is to design a study to closely match the theoretical with the obtained results for a statistical test in a research study. Our example specified no difference with a large sample size. If we decrease the sample size, the obtained results will be greater than the true results, indicating more Type II error. We wish to minimize the Type II error, which implies that a null hypothesis has been retained (accepted), but erroneously so.

The probability of a Type II error is denoted by the symbol β and decreases if

- α increases from .01 to .05,
- N increases,
- the population variance decreases, or
- the effect size is larger (the true mean is farther from the hypothesized mean in the direction of the alternative hypothesis).

When a Type II error decreases, power increases (power is the probability of rejecting a null hypothesis that is false). When the null hypothesis is false, power is equal to $1 - \beta$; but when the null hypothesis is true, power is equal to α.

You can also examine the Type II error by selecting certain values and running a few R commands. For example, if you specify $\alpha = .05$, standard deviation = 5, population mean = 100, and sample mean = 105, then the beta value and power can be computed as follows:

```
> options(scipen = 999)   # stops scientific notation in output
> S = 5
> pop = 100
> sample = 105

> low05 = qnorm(.025, mean = pop, sd = s)
> high05 = qnorm(.975, mean = pop, sd = s)
> top05 = pnorm(high05, mean = sample, sd = s)
> bottom05 = pnorm(low05, mean = sample, sd = s)
```

```
> beta = top05 - bottom05
> beta
> power = 1 - beta
> power
```

The results are printed as

```
> beta
[1] 0.829925
> power = 1 - beta
> power
[1] 0.170075
```

The power = .17, which is low for detecting a 5-point difference. This simple exercise shows us that determining the beta value and power requires selection of certain criteria, namely, the alpha level, the standard deviation, the directional nature of the hypothesis (one- or two-tailed), and the effect size. The directional nature of the hypothesis is determined by the alpha values used in the *qnorm()* function. The effect size is the difference you wish to detect. In this example, it is 105 − 100, a 5-point difference, which indicates 1 standard deviation from the population mean. The alpha values of .025 and .975 indicate a one-tailed directional hypothesis test.

If we increase the effect size to 15 points, the power to detect a difference increases to an acceptable level:

```
> beta
[1] 0.1491612

> power = 1 - beta
> power

[1] 0.8508388
```

If we increase $\alpha = .01$ (.005 and .995) with a 15-point effect size difference, the results are as follows:

```
> beta
[1] 0.3357207

> power = 1 - beta
> power

[1] 0.6642793
```

Power = .66 indicates a decrease below an acceptable level for detecting the 15-point effect size difference. Power = .80 is the acceptable level a researcher typically desires to control the Type II error rate.

A researcher is generally interested in the sample size needed to conduct the research study, in addition to the power to detect a difference (effect size) when one truly exists. The above set of R commands can be updated to also include sample size, which is the final criterion one needs for power determination. For example, if sample size were $n = 100$, the standard error of the mean could be changed. The standard error of the mean is the value affected by the sample size; thus, in the R commands you would divide the value S by the square root of n:

$$S = \frac{S}{\sqrt{n}} = \frac{5}{\sqrt{100}} = \frac{5}{10} = 0.5.$$

Setting $S = .5$, effect size $= 5$ (100 vs. 105), and $\alpha = .01$ (.005, .995), the results would be as follows:

```
> beta
[1]  0.00000000000005674436

> power = 1 - beta

> power
[1]  1
```

Note: Software is available that does these calculations for different statistical tests (Faul, Erdfelder, Buchner, & Lang, 2009; Faul, Erdfelder, Lang, & Buchner, 2007).

● CONFIDENCE INTERVALS AND CONFIDENCE LEVELS

In Chapter 6, the concept of confidence intervals was introduced. We revisit the importance of confidence intervals because when reporting hypothesis-testing results, the researcher should state the null and alternative hypotheses, sample size, power, effect size, and confidence interval for the research study. The standard error of the statistic is used to establish the confidence interval around a sample statistic that captures the population parameter. Based on the confidence level (alpha), we can determine how precise our sample statistic is as an estimate of the population parameter. It also indicates how much the sample estimate of our population parameter may vary from study to study because the population values are captured within confidence intervals around the sample statistic for a given confidence level.

Confidence intervals can be computed for many different population parameters by using the standard error of the statistic and the confidence level. The standard error of the statistic was described earlier, for example, the standard error of the mean. The variance of a sampling distribution indicates the amount of error in estimating the population parameter. A smaller sampling variance reflects less error in estimating the population parameter. The standard error of a statistic is computed as the standard deviation of the sampling distribution divided by the square root of the sample size. Consequently, as the sample size increases, the standard error of the statistic decreases. A confidence interval is computed using the sample statistic and the standard error of the statistic (standard deviation of the statistic in the sampling distribution). The confidence interval around the sample statistic is a range of values that should contain the population parameter.

A confidence level is used that defines how confident we are that the interval around the sample statistic contains the parameter being estimated. The confidence interval is determined by picking an area in the tail of the sampling distribution in which the value of the statistic is improbable. Recall that a sampling distribution is a frequency distribution; therefore, we could pick a 5% probability area, leaving 95% of the sample statistics in the frequency distribution as plausible estimates of the population parameter.

The confidence interval around a sample statistic is computed by using the standard error of the statistic. The confidence interval indicates the precision of the sample statistic as an estimate of the population parameter. The confidence interval around the sample statistic is said to include the population parameter with a certain level of confidence. It should be common practice to report confidence intervals for various population parameters, such as proportions, means, or correlations. The confidence interval contains a high and a low score, above and below the sample statistic, between which we feel confident that the population parameter occurs. Confidence levels are used to determine the width of the confidence interval. Commonly used confidence levels are 90%, 95%, and 99%. These confidence levels for sample data are indicated by critical t values of 1.65 (10% probability area), 1.96 (5% probability area), and 2.58 (1% probability area), respectively, which are given in Table 2 in Appendix A (Distribution of t for Given Probability Levels).

The 95% confidence interval for the population mean is computed as

$$\bar{X} \pm 1.96(S / \sqrt{N}),$$

where S = sample standard deviation and n = sample size. The value of 1.96 corresponds to the t value that contains 5% of the sample means in the tail of the sampling distribution that are improbable. This implies that 5 times out of 100 replications, a confidence interval for a sample mean may not contain the population mean. In contrast, 95 times out of 100, the confidence interval around the sample mean will contain the population mean. Stated differently, 5% of the time the sample mean will not be a good estimate of the population mean, or conversely, 95% of the time we are confident that the sample mean will be a good estimate of the population mean.

If the sample mean was 50, sample standard deviation 10, the sample size 100, and we wanted to be 95% confident that the confidence interval captured the population mean, then the confidence interval around the sample mean would range between 48.04 and 51.96. This range of values is computed as

$$CI_{.95} = \bar{X} \pm t(\frac{S}{\sqrt{n}}) = 50 \pm 1.96(\frac{10}{\sqrt{100}}) = 50 \pm 1.96$$

$$CI_{.95} = (48.04; 51.96).$$

If we replicated our sampling 10 times, we would expect the population mean to fall in the confidence interval range of values approximately 95% of the time (5 times out of 100 the confidence intervals would not contain the population mean).

The *confidence interval function* in the script file (chap10d.r) simulates random samples and computes the confidence intervals around the sample mean (the process is the same for other population parameters because it would be based on the sampling distribution of the statistic). A population with a normal distribution ($\mu = 50$ and $\sigma = 10$) will be sampled. When entering different sample sizes and confidence levels, the effect on estimating the confidence interval is output. The function uses the population standard deviation rather than the sample standard deviation in the confidence interval formula because it is known. The 95% confidence interval would be computed as:

$$\bar{X} \pm 1.96(\sigma / \sqrt{N}).$$

If the population standard deviation is known, one would use the population standard deviation with a z value for the confidence interval. If the population standard deviation is *not* known, one would use a sample standard deviation estimate with a critical t value for the confidence interval. The sampling distribution of the mean will be based on 20 replications. For each sample mean, the 95% confidence interval around the mean will be computed, and the function will check to see whether or not the population mean of 50 is contained in the confidence interval. Due to sampling error, one may not achieve the exact percent of confidence intervals that contain the population mean as indicated by the confidence level, that is, 95%.

You will need to enter the following values for the function prior to running it:

```
> SampleSize = 100
> PopMean = 50
> PopSD = 10
> NumRep = 20
# Zvalue = 1.65(90%), Zvalue = 1.96(95%), or Zvalue = 2.58(99%)
> Zvalue = 1.96
> chap10d(SampleSize, PopMean, PopSD, NumRep, Zvalue)
```

The results will first list the values you entered, then show the sample means for the 20 replications, with their confidence intervals and a decision of whether the population mean fell within the confidence interval.

```
PROGRAM OUTPUT

                 Results
Sample Size   = 100.00
Pop Mean      =  50.00
Pop SD        =  10.00
Replications  =  20.00
Z value       =   1.96

Confidence Intervals That Contain Population Mean = 19/20 = 95%

Sample Mean (low - high)CI Pop Mean Within CI
   49.96          48    - 51.92    50        Yes
   49.12         47.16 - 51.08    50        Yes
   49.5          47.54 - 51.46    50        Yes
   49.95         47.99 - 51.91    50        Yes
```

49.74	47.78	-	51.7	50	Yes
50.96	49	-	52.92	50	Yes
48.78	46.82	-	50.74	50	Yes
50.23	48.27	-	52.19	50	Yes
49.58	47.62	-	51.54	50	Yes
50.24	48.28	-	52.2	50	Yes
49.27	47.31	-	51.23	50	Yes
49.08	47.12	-	51.04	50	Yes
51.6	49.64	-	53.56	50	Yes
50.16	48.2	-	52.12	50	Yes
50.94	48.98	-	52.9	50	Yes
49.72	47.76	-	51.68	50	Yes
50.93	48.97	-	52.89	50	Yes
47.45	45.49	-	49.41	50	No
51.21	49.25	-	53.17	50	Yes
49.33	47.37	-	51.29	50	Yes

The confidence intervals above reflect a range of values (low–high) around the sample mean for the 95% level of confidence. These confidence intervals indicate the precision of a sample statistic (mean) as an estimate of a population parameter (mean). Since the confidence interval has a 95% level of confidence, it indicates that approximately 95 out of 100 confidence intervals around the sample statistic will contain the population parameter. Our results indicated that for $z = 1.96$ (95% confidence level), 19 out of 20 replications contained the population mean within the confidence interval, that is, $19/20 = 95\%$. The remaining 5% (1/20) of the confidence intervals did not contain the population mean. This remaining 5% is associated with the Type I error rate and specified by the level of significance (alpha). If the confidence level remains the same but the sample size increases, then the width of the confidence interval decreases, indicating a more precise estimate of the population parameter.

● CRITERIA FOR STATISTICAL TESTS

The statistical assumptions for the various statistical tests and the selection of power, sample size, alpha, and effect size are covered in this section. The different effect size values for the statistics and the creation of sample size and power plots are also covered in this section. Researchers often dismiss these issues when conducting their research, often because they do not have the tools to readily determine the appropriate criteria for testing their statistical hypothesis. Today, much of our research and publication endeavours require addressing and reporting of these criteria.

Statistical Assumptions

The statistical tests covered in this book have assumptions, which when not met, usually cause problems in the robustness of the statistic and the interpretation of the results. A list of the assumptions for the various statistical tests are listed below, all of them basically requiring a random sample from a population:

Chi-square: A minimum of five expected observations per cell in the crosstab table

z test: Normality, independence

t test: Normality, independence, equal variances in the two groups

r test: Normality, linear relationship, no restriction of range, no missing data, no outliers

R: Normality, no multicollinearity, no outliers, homogeneity of variance

F test: Normality, independence, equal variances across three or more groups

The assumptions fall into the categories of random sample, normality, independence, and homogeneity of variance. They relate to issues of whether variable relations are linear and errors are independent, that is, not correlated with variables (correlation, regression) or whether errors are normally distributed in groups and there are equal variances across groups (*t* test, analysis of variance [ANOVA]). Many of these assumptions can be checked using R functions. They are listed below and then run with a sample set of data.

Function	Description
skewness()	Shape of sample distribution, e.g., asymmetrical or skewed
kurtosis()	Shape of sample distribution, e.g., leptokurtic or peaked
hist()	Histogram
boxplot()	Outliers
shapiro.test()	Normality test in {base} package; {nortest} package has others
leveneTest()	Equal variances in {cars} package

The *stat.desc()* function in the *pastecs* package and the *describe()* function in the *psych* package provide skewness and **kurtosis** values, which indicate the degree of skew and flatness, respectively. The *hist* and *boxplot* functions provide a visual examination of data in a graph. The *shapiro.test()* function is a test of normality with associated *p* value. There are several tests of equal variance: Bartlett chi-square (1937), Hartley F_{max} (1940, 1950), Cochran *C* (1941), and Levene (1960). The *leveneTest()* function is recommended because it is less sensitive to nonnormality than the others and uses median values. The *leveneTest()* function compares the means of the absolute values of deviations from the median value.

It is important to know your data, that is, understand whether your data meet the basic assumptions for the statistical test. Prior research has shown that these tests are robust to violations of the assumptions; however, they have also formed the basis for other nonparametric statistics and robust statistical tests to be created. For example, the Pearson correlation is for interval data, so the Phi was created for nominal data and Spearman rank for ordinal data (Chen & Popovich, 2002). In multiple regression, the basic ordinary least squares regression has been expanded to include logistic regression, log-linear regression, ordinal regression, robust regression, and so on. When assumptions are not met (severely violated), it is recommended that you use nonparametric statistics or robust statistical procedures, which are beyond the scope of this book.

An example will demonstrate how to obtain the descriptive statistics. I first installed the *psych* package and used the *library()* function to load the package. Next, I put test scores into a data vector, *test*. The *describe()* function can now be used to obtain the descriptive statistics.

```
> install.packages("psych")
> library(psych)
> test = c(99,98,97,97,95,96,91,90,89,85,70,50,20,10)
> describe(test)
```

var	n	mean	sd	median	trimmed	mad	min	max	range	skew	kurtosis	se
1	1	14 77.64	29.73	90.5	81.5	9.64	10	99	89	−1.28	0.06	7.95

The results indicate that the tests scores are skewed (−1.28) but not kurtotic (.06). We can see that the mean = 77.64 ~ 78 and median = 90.5 ~ 91, which further supports our understanding of a nonnormal, skewed distribution of test scores.

The *pastecs* package was also installed and loaded to show the results, using the *stat.desc()* function. This function provides an additional test of normality along with median, mean, skewness, and kurtosis.

```
> install.packages("pastecs")
> library(pastecs)
> stat.desc(test)
```

median	mean	SE.mean	CI.mean.0.95	var
90.5000000000	77.6428571429	7.9466677949	17.1677320274	884.0934065934

std.dev	coef.var	skewness	skew.2SE	kurtosis
29.7337082550	0.3829548441	−1.2835335716	−1.0743026098	0.0616743802

kurt.2SE	normtest.W	normtest.p
0.0267208355	0.7183102217	0.0005755458

The mean, median, skewness, and kurtosis values are the same as those returned from the *describe()* function. In addition, the *normtest.W* value of 0.718 ($p = .0005$) is statistically significant, indicating a nonnormal distribution. This reported value is also the Shapiro test of normality, which can be obtained by the *shapiro.test()* function:

```
> shapiro.test(test)

Shapiro-Wilk normality test

data: test
W = 0.7183, p-value = 0.0005755
```

A visual display of the data provides visual evidence of the skewness or kurtosis of the data. The histogram shows more bars (frequency) to the right and does not have the appearance of a normal distribution:

```
> hist(test)
```

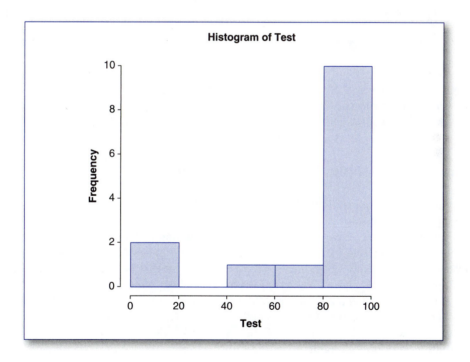

The *boxplot()* function also provides information about outliers and score distribution:

```
> boxplot(test)
```

The box plot shows two extreme values (circles) below the lower box whisker (test scores = 20 and 10). The median value in the box also does not divide the scores into equal 25% areas. Recall

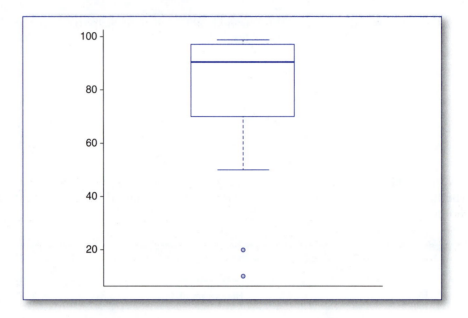

that the box represents 50% of the score distribution. Its appearance further shows a skewness toward the top or upper end of the score distribution.

Note: It is important to run these R functions on the variables in your data set to determine if they meet the assumptions for conducting the statistical tests in this book.

Selecting Power, Sample Size, Alpha, and Effect Size

The basic task a researcher must undertake when conducting a statistical test is to determine the power, sample size, alpha level (level of significance), direction of the hypothesis (one- or two-tailed test), and effect size. Power is the probability of finding a difference or effect when it truly exists. When the sample size increases, it provides better estimates of population parameters. The alpha level is the probability of finding a difference or effect that is *not* present. The direction of the hypothesis affects this alpha level based on the probability area underneath the sampling distribution. The effect size is the amount of difference we want to detect. A large effect size is easier to detect (like the Grand Canyon) than a small effect size (like a needle in a haystack).

A researcher would select four out of the five above criteria to determine the value of the remaining fifth criterion. For example, setting sample size = 100, alpha = .05, direction = one-tail test, and effect size = 0.2, a power value is determined. Likewise, setting power = .80, alpha = .05, direction = one-tail test, and effect size = 0.2, a sample size is determined. These criteria values are established a priori, that is, when planning a research study. After the study is completed, posterior or actual values are used to determine the criteria for the study. In R power analysis functions, the direction of the hypothesis is left out, leaving it up to the researcher to divide, say, .05/2 = .025 for a two-tailed test.

Kabacoff (2012) has developed a website called Quick-R, which is a valuable resource to explore and understand power analysis in R. In R, various power functions are available, which require entering the four criteria values: power, sample size, significance level, and effect size. For each of these functions, you enter three of the criteria to obtain the value of the remaining fourth criterion. The significance level defaults to .05, so when wanting to obtain that criterion given the power, sample size, and effect size, use the option, *sig.level = NULL*.

The R package is *pwr*, which follows the work by Cohen (1988). The functions are as follows:

Function Name	Description
pwr.p.test	Percent: proportion (one sample)
pwr.2p.test	Percent: difference between two proportions (equal *n*)
pwr.2p2n.test	Percent: difference between two proportions (unequal *n*)
pwr.chisq.test	Chi-square: independence of row and column cells
pwr.t.test	*t* Test: mean difference (one sample, two samples, paired samples)
pwr.t2n.test	*t* Test: mean difference (two samples—unequal *n*)
pwr.anova.test	Analysis of variance: one way (balanced design—equal *n*)
pwr.r.test	Correlation: Pearson bivariate relationship
pwr.f2.test	Regression: general linear model

Install the R *pwr* package by entering the *Install.packages()* function in the R Gui window:

```
> Install.packages("pwr")
```

A dialog box will open, then select a CRAN mirror site. After a "successful download" message appears, enter the *library()* function to load the package:

```
> library(pwr)
```

To obtain the arguments for any of the power functions, simply place a ? in front of the function name, and an Internet window will open with R documentation. For example,

```
> ? pwr.2p.test
```

When planning a research study, the investigator is usually interested in determining the required sample size. The rationale for this selection is that the sample size determines the duration and cost of the study and has a bearing on obtaining institutional review board (human subjects) approval for the research. We would therefore select values for power, alpha significance level, and effect size. A researcher planning a study would usually set power = .80 $(1 - \beta)$, where β is the Type II error rate. This reflects a 20% chance of making the wrong decision about the outcome of the study results. Recall that a Type II error occurs when a false null hypothesis is retained, that is, we conclude that there is no difference in the population parameters but a difference does exit. A Type II error generally occurs when we have insufficient data to reject the null hypothesis, that is, our sample size is too small. The alpha or significance level for the statistical test (one- or two-tailed) is also generally selected when planning a study. The significance level is usually set at .05, which establishes a Type I error rate, or the probability of rejecting the null hypothesis when it is true. A researcher in this case is willing to accept a 5% chance that the null hypothesis would be rejected when in fact it is the true outcome—that is, no difference exists. The third a priori decision in planning a research study is to establish the amount of difference you want to detect. This can be small, medium, or large. Cohen (1988) indicated a rule of thumb that 0.2 (small), 0.5 (medium), and 0.8 (large) were reasonable standardized values for his effect size of the mean difference between treatment and control groups in an experimental design. Many researchers conducting experimental designs quote these values, but actually one should determine what the effect sizes are given the prior research studies published on the topic. Every academic discipline and each area researched will have different effect sizes. It is best to look for **meta-analysis** articles that summarize the effect sizes of multiple research studies on your topic (see Chapter 21 for more insight on meta-analysis).

The sample size affects the power of a statistical test (the ability to detect a difference), the Type II error rate (the probability of making an incorrect decision), and the Type I error rate (the probability of making a correct decision). The use of R power functions for a given statistical test is therefore very important to know and understand when conducting a research study. An example, will illustrate one of the power functions, while the others are demonstrated in their respective chapters for the different statistics.

A researcher wishes to test the percent (%) difference between high school boys and girls who smoke cigarettes. The research question: Is there a statistically significant average percent difference between high school boys and girls who smoke cigarettes? In planning to conduct this study, the researcher wishes to know how many students should be randomly sampled. The *pwr.2p.test* power function is used for the difference of proportion given a binomial distribution. The arguments are h = 0.2 (the effect size for a 20% difference), power = .80 (the Type II error rate), sig.level = .05 (the Type I error rate), and n = NULL (to determine the total sample size for both groups).

```
> library(pwr)
> pwr.2p.test(h = .2, n = NULL, power = .80, sig.level =.05)
```

The results indicate that the total sample size would be N = 392, or 196 boys and 196 girls, to have an equal number of students in each group. The results also indicate a two-sided hypothesis, which means that you are testing a percent difference between the groups, rather than stating that boys smoke more cigarettes than girls in high school.

```
Difference of proportion power calculation for binomial distribution
(arcsine transformation)
n = 392.443
sig.level = 0.05
power =   0.8
```

```
alternative = two.sided
NOTE: same sample sizes
```

If you want to test a one-sided statistical hypothesis, simply change this argument in the power function (?pwr.2p.test provides the arguments with examples and documentation). For example,

```
> pwr.2p.test(h = .2, n = NULL, sig.level = .05, power = .80, alternative = "greater")
```

The results now show that the sample size is smaller, that is, $N = 309$ students, or roughly 155 boys and 155 girls. We obtain the same power, significance level, and effect size, but with a smaller sample size based solely on a directional rather than a nondirectional hypothesis.

```
     Difference of proportion power calculation for binomial distribution
(arcsine transformation)

     h = 0.2
     n = 309.1279
     sig.level = 0.05
     power = 0.8
     alternative = greater

     NOTE: same sample sizes
```

It is possible to establish a table with different power, significance level, and effect size values to determine the sample size that is reasonable given your time and budget. This activity also reveals how these values interplay when determining the sample size. Another activity would be to determine power values given your selection of the significance level, sample size, and effect size. Doing these activities is very rewarding and an integral part of your conducting a statistical test to answer your research questions. Once a researcher finds a set of values that work, given the study requirements, these criteria should be reported.

Effect Size Values for Statistical Tests

There are different effect size measures for the different statistical tests covered in the next chapters. Effect size measures indicate the magnitude of difference detected in the statistical analysis. The power functions are used to a priori plan for the expected results before conducting your study. You can also use these power functions *posteriorly*, that is, after the study has been completed. You simple insert the values from the study into the function to report the actual values. The statistical formulas for effect size are outlined below for the different types of statistical tests.

Chi-Square. The effect size w argument in the power function is determined by

$$w = \sqrt{\sum_{i=1}^{m} \frac{(p0_i - p1_i)^2}{p0_i}},$$

where

$p0_i$ = cell probability in the ith cell under H_0

$p1_i$ = cell probability in the ith cell under H_1.

This takes into account the expected cell frequency versus the observed cell frequency in the cross-tabulated chi-square table.

z Test. When comparing two proportions, h is the effect size value for setting the magnitude of difference you want to detect. The effect size for proportions is determined by an arcsine transformation as follows:

$$h = 2\arcsin(\sqrt{p_1}) - 2\arcsin(\sqrt{p_2}).$$

t Test. The effect size for the mean difference between two groups, d, commonly referred to as Cohen's d, is determined by

$$d = \frac{|\mu_1 - \mu_2|}{\sigma},$$

where

μ_1 = mean of Group 1,

μ_2 = mean of Group 2, and

σ^2 = common error variance.

In practice, we do not know the population standard deviation, σ, so the sample standard deviation, S, is used. This can be either the standard deviation of the entire sample (treatment and control group scores) or just the standard deviation of the control group scores. The standard deviation of the control group scores is argued to be preferred because the scores have not been affected by the treatment intervention.

Analysis of Variance. The effect size for the mean differences in three or more groups, f, is determined by

$$f = \sqrt{\frac{\sum_{i=1}^{k} p_i * (\mu_i - \mu)^2}{\sigma^2}},$$

where

$p_i = n_i/N$,

n_i = number of observations in group i,

N = total number of observations,

μ_i = mean of group i,

μ = grand mean, and

σ^2 = error variance within groups.

Once again, in practice, we would use the sample group standard deviations. In this case, it is usually the standard deviation of all scores from all groups. In practical applications, mean difference tests are conducted post hoc, that is, after an overall test for the existence of at least one pair of means that are different between groups. We will explore these post hoc tests of mean difference in Chapter 14 on analysis of variance.

Correlation. The sample correlation coefficient is an estimate of the population correlation (ρ) effect size. Cohen suggests that sample r values of .1, .3, and .5 represent small, medium, and large effect sizes, respectively. However, it is prudent to know what the effect size levels are in your area of research. They will most likely be different, and this will allow you to compare your research study's effect size with those found in previous research studies (see Chapter 21 on meta-analysis for more detailed information).

Regression. The effect size measure is f^2, where it can reflect the R^2, the squared multiple correlation, from a single study or from the difference between two regression equations (full- vs. restricted-model R^2). This is further explained in the chapters on regression.

$$f^2 = \frac{R^2}{1 - R^2},$$

where R^2 is the population squared multiple correlation.

$$f^2 = \frac{R^2_{AB} - R^2_A}{1 - R^2_{AB}},$$

where R^2_A is the variance accounted for in the population by the variable set A and R^2_{AB} is the variance accounted for in the population by the variable sets A and B together.

Creating Sample Size and Power Plots

The functions in the pwr package can also be used to create power and sample size graphs. Kabacoff (2012) has provided an excellent set of R code that produces the power curves for the correlation coefficient, given different power values and sample sizes. One of the great features of R is that you can cut R code you find or discover on websites, paste it in the RGui window, and run it. More important, these websites provide a template that you can modify or change to meet your particular needs. I have modified Kabacoff's code with a few of my own changes in the Power R script file (chap10e.r) and then printed the newly created graph below.

The graph displays the .7, .8 and .9 power curves at the .05 level of significance for the sample sizes and range of correlation coefficients. I have chosen different types of lines when plotting the different power curves to show that as the sample size increases, the power curve increases.

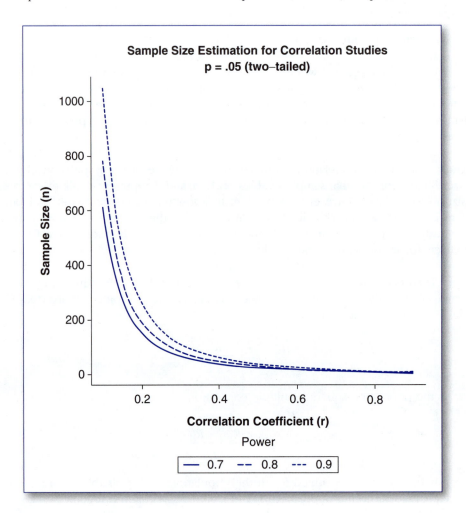

● INTERPRETATION OF HYPOTHESIS-TESTING RESULTS

The concerns in research for having an adequate sample size, the nature of Type I and Type II errors, the power of a test, and the selection of alternative values for the population parameters, called effect size, form the basis of hypothesis testing. The hypothesis-testing theory, known as the Neyman-Pearson hypothesis-testing theory, formulates the relationship between these concerns. In practice, we might select power equal to .80, use a .05 level of significance, and frame a directional hypothesis to test our statistical hypothesis. The effect size or magnitude of difference between the population parameters also affects the power of the test. If a small difference must be detected, then the sample size, level of significance, and power must be increased. We also generally know that the power of a test increases as the sample size increases, and the power of a test increases as the level of significance is decreased, that is from .01 to .05. All of these values are interrelated such that increasing or decreasing one affects the others. There are software programs available on the Internet (e.g., G*Power 3: http://www.psycho.uni-duesseldorf.de/abteilun gen/aap/gpower3/) that help in selecting the sample size or power for different statistical tests (Faul et al., 2007).

The research process, to be peer reviewed, should provide sufficient information for others to judge the outcome and decision made. This requires the researcher to provide a description of the population, the sampling, and the statistical hypotheses. Research results should include the alpha level (Type I error rate), power (Type II error rate), effect size (sample statistic – population parameter), and statistical test (point estimate), with the associated *p* value and confidence interval. Our understanding of the results (outcome and decision) can then be interpreted with our knowledge of the amount of error in making a decision (Type I and Type II), how much the sample statistic might vary if the study is replicated (confidence interval), the ability to detect a difference (power), and the probability of obtaining the statistical value from the sample data (the *p*-value area in the statistical distribution). These ideas and findings will be further explained in the next several chapters that cover the statistical tests.

TIP

✔ Use the following R statements

- to view the arguments of a function, for example,

```
> ?t.test
```

```
> ?var
```

```
> ?cor
```

- to find the library packages that use these functions:

```
>??t.test
```

```
>??var
```

```
>??cor
```

✔ Use the following command(s) to view the R source code of a statistics function, for example, *t.test()*:

```
> stats:::t.test.default *Required command that is different
from the rest*
```

```
> stats::power.t.test
```

```
> stats::chisq.test
```

(Continued)

(Continued)

```
> stats::fisher.test

> stats::pairwise.t.test
```

✓ The *fix* command also works to show the source code of functions (except for the *t.test* function), for example,

```
> fix(chisq.test)

> fix (fisher.test)

> fix(pairwise.test)
```

NOTE: > ??t.test can be used to find the correct package and expression to use.

✓ For some commands, simply enter the command to see the source code, for example,

```
> sort

> cor

> var

> cov
```

✓ For some commands, use the *name.default* format, for example,

```
> mean.default
```

SUMMARY

This chapter has covered the important concepts related to hypothesis testing. It describes the five steps that are used in the hypothesis-testing process to conduct the various tests of statistical hypotheses. More important, the chapter discusses the criteria that affect the statistical significance of the test: the sample size, power, alpha level, directional nature of the hypothesis, and effect size. These criteria are not only important in planning a study, but they also should be reported after you have collected the data and conducted the statistical test for your hypothesis.

The role probability plays in the statistical test was also discussed in the chapter as it relates to Type I and Type II errors. Our decision is not 100% accurate; rather, a certain amount of uncertainty in the outcome is always present. We establish some degree of certainty, for example, 95% confidence with 5% error, when making a decision that our alternative statistical hypothesis is correct. We have the ability to change the criteria in statistical hypothesis testing to have a more confident decision, for example, 99% confidence with 1% error. This requires changing some of the criteria (alpha, sample size) and establishing a directional hypothesis. We have also learned that changing the effect size and power would also affect our ability to detect a difference. It is therefore important to not only express our decision outcome with a test of statistical significance but also establish a confidence interval around the sample statistic.

The background information in research methods, probability, sampling, and populations in the earlier chapters provided a basis for our understanding of hypothesis testing. The central limit theorem, sampling distributions, and statistical distributions provide the knowledge required to understand the basis for conducting a test of a statistical hypothesis. Depending on the data (frequency, mean, correlation), the type of statistic used will be different, but the process of determining whether the sample statistic is beyond a chance level of probability, given the sampling distribution of the statistic, remains the same. When conducting statistical tests, we also learned that certain assumptions should be made so that the test is fair, robust, and valid.

The graphing of data and measures of central tendency and dispersion presented in earlier chapters also highlight the importance of examining your sample data. The visual display of data can quickly show characteristics that may affect your statistical test (skewness, restriction of range, outliers). The measures of central tendency and dispersion are also important to understand because they provide meaningful information about the sample data. They provide an understanding of whether the data are normally distributed and how much variation is present around the central tendency (mean). In some cases, data transformation may be necessary to meet the assumptions required for a statistical test.

The previous chapters provided the information, background, and examples that formed the basis for our understanding of the research process and hypothesis testing. This chapter and the next chapters now present the various statistics a researcher would use depending on the level of measurement of the variables. There are many different types of research questions and data, and thus many different types of statistical tests. Appendix B contains a summary of this information in the "Guide to Selecting a Statistical Test." The guide summarizes this information for the following chapters, which cover chi-square, z, t, F, correlation, linear regression, multiple regression, logistic regression, and log-linear regression.

EXERCISES

1. Explain the null and alternative hypotheses format in a few sentences.
2. Explain Type I and Type II error in a few sentences.
3. Is the Oregon State average SAT score statistically greater than the national average SAT? Use a t test at the $p = .05$ level of probability. Oregon average SAT = 700, $S = 50$, $N = 121$. National average SAT = 650. State the null and alternative hypotheses. Show the work.
4. Which five basic principles does the scientific research process involve?
5. What factors affect the Type II error in a study?
6. Define power.
7. Compute the 95% confidence interval given mean = 50, $S = 10$, $n = 100$. Interpret the results.
8. What information should a researcher report when conducting a scientific research study?

TRUE OR FALSE QUESTIONS

T   F   a.   The null and alternative hypotheses are the same.

T   F   b.   The Type I error is the probability of retaining the null when it is false.

T   F   c.   The confidence interval indicates the probability of making a Type I error.

T   F   d.   Power affects the Type I error rate.

T   F   e.   The standard error of the statistic is used to establish the confidence interval around a sample statistic that captures the population parameter.

WEB RESOURCES

Chapter R script files are available at http://www.sagepub.com/schumacker

Confidence Interval Function R script file: chap10d.r

Hypothesis Test Function R script file: chap10a.r

Power R script file: chap10e.r

Type I Error Function R script file: chap10b.r

Type II Error Function R script file: chap10c.r

G*Power 3: http://www.psycho.uni-duesseldorf.de/abteilungen/aap/gpower3/

Quick-R: http://www.statmethods.net/stats/

## CHAPTER 11

CHI-SQUARE TEST FOR CATEGORICAL DATA

O ur intuition guides our desire to know if events are independent or related. When our questions involve categorical variables, we can observe what happens and compare it with what is expected, that is, the probability of occurrence. The chi-square statistic is used for testing the independence (or dependence) of two events that are categorical—for example, "Do you smoke cigarettes?" (yes or no) and "Are you male or female?" (male or female). These two events or questions can be cross-tabulated, thus providing the basis for computing a chi-square statistic.

The chi-square statistic was developed by Karl Pearson to test whether two categorical variables were independent of each other. A research question involving two categorical variables would take the following form: Is eating junk food independent of exercising? A researcher would gather data on both variables in a yes/no format, then cross-tabulate the data. The cross-tabulation of the data for this research question would look like the following:

		Do you eat junk food?	
		Yes	No
Do you exercise?	Yes		
	No		

Individuals would be asked both questions and their separate responses recorded. The cross-tabulation of the data would permit a count of the number of people who *did* exercise and *did* eat junk food, the number of people who *did* not exercise and *did not* eat junk food, the number of people who *did not* exercise and *did* eat junk food, and the number of people who *did not* exercise and *did not* eat junk food. Consequently, four possible outcomes are represented by the cross-tabulation of the yes/no responses to the two questions.

The chi-square statistic is computed by taking the sum of the observed frequency (O) minus the expected frequency (E) squared in each cell and dividing this value by the expected frequency (E) of each in the four cells. The chi-square formula is expressed as

$$\chi^2 = \sum_{i=1}^{4} \frac{(O - E)^2}{E}.$$

Multiplying the respective row and column sums and dividing by the total number of individuals yields the expected frequencies (E) in each of the four cells. The calculation of the difference between what is observed (O) and what is expected (E) by chance alone forms the basis for the chi-square test of independence between two categorical variables. The *expected cell frequencies* are based on the two categorical variables being independent. An example will help illustrate how to calculate the expected frequencies and the chi-square statistic.

● CHI-SQUARE EXAMPLE

A school district is interested in having parents participate in activities at a new high school. The superintendent decides to conduct a preliminary poll of parents to see if they would be interested in volunteering at the new high school. The superintendent is also concerned about whether men and women would participate equally at the high school. Consequently, 600 parents (300 men and 300 women) in the school district were randomly selected and telephoned to collect the data. Each parent was asked his or her gender and whether he or she would volunteer at the new high school. The responses are cross-tabulated below, with expected frequencies (E) of each cell in parentheses.

	Volunteer		
Gender	Yes	No	Total
Men	140 (160)	160 (140)	300
Women	180 (160)	120 (140)	300
Total	320	280	600

The observed values indicate that 140 out of 300 (47%) men and 180 out of 300 (60%) women said yes to volunteering at the new high school, while 160 out of 300 (53%) men and 120 out of 300 (40%) women said that they would not have time to volunteer. If the null hypothesis is true (no difference between men and women), then we would expect the percentages to be the same for both men and women. So out of the 320 observed in favor, one half or 160 individuals would be expected in each gender cell, and out of the 280 observed who would not volunteer, one half or 140 individuals would be expected in each gender cell. The expected cell frequencies are what would be expected if gender and volunteer were independent.

The most convenient way to calculate the expected cell values is to multiply the corresponding row and column sums and divide by the total sample size. For men, the first expected cell value is $(300 \times 320)/600 = 160$. The other expected cell value is $(300 \times 280)/600 = 140$. For women, the first expected cell value is $(300 \times 320)/600 = 160$. The other expected cell value is $(300 \times 280)/600 = 140$. The expected cell values are in parentheses in the table. The expected cell values should always add up to the total for each row and/or column.

The chi-square statistic compares the corresponding observed and expected values in the cells of the table under the assumption that the categorical variables are independent, that is, the null hypothesis is true. If the row and the column variables are independent, then the proportion observed in each cell should be similar to the proportion expected in each cell. The chi-square test determines if the difference between what we observed and expected in the four cells is statistically different or due to random chance. A decision about the null hypothesis is made on the basis of the chi-square statistic at a given level of significance, which is computed as follows.

$$\chi^2 = \sum_{i=1}^{4} \left(\frac{(140 - 160)^2}{160} + \frac{(160 - 140)^2}{140} + \frac{(180 - 160)^2}{160} + \frac{(120 - 140)^2}{140} \right)$$

$$\chi^2 = \sum_{i=1}^{4} \left(2.5 + 2.857 + 2.5 + 2.857 \right) = 10.714.$$

The computed chi-square value is compared with a tabled chi-square value in Appendix A for a given degree of freedom (level of significance). The degrees of freedom are always determined by the number of rows minus one $(r - 1)$ times the number of columns minus one $(c - 1)$. This can be expressed as $df = (r - 1) * (c - 1)$. Since there are two rows and two columns, the degree of freedom is $df = (2 - 1) * (2 - 1) = 1$. The tabled chi-square value for $df = 1$ at the .05 level of significance is 3.84. Since the computed chi-square value of 10.714 is greater than the tabled chi-square value of 3.84, the two events are not independent, so we reject the null hypothesis in favor of the alternative hypothesis that men and women differ in the percentage of who would volunteer at the new high school. The women indicated a higher percentage (60%) than the men (47%) when asked if they would volunteer at the new high school.

TIP

✓ Many statistics are calculated using the basic math operations of adding, subtracting, multiplying, dividing, and/or taking a square root.

✓ The statistic you calculate is compared with the expected statistic found in the sampling distribution at a specified probability level.

✓ If the statistic you calculated is greater than the expected statistic, it falls in the probability area under the sampling distribution, called the region of rejection for the null hypothesis of no difference.

● INTERPRETING THE CHI-SQUARE STATISTIC

The chi-square statistic is computed by summing the difference between what is observed and what is expected for all cells, therefore a significant chi-square doesn't specify which cells may have contributed the most to the significance of the overall chi-square statistic. Our interpretation of the overall chi-square result is greatly enhanced by realizing that each cell value is itself an individual chi-square value. Consequently, we can interpret each cell value individually and compare it with the tabled chi-square value of 3.84 with $df = 1$. Each cell chi-square is converted to a residual value for interpretation. If the standardized residual for each cell is greater than 2.0 (absolute value), then it makes a significant contribution to the overall chi-square. The formula for computing the standardized residual is

$$R = \frac{O - E}{\sqrt{E}}.$$

The four standardized residual values for the chi-square statistic were

(1) $R = \dfrac{O - E}{\sqrt{E}} = \dfrac{140 - 160}{\sqrt{160}} = \dfrac{-20}{12.64911} = -1.58.$

(2) $R = \dfrac{O - E}{\sqrt{E}} = \dfrac{160 - 140}{\sqrt{140}} = \dfrac{20}{11.832159} = 1.69.$

(3) $R = \dfrac{O - E}{\sqrt{E}} = \dfrac{180 - 160}{\sqrt{160}} = \dfrac{20}{12.64911} = 1.58.$

(4) $R = \dfrac{O - E}{\sqrt{E}} = \dfrac{120 - 140}{\sqrt{140}} = \dfrac{-20}{11.832159} = -1.69.$

Since no single standardized residual value for the four cells exceeded 2.00, we would conclude that no one cell was a major contributor to the statistical significance of the overall chi-square statistic. Although, no single cell emerged as a predominant contributor in this case, you should still conduct this important step for interpreting a chi-square test.

Note: If each expected cell frequency is not greater than 5 to meet the assumption for computing the chi-square statistic, a Yates correction by subtracting .5 from each cell computation has been recommended (Cochran, 1954); however, Camilli and Hopkins (1978) have determined that the Yates correction is *not* recommended for chi-square 2 × 2 tables because of a tendency to not reject the null hypothesis when it is false.

Another helpful approach to interpreting the overall chi-square statistic is to take each individual chi-square cell value as a percent of the overall chi-square statistic. This provides a variance accounted for interpretation. In our example, 2.5/10.714 = 23.33%, 2.857/10.714 = 26.67%, 2.5/10.714 = 23.33%, and 2.857/10.714 = 26.67%. The sum of these cell percents must always equal 100%. Our interpretation would then be based on which cell or cells contributed the most to the overall chi-square statistic based on a variance contribution. In this example, the cell percents for the men and women who did not volunteer contributed slightly more than for the men and women who did volunteer.

The chi-square statistic will be small if there are small differences between the observed and the expected values in each cell, and it will be larger if there are larger differences. A single cell could be a major contributor to the statistically significant chi-square value, so the residual cell chi-square values and the variance contribution of each cell are important to determine because they aid our interpretation of an overall statistically significant chi-square statistic.

The chi-square statistic for a 2 × 2 table is distributed as a theoretical chi-square sampling distribution with 1 degree of freedom. Therefore, the theoretical chi-square distribution can be used to determine the probability area for the region of rejection of the null hypothesis. The region of rejection includes any chi-square statistic greater than the $1 - \alpha$ percentile of the theoretical chi-square distribution with $df = (r - 1) * (c - 1)$. Consequently, the chi-square test of independence can be performed on tables of any dimension, that is, varying numbers of rows and columns for categorical variables. The critical chi-square statistic table in Appendix A provides the expected chi-square values for the varying degrees of freedom.

● HYPOTHESIS-TESTING STEPS

When we ask a question, gather data, and then determine if our results are significant beyond a chance probability level, the scientific method is undertaken. There are five basic steps researchers can use to conduct their hypothesis testing. This five-step hypothesis testing approach is outlined below.

Step 1. State the research question in a directional or nondirectional statistical hypothesis format.

If we hypothesize that women will have a higher percent (P_1) than men (P_2) in favor of volunteering at the new high school, an alternative hypothesis (H_A) would specify the *directional* (one-tailed) nature of the statistical hypothesis:

$$H_0: P_1 \leq P_2 \text{ (or } P_1 - P_2 \leq 0)$$

$$H_A: P_1 > P_2 \text{ (or } P_1 - P_2 > 0).$$

If we hypothesize that women and men will differ in their percentage in favor of volunteering at the new high school, an alternative hypothesis (H_A) would specify the *nondirectional* (two-tailed) nature of the statistical hypothesis:

$$H_0: P_1 = P_2 \text{ (or } P_1 - P_2 = 0)$$

$$H_A: P_1 \neq P_2 \text{ (or } P_1 - P_2 \neq 0).$$

The *directional* statistical hypothesis invokes the probability area in only one tail of the sampling distribution of the statistic, for example, by selecting $\alpha = .05$, or 5%. The null hypothesis in the *directional* statistical hypothesis includes the rest of the probability area, that is, $1 - \alpha$, or 95%. A *nondirectional* statistical hypothesis involves the probability area in both tails (two-tailed) of the sampling distribution of the statistic, for example, by selecting α = .05; .025 or 2.5% will be in each tail. A researcher generally chooses a *directional* statistical hypothesis based on findings from prior research, otherwise a *nondirectional* statistical hypothesis is made to allow for both probability outcomes (women having a higher percent than men or men having a higher percent than women). A researcher would specify the *nondirectional* statistical hypothesis when uncertain about the preference of men and women regarding volunteering at the new high school.

Step 2. Determine the criteria for rejecting the null hypothesis and accepting the alternative hypothesis.

We have learned from previous chapters that a statistic has a sampling distribution based on the sample size (or degrees of freedom) and the level of significance for the Type I error rate (alpha). When testing the probable outcome of our statistical hypothesis, we need to establish the criteria for rejecting the null hypothesis of no difference. This is done when we select our level of significance (α = 0.05) and sample size (or degrees of freedom for a statistic). In our example, α = 0.05 and df = 1, so from Table 4 (Appendix A) we located χ^2 = 3.841. This chi-square value in the sampling distribution for df = 1 designates a cut-off point for the probability area where a larger computed chi-square value would not be expected by chance. We specify this area as a region of rejection for the null hypothesis of no difference:

$$\text{Region of rejection}_{.05,DF} = 1: \chi^2 = 3.841.$$

If the computed chi-square is greater than this tabled chi-square value, we would reject the null hypothesis and accept the alternative hypothesis.

Step 3. Collect the sample data, and compute the chi-square test statistic.

A random sample of data would be collected for two events or questions that were categorical in nature. In our example, one categorical variable was *Gender* (men vs. women), while the other categorical variable was *Volunteer* (yes vs. no). Data were gathered and cross-tabulated, then the chi-square statistic was computed. Our results indicated that the computed chi-square value for the random sample of data was = 10.714. A Yates correction was not made on each cell value computation.

Step 4. Interpret the region of rejection for chi-square.

We interpret the computed χ^2 = 10.714 value for our sample data by comparing it with the region of rejection for the null hypothesis. Since the computed χ^2 = 10.714 is greater than χ^2 = 3.841, it falls in the 5% probability area established for the Type I error rate. This means that the chi-square value is statistically significant, that is, the chi-square statistic occurs beyond a chance probability level.

Step 5. Interpret the chi-square test statistic results.

We have determined that the chi-square value is statistically significant at the 0.05 level of significance. What does this mean? First, a significant chi-square statistic indicates that men and women are *not* the same in their willingness to volunteer at the new high school. A nonsignificant chi-square result would have implied that men and women had the same percentage (retain the null hypothesis of no difference). Second, by interpreting each cell's standardized residual value, no single cell made a major contribution to the overall chi-square value. Finally, a variance contribution of each cell indicated that a slightly larger contribution was made by the men and women who indicated their unwillingness to volunteer. The cell percent interpretation provides a practical interpretation to the research question above and beyond the statistical determination based on the chance probability of obtaining the overall chi-square value.

We can examine the power and effect size of our chi-square test by using the *pwr.chisq.test()* function. Power indicates the ability to detect a difference when one exists, thus controlling for Type II error (falsely rejecting the null hypothesis). Recall from the chapter "Hypothesis Testing" that the *pwr* package contains the functions (*??pwr*), which can be loaded and listed by

```
> library(pwr);??pwr
> ?pwr.chisq.test
```

I selected the power function for chi-square, which is

```
pwr.chisq.test(w = 3.84, N = NULL, df = NULL, sig.level = 0.05, power = NULL)
```

Arguments

W	Effect size
N	Total number of observations
df	degree of freedom (depends on the chosen test)
sig.level	Significance level (Type I error probability)
Power	Power of test (1 minus Type II error probability)

For the chi-square test, w = the tabled chi-square value, $N = 200$ total observations, $df = 1$, sig.level = .05, and power = NULL (this means that power will be calculated given the other arguments).

```
> pwr.chisq.test(w = 3.84, N = 200, df = 1, sig.level = .05, power
= NULL)
   Chi squared power calculation

   w = 3.84
   N = 200
   df = 1
   sig.level = 0.05
   power = 1
```

Note: N is the number of observations.

Since power = 1.0, we have sufficient power to detect the independence of the two variables and thus reject the null hypothesis given our significant chi-square.

● CHI-SQUARE TEST

The *stats* package, which is loaded by *library(stats)* contains various statistical functions, including one that computes the chi-square statistic, *chisq.test()*. The chi-square function requires providing certain arguments or values in the parentheses. To learn what arguments are required, open the Internet documentation file for the *chisq.test()* function by issuing the following command in the RGui dialog box:

```
> ?chisq.test
```

The following documentation is then opened in an Internet html file:

chisq.test {stats}	*R Documentation*

Pearson's Chi-squared Test for Count Data
Description
chisq.test performs chi-squared contingency table tests and goodness-of-fit tests.

Usage
```
chisq.test(x, y = NULL, correct = TRUE,
        p = rep(1/length(x), length(x)), rescale.p = FALSE,
        simulate.p.value = FALSE, B = 2000)
```

Arguments

X	a numeric vector or matrix. x and y can also both be factors.
Y	a numeric vector; ignored if x is a matrix. If x is a factor, y should be a factor of the same length.
Correct	a logical indicating whether to apply continuity correction when computing the test statistic for 2 by 2 tables: one half is subtracted from all $|O - E|$ differences. No correction is done if simulate.p.value = TRUE.
P	a vector of probabilities of the same length of x. An error is given if any entry of p is negative.
rescale.p	a logical scalar; if TRUE then p is rescaled (if necessary) to sum to 1. If rescale.p is FALSE, and p does not sum to 1, an error is given.
simulate.p.value	a logical indicating whether to compute p-values by Monte Carlo simulation.
B	an integer specifying the number of replicates used in the Monte Carlo test.

```
Details

If x is a matrix with one row or column, or if x is a vector and y is
not given, then a goodness-of-fit test is performed (x is treated as a
one-dimensional contingency table). The entries of x must be non-negative
integers. In this case, the hypothesis tested is whether the population
probabilities equal those in p, or are all equal if p is not given.
If x is a matrix with at least two rows and columns, it is taken as a
two-dimensional contingency table: the entries of x must be non-negative
integers. Otherwise, x and y must be vectors or factors of the same
length; cases with missing values are removed, the objects are coerced
to factors, and the contingency table is computed from these. Then
Pearson's chi-squared test is performed of the null hypothesis that the
joint distribution of the cell counts in a 2-dimensional contingency
table is the product of the row and column margins.
If simulate.p.value is FALSE, the p-value is computed from the
asymptotic chi-squared distribution of the test statistic; continuity
correction is only used in the 2-by-2 case (if correct is TRUE, the
default). Otherwise the p-value is computed for a Monte Carlo test
(Hope, 1968) with B replicates.
In the contingency table case simulation is done by random sampling from
the set of all contingency tables with given marginals, and works only
if the marginals are strictly positive. (A C translation of the
algorithm of Patefield (1981) is used.) Continuity correction is never
used, and the statistic is quoted without it. Note that this is not the
usual sampling situation assumed for the chi-squared test but rather
that for Fisher's exact test.
In the goodness-of-fit case simulation is done by random sampling from
the discrete distribution specified by p, each sample being of size n =
sum(x). This simulation is done in R and may be slow.
```

For simplicity, we can cut and paste the *chisq.test()* function into a new script window and then create matrix *x*, which is a required argument for the function. If you need information for the *matrix()* function arguments, use *?matrix* to also open its Internet html documentation. Now copy the matrix and chi-square functions into a new script dialog box using the main menu commands File, New Script; then make the following changes to each of them, and copy–paste commands into the RGui dialog box to run.

Note: The > symbol is inserted when running the command lines, so do not put them in the script file. The script file can also be saved using the file extension *r*, for example, *chisq.r*.

```
> x = matrix(c(140,160,180,120), nrow = 2, ncol = 2, byrow = TRUE,
dimnames  = list(c("men","women"), c("yes","no")))
> x
> chisq.test(x, y = NULL, correct = FALSE, p = rep(1/length(x),
```

```
length(x)), rescale.p =
FALSE, simulate.p.value = FALSE, B = 2000)
```

Note: The *correct = TRUE* statement was changed to *correct = FALSE* because our hand calculations did not perform a Yates correction (subtraction of 0.5 from the absolute value of $|O - E|$). The command lines also wrap around on the page given the number of arguments, but they must be on the same command line in the RGui dialog box.

The RGui output when running the matrix and chi-square function is

```
          yes    no
men       140    160
women     180    120


Pearson's Chi-squared test
data: x
X-squared = 10.7143, df = 1, p-value = 0.001063
```

$\chi^2 = 10.7143$, which is within rounding error of our hand-calculated value (10.714) with $df = 1$. Notice that the *p* value given is the actual *p* value for the calculated chi-square value (not 3.841, which was selected for $\alpha = .05$, Type I error rate). Also notice that the *p* value is not in scientific notation; recall that the *options (scipen=999)* could be used if this occurs. $\chi^2 = 10.714$ falls in the probability area of the tail of the sampling distribution, where we would reject the null statistical hypothesis and accept the alternative statistical hypothesis.

● CHI-SQUARE DISTRIBUTION PLOT

The *base* package has the *plot()* and *polygon()* functions, which can be used to graph the chi-square distribution for a given number of degrees of freedom and then plot the region of rejection. The base package does not have to be loaded using the *library()* function. For example, we can first generate the chi-square sampling distribution for $df = 1$, then graph in a gray color for the region of rejection that corresponds to $\alpha = .05$. The chi-square value at $p = .05$ with $df = 1$ is $\chi^2 = 3.84$. The following commands are in the Chi-Square Density Function R script file (chap11a.r). The following *plot()* function generates the density function for this chi-square sampling distribution:

```
> x= seq(0,30)
> df = 1
> chisqvalues = dchisq(x, df)
> plot(x, chisqvalues, type = "l", main = "Density Plot of Chi-square values", xlab
= paste("Chi-square values, df =", df), ylab = "Frequency - Chi-square values")
```

These R commands will create a polygon with the gray area for the region of rejection. It is overlaid onto the chi-square density plot.

```
> x = seq(3.84,30)
> df = 1
> y = dchisq(x, df)
> polygon(c(3.84,x,30), c(0,y,0), col = "gray")
```

The *polygon()* function fills in the area beyond $\chi^2 = 3.84$, which is the region for rejecting the null hypothesis. If our computed chi-square statistic is greater than 3.84, we would reject the null and accept the alternative hypothesis because it indicates an unlikely probability outcome. These combined plots should look this:

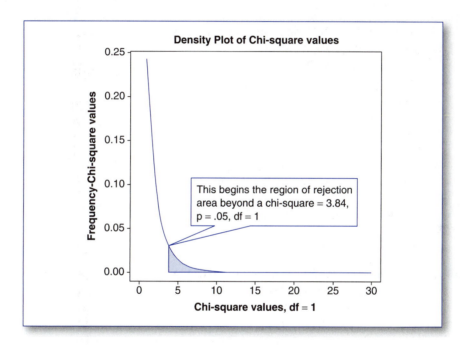

● CHI-SQUARE SIMULATION

The *chi-square simulation function* in the script file (chap11b.r) will help us understand how the chi-square statistic and *p* values change for a two-by-two table using randomly sampled data from a population. The function selects a random sample of size *N*, then uses the *chisq.test()* function to compute the chi-square statistic and associated *p* value. The *chisq.test()* function will use the Yates correction, which uses real limits around numbers, for example, real limits of 5 is 4.5 to 5.5. The four cell percents that are input will be printed along with the observed and expected values. A chi-square statistic will be computed and printed with the degrees of freedom and probability value. The results will change each time the function is run unless you specify a seed number using the *set.seed()* function. (Use >?set.seed in the RGui dialog box for function arguments.)

A decision can then be made about whether to retain or reject the null hypothesis based on the probability value $p < .05$ and $\chi^2 = 3.841$. A Type I error will occur when the rows and columns are independent, that is, the null hypothesis is rejected when it is true. A Type II error will occur when the rows and columns are dependent, that is, the null hypothesis is retained when it is false. The standardized residual cell values and the percent contribution of each cell to the overall chi-square value are not given. You will need to enter the cell probabilities and sample size, then run the function

```
> cellProbs=c(.10,.15,.30,.45)  # cell percents should sum to 1.00
> sample = 100
> chap11b(cellProbs, sample)
```

The output will show the population cell values you entered along with the observed and expected cell frequencies for calculating the chi-square value. The chi-square statistic is reported along with the associated degrees of freedom and *p* value.

```
PROGRAM OUTPUT

 Population Proportions
     X       Y
A 0.10    0.15
B 0.30    0.45

 Observed Proportions
     X       Y
A 0.09    0.09
B 0.33    0.49

 Expected Proportions
     X    Y
A 0.08 0.10
B 0.34 0.48


     Pearson's Chi-squared test with Yates' continuity correction

data: testMatrix
X-squared = 0.2457, df = 1, p-value = 0.6201
```

TIP

✓ An advanced R programmer would modify the *chisq.test()* function, which has more programming elements—possibly to include the residual cell values and the percent contribution as output. The R command to obtain the entire function arguments is

```
> stats::chisq.test
```

● BASIC CHI-SQUARE EXAMPLE

Agresti (2007) provides the basic R commands to create a row by column ($R \times C$) cross-tabulated table with the chi-square statistical test, the observed and expected cell counts, the Pearson residuals, and the standardized residuals. The standardized residuals would aid our interpretation of each cell's contribution to the overall chi-square statistic. The example given in R for the *chisq.test()* function was

```
## From Agresti(2007) p.39

M <- as.table(rbind(c(762,327,468), c(484,239,477)))
    dimnames(M) <- list(gender = c("M","F"),
    party = c("Democrat","Independent","Republican"))
    (Xsq <- chisq.test(M)) # Prints test summary

Xsq$observed  # observed counts (same as M)
Xsq$expected  # expected counts under the null
Xsq$residuals # Pearson residuals
Xsq$stdres    # standardized residuals
```

The output provides the detailed results for gender (male and female) cross-tabulated with political party (Democrat, Independent, and Republican). The chi-square value is 30.07, with $df = 2$ ($R - 1$ times $C - 1$), which is statistically significant at the .05 level of probability. Standardized residuals indicated that more males belong to the Democratic Party (residual = 4.50) while more females favor the Republican Party (residual = 5.31).

```
Pearson's Chi-squared test

data: M
X-squared = 30.0701, df = 2, p-value = 2.954e-07

> Xsq$observed  # observed counts (same as M)
    party

gender Democrat Independent Republican
    M      762         327        468
    F      484         239        477

> Xsq$expected  # expected counts under the null
                party

gender Democrat  Independent  Republican
    M   703.6714    319.6453    533.6834
    F   542.3286    246.3547    411.3166
```

```
> Xsq$residuals # Pearson residuals
    party

gender    Democrat    Independent   Republican
    M    2.1988558    0.4113702    -2.8432397
    F   -2.5046695   -0.4685829     3.2386734

> Xsq$stdres    # standardized residuals
    party

gender   Democrat   Independent   Republican
    M   4. 5020535    0.6994517   -5.3159455
    F  -4. 5020535   -0.6994517    5.3159455
```

The standardized residuals (*Xsq$stdres*) show that the male Democrats (4.5) and female Republicans (5.31) contributed the most to the chi-square statistic, namely, 30.07.

TIP

✓ Three options are possible for computing statistical tests:

1. Write your own R function.

2. Use an existing function in an R {stats} library. The list of functions is made available by issuing the following command in the RGui dialog box:

   ```
   > library(help="stats").
   ```

3. Modify an existing function in an R package or find one on the Internet, then modify or save as your own R function in a script file, for example, *mystat.r*.

✓ Many R functions can be simply created by cutting and pasting the syntax, then saving it in a new script file.

✓ Many R functions and information are available on the Internet in tutorials, for example, http://ww2.coastal.edu/kingw/statistics/R-tutorials/index.html.

SUMMARY

This chapter has outlined how to hand calculate the chi-square statistic from cross-tabulated categorical data. It further presented a five-step hypothesis-testing approach that is used in conducting scientific inquiry. The *chisq.test()* function in the R stats package provided the calculation for a chi-square statistic with sample data. A *chi-square simulation* function was provided to permit further investigation into how the chi-square statistic performs when the population cell values are known and a Yates correction is performed.

Several important concepts were introduced when using a chi-square statistic to test research questions involving cross-tabulated categorical variables. First, the overall chi-square statistic is computed by summing the individual cell chi-square values in a cross-tabulated table. Second, the degrees of freedom for a cross-tabulated table are row minus one times column minus one, that is, $df = (R - 1) * (C - 1)$. A chi-square test of independence is used to determine whether or not the rows and columns are independent. If the null hypothesis is true, it is still possible that the chi-square test could lead to a rejection of the null hypothesis (Type I error). If the null hypothesis is false, it is still possible that the chi-square test could lead to retaining the null hypothesis (Type II error). The chi-square test is therefore based on the probability of obtaining a chi-square value beyond a chance level of probability. Finally, the ratio of each cell value to the overall chi-square value provides a variance accounted for interpretation of how much each cell contributed to the overall chi-square value. This aids our practical interpretation of the statistically significant chi-square statistic.

EXERCISES

1. A researcher wanted to test the question "Do you attend college?" for independence between males and females. State the null hypothesis and alternative hypothesis.

2. Compute the expected cell frequencies (E) in the following 2 × 2 cross-tabulated table.

Do you attend college?	Male	Female	Total
Yes	O = 25, E =	O = 125, E =	150
No	O = 125, E =	O = 25, E =	150
Total	150	150	300

3. Compute the chi-square statistic for the 2 × 2 cross-tabulated table in #1.

4. Is $\chi^2 = 133.33$ statistically significant at $p = .05$ level of probability? Report the tabled chi-square values and degrees of freedom in your answer.

5. List the five basic steps in hypothesis testing.

6. Run the *chisq.test()* function given the following row-by-column matrix. Do males and females differ in their percentage of cigarette smokers? Interpret the results.

```
out = rbind(c(50,100), c(10,10))
dimnames(out) = list(gender = c("M","F"), smoke = c("Yes","No"))
```

TRUE OR FALSE QUESTIONS

T   F   a.   Chi-square statistic tests the independence of two categorical events.

T   F   b.   The chi-square degrees of freedom is (row − 1) * (column − 1).

T   F   c.   The chi-square statistics do not use a sampling distribution.

T   F   d.   A chi-square statistical test is used with ordinal data.

T   F   e.   The overall chi-square value indicates which cells contribute to a statistically significant finding.

WEB RESOURCES

Chapter R script files are available at http://www.sagepub.com/schumacker

Chi-Square Density Function R script file: chap11a.r

Chi-Square Simulation Function R script file: chap11b.r

## CHAPTER 12

Z TEST FOR DIFFERENCES IN PROPORTIONS

C ounting is a basic part of the human condition. We count just about everything from our money to the number of steps from our car to our house. We ask all types of questions related to this basic activity, for example, "How many TV sets do you own?" or "How many songs do you have on your iPod?" The count easily becomes a percentage, for example, household expenses are broken down into mortgage payments, car payments, insurance payments, and food and utility payments. If we take each dollar amount over the total spent, we quickly ponder over the percentage spent on each from our total monthly income.

Many research questions involve testing how much of something we have, that is, a count (percent). We could be interested in whether there are percent differences between a single sample and a population or between two groups. The research question for percent differences between groups pertains to the difference in percentage between two population proportions—for example, "Is there a significant difference between the proportion of girls and boys who smoke cigarettes in high school?" or "Is there a significant difference in the proportion of foreign and domestic automobile sales?" or "Is there a significant difference in the proportion of girls and boys passing the Iowa Test of Basic Skills?"

Research questions using the z test can involve testing the difference between a single-sample percent and a known population percent or the difference in population proportions between two independent groups. Other types of research questions can involve differences in population proportions between related or dependent groups—for example, "Is there a significant difference in the proportion of adults smoking cigarettes before and after attending a 'Stop Smoking' clinic?" or "Is there a significant difference in the proportion of foreign automobiles sold in the United States between the years 1999 and 2000?" or "Is there a significant difference in the proportion of girls passing the Iowa Test of Basic Skills between the years 1980 and 1990?"

The z-test statistic can answer research questions involving a single percentage, differences in percentages between independent groups, and differences in percentages that are dependent (pre to post; Time 1 vs. Time 2, etc.). Our understanding of sampling distributions, the central limit theorem, confidence intervals, Type I error, Type II error, and hypothesis testing will be useful in knowing how the z test works in testing differences in percentages. The z test presented in this chapter depends on the level of measurement being nominal (count), with one of several types of research designs that help formulate the research question. There are other categorical data analysis techniques beyond the scope of this book (Agresti, 1996; Upton, 1978). A basic five-step hypothesis testing strategy will be presented to better understand the research design and accompanying research question.

● SINGLE-SAMPLE Z TEST

A single-sample z test would involve a research design where a single-sample percent is compared with a known population percent. Our research question of interest is whether the sample percent is statistically different from the population percent. The research question for our example is "Do a greater proportion of high school students in Tennessee smoke cigarettes than in the U.S. population of high school students?" This is a directional research question. The five-step hypothesis-testing approach to this research question is outlined below.

Step 1. State the directional research question in a statistical hypothesis format.

$$H_0: P_1 \leq P_0 \text{ (or } P_1 - P_0 \leq 0)$$

$$H_A: P_1 > P_0 \text{ (or } P_1 - P_0 > 0).$$

The P_1 value represents the population percent of high school students in Tennessee who smoke cigarettes, while the P_0 value represents the population percent of high school students in the United States who smoke cigarettes. The null hypothesis (H_0) indicates that the population percent of high school students in Tennessee is less than or equal to the population percent in the United States. In contrast, the alternative hypothesis (H_A) indicates that the population percent of high school students in Tennessee is greater than the population percent in the United States (directional hypothesis). Recall that together these probabilities equal 100% under the sampling distribution of the z-test statistic.

> **TIP**
>
> The "H" stands for "hypothesis," with the subscripts "0" for the null statistical hypothesis and "A" for the alternative statistical hypothesis. The alternative statistical hypothesis is stated to reflect the research question. In this example, the alternative statistical hypothesis indicates the directional nature of the research question, that is, the P_1 population proportion of high school students who smoke cigarettes in Tennessee is greater than the P_0 population proportion of high school students who smoke cigarettes in the United States.

Step 2. Determine the criteria for rejecting the null hypothesis and accepting the alternative hypothesis.

Given $\alpha = .01$, we select the corresponding z value from Table 1 (Appendix A), which is the closest to 1% of the area under the normal curve. If our computed z-test statistic is greater than this tabled z value, we would reject the null hypothesis in favor of the alternative hypothesis. This establishes our region of rejection, or the probability area under the normal curve where differences in sample proportions are unlikely to occur by random chance.

Region of rejection: $z > 2.33$.

TIP

Notice that in Table 1 (Appendix A), the first column indicates $z = 2.3$ with the other column indicating the 3 in the hundredths decimal place. Also, notice that the percentage 0.4901 is the closest to 49%, which leaves 1% area under the normal curve. In Table 1, only one half of the normal curve is represented, so 50% is automatically added to the 49% to get 99%, which reflects the one-tailed probability for the directional alternative statistical hypothesis. If our computed sample z is greater than 2.33, we would reject the null and accept the alternative hypothesis.

Step 3. Collect the sample data, and compute the z-test statistic.

A random sample of 1,000 high school students in Tennessee were selected and asked if they smoked cigarettes; $n_1 = 250$, or 25%, said yes ($250/1000 = 0.25$). The Smoking Ad Council published the population percent of 20,000 high school students who smoked cigarettes as 15% nationwide; $n_2 = 3,000$, or 15%, said yes ($3000/20000 = 0.15$). The proportions therefore were

$P_1 = 0.25$ (25% of the Tennessee high school students smoke cigarettes)

$P_0 = 0.15$ (15% of U.S. high school students smoke cigarettes).

The standard deviation of the sampling distribution for the z-test statistic is called the standard error of the difference between proportions. This value is needed to compute the z-test statistic. The formula is

$$S_{P_1 - P_0} = \sqrt{\frac{pq}{N}},$$

where

$p = (n_1 + n_2)/N = (250 + 3000)/21000 = 0.155,$

$q = 1 - p = 1 - 0.155 = 0.845,$

n_1 = number of students in the first sample = 250,

n_2 = number of students in the second sample = 3,000, and

N = total sample size taken = $20000 + 1000 = 21000$.

$$S_{P_1 - P_0} = \sqrt{\frac{0.155(0.845)}{21000}} = 0.0025.$$

The z test can now be computed as

$$z = \frac{P_1 - P_0}{S_{P_1 - P_0}} = \frac{0.25 - 0.15}{0.0025} = \frac{0.10}{0.0025} = 40.$$

TIP

To test a statistical hypothesis, we need to know the sampling distribution of the statistic. The sampling distribution for the z test is normally distributed when sample sizes are greater than five, so we can use the normal distribution of z values to test our statistical hypothesis.

Step 4. Interpret the region of rejection, and compute the confidence interval around z.

The region of rejection (Step 2) was determined based on a Type I error rate of 1% or α = .01, so $z > 2.33$ yields 1% of the probability area in the sampling distribution. If our computed z value is greater than this tabled z value in the sampling distribution (normal distribution), then 1 out of 100 times we would falsely reject the null and accept the alternative hypothesis. Our computed $z = 40$ is greater than $z = 2.33$, which established our region of rejection, so we reject the null hypothesis and accept the alternative hypothesis. We conclude that the sample proportion of high school students smoking cigarettes in Tennessee is greater than the U.S. population proportion, $H_A: P_1 > P_0$ (or $P_1 - P_0 > 0$).

A confidence interval around the percent difference ($P_1 - P_0 = 0.10$) can be computed using a tabled z value corresponding to an alpha level for a two-tailed region of rejection ($z = 2.58$) and the standard error of the difference (standard deviation of the sampling distribution: $S_{P_1 - P_0} = 0.0025$).

$$CI_{99} = 0.10 \pm (2.58)(0.0025)$$

$$CI_{99} = 0.10 \pm (0.00645)$$

$$CI_{99} = (0.0936, 0.1064).$$

The 99% confidence interval indicates that 99 times out of 100, the percent difference in smoking between the high school students in Tennessee and the U.S. population would range between 9.5% (0.095 × 100) and 10.5% (0.105 × 100).

TIP

The tabled z value selected for determining the confidence interval around the computed z-test statistic is based on a two-tailed interpretation because it produces a lower and an upper percentage. The alternative statistical hypothesis used a one-tailed probability because of the directional nature of the research question.

Step 5. Interpret the z-test statistic results.

Our practical interpretation is based on a test of the null hypothesis and a 99% confidence interval around the computed z-test statistic. Since the computed $z = 40$ is greater than the tabled z value, $z = 2.33$ at the .01 level of significance, we reject the null statistical hypothesis in favor of the alternative statistical hypothesis. The probability that the observed difference in the sample proportions of 10% would have occurred by chance is less than .01 or 1%. We can therefore conclude that the high school students in Tennessee had a greater percentage smoking cigarettes than the U.S. population of high school students. The Type I error was set at .01, so we can be fairly confident in our interpretation.

The confidence interval was computed as 0.095 to 0.105, indicating that we can be 99% confident that this interval contains the difference between the population proportions. Moreover, the narrowness of the confidence interval gives us some idea of how much the difference in proportions might vary from random sample to random sample from the population. Consequently, we can feel fairly confident that a 9.5% (0.095) to 10.5% (0.105) difference would exist for Tennessee high school students smoking cigarettes on repeated sampling.

The *single sample z-test function* in the script file (chap12a.r) requires the single-sample size and the number of those who smoked cigarettes, as well as the known population size and the number who smoked cigarettes. The function then computes the z statistic as the difference in the percentages divided by the standard error of the z statistic, followed by the confidence interval given the specified alpha level. The results should be the same as those computed above. You will need to enter the critical value for z, the two population sizes, and the sample sizes for each prior to running the function.

```
> zCrit = 2.58 # 90% = 1.645, 95% = 1.96, 99% = 2.58 CI (two-tailed)
> size1 = 1000
> size2 = 20000
> num1 = 250
> num2 = 3000
> chap12a(zCrit, size1, size2, num1, num2)
```

The output will first list the values you entered, then show the difference in percentages, standard error, z statistic, and confidence interval. If you divide the percent difference by the standard error, you should obtain the z statistic.

```
PROGRAM OUTPUT

z CI = 2.58
size1 = 1000
size2 = 20000
num1 = 250
num2 = 3000
P1 = 0.25
P0 = 0.15
N = 21000
```

```
p = 0.1547619
q = 0.8452381

Difference in percents = 0.1
Standard Error of z = 0.0025
z Statistic = 40
Confidence Interval = (0.0936, 0.1064)
```

The power of our z test can be computed using the *pwr.p.test()* function from *library(pwr)*.

```
> library(pwr); ??pwr
> ?pwr.p.test

pwr.p.test(h = NULL, n = NULL, sig.level = 0.05, power = NULL,
alternative = c("two.sided","less","greater"))
```

Arguments

H	Effect size
n	Number of observations
sig.level	Significance level (Type I error probability)
power	Power of test (1 minus Type II error probability)
alternative	a character string specifying the alternative hypothesis, must be one of "two.sided" (default), "greater" or "less"

The arguments are $b = 0.10$ for the difference between Tennessee cigarette smokers and the national population (effect size), $n = 1,000$ for the number of students, sig.level = .01 for the Type I error rate, power = NULL (we want this to be estimated), and alternative = "greater" based on the alternative hypothesis. The R command is then run as

```
> pwr.p.test(h = .10, n = 1000, sig.level = .01, power = NULL,
alternative = "greater")

    proportion power calculation for binomial distribution (arcsine
transformation)

    h = 0.1
    n = 1000
    sig.level = 0.01
    power = 0.7984028
    alternative = greater
```

Power = .798 ~ .80, which indicates a desired level against a Type II error. If we change alpha level to *sig.level* = .05, then power = .935. You may recall that several criteria affect power calculations, including the alpha level used to test the null hypothesis.

● INDEPENDENT-SAMPLES *Z* TEST

A second research design tests whether population percents differ between two independent groups, that is, we would compute a *z* test for differences in proportions between two independent samples. The type of research question for this research design would be "Do a greater proportion of male high school students than female high school students smoke cigarettes in Tennessee?" This is a directional research question. Once again, we can follow a five-step approach to test this research question.

Step 1. State the directional research question in a statistical hypothesis format.

$$H_0: P_1 \leq P_2 \ (\text{or } P_1 - P_2 \leq 0)$$
$$H_A: P_1 > P_2 \ (\text{or } P_1 - P_2 > 0).$$

P_1 is the percentage of male high school students in Tennessee who smoke cigarettes, and P_2 is the percentage of female high school students in Tennessee who smoke cigarettes. The alternative hypothesis (H_A) states that the percentage of males is greater than the percentage of females who smoke cigarettes.

Step 2. Determine the criteria for rejecting the null hypothesis and accepting the alternative hypothesis.

Given $\alpha = .05$, we select the corresponding *z* value from Table 1 (Appendix A), which is the closest to 5% of the area under the normal curve. If our computed *z*-test statistic is greater than this tabled *z* value, we would reject the null hypothesis in favor of the alternative hypothesis. This establishes our region of rejection, or the probability area under the normal curve where differences in sample proportions are unlikely to occur by random chance.

Region of rejection: $z > 1.65$.

TIP

Table 1 (Appendix A) is used to find $z = 1.65$. The first column indicates $z = 1.6$, with the other column indicating the *5* in the hundredths decimal place. The percentage = 0.4505, which is the closest to 45%, leaving 5% probability area under the normal curve. Notice only one half of the normal curve is represented, so 50% is automatically added to the 45% to get 95%, which reflects the one-tailed probability for the directional alternative statistical hypothesis.

Step 3. Collect the sample data, and compute the *z*-test statistic.

A random sample of 5,000 male high school students and 5,000 female high school students were selected in Tennessee. Of the male high school students, 1,000 replied that they smoked cigarettes (20% = 1000/5000), and of the female high school students, only 250 stated that they smoked cigarettes (5% = 250/5000). The proportions were

$P_1 = 0.20$ (20% of the boys in the sample of high school students smoked cigarettes)

$P_2 = 0.05$ (5% of the girls in the sample of high school students smoked cigarettes).

The standard deviation of the sampling distribution is called the standard error of the difference between independent-samples proportions. This value is needed to compute the z-test statistic. The formula is

$$S_{P_1-P_2} = \sqrt{\frac{pq}{N}},$$

where

$p = (n_1 + n_2)/N = (1000 + 250)/10000 = 0.125,$

$q = 1 - p = 1 - 0.125 = 0.875,$

n_1 = number of students in the first sample = 1,000,

n_2 = number of students in the second sample = 250, and

N = total sample size taken = (5000 + 5000) = 10000.

$$S_{P_1-P_2} = \sqrt{\frac{0.125(0.875)}{10000}} = 0.0033.$$

The z test can now be computed as

$$z = \frac{P_1 - P_2}{S_{P_1-P_2}} = \frac{0.20 - 0.05}{0.0033} = \frac{0.15}{0.0033} = 45.45.$$

Step 4. Interpret the region of rejection, and compute the confidence interval around z.

A confidence interval is computed by using the percent difference between the two independent groups ($P_1 - P_2 = .15$), the tabled z value corresponding to a given alpha level for a two-tailed region of region ($z = \pm 1.96$), and the standard deviation of the sampling distribution or standard error of the test statistic ($S_{P_1-P_2} = 0.0033$).

$$CI_{95} = .15 \pm (1.96)(0.0033)$$

$$CI_{95} = .15 \pm (0.00588)$$

$$CI_{95} = (0.1435, 0.1565).$$

TIP

The tabled z value selected for determining the confidence interval around the computed z-test statistic is not the same because the confidence interval is based on a two-tailed interpretation. The alternative statistical hypothesis used a one-tailed probability because of the directional nature of the research question.

Step 5. Interpret the z-test statistic results.

Our interpretation of the results is based on a test of the null hypothesis and a 95% confidence interval around the computed z-test statistic. Since the computed $z = 45.45$ is greater than the tabled z value ($z = 1.96$ at the .05 level of significance) we reject the null statistical hypothesis in favor of the alternative statistical hypothesis. The probability that the observed difference in the sample proportions of 15% would have occurred by chance is less than .05. We can therefore conclude that in Tennessee male high school students had a greater percentage of those smoking cigarettes than female high school students. The Type I error rate was set at .05, so there is only a 5% chance of error in rejecting the null hypothesis when it is actually true.

The confidence interval was computed as 0.1435 to 0.1565, indicating that we can be 95% confident that this interval contains the difference between the population proportions from which the two samples were taken. The narrowness of the confidence interval gives us some idea of how much the difference in independent-samples proportions might vary from random sample to random sample. Consequently, we can feel fairly confident that a 14.35% (0.1435) to 15.65% (0.1565) difference would exist between male and female high school students smoking cigarettes on repeated sampling of their population.

The *independent-samples z-test function* in the script file (chap12b.r) is similar to the single-sample function, except that now we have two independent sample percents representing their respective populations. The research design and hypothesis are therefore different from the single-sample design. The function inputs the critical z value for the confidence interval, the sizes for both populations, and the sample sizes for each group. The difference in percentages and the standard error of the z statistic are reported, followed by the z statistic and the confidence interval around the z statistic given the critical z value (based on alpha level and directional nature of the hypothesis). You will enter the critical z value, two population sizes, and the sample size for each and then run the function.

```
> zCrit = 1.96 # 90% = 1.645, 95% = 1.96, 99% = 2.58 CI (two-tailed)
> size1 = 5000
> size2 = 5000
> num1 = 1000
> num2 = 250
> chap12b(zCrit, size1, size2, num1, num2)
```

The results will first list the values you entered, then the difference in percentages, standard error, z statistic, and confidence interval. Once again, dividing the percent difference by the standard error will compute the z statistic.

```
PROGRAM OUTPUT

z CI = 1.96
size1 = 5000
size2 = 5000
num1 = 1000
num2 = 250
P1 = 0.2
P2 = 0.05
N = 10000
```

```
p = 0.125
q = 0.875

Difference in percents = 0.15
Standard Error of z = 0.0033
z Statistic = 45.4545
Confidence Interval = (0.1435, 0.1565)
```

Power for the independent-samples z test is computed using the *pwr.2p.test()* function because the sample sizes are equal.

```
> ?pwr.2p.test
pwr.2p.test(h = NULL, n = NULL, sig.level = 0.05, power = NULL,
alternative = c("two.sided","less","greater"))
```

Arguments

H	Effect size
N	Number of observations (per sample)
sig.level	Significance level (Type I error probability)
power	Power of test (1 minus Type II error probability)
Alternative	a character string specifying the alternative hypothesis, must be one of "two.sided" (default), "greater" or "less"

The arguments in the function would be $h = 0.15$ (detect a 15% difference), $n = 5,000$ (sample size of each group), *sig.level* = 0.05, power = NULL, alternative = "greater"):

```
> pwr.2p.test(h = .15, n = 5000, sig.level = .05, power = NULL,
alternative = "greater")
```

```
Difference of proportion power calculation for binomial
distribution (arcsine transformation)
h = 0.15
n = 5000
sig.level = 0.05
power = 1
alternative = greater
```

Note: Same sample sizes.

Power = 1, which indicates sufficient protection against a Type II error when testing for a difference of 15% between males and females smoking cigarettes in Tennessee.

● DEPENDENT-SAMPLES Z TEST

A third type of research design that tests for differences in proportions is based on dependent (paired or repeated) samples. The null hypothesis would be that there is no difference between the two population proportions for the dependent samples. This research design would involve obtaining percentages from the same sample or group twice. The research design would therefore have paired observations. Listed below are some examples of when this occurs:

1. Test differences in proportions of agreement in a group before and after a discussion of the death penalty

2. Test differences in percent passing for students who take two similar tests

3. Test differences in the proportion of employees who support a retirement plan and the same employee proportion that support a company daycare

Our research design example involves studying the impact of diversity training on the proportion of company employees who would favor hiring foreign workers. Before and after diversity training, employees were asked whether or not they were in favor of the company hiring foreign workers. The research question would be stated as follows: Are the proportions of company employees who favor hiring foreign workers the same before and after diversity training? This is a nondirectional research question, or two-tailed hypothesis. The five-step approach will once again guide our understanding of how to conduct the hypothesis testing for this type of research design.

Step 1. State the nondirectional research question in a statistical hypothesis format.

$$H_0: P_{1A} = P_{1B} \text{ (or } P_{1A} - P_{1B} = 0)$$

$$H_A: P_{1A} \neq P_{1B} \text{ (or } P_{1A} - P_{1B} \neq 0).$$

P_{1A} represents the proportion of employees who favor hiring foreign workers before diversity training, and P_{1B} represents the proportion who favor hiring foreign workers after diversity training. The alternative hypothesis (H_A) states that we expect a difference between these two percentages, however, we do not know if it will be higher before or after diversity training, hence the nondirectional two-tailed test.

TIP

In this example, we are interested in testing the null hypothesis of no difference between the population proportions against the nondirectional alternative hypothesis, which indicates that the proportions are different. The alternative statistical hypothesis is stated to reflect the nondirectional research question.

Step 2. Determine the criteria for rejecting the null hypothesis and accepting the alternative hypothesis.

Given $\alpha = .05$, we select the corresponding z value from Table 1 (Appendix A), which is the closest to 5% of the area under the normal curve (2.5% in each tail of the normal curve for the two-tailed test). If our computed z-test statistic is greater than this tabled z value, we would reject the null hypothesis and accept the alternative hypothesis. This establishes our region of rejection, or the probability areas under the normal curve where differences in sample proportions are unlikely to occur by random chance.

$$\text{Region of rejection}_{\alpha/2}: z = \pm 1.96.$$

TIP

In Table 1 (Appendix A), the first column indicates $z = 1.9$, with the other column indicating the 6 in the hundredths decimal place. The percentage is 0.4750, which indicates that the .025 probability area under the normal curve is only one-tailed. In Table 1, only one half of the normal curve is represented, but .025 in both tails of the normal curve would equal 5%. If we add 0.4750 + 0.4750, it would equal 0.95, or 95%, which indicates the remaining percentage under the normal curve. The region of rejection indicates two z values, +1.96 and −1.96 ($\pm$), for rejecting the null hypothesis, which reflects testing a nondirectional research question.

Step 3. Collect the sample data, and compute the z-test statistic.

A random sample of 100 employees from a high-tech company were interviewed before and after a diversity training session and asked whether or not they favored the company hiring foreign workers. Their sample responses before and after diversity training were as follows:

Before Diversity Training	After Diversity Training		Total
	No	Yes	
Yes	P_{11} = 10 (0.10)	20 (0.20)	**30 (0.30)**
No	50 (0.50)	P_{12} = 20 (0.20)	70 (0.70)
Total	60 (0.60)	**40 (0.40)**	100 (1.00)

NOTE: The order of data entry in the cells of this table indicates agreement and disagreement before and after diversity training.

The sample data (*boldfaced in table above*) indicated the following proportions:

$$P_{1A} = \text{proportion in favor before diversity training} = 0.30, \text{ or } 30\%$$

$$P_{1B} = \text{proportion in favor after diversity training} = 0.40, \text{ or } 40\%.$$

The standard deviation of the sampling distribution is called the standard error of the difference between dependent-samples proportions. This value is needed to compute the z-test statistic. The formula uses the percent change from before to after diversity training, that is, cells P_{11} and P_{12}:

$$S_{P_{1A}-P_{1B}} = \sqrt{\frac{p_{11} + p_{12}}{N}},$$

where

p_{11} = percent change from before to after training (yes→no) = 0.10,

p_{12} = percent change from before to after training (no→yes) = 0.20, and

N = total sample size = 100.

$$S_{P_{1A}-P_{1B}} = \sqrt{\frac{0.10 + 0.20}{100}} = 0.0548.$$

The z test can now be computed as

$$z = \frac{P_{1A} - P_{1B}}{S_{P_{1A}-P_{1B}}} = \frac{0.30 - 0.40}{0.0548} = \frac{-0.10}{0.0548} = -1.82.$$

TIP

Our understanding from previous chapters helps us know that to test a statistical hypothesis we need to use the sampling distribution of the statistic. The sampling distribution of the difference between two dependent proportions is normally distributed when the sum of the sample sizes in the diagonal cells is greater than 10. Thus, we can use the normal distribution z statistic to test our statistical hypothesis.

Step 4. Interpret the region of rejection, and compute the confidence interval around z.

The computed $z = -1.82$ indicates that the percentage after diversity training was higher because of the negative sign. When we compare the computed $z = -1.82$ with the region of rejection z values ($z = \pm 1.96$) the results indicate that -1.82 is not greater than -1.96 in that tail of the distribution, so the findings are not statistically significant. The percent difference before and after diversity training is not statistically significant different at the .05 level of significance for a two-tailed test. We are confident that our decision to retain the null hypothesis would result in a Type I error rate only 5% of the time.

A confidence interval further helps our understanding of the findings. The confidence interval is computed by using the percent difference before and after diversity training for the employees ($P_{1A} - P_{1B} = -0.10$), the tabled z value corresponding to the alpha level for the two-tailed region of rejection ($z = \pm1.96$), and the standard deviation of the sampling distribution or standard error of the test statistic ($S_{P1A-P1B} = 0.0548$). The 95% confidence interval is computed as

$$\text{CI}_{95} = -0.10 \pm (1.96)(0.0548)$$

$$\text{CI}_{95} = -0.10 \pm (0.1074)$$

$$\text{CI}_{95} = (-0.2074, 0.0074).$$

TIP

The tabled z value selected for determining the confidence interval around the computed z-test statistic is the same because the confidence interval is also based on a two-tailed interpretation. The null hypothesized parameter of zero (no difference in proportions) is contained in the confidence interval, which is consistent with retaining the null hypothesis.

Step 5. Interpret the z-test statistic results.

Our interpretation of the findings is once again based on a test of the null hypothesis, but this time using a 95% confidence interval around the computed z-test statistic because of the nondirectional nature of the research question. Since the computed $z = -1.82$ is more than the tabled z value ($z = -1.96$ at the .05 level of significance), we retain the null statistical hypothesis. The probability that the observed difference in the sample proportions of 10% would have occurred by chance is greater than .05. We therefore cannot conclude that the percentage of company employees in favor of hiring foreign workers was different after diversity training. The Type I error was set at .05, so we would only make an error in our decision to retain the null hypothesis 5% of the time, thus 95% confident in our decision.

The confidence interval was computed from −0.2074 to 0.0074, indicating that we can be 95% confident that this interval contains the null hypothesis parameter of zero difference in percentages between the population proportions. Moreover, the spread in the confidence interval gives us some idea of how much the difference in the dependent-samples proportions might vary from random sample to random sample. Consequently, we should be sensitive to a research design factor that may have affected the statistical test, which is the duration and intensity of the diversity training. Obviously a 1-hour training session involving watching a short slide presentation might have less of an impact on employees than a 6-week training session involving role modeling with foreign workers on the job.

The *dependent-samples z-test function* in the script file (chap12c.r) inputs the table z critical value for a two-tailed test and the number who agreed and then disagreed before and after diversity training. These values are then used to compute the percentage before and after diversity training who favored the company hiring foreign workers as well as the standard error of the z statistic for differences in proportions. The function outputs these values plus the difference in proportions, the standard error of the difference, the z statistic, and the confidence interval around the z statistic. You will need the critical value for z and the cell numbers prior to running the function:

```
> zCrit = 1.96 # 90% = 1.65,  95% = 1.96,  99% = 2.58 (two-tailed)
> num11 = 10
> num12 = 20
> num21 = 50
> num22 = 20
> chap12c = function(zCrit, num11, num12, num21, num22)
```

The results show not only the critical z value but also the sample size, change in answers, and percentages before and after. This difference in proportions and standard error are used to compute the z statistic. The z statistic should be the same as the one we calculated by hand. The difference in proportions (−0.10) falls within the confidence interval (−0.20, 0.007).

```
PROGRAM OUTPUT

z CI = 1.96
N = 100
Change yes to no = 0.1
Change no to yes = 0.2
Percent before = 0.3
Percent after = 0.4

Difference in proportions = -0.1
Standard Error of Diff = 0.0548
z Statistic = -1.8248
Confidence Interval = (-0.2074, 0.0074)
```

The power calculation can be accomplished using the *pwr.p.test()* function. The arguments would be $h = 0.10$ (10% improvement), $n = 100$ (number of subjects), *sig.level* = .05 (Type I error rate), power = NULL (the value we desire to compute), and alternative = "greater" (hypothesized improvement). The R command is

```
> pwr.p.test(h = .10, n = 100, sig.level = .05, power = NULL, alter-
native = "greater")

    proportion power calculation for binomial distribution (arcsine
transformation)

    h = 0.1
    n = 100
    sig.level = 0.05
    power = 0.259511
    alternative = greater
```

The power of .259 is lower than our desired .80, thus the ability to detect a true difference is subject to a Type II error. Changing our sample size to $n = 650$, yields power = .817, which provides for a better test of the null hypothesis. The power results indicate that our conclusion of no difference in diversity training before and after may be due to a low sample size to detect a percent difference. In other words, a percent difference may exist, but we failed to gather enough data to detect the difference.

● R *prop.test()* FUNCTION

The *stats* package has a *prop.test()* function that computes a two-sided, "less than," or "greater than" test of proportions for single-sample and difference-in-independent-samples proportions. The R function with arguments is

```
prop.test(x, n, p = NULL, alternative = c("two.
sided","less","greater"), conf.level = 0.95,correct = TRUE)
```

The R function with an explanation of the arguments can be obtained from the R command:

```
> ?prop.test
```

Usage

```
prop.test(x, n, p = NULL,
alternative = c("two.sided","less","greater"),conf.level = 0.95, correct = TRUE)
```

Arguments

X	a vector of counts of successes, a one-dimensional table with two entries, or a two-dimensional table (or matrix) with 2 columns, giving the counts of successes and failures, respectively.
N	a vector of counts of trials; ignored if x is a matrix or a table.
P	a vector of probabilities of success. The length of p must be the same as the number of groups specified by x, and its elements must be greater than 0 and less than 1.
Alternative	a character string specifying the alternative hypothesis, must be one of "two.sided" (default), "greater" or "less". You can specify just the initial letter. Only used for testing the null that a single proportion equals a given value, or that two proportions are equal; ignored otherwise.
conf.level	confidence level of the returned confidence interval. Must be a single number between 0 and 1. Only used when testing the null that a single proportion equals a given value, or that two proportions are equal; ignored otherwise.
Correct	a logical indicating whether Yates' continuity correction should be applied where possible.

NOTE: The proportion test calculates a chi-square statistic rather than a *z* statistic. The traditional *z* test of a proportion is not implemented in R, but the two tests are equivalent. The correction for continuity can be nullified by setting the "correct=" option to FALSE. This value must be set to FALSE to make the test mathematically equivalent to the *z* test of a proportion.

Single-Sample Proportion Test

A person rolls a set of dice 20 times, recording each time the sum of the two dice. The person expects a sum of 6 for the two dice 50% of the time. The observed results indicated that 12 out of the 20 rolls of the two dice yielded a sum of 6. We wish to test the probability of this sample proportion being greater than 0.5, or 50%. A single-sample proportion test can be conducted without the Yates correction using the *prop.test()* function as follows:

```
> prop.test(x = 12, n = 20, p = .5, alternative = "greater", conf.
level = 0.95, correct = FALSE)

PROGRAM OUTPUT

1 - sample proportions test without continuity correction

data: 12 out of 20, null probability 0.5
X-squared = 0.8, df = 1, p-value = 0.1855
alternative hypothesis: true p is greater than 0.5
95 percent confidence interval:
 0.4185559 1.0000000
sample estimates:
 p
0.6
```

The actual proportion is $p = .6$ (12 out of 20), but this was not statistically greater than the true $p = .5$, as indicated by the nonsignificant $\chi^2 = 0.8$, $df = 1$, $p = .1855$.

Two-Independent-Samples Proportion Test

A test of the difference in proportions between two independent groups can also be conducted using the *prop.test()* function. For example, a random sample of 500 adults from Tennessee indicated that 125 people drank moonshine, compared with a random sample of 700 adults from Texas, which indicated that only 100 people drank moonshine. Is the proportion of adults who drank moonshine in Tennessee different from the proportion of adults in Texas? We can test the difference in proportions at the $\alpha = .01$ level of significance as follows:

```
> prop.test(x = c(125,100), n = c(500,700), alternative = "two.sided",
conf.level = .99, correct = FALSE)

Program Output

2-sample test for equality of proportions without continuity correction
```

```
data: c(125,100) out of c(500,700)
X-squared = 21.978, df = 1, p-value = 2.758e-06
alternative hypothesis: two.sided
99 percent confidence interval:
 0.04673831 0.16754741
sample estimates:
 prop 1    prop 2
0.2500000 0.1428571
```

Note: Enter number of successes in the first vector, x, and the sample sizes into the second vector, n. The Yates continuity correction is nullified by *correct = FALSE*. A two-sided alternative hypothesis was specified with a 99% confidence interval.

   Of the Tennessee adults, 25% drank moonshine (125/500), while the Texas adults had 14% who drank moonshine (100/700). The chi-square test was statistically significant ($\chi^2 = 21.978$, $df = 1$, $p = .000002758$), indicating that we would reject the null hypothesis of no difference and accept the alternative hypothesis that the two groups had different percentages. The Tennessee and Texas adults did differ in their proportions (percentages) of those who drank moonshine. The Tennessee adults (25%) had a higher percentage than the Texas adults (14%). The 99% confidence interval indicates that this percent difference could fluctuate between 5% (0.0467) and 17% (0.1675).

● R COMMANDS FOR AREA UNDER THE NORMAL CURVE

A few simple R commands can be used to determine the area under the normal distribution curve. You recall from Chapter 5 that the normal distribution can be expressed by the following functions: *dnorm()*—density, *pnorm()*—probability, *qnorm()*—quantiles, and *rnorm()*—random numbers. We can use the *pnorm()* function to determine the area under the normal curve. The various possibilities are expressed below:

```
# Find area below z = 1.96
> pnorm(1.96)
[1] 0.9750021
```

This indicates that .025 of the scores fall in the tail of the normal distribution.

```
# Find area between z = -1 and z = + 1
> pnorm(1.00)-pnorm(-1.00)
[1] 0.6826895
```

Recall that 68% of the scores fall between ±1 standard deviation in a normal distribution.

   We can also determine the probability area between two scores; for example, in a set of exam scores with mean = 80 and standard deviation = 5, the R command would be

```
# Find area between scores of 70 and 90 with mean = 80, and standard
deviation = 5
> pnorm(90, mean = 80, sd = 5)-pnorm(70, mean = 80, sd = 5)
[1] 0.9544997
```

The results indicate that 95% of the scores fall between 70 and 90 in a score distribution with mean = 80 and standard deviation = 5. This should not be surprising because 2 standard deviations above and below the mean would capture approximately 95% of the scores in a normal distribution.

SUMMARY

The z test can be used in three different types of research designs to test hypotheses about differences in proportions. The first research design tested the difference between a single-sample percent and a known population percent. The second research design tested the difference between two independent sample percents. The third research design tested the difference between two percentages from the same group or sample. The *prop.test()* function can be used for the single-sample and two-independent-samples tests of proportions but not for the dependent-samples proportion test. The function does not report a z statistic, so I choose to write my own function to make the computations.

The *z test* uses the probability area under the normal distribution to determine if a computed z value falls in an area of rejection. The region of rejection or area under the normal distribution is based on the alpha level selected (Type I error rate) and the directional nature of the research questions (one tailed or two tailed). You also have the option of using the *prop.test()* function and the chi-square sampling distribution.

A statistically significant difference in proportions indicates that, beyond a random chance level, the proportions are different. A confidence interval around the z-test statistic indicates the amount of difference in the group proportions one can expect on repeated sampling. The confidence interval captures the null hypothesis parameter of zero when proportions are not statistically significantly different.

TIP

The R {stats} library has many different statistical tests, which are performed by functions. Use the following command in the RGui dialog window to obtain a list of the statistical functions:

```
> library(help = "stats")
```

EXERCISES

1. For the following hypothesis, calculate the single sample z test statistic. Is there a statistically significant difference in the percentage of automobile accidents in Texas compared with the

percentage nationwide. State the statistical hypothesis, show your work, and interpret the results given a 0.05 level of probability.

$$H_0: P_1 = P_0 \text{ (or } P_1 - P_0 = 0)$$
$$H_A: P_1 \neq P_0 \text{ (or } P_1 - P_0 > 0).$$

The following results are given:

$P_1 = 0.45$ (percentage of automobile accidents in Texas)

$P_0 = 0.30$ (percentage of automobile accidents nationwide)

$S_{P_1 - P_0} = 0.05$.

2. Calculate the 95% confidence interval for the results in #1. Show your work. What would you conclude?

3. For the following hypothesis, calculate the dependent-samples z-test statistic. The percentage who favor nationwide health care before attending an informative workshop will be statistically significantly lower than the percentage who favor nationwide health care after attending the informative workshop. State the statistical hypothesis, show work, and interpret results given a 0.05 level of probability.

$$H_0: P_{Before} \geq P_{After} \text{ (OR } P_{Before} - P_{After} \geq 0)$$
$$H_A: P_{Before} < P_{After} \text{ (OR } P_{Before} - P_{After} < 0)$$

The following results are given:

$P_{Before} = 0.25$ (percentage in favor of nationwide healthcare before workshop)

$P_{After} = 0.65$ (percentage in favor of nationwide healthcare after workshop)

$S_{P_{Before} - P_{After}} = 0.10$.

4. Use the *prop.test()* function to test a single sample proportion without Yates correction. Results indicated that 75 people ($x = 75$) bought tickets out of 100 possible sales ($n = 100$). Given a 50% expected sales rate, are the ticket sales greater than 50% at the 0.05 level of probability? What would you conclude?

TRUE OR FALSE QUESTIONS

T   F   a. The standard error of the difference in percentages is based on the standard deviation of the sampling distribution for the z statistic.

T   F   b. A z test can be computed for independent or dependent related samples.

T   F   c. The R command *library(help = "stats")* provides a list of statistical functions.

T   F   d.   The *prop.test()* function can be used to test single-sample, independent-samples, and dependent-samples differences in proportions.

T   F   e.   The *prop.test()* function yields a *z* value when testing differences in percentages.

WEB RESOURCES

Chapter R script files are available at http://www.sagepub.com/schumacker

Dependent Samples *z* Test Function R script file: chap12c.r

Independent Samples *z* Test Function R script file: chap12b.r

Single Sample *z* Test Function R script file: chap12a.r

## CHAPTER 13

T TEST FOR MEAN DIFFERENCES (TWO GROUPS)

The *t* test is used to conduct tests of mean differences between two groups. Recall that the *t*-sampling distribution is peaked or leptokurtic, so adjustments are made for the probability area in the tails of the distribution. As the sample size increases, the *t*-sampling distribution becomes normally distributed, thus a *t* value equals a *z* value. For example, Table 2 (Appendix A) indicates the *t* values for one-tailed and two-tailed hypotheses. If we select $\alpha = .05$, one-tailed test, degrees of freedom (df) = ∞ (infinity), the *t* value = 1.645, which is the same as the *z* value in the normal distribution. However, notice that the *t* values start out larger at $df = 1$ ($t = 6.314$) and decrease as the sample size (degrees of freedom) becomes larger, that is, $df = 120$ ($t = 1.658$). So if the sample size is greater than $N = 120$, the *t* value should be fairly close to a *z* value, that is, $t = z = 1.645$. The same is true for the other one-tailed and two-tailed probability levels. Generally, a researcher will report the *t* statistic when testing mean differences for a single sample, the difference between the means of two independent samples, or the difference between the means of dependent (paired) samples.

In this chapter, we extend our understanding of statistical tests beyond the chi-square test and *z* test that was used for counts or percentages. The five-step hypothesis-testing format can be used for testing mean differences, similar to testing for percent differences. Our understanding of the sampling distribution of a statistic will also be applied to selecting a region of rejection, or the probability area for rejecting the null hypothesis of no mean difference. If the computed *t* statistic from sample data is greater than the critical *t* value in the table at a selected probability level, then we reject the null hypothesis and accept the alternative hypothesis. We therefore apply the sampling distribution of the mean that provides the probability area to test our statistical hypotheses. A **one-sample *t* test** for the mean given small sample size is presented, followed by a two-sample independent *t* test, and then a dependent (paired)-sample *t* test.

Sampling distributions are frequency distributions of a statistic, which are generated to make an inference between the sample statistic and its corresponding population parameter. The average (mean) statistical value in the sampling distribution is the expected value of the population parameter. The variance of the sampling distribution is used to calculate the standard error of the statistic. The standard error of the statistic is a function of sample size and is used to calculate confidence intervals around the sample statistic, which provides the basis for testing statistical hypotheses. These concepts from earlier chapters will be further explained and clarified in this chapter.

The distribution theory that led to a solution of the problem of estimating the population mean, μ, when the population variance was unknown, σ^2, was due to William S. Gossett, a chemist, who in 1908 wrote under the pseudonym "Student" (Pearson, 1939, 1990). Gossett, who worked for a brewery, in Dublin, Ireland, determined that when the sample size was large, the sampling distribution of the z statistic was normal; however, when the sample size was small, the sampling distribution was leptokurtic or peaked. He referred to this slightly nonnormal distribution as the t distribution. Gossett further discovered that as he increased the sample sizes, the sampling distribution became normal, and therefore the t values equaled the z values. Gossett signed his pivotal work "Student," and today small sample tests of mean differences are referred to as the *Student t test* or simply the *t test*. Sir Ronald Fisher, using his earlier work, extended the *t test* into the analysis of variance techniques, which are covered in the next chapter.

● R *t.test()* FUNCTION

The *stats* package has a *t.test()* function that permits the individual test of mean differences for single-sample means, two-group independent means, or paired-sample dependent means. You can use the *t.test()* function by itself to run each of the *t*-test examples in this chapter. The arguments required for the *t.test()* function are given by the following command in the RGui window:

```
> ?t.test()
```

Usage

```
t.test(x, ...)

## Default S3 method:
t.test(x, y = NULL, alternative = c("two.sided","less","greater"), mu = 0,
paired = FALSE, var.equal = FALSE, conf.level = 0.95, ...)

## S3 method for class 'formula'
t.test(formula, data, subset, na.action, ...)
```

Arguments

X	a (non-empty) numeric vector of data values.
y	an optional (non-empty) numeric vector of data values.
Alternative	a character string specifying the alternative hypothesis, must be one of "two.sided" (default), "greater" or "less". You can specify just the initial letter.

(Continued)

(Continued)

Mu	a number indicating the true value of the mean (or difference in means if you are performing a two sample test).
Paired	a logical indicating whether you want a paired t-test.
var.equal	a logical variable indicating whether to treat the two variances as being equal. If TRUE then the pooled variance is used to estimate the variance otherwise the Welch (or Satterthwaite) approximation to the degrees of freedom is used.
conf.level	confidence level of the interval.
formula	a formula of the form lhs ~ rhs where lhs is a numeric variable giving the data values and rhs a factor with two levels giving the corresponding groups.
Data	an optional matrix or data frame (or similar: see model.frame) containing the variables in the formula formula. By default the variables are taken from environment(formula).
Subset	an optional vector specifying a subset of observations to be used.
na.action	a function which indicates what should happen when the data contain NAs. Defaults to getOption("na.action").
...	further arguments to be passed to or from methods.

An example of how to use the *t.test()* function for each of the different types of *t* tests presented above is presented next.

● SINGLE-SAMPLE *T* TEST

The sampling distribution of the mean can be used to determine the expected value of the population mean and variance when they are unknown. The central limit theorem supports this assumption because as the sample size increases, the sampling distribution of the mean becomes more normally distributed, with mean = μ and variance = σ^2/N. Knowledge of this theorem permits us to test whether the sample mean is statistically different from the population mean. The test is called a single-sample *t* test, which is computed as follows.

$$t = \frac{\bar{X} - \mu}{\sqrt{\dfrac{s^2}{N}}} = \frac{\bar{X} - \mu}{S / \sqrt{N}}$$

Suppose a class of 20 students were given instruction using computer lab software, and then they took a nationally standardized achievement test. If the computer lab software leads to better learning in the population, then this sample of 20 students should perform better on the achievement test than students in the larger population who learned without the computer lab software. Assume that the 20 students had a mean achievement score of 120 with a standard deviation of 10. The mean achievement score for students in the population taking regular classes was 100. What is the probability that a random sample of this size would have a sample mean of 120 or higher? This research question can be tested using a one-sample *t* test that follows a five-step hypothesis-testing format.

Step 1. State the directional research question in a statistical hypothesis format.

$$H_0: \mu_1 \leq \mu_0 \text{ (or } \mu_1 - \mu_0 \leq 0)$$
$$H_A: \mu_1 > \mu_0 \text{ (or } \mu_1 - \mu_0 > 0).$$

μ_1 represents the achievement test mean for the random sample of 20 students who learned using computer lab software, while μ_0 indicates the population mean achievement test score. The null hypothesis (H_0) indicates that the sample mean is expected to be less than or equal to the population mean. In contrast, the alternative hypothesis (H_A) indicates that the sample mean is greater than the population mean (directional hypothesis). Recall that together these probabilities equal 100% under the sampling distribution of the *t*-test statistic.

> **TIP**
>
> The "H" stands for "hypothesis," with the subscripts "0" for the null statistical hypothesis and "A" for the alternative statistical hypothesis. The alternative statistical hypothesis is stated to reflect the research question. The following research question reflects a directional one-tailed hypothesis: Is the achievement test mean for students learning with computer lab software significantly higher than the population mean on the achievement test?

Step 2. Determine the criteria for rejecting the null hypothesis and accepting the alternative hypothesis.

Given $\alpha = .01$, a one-tailed test, and $df = 19$ ($N - 1$), we select the corresponding t value from Table 2 (Appendix A), which is $t = 2.539$. If our computed *t*-test statistic is greater than this tabled t value, we would reject the null hypothesis in favor of the alternative hypothesis. This establishes our region of rejection, or the probability area under the t distribution where differences in sample means are unlikely to occur by random chance.

Region of rejection: $t > 2.539$.

The t distribution with 1% probability area for the one-tailed test (region of rejection) can be plotted by the following *t-distribution function* (one-tailed test) in the script file (chap13a.r). You will only need to enter the degrees of freedom (recall that this is used to determine the region of rejection for different sample sizes).

```
> df = 19
```

```
Plot Output
```

Step 3. Collect the sample data, and compute the single-sample *t*-test statistic.

A random sample of 20 students who participated in learning using computer lab software were given the national achievement test. The mean of their scores was 120 and the standard

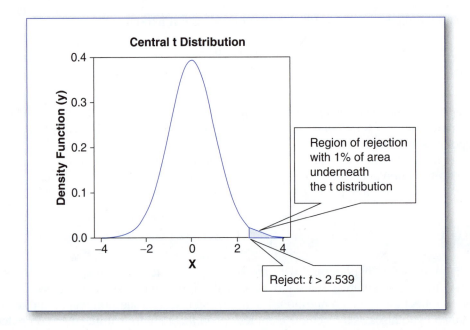

deviation, 10. The national average for the mathematics test was 100. The *t* test of mean difference is computed as

$$t = \frac{120 - 100}{10 / \sqrt{20}} = \frac{20}{10 / 4.47} = \frac{20}{2.237} = 8.94.$$

The standard deviation of the sampling distribution for the *t*-test statistic is called the standard error of the difference between means. This value is needed to compute the *t*-test statistic. The formula is

$$S_{\mu_1 - \mu_2} = \frac{s}{\sqrt{N}} = \frac{10}{\sqrt{20}} = \frac{10}{4.47} = 2.237,$$

where

   s = the sample standard deviation and

   N = the sample size.

TIP

To test a statistical hypothesis, we need to know the sampling distribution of the statistic. The sampling distribution for the *t* test is peaked or leptokurtic when sample sizes are small but becomes more normally distributed and similar to *z* values as the sample size increases.

Step 4. Interpret region of rejection, and compute confidence interval around *t*.

The region of rejection (Step 2) was determined based on a Type I error rate of 1%, or $\alpha = .01$, so $t > 2.539$ yields 1% of the probability area in the sampling distribution, the region of rejection. If our computed *t* value is greater than this tabled *t* value in the sampling distribution (*t* distribution), then only 1 out of 100 times would we falsely reject the null and accept the alternative hypothesis. Our computed $t = 8.94$ is greater than $t = 2.539$, which established our region of rejection, so we reject the null hypothesis and accept the alternative hypothesis. The sample mean is statistically significantly higher than the population mean, so we accept the alternative hypothesis, H_A: $\mu_1 > \mu_0$ (or $\mu_1 - \mu_0 > 0$).

A confidence interval around the mean difference ($\mu_1 - \mu_0 = 120 - 100 = 20$) can be computed using a tabled *t* value corresponding to an alpha level for a two-tailed region of rejection ($t = 2.861$) and the standard error of the difference (standard deviation of the sampling distribution; $S_{\mu_1 - \mu_0} = 2.237$).

$$CI_{99} = 10 \pm (2.861)(2.237)$$

$$CI_{99} = 10 \pm (6.40)$$

$$CI_{99} = (3.6, \ 16.40).$$

The 99% confidence interval indicates that 99 times out of 100, the mean difference in achievement test scores between the random sample of students and the population would range between 4 and 16 score points on average.

TIP

The tabled *t* value selected for determining the confidence interval around the computed *t*-test statistic is based on a two-tailed interpretation because it produces a lower and an upper mean. The alternative statistical hypothesis used a one-tailed probability because of the directional nature of the research question.

Step 5. Interpret the *single sample t-test* statistic results.

Our statistical interpretation is based on a test of the null hypothesis for the computed *t*-test statistic. Since the computed $t = 8.94$ is greater than the tabled *t* value ($t = 2.539$ at the .01 level of significance for a one-tailed test), we reject the null statistical hypothesis in favor of the alternative statistical hypothesis. The probability that the observed difference in the means would have occurred by chance is less than .01, or 1%. We can therefore conclude that the students using the computer lab software had a statistically significantly higher achievement test mean than the population of students. The Type I error was set at .01, so we can be fairly confident in our interpretation.

Our practical interpretation is based on the 99% confidence interval around the mean difference. The 99% confidence interval ranged from 4 points to 16 points on average, indicating that we can be 99% confident that this interval contains the difference between the sample and population mean. The confidence interval is wide and provides us some idea of how much the mean difference might vary from random sample to random sample. Our results indicate that we might find a mean difference of only 4 points or as much as 16 points if we conducted the study again. A 4-point mean difference on a test (4 test questions) would not have as much practical importance as a 16-point difference (16 test questions).

The power of our *t* test to detect a mean difference can be computed using the *pwr.t.test()* function in *library(pwr)*.

```
> library(pwr)
> ?pwr.t.test
```

```
pwr.t.test(n = NULL, d = NULL, sig.level = 0.05, power = NULL,
type = c("two.sample","one.sample","paired"), alternative = c("two.
sided","less","greater"))
```

Arguments

N	Number of observations (per sample)
d	Effect size
sig.level	Significance level (Type I error probability)
power	Power of test (1 minus Type II error probability)
type	Type of t test : one- two- or paired-samples
alternative	a character string specifying the alternative hypothesis, must be one of "two.sided" (default), "greater" or "less"

For the single-sample *t* test, the arguments would be $n = 20$ (number of students), $d = 20$ (20-point difference in average test scores), *sig.level* = .01, power = NULL, type = "one.sample" (one-sample *t* test), alternative = "greater" (directional hypothesis).

```
> pwr.t.test(n = 20, d = 20, sig.level = 0.01, power = NULL, type
= "one.sample",
alternative = "greater")

One-sample t test power calculation

n = 20
d = 20
sig.level = 0.01
power = 1
alternative = greater
```

Power = 1, which indicates sufficient protection against a Type II error when testing for a 20-point difference in average achievement test scores between students and the national average.

Because the *t* distribution is leptokurtic or peaked for small samples, the probabilities in the tails of the *t* distribution are greater than the probabilities in the normal distribution. When

Gossett discovered this, he made an adjustment for small sample sizes by entering larger tabled *t* values from the sampling distribution of the *t* values. By adjusting the *t* values, he compensated for the greater probability area under the sampling distributions. Once again, if you examine the last row in the *t* table (Table 2, Appendix A) for $\alpha = .01$, one-tailed test, $df = 19$, you will find that the *t* value is 2.539, which is larger than the *t* value under the normal distribution ($t = z = 2.326$, $df = \infty$). In practice, we use the *t* test rather than the *z* test for testing mean differences because it applies to both small and large samples.

Single-Sample *t* Test: *rnorm()* Function

This example has a random sample of 25 subjects with an estimated mean = 110 and standard deviation = 10—obtained from using the *rnorm()* function (actual values will vary unless we specify the *set.seed()* function). Next, a single-sample *t* test, two-tailed, with population mean = 100 will be conducted using the *t.test()* function. The results indicate that the sample mean of 108.97 is statistically significantly different from the population mean of 100 ($t = 5.2519$, $df = 24$, $p = .00002199$—given by not showing the scientific notation, using the *options(scipen = 999)* function).

```
> set.seed(13579)
> sample = rnorm(25,110,10)
> options(scipen = 999)
> t.test(sample, alternative = "two.sided", mu = 100)
```

The output shows the results of the one-sample *t* test and the data set used, along with the computed *t*, *df*, and *p* value. The results also show the 95% confidence interval and sample mean estimate.

```
Program Output

One Sample t-test

data: sample
t = 4.1606, df = 24, p-value = 0.0003509

alternative hypothesis: true mean is not equal to 100

95 percent confidence interval:
 104.1815 112.4135

sample estimates:
mean of x
108.2975
```

> **TIP**
>
> You will get different results each time you execute the *rnorm()* function unless the *set.seed()* function is used.

Single-Sample *t* Test: Sample Data

This example uses a set of SAT test scores for a classroom of students at the Academy High School. The teacher wants to test whether her students on average scored higher than the overall SAT 2012 national norms (population mean). The overall population mean = 1,498 from fall 2011 to June 2012 (Roell, 2012). She recorded the students' overall SAT scores in a data vector, *SAT*. Next, the teacher ran the *t.test()* function to test whether the class sample mean was greater than the SAT national average, a one-tailed test.

```
> SAT = c(1525,1400,1550,1500,1495,1575,1600,1535,1565,1475)
> options(scipen = 999)
> t.test(SAT, alternative = "greater", mu = 1498)


One Sample t-test

data: SAT
t = 1.3143, df = 9, p-value = 0.1106
alternative hypothesis: true mean is greater than 1498
95 percent confidence interval:
 1488.527    Inf
sample estimates:
mean of x
    1522
```

The teacher thought that because her classroom SAT average = 1,522, or 24 points higher than the SAT national average (1522 − 1498 = 24), her classroom mean would be statistically significantly greater. The *t* test, however, indicated $t = 1.31$, $df = 9$, $p = .11$, which is not statistically significant. The teacher calculated the standard deviation of the class SAT scores and then hand calculated the single-sample *t*-test value just to be certain:

```
> sd(SAT)
[1] 57.74465
```

The teacher's calculations indicated the same $t = 1.31$ that was computed using the *t.test()* function:

$$t = \frac{(1522 - 1498)}{57.7446 / \sqrt{10}} = \frac{24}{18.26} = 1.31.$$

The teacher also wanted to make sure that she had a sufficient sample size and power to detect a difference, so she ran the *pwr.t.test()* function. She entered the following arguments: $n = 10$ students, effect size = 24 points higher, $\alpha = .05$ (Type I error), power = NULL (value to be estimated), type = "one.sample" (comparison to population), and alternative = "greater" (test of null hypothesis).

```
> pwr.t.test(n = 10, d = 24, sig.level = .05, power = NULL, type =
"one.sample", alternative = "greater")

One-sample t test power calculation

n = 10
d = 24
sig.level = 0.05
power = 1
alternative = greater
```

The results indicated that 10 students was a sufficient sample size for power to detect a mean difference, if a difference existed, which it did not.

> **TIP**
>
> You do not need the *set.seed()* function when using real data sets.

● INDEPENDENT *T* TEST

The sampling distribution of the difference between the means of two independent samples provides the basis for testing the mean differences between two independent groups. Taking a random sample from one population, a second random sample from another population, and then computing the difference in the means provides the basis for the sampling distribution. The process is repeated several times, and the mean differences are graphed in a frequency distribution. Under the assumption of no difference between the means (null hypothesis), the mean of the sampling distribution of differences in means is zero.

A typical research situation in which one would use the independent *t* test might involve an experimental group receiving treatment and a control group *not* receiving treatment. The number of positive behaviors for each group is recorded and averaged. The null hypothesis would be stated as H_0: The average numbers of positive behaviors for the two groups are equal. An alternative hypothesis would be stated as H_A: The average numbers of positive behaviors for the two groups are *not* equal. The alternative hypothesis reflects a nondirectional, two-tailed test. The five-step hypothesis-testing approach can be used to conduct our independent *t* test.

Step 1. State the nondirectional research question in a statistical hypothesis format.

$$H_0: \mu_1 = \mu_2 \text{ (or } \mu_1 - \mu_2 = 0)$$

$$H_A: \mu_1 \neq \mu_2 \text{ (or } \mu_1 - \mu_2 \neq 0).$$

μ_1 represents the average number of positive behaviors for the group receiving treatment, and μ_2 indicates the average number of positive behaviors for the group that did not receive treatment. The null hypothesis (H_0) indicates that the sample means are equal, and the alternative hypothesis (H_A) indicates that the sample means are not equal (nondirectional hypothesis).

Step 2. Determine the criteria for rejecting the null hypothesis and accepting the alternative hypothesis.

If we select $\alpha = .05$ for a two-tailed test with $N = 200$ participants, the corresponding t value from Table 2 (Appendix A) would be $t = \pm 1.960$ ($df = \infty$). If our computed t-test statistic is greater than the tabled t value (± 1.960), we would reject the null hypothesis in favor of the alternative hypothesis. This establishes our region of rejection, or the probability area under the t distribution where differences in sample means are unlikely to occur by chance. The region of rejection is 0.025, or 2.5%, in each tail of the t distribution.

Region of rejection: $t > \pm 1.960$.

The t distribution with 2.5% probability area in each tail of the t distribution (regions of rejection) can be plotted by the following *t-distribution function* (two-tailed test) in the script file (chap13b.r). You will only need to enter the degrees of freedom prior to running the function:

```
> df = 198
```

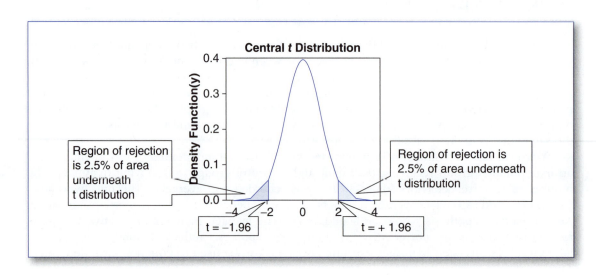

Step 3. Collect the sample data, and compute the independent *t*-test statistic.

The following sample data for the two groups were recorded: Experimental: mean = 50, standard deviation = 10, *n* = 100; Control: mean = 40, standard deviation = 10, *n* = 100. The independent *t* test would be computed as the difference between the means of the two independent groups in the numerator of the formula and the standard error of the *t* statistic (standard deviation of the sampling distribution of mean differences) in the denominator. The independent *t*-test formula is written as

$$t = \frac{\bar{X}_1 - \bar{X}_2}{S_{\bar{x}_1 - \bar{x}_2}}.$$

The standard error of the statistic (standard deviation of the sampling distribution) is computed using the sample size and variance for each group. The equation uses information from both samples to estimate a common population variance, which is referred to as pooling the variances or averaging the sample variances. Our pooled variance is the average of the two sample variances, S_p^2 (10^2), which is 100. The square root of this pooled variance estimate times a sample size adjustment $\left(\frac{1}{n_1} + \frac{1}{n_2}\right)$ is the standard error of the statistic (or sampling distribution of the statistic). The standard error of the difference between two means can now be computed as

$$S_{\bar{x}_1 - \bar{x}_2} = \sqrt{S_p^2 \left(\frac{1}{n_1} + \frac{1}{n_2}\right)}$$

$$= \sqrt{\frac{(n_1 - 1)s_1^2 + (n_2 - 1)s_2^2}{n_1 + n_2 - 2} \left(\frac{1}{n_1} + \frac{1}{n_2}\right)}$$

$$= \sqrt{\frac{(100 - 1)10_1^2 + (100 - 1)10_2^2}{n_1 + n_2 - 2} \left(\frac{1}{100} + \frac{1}{100}\right)}$$

$$= \sqrt{100(.02)}$$

$$= 1.4142.$$

The independent *t* test for the mean difference between the two groups can now be computed as follows:

$$t = \frac{50 - 40}{1.4142} = 7.07.$$

Step 4. Interpret the region of rejection, and compute the confidence interval around the *t* value.

Referring to the table of *t* values (Table 2, Appendix A), we find that the computed *t* value of 7.07 exceeds the tabled *t* value of ±1.960, for *df* = 198 (*df* = ∞) and *p* = .05 (two-tailed test). We would reject the null hypothesis of no mean difference and accept the alternative hypothesis that the two groups differed in their average number of positive behaviors because a *t* value of 7.07 falls in the region of rejection for one of the tails. This is considered a statistically significant finding because the mean difference was beyond a chance occurrence at the probability level selected.

A confidence interval around the mean difference ($\mu_1 - \mu_2 = 50 - 40 = 10$) can be computed using a tabled t value corresponding to an alpha level for a two-tailed region of rejection ($t = 1.960$) and the standard error of the difference (standard deviation of the sampling distribution: $S_{\mu_1-\mu_2} = 1.4142$).

$$CI_{99} = 10 \pm (1.960)(1.4142)$$

$$CI_{99} = 10 \pm (2.77)$$

$$CI_{99} = (7.23, 12.77).$$

The 95% confidence interval indicates that 95 times out of 100, the mean difference in positive behaviors between the two groups would range between 7 and 13 on average.

> **TIP**
>
> The tabled t value selected for determining the confidence interval around the computed t-test statistic is the same as the statistical hypothesis because the alternative statistical hypothesis used a two-tailed probability for the nondirectional research question.

Step 5. Interpret the *independent t-test* statistic results.

Our statistical interpretation is based on a test of the null hypothesis for the computed t-test statistic. Since the computed $t = 7.07$ was greater than the tabled t value ($t = 1.960$ at the .05 level of significance for a two-tailed test), we reject the null statistical hypothesis in favor of the alternative statistical hypothesis. The probability that the observed difference in the means would have occurred by chance is less than .05, or 5%. We would conclude that the experimental group that received treatment on average had a statistically significantly higher number of positive behaviors than the control group that received no treatment.

Our practical interpretation is based on the 95% confidence interval around the mean difference. The 95% confidence interval ranged from 7 to 13 positive behaviors on average, indicating that we can be 95% confident that this interval contains the mean number of positive behavior difference between the two groups. The confidence interval is narrow and gives some idea of how much the mean number of positive behavior difference might vary from random sample to random sample. This provides a practical interpretation, which can help us decide if funding for treatment should be continued.

The power value for the independent t test can be computed using the *pwr.t.test()* function. The arguments would be $n - 100$ (subjects per group), $d = 10$ (mean difference tested), *sig.level* = .05 (Type I error), power = NULL (value to be estimated), type = "two.sample" (independent t test), and alternative = "two.sided" (test of null hypothesis).

```
> pwr.t.test(n = 100,d = 10,sig.level = 0.05,power = NULL, type =
"two.sample", alternative = "two.sided")
```

```
Two-sample t test power calculation


n = 100
d = 10
sig.level = 0.05
power = 1
alternative = two.sided
```

Note: n is the number in each group.

Power is sufficient to detect a true difference between the two independent groups, that is, control for a Type II error.

Independent *t* Test: *rnorm()* Function

This example uses two sets of independent sample data using the *rnorm()* function. For the first group (*X*), *N* = 20, mean = 55, and standard deviation = 10. For the second group (*Y*), *N* = 20, mean = 50, and standard deviation = 10. The *set.seed()* function was used so that these results can be replicated. The R commands are as follows:

```
> set.seed(13579)
> SizeX = 20
> MeanX = 55
> SDX = 10
> SizeY = 20
> MeanY = 50
> SDY = 10
> sampleX = rnorm(SizeX, MeanX, SDX)
> sampleY = rnorm(SizeY, MeanY, SDY)
> t.test(sampleX, sampleY, alternative = "two.sided", paired = F)
```

A Welch two-sample *t*-test result is indicated for *t*, *df*, and *p* value given the two samples (*sampleX* and *sampleY*).

```
Program Output


Welch Two Sample t-test


data: sampleX and sampleY
t = 0.6061, df = 37.888, p-value = 0.548


alternative hypothesis: true difference in means is not equal to 0
```

```
95 percent confidence interval:
 -4.607060 8.544565
sample estimates:
mean of x mean of y
  53.40591 51.43716
```

The mean of group X was not statistically different from the mean of group Y at the .05 level of probability (t = .6061, df = 37.889, p value = .548). The mean difference was 53.40591 − 51.43716 = 1.96875, which was less than 2 points.

Note: The sample sizes and standard deviations do not have to be the same for the two groups for the independent t test to be calculated. Removing the *set.seed()* function will provide different sets of randomly sampled data.

Independent t Test: Sample Data

This example used Air Force data where two methods of flight training were conducted (Roscoe, 1975, p. 222). The first method used computer-simulated flight training, and the second method used traditional classroom instruction. Initially, a random sample of 10 students was selected for each group, but the computer-simulated training group had two students drop out due to chicken pox. When missing data are present, use the *NA* value. The criterion test scores for the two groups and the *t.test()* function were as follows:

```
> exper = c(2,5,5,6,6,7,8,9,NA,NA)
> trad = c(1,2,2,3,4,4,5,5,6,8)
> t.test(exper, trad, alternative = "greater", paired = F)
```

The results indicated that the average criterion score for pilot-training students in the experimental method (mean = 6) was statistically significantly higher than for students trained in the traditional method (mean = 4). The Welch two-sample t test indicated that t = 1.98, df = 15.045, and p = .03. The Welch test was used because of unequal sample sizes, and it adjusts the degrees of freedom accordingly. Boneau (1960) reported on the robustness of the t test given violations of assumptions (unequal group sizes, unequal group variances), which is why the Welch t test was computed.

```
Welch Two Sample t-test

data: exper and trad
t = 1.9843, df = 15.045, p-value = 0.03289
alternative hypothesis: true difference in means is greater than 0
95 percent confidence interval:
 0.2334366     Inf
sample estimates:
mean of x mean of y
      6         4
```

The *pwr.t2n.test()* function will report the power of an independent *t* test when the sample sizes for the two groups are different. The function arguments are

```
> ?pwr.t2n.test

pwr.t2n.test(n1 = NULL, n2 = NULL, d = NULL, sig.level = 0.05,
power = NULL, alternative = c("two.sided","less","greater"))
```

Arguments

n1	Number of observations in the first sample
n2	Number of observations in the second sample
d	Effect size
sig.level	Significance level (Type I error probability)
power	Power of test (1 minus Type II error probability)
Alternative	a character string specifying the alternative hypothesis, must be one of "two.sided" (default), "greater" or "less"

The power is calculated as

```
> pwr.t2n.test (n1 = 8, n2 = 10, d = 2, sig.level = .05, power =
NULL, alternative = "greater")

t test power calculation

n1 = 8
n2 = 10
d = 2
sig.level = 0.05
power = 0.9914497
alternative = greater
```

Power = .99, which protects against a Type II error when testing for a 2-point difference between the computer-simulated and traditional methods.

● DEPENDENT *T* TEST

The *dependent t test* is sometimes referred to as the *paired t test* or the *correlated t test* because it uses two sets of scores on the same individuals. The sampling distribution of the difference between the means of two related (paired) samples is obtained by taking a single random sample, taking two measures on each person, then subtracting these two related measures, and graphing the difference. The expected average difference between the related measures is zero under the null hypothesis.

A typical research situation that uses the dependent t test involves a repeated measures design with one group. For example, a psychologist is studying the effects of treatment counseling on the reduction in cigarette smoking. The psychologist hypothesizes that treatment counseling will cause patients to reduce their incidence of smoking cigarettes. A random sample of 10 patients record the number of times they smoked over the past month. Next, the 10 patients receive treatment counseling to reduce the incidence of cigarette smoking for 1 hour per day for 1 week. The 10 patients then record their number of times of smoking over the next month.

Dependent t Test: Sample Data

We can use the five-step hypothesis-testing approach to conduct our test of whether the mean number of cigarettes smoked in 1 month changes after counseling treatment. We are testing the mean difference to determine if on average the difference is statistically significant beyond a chance level (directional hypothesis).

Step 1. State the directional research question in a statistical hypothesis format.

$$H_0: \mu_{after} \geq \mu_{before} \text{ (or } \mu_{after} - \mu_{before} \geq 0)$$
$$H_A: \mu_{after} < \mu_{before} \text{ (or } \mu_{after} - \mu_{before} < 0).$$

μ_{after} represents the average number of cigarettes smoked after counseling treatment, while μ_{before} indicates the average number of cigarettes smoked before counseling treatment. The null hypothesis (H_0) indicates that the mean after counseling treatment is expected to be greater than or equal to the mean before counseling treatment. In contrast, the alternative hypothesis (H_A) indicates that the mean number of cigarettes smoked after treatment counseling is less than the mean number of cigarettes smoked before counseling treatment (directional hypothesis).

Step 2. Determine the criteria for rejecting the null hypothesis and accepting the alternative hypothesis.

If we select $\alpha = .01$ for a one-tailed test with $N = 10$ patients, the corresponding t value from Table 2 (Appendix A) would be $t = 2.821$ ($df = 9$). If our computed t-test statistic is less than this tabled t value, we would reject the null hypothesis in favor of the alternative hypothesis. Notice that we are in the negative tail of the t distribution based on our directional hypothesis. This establishes our region of rejection, or the probability area under the t distribution where differences in sample means are unlikely to occur by random chance. The region of rejection is .01 or 1% probability area in the right tail of the t distribution.

Region of rejection: $t < -2.821$.

The t distribution with 1% probability area in the tail of the t distribution (region of rejection) can be plotted by the following *dependent t-distribution function* (one-tailed test) in the script file (chap13c.r). You only need to specify the degrees of freedom prior to running the function.

```
> df = 9
```

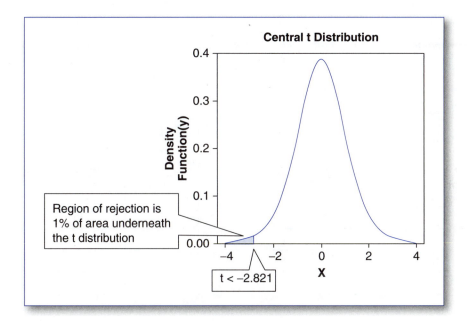

Step 3. Collect the sample data, and compute the *dependent t-test* statistic.

The average number of cigarettes for the month before counseling treatment was 73, but after counseling treatment, the average number of cigarettes smoked during a 1-month period was 67.5, a decrease on average of 5.5 cigarettes. The mean difference in the average number of cigarettes smoked is used in the numerator of the dependent *t* test. The denominator of the dependent *t*-test formula uses the standard error of the dependent *t* test. The standard error is computed by squaring the score differences, summing them to calculate the sum of squared differences, and then taking the square root of the sum of squared differences divided by $N(N-1)$.

The dependent *t*-test formula to investigate whether the patients' average number of cigarettes smoked in a month was different is computed as

$$t = \frac{\bar{D}}{S_{\bar{D}}}.$$

The numerator in the formula is the average difference between the after and before mean scores, which is $67.5 - 73 = -5.5$. The standard error in the denominator is calculated as

$$S_{\bar{D}} = \sqrt{\frac{\sum d^2}{N(N-1)}},$$

where the $\sum d^2$ is computed as

$$\sum d^2 = \sum D^2 - \frac{\sum D^2}{N}.$$

The sample data of the 10 patients are given below to calculate these values and the dependent *t* test.

Student	Post	Pre	D	D^2
1	70	75	−5	25
2	60	70	−10	100
3	85	80	+5	25
4	50	65	−15	225
5	65	75	−10	100
6	80	70	+10	100
7	90	95	−5	25
8	70	80	−10	100
9	40	55	−15	225
10	65	65	0	0
	$D_2 = 67.5$	$D_1 = 73.0$	$\Sigma D = 55$	$\Sigma D^2 = 925$

The denominator of the formula can be hand calculated as follows:

$$\Sigma d^2 = \Sigma D^2 - \frac{(\Sigma D)^2}{N} = 925 - \frac{(55)^2}{10} = 925 - 302.5 = 622.5.$$

Then,

$$S_{\bar{D}} = \sqrt{\frac{\Sigma d^2}{N(N-1)}} = \sqrt{\frac{622.5}{10(9)}} = 2.6299.$$

The dependent *t* test can now be calculated as

$$t = \frac{\bar{D}}{S_{\bar{D}}} = \frac{\bar{D}_2 - \bar{D}_1}{S_{\bar{D}}} = \frac{-5.5}{2.6299} = -2.0913.$$

Step 4. Interpret the region of rejection, and compute the confidence interval around *t*.

The dependent *t* test was calculated as $t = -5.5/2.6299 = -2.0913$. This value is compared with the tabled *t* value for $df = 9$ for a one-tailed test with $p = .01$ (probability value), which is $t = 2.821$. Since the computed $t = -2.0913$ does *not* exceed the tabled $t = 2.821$, we retain the null hypothesis of no difference in the average number of cigarettes smoked during 1 month before and after counseling treatment. The counseling treatment for 1 hour a day for 1 week was not effective in reducing the average number of cigarettes smoked in 1 month beyond a chance level.

The power for this dependent *t* test can be calculated using the *pwr.t.test()* function. The arguments for the function indicate the number of paired scores (*n* = 10), effect size to detect (*d* = 5.5), alpha level (.01), type of test (paired *t* test), and directional hypothesis:

```
> pwr.t.test(n = 10, d = 5.5, sig.level = .01, power = NULL, type
= "paired", alternative = "greater")

Paired t test power calculation

n = 10
d = 5.5
sig.level = 0.01
power = 1
alternative = greater
```

Note: n is the number of pairs.

Results indicate that power = 1, which provides protection against a Type II error. We therefore assume that we had sufficient power to detect a mean difference if it existed in the population.

I should mention a few key points at this time. First, notice that in calculating the dependent *t* test, the sum of the differences between the before and after test scores took into account whether the difference was positive or negative. We were testing for a reduction in the average number of cigarettes smoked, thus a negative difference. Also, notice that the computation formula makes the sum of squared difference scores easy to calculate. Finally, the importance of the standard error of the sampling distribution is once again illustrated in determining whether the sample statistic is significant.

Dependent *t* Test: *t.test()* Function

The sample data from the study can be run using the *t.test()* function. The function now sets the argument *paired* = *T*, which indicates that scores are paired for purposes of computing the dependent *t* test. The set of R commands are as follows:

```
> before = c(70,60,85,50,65,80,90,70,40,65)
> after = c(75,70,80,65,75,70,95,80,55,65)
> mean(before)
> mean(after)
> t.test(before, after, alternative = "two.sided", paired = T)

> mean(before)
[1] 67.5
> mean(after)
[1] 73

    Paired t-test
```

```
data: before and after
t = -2.0913, df = 9, p-value = 0.06605
alternative hypothesis: true difference in means is not equal to 0
95 percent confidence interval:
 -11.449373  0.449373
sample estimates:
mean of the differences
          -5.5
```

TIP

The *t.test()* function places the before data vector first so that the mean subtraction yields the correct −5.5 mean difference.

Step 5. Interpret the dependent *t*-test statistic results.

The dependent *t* test was *not* statistically significant beyond a 1% probability level, as shown by both the hand calculations and the *t.test()* function. We would therefore conclude that counseling treatment did not reduce the number of cigarettes smoked. The paired *t* results provide the actual *p* value for the calculated *t* (paired *t* = 2.0913, *df* = 9, *p* = .066). The mean difference of −5.5 (an average of six cigarettes less after counseling treatment) would not have occurred beyond the .05 chance level of probability.

● VIOLATION OF ASSUMPTIONS

The previous *t*-test examples have shown that when missing data and unequal variances are present, the *t.test()* function reports the Welch test results, which adjusts the degrees of freedom to control for violations of assumptions. Boneau (1960) has reported that the *t* test is robust to these violations of assumptions. Another test, the *Levene* test, is used to check for the violation of equal variance assumption between groups prior to testing for mean differences.

The Levene test is recommended over other available tests and is conducted using the *levene. test()* function. Levene (1960) proposed a test for homogeneity of variances in *k* groups, which is based on the analysis of variance statistic applied to absolute deviations of observations from the corresponding group mean. The robust Brown-Forsythe version of the Levene-type test substitutes the group mean with the median value. The third option is to consider the analysis of variance applied to the absolute deviations of observations from the group trimmed mean instead of the group means.

Note: The equality-of-variance assumption is also required in the analysis of variance covered in the next chapter.

levene.test() Function

The *levene.test()* function is in the *lawstat* package. You should only have to issue the command *library(lawstat)* to load the package. The arguments in the *levene.test()* function can now be indicated by *?levene.test*.

```
> library(lawstat)
> ?levene.test
```

```
levene.test(y, group, location = c("mean","median","trim.mean"), trim.
alpha = 1)
```

Y	Data
Group	factor of the data
Location	The option must be "mean" corresponding to classical Levene's test (default), "median" corresponding to the robust Brown-Forsythe Levene-type test or "trim.mean" corresponding to the robust Levene-type test using the trimmed mean.
trim.alpha	the fraction (0 to 0.5) of observations to be trimmed from each end of 'x' before the mean is computed.

The following example demonstrates the use of the Levene test of equal variances between groups. First load the package, *library(lawstat)*. Next create a data vector *test*, which represents a set of student test scores. Also, create the variable *gender* and declare it as a *factor* variable (group variable) using the *gl()* function. The *levene.test()* function can now be run with the data (test), the group factor (gender), and the location, indicating the classical Levene test.

```
> library(lawstat)
> test=c(99,98,97,97,95,96,91,90,89,85,70,50,20,10)
> gender = gl(2,7)
> gender = factor(gender)
> levene.test(test, gender, location = "mean")
```

The Levene test = 22.64 and p = .0004, which indicates that the two groups do not have equal variances.

```
classical Levene's test based on the absolute deviations from the
mean (none not applied because the location is not set to median)
```

```
data: test
Test Statistic = 22.6427, p-value = 0.0004654
```

The robust Brown-Forsythe test is given by changing the location to "median." The results also indicate that the group variances are not equal.

```
> levene.test(test, gender, location = "median")
```

```
modified robust Brown-Forsythe Levene-type test based on the absolute devi-
ations from the median
```

```
data: test
Test Statistic = 9.48, p-value = 0.009556
```

When group variances are unequal, a test of mean differences is not recommended. In current practice, an adjustment is made in the degrees of freedom to conduct a test of mean difference in the presence of unequal variance in the groups. A researcher should, however, first examine any possible reasons behind the difference in variance, for example, outliers, and make any necessary adjustments.

t.test() Function

We now revisit the use of the *t.test()* function. Recall that the *?t.test* command shows the arguments used in the function. The argument *var.equal = FALSE* would be used when testing for mean differences between two groups with unequal group variances. The argument *var.equal=TRUE* would be used when the group variances are equal. I ran the *t.test()* function both ways to show the difference in output results. Basically when unequal variances are present, the degrees of freedom are adjusted giving a smaller probability level for statistical significance.

```
t.test(x, y = NULL, alternative = c("two.sided","less","greater"), mu = 0,
paired = FALSE, var.equal = FALSE, conf.level = 0.95, ...)


> t.test(test~gender, alternative = "two.sided", var.equal = FALSE)

  Welch Two Sample t-test

data: test by gender
t = 2.9291, df = 6.074, p-value = 0.02595
alternative hypothesis: true difference in means is not equal to 0
95 percent confidence interval:
 6.181453 67.818547
sample estimates:
mean in group 1 mean in group 2
      96.14286      59.14286
```

Incorrect t-test results would occur if setting *var.equal = TRUE*:

```
> t.test(test~gender, alternative = "two.sided", var.equal = TRUE)
Two Sample t-test

data: test by gender
t = 2.9291, df = 12, p-value = 0.01263
alternative hypothesis: true difference in means is not equal to 0
95 percent confidence interval:
 9.477478 64.522522
```

```
sample estimates:
mean in group 1 mean in group 2
      96.14286      59.14286
```

TIP

The *t.test()* function can be used separately to conduct the three different types of *t* tests.

Individual script commands can be placed in an R Editor window, then run and/or saved as a script file.

Use *set.seed()* function to obtain the same results each time.

For a dependent *t* test, specify the second sample mean first in the *t.test()* function, so mean difference = after mean − before mean.

SUMMARY

In this chapter, a one-sample *t* test, a two-sample independent *t* test, and a dependent *t* test have been presented for different research situations. Two important statistical concepts from earlier chapters were emphasized, namely, sampling distribution of a statistic and the standard error of the sampling distribution of a statistic. An understanding of the sampling distribution of a statistic is important in making inferences about the corresponding population parameter. An understanding of the standard error of the sampling distribution of a statistic is important in testing whether the sample statistic is statistically different from the population parameter.

A table of *t* values has been created for various sample sizes (degrees of freedom) and probability areas under the *t* distribution. Each *t* value indicated in Table 2 (Appendix A) was obtained by creating a sampling distribution for that probability level and degree of freedom. These tabled *t* values are expected by chance for each probability and degree of freedom combination and allow a test of whether our computed sample *t* statistic could occur beyond this level of probability or chance occurrence.

The one-sample *t* test is useful for testing whether a sample mean is statistically different from the population mean. The two-sample independent *t* test is useful for testing whether the means of two independent groups are the same or different. The dependent *t* test is useful for testing whether the means before and after some intervention in a single group are statistically different. The assumption of equal group variance is important when testing for group mean differences.

The *t* distribution is not normally distributed for small sample sizes, therefore *t* values are larger than *z* values in the normal distribution. The *t* values are adjusted for small sample sizes by adjusting the probability area under the *t* distribution. However, as the sample size (degrees of freedom) increases, the *t* value more closely approximates a *z* value in the normal distribution. The probability area therefore becomes similar as the degrees of freedom (sample size) increases. Researchers typically report the *t*-statistical value rather than a *z* value. Computer calculations and computer output now routinely print the actual *p* value for the computed sample *t* statistic, making interpretation and comparison with a tabled *t* value easier.

EXERCISES

1. For the following hypothesis, calculate the single-sample t-test statistic. Is there a statistically significant mean difference between the Ridgewood H.S. average SAT and the Tennessee average SAT? Ridgewood H.S. average SAT = 650, S = 50, N = 100. Tennessee average SAT = 600. State the statistical hypothesis, show your work, and interpret the results given a .05 level of probability.

$$H_0: \mu_{H.S.} = \mu_{TN} \text{ (or } \mu_{H.S.} - \mu_{TN} = 0)$$

$$H_A: \mu_{H.S.} \neq \mu_{TN} \text{ (or } \mu_{H.S.} - \mu_{TN} > 0)$$

The following results are given:

$\text{Mean}_{H.S.}$ = 650 (average SAT score for Ridgewood H.S.)

Mean_{TN} = 600 (average SAT score for Tennessee)

$SE = SE = \dfrac{50}{\sqrt{100}} = 5.$

2. Use the five-step hypothesis-testing approach when conducting the following independent t test at the .05 level of probability. Is there a statistically significant mean difference in the algebra exam scores between boys and girls in the ninth grade?

Data for a Ninth-Grade Algebra Exam

Gender	Mean	S	N
Boys	92	5	12
Girls	90	4	15

Step 1. State the nondirectional research question in a statistical hypothesis format.

Step 2. Determine the criteria for rejecting the null hypothesis and accepting the alternative hypothesis.

Step 3. Collect the sample data, and compute the independent t-test statistic.

Note:

$$S_{\bar{x}_1 - \bar{x}_2} = \sqrt{S_p^2 \left(\frac{1}{n_{boy}} + \frac{1}{n_{girl}} \right)}.$$

Step 4. Interpret the region of rejection, and compute the confidence interval around t.

Step 5. Interpret the independent t-test statistic results.

3. Use the *t.test()* function to compute the following dependent (paired) *t* test. The numbers of automobile car sales by salesmen before and after the economic recession in Mississippi are indicated in the table below. Was there a statistically significant mean drop in the average number of automobile sales after the recession in Mississippi?

Car Salesman	Before	After
John	5	2
Sue	4	2
Juan	10	8
Mark	9	5
Steve	3	3
Mary	7	6
Sam	9	7
Jill	12	6

TRUE OR FALSE QUESTIONS

T   F   a.   The *t* test is used to conduct tests of mean differences between two groups.

T   F   b.   As the sample size increases, the *t* value becomes a *z* value under the normal curve.

T   F   c.   Use the *set.seed()* function in R script file to obtain the same results each time.

T   F   d.   The *t.test()* function can conduct single-sample, independent-samples, and dependent-samples *t* tests.

T   F   e.   A table of *t* values has been created for various sample sizes (degrees of freedom) and probability areas under the *t* distribution.

WEB RESOURCES

Chapter R script files are available at http://www.sagepub.com/schumacker

Dependent *t* Distribution Function (one-tailed test) R script file: chap13c.r

t Distribution Function(one-tailed test) R script file: chap13a.r

t Distribution Function (two-tailed test) R script file: chap13b.r

## CHAPTER 14

F TEST FOR MEAN DIFFERENCES (THREE OR MORE GROUPS)

The *F* test extends the *t* test from two groups to a test of mean differences in three or more groups. The *F* test is used in one-way analysis of variance, analysis of covariance, fixed factor analysis of variance, and **repeated measures analysis of variance**. Once the *F* test is conducted, a comparison of the pairs of group means is conducted via a post hoc test, which is similar to a *t* test, to determine which means are different. The *F* test has also become useful in testing the equality of group variances, which is an assumption that should be met before testing for mean differences between groups. These *F*-test applications for the different research designs are covered in this chapter.

● CONCEPT OF ANALYSIS OF VARIANCE

On discovering the work of W. S. Gossett (who developed a test of mean differences between two groups, the Student *t* test, or simply the *t test*), Sir Ronald Fisher extended it into his idea for an analysis of variance (ANOVA) technique (Box, 1978; Fisher, 1925). The analysis of variance technique was based on the idea that variation (variance) could be used to indicate whether sample means were different. For example, if three groups had the same average math score, the variation of the group means would be zero, implying that the means do not vary (differ). As the sample means become more different, the variation of the group means will increase. When sample means are similar in value, they are called *homogeneous*; when they become more different in value, they are called *heterogeneous*.

The basic idea of how variation indicates sample mean differences can be understood using the following two sets of data means, which indicate similar grand means (average of the sample means divided by 3) but different sample means in Set A and Set B.

	Set A			Set B		
Population	N	*Mean*	*Variance*	N	*Mean*	*Variance*
Sample mean 1	10	4	2	10	3	2
Sample mean 2	10	4	2	10	4	2
Sample mean 3	10	4	2	10	5	2
Grand mean		4			4	
Variance		0			1	

The three sample means are all the same in Set A; hence, the variation around the grand mean is zero (variance = 0). The three sample means are different in Set B; hence, the variation increases and is greater than zero (variance = 1). As sample means become more different in value, the variance value will become larger. Fisher realized that the calculation of variance, which was typically computed as individual scores varying around the sample mean, could also be applied to sample means varying around a grand mean (the average of the sample means).

Fisher understood that the variance of sample means around a common mean (grand mean) could be calculated by determining the sum of squared deviations (SS_B) of the sample means around the grand mean divided by the degrees of freedom (number of groups minus 1). Fisher called this average variance a **mean square between groups**; therefore, $MS_B = SS_B/df_B$. This follows the basic formula for computing variance, but it uses sample means rather than individual scores.

For Set A, MS_B would be as follows:

$$MS_B = \frac{SS_B}{df_B}$$

$$= \frac{\Sigma\left[(4-4)^2 + (4-4)^2 + (4-4)^2\right]}{3-1} = \frac{0}{2} = 0.$$

For Set B, MS_B would be as follows:

$$MS_B = \frac{SS_B}{df_B}$$

$$= \frac{\Sigma\left[(3-4)^2 + (4-4)^2 + (5-4)^2\right]}{3-1} = \frac{2}{2} = 1.$$

Fisher also used the variance of scores within a group, which followed the typical way variance was calculated for a sample of data, and calculated MS_W as a sum of the individual group variations. MS_W was calculated by determining the sum of squared deviations of the scores around each group mean (SS_W), divided by the degrees of freedom (number of scores in a group minus 1). Each group variance is therefore computed as $SS/(n-1)$. Fisher determined that the sum of squares for each group could be summed, then averaged across three or more groups. He called this average variance a **mean square within groups**; therefore, $MS_W = SS_W/df_W$. The degrees of freedom (df_W) is computed as the number of total subjects (N) minus the number of groups (k).

For Set A, MS_W would be as follows:

$$MS_W = \frac{SS_W}{df_W}$$

$$= \frac{\sum\left[\left((n_1 - 1)S_1^2\right) + \left((n_2 - 1)S_2^2\right) + \left((n_3 - 1)S_3^2\right)\right]}{N - k}$$

$$= \frac{\sum[((9)2) + ((9)2) + ((9)2)]}{30 - 3}$$

$$= \frac{\sum[(18) + (18) + (18)]}{27}$$

$$= \frac{54}{27} = 2.$$

For Set B, MS_W would be as follows:

$$MS_W = \frac{SS_W}{df_W}$$

$$= \frac{\sum\left[\left((n_1 - 1)S_1^2\right) + \left((n_2 - 1)S_2^2\right) + \left((n_3 - 1)S_3^2\right)\right]}{N - k}$$

$$= \frac{\sum[((9)2) + ((9)2) + ((9)2)]}{30 - 3}$$

$$= \frac{\sum[(18) + (18) + (18)]}{27}$$

$$= \frac{54}{27} = 2.$$

This shows that the mean square variance in the groups (variance of scores around each sample mean) can be the same, thus meeting the assumption of equal group variance, but the group means can vary around the grand mean.

Note: We can calculate each group's sums of square deviation without having the individual scores for each group. This is accomplished by multiplying $(n - 1)$ times the group variance to obtain the sum of squared deviations (SS). The SS values for each group can then be added to obtain the SS_W value for all groups. Recall the following variance formula:

$$S^2 = \frac{\sum(X - \bar{X})^2}{n - 1} = \frac{SS}{n - 1}.$$

So with a little math,

$$S^2 = \frac{SS}{n-1} \times \frac{n-1}{1}$$

equals

$$(n-1)S^2 = SS.$$

Fisher developed the *F*-test to test whether the variance of sample means around the grand mean was greater than the variance of individual scores around each sample mean. The *F* test was computed as $F = MS_B/MS_W$. The *F* test would be zero, $F = 0$, if all sample means were identical, otherwise the sum of square deviations would increase in value as the sample means varied more around their grand mean. In some research situations, more variance exists within the groups (MS_W) than between the groups (MS_B), which results in *F* values being less than one ($F < 1$). This is not an expected result when testing for group mean differences; rather, we expect the *F* test to yield larger positive values as group means become more different.

The *stats* library has various functions that compute the *F* test, depending on the research design. Examples will be provided for different research designs with basic calculations and formula, followed by the use of the corresponding R function. This will permit an understanding of the *F* test, as well as how to run the *F* test using the R functions. The statistical significance of the *F* test is based on the *F* sampling distribution, which is created for various combinations of degrees of freedom between groups (df_B) and degrees of freedom within groups (df_W) to provide the expected probability *F* values, which are shown in Table 5 in Appendix A. These tabled *F* values are used to determine if the *F* value you calculate from sample data is larger than the *F* value expected by chance. If your *F* value is larger than the tabled *F* value, the group means are considered statistically significantly different.

● ONE-WAY ANALYSIS OF VARIANCE

The **one-way analysis of variance** extends the independent *t*-test comparison of two group means to three or more group means. In my first example, the high school exam scores for freshman, sophomore, junior, and senior students yielded the following group sample sizes, means, and variances. I wish to determine if there is a statistically significant mean difference in exam scores between the high school grade levels.

Group	N	Mean	Variance
Freshman	30	70	8
Sophomore	30	80	7
Junior	30	85	10
Senior	30	90	5

We can compute the MS_B for our high school example data after calculating the grand mean. The grand mean is $((70 + 80 + 85 + 90)/4)) = 81.25$. The MS_B is computed as follows:

$$MS_B = \frac{SS_B}{df_B}$$

$$= \frac{\Sigma\left[(70 - 81.25)^2 + (80 - 81.25)^2 + (85 - 81.25)^2 + (90 - 81.25)^2\right]}{4 - 1}$$

$$= \frac{\Sigma(126.5625) + (1.5625) + (14.0625) + (76.5625)}{3}$$

$$= \frac{218.75}{3} = 72.916.$$

Note: Sample means that have a greater distance from the grand mean have a larger sum of squared deviations, thus indicating that the means vary more from the grand mean. For example, the sample mean 70 varies more than the sample mean 80 from the grand mean of 81.25.

For our high school example, MS_W is computed as follows:

$$MS_W = \frac{SS_W}{df_W}$$

$$= \frac{\Sigma\left[\left((n_1 - 1)S_1^2\right) + \left((n_2 - 1)S_2^2\right) + \left((n_3 - 1)S_3^2\right) + \left((n_4 - 1)S_4^2\right)\right]}{N - k}$$

$$= \frac{\Sigma((29)8) + ((29)7) + ((29)10) + ((29)5)}{120 - 4}$$

$$= \frac{\Sigma(232) + (203) + (290) + (145)}{116}$$

$$= \frac{870}{116} = 7.5.$$

The *F*-test ratio can now be computed given the MS_B and MS_W values:

$$F = \frac{MS_B}{MS_W} = \frac{72.916}{7.5} = 9.72.$$

We compare this *F*-test value with the critical *F* value at the .05 level of significance for 3 (df_B) and 116 (df_W) degrees of freedom (Table 5, Appendix A) to determine if our computed *F* value is beyond a chance level of probability. The tabled $F_{.05} = 2.76$ for 3, 60 degrees of freedom and $F_{.05} = 2.68$ for 3, 120 degrees of freedom. We can therefore conclude that our computed *F* is greater than the tabled *F*, so it occurs beyond a chance level of probability. In practical terms, this indicates that the mean exam scores are different between the four high school grade levels.

Another example will provide additional understanding in the testing of mean differences in one-way analysis of variance. The numbers of purchases in three different stores are compared to determine if they are significantly different. The numbers of purchases for each store were as given in the following table.

	Store A	Store B	Store C	Grand Values (Total Purchases)
	30	25	15	
	30	20	20	
	40	25	25	
	40	30	20	
Sum	140.00	100.00	80.00	320.00
Mean	35.00	25.00	20.00	26.67
SD	5.77	4.08	4.08	7.785

The number of purchases on average for Store A (mean = 35) was higher than for Store B (mean = 25); likewise, Store B had more purchases on average than Store C (mean = 20). The *F* test (one-way analysis of variance) can determine whether the mean differences in purchases between the stores are statistically significant. To calculate the *F* test, we must first compute the variance of the sample means around the grand mean using the following steps (*Note: n_j = number of stores*):

1. $SS_B = n_j$ (Store mean – Grand mean)².
2. $SS_B = 4(35 – 26.67)^2 + 4(25 – 26.67)^2 + 4(20 – 26.67)^2$.
3. $SS_B = 466.67$.
4. $df_B = (j – 1) = (3 – 1) = 2$.
5. $MS_B = SS_B/df_B = (466.67/2) = 233.33$.

The sum of squares between the stores (SS_B) indicates the sum of the deviation from the grand mean (common mean for all the sample means), which is squared and weighted (multiplied by the sample size) for each store (Steps 1–3 above). The degree of freedom is simply the number of stores minus 1 (Step 4 above). The mean square between the stores, which is used in the *F*-test formula to indicate mean differences in the stores, is the average sum of squares between the groups divided by the degrees of freedom (Step 5 above).

Next, we compute the variance of the number of purchases around each store mean using the following steps (*Note: j = Number of stores*):

1. $SS_W = \Sigma_j$ [(Number of purchases – Store mean)²].
2. $SS_W = [(30 – 35)^2 + (30 – 35)^2 + (40 – 35)^2 + (40 – 35)^2 + (25 – 25)^2 + (20 – 25)^2 + (25 – 25)^2$
   $+ (30 – 25)^2 + (15 – 20)^2 + (20 – 20)^2 + (25 – 20)^2 + (20 – 20)^2]$.
3. $SS_W = 200.00$.
4. $df_W = (Sample size – j) = (12 – 3) = 9$.
5. $MS_W = SS_W/df_W = (200/9) = 22.22$.

The sum of squares within the stores (SS_W) indicates the sum of the purchases minus the store mean, which is squared (Steps 1–3 above). The degrees of freedom equals the total sample size minus the number of stores (Step 4 above). The mean square within the stores, which is used in the F-test formula to indicate the variance within the stores, is the average sum of squares within the groups divided by the degrees of freedom (Step 5 above). This averaging of the sum of squares within the stores is sometimes referred to as *pooling* the sum of squares within the groups (stores).

The *F test* (ratio) can now be calculated as

$$F = \frac{MS_B}{MS_W}$$
$$= \frac{233.33}{22.22}$$
$$= 10.50.$$

The F test indicates the *ratio* of the variance between the stores over the variance within the stores. If the store means are more different, that is, they vary more between stores than the number of purchases varies within each store, the F-test ratio would be greater than the tabled F value expected by chance. We therefore compare the computed F value, $F = 10.50$, with a tabled F value in Appendix A (Table 5) for $df_B = 2$ and $df_W = 9$ at the .05 chance level (5% chance our comparison might not yield a correct decision). The computed F value of 10.50 is greater than the tabled F value of 4.26 (the value expected by chance), which indicates that the average numbers of purchases per store are significantly different, that is, the store means are statistically different.

The results of all the calculations are traditionally placed in a summary table, which in itself has meaningful interpretation. For example, we can easily inspect the division of the sums of squares by the degrees of freedom to obtain each **mean square** value. It is also easy to see that $F = MS_B/MS_W$ from the summary tabled values. Another interesting result from the summary tabled values is that the total sums of squares (666.67) divided by the total degrees of freedom (11) is the variance of the dependent variable, that is,

$$S_Y^2 = \frac{666.67}{11} = 60.606.$$

The variance in Y can also be easily calculated as the standard deviation squared: $S_Y^2 = SD^2 = 7.785^2 = 60.606$. Our interest in conducting analysis of variance is to explain this variation in Y due to independent variables or factors, which in this example was store differences. The results are then neatly summarized in an analysis of variance summary table.

Analysis of Variance Summary Table

Source	Sum of Squares (SS)	Degrees of Freedom (df)	Mean Square (MS)	F
Between groups	466.67	2	233.33	10.50
Within groups	200.00	9		22.22
Total	666.67	11		

Five-Step Hypothesis-Testing Approach

The five-step hypothesis-testing approach can be used to organize our research efforts when testing the mean differences between groups for statistical significance. The five steps are outlined as follows:

Step 1. State the research question in a statistical hypothesis format.

Our research question would be "Is the average number of purchases for each store different?"—which is converted into a statistical hypothesis.

$$\text{Null hypothesis } (H_0)\text{: } \mu_i = \mu_j$$

$$\text{Alternative hypothesis } (H_A)\text{: } \mu_i \neq \mu_j.$$

The subscripts i and j are used to denote pairs of store means that can be tested for a difference. The alternative hypothesis is stating that at least one store mean is different from the other store means.

Step 2. Determine the criteria for rejecting the null hypothesis and accepting the alternative hypothesis.

Given $\alpha = .05$, with $df_1 = 2$ (numerator degrees of freedom for between groups) and $df_2 = 9$ (denominator degrees of freedom for within groups), the tabled F value (Table 5, Appendix A) is $F = 4.26$. The region of rejection for the null hypothesis or probability area in the F distribution is beyond this value, which is written as

$$\text{Region of rejection: } F > 4.26.$$

The *F density plot function*, in the script file (chap14a.r), shows the F sampling distribution with the region of rejection highlighted in gray (text box added in MS Word). You only need to enter x (a sequence of numbers from 0 to 10 increasing by 0.1) and the 2 degrees of freedom for the F test prior to running the function.

```
> x = seq(0,10, by = .1)
> df1 = 2
> df2 = 9
> chap14a(x, df1, df2)
```

Step 3. Collect the sample data and compute the F test statistic.

F test:

$$SS_B = 466.67 \text{ and } df_B = 2; \ MS_B = SS_B/df_B = (466.67/2) = 233.33.$$

$$SS_W = 200.00 \text{ and } df_W = 9; \ MS_W = SS_W/df_W = 22.22.$$

$$F = \frac{MS_B}{MS_W} = \frac{233.33}{22.22} = 10.50.$$

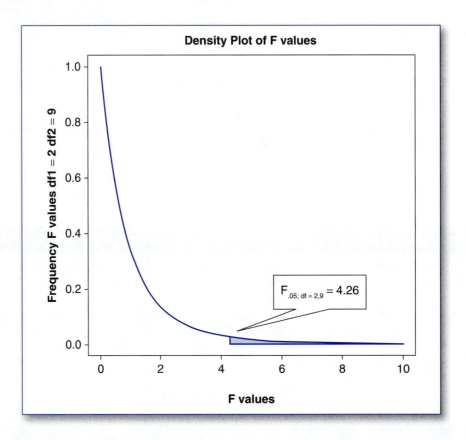

Density Plot of F values

$F_{.05;\ df = 2,9} = 4.26$

Sample data:

	Store A	Store B	Store C	Grand Values (Total Purchases)
	30	25	15	
	30	20	20	
	40	25	25	
	40	30	20	
Sum	140.00	100.00	80.00	320.00
Mean	35.00	25.00	20.00	26.67
SD	5.77	4.08	4.08	7.79

The results of these calculations should be organized in a summary table. The analysis of variance summary table indicates that both of the sums of squared deviations can be added together to yield a total sum of squared deviations for all scores ($SS_T = SS_B + SS_W$). Likewise, the degrees of freedom from both calculations can be added together to yield the sample size minus

1 ($df_T = N - 1$). The SS_T value divided by df_T yields the total variance in purchases, which has been partitioned into the variance between groups and the variance within groups. The variance for the total number of purchases is computed as $SS_T/df_T = 666.67/11 = 60.606$. The standard deviation of the total number of purchases is simply the square root of this variance, which is equal to 7.785 (rounded to 7.79 in summary statistics above). This indicates that the sum of squares total divided by the sample size minus 1 is actually the variance of all the scores. The square root of this variance is the standard deviation of all the scores. The key point is that the analysis of variance procedure partitions the variance of *all* the scores based on group membership. The dependent variable is the number of purchases, while the independent variable is the type of store, so a one-way analysis of variance is used to determine if variation in the dependent variable can be attributed to the independent variable—type of store.

Analysis of Variance Summary Table

Source	Sum of Squares (SS)	Degrees of Freedom (df)	Mean Square (MS)	F	p
Between groups	466.67	2	233.33	10.50	.0044
Within groups	200.00	9		22.22	
Total	666.67	11			

Step 4. Interpret the region of rejection for computed F.

Since the computed F value of 10.50 is greater than the tabled F value of 4.26, we would reject the null hypothesis of no mean differences and accept the alternative hypothesis that the store means differ. The computed F value falls within the region of rejection at the .05 level of probability for the F distribution with the specified degrees of freedom. Although the tabled F value for the specified alpha and probability level allowed us to make this comparison, the analysis of variance summary table will provide a p value for our computed F value, that is, $p = .0044$, even though we are originally stating that $p < .05$ level of significance for testing our statistical hypothesis. Researchers commonly report the actual p value obtained for the computed F value.

Step 5. Interpret the F-test statistic results.

The computed F value of 10.50 was greater than the tabled F value of 4.26, which occurs at the .05 level of probability. The statistically significant F value indicates that at least one of the store means is different from the other store means. The F value does not indicate which store means differ.

We need to conduct a post hoc test procedure that will compare pairs of store means to determine which ones are different. Therefore, a sixth step is added to the hypothesis-testing approach, which conducts a post hoc test to compare the pairs of store means.

The one-way analysis of variance F test has a power and effect size that can be calculated using the *pwr.anova.test()* function when groups have equal sample sizes. The function is in the *library(pwr)* and has the following arguments:

```
pwr.anova.test(k = NULL, n = NULL, f = NULL, sig.level = 0.05, power = NULL)
```

Arguments

K	Number of groups
N	Number of observations (per group)
F	Effect size
sig.level	Significance level (Type I error probability)
Power	Power of test (1 minus Type II error probability)

For the one-way analysis of variance example, the arguments would be $k = 3$ (three stores), $n = 4$ (number of data values), $f = 5$ (detect an average 5-point difference), and $sig.level = .05$ (Type I error). The function is run as follows:

```
> pwr.anova.test(k = 3, n = 4, f = 5, sig.level = 0.05, power = NULL)

Balanced one-way analysis of variance power calculation

     k = 3
     n = 4
     f = 5
     sig.level = 0.05
     power = 1
```

Note: n is the number in each group.

The results indicate that the one-way analysis of variance has sufficient power to detect an average 5-point difference between the stores.

R aov() Function

The one-way analysis of variance can be conducted using R commands and the *aov()* function with a suitable data set (no missing data; balanced design—equal group sizes). The following R commands and *aov()* function will produce the same results as those calculated by hand above. The *anova()* function produces the analysis of variance summary table. The *data.frame()* function is the essential and necessary file structure for conducting these statistical tests (Kabacoff, 2012). The *data.frame()* file structure is similar to the type of data sets found in SPSS, SAS, SPlus, STATA, and Excel, where variable labels and data characteristics are included as part of the data set.

To create the data set, we must first enter the number of purchases into a data vector, *data*. Next, the store names are entered into a data vector, *store*, that is, Store A, Store B, and Store C. The first data vector, *data*, contains the number of purchases per store and the second data vector, *store*, contains the name of each store. These two data vectors are then combined as a *data.frame()* file structure, *y*. The data set is printed out using the R command *print(y)*. The *store* data vector *must be* defined as a factor, which has a unique group or category property that is important for defining groups using the *factor()* function. The factor variable, *score*, defines the three groups for comparison of mean differences.

Note: If you do not declare the *score* variable as a factor, the one-way analysis of variance results will issue a warning message.

Note: The store name was easily repeated as a character string, rather than entering the store name repeatedly in the data vector by using the following command:

```
store = rep(c("Store A","Store B","Store C"), c(4,4,4))
```

The *aov()* function is now run and assigned to the object, *out*. The *print()* function lists the data set, and the *anova()* function lists a summary table. Results indicate that $F = 10.50$, $df = 2, 9$ with $p = .004437$ (the probability level associated with the computed F value). The *one-way ANOVA function* in the script file (chap14b1.r), outputs the following results for the data vector *data*.

```
> data = c(30,30,40,40,25,20,25,30,15,20,25,20)
> store = rep(c("Store A","Store B","Store C"), c(4,4,4))
> chap14b1(data, store)
```

The results print the data values by store, then show the analysis of variance summary table. The three store means are statistically different ($F = 10.5$, $df = 2, 9$, $p = .0044$), which are the results we obtained with our hand calculations.

```
PROGRAM OUTPUT

      data  store
 1 30    Store A
 2 30    Store A
 3 40    Store A
 4 40    Store A
 5 25    Store B
 6 20    Store B
 7 25    Store B
 8 30    Store B
 9 15    Store C
10 20    Store C
11 25    Store C
12 20    Store C

Analysis of Variance Table

Response: data
          Df Sum Sq Mean Sq F value Pr(>F)
store      2 466.67 233.333   10.5  0.004437 **
Residuals  9 200.00  22.222

Signif. codes:  0 '***' 0.001 '**' 0.01 '*' 0.05 '.' 0.1 ' ' 1
```

> **TIP**

> ✓ You have multiple options for getting data into R and printing the results of an analysis of variance.
>
> ```
> > my.data = read.table(file.choose(), header = T) # locate your
> data file and click on it
> > my.data # list data set
> > attach(my.data) # open data set in R workspace
> > group = factor(group) # define variable as factor, e.g.,
> group variable
> > out = aov(y ~ group, intercept = F) # conduct ANOVA without
> the intercept term
> > anova(out) # print ANOVA summary table
> > summary(out) # Optional print ANOVA summary table
> ```

Tukey Post Hoc Test

Step 6. Conduct a post hoc test.

The *F* test doesn't reveal *which* store means are different, only that the three store means are different. Consequently, a post hoc test (multiple-comparison test) is needed to determine which store means are different. There are many different types of multiple-comparison tests depending on whether the group sizes are equal or unequal, whether all group means are compared (pairwise) or combinations of group means are compared (complex contrasts), and whether group mean differences are specified in advance (a priori planned comparison) or after the statistical test (posterior comparison). There are more than 32 multiple-comparison tests to choose from for comparing group means, with a key distinction being whether sample sizes are equal or unequal (Hinkle et al., 2003). A discussion and presentation of the many different multiple-comparison tests is beyond the scope of this book (see Hsu, 1996, for a complete coverage; Scheffé, 1953, for complex contrasts).

We will only focus on one type of multiple-comparison test, called the *Tukey HSD post hoc* test (Tukey, 1949), named after John Tukey, which compares all possible pairs of means and is based on a *studentized range* distribution Q (this distribution is similar to the distribution of t from the t test). The Tukey HSD test compares all possible pairs of means controlling for the Type I error rate. The test identifies whether the difference between two means ($\bar{X}_{max} - \bar{X}_{min}$) is greater than the standard error $\left(\sqrt{MS_W / n}\right)$. The confidence interval for all mean comparisons, when sample sizes are equal, is exactly $1 - \alpha$. For unequal sample sizes, the confidence interval is greater than $1 - \alpha$, so the Tukey HSD test is considered more conservative when groups have unequal sample sizes.

Tukey based his formula on the t test, so it is essentially a t test, except that it corrects for **experiment-wide error rate**. Experiment-wide error rate occurs when conducting multiple tests using the same alpha level. When there are multiple comparisons being made, the probability of making a Type I error increases, but the Tukey HSD test corrects for this, so it is more suitable for making multiple comparisons of mean differences than doing several t tests. When we conduct a single *t test* with α = .05, it implies a 5% probability level of making a Type I error. However, when conducting two *t* tests, we increase our chances of finding a difference, so the α = .05 would be inflated. A better alpha specification would be .05/2 = .025 for each *t test*. If we conducted three *t tests*, α = .05 would once again be an inflated probability level. A better alpha specification would be .05/3 = .0167. As we add more *t tests*, we need to control for the experiment-wide error rate by increasing the alpha level for each individual test of mean difference. The basic calculation for adjusting the alpha probability level when running multiple tests is

$$\alpha' = \frac{\alpha}{n}.$$

The formula for Tukey's test, which subtracts the largest group mean from the smallest group mean (hence is considered a *studentized range* test) divided by the standard error is

$$q_s = \frac{\bar{X}_{max} - \bar{X}_{min}}{\sqrt{MS_W / n}}.$$

Since the null hypothesis for Tukey's HSD test states that all means being compared are from the same population, that is, $\mu_i = \mu_p$, the means should be normally distributed according to the central limit theorem, which yields the normality assumption of the Tukey HSD test.

The *TukeyHSD()* function in the script file (chap14b2.r) computes the multiple comparisons of mean differences controlling for the Type I error rate and provides an adjusted *p* value for the three pairs of mean comparisons: Store A versus Store B, Store A versus Store C, and Store B versus Store C. You will only need to enter the data set name and the confidence interval in the function.

```
> TukeyHSD(out, conf.level = .95)
```

The results show the mean difference between the pairs of stores with the confidence interval and *p* values for the Tukey test. The individual Tukey test values are not indicated but can be computed given the mean difference and the standard error. The standard error is

$$\text{Standard error} = \sqrt{\frac{MS_W}{n}} = \sqrt{\frac{22.22}{10}} = 1.49.$$

Therefore, each Tukey test value is the mean difference divided by the standard error. For example, Tukey (Store B − Store A)/Standard error = (25 − 35)/1.49 = −10/1.49 = −6.71, indicating that Store A has a statistically significantly higher mean than Store B. Tukey (Store C − Store A)/Standard error = (20 − 35)/1.49 = −15/1.49 = −10.067, indicating that Store A has a statistically significantly higher mean than Store C. Finally, Tukey (Store C − Store B)/Standard error = (20 − 25)/1.49 = −5/1.49 = −3.355, indicating that Store B and Store C did not have a statistically significantly mean difference. The critical Tukey value for making these comparisons between the pairs of means would be obtained from a table of percentage points for the studentized range test, which is the *Q* distribution (see Hinkle et al., 2003, table C.8). The region of rejection is Tukey > 3.95, for *r* = 3 (number of means) and *df* = 9 (residual error) at the .05

level of significance. The function does provide the mean difference for each pair, a confidence interval, and a p value to indicate whether the mean difference was statistically significant. A researcher would report these values, so looking up a tabled critical value is not essential when conducting the post hoc test.

```
Tukey multiple comparisons of means
95% family-wise confidence level

Fit: aov(formula = data ~ store)

$store
      diff      lwr       upr          p          adj
Store B-Store A -10 -19.30669 -0.6933146 0.0361479
Store C-Store A -15 -24.30669 -5.6933146 0.0038138
Store C-Store B  -5 -14.30669  4.3066854 0.3357776
```

Note: The analysis of variance results do not print when inserting the *TukeyHSD()* function.

The results indicate that the mean difference between Store B and Store A (25 − 35 = −10; p = .036) and Store A and Store C (20 − 35 = −15; p = .0038) are statistically significantly different. The mean difference between Store B and Store C (20 − 25 = −5; p = .335) was not statistically significant. The Tukey HSD post hoc test reports a p value to indicate where the group mean differences are located after conducting an F test.

Note: The computed Tukey values for each pair of means and the Tukey critical table value are not printed out in the *TukeyHSD()* function. I do not know why the R function could not report the critical Tukey value along with the computed Tukey test value for each mean difference comparison. Here is a good example of where you could modify the function and save these calculations and output.

The 95% confidence interval can be graphed to show the range of lower and upper values for the mean differences of each pair of comparisons. The R command is

```
> plot(TukeyHSD(aov(data ~ store), conf.level = .95)); abline(v = 0)
```

Note: You will need to replace the *TukeyHSD()* function with this plot command. No analysis of variance results are printed. A second command, *abline()*, can be included on the same line using the special semicolon syntax (;).

The graph shows that the mean difference between Store B and Store A could range from −19.30 to −.69. The mean difference between Store C and Store A could range from −24.30 to −5.69. Both of these 95% confidence intervals do not overlap with the null hypothesis, where μ_1 − μ_2 = 0. The 95% confidence interval for Store C–Store B ranges from −14.30 to 4.30, which contains the probability of no mean difference, that is, mean difference = 0. If the confidence interval contains the value of zero, this indicates that a mean difference could be zero, which is the null hypothesis. So you would retain the null hypothesis of no mean difference between Store B and Store C.

● ANALYSIS OF COVARIANCE

The research design and accompanying research question in one-way analysis of variance are centered on testing the mean differences between three or more groups to explain the variation in the dependent variable. The group or factor variable (store) was included to determine if the variation in the dependent variable could be attributed to the type of store. This type of research can involve an **experimental design**, with random assignment of subjects to groups and a treatment given to one or more groups with a control or placebo group. The manipulation of the independent variable would result in a cause-and-effect outcome. For example, a randomly assigned group of shoppers could have been provided discount coupons or other incentives to shop. The study could have been designed to see which type of store would have more purchases based on the manipulation of incentives. A comparison of shoppers with discount coupons and those without (control group) would indicate whether discount coupons increased the number of purchases.

Sometimes the research design explains the variation in the dependent variable by **statistical control**. Statistical control is used when experimental control has not been implemented in the research design; this typically occurs after the study is completed and is referred to as a **quasi-experimental design**. In this type of research design, an experimental group and a comparison group, rather than a control group, are formed. The quasi-experimental design does not randomly assign subjects to groups. The analysis of covariance statistical method bridges the gap between analysis of variance (experimental design) and multiple regression (statistical control in a quasi-experimental design). See Shadish, Cook, and Campbell (2001) for more detailed information on experimental and quasi-experimental designs and assumptions.

Analysis of covariance adjusts the group means for any influence by other variables not controlled in the study, which are referred to as extraneous variables. The rationale is that **extraneous variables** are influencing the variation in the dependent variable and should be controlled by statistical adjustment, since the variable is not controlled in the research design by random assignment. Random assignment in an experimental design controls for bias in subject selection, attrition, maturation, and so on, which are referred to as threats to design validity. This is not present in the quasi-experimental design.

Analysis of covariance is a statistical procedure to control for extraneous variables, called *covariates*. The statistical analysis *partitions* out variance from the total sum of squares due to the covariate and thus tests the effects of the independent variable on the dependent variable controlling for the covariate variable. Ideally, the covariate variable is related (correlated) to the dependent variable, is not affected by the independent variable(s), and has the effect of reducing the error sums of squares (variation not explained by the independent variables). Group differences that explain the variation in the dependent variable (number of purchases) are represented by SS_B and the unexplained variation or error sums of squares by SS_W. Our goal in conducting the analysis of covariance is to reduce the SS_W by explaining some of the variation due to a covariate variable. A pie chart diagram visually shows how the dependent variable variance ($S^2 = SS_T/df_T$) is partitioned into the variation due to group differences (SS_B) and the leftover unexplained variation (SS_W), which could be due to other factors (other independent variables) or a covariate variable that influences the dependent variable. The dependent variable variance is partitioned into these parts using sums of squares because the values can be summed for each effect, yielding the total sums of squares (SS_T).

An example will illustrate how adding a covariate can reduce the SS_W, thus providing a statistical control that reduces the error variance (unexplained SS). In our previous example, the three stores had statistically significant mean differences. What if the number of purchases was affected by the number of miles a person drove to the store? If we controlled for this covariate, maybe the significance of our group mean differences would increase, that is, *F test* would increase.

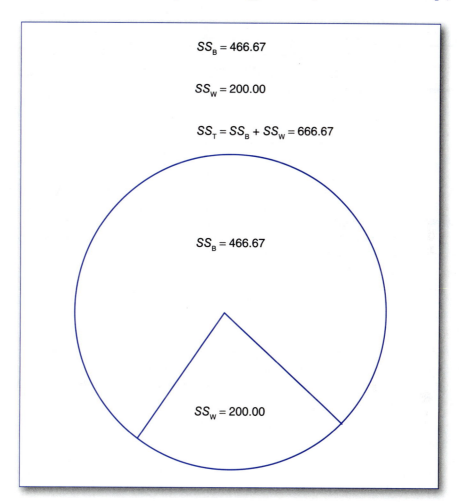

$SS_B = 466.67$

$SS_W = 200.00$

$SS_T = SS_B + SS_W = 666.67$

$SS_B = 466.67$

$SS_W = 200.00$

The data set with the covariate variable values is listed below:

Number of Purchases	Store	Number of Miles to Store
30	A	5
30	A	6
40	A	7
40	A	8
25	B	9
20	B	10

(Continued)

(Continued)

Number of Purchases	Store	Number of Miles to Store
25	B	11
30	B	12
15	C	13
20	C	14
25	C	15
20	C	16

NOTE: The R *aov()* function does not work in analysis of covariance, although it is a balanced design (equal group sizes), because the covariate variable is not a factor (group) variable. We must therefore use the *lm()* function or other general linear model function.

R *lm()* Function

The *lm()* function is used when conducting analysis of covariance because the *aov()* function does not work correctly. The *aov()* function only uses group variables (factors), so the covariate variable adjustment to the dependent variable is done incorrectly. An example of the correct and incorrect use of the *aov()* function is shown next.

Correct Use of aov() in One-Way Analysis of Variance, No Covariate

```
store = factor(store)
out = aov(data ~ store)
anova(out)
```

```
Analysis of Variance Table
```

```
Response: data
          Df Sum Sq Mean Sq F value Pr(>F)
store      2 466.67 233.333   10.5   0.004437   **
Residuals  9 200.00  22.222
```

Incorrect Use of aov(), Treating the Covariate as a Factor

```
store = factor(store)
drive = factor(drive)
out = aov(data ~ store + drive)
anova(out)
```

```
Analysis of Variance Table

Response: data
          Df Sum Sq Mean Sq F value Pr(>F)
store      2 466.67 233.333 18.667  0.1615
drive      8 187.50  23.438  1.875  0.5140
Residuals  1  12.50  12.500
```

Correct Use of lm() With Covariate

The variable store is defined as a factor but not drive.

```
store = factor(store)
out = lm(data ~ store + drive)
anova(out)

Analysis of Variance Table

Response: data
          Df Sum Sq  Mean Sq F value Pr(>F)
Store      2 466.67  233.333 20.3951 0.0007228 ***
drive      1 108.47  108.475  9.4815 0.0151352 *
Residuals  8  91.53   11.441
```

The analysis of variance summary table indicates that the covariate variable, *drive,* is statistically significant. Therefore, mean differences in store purchases are influenced by the distance a shopper must drive to the store.

Analysis of Covariance Function

The *analysis of covariance function* in the script file (chap14c.r) combines all of the commands to read in the data, calculates the analysis of covariance results, and prints the results in an analysis of variance summary table. You will need to enter the data vectors *data* and *drive*, with the creation of the factor *store*, prior to running the function.

```
> data = c(30,30,40,40,25,20,25,30,15,20,25,20)
> drive = c(5,6,7,8,9,10,11,12,13,15,15,16)
> store = rep(c("Store A","Store B","Store C"), c(4,4,4))
> chap14c(data, drive, store)
```

The results will first print out the data set with the three variables, followed by the analysis of variance summary table.

```
PROGRAM OUTPUT

     data   store     drive
 1 30     Store A     5
 2 30     Store A     6
 3 40     Store A     7
 4 40     Store A     8
 5 25     Store B     9
 6 20     Store B    10
 7 25     Store B    11
 8 30     Store B    12
 9 15     Store C    13
10 20     Store C    15
11 25     Store C    15
12 20     Store C    16


Analysis of Variance Table

Response: data
             Df Sum Sq Mean Sq F value Pr(>F)
store         2 466.67 233.333 20.3951 0.0007228 ***
drive         1 108.47 108.475  9.4815 0.0151352 *
Residuals     8  91.53  11.441


Signif. codes: 0 `***' 0.001 `**' 0.01 `*' 0.05 `.' 0.1 ` ' 1
```

The analysis of covariance summary table indicates that the SS_B (store) = 466.67 but the SS_W (error or residual) has been reduced due to a covariate variable (*drive*: number of miles to the store), SS_{cov}. The reduction in SS_W has the effect of reducing the MS_W in the F-test formula, so the F value becomes larger ($F = MS_B/MS_W$). $F_{.05;df=2,9} = 10.50$ with $p = .004$ in the previous one-way analysis of variance for testing store mean differences is now $F_{.05;df=2,8} = 20.39$ with $p = .0007$ when statistically controlling for an extraneous variable that affects the dependent variable. The covariate variable *drive* is also indicated in the analysis of variance summary table as being a significant covariate ($F = 9.4815$; $p = .015$), which reflects the fact that the sums of squares removed from SS_W were statistically significant. Notice also that a covariate variable has 1 degree of freedom associated with this reduction in the sums of squares. The one-way analysis of variance results showed significant store mean differences, but sometimes we might not find a significant mean difference if we have not statistically controlled for an extraneous variable (covariate) that affects the dependent variable. We do need to exercise caution, however, in using analysis of covariance in the statistical control of covariate variable effects on a dependent variable. It is possible that the covariate sum of squares does not reduce the SS_W but rather reduces SS_B or both. If a covariate reduces SS_B, it affects the significance of the independent variable.

TIP

✓ *Caution:* Analysis of covariance can reduce the SS_B rather than the SS_W, which would have a negative impact on the *F* test.

Advice: Run an analysis of variance, then run an analysis of covariance to see how the sum of squares (*SS*) is partitioned for the independent and covariate variable.

Venn or Ballentine Diagram

We can show the analysis of covariance partitioning of the sums of squares for the dependent variable in a pie chart diagram as follows:

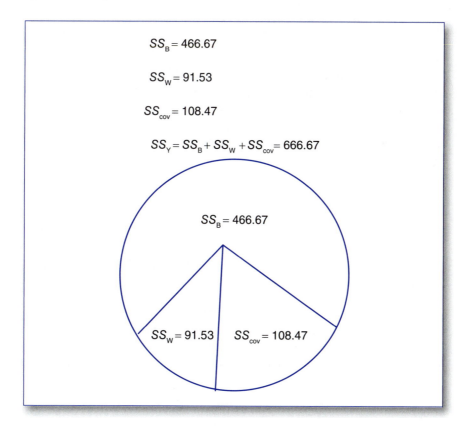

The total sum of squares (SS_T) is now partitioned into three areas corresponding to the sum of squares for store differences (SS_B), the sum of squares for the covariate variable—number of miles to the store (SS_{cov}), and the sum of squares residual or unexplained error (SS_W). We should also see that the partitioned sums of squares (SS_{cov}, SS_B, SS_W) always add up to the total sum of squares (SS_T).

Adjusted Means in Analysis of Covariance

When a statistically significant covariate variable is present, the SS_w should be reduced, because the dependent variable is affected by the extraneous variable. In analysis of covariance, we use a multiple regression procedure to compute the adjusted means based on the covariate variable (correlation and regression are presented in the next two chapters). The adjusted dependent variable means reflect the statistically significant mean differences after a covariate variable adjustment—not the original dependent variable group means.

The adjusted group means are computed using the correlation between the covariate variable and the dependent variable. The *cor.test()* function in R is used to obtain the correlation:

```
> r = cor.test(data, drive, alternative = c("two.sided"), method = c("pearson"))
> r


cor
-0.6515496
```

The negative relationship (correlation), $r = -.65$, suggests that as the number of miles to the store decreases, the number of purchases per store increases. So the covariate variable did significantly affect the dependent variable—number of purchases per store. The adjusted dependent variable means can now be computed as follows:

$$Y'_j = \bar{Y}_j - b_W(\bar{X}_k - \bar{X}),$$

where

Y'_j = adjusted group mean on the dependent variable,

$\bar{Y}_j$ = original group mean on the dependent variable,

b_W = regression coefficient indicating correlation between the dependent variable and the covariate,

$\bar{X}_k$ = group mean on the covariate variable, and

$\bar{X}$ = grand mean on the covariate variable.

We put all the pieces of the equation together to compute the adjusted dependent variable means:

$$Y'_A = \bar{Y}_A - b_W(\bar{X}_k - \bar{X}) = 35 - (-0.65)[6.5 - 10.58] = 35 - 2.652 - 32.348.$$

$$Y'_B = \bar{Y}_B - b_W(\bar{X}_k - \bar{X}) = 25 - (-0.65)[10.5 - 10.58] = 25 - 0.052 = 24.948.$$

$$Y'_C = \bar{Y}_C - b_W(\bar{X}_k - \bar{X}) = 20 - (-0.65)[14.75 - 10.58] = 20 - (-2.7105) = 22.7105.$$

We should table these original and adjusted means on the dependent variable, so that we can compare the adjustment means based on the covariate variable and interpret the adjusted means for statistically significant mean differences. The following table includes these two sets of dependent variable means.

Descriptive Statistics for the Number
of Purchases per Store Controlling for Distance

Store	N	Original Mean	Adjusted Mean
A	4	35	32.35
B	4	25	24.95
C	4	20	22.71

TIP

✓ You can get the means and standard deviations from R commands.

```
> mean(data[1:4]); sd(data[1:4]); mean(drive[1:4]) # Store A
    dependent and covariate

[1] 35
[1] 5.773503
[1] 6.5

> mean(data[5:8]); sd(data[5:8]); mean(drive[5:8]) # Store B
    dependent and covariate

[1] 25
[1]  4.082483
[1] 10.5

> mean(data[9:12]); sd(data[9:12]); mean(drive[9:12]) # Store C
    dependent and covariate

[1] 20
[1]  4.082483
[1] 14.75

> mean(data); sd(data); mean(drive) # Total dependent and
    covariate

[1] 26.66667
[1]  7.784989
[1] 10.58333
```

● FIXED FACTOR ANALYSIS OF VARIANCE

The one-way analysis of variance example had a single factor or group variable. It is possible to add a second factor (variable) and then partition the variance of Y into both factors, or independent variables. For example, we might have mean differences in the number of purchases per store but could also include whether customers were male or female, thus including a *gender* factor variable. Since the levels for *store* and *gender* are fixed, that is, only specific levels for the variables are selected, we refer to this as a **fixed factor** analysis of variance. When including a second factor variable, it is customary to test whether they interact. Therefore, our discussion will include not only the **main effects** of two fixed factor variables but also their **interaction effect**. The main effects would test the group mean differences for each of the factor group variables separately, while the interaction effect would test the joint cell means of the two group variables (factors). An example will present and clarify the analysis of data when more than one fixed factor variable is investigated.

Fixed Analysis of Variance Examples

Two-by-Three Analysis of Variance: Two Main Effects, No Interaction

We will first add the second factor, *gender*, to our *data.frame()* file *y* and print the data file. The set of R commands to do this are as follows:

```
> number = c(30,30,40,40,25,20,25,30,15,20,25,20)
> store = rep(c("Store A","Store B","Store C"), c(4,4,4))
> gender = rep(c("Female","Male"), c(2,2))
> y = data.frame(data, store, gender)
```

The data set now contains the number of purchases (*number*), the store name (*store*), and the gender (*gender*).

The two group variables are defined as factors by the following R commands:

```
> store = factor(store)
> gender = factor(gender)
```

We are now ready to conduct the fixed factor analysis of variance and print the results in an analysis of variance summary table. The R commands are

```
> out = aov(number ~ store * gender, data = y)
> anova(out)
```

or, optionally, the equation can be written out as

```
> out = aov(number ~ store + gender + store*gender, data = y)
> summary(out)
```

We can also print the analysis of variance model means for the main effects of *store* and *gender*, as well as the interaction effect cell means, with the following R command:

```
> print(model.tables(out, "means"), digits = 3)
```

The *fixed factor analysis of variance function* in the script file (chap14d1.r) combines all of these individual R commands into a single R function, with some formatting for printing the output of results. You therefore only need to enter the data vector, *number*, along with the factor variables, *store* and *gender*, as follows, prior to running the function:

```
> number = c(30,30,40,40,25,20,25,30,15,20,25,20)
> store = rep(c("Store A","Store B","Store C"), c(4,4,4))
> gender = rep(c("Female","Male"), c(2,2))
> chap14d1(number, store, gender)
```

The output from the fixed factor analysis of variance lists the data set values, followed by the grand mean, main effect means, and joint cell means (interaction effect) for the *store* and *gender* factor variables. The mean for Store A is 35, which is the average of the *Female* and *Male* means at the store, that is, 35 = (30 + 40)/2. The other *store* means are also averages of their *gender* means. Similarly, the *gender* means are the average of the *store* means. For example, the *Female* mean = 23.33 = (30 + 22.5 + 17.5)/3. This reveals that the data are partitioned into the levels for each of the grouping variables (*store* and *gender*).

The fixed factor analysis of variance summary table displays the degrees of freedom, the sum of squared deviations (SS_B), the mean square (MS_W), F, and p values for the main effects and the interaction effect. The degrees of freedom for the two factor variables are calculated as $j - 1$ (store: $3 - 1 = 2$) and $k - 1$ (gender: $2 - 1 = 1$). The interaction effect $df = (j - 1)(k - 1) = (2)(1) = 2$. The residual $df = jk(n - 1) = 3(2)(2 - 1) = 6$, where n = a cell sample size. The results indicated that the *store* means are statistically different ($F = 28, p = .0009$) and the *gender* means are also statistically different ($F = 16, p = .007$). The *store:gender* interaction effect (joint cell means), however, was not statistically different ($F = 1, p = .421$).

```
Data Set for Fixed Factor ANOVA

    data    store     gender
1   30    Store A    Female
2   30    Store A    Female
3   40    Store A    Male
4   40    Store A    Male
5   25    Store B    Female
6   20    Store B    Female
7   25    Store B    Male
8   30    Store B    Male
9   15    Store C    Female
10  20    Store C    Female
11  25    Store C    Male
12  20    Store C    Male
```

```
PROGRAM OUTPUT

Tables of means
Grand mean

26.66667

  store
store
Store A Store B Store C
   35      25      20

  gender
gender
Female    Male
23.33    30.00

  store:gender
  gender
store     Female   Male
Store A    30.0    40.0
Store B    22.5    27.5
Store C    17.5    22.5

Fixed Factor Analysis of Variance Summary Table

                Df Sum Sq Mean Sq   F value Pr(>F)
store            2 466.67 233.333     28    0.0009063 ***
gender           1 133.33 133.333     16    0.0071190 **
store:gender     2  16.67   8.333      1    0.4218750
Residuals        6  50.00   8.333

Signif. codes: 0 '***' 0.001 '**' 0.01 '*' 0.05 '.' 0.1 ' ' 1
```

The fixed factorial analysis of variance falls under what is now called the general linear model in statistics packages.

The power for testing the null hypothesis of no mean difference in *store* and *gender* is possible using the *pwr.f2.test()* function in the *pwr* package. We would load the pwr package and identify the needed arguments as

```
> library(pwr)
> ?pwr.f2.test

pwr.f2.test(u = NULL, v = NULL, f2 = NULL, sig.level = 0.05, power = NULL)
```

Arguments

u	Degrees of freedom for numerator
v	Degrees of freedom for denominator
f2	Effect size
sig.level	Significance level (Type I error probability)
Power	Power of test (1 minus Type II error probability)

For the fixed factorial analysis of variance, the arguments would be as follows: $u = 2$ (degrees of freedom for the numerator of *store* differences), $v = 6$ (degrees of freedom for the denominator of residual error), $f2 = 5$ (average 5-point difference), *sig.level* = .05 (Type I error), and power = NULL (the value to be estimated). I chose the numerator degrees of freedom for *store* because the interaction term was nonsignificant.

```
> pwr.f2.test(u = 2, v = 6, f2 = 5, sig.level = 0.05, power = NULL)

Multiple regression power calculation

    u = 2
    v = 6
    f2 = 5
    sig.level = 0.05
    power = 0.9961437
```

Results indicate that power = .99, which is sufficient to protect against a Type II error. We can also run this for *gender* ($u = 1$), which yielded power = 1.

TIP

✓ The *summary()* function does not give the total degrees of freedom and sums of squares in the summary table. You will need to compute these values for the table.

✓ The dependent variable S^2 (number) = SS_T/df_T, which is the total *df* and *SS* you get when summing the values in the table:

$$SS_T = 666.67 \text{ and } df_T = 11$$

$$S^2 \text{ (number)} = SS_T/df_T = 666.67/11 = 60.606363 = 60.61.$$

So the grand mean is 26.6667, and $S = \sqrt{S^2} = 7.785$, also given by

```
> mean(data); sd(data)
```

Tukey HSD Post Hoc Test

There were statistically significant main effects for both *store* and *gender* but no interaction effect. The main effect for *gender* has two levels (female, male), and therefore, no post hoc test is required. We simply compare the two means, which show that males on average (mean = 30) had a higher number of store visits than females (mean = 23). *Store* has three levels, so a post hoc test is required to determine which pairs of means are statistically different. Store A mean = 30, followed by Store B mean = 22.5 and Store C mean = 17.5. A one-way analysis of variance would be conducted, followed by a post hoc test (Tukey HSD); however, recall that you must run two separate analyses: an analysis of variance first to obtain results, then the post hoc commands. The R commands for *store* post hoc mean differences in the R script file (chap14d1.r) are

```
> post = TukeyHSD(aov(number ~ store), conf.level = .95)
> print (post)
> plot(TukeyHSD(aov(number ~ store), conf.level = .95));
  abline(v = 0)
```

The results indicate the following:

```
Tukey multiple comparisons of means
95% family-wise confidence level
$store
          diff       lwr       upr          p          adj
Store B - Store A   -10  -19.30669  -0.6933146  0.0361479
Store C - Store A   -15  -24.30669  -5.6933146  0.0038138
Store C - Store B    -5  -14.30669   4.3066854  0.3357776
```

The 95% confidence interval graph shows that the mean difference between Store C and Store B does not fall outside the confidence interval, that is, it overlaps or contains the value of zero, indicating no mean difference in stores. In contrast, the other two comparisons, Store C versus Store A and Store B versus Store A, fall outside the confidence interval; thus, they do not contain the zero value. The p values from the Tukey HSD mean comparisons also indicated that these comparisons have statistically significant mean differences, $p = .0361$ and $p = .0038$, respectively.

Two-by-Two Analysis of Variance: One Main Effect, No Interaction

A second fixed factor analysis of variance example is given using the *blink function* in the R script file (chap14d2.r). The data come from Roscoe (1975, p. 344). The fixed effects analysis of variance examines the effects of *shock* and *drugs* on the number of eye blinks (dependent variable). *Shock* has two levels (*yes* or *no*) and *drug* has two levels (*drug* or *no drug*).

You would enter the data vector, *blinks*, and create the two factor variables, *shock* and *drug*, prior to running the function.

```
> blinks = c(2,3,3,4,0,1,2,3,1,2,2,3,0,1,1,2)
> shock = rep(c("Yes","No"), c(4,4))
> drug = rep(c("Drug","No Drug"), c(8,8))
> chap14d2(blinks, shock, drug)
```

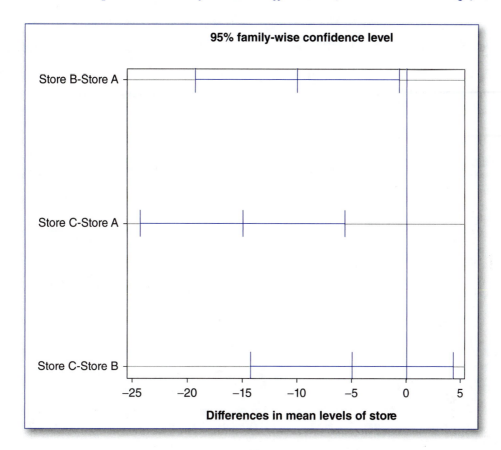

The results would first print out the data set, then report the main effect means and interaction cell means followed by the analysis of variance summary table.

```
PROGRAM OUTPUT

     blinks  shock   drug
  1    2      Yes     Drug
  2    3      Yes     Drug
  3    3      Yes     Drug
  4    4      Yes     Drug
  5    0      No      Drug
  6    1      No      Drug
  7    2      No      Drug
  8    3      No      Drug
  9    1      Yes     No Drug
 10    2      Yes     No Drug
 11    2      Yes     No Drug
 12    3      Yes     No Drug
```

```
13  0    No      No Drug
14  1    No      No Drug
15  1    No      No Drug
16  2    No      No Drug
```

```
Tables of means
Grand mean
```

```
1.875
```

```
 shock
shock
 No    Yes
1.25   2.50
```

```
 drug
drug
 Drug   No Drug
 2.25    1.50
```

```
 shock:drug
 drug
shock Drug No Drug
 No    1.5    1.0
 Yes   3.0    2.0
```

```
Fixed Factor Analysis of Variance Summary Table
           Df Sum Sq Mean Sq F value Pr(>F)
shock       1   6.25   6.250   6.818  0.0228  *
drug        1   2.25   2.250   2.455  0.1432
shock:drug  1   0.25   0.250   0.273  0.6110
Residuals  12  11.00   0.917
```

```
Signif. codes: 0 `***' 0.001 `**' 0.01 `*' 0.05 `.' 0.1 ` ' 1
```

Results in the summary table show that there is no *shock*-by-*drug* interaction effect (*shock:drug*). Examining the main effects, we see that *drug*, *drug/no drug* condition, had no statistically significant main effect on eye blinking. The main effect for *shock*, *shock/no shock* condition, was statistically significant ($F = 6.818$, $df = 1, 12$, $p = .02$). We would conclude that shocking a person caused more eye blinking. We would *not* conduct a post hoc test for the *shock* main effect because it contains only two levels. Examining the two means indicates that subjects who received a shock had a higher mean number of blinks (mean = 2.5) compared with those subjects who did not receive a shock (mean = 1.25).

2 × 3 Analysis of Variance: Interaction Effect

The researcher decided to expand the previous experiment by including three treatment levels for shock: (1) placebo, (2) a 5-volt shock, and (3) a 10-volt shock. The second factor was kept at two levels, *drug* or *no drug*, where one group of subjects received Dramamine and the other did not. Dramamine is used for motion sickness, but it also causes drowsiness or a sleeplike state when taken. The *second blink function* is in a script file (chap14d3.r), which conducts the 2 × 3 fixed factor analysis of variance. Notice that the numbers (2 × 3) indicate the levels of the independent variables. You will once again enter the data vector, *blinks*, followed by the factor variables, *shock* and *drug*, prior to running the function.

```
> blinks = c(0,1,2,2,0,4,3,4,3,3,1,2,3,1,2,0,2,2,1,0,0,2,2,1,0,5,4,5,3,4)
> shock = rep(c("Placebo","5 Volt","10 Volt"), c(5,5,5))
> drug = rep(c("Drug","No Drug"), c(5,5))
> chap14d3(blinks, shock, drug)
```

The results will first print the data set followed by the main effect means and interaction means. The analysis of variance summary table reports the results of the *F* test for main effects and interaction effects.

PROGRAM OUTPUT

	blinks	shock	drug
1	0	Placebo	Drug
2	1	Placebo	Drug
3	2	Placebo	Drug
4	2	Placebo	Drug
5	0	Placebo	Drug
6	4	5 Volt	No Drug
7	3	5 Volt	No Drug
8	4	5 Volt	No Drug
9	3	5 Volt	No Drug
10	3	5 Volt	No Drug
11	1	10 Volt	Drug
12	2	10 Volt	Drug
13	3	10 Volt	Drug
14	1	10 Volt	Drug
15	2	10 Volt	Drug
16	0	Placebo	No Drug
17	2	Placebo	No Drug
18	2	Placebo	No Drug
19	1	Placebo	No Drug
20	0	Placebo	No Drug
21	0	5 Volt	Drug
22	2	5 Volt	Drug
23	2	5 Volt	Drug
24	1	5 Volt	Drug

```
25  0   5 Volt     Drug
26  5  10 Volt     No Drug
27  4  10 Volt     No Drug
28  5  10 Volt     No Drug
29  3  10 Volt     No Drug
30  4  10 Volt     No Drug


Tables of means

Grand mean

2.066667
 shock
shock
10 Volt   5 Volt   Placebo
 3.0       2.2       1.0


drug
 Drug    No Drug
 1.267    2.867

 shock:drug
 drug
shock     Drug   No Drug
10 Volt   1.8      4.2
 5 Volt   1.0      3.4
Placebo   1.0      1.0


 Fixed Factor Analysis of Variance Summary Table
            Df  Sum Sq  Mean Sq  F value   Pr(>F)
shock        2   20.27  10.133   12.936   0.000154   ***
drug         1   19.20  19.200   24.511   0.0000471  ***
shock:drug   2    9.60   4.800    6.128   0.007081   **
Residuals   24   18.80   0.783


Signif. codes: 0 `***' 0.001 `**' 0.01 `*' 0.05 `.' 0.1 ` ' 1
```

Results indicated that the interaction effect (*shock:drug*) was statistically significant. We do not interpret the main effects for *shock* and *drug* when an interaction effect is statistically significant. We also do not conduct a post hoc test. Instead, we examine the cell means to interpret the interaction effect. The average numbers of eye blinks for those receiving a drug at each shock level were 1.0, 1.0, and 1.8, respectively. Therefore, the Dramamine drug maintained a low level of eye blinks. For those receiving no drug, the number of eye blinks increased from 1.0 to 3.4 to 4.2 across the shock levels.

Interaction Effect Graph: Ordinal

Statistically significant interaction effects are best seen visually in a graph. Nonintersecting lines are referred to as a *disordinal* interaction because the lines do not remain parallel. The lines in a disordinal interaction flare out similar to a funnel appearance, which indicates one group increasing and the other remaining fairly constant. The other type of interaction is called *ordinal*, where the lines cross to form an *X* in the graph. This signifies that one group increases while another group decreases across levels of the second factor.

The *interaction.plot()* function in the script file (chap14d4.r) was used to create the two-way interaction graph for the *shock* and *drug* fixed factors. The arguments and further documentation are obtained by issuing the command *?interaction.plot()* in the RGui window. Also, *Quick-R* (Kabacoff, 2012) has examples for creating interaction plots in R. The R commands I used to draw the interaction plot are as follows:

```
# Two-way Interaction Plot - Chap14d4.r

> blinks = c(1.0,1.0,1.8,1.0,3.4,4.2)
> shock = c(0,5,10,0,5,10)
> drug = c(1,1,1,0,0,0)
> shock = factor(shock)
> drug = factor(drug)
> grp = c("No Drugs","Drugs")

> interaction.plot(shock, drug, blinks, type = "l", legend = "FALSE",
> ylab = "Mean Blinks",
> xlab = "Treatment Conditions",
> main = "Plot of Interaction Effect",
> sub = "(Placebo 5V 10V)")
> legend("topleft", title = "Group", as.character(grp), lty = c(1,2))
```

The cell means for number of blinks are input into a data vector, *blinks*. The group member-ship variables, *shock* and *drug*, must contain the same number of elements in their data vectors and match the number of means to be graphed, that is, six elements to represent the six cell means. The data for the *interaction.plot()* function is entered to reflect this pairing of the cell means with the treatment conditions (factors). The data structure is shown below in a data frame, *mydata*, with the variables.

```
# Data set for plotting

> mydata = data.frame(blinks, shock, drug)
> mydata

  blinks shock drug
1  1.0     0    1
2  1.0     5    1
3  1.8    10    1
4  1.0     0    0
5  3.4     5    0
6  4.2    10    0
```

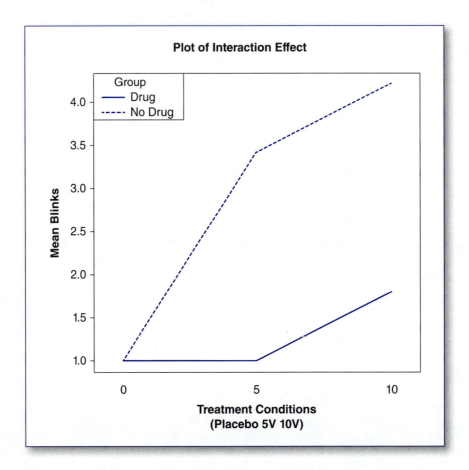

The groups in analysis of variance, called factors, must be also identified as such: *shock = factor(shock)* and *drug = factor(drug)*. The *legend()* function provides identification of each group and their line type. The interaction plot visually shows that subjects receiving a Dramamine drug had lower mean blinks (1.0, 1.0, and 1.8) across the shock conditions than subjects who did not receive a drug (1.0, 3.4, and 4.2).

When interaction effects are statistically significant, it is prudent to graph the cell means to visually determine if a disordinal or ordinal interaction is present. Also, no post hoc tests are required when your results indicate a statistically significant interaction effect. Post hoc tests are only conducted when the main effects are statistically significant and the factor variable (group variable) has three or more levels.

The Sixth Step in Hypothesis Testing

We revisit the 2 × 3 fixed factor analysis of variance example where *store* and *gender* were the two fixed factors. *Gender* had two levels, and *store* had three levels, hence the reference to a 2 × 3 fixed factor analysis of variance. The hypothesis-testing steps are presented for the statistical analysis of the data; however, I have added a sixth step, which addresses the interpretation of the post hoc test results.

Step 1. State the research question in a statistical hypothesis format.

Our research question—Is there a mean difference in the number of purchases based on the type of store and gender?—contains two fixed factor variables. Therefore our statistical hypothesis must first test for an interaction between these two factors (*store* and *gender*) before examining any main effects for the individual factor variables. Three statistical hypotheses are formulated to cover the test of interaction effect and the two main effects.

A. Interaction statistical hypothesis (cell means)

$$\text{Null hypothesis } (H_0): \mu_{ij} = \mu_{ji}$$

$$\text{Alternative hypothesis } (H_A): \mu_{ij} \neq \mu_{ji}.$$

The subscripts i and j are used to denote pairs of cell means that can be tested for a mean difference. In an interaction statistical hypothesis, the i and j subscripts refer to cell means. The alternative hypothesis states that at least one cell mean is different from another cell mean.

B. Main effect statistical hypothesis (*store*)

$$\text{Null hypothesis } (H_0): \mu_i = \mu_j$$

$$\text{Alternative hypothesis } (H_A): \mu_i \neq \mu_j.$$

The subscripts i and j denote pairs of group means that can be tested for a difference. In the main effects statistical hypothesis, the groups to be tested for mean difference are represented by each store type. The alternative hypothesis states that at least one *store* mean is different from another.

C. Main effect statistical hypothesis (*gender*)

$$\text{Null hypothesis } (H_0): \mu_i = \mu_j$$

$$\text{Alternative hypothesis } (H_A): \mu_i \neq \mu_j.$$

The subscripts i and j denote a pair of group means that can be tested for a difference. In the main effects statistical hypothesis, the groups to be tested for mean differences are represented by each gender type. The alternative hypothesis states that the female and male group means are different.

Step 2. Determine the criteria for rejecting the null hypothesis and accepting the alternative hypothesis for each statistical hypothesis.

The criteria for testing mean differences depend on the number of groups and the alpha probability level, so each test can have a different F value associated with the degrees of freedom. The three F values for $\alpha = .05$ are listed for each statistical hypothesis.

A. Interaction statistical hypothesis

Region of rejection: $F > 5.14$, $df = 2, 6$; $p = .05$

B. *Store* main effect statistical hypothesis

Region of rejection: $F > 5.14$, $df = 2, 6$; $p = .05$

C. *Gender* main effect statistical hypothesis

Region of rejection: $F > 5.99$, $df = 1, 6$; $p = .05$

Step 3. Collect the sample data, and compute the F-test statistic.

The sample data are in the *data.frame()* file y, which was created from three individual data vectors. The data set is viewed by the R command $>$ `print(y)`.

A fixed factor analysis of variance function was run to produce the following analysis of variance table:

```
Fixed Factor Analysis of Variance Summary Table

              Df Sum Sq Mean Sq F value   Pr(>F)
store          2 466.67 233.333    28    0.0009063  ***
gender         1 133.33 133.333    16    0.0071190  **
store:gender   2  16.67   8.333     1    0.4218750
Residuals      6  50.00   8.333

Signif. codes:  0 `***' 0.001 `**' 0.01 `*' 0.05 `.' 0.1 ` ' 1
```

TIP

✓ *Note:* The R *aov()* function is used for a balance design (equal sample sizes in groups with no missing data); use *lm()* for unbalanced group sizes, with *anova()* to list the summary table.

Type III sums of squares solution should be used when testing interaction effects.

Step 4. Interpret the region of rejection for computed F values.

The regions of rejection for the different degrees of freedom at the .05 level of probability of each statistical hypothesis are stated as follows:

A. Interaction effect statistical hypothesis

Region of rejection: $F > 5.14$, $df = 2, 6$; $p = .05$

B. *Store* main effect statistical hypothesis

Region of rejection: $F > 5.14$, $df = 2, 6$; $p = .05$

C. *Gender* main effect statistical hypothesis

Region of rejection: $F > 5.99$, $df = 1, 6$; $p = .05$

Since there are two main effects and one interaction effect, we can quickly determine from the summary table which F values fall in the region of rejection. The interaction effect (*store* by *gender*) had $F = 1$, which is less than the tabled $F = 5.14$ and so is *not* statistically significant (we also know this by the summary table p value = .421). Next, we examine the main effect for *store*, which has $F = 28$ compared with the tabled $F = 5.14$, which is statistically significant (we also know this by the summary table p value, .0009). Finally, we examine the main effect for *gender*, which has $F = 16$, compared with the tabled $F = 5.99$, which is statistically significant (we also know this by the summary table p value, .007). The interaction hypothesis was not statistically significant, while both the main effect variables had F values that indicated the presence of statistically significant mean differences.

Step 5. Interpret the F-test statistic results.

The computed F values are indicated for each effect listed in the analysis of variance summary table. The interaction effect (*store* by *gender*) was not statistically significant. Therefore, the numbers of purchases in each combination of store type and gender type (cell means) on average were not different. However, both main effects were statistically significant. The F value for the *store* main effect indicated mean differences, but not which stores differ, and we must conduct a post hoc test to determine which pairs of store means differ. The F value for the *gender* main effect indicated mean differences, but it does not require a post hoc test because we can simply interpret the two means. The number of female purchases on average at all three stores was 23.33, while the number of male purchases was 30.00. The number of male purchases on average per store was higher than the average number of female purchases.

Step 6. Conduct post hoc tests.

The interaction effect was not statistically significant. Although the main effect for *gender* was statistically significant, a comparison of the two means provides an adequate interpretation. The F test for *store*, however, doesn't reveal *which* store means are different, only that the *store* means *are* different. Consequently, a post hoc test (multiple-comparison test) is needed to determine which *store* means are different. The Tukey HSD multiple-comparison test was conducted using the *aov()* function and a one-way analysis of variance model for a balanced design (equal sample sizes). Results for the three *store* group mean comparisons were as follows:

```
Tukey multiple comparisons of means
  95% family-wise confidence level

Fit: aov(formula = number ~ store)

$store
```

```
            diff        lwr   upr          p         adj
Store B-Store A  -10  -19.30669 -0.6933146 0.0361479
Store C-Store A  -15  -24.30669 -5.6933146 0.0038138
Store C-Store B   -5  -14.30669  4.3066854 0.3357776
```

We interpret that Store B was higher than Store A, and Store C was higher than Store A, but Store C and Store B did not differ. This was also shown in the 95% confidence interval graph presented earlier.

It is important to follow the five-step hypothesis-testing approach or the six-step approach when post hoc testing is required. This structure lays out the decisions and format that a researcher should follow, from stating a research question to answering the research question. The hypothesis-testing information and results are typically reported when publishing the results.

Saving the Data File and R Script Files

When you create R functions, they should be saved along with any R data files. I have created R script files for this book that include the values entered in each function. You can also save the data input file commands and other comments as needed in R script files. The data set itself is also important to save with the R script file or function.

In our example above, the data set, *y*, was saved to the current directory on the computer. The directory can be changed or selected from the File menu. The saved data set can be imported into other statistical packages, for example, SPSS, and the results compared. The following R command writes out the data with spaces between variables to a file named Rdata.txt.

```
> write.table(y, "Rdata.txt", sep = " ", row.names = FALSE)
```

Note: The *row.names = FALSE* argument is included to prevent hidden row names in the data file output, which causes a misalignment when reading the data column variables into SPSS. The data set is saved on your computer in the current directory, but it can be changed under the File menu in the main RGui window.

● REPEATED MEASURES ANALYSIS OF VARIANCE

The repeated measures analysis of variance technique extends the **dependent *t* test** to three or more groups. The *dependent t test* is appropriate in research settings where you measure the same subjects twice and test whether the average scores change—that is, increase or decrease in a hypothesized direction. In the case of repeated measures analysis of variance, subjects are measured on three or more occasions (typically over time or under different experimental conditions), with the same idea of testing whether average scores change in a hypothesized direction.

The following repeated measures example indicates the number of children per family for four different families measured over a 3-year time period to test whether family size increased or remained the same. The following data were collected:

Average Number of Children per Family (X)			
ID	1995	1996	1997	Total (T)
1	2	5	5	12
2	2	7	5	14
3	3	2	6	11
4	1	2	4	7
⋮	⋮	⋮	⋮	⋮
n	4	4	4	N = 12
Sum	8	16	20	ΣT = 44
Mean	2	4	5	

The repeated measures analysis of variance partitions the total sum of squared deviations around the grand mean into three component variances: *ID*, *Year*, and remaining Residual (*Error*) variance. The hand calculations obtain the sums of squares as follows:

Total sum of squares:

1. $SS_{Total} = \Sigma[(X)^2] - [(\Sigma T)^2/N]$.

2. $SS_{Total} = \Sigma[(2^2) + (2)^2 + (3)^2 + (1)^2 \cdots + (4)^2] - [(44)^2/12]$.

3. $SS_{Total} = 202 - 161.33 = 40.667$.

ID sum of squares:

1. $SS_{Individual} = \Sigma[(T)^2/k] - [(\Sigma T)^2/N]$

2. $SS_{Individual} = \Sigma[(12)^2/3 + (14)^2/3 + (11)^2/3 + (7)^2/3] - [(44)^2/12]$

3. $SS_{Individual} = 169.99 - 161.33 = 8.66$

Year sum of squares:

1. $SS_{Year} = \Sigma[(T_k)^2/n] - [(T)^2/N]$.

2. $SS_{Year} = \Sigma[(8)^2/4 + (16)^2/4 + (20)^2]/4] - [(44)^2/12]$.

3. $SS_{Year} = 180 - 161.33 = 18.667$.

Error sum of squares:

1. $SS_E = SS_{Total} - SS_{Error(ID)} - SS_{Year.}$

2. $SS_E = 40.667 - 8.66 - 18.667$.

3. $SS_E = 13.33$.

The degrees of freedom associated with each of these sums of squares are as follows:

$$df_{\text{Total}} = N - 1 = 12 - 1 = 11.$$

$$df_{\text{ID}} = n - 1 = 4 - 1 = 3.$$

$$df_{\text{Year}} = k - 1 = 3 - 1 = 2.$$

$$df_{\text{Error}} = (k - 1)(n - 1) = 6.$$

The repeated measures analysis of variance partitions out the sum of squares due to individual differences; thus, the SS_E and the resulting MS_W values are different in the F-test formula from the one-way analysis of variance and fixed factor analysis of variance calculations; that is, $F = MS_o/df_E$, where the subscript "o" represents time or occasions. The results are neatly summarized in the analysis of variance table below:

Repeated Measures Analysis of Variance Summary Table				
Source	Sum of Squares (Type I SS)	Degrees of Freedom (df)	Mean Squares (MS)	F
ID	8.67	3	2.89	
Year	18.67	2	9.33	4.2
Error	13.33	6	2.22	
Total	40.67	11		

The F test in this repeated measures design is *only* calculated for the variable that is measured over time (*Year*). In this case, the F test is a test of whether the average birth rate is different over the 3 years. We would compare the computed $F = 4.2$ with a tabled F in Appendix A (Table 5), with $df = 2, 6$ at the .05 level of significance; which is $F = 5.14$. Since the computed $F = 4.2$ is less than the tabled $F = 5.14$, we conclude that the average birth rates across the 3 years do not differ. The average birth rate increased from 2 per family to 5 per family from 1995 to 1997. The mean birth rate, however, did not increase enough across the years to warrant a beyond chance statistically significant finding.

R *aov()* Function

The *aov()* function used in the *one-way repeated measures of variance function* in the script file (chap14e.r) reports a *Type III SS* solution, which is appropriate due to a balanced design (equal group sizes) and yields the same results as the hand calculations. You will need to enter the data vector and the birth and factor variables, *id* and *year*, prior to running the function.

```
> birth = c(2,5,5,2,7,5,3,2,6,1,2,4)
> id = rep(c(1,2,3,4),  c(3,3,3,3))
> year = rep(c("1995","1996","1997"),  c(1,1,1))
> chap14e(birth, id, year)
```

The results first print the data set followed by the repeated measures analysis of variance results.

Program Output

```
id year birth
1   1995   2
1   1996   5
1   1997   5
2   1995   2
2   1996   7
2   1997   5
3   1995   3
3   1996   2
3   1997   6
4   1995   1
4   1996   2
4   1997   4
```

Repeated Measures Analysis of Variance

Error: id

```
            Df Sum Sq Mean Sq F value Pr(>F)
Residuals 3 8.667   2.889
```

Error: Within

```
            Df Sum Sq Mean Sq F value Pr(>F)
year         2 18.67   9.333    4.2   0.0723
Residuals 6 13.33   2.222
```

Signif. codes: 0 `***' 0.001 `**' 0.01 `*' 0.05 `.' 0.1 ` ' 1

The summary tables indicate that the repeated measures variable, *year*, is not statistically significant, $p = .0723$. Therefore, we would conclude that the average number of births per family did not increase for the years indicated. We can follow a five-step hypothesis-testing format to conduct our repeated analysis of variance for differences across years in birth rates.

Step 1. State the research question in a statistical hypothesis format.

The research question was "Is there a mean difference in the average birth rate per family across 3 years?" The statistical hypothesis to test for the trend or change in average birth rate is stated as follows:

$$\text{Null hypothesis } (H_0): \mu_{1995} = \mu_{1996} = \mu_{1997}$$

$$\text{Alternative hypothesis } (H_A): \mu_{1995} \neq \mu_{1996} \neq \mu_{1997}.$$

The subscripts indicate the years in which the average birth rate was recorded. The null hypothesis states that there is no mean difference from year to year. The alternative hypothesis states that the average birth rate will be different year to year.

Step 2. Determine the criteria for rejecting the null hypothesis.

The criteria for testing mean differences depend on the number of time periods ($j - 1$), which is 2; the degrees of freedom for residual error, which is 6; and the alpha probability level. The tabled F value = 5.14 for df = 2, 6 and p = .05.

$$\text{Region of rejection: } F > 5.14, \; df = 2, 6; \; p = .05.$$

Step 3. Collect the sample data and compute the F test statistic.

The sample data were created in the *data.frame()* file *mydata*, which is viewed by the R command

```
> print(mydata)
```

The repeated measures analysis of variance function was run using the R *aov()* function with a Type III *SS* solution to produce the following analysis of variance table:

```
Repeated Measures Analysis of Variance

Error: id
            Df  Sum Sq  Mean Sq  F value  Pr(>F)
Residuals    3   8.667    2.889

Error: Within
            Df  Sum Sq  Mean Sq  F value   Pr(>F)
year         2   18.67    9.333    4.2     0.0723
Residuals    6   13.33    2.222

Signif. codes:  0 `***' 0.001 `**' 0.01 `*' 0.05 `.' 0.1 ` ' 1
```

Step 4. Interpret the region of rejection for the computed F value.

The computed F value = 4.2, which is less than the tabled F value = 5.14, df = 2, 6 at the .05 level of probability, so we retain the null hypothesis of no mean difference. A researcher would report the F and the actual p value in the summary table.

Step 5. Interpret the F-test statistic results.

The computed F value is not statistically significant (F = 4.2, p = .07), indicating that the average birth rates do not change over the 3-year period. The average birth rate increase from 2 in 1995 to 5 in 1997 was not statistically significant at the .05 level of probability.

One-Way Repeated Measures Analysis of Variance

A second *one-way repeated measures analysis of variance function* in the R script file (chap14f.r) uses the *aov()* function in a one-way repeated measures example using data from Hinkle et al.

(2003, p. 360). The data represent 10 persons who were measured on three test occasions. The entire set of scores is entered into the data vector *total*. The testing occasions are in the data vector *test*. Finally, the data for person ids are in the vector *id*. A data frame, *out*, must be created with these data values and variable names. The data output shows the *id* variable repeated three times, once for each test occasion with the corresponding score.

Note: These R commands produce a special type of person–period data set required for conducting repeated measures analysis of variance.

Before running the repeated measures analysis of variance, certain variables must be defined as factors for use in the *aov()* function. The *id* and *test* variables are defined as factors. Finally, the *aov()* function is run with residual error indicated as the *id* variable, so *df* = 10 − 1, which is correctly estimated in a balanced design using a Type III solution. The commands in the script file are as follows:

```
# chap14f.r - Hinkle, Weirsma, Jurs (2003), p. 360 data

> total =
c(6,12,18,9,14,16,4,8,15,3,10,12,1,6,10,7,15,20,8,8,15,9,11,18,8,12
,13,6,10,16)
> test = rep(c("1","2","3"), c(1,1,1))
> id = rep(c(1,2,3,4,5,6,7,8,9,10), c(3,3,3,3,3,3,3,3,3,3))

> out = data.frame(id, test, total)
> names(out)=c("id","test","total")
> out

# convert variables to factors
> out = within(out, {
 id = factor(id)
 test = factor(test)
})

> result = aov(total ~ test + Error(id), data = out)
> summary(result)
```

The *summary()* function prints out the data set followed by the repeated measures analysis.

	id	test	total
1	1	1	6
2	1	2	12
3	1	3	18
4	2	1	9
5	2	2	14
6	2	3	16
7	3	1	4
8	3	2	8
9	3	3	15
10	4	1	3
11	4	2	10

```
12   4   3      12
13   5   1       1
14   5   2       6
15   5   3      10
16   6   1       7
17   6   2      15
18   6   3      20
19   7   1       8
20   7   2       8
21   7   3      15
22   8   1       9
23   8   2      11
24   8   3      18
25   9   1       8
26   9   2      12
27   9   3      13
28  10   1       6
29  10   2      10
30  10   3      16
```

```
Error: id
           Df Sum Sq Mean Sq F value Pr(>F)
Residuals  9 167.3   18.59
```

```
Error: Within
           Df Sum Sq Mean Sq F value   Pr(>F)
test        2 423.3   211.63   76.09  1.66e-09   ***
Residuals  18  50.1     2.78
```

```
Signif. codes:  0 '***' 0.001 '**' 0.01 '*' 0.05 '.' 0.1 ' ' 1
```

The repeated measures analysis of variance results indicate that *test* was statistically significant (F = 76.09, p = 1.66e–09) across the three testing occasions (use *options(scipen = 999)* to not have the p value printed in scientific notation). No F value is reported for the *Error:id* effect, as expected. Typically, we would place the *Error:id* values in the body of the summary table so that the degrees of freedom, sums of squares, and mean square values would sum together in the repeated measures summary table as shown below:

Repeated Measures Analysis of Variance Table

Variable	SS	df	MS	F	p
ID	167.3	9	18.59		
Test	423.3	2	211.63	76.09	.0001
Residuals	50.1	18	2.78		
Total	640.7	29			

The power calculations can be computed using the *pwr.f2.test()* function for the general linear model. The arguments specify that $u = 2$ (*df* for Test), $v = 18$ (*df* for Residuals), $f2 = 5$ (5-point difference), and $\alpha = .05$, which are as follows:

```
> pwr.f2.test(u = 2, v = 18, f2 = 5, sig.level = 0.05, power = NULL)
Multiple regression power calculation

     u = 2
     v = 18
    f2 = 5
sig.level = 0.05
 power = 1
```

Since power = 1, there is sufficient protection against a Type II error. Recall that power indicates whether we have sufficient data to detect a difference if one exists, thus protecting against falsely rejecting the null hypothesis when it is really true.

Fixed Factor Repeated Measures Analysis of Variance

Repeated measures can also be used with a factor (group) variable when testing for differences across time. The next example tests whether males and females differ across three time periods in their weight. Our research question is "Do men and women (gender) have different weight gain over time?" The repeated measures data set looks different from other data sets because a variable indicating time (*Time*) must be coded repeatedly with dependent variable values at each time point. The small sample data set shows that eight individuals (*id*) of different gender (*gender*, M/F) were measured at three time points (*time*) and their weight recorded (*weight*), which is the dependent variable. We are able to examine gender differences in weight across time because of including a group variable (factor) coded for *gender*. The small sample data set is coded as seen here:

This data set shows that a person ID is repeated three times for the repeated measures variable, *time*, with each time (1, 2, and 3) indicating the person's weight. Once the data set is created, the variables are defined as factors, prior to running the *aov()* function. Results are printed via the *summary()*

ID	Gender	Time	Weight
1	M	1	115
1	M	2	120
1	M	3	125
2	M	1	120
2	M	2	125
2	M	3	130
3	M	1	117
3	M	2	122
3	M	3	125
4	M	1	145
4	M	2	150
4	M	3	155
5	F	1	120
5	F	2	115
5	F	3	110
6	F	1	130
6	F	2	120
6	F	3	110
7	F	1	140
7	F	2	125
7	F	3	115
8	F	1	135
8	F	2	125
8	F	3	115

function. The data set is listed using the *print()* function with *row.names = FALSE*, so hidden row numbers are not listed in the output, that is, *print(out, row.names = FALSE)*. The *aov()* function for conducting the repeated measures analysis of variance is used because of a balanced design and a Type III solution. The *summary()* function is used to print out an analysis of variance–style summary table.

The *fixed factor repeated measures function* in the script file (chap14g.r) contains the data for *id, gender, time,* and *weight.* You would enter these data prior to running the function.

```
> weight = c(115,120,125,120,125,130,117,122,125,145,150,155,120,115,110,1
30,120,110,140,125,115,135,125,115)
> gender = rep(c("M","F"), c(12,12))
> time = rep(c("1","2","3"), c(1,1,1))
> id = rep(c(1,2,3,4,5,6,7,8), c(3,3,3,3,3,3,3,3))
> chap14g(weight, gender, time, id)
```

The results would list the data set values followed by the repeated measures analysis.

Program Output

id	gender	time	weight
1	M	1	115
1	M	2	120
1	M	3	125
2	M	1	120
2	M	2	125
2	M	3	130
3	M	1	117
3	M	2	122
3	M	3	125
4	M	1	145
4	M	2	150
4	M	3	155
5	F	1	120
5	F	2	115
5	F	3	110
6	F	1	130
6	F	2	120
6	F	3	110
7	F	1	140
7	F	2	125
7	F	3	115
8	F	1	135
8	F	2	125
8	F	3	115

```
Repeated Measures Analysis of Variance

Error: id
        Df  Sum Sq  Mean Sq
gender  1  0.33532  0.33532

Error: With in
             Df  Sum Sq  Mean Sq   F value   Pr(>F)
gender        1  1464.38  1464.38  25.6624  0.0000955  ***
time          2    85.75    42.87   0.7514  0.48676
gender:time   2   799.08   399.54   7.0017  0.00605    **
Residuals    17   970.08    57.06

Signif. codes:  0 '***' 0.001 '**' 0.01 '*' 0.05 '.' 0.1 ' ' 1
```

The results indicate that *gender* is a statistically significant main effect, which means that the difference between males and females in *weight* and *time* was not statistically significant ($p = .48676$). However, in the presence of a statistically significant interaction effect (*gender:time*, $p = .00605$), we would not interpret any main effects. The interaction of *gender* by *time* was statistically significant beyond a .05 level of probability, so the cell means are different. Graphing the results will help us visualize the trend in the cell means across *time* for the two groups (males and females).

The power calculations for detecting the interaction effect would be as follows:

```
> pwr.f2.test(u = 2, v = 17, f2 = 5, sig.level = 0.05, power = NULL)
Multiple regression power calculation
u = 2
v = 17
f2 = 5
sig.level = 0.05
power = 1
```

Power = 1, which provides sufficient protection against a Type II error rate, so we can be confident that we are not falsely rejecting the null hypothesis. Our statistical test is suitable for detecting a 5-pound difference over time between males and females.

Interaction Effect Graph: Disordinal

The optional R commands in the script file (chap14g.r) plot the interaction effect:

```
> par(cex = .6)
> with(out, interaction.plot(time, gender, weight, ylim = c(90,110), lty = c(1,12),
lwd = 3, ylab = "weight in lbs", xlab = "time", trace.label = "gender"))
```

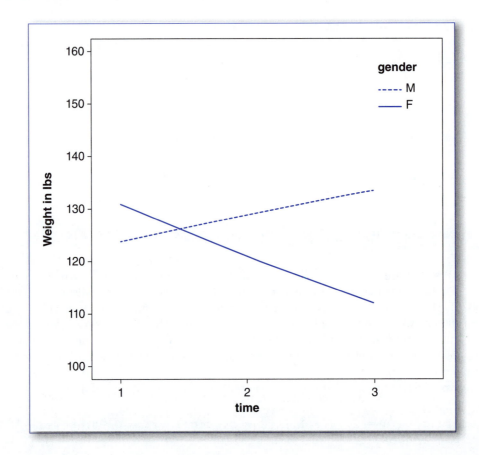

The graph displays a *disordinal* interaction effect (lines cross) for *gender × time*. The graph shows that males gained weight across the three time periods (*dashed line*), while females lost weight across the time periods (*solid line*). Recall that an ordinal interaction occurs when the lines flare out and do not cross. Also, when the lines are parallel for the groups, no interaction or main effects exists.

● EQUALITY OF GROUP VARIANCE ASSUMPTION

An important assumption in analysis of variance prior to testing for group mean differences is that the group variances are approximately equal. Several tests have been created to test for the equality of k group variances. Some of the most notable are Bartlett's chi-square test (1937), Hartley's F_{max} test (1940, 1950), Cochran's C test (1941), and Levene's test (1960). Bartlett's chi-square test, Hartley's F_{max} test, and Cochran's C test are sensitive to departures from normality in the data. Levene's test is less sensitive to nonnormality in the data and uses the median value or trimmed mean value in the function.

Since Hartley's F_{max} is the easiest to understand and compute, it will be covered in more detail. In contrast, Levene's test will also be covered because it is less sensitive to departures from normality and it compares the means of the absolute values of deviations from the medians. Hartley's F_{max} and Levene's test will therefore give contrasting results depending on the departure from normality in the data.

Hartley's F_{max} Test

Hartley (1950) discovered that the *F* test could be used to form a test of whether the range of group variances were similar or different. It is so easy to calculate that no R function is really necessary. The null and alternative statistical hypotheses would be stated as follows:

$$\text{Null hypothesis } (H_0): \sigma_i^2 = \sigma_j^2$$

$$\text{Alternative hypothesis } (H_A): \sigma_i^2 \neq \sigma_j^2.$$

The subscripts *i* and *j* are used to denote pairs of group variances that can be tested for a difference. The alternative hypothesis states that at least one group variance is different from the other group variances. Hartley's F_{max} formula shows that the group with the largest variance (max S^2) is divided by the group with the smallest or minimum variance (min S^2). The F_{max} formula is

$$F_{max} = \frac{\max S^2}{\min S^2}.$$

The F_{max} value has an expected value of 1.0 when the ratios of the largest to smallest sample variances are equal. When the two sample variances are not equal, F_{max} will increase. To test the null hypothesis of no difference in the two sample variances, we compare the calculated F_{max} value with the critical tabled *F* value in Table 6 in Appendix A for $\alpha = .05$ or .01, $df = n - 1$, and $k =$ number of variances compared. The sample size, *n*, would be chosen for the group with the largest sample size, if the sample sizes were different.

A research example will illustrate how the F_{max} formula is used and the results interpreted. In my study, the high school exam scores for freshmen, sophomores, and junior and senior students yielded the following group sample sizes, means, and variances:

Group	N	Mean	Variance
Freshman	30	70	8
Sophomore	30	80	7
Junior	30	85	10
Senior	30	90	5

We wish to test whether the group variances are statistically different. The F_{max} calculation to test the null hypothesis using the largest and smallest group variances is as follows:

$$F_{max} = \frac{\max S^2}{\min S^2} = \frac{10}{5} = 2.0.$$

In Table 6 (Appendix A), we use $df = 30$ ($n - 1 = 30 - 1 = 29$), $\alpha = .05$, and $k = 4$ (number of group variances) and find that $F_{.05,k=4} = 2.61$. Since $F_{max} = 2.0$ is less than the tabled $F_{.05,k=4} = 2.61$, we retain the null hypothesis of no difference in the four group variances. This is a time when we do not want the group variances to be statistically different. When the group variances are equal, we meet the assumption of equal group variance required to test for mean differences.

Levene's Test

I introduced the *levene.test()* function in the previous chapter when we compared the means of two independent groups. *Levene's* test is for k groups, so it can be used in analysis of variance where the means of three or more groups are tested for statistical significance. Recall that to use the function, we must first load the *lawstat* package. Then the R command *?levene.test()* will provide the arguments and documentation.

```
> library(lawstat)
> ?levene.test()

levene.test(y, group, location = c("median","mean","trim.mean"), trim.alpha = 0.25)
```

Y	A numeric vector of data values
Group	Factor of the data
Location	The default option is "median" corresponding to the robust Brown-Forsythe Levene-type procedure; "mean" corresponds to the classical Levene's procedure, and "trim.mean" corresponds to the robust Levene-type procedure using the group trimmed means
trim.alpha	The fraction (0 to 0.5) of observations to be trimmed from each end of "x" before the mean is computed

Using data from our previous example, we can test the equality of variance assumption across the three groups. The data were as follows:

	Store A	Store B	Store C
	30	25	15
	30	20	20
	40	25	25
	40	30	20
Mean	35.00	25.00	20.00
SD	5.77	4.08	4.08

These data are entered into a data vector *number*, which represents the number of purchases in each store. The *gl()* function is used to create the sets of scores for the three groups, where *gl(3,4)* is entered to indicate three groups of 4 scores. The 4 scores out of the 12 scores are consecutively assigned to each group. The variable *grp* must also be designated as a factor variable (*group*). The *Levene* test is then computed. The R commands can be executed in the RGui window as follows:

```
> number = c(30,30,40,40,25,20,25,30,15,20,25,20)
> grp = gl(3,4)
> grp = factor(grp)
> levene.test(number, grp, location = "mean")
```

The results indicate the data set and the Levene test statistic with the *p* value.

```
classical Levene's test based on the absolute deviations from the mean
(none not applied because the location is not set to median)

data: number
Test Statistic = 1.5, p-value = 0.274
```

The results indicate that the assumption of equal variances has been met when conducting the one-way analysis variance ($p = .274$). Recall that the standard deviation squared is the variance. The group variances were 33.29, 16.65, and 16.65, respectively.

If we change the central tendency value to the median for the robust Brown-Forsythe test, the results are the same:

```
> levene.test(number, grp, location = "median")

modified robust Brown-Forsythe Levene-type test based on the absolute
 deviations from the median

data: number
Test Statistic = 1.5, p-value = 0.274
```

A researcher would report the results of one of these tests of equal variance when conducting *t* tests or analyses of variance. This informs the reader that you have met the assumption of equal group variances when testing for mean differences. Although research has shown that analysis of variance is robust to this violation of assumption, it is prudent to know that you are conducting a fair, unbiased test of mean differences when the equal variance assumption is met.

● TYPES OF SUMS OF SQUARES

This chapter briefly addressed some very important issues to consider when conducting analysis of variance, namely, differences in how the sums of squares are calculated in the different research designs (Types I, II, III sums of squares) and whether research designs were balanced (equal sample sizes) or unbalanced (unequal sample sizes due to missing data, attrition, etc.). These two issues surfaced when using the *aov()* and *lm()* functions in analysis of variance. The *aov()* function analyzes data that must have equal group sizes (balanced design) and calculates Type I sums of squares. The *lm()* function is preferred when analyzing data from an unbalanced design (unequal group sizes), and it calculates Type III sums of squares by default, with the *anova()* function printing the familiar analysis of variance summary table. We will learn more about the *lm()* function in Chapter 17 on multiple regression.

The different types of sums of squares (I, II, III) are calculated differently depending on the analytic approach used in testing different statistical hypotheses. A brief description of each is provided, where *A* and *B* represent factor or group variables:

Type I *SS*: Sequential calculation of sums of squares, first *A*, then *B*, then *AB* interaction (balanced design)

SS(*A*) for factor *A*

SS (*B*|*A*) for factor *B*—after factor *A* is removed

SS(*AB*|*B, A*) for interaction *AB*—after factors *B* and *A* are removed

Type II *SS*: Calculation of sums of squares when the *AB* interaction is not significant (balanced design)

SS(*A*|*B*) for factor *A*

SS(*B*|*A*) for factor *B*

Type III *SS*: Calculation of sums of squares when the *AB* interaction is significant (balanced or unbalanced design)

SS(*A*|*B, AB*) for factor *A*

SS (*B*|*A, AB*) for factor *B*

Note: If your research design is balanced and the factors are orthogonal (independent), then Types I, II, and III all give the same results.

TIP

✓ In repeated measures analysis of variance, make sure the degrees of freedom are correct.

✓ When testing interaction effects, use Type III sums of squares solutions.

A researcher can choose several approaches to analyze repeated measures data. In most cases, it is important to report an epsilon correction, Huynh-Feldt, Greenhouse-Geisser, Wilks's lambda, or Hotelling's trace. The *Anova(mod, idata, idesign)* function from the *car* package conveniently yields all of the relevant repeated measures information.

✓ Install *library(car)* to use the *Anova(mod, idata, idesign)* function.

?*Anova(mod, idata, idesign)* provides arguments for the function.

ACCESS R DATA SETS ●

There are several existing data sets in the *datasets* package for conducting statistical analyses. These can be listed by issuing the following R command:

```
> library(help = "datasets")
```

A dialog window will open and list many different types of data sets in the *base* package.

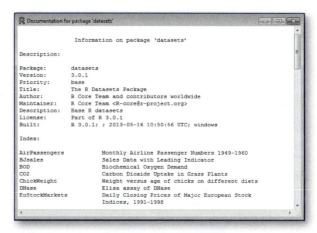

I selected the *mtcars* data set, which contains the Motor Trend Car Road Tests. The first action required is to use the *attach()* function to obtain this data set and the *print()* function to view the names of the variables and raw data in the file. These two R commands can be issued in the RGui window.

```
> attach(mtcars)
```

```
> print (mtcars)
```

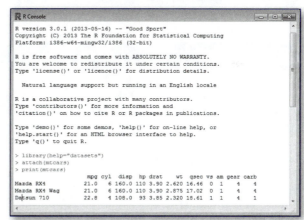

Once the data set is attached and you are familiar with the variables, many of the statistical functions in R can be performed. For example, the mean or average miles per gallon (mpg) is 20:

```
> mean(mpg)
[1] 20.09062
```

TIP

✓ Critical information on the R Data Import/Export menu is available in the R manual documentation at http://cran.r-project.org/doc/manuals/R-data.html#dir

✓ You can save data files in the R library to other statistical packages; for information, visit http://www.statmethods.net/input/exportingdata.html

(Continued)

(Continued)

✓ You can use the R command *write.table* to save space-separated, comma-separated, or tab-delimited files to the current directory in R, then open them using SPSS, SAS, and so on. For example,

```
> attach(mtcars)
> write.table(mtcars, "Rdata", sep = " ")
```

✓ You can access data files stored on the Internet by using the following R command:

```
> demo1 = read.csv("http://www.ats.ucla.edu/stat/data/demo1.csv")
> demo1
```

or

```
> dfilename = "http://personality-project.org/R/datasets/R.appendix1.data"
> dfilename = read.table(dfilename, header = T) #read the data into a table
> dfilename
```

SUMMARY

This chapter covered several research designs that use the *F* test. The *one-way analysis of variance* design uses an *F* test to determine if three or more group means differ. The *analysis of covariance* design uses an *F* test to determine if a covariate is statistically significant in affecting the dependent variable and whether any factor is significant after the adjustment to the error sums of squares. A *fixed factor analysis of variance* uses the *F* test to determine if an interaction between two factors is statistically significant, and if not, then it is used for interpreting the significance of the main effects. We also covered the use of the *F* test in *repeated measures analysis of variance*—first with a single measure repeated over time (birth rate) and then to test for group differences (male vs. female) in weight gain across time. The *F* test is a versatile statistic used in many research designs. The research designs can involve *experimental control* of extraneous variables that affect the dependent variable or *statistical control* using the analysis of covariance technique.

The chapter also described how to calculate the sums of squares (SS) to show how the total sums of squares (SS_T) is partitioned into explanatory factors (SS_B) and residual error (SS_E). This partitioning of the total sums of squares for the dependent variable was different depending on the research design. The degrees of freedom was also calculated differently based on the type of analysis conducted. These differences appeared in the different analysis of variance summary tables. We also learned that the *F* test only indicates that a statistically significant mean difference exists but does not indicate which group means are different. We need a post hoc test to further investigate which group means are different. The Tukey HSD was presented because of equal sample sizes or group sizes, and it parallels the *t*-test approach in testing the difference in group means. Finally, the five-step hypothesis-testing approach was followed to provide guidance on the steps a researcher would take when testing and interpreting the *F*-test results.

Several important concepts and points were made in this chapter. They are as follows:

- The one-way analysis of variance procedure is an extension of the independent *t* test for testing the differences in three or more sample means.
- The repeated measures analysis of variance procedure is an extension of the dependent *t* test for testing the differences in three or more sample means over time.
- The total variance of all scores is partitioned into the sum of squares between groups and the sum of squares within groups.
- The degrees of freedom for the sum of squares between groups is the number of groups minus 1.
- The degrees of freedom for the sum of squares within groups is the total sample size minus the number of groups.
- The *F* test is computed as a ratio of the mean square between to the mean square within.
- Analysis of variance summary tables neatly organize the between-group, within-group, and total sum of squared deviation scores, degrees of freedom, and mean of the squared values for the *F*-test results.
- A post hoc test determines which sample means are different between groups after conducting an analysis of variance procedure with a statistically significant *F* test.

EXERCISES

1. Compute an *F* test for the one-way analysis of variance data below. Show your work using R commands and the *aov()* function. Interpret your results using the *anova()* function to output the analysis of variance summary table. Do the average air temperatures differ by season?

Season	Data: Air Temperature
Fall	60, 65, 62, 64, 63
Spring	80, 85, 82, 84, 83
Summer	90, 95, 101, 99, 100

R Commands:

```
data = c(60,65,62,64,63,80,85,82,84,83,90,95,101,99,100)
season = rep(c("Fall","Spring","Summer"), c(5,5,5))
```

Output:

Interpretation:

2. Conduct a post hoc test using the *TukeyHSD()* function for the results in #1 given a 95% family-wide confidence level. Calculate the means for each season. Show the R commands and results. Interpret the post hoc mean comparisons for the three seasons.

R Commands:

Output:

Interpretation:

3. A colleague has challenged your statistical analysis of the air temperature data. She believes that you should have controlled for wind speed when testing for mean differences in seasonal air temperatures. She has provided you the additional wind speed data for conducting an analysis of covariance. Show your work using R commands and the *lm()* function. Interpret your results using the *anova()* function to output the analysis of variance summary table. Do the average air temperatures differ by season when controlling for wind speed?

R Commands:

```
data = c(60,65,62,64,63,80,85,82,84,83,90,95,101,99,100)
wind = c(10,15,20,15,18,25,15,20,30,25,15,30,40,30,35)
season = rep(c("Fall","Spring","Summer"), c(5,5,5))
```

Output:

Interpretation:

4. Use the *cor.test()* function to test whether the dependent variable (data) and the covariate (wind) are related in #3. Is there a statistically significant correlation between *data* and *wind*? Show the R commands and output, and interpret the results.

5. Using the $r = .77$ correlation between the dependent variable and the covariate, compute the adjusted means for the analysis of covariance in #3. Show the R commands. Compute the adjusted seasonal means, complete the comparison table, and interpret the results.

$$Y'_j = \bar{Y}_j - b_W(\bar{X}_k - \bar{X}).$$

R Commands:

Output:

Interpretation:

Comparison Table			
Season	N	Original Mean	Adjusted Mean
Fall	5		
Spring	5		
Summer	5		

6. Compute an *F* test for the fixed factor analysis of variance data below. Show your work using the R commands and *aov()* function. Interpret your results using the *anova()* function to output the analysis of variance summary table. Is there a statistically significant interaction between school type (high school vs. college) and country (the United States, Asia, Europe) in time (in hours) spent watching TV?

R Commands:

```
data = c(30,30,40,40,15,20,25,10,30,20,25,20)
country = rep(c("US","Asia","Europe"), c(4,4,4))
school = rep(c("H.S.","College"), c(2,2))
```

Output:

Interpretation:

7. Use the *print()* function with the argument *model.tables* to output the main effect and interaction means in #6. Use the *TukeyHSD()* function to compute the post hoc test for mean differences in the country main effect in #6. Show the R commands and output. Interpret the results.

R Commands:

Output:

Interpretation:

8. As a reviewer for a journal, you noticed that an article did not have all the values in the analysis of variance table. What are the missing values for a, b, and c in the table?

Analysis of Variance Summary Table

Source	Sum of Squares (SS)	Degrees of Freedom (df)	Mean Square(MS)	F
Between groups	500.00	3	b	7.50
Within groups	200.00	9	c	
Total	a	12		

a

b

c

9. Conduct a repeated measures analysis of variance using the *aov()* and *summary()* functions. The university enrollment from 2009 to 2011 for four universities is given below, with the data

reported in thousands, that is, 25,000 = 25. Show the R commands and output, and interpret the results. Have the enrollments increased over the time period from 2009 to 2011?

Data:

```
    id  year enroll
 1  1   2009   15
 2  1   2010   20
 3  1   2011   25
 4  2   2009   12
 5  2   2010   17
 6  2   2011   20
 7  3   2009   12
 8  3   2010   15
 9  3   2011   26
10  4   2009   10
11  4   2010   12
12  4   2011   14
```

R Commands:

```
enroll = c(15,20,25,12,17,20,12,15,26,10,12,14)
id = rep(c(1,2,3,4), c(3,3,3,3))
year = rep(c("2009","2010","2011"), c(1,1,1))
```

Output:

Interpretation:

TRUE OR FALSE QUESTIONS

T F a. The F test extends the t test from two groups to a test of mean differences in three or more groups.

T F b. An important assumption in computing the F test is the equality of group variances.

T F c. The *aov()* function can be used when conducting analysis of covariance.

T F d. The adjusted group means are computed using the correlation between the covariate variable and the dependent variable.

T F e. A fixed factor analysis of variance is conducted to test an interaction hypothesis.

T F f. Repeated measures data must be formatted differently for statistical analysis.

WEB RESOURCES

Chapter R script files are available at http://www.sagepub.com/schumacker

Analysis of Covariance Function R script file: chap14c.r

Blink Function R script file: chap14d2.r

F Density Plot Function R script file: chap14a.r

Fixed Factor Analysis of Variance Function R script file: chap14d1.r

Fixed Factor Repeated Measures Function R script file: chap14g.r

Interaction Plot Function R script file: chap14d4.r

One-Way Analysis of Variance Function R script file: chap14b1.r

One-Way Repeated Measures Function R script file: chap14e.r

Second Blink Function R script file: chap14d3.r

Second One-Way Repeated Measures Function R script file: chap14f.r

Tukey HSD Function R script file: chap14b2.r

## CHAPTER 15

CORRELATION TESTS
OF ASSOCIATION

I n 1869, Sir Francis Galton demonstrated that the mathematics scores of students at Cambridge University and the admissions exam scores at the Royal Military College were normally distributed. In 1889, Galton published *Natural Inheritance*, which summarized his work on correlation and regression, suggesting the idea for examining how two hereditary traits varied together (covariance). This effort resulted in the first use of the term *regression*, which he earlier had called reversion, implying the tendency for his measures to regress toward the mean or average.

Note: Galton was also interested in studying individual differences in heredity based on the work of his half cousin Charles Darwin and his travels to other countries, which led to his book on *Finger Prints* (Galton, 1892). He discovered that even as we get older, our fingerprints remain uniquely individual and the same, which culminated in a second book, *Fingerprint Directories* (Galton, 1895). You can read more about Galton at http://galton.org.

Karl (formerly Carl) Pearson in 1898, based on the suggestions made by Galton in *Natural Inheritance*, investigated the development of a statistical formula that would capture the relationship between two variables (Pearson, 1938). During this time, he was acutely aware of the work by Sir Ronald Fisher because of his earlier involvement with William Gossett Jr. on small-sample distributions related to beer quality and production. Pearson, however, was interested in large populations, random samples, and making inferences in the field of heredity, whereas Fisher was interested in the design of experiments, small samples, and making cause-and-effect conclusions in the field of agriculture.

Pearson and Fisher forged two very different approaches to the statistical analysis of data that remain in effect today: one based on *inference* (correlation, regression) and the other on *cause and effect* (experimental design). We have scholars in many academic disciplines that embrace the experimental design using random assignment of subjects to groups (treatment vs. control), experimental control of variables, and smaller samples in casual comparative designs or laboratory settings to achieve results that indicate cause-and-effect conclusions. In contrast, many scholars in other academic disciplines embrace correlation research from the perspective that infinitely large populations exist, requiring random sampling of subjects, multiple measured or observed variables, and sample statistics as estimates that permit making an inference from sample statistics to the corresponding population parameters. Extraneous variables that might affect the study results can be controlled in an experimental design by random selection and random assignment of subjects to groups. In correlation research, the control of extraneous variables that might affect the study results is accomplished by computing a semipartial or partial correlation (see Chapter 17). Scholars also implemented statistical control using the analysis of covariance method when extraneous variables affected the variation in the dependent variable. Analysis of covariance included both the experimental and the correlation method by using the quasi-experimental design with no random assignment of subjects and using correlation to statistically control for covariates (extraneous variables).

The experimental design and correlation methods for statistical analysis of data were differentiated in statistics books in the past by separate chapters on analysis of variance and correlation/regression. Today, textbooks on multiple regression are popular because they extend the analysis-of-variance approach to data analysis to other general linear model types (logistic regression, log-linear regression, etc.). Gosset was instrumental in influencing the development of the F test by Fisher and his subsequent use of many different types of experimental designs. Pearson with his Pearson correlation coefficient went on to influence the development of many correlation-based statistical methods, including multiple regression and factor analysis, to name a few, which are correlation-based statistical approaches. Today, approaches based on experimental design with analysis of variance and correlation with multiple regression have merged into what is called the *general linear model*.

● PEARSON R

The Pearson r coefficient formula embraced the idea of how to determine the degree to which two things went together—that is, how two things varied together. The concept was simple enough in principle: Take measurements on two variables, order the measurements of the two variables, and then determine if one set of measurements increased along with the second set of measurements. In some cases, the measurements of one variable might decrease, while the other increased. The basic assumption Pearson made was that the measurements needed to be linear and continuous. He quickly determined that how two things covary divided by how they individually vary would yield a statistic that was bounded by +1 and −1 depending on the relation of the two measurements. The conceptual formula he developed, which took into account the covariance between two variables divided by the square root of the variance of the two variables, was defined as follows (the square root in the denominator provides a standardized solution):

$$\text{Pearson } r = \frac{\text{Covariance } XY}{\sqrt{(\text{Var } X)(\text{Var } Y)}}.$$

In 1927, after L. L. Thurstone developed the concept of a **standard score** (z score) as the deviation of a raw score from the mean divided by the standard deviation, the Pearson correlation formula was further defined as the average product of standard scores:

$$\text{Pearson } r = \frac{\sum z_x z_y}{N}.$$

An example of the relationship between two continuous variables will better illustrate how the bivariate (two variable) relationship is established. A typical research question for a group of students can be stated as "Is there a significant relationship between the amount of time spent reading and the time spent watching television?" The data for these two linear continuous variables measured in hours are ordered by time spent reading (see Table 15.1).

A computational version of the correlation formula makes the calculation easier and uses the following summary values:

$$\sum Y = 34$$

$$\sum Y^2 = 140$$

$$\sum X = 745$$

$$\sum X^2 = 57225$$

$$\sum XY = 2340.$$

The computational Pearson correlation coefficient formula is as follows:

$$\text{Pearson } r = \frac{SP}{\sqrt{SS_x SS_y}}.$$

Table 15.1 Pearson r Data

Time Spent Reading (Y) (hr)	Time Spent Watching TV (X) (hr)
1	90
2	95
2	85
2	80
3	75
4	70
4	75
5	60
5	65
6	50

The expression SP is defined as the sum of the cross products for X and Y, which captures how two variables covary (positively or negatively). The expression SS_x is the sum of squares of X, which captures the deviations of each X score from the mean of X. The expression SS_y is the sum of squares of Y, which captures the deviations of each Y score from the mean of Y. These values are computed for each expression in the correlation coefficient formula as follows:

$$SP = \sum XY - \frac{(\sum X)(\sum Y)}{N} - 2340 - \frac{(745)(34)}{10} = -193.$$

$$SS_x = \sum X^2 - \frac{(\sum X^2)}{N} = 57225 - \frac{(745)^2}{10} = 1722.5.$$

$$SS_y = \sum Y^2 - \frac{\left(\sum Y^2\right)}{N} = 140 - \frac{(34)^2}{10} = 24.4.$$

These values are substituted in the Pearson correlation coefficient formula to yield the following:

$$\text{Pearson } r = \frac{SP}{\sqrt{SS_x SS_y}} = \frac{-193}{\sqrt{1722.5(24.4)}} = \frac{-193}{205} = -.94.$$

The value $r = -.94$ indicates a negative relation between the two variables, implying that as the amount of study time spent reading increases, the amount of time watching television decreases. The sign of the correlation coefficient indicates the direction of the correlation—that is, a positive relationship is present when the two sets of scores increase together. A negative direction or negative relationship would have a minus sign in front of the r coefficient, which would indicate that as one set of scores increases, the other set of scores decreases. The SP in the numerator of the formula determines if the direction of the correlation is positive or negative—that is, covariance between two variables can be positive or negative in direction. The correlation coefficient also indicates the *magnitude* of the relationship between two variables. If the r coefficient is approaching ±1.0, then a stronger relationship exists. A correlation coefficient of −1.0 would indicate a perfect negative relationship, which indicates that as time spent reading increased, the time spent watching television decreased. In this example, there is a negative relation, indicating that as time spent reading increased, a person watched less television. This makes practical sense, but now we have a way to test our theory.

● Correlation and Levels of Measurement

The Pearson r was developed by Pearson to indicate how two linear continuous variables covary. However, not all variables are measured as continuous variables. In fact, not long after Pearson formulated his coefficient, scholars were debating the idea of measurement, not only in the physical sciences (physics, genetics, astronomy) but also in the emerging social sciences (psychology, sociology). An operational theory of measurement was undertaken in reaction to the conclusions of a committee established in 1932 by the British Association for the Advancement of Science, which investigated the possibility of genuine scientific measurement in the psychological and behavioral sciences. This committee, which became known as the Ferguson Committee, published its final report (Ferguson et al., 1940), which criticized Stanley Smith Stevens's use of his *Sone* scale of loudness based on it lacking permissible mathematical operations (Stevens & Hallowell, 1938). Stevens's reaction to their findings was to publish an article outlining eight psychosocial properties of scale—basically stating that measurement is defined as the assignment of numbers to objects and events according to rules (Stevens, 1946, p. 677). Stevens[1] is referenced in many statistics books as formulating the measurement properties of scale; however, only four such properties are typically listed. They are outlined in Table 15.2.

Table 15.2   Levels of Variable Measurement

Variable Measurement Scale	Characteristic of Scale	Variable Examples
Nominal	Unique, mutually exclusive categories	Country, gender, automobile manufacturer
Ordinal	Unique, mutually exclusive ordered categories	High school class rank, countries' gross national product, Olympic races
Interval	Continuous data with an arbitrary zero point	Test scores (ACT, SAT), survey data
Ratio	Continuous data with a true zero point	Temperature, height, weight, age, income

The statistics community recognized that the Pearson r coefficient was for computing the correlation between two linear continuous variables. Consequently, other scholars over the years have developed different correlation formula for the relations among variables with different measurement scales. The Phi coefficient was developed for correlating two variables that are measured at the nominal measurement scale; the point biserial was developed for correlating two variables, one dichotomous and the other continuous; and the Spearman coefficient was developed for correlating two variables measured at the ordinal measurement scale. The Kendall tau correlation coefficient was created to correlate a nominal variable with an ordinal variable. Many other types of correlations have been developed and used over the years. Unfortunately, most statistical packages do not have a pull-down menu for calculating these different types of correlation coefficients based on levels of measurement of observed variables. I have summarized many of the correlation coefficient types created for the different levels of variable measurement in Table 15.3.

Table 15.3   Correlation Type by Levels of Measurement

	Nominal	Ordinal	Interval/Ratio
Nominal	Phi coefficient, contingency coefficient, tetrachoric coefficient		Point biserial/biserial
Ordinal	Rank biserial	Spearman coefficient, Kendall tau, gamma polychoric coefficient	
Interval/ratio	Point-biserial coefficient, biserial coefficient, eta coefficient	Polyserial coefficient	Pearson coefficient

Table 15.4	Explanation of Correlation Types by Level of Measurement

Correlation Coefficient	Level of Measurement
Biserial	One variable interval, one variable artificial[a]
Polyserial	One variable interval, one variable ordinal with underlying continuity[b]
Tetrachoric	Both variables dichotomous (one nominal and one artificial)
Polychoric	Both variables ordinal with underlying continuities

a. "Artificial" refers to recoding the variable values into a dichotomy.

b. "Continuity" refers to an underlying continuous measurement scale for dichotomous or ordinal data.

Some correlation coefficients use a recoded variable so that the level of measurement is considered artificial or assume an underlying continuity for the variable measurement scale in the presence of dichotomous or ordinal data. This is further explained in Table 15.4.

● R *COR.TEST()* FUNCTION

The *stats* package has a *cor.test()* function, which performs a test of significance for the Pearson, Kendall, or Spearman correlation coefficients. The basic arguments for this function can be obtained by specifying *?cor.test* in the R Console window, which opens an Internet window with a description of the function and arguments.

```
> ?cor.test()

cor.test (x, y)
alternative = c("two.sided","less","greater")
method = c("pearson","kendall","spearman")
exact = NULL, conf.level = 0.95, continuity = FALSE, ...
```

Pearson Correlation

We compute the Pearson correlation coefficient for the reading time and television time using the *Pearson function* in the script file (chap15a.r), where you only have to enter the data vectors, *read* and *tv*, prior to running the function.

```
> read = c(1,2,2,2,3,4,4,5,5,6)
> tv = c(90,95,85,80,75,70,75,60,65,50)
> chap15a(tv, read)
```

The output shows the Pearson correlation and a plot of the *read* and *tv* values:

```
Pearson's product-moment correlation

data: tv and read
t = -7.8957, df = 8, p-value = 4.799e-05

alternative hypothesis: true correlation is not equal to 0
95 percent confidence interval:
-0.9863776 -0.7655890
sample estimates:
cor
-0.9414186
```

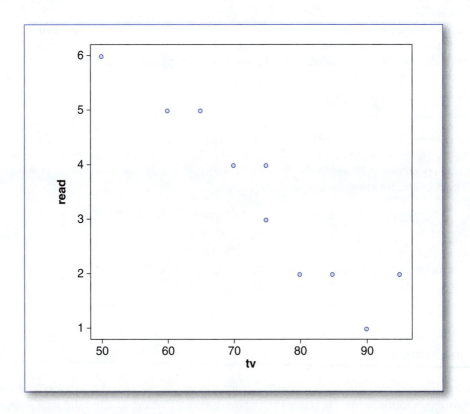

The Pearson correlation coefficient value is −.94, which matches our hand calculations. The plot of the *read* and *tv* values visually shows the negative association—that is, as *read* increases, *tv* decreases.

Note: The *set.seed()* function was used so that these results will be replicated each time.

The significance of *r* is tested in the function using a *t test*. The *r* sampling distribution with $n - 1$ degrees of freedom also has a *t* sampling distribution with $n - 2$ degrees of freedom. The *t* test for the correlation of exam score and time spent studying would be computed as follows:

$$t = r\sqrt{\frac{n-2}{1-r^2}} = -.94\sqrt{\frac{10-2}{1-(-.94)^2}} = -.94(8.387) = -7.89.$$

$t = -7.89$ with $df = 10 - 2 = 8$ is statistically significant beyond the .05 level, and $p = .00047$ (4.799e– 05). The 95% confidence interval (−.986, −.765) suggests that we could obtain a Pearson correlation between these two values if another sample of data were collected and analyzed.

We have the option of using Table 3 (Appendix A), which gives the *r* values in the sampling distribution for different degrees of freedom, the alpha (α) level, and one or two-tailed test, or we can use the *t* values for the sampling distributions in Table 2 (Appendix A) with $n - 2$ degrees of freedom. Given that Table 3 is provided, the region of rejection for the null hypothesis is readily available; however, the R function will only provide a *t* test for the correlation coefficient. Table 3 would indicate a region of rejection as follows: $p > -.602$, for our sample data given a two-tailed test, $\alpha = .05$, $df = n - 1 = 9$. Table 2 would indicate a region of rejection as follows: $t > -2.306$, for the sample data given a two-tailed test, $\alpha = .05$, but $df = n - 2 = 8$. In both cases, the sample $r = -.94$ is greater than the tabled $r = -.602$, and the sample $t = -7.89$ is greater than the tabled $t = -2.306$.

The power for the correlation coefficient is calculated using the *pwr.r.test()* function loaded by *library(pwr)*. The arguments for the power function are as follows:

```
> library(pwr)
> ?pwr.r.test

pwr.r.test(n = NULL, r = NULL, sig.level = 0.05, power = NULL,
alternative = c("two.sided","less","greater"))
```

Arguments

N	Number of observations
R	Linear correlation coefficient
sig.level	Significance level (Type I error probability)
Power	Power of test (1 minus Type II error probability)
Alternative	a character string specifying the alternative hypothesis, must be one of "two.sided" (default), "greater" or "less"

For the Pearson correlation coefficient sample estimate, the arguments would be as follows: $n = 10$ (pairs of scores), $r = .94$ (Pearson correlation), sig.level = .05 (TYPE I error), power = NULL (value to be estimated, and alternative = "greater" (one-tailed test)). The R commands are as follows:

```
> library(pwr)
> options(scipen = 999)
> pwr.r.test(n = 10, r = .94, sig.level = 0.05, power = NULL, alternative = "greater")

approximate correlation power calculation (arctangh transformation)

n = 10
r = 0.94
sig.level = 0.05
power = 0.9987454
alternative = greater
```

Since power = .99, we have sufficient sample size and protection against a Type II error for the statistical significance of the Pearson correlation coefficient.

Note: The *pwr()* function only inputs a positive value for the *r* correlation value. If you insert the negative correlation coefficient, the result is 1 − power. Also, you must load the *pwr* package and use the *options(scipen = 999)* function—otherwise scientific notation is reported.

Spearman Correlation

The Spearman correlation is computed when one or both variables are on the ordinal scale of measurement. The Spearman correlation coefficient is considered a *nonparametric* statistic. The Spearman correlation coefficient is questionable when a large number of the ranks are tied—that is, they have the same rank on both variables. Each variable must have N ranks that range from 1 to N. The formula is as follows:

$$r_s = 1 - \frac{6\Sigma d_i^2}{N^3 - N},$$

where d_i represents the difference in the two ranks assigned to the *i*th individual. An example using the following data will provide hand calculations.

X_i	Y_i	d_i	d_i^2
1	3	−2	4
2	1	1	1
3	4	−1	1
4	2	2	4
5	5	0	0

$$r_s = 1 - \frac{6(10)}{125 - 5} = .50.$$

I entered the rank data in the *cor.test()* function and specified the Spearman method.

```
> X = c(1,2,3,4,5)
> Y = c(3,1,4,2,5)
> cor.test(X, Y, method = "spearman")
```

Results indicate that the correlation of the X and Y ranks ($r_s = .50$) is not statistically significant ($\rho = .5$, $p = .45$).

```
Spearman's rank correlation rho

data: X and Y
S = 10, p-value = 0.45

alternative hypothesis: true rho is not equal to 0
sample estimates:
rho
0.5
```

Kendall tau Correlation

The Kendall correlation coefficient is an alternative to the Spearman rank correlation coefficient. The computations for this coefficient, however, determine the number of consistent ranks minus the number of discrepancies in the paired ranks, S. The optimum value of S, that is, the value when perfect correspondence (correlation) exists, is computed as $1/2N(N-1)$. The ratio of these two values is the Kendall tau (τ) correlation coefficient:

$$\tau = \frac{S}{\frac{1}{2}N(N-1)} = \frac{8}{20} = .40.$$

The *cor.test()* function can be used to easily compute the Kendall correlation coefficient value:

```
> X = c(1,2,3,4,5)
> Y = c(3,1,4,2,5)
> cor.test(X, Y, method = "kendall")

Kendall's rank correlation tau

data: X and Y
T = 7, p-value = 0.4833

alternative hypothesis: true tau is not equal to 0
sample estimates:
tau
0.4
```

This correlation value is lower than the Spearman correlation coefficient for the same data (.50 vs. .40). The Kendall tau correlation coefficient, however, has the advantage of being a partial correlation coefficient for rank data. A third variable ranking can therefore be controlled when computing the bivariate Kendall correlation.

● PHI CORRELATION

The Phi coefficient correlation (Φ) is a measure of the association between two nominal variables, for example, gender (1 = *boy*, 2 = *girl*) and whether the students smoked cigarettes or not (1 = *yes*, 2 = *no*).

The following data set indicates gender and whether the students smoked cigarettes or not:

Gender	Do You Smoke Cigarettes?
Boy	Yes
Boy	Yes
Boy	Yes
Boy	Yes
Boy	Yes
Boy	Yes
Boy	Yes
Boy	No
Boy	No
Boy	No
Girl	Yes
Girl	Yes
Girl	Yes
Girl	Yes
Girl	Yes
Girl	No
Girl	No
Girl	No
Girl	No
Girl	No

R *assocstats()* Function

The *vcd* package has the *assocstats()* function, which calculates the Phi correlation coefficient. Once the vcd package has been installed and loaded, the Phi correlation coefficient can be computed using the *assocstats()* function; use *?assocstats()* to obtain arguments and documentation.

```
> install.packages("vcd")
> library(vcd)
```

A matrix must be used as the input data format. The matrix, *study*, is in the form of a 2 × 2 matrix for input into the function, where the values indicate the frequency counts for a row-by-column table. The matrix arguments are read in the cell frequencies by row: *byrow = TRUE*. The cell frequency counts must sum to the total pairs of numbers, $N = 20$ in this case.

```
> study = matrix(c(7,3,5,5), nrow =
2, ncol = 2, byrow = TRUE, dimnames =
list(c("boy","girl"), c("yes","no")))
> study
> assocstats(study)
```

The results show a contingency table with the number in each cell followed by several measures of association. For our purposes, we report the Phi coefficient:

```
      yes no
boy   7 3
girl  5 5

X^2 df P(> X^2)
Likelihood Ratio 0.84024 1 0.35933
Pearson          0.83333 1 0.36131

Phi-Coefficient: 0.204
Contingency Coeff.: 0.2
Cramer's V: 0.204
```

The results show the cell frequencies for *gender* by *smoking* in the form of a 2 × 2 table, which matches up with our data. The Pearson chi-square test indicates that $\chi^2 = 0.83$ and $p = .36$, which also implies that the Phi correlation coefficient is nonsignificant. Ironically, no p values are reported for the measures of association (Phi, contingency coefficient, Cramer's *V*)—which are not necessary, as explained next.

Phi and Chi-Square Formula

In most software packages (SPSS, SAS), the Phi correlation coefficient is output when running a chi-square test of independence for two crosstab variables. The computational relation is expressed as

$$\chi^2 = N\varphi^2$$

and

$$\varphi = \sqrt{\frac{\chi^2}{N}}.$$

In our results, the Pearson chi-square value (0.83) and Phi coefficient (.204) are both reported:

$$\chi^2 = N\varphi^2 = 20(.204)^2 = 0.83$$

and

$$\varphi = \sqrt{\frac{\chi^2}{N}} = \sqrt{\frac{.83}{20}} = .204.$$

The ability to convert the Phi correlation coefficient into a chi-square statistic negates the necessity of having a separate critical table of Phi correlation coefficients for testing statistical significance.

● POINT-BISERIAL/BISERIAL CORRELATION

The point-biserial correlation is a measure of association between a dichotomous variable and a continuous variable. The dichotomous variable can be treated as a factor (group membership) or a numeric vector in computing a point-biserial correlation. When the dichotomous variable is treated as a factor (group), it is reported in the chi-square analysis as a measure of association. When the dichotomous variable is treated as a numeric vector, the point-biserial and biserial correlations are reported in measurement software as an index of item discrimination. The biserial correlation assumes that the dichotomous numeric vector is normally distributed. This assumption is what distinguishes it from the point-biserial correlation.

ltm Package

The ltm package contains the *biserial.cor()* function for computing either the point-biserial or the biserial correlation. You will need to load the ltm package prior to using the *biserial.cor()* function.

```
> install.packages("ltm")
> library(ltm)
```

biserial.cor() Function

The *biserial.cor()* function and required arguments can be obtained using the following R command after installing the ltm package. It is important to examine what information and type must be supplied in a function. You should notice that x is a data vector that contains the continuous variable and y is a data vector that contains the dichotomous variable. Also, the *use* argument determines how missing data are treated in the computation of the correlation coefficient. Finally, the *level* argument is required to specify whether the dichotomous variable should be treated as a group (factor) or a numeric variable. The R command to obtain these arguments is

```
> ?biserial.cor()
```

Description

```
Computes the point-biserial correlation between a dichotomous and a continuous variable.
```

Usage

```
biserial.cor(x, y, use = c("all.obs","complete.obs"), level = 1)
```

Arguments

x	a numeric vector representing the continuous variable.
y	a factor or a numeric vector (that will be converted to a factor) representing the dichotomous variable.
use	If use is "all.obs", then the presence of missing observations will produce an error. If use is "complete.obs" then missing values are handled by casewise deletion.
level	which level of y to use.

A simple data set example will illustrate the computation of the point-biserial correlation. Notice that y represents the dichotomous variable and x indicates the continuous variable in the argument section of the function. The dichotomous variable, y, represents whether a student got a question right (1) or wrong (0). The continuous variable, x, represents the student's test scores. This point-biserial correlation is normally output in measurement software as a measure of item discrimination. This would involve correlating each item's dichotomous responses (0,1) with the vector of test scores, so we want to treat the dichotomous variable as a numeric vector.

```
> y = c(0,1,1,0,1,1,0,1,1,1)
> x = c(55,80,87,60,77,82,66,90,95)
> biserial.cor(x, y, level = 2)
[1] 0.4240984
```

You will get either a negative point-biserial correlation (level = 1) or a positive point-biserial correlation (level = 2) depending on whether the y variable is designated as a factor or a numeric vector. A numeric vector is specified (level = 2), which indicates a positive item discrimination. If you examine the relationship between the 0/1 item responses and the test scores, you would see that students with higher scores got the question correct, hence a positive item discrimination. A biserial correlation will also use a dichotomous and a continuous variable; however, it assumes that the dichotomous variable is normally distributed. This assumption is the basic difference between a point-biserial correlation coefficient and a biserial correlation coefficient.

Summary

The *cor.test()* function only computes the Pearson, Spearman, and Kendall tau correlation coefficients, so other functions or hand calculations are needed to compute the other correlation types in Tables 15.3 and 15.4. The ltm package includes some of these other correlation types, for example, the *biserial.cor()* function. The types of correlation coefficients that were created for the different combinations of variable measurement scale demonstrate the interest statisticians took in the bivariate correlation of variables. In turn, these correlations have been used in specific applications of psychometric or statistical analysis. For example, the *point-biserial* correlation is used to establish item discrimination in the field of test and measurement by correlating each item response (nominal: 0 = *incorrect*, 1 = *correct*) to the total test score (interval: continuous data with an arbitrary zero point). The Phi correlation is reported as a measure of association along with the chi-square statistic when testing the independence of two variables (gender [male, female] vs. country [United States, Canada]), or it is used in the correlation of two test items that are dichotomously scored 1 = *correct* and 0 = *incorrect*. Measurement software usually computes these two types of correlations, but many statistical software packages report these in the crosstab or chi-square analysis section.

● FACTORS AFFECTING THE PEARSON CORRELATION

The Pearson correlation coefficient is the most commonly used type of correlation in statistics. We will be using this correlation coefficient in the next chapter, and therefore, we will explore the assumptions or factors that affect the Pearson correlation coefficient. The level of variable measurement was just one factor, and it formed the basis for developing the other correlation coefficients. The other factors that also affect the value of the Pearson r coefficient are listed below:

Factors Affecting the Pearson Correlation Coefficient

1. Level of variable measurement

2. Nonlinear data

3. Missing data

4. Range of data values

5. Sampling effect

6. Outliers

The easiest way to understand how the Pearson r is affected by these factors would be to calculate the Pearson correlation coefficient given the data for each of these situations. The following examples of data begin with a *Complete Data* set that is linear and continuous, which meets the assumptions of the Pearson r correlation. The other data sets do not meet the assumptions of the Pearson r coefficient, so the r values should be different. How do these factors affect the Pearson r coefficient value? The Pearson correlation for the complete data is $r_{yx} = .782$. The Pearson correlation for nonlinear data is $r_{yx} = 0$, which indicates no relationship when the data are nonlinear. When missing data are present, $r_{yx} = .659$, which is less than $r_{yx} = .782$. We would therefore expect the missing data to reduce the correlation coefficient. When the range of the data values is restricted, for example, using scales for questions on a survey questionnaire that range from 1 to 5, the correlation coefficient would be $r_{yx} = 0$. If one is not taking a representative random sample from the population, $r_{yx} = -1.00$, which is in the opposite direction of the Pearson correlation coefficient in the complete data set. Outliers, or a single extreme score in a data set, could also dramatically change the correlation to $r_{yx} = -.189$. It becomes very clear that a researcher should take into consideration these factors when gathering data for their research studies. Failure to do so can have a dramatic effect on the Pearson correlation coefficient value and interpretation, and thus the statistical analysis methods that use correlation.

Table 15.6   Sample Data Sets for the Pearson Correlation

Complete Data		Non-Linear data		Missing Data	
Y	X	Y	X	Y	X
8.00	6.00	1.00	1.00	8.00	--
7.00	5.00	2.00	2.00	7.00	5.00
8.00	4.00	3.00	3.00	8.00	--
5.00	2.00	4.00	4.00	5.00	2.00
4.00	3.00	5.00	5.00	4.00	3.00
5.00	2.00	6.00	5.00	5.00	2.00
3.00	3.00	7.00	4.00	3.00	3.00
5.00	4.00	8.00	3.00	5.00	--
3.00	1.00	9.00	2.00	3.00	1.00
2.00	2.00	10.00	1.00	2.00	2.00
$r_{yx} = .782$		$r_{yx} = 0$		$r_{yx} = .659$	

Range of data values		Sampling effect		Outliers	
Y	X	Y	X	Y	X
3.00	1.00	8.00	3.00	8.00	6.00
3.00	2.00	9.00	2.00	7.00	5.00
4.00	3.00	10.00	1.00	8.00	4.00
4.00	4.00			5.00	2.00
5.00	1.00			4.00	3.00
5.00	2.00			5.00	2.00
6.00	3.00			3.00	3.00
6.00	4.00			5.00	4.00
7.00	1.00			3.00	1.00
7.00	2.00			52.00	2.00
$r_{yx} = 0$		$r_{yx} = -1.00$		$r_{yx} = -.189$	

● PEARSON *R* IN STATISTICS

The Pearson correlation coefficient has become very useful in the field of statistics. We can test the significance of the Pearson *r* because its sampling distribution permits the determination of the *r* value that occurs at a given probability area under its sampling distribution. Table 3 in Appendix A provides the *r* values for given degrees of freedom, the one or two-tailed test, and a few probability levels for the different sampling distributions. We can also use the Pearson *r* correlation to determine the amount of variance explained, which is similar to what we have learned in analysis of variance. Since the Pearson correlation indicates how two variables vary together, we can also graph the relationship between the data points in a scatterplot to visually see the trend of the relationship. This also demonstrates that we can use the Pearson correlation coefficient in prediction—that is, to predict one variable (Y) from our knowledge of another (X), which is discussed in the next chapter. The three uses for the Pearson correlation coefficient therefore are as follows:

1. Test for significance

2. Explanation (variance explained)

3. Prediction

Test of Significance

To test the significance of the Pearson correlation coefficient, we use our standard five-step hypothesis-testing approach:

Step 1. State the null and alternative hypothesis using the population parameters.

H_0: $\rho = 0$ (no correlation)

H_A: $\rho \neq 0$ (correlation exists)

Step 2. Choose the appropriate statistic, and state the sample size obtained.

Pearson correlation coefficient for continuous variables

Sample size, $N = 10$

Step 3. State the level of significance, direction of the alternative hypothesis, and region of rejection.

Level of significance (α) = .05

Alternative hypothesis: nondirectional (two-tailed test)

For $N = 10$, $df = N - 1 = 9$

R: $r_{tabled} > -.602$

Step 4. Collect data, and calculate the sample correlation statistic.

Continuous variables: Time spent reading and time spend watching TV, $N = 10$ pairs of data

$r = -.94$

Step 5. Test the statistical hypothesis, and interpret the results.

Since the computed $r = -.94$ is greater than the tabled $r = -.602$ at the .05 level of significance for a two-tailed test, reject the null hypothesis, and accept the alternative hypothesis. There is a statistically significant negative relationship between the amount of time spent reading and time spent watching TV.

Explanation

The second approach to interpreting the Pearson correlation coefficient is to square the sample correlation value. The r^2 value is $(-.94)^2 = .88$. This implies that 88% of the variability in time spent reading is accounted for by knowledge of how much time a person spent watching TV. This also implies that 12% of the variability in time spend reading is due to other variable relationships or unexplained variance. The amount of variance explained (88%) and the amount of variance unexplained (12%) always adds up to 100%.

The average number of hours spent reading was 3.4, with a standard deviation of 1.639. The average number of hours spent watching TV was 74.5, with a standard deviation of 13.83. The interpretation of the amount of variance explained is linked to the variance of the time spent reading (Y), hence $S_Y^2 = (1.639)^2 = 2.686$. We would state that 88% of 2.686 is the explained variability $\left(S_{explained}^2 = 2.63\right)$ and 12% of 2.686 is the unexplained variability $\left(S_{unexplained}^2 = 0.056\right)$, given the knowledge of how much time a student spent watching TV. These two variances, explained (2.63) and unexplained (0.056), should add up to the total variance (2.686) in time spent reading.

We can also depict this relationship using a *Venn* or *Ballentine* diagram.

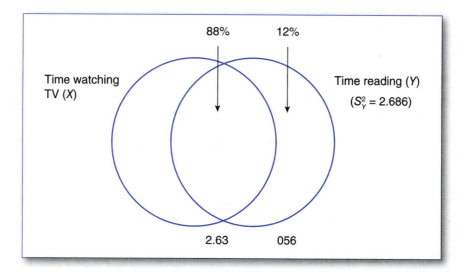

Prediction

The third approach to interpreting the correlation coefficient obtained from sample data is to graph the data points of the two variables. The scatterplot is used for this purpose. We draw a y-axis for the time spent reading and an x-axis for the amount of time spent watching TV. We label and scale these two axes to provide a grid such that the pairs of data points can be graphed. A visual look at the trend of the pairs of data points helps in interpreting whether a positive or negative direction exists for the correlation coefficient. Scatterplots can display an upward trend (positive relationship), a downward trend (negative relationship), or a curvilinear trend (one half is positive and the other half negative). If a curvilinear relationship exists, one half cancels the other half out, so the correlation coefficient would be 0 and the interpretation of the correlation coefficient meaningless. This is why Pearson made the assumption of linear data. A scatterplot of the data points visually reveals the negative downward trend expected from $r = -.94$.

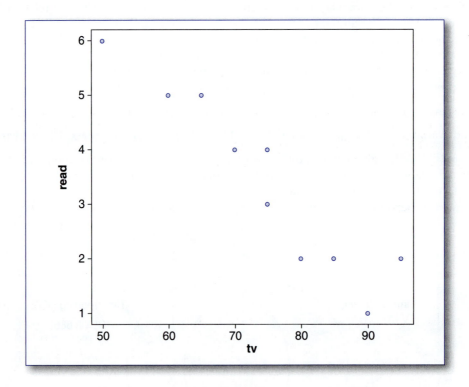

The Pearson correlation coefficient in determining the linear relationship between two continuous variables provides both a measure of the strength of the relationship as well as the direction of the relationship. In our example, the time spent reading was negatively related to the time spent watching TV. The strength of the relationship was indicated by a value close to -1.0 and the direction of the relationship by the negative sign. We are also able to explain the variability in the time spent reading by squaring the correlation coefficient. In other words, why didn't all the people have the same amount of time spent reading? Well, because they had different amounts of time spent watching TV. This association can be presented in a diagram and depicted as a percentage of the variance of the exam scores that can be explained. A scatterplot is the best visual aid to understanding the trend in the pairs of scores with regard to both magnitude and direction.

The correlation approach assumes that both the X and the Y variables are random and have a distribution known as the bivariate normal distribution. In the bivariate normal distribution, for any given X value the Y values have a normal distribution in which the mean and the standard deviation depend on the value of X and the strength of the relationship between X and Y. The strength of the relationship between X and Y is measured by a population parameter ρ

(pronounced "rho"), which can range from −1 through 1. If ρ = 0, there is either no relationship between *X* and *Y* or a curvilinear relationship that the Pearson correlation coefficient doesn't detect. If ρ = 1, there is a perfect *positive* linear relationship between the two variables, and if ρ = −1, there is a perfect *negative* linear relationship between the variables. A value of ρ close to 0 indicates a weak relationship (assuming linear data), and a value close to either +1 or −1 indicates a strong relationship. Consequently, *r* = −.90 is a stronger relationship than *r* = +.50 for the same sample size.

> **TIP**
>
> Pearson correlation values form an ordinal scale, so we do not compare the distances between two correlation values. For example, if a correlation of *r* = +.50 was obtained in one sample and a correlation of *r* = +.60 in a second sample, you *would not* indicate that the second correlation was .10 higher than the first.

● CORRELATION FUNCTION

The *correlation function* in the script file (chap15b.r) uses the bivariate normal distribution to specify the value of rho (ρ) in the population. The function selects values for *X* at random from a normal distribution with a mean of 10 and a standard deviation of 3. Values for *Y* are selected at random from a normal distribution with a mean of 5 and a standard deviation of 1, given the population rho value specified and the *X* distribution of scores. The function will repeat to obtain 20 pairs of *X*,*Y* scores; calculate Pearson *r*; and then output a scatterplot. By varying rho in the program, different scatterplots of data will be produced, which arise because rho has different values in the population. You only need to enter the population correlation value, rho, and the sample size prior to running the function.

```
> rho = .60
> sampleSize = 20
> chap15b(rho, sampleSize)
```

Note: I used the *set.seed()* function, so the results will be replicated each time. Remove the function or comment it out (# symbol) to obtain different results.

The results report the *t*-test value for the Pearson *r*, the confidence interval, and the sample Pearson *r* value. The graph shows the scatterplot of the pairs of scores.

```
Program Output

Pearson's product-moment correlation

data: sampleX and sampleY
t = 3.2182, df = 18, p-value = 0.004767
```

```
alternative hypothesis: true correlation is not equal to 0

95 percent confidence interval:
0.2209080 0.8259742

sample estimates:
cor
0.6043498
```

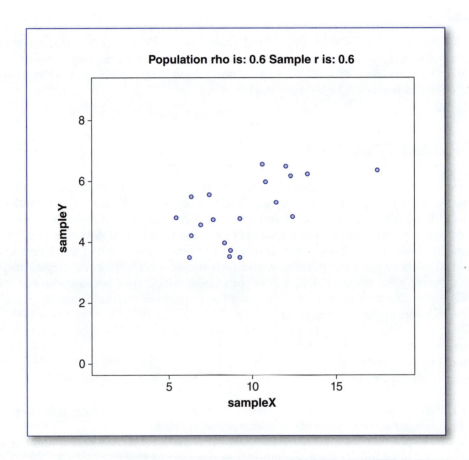

The Pearson correlation coefficient is statistically significant at the .05 level based on the t test ($t = 3.2182$, $df = 18$, $p = .004767$). We also know that the Pearson correlation coefficient could range from $r = 0.2340480$ to $r = 0.8303275$ in another sample of data at the 95% confidence level. However, since we know the population correlation, $\rho = .60$, our sample correlation estimate, $r = .60$, is a good sample statistic estimate of the population parameter. In actual practice, we would not know the population correlation rho, so we must rely on the test of statistical significance and confidence interval at a specified alpha level for a meaningful interpretation of the sample correlation estimate.

TIP

✓ You can use Table 3 (Appendix A) to determine if $r = .61$ is statistically significant for $df = n - 1 = 19$, $\alpha = .05$, two-tailed test. Region of rejection: $p > .433$.

✓ You can use Table 2 (Appendix A) to determine if $t = 3.29$ is statistically significant for $df = n - 2 = 18$, $\alpha = .05$, two-tailed test. Region of rejection: $t > 2.101$.

SUMMARY

Pearson's correlation coefficient was one of the most important discoveries in the field of statistics because numerous other statistical techniques such as multiple regression, path analysis, factor analysis, cluster analysis, discriminant analysis, canonical correlation, and structural equation modeling are based on this coefficient and interpretative understanding. More than 100 years later, the examination of variable relationships is the single most important analysis conducted in education, psychology, business, medicine, and numerous other disciplines. As noted in the chapter, many different types of correlation coefficients were later developed depending on the level of measurement and found applications in categorical data analysis and measurement.

The Pearson correlation coefficient indicates the linear relationship between two continuous variables that have a bivariate normal distribution where X and Y are random variables. The Pearson correlation coefficient indicates both the magnitude and the direction of the relationship between two linear continuous variables. A Pearson correlation coefficient of $r = 0$ indicates no linear relationship between two variables. The Pearson correlation coefficient can be interpreted in three ways: (1) test of significance, (2) variance accounted for, and (3) a diagram of trend in the paired data points. The sample correlation coefficient, r, is an estimate of the population correlation coefficient, rho. If $\rho = 0$, then the sample data points will have a random scatterplot. As ρ approaches $+1$ or -1, the sample data points appear to form a line. If $\rho = +1$ or -1, then the sample data points form a single straight line.

In this chapter, we have learned when the Pearson bivariate correlation coefficient originated, how the Pearson correlation coefficient is computed, and the interpretation of the magnitude and direction of the Pearson correlation coefficient. The Pearson correlation coefficient permits a test of the significance, a variance explained interpretation, and the visual display of a scatterplot of the bivariate data relationship, useful in prediction. We have also learned that the sample Pearson correlation coefficient, r, is a sample estimate of the population correlation coefficient, rho.

EXERCISES

1. The Pearson correlation between test score (Y) and time spent studying (X) was $r_{yx} = .50$, $df = 30$. Is the positive correlation between test score and time spent studying statistically significant at the one-tail, .05 level of probability? Report the tabled r value in your answer.

2. Using the *cor.test()* function, compute the Pearson correlation coefficient and the 95% confidence interval for the following data. Conduct your test using a two-tailed hypothesis. Show your work, and interpret the results.

Y	X
10	20
8	15
7	17
5	12
3	10

Y	X
10	200
8	15
7	17
5	12
3	10

R commands:

Output:

Interpretation:

3. Using the *cor.test()* function, compute the Pearson correlation coefficient and 95% confidence interval for the following data with an outlier, $X = 200$. Conduct your test using a two-tailed hypothesis, the same as in #2. Show your work and interpret results.

R commands:

Output:

Interpretation:

4. Given $r_{yx} = +.90$, $df = 30$ for a one-tailed hypothesis with a .05 level of probability, explain three ways the Pearson correlation coefficient can be used in a few sentences.

TRUE OR FALSE QUESTIONS

T   F   a.   Pearson correlation is computed as the average product of z scores on Y and X.

T   F   b.   Pearson correlation is computed using nonlinear, ordinal pairs of data.

T   F   c.   Interval and ratio levels of measurement differ based on whether they have an arbitrary or a true zero point, respectively.

T   F   d.   Spearman correlation is computed using ordinal variables.

T   F   e.   Outliers do not affect the correlation coefficient.

T   F   f.   Pearson correlation can be tested for statistical significance, interpreted as variance explained, and used in prediction.

NOTE

1.   Future authors of textbooks conveniently dropped the other four psychosocial properties of scale. Today, however, there is an understanding that a loss of information occurs when going from a ratio to a nominal level of measurement, and only certain permissible mathematical operations are possible.

WEB RESOURCES

Chapter R script files are available at http://www.sagepub.com/schumacker
    Pearson Function R script file: chap15a.r
    Correlation Function R script file: chap15b.r

## CHAPTER 16

LINEAR REGRESSION TESTS OF PREDICTION

I n the late 1950s and early 1960s, the mathematics related to solving a set of simultaneous linear equations was introduced to the field of statistics in the United States. In 1961, Franklin A. Graybill published a definitive text on the subject, *An Introduction to Linear Statistical Models*, which piqued the curiosity of several scholars. A few years later, in 1963, Robert A. Bottenberg and Joe H. Ward Jr., who worked in the Aerospace Medical Division at Lackland Air Force Base in Houston, Texas, applied the linear regression technique using basic algebra and the Pearson correlation coefficient. Norman R. Draper and Harry Smith Jr. published in 1966 one of the first books on the topic, *Applied Regression Analysis*. In 1967, under a funded project by the U.S. Department of Health, Education, and Welfare, W. L. Bashaw and Warren G. Findley invited several scholars to the University of Georgia for a symposium on the general linear model approach to the analysis of experimental data in educational research. The five speakers invited were Franklin A. Graybill, Joe H. Ward Jr., Ben J. Winer, Rolf E. Bargmann, and R. Darrell Bock. Dr. Graybill presented the theory behind statistics, Dr. Ward presented the regression models, Dr. Winer discussed the relationship between the general linear regression model and the analysis of variance, Dr. Bargmann presented applied examples that involved interaction and random effects, and Dr. Bock critiqued the concerns of the others and discussed computer programs that would compute the general linear model and analysis of variance. Since the 1960s, numerous textbooks and articles in professional journals have painstakingly demonstrated that the linear regression technique, presented by Bottenberg and Ward, is the same as the analysis of variance. In recent years, multiple regression techniques have proven to be more versatile than analysis of variance, hence the two methods today are combined into the general linear model framework (McNeil, Newman, & Fraas, 2012).

● GAUSS-MARKOV THEOREM

Linear regression is based on the Gauss-Markov theorem, which states that if the errors of prediction are independently distributed, sum to zero, and have constant variance, then the least squares estimation of the **regression weight** (*b*) is the best linear unbiased estimator of the population B. The least squares criterion is sometimes referred to as BLUE, or best linear unbiased estimator. Basically, of all unbiased estimators that are **linear functions** of the observations, the least squares estimation of the regression weight yields the smallest sampling variance or errors of prediction.

We will demonstrate linear regression in this chapter and apply the least squares estimation method to determine the regression weight in the equation. This approach will also be applied in the next chapter on multiple regression, termed ordinary least squares regression. The individual observation on Y_i is composed of a constant value assigned to all individuals (a), plus a common regression weight (b) applied to each individual corresponding X_i value, with a residual or error term (e). Each individual observation, Y_i, is the sum of a plus bX_i plus e, which is expressed in equation format as $Y_i = a + bX_i + e$. The selection of a value for b (regression weight) is done to minimize the error (e). The error is the difference between the original individual observation Y_i and what the linear regression equation would predict for each individual, denoted by $\hat{Y}_i$. The error term is therefore computed as $e = Y_i - \hat{Y}_i$. The Gauss-Markov theorem provides the rule that justifies the selection of a regression weight based on minimizing the error of prediction, which gives the best prediction of Y. We refer to this as the *least squares criterion*, that is, selecting regression weights based on minimizing the sum of squared errors of prediction.

● LINEAR REGRESSION EQUATION

The linear regression equation used by Bottenberg and Ward was expressed as

$$Y = a + bX + e.$$

The Y variable represents a continuous measure that was referred to as the *dependent variable*. The X variable represents a continuous measure that was called an independent variable but was later referred to as a *predictor variable*. The value a was termed the *intercept* and represented the value on the y-axis where the regression line crossed. The b value was a weight, later referred to as a *regression weight* or coefficient. The value e was referred to as *prediction error*, which is calculated as the difference between the Y variable and the predicted Y value ($\hat{Y}$) from the linear regression equation. The predicted Y value is computed based on the values of the intercept and regression weight. An example will illustrate the logic behind the linear regression equation.

Given the data pairs (to the left) on the amount of time, in hours, spent studying (X) and the corresponding exam scores (Y), a linear regression equation can be created:

Time Spent Studying (X)	Exam Scores (Y)
1	70
2	75
3	80
4	85
5	85
6	90
7	98

The regression intercept (*a*) indicates the point on the *y*-axis where a regression line crosses in a scatterplot. The regression weight (*b*) determines the rate of change (sometimes called *rise* and *run*), which can be seen by the slope of the regression line in the scatterplot. Given the correlation and standard deviation values for *X* and *Y*, the **intercept** and **slope** (regression weight) for the data can be calculated:

$$b = r_{XY} \frac{S_Y}{S_X}$$

$$a = \bar{Y} - b\bar{X}.$$

The prediction of *Y* given knowledge of *X* is expressed in a linear regression prediction equation as

$$\hat{Y} = a + bX.$$

Notice that the error (*e*) is not expressed in the linear regression prediction equation. We predict *Y* ($\hat{Y}$) given the correlation of *X* with *Y*, so $e = Y - \hat{Y}$, which occurs when the Pearson correlation is not +1.00 or −1.00. When Pearson $r = +1.00$ or Pearson $r = -1.00$, then no prediction error exists, that is, $Y = \hat{Y}$, and prediction error = 0.

TIP

✓ The linear regression equation only relates to the range of values for the pairs of *Y* and *X* scores used to calculate the slope or regression weight (*b*) and the intercept (*a*).

✓ $R = r$ (Pearson correlation) when using a single predictor—called multiple correlation coefficient.

✓ $R = r (Y, \hat{Y})$—correlation between *Y* and predicted *Y* values.

✓ R^2 = Multiple correlation coefficient—coefficient of determination squared.

NOTE: Do not confuse the use of R in linear regression with the R software notation.

The calculation of the regression weight (*b*) requires the computation of the Pearson correlation coefficient and the standard deviation of scores on *Y* and *X*. The calculation of the intercept (*a*) requires the use of the regression weight (*b*) and the mean values for the *Y* and *X* scores. The intercept calculation should give us a clue—that if we only have the *Y* scores and no knowledge of *X*, then our best prediction of *Y* is the mean of *Y*. It is only when we have additional variables that correlate with *Y* that we can be predict variability in the *Y* scores.

The linear regression equation calculations for number of hours spent studying (*X*) predicting the exam score (*Y*), given the Pearson correlation, means, and standard deviations of *X* and *Y*, are

$$rXY = +0.983$$

$$\bar{Y} = 83.286, \quad SD(Y) = 9.34$$

$$\bar{X} = 4, \quad SD(X) = 2.16$$

$$b = r_{XY} \frac{S_Y}{S_X} = +0.983 \left(\frac{9.34}{2.16} \right) = 4.25$$

$$a = \bar{Y} - b\bar{X} = 83 - 4.25(4) = 83.286 - 17 = 66.286.$$

The linear regression prediction equation is then created as

$$\hat{Y} = 66.286 + 4.25(X).$$

The linear regression prediction equation contains error (e) because the correlation between X and Y is not perfect. We use the equation to predict a Y score given the value of X. For example,

$$\hat{Y} = 66.286 + 4.25(X)$$
$$\hat{Y} = 66.286 + 4.25(1)$$
$$\hat{Y} = 70.536.$$

This indicates that for 1 hour of study time, the predicted exam score would be 70.536. The actual Y score was 70, so the linear regression equation overpredicted; that is, error = −0.536. The error is determined by $Y - \hat{Y}$. I have placed the Y, predicted Y, and error value in the table below for each value of X.

Y	$\hat{Y}$	Error
70	70.536	−0.536
75	74.786	0.214
80	79.036	0.964
85	83.286	1.714
85	87.536	−2.536
90	91.786	−1.786
98	96.036	1.964

Notice that the sum of the errors (*Error*) will always be 0. The reason is that some of the predictions are more than the actual Y value and some are less, but on average they will cancel out to zero.

A scatterplot of these data values would indicate the intercept and slope (rise and run) of this relationship, with the intercept intersecting the y-axis at $a = 66.286$. Perfect relationships between variables do not usually occur with real data, so the prediction of *Y* will generally involve some error of prediction. The predicted *Y* values form the regression line on the graph. The actual *Y* values fall near and far from this fitted regression line depending on the amount of error, or the difference between *Y* and the predicted *Y* value. The distance from the line for each *Y* therefore visually shows the amount of error in prediction.

We can see the linear relationship of *X* and *Y* by using a few R commands to create a scatterplot of the *X* and *Y* values with the linear regression line. After *X* and *Y* are placed in data vectors, the linear regression is computed, with the output saved in the file *model* using the *lm()* function. The *plot()* function graphs the *X* and *Y* values. The *abline()* function takes the *a* (intercept) and *b* (slope) values from the regression equation and uses them to draw a fitted regression line in the graph. The set of R commands are as follows:

```
> x = c(1,2,3,4,5,6,7)
> y = c(70,75,80,85,85,90,98)
> model = lm(y ~ x)
> plot(x,y)
> abline(model)
```

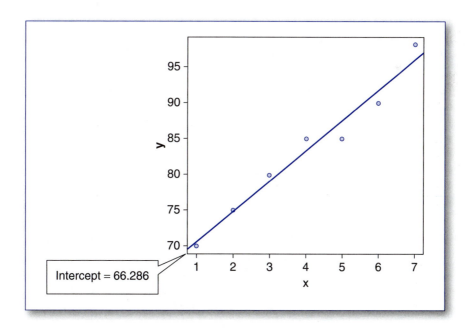

Intercept = 66.286

● LINEAR REGRESSION BY CALCULATOR

Another example will help demonstrate the linear regression prediction equation based on using summary values and a calculator. The data for 20 student math achievement scores (*Y*) and days absent from school (*X*) during the week are summarized below:

Student	X	Y	X^2	Y^2	XY
1	2	90	4	8,100	180
2	4	70	16	4,900	280
3	3	80	9	6,400	240
4	5	60	25	3,600	300
5	1	95	1	9,025	95
6	2	80	4	6,400	160
7	5	50	25	2,500	250
8	3	45	9	2,025	135
9	2	75	4	5,625	150
10	4	65	16	4,225	260
11	5	45	25	2,025	225
12	1	80	1	6,400	80
13	4	80	16	6,400	320
14	5	60	25	3,600	300
15	1	85	1	7,225	85
16	0	90	0	8,100	0
17	5	50	25	2,500	250
18	3	70	9	4,900	210
19	4	40	16	1,600	160
20	0	95	0	9,025	0
Σ	59	1,405	231	104,575	3,680

The summary statistics for these data can be calculated by hand as follows:

$$\bar{X} = \frac{\Sigma X}{N} = \frac{59}{20} = 2.95 \qquad S_x = \sqrt{\frac{SS_x}{N-1}} = \sqrt{\frac{56.95}{19}} = 1.73$$

$$\bar{Y} = \frac{\Sigma Y}{N} = \frac{1405}{20} = 70.25 \qquad S_y = \sqrt{\frac{SS_y}{N-1}} = \sqrt{\frac{5873.75}{19}} = 17.58$$

$$r = \frac{SP}{\sqrt{SS_X SS_Y}} = \frac{-464.75}{\sqrt{56.95(5873.75)}} = -.804.$$

TIP

✓ Recall from the previous chapter that the sum of products and sum of squares

$$SP = \Sigma XY - \frac{(\Sigma X)(\Sigma Y)}{N} = 3680 - \frac{(59)(1405)}{20} = -464.75$$

$$SS_Y = \Sigma Y^2 - \frac{(\Sigma Y)^2}{N} = 104575 - \frac{(1405)^2}{20} = 5873.75$$

$$SS_X = \Sigma X^2 - \frac{(\Sigma X)^2}{N} = 231 - \frac{(59)^2}{20} = 56.95$$

of X and sum of squares of Y were used in computing the correlation coefficient.

The intercept (*a*) and slope (*b*) in the linear regression prediction equation can now be computed:

$$b = r_{XY} \frac{S_Y}{S_X} = -0.804 \left(\frac{17.58}{1.73} \right) = -8.16$$

$$a = \bar{Y} - b\bar{X} = 70.25 - [(-8.16)(2.95)] = 70.25 + 24.07 = 94.32.$$

The prediction of *Y* (math scores) given knowledge of *X* (days absent) is now possible, using the intercept and slope values, in the following linear regression prediction equation:

$$\hat{Y} = 94.32 + -8.16X.$$

To determine the predicted *Y* values, we would substitute each value of *X* into the linear regression equation. The resulting values for *Y* and *Ŷ* and the errors of prediction are given below in a table format:

Student	X	Y	$\hat{Y}$	e
1	2	90	78	12
2	4	70	61.68	8.32
3	3	80	69.84	10.16
4	5	60	53.52	6.48
5	1	95	86.16	8.84
6	2	80	78.00	2.00

(Continued)

(Continued)

Student	X	Y	$\hat{Y}$	e
7	5	50	53.52	−3.52
8	3	45	69.84	−24.84
9	2	75	78.00	−3.00
10	4	65	61.68	3.32
11	5	45	53.52	−8.52
12	1	80	86.16	−6.16
13	4	80	94.32	18.32
14	5	60	53.52	6.48
15	1	85	86.16	−1.16
16	0	90	94.32	−4.32
17	5	50	53.52	−3.52
18	3	70	69.84	0.16
19	4	40	61.68	−21.68

NOTE: Errors of prediction can be positive or negative, but the sum (and mean) of the errors of prediction should be zero, $\Sigma e = 0$.

In this sample data set, the correlation coefficient is negative ($r = -.804$), which indicates that as the number of days absent during the week increases (X), the math achievement score (Y) decreases. We would conclude that absenteeism from school affects student test scores, which makes theoretical sense. This relationship would be depicted as a downward trend in the data points on a scatterplot. Also notice that the data points go together (covary) in a negative or inverse direction, as indicated by the negative sign for the sum of products in the numerator of the correlation coefficient formula.

The set of R commands to analyze and verify our hand calculations would be as follows:

```
> absent = c(2,4,3,5,1,2,5,3,2,4,5,1,4,5,1,0,5,3,4,0)
> math = c(90,70,80,60,95,80,50,45,75,65,45,80,80,60,85,90,50,70,40,95)
> results = lm(math ~ absent)
> summary(results)

Call:
lm(formula = math ~ absent)

Residuals:
   Min      1Q    Median     3Q      Max
-24.842  -3.721    0.417   6.939   18.319
```

```
Coefficients:
              Estimate Std. Error t value Pr(>|t|)
(Intercept)     94.324     4.842   19.479 1.52e-13 ***
absent          -8.161     1.425   -5.727 1.98e-05 ***
---
Signif. codes:   0 `***' 0.001 `**' 0.01 `*' 0.05 `.' 0.1 ` ' 1

Residual standard error: 10.75 on 18 degrees of freedom
Multiple R-squared: 0.6457,  Adjusted R-squared: 0.626
F-statistic:  32.8 on 1 and 18 DF,  p-value: 1.979e-05
```

The intercept (94.32) and regression weight (–8.16) match our hand calculations. Next, use the following R commands to plot the X and Y values and include the regression prediction line:

```
> plot(absent, math)
> abline(results)
```

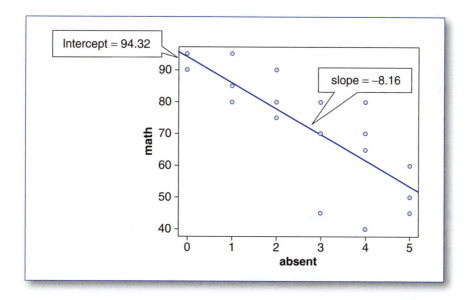

We square the correlation coefficient value to obtain a variance accounted for interpretation; that is, $r = -.804$, so the multiple R-squared (R^2) value = $r^2 = .6457$. Knowledge of the number of days absent accounts for 64.6% of the variance in the math achievement scores. The variance of the math achievement scores is $S_Y^2 = (17.58)^2 = 309.0564 \sim 309.06$, so the amount of variance explained is $0.646 * 309.0564 = 199.65$. The amount of variance not explained is $(1 - r^2) \times S_Y^2 = 0.354 \times 309.0564 = 109.41$. The total S_Y^2 = %Explained + %Unexplained = 199.65 + 109.41 = 309.6. The errors of prediction help identify the accuracy of the regression equation. If the errors of prediction are small, the amount of variance unexplained is less; thus, more variance in Y is explained. Our results show 64.6% explained and 35.4% unexplained variance, most likely due to another predictor variable.

We expect the Y scores to be normally distributed around each predicted Y value for a given value of X, so that the variability of the errors of prediction indicates the standard deviation of the Y scores around the predicted Y value for each value of X. The standard deviation of the Y scores around each predicted Y value is called a *standard error of estimate*, or **standard error of pre-diction**. It is computed as

$$S_{Y.X} = \sqrt{\frac{\sum e^2}{n-2}} = \sqrt{\frac{2081.08}{18}} = 10.75.$$

Another approach, using the standard deviation of Y, the correlation coefficient, and the sample size, computes the standard error of estimate as follows:

$$S_{Y.X} = S_Y \sqrt{1-r^2} \sqrt{(n-1)/(n-2)}$$
$$S_{Y.X} = 17.58\sqrt{1-(-0.804)^2} \sqrt{(20-1)/(20-2)}$$
$$S_{Y.X} = 10.75.$$

Note: The S_{YX} value is reported in the output as "Residual standard error: 10.75 on 18 degrees of freedom."

● GRAPH OF THE FITTED REGRESSION LINE

A graph of each frequency distribution of Y scores around each predicted Y value for each individual X score aids in the interpretation of the standard error of estimate. For each value of X, there is a distribution of Y scores around the predicted Y value. This standard deviation is assumed to be the same for each distribution of Y scores along the regression line, which is referred to as the **homoscedasticity of variance** along the regression line (equal variance of Y scores around a predicted Y value for each X score along the regression line). For the sample of data, $S_{YX} = 10.75$, which is the standard deviation of the Y scores around the predicted Y value for each X score—assumed to be the same for each frequency distribution along the regression line—and is formed by

$$\hat{Y} = 94.32 + (-8.16)X.$$

The predicted Y value is the mean of the distribution of Y scores for each value of X. The predicted Y values are also used to draw the regression prediction line through the scatterplot of data points for X and Y. Since it is assumed that different values of Y vary in a normal distribution around the predicted Y values, the assumption of equal variance in Y across the regression line is important when using the regression prediction equation to predict Y for a given X value.

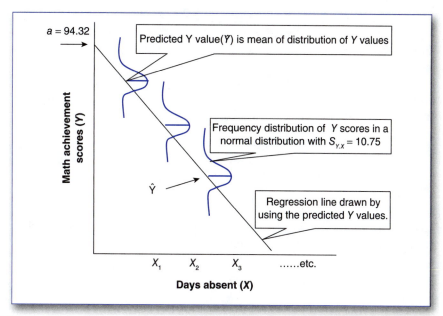

● LINEAR REGRESSION FUNCTION

The linear regression function in the script file (chap16a.r) involves taking a random sample of data and calculating a regression equation. The sample estimates for the intercept and slope are inferred to be the corresponding population parameters. A researcher typically does not know the true population parameters, which is why a random sample of data is used to provide estimates of the population parameters. The function permits a hypothetical comparison between a known population regression equation and the sample regression equation. You will need to enter the true values for the slope (*bTrue*) and intercept (*aTrue*) along with the sample size prior to running the function.

```
> bTrue = .25
> aTrue = 3
> sampleSize = 20
> chap16a(bTrue,aTrue,sampleSize)
```

The function will list the data points, the mean of *X* and *Y*, and the Pearson correlation with degrees of freedom and then compare the true regression equation (population) with the sample regression equation. The sample intercept and slope values are estimates of the population intercept and slope values. In practice, a researcher would not know the true population parameter values but would instead interpret the sample statistics as estimates of the population intercept and slope values.

```
Scatterplot Data Points

   X    Y
1.98 4.24
8.91 5.70
```

```
1.95 2.72
9.12 4.84
4.60 3.68
3.91 3.42
1.57 2.18
9.75 5.68
8.77 4.33
2.00 4.16
9.94 5.45
8.81 4.25
8.04 3.31
6.37 5.49
6.17 5.26
8.27 4.90
2.37 2.83
7.41 6.66
4.59 4.39
2.67 3.57


   Descriptive Statistics


     Mean     SD
X  5.860  3.037
Y  4.353  1.160


Pearson r =              0.684
Degrees of Freedom =   19.000


True Regression line is: y = 3 + 0.25x
Data Regression line is: y = 2.82 + 0.26x
```

Note: I used the *set.seed()* function so that you can replicate these results. Remove this function to obtain different results each time you run the function.

The *linear regression function* lists the sample data linear regression equation, while the output provides the true population values for the equation. This permits a comparison of how a random sample of data can provide a good estimate of population parameters.

● LINEAR REGRESSION WITH STANDARD SCORES

In some instances, the Y and X scores are converted to z scores or standard scores to place them both on the same measurement scale. This permits an equivalent interpretation of the change or

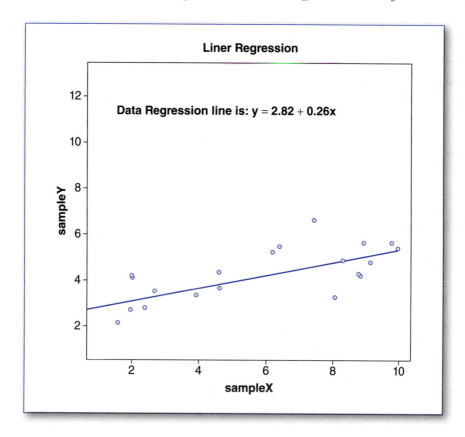

Liner Regression

Data Regression line is: y = 2.82 + 0.26x

slope of z values for Y and X starting at 0. The z-score formula subtracts the mean from each score and divides by the standard deviation. The formula, you may recall, is

$$z_{X_i} = \frac{X_i - \bar{X}}{S_X}$$

and

$$z_{Y_i} = \frac{Y_i - \bar{Y}}{S_Y}.$$

The standard scores (z scores) can be converted back to their respective raw scores by computing

$$X_i = \bar{X} - S_X(z_{Xi})$$

and

$$Y_i = \bar{Y} - S_Y(z_{Yi}).$$

As a result of placing Y and X scores on the z-score scale, the intercept (a) and slope (b) in the linear regression equation are simplified because the mean values for X and Y are 0 and the standard deviations for X and Y are 1. This is indicated in their calculations:

$$a = \bar{Y} - b\bar{X} = (0) - b(0) = 0$$

and

$$b = r_{XY} \frac{S_Y}{S_X} = -0.804 \left(\frac{1}{1}\right) = -0.804.$$

Because the mean and standard deviation of the X and Y z scores are 0 and 1, respectively, the regression line will pass through the origin of the scatterplot, where $Y = 0$ and $X = 0$, with the Y and X axes labeled in z-score units rather than raw score units.

The correlation coefficient captures the slope of the regression prediction line. The regression prediction equation in z-score form is

$$Z_{Y_i} = \beta Z_{X_i}$$

$$Z_{Y_i} = -0.804(Z_{X_i}),$$

where b (the raw score regression weight) is replaced with β (the standard score regression weight).

β will always equal the Pearson correlation coefficient in a single-predictor equation.

The use of linear regression in applied research is very popular. For example, admission to graduate school is based on the prediction of grade point average using the Graduate Record Exam score. Colleges and universities predict budgets and enrollment from one year to the next based on previous attendance data. The Pearson correlation coefficient plays an important role in making these predictions possible.

A statistically significant correlation between Y and X will generally indicate that a good prediction is possible, because the difference between the observed Y values and the predicted Y ($\hat{Y}$) values are kept to a minimum. The least squares line is fitted to the data to indicate the prediction trend. The least squares line is a unique fitted regression line based on minimizing the sum of the squared differences between the observed Ys and the predicted Ys, thus keeping prediction error to a minimum by the selection of values for the intercept (a) and slope (b). In the single-predictor regression formula that uses z scores, we see the unique role that the Pearson correlation coefficient plays as the slope value. A researcher should report the unstandardized linear regression values for the intercept (a) and slope (b) that we previously calculated, as well as the standardized regression weight (β).

● R FUNCTIONS FOR LINEAR REGRESSION

The *stats* package contains two different functions that can be used to estimate the intercept and slope in the linear regression equation. The two different R functions are *lm()* and *lsfit()*. The *lm()* function is preferred over the *lsfit()* function. The *lm()* function uses a data frame, whereas the *lsfit()* function uses a matrix or data vector. Also, the *lm()* function outputs an intercept term, which has meaning when interpreting results in linear regression. The linear regression command will therefore be of the form

```
> sampleReg = lm(sampleY ~ sampleX, data = out1)
```

The *lm()* function can also specify an equation with *no intercept* of the form

```
> sampleReg = lm(sampleY ~ 0 + sampleX, data = out1)
```

or

```
> sampleReg = lm(sampleY ~ sampleX - 1, data = out1)
```

The *lm()* function with *X* and *Y* data will be used in a single-predictor regression equation with and without an intercept term in the next two sections.

Linear Regression With Intercept

The *summary()* function returns the results of the linear regression equation. The intercept value of 94.32 is reported in the output.

```
> library(stats)
> sampleX = c(2,4,3,5,1,2,5,3,2,4,5,1,4,5,1,0,5,3,4,0)
> sampleY = c(90,70,80,60,95,80,50,45,75,65,45,80,80,60,85,90,50,70,40,95)
> sampleReg = lm(sampleY ~ sampleX)
> summary(sampleReg)

Call:
lm(formula = sampleY ~ sampleX)

Residuals:
    Min      1Q    Median    3Q       Max
 -24.842  -3.721   0.417    6.939    18.319

Coefficients:
               Estimate   Std. Error   t value   Pr(>|t|)
(Intercept)     94.324       4.842      19.479   1.52e-13  ***
sampleX         -8.161       1.425      -5.727   1.98e-05  ***
---
Signif. codes:  0 '***' 0.001 '**' 0.01 '*' 0.05 '.' 0.1 ' ' 1

Residual standard error: 10.75 on 18 degrees of freedom
Multiple R-squared: 0.6457, Adjusted R-squared: 0.626
F-statistic:  32.8 on 1 and 18 DF,  p-value: 1.979e-05
```

Linear Regression Without Intercept

The *lm()* function now contains the prediction equation with 0 as the intercept term. The *summary()* function now outputs results that do not contain the intercept value. Notice that the regression weight does not equal the correlation coefficient (−.8035), which can be obtained from the *cor(sampleX, sampleY)* command. You would need to use *z* scores for the *X* and *Y* values to achieve this standardized linear regression solution.

```
> library(stats)
> sampleX = c(2,4,3,5,1,2,5,3,2,4,5,1,4,5,1,0,5,3,4,0)
> sampleY = c(90,70,80,60,95,80,50,45,75,65,45,80,80,60,85,90,50,70,40,95)
> sampleReg = lm(sampleY ~ 0 + sampleX)
> summary(sampleReg)
```

These results would not be correct because standardized values for *X* and *Y* should be used.

```
Call:
lm(formula = sampleY ~ 0 + sampleX)

Residuals:
    Min     1Q   Median    3Q     Max
 -34.65 -19.65   19.24   59.62   95.00

Coefficients:
          Estimate Std. Error t value Pr(>|t|)
sampleX     15.931      3.236   4.924 9.43e-05 ***
---
Signif. codes:   0 '***' 0.001 '**' 0.01 '*' 0.05 '.' 0.1 ' ' 1

Residual standard error: 49.18 on 19 degrees of freedom
Multiple R-squared: 0.5606, Adjusted R-squared: 0.5375
F-statistic: 24.24 on 1 and 19 DF,  p-value: 9.433e-05
```

The linear regression analysis with an intercept matches the previous example. The linear regression analysis without an intercept term does not yield the correct results. We would expect a standardized beta weight to equal the Pearson correlation coefficient in a single-predictor case. Another example will further demonstrate the use of the *lm()* linear regression function.

Linear Regression Example

The *linear regression example function* in the script file (chap16b.r) uses the 20 student math achievement scores (*Y*) and the number of days absent from school during the week (*X*). The function will list the *X* and *Y* values, calculate the descriptive statistics (mean and standard deviation), calculate the Pearson *r* and degrees of freedom, and finally list the linear regression equation with the intercept and slope values. The results should be exactly the same as those calculated before by hand. You will need to enter the data vectors *sampleX* and *sampleY* prior to running the function.

```
> sampleX = c(2,4,3,5,1,2,5,3,2,4,5,1,4,5,1,0,5,3,4,0)
> sampleY = c(90,70,80,60,95,80,50,45,75,65,45,80,80,60,85,90,50,70,40,95)
> chap16b(sampleX,sampleY)
```

The results list the pairs of X and Y data values followed by the descriptive statistics and Pearson r value. The linear regression equation is then printed with the intercept and slope value. Finally, a scatterplot of the X and Y data values with the regression line is shown.

```
PROGRAM OUTPUT

Scatterplot Data Points

   X Y
   2 90
   4 70
   3 80
   5 60
   1 95
   2 80
   5 50
   3 45
   2 75
   4 65
   5 45
   1 80
   4 80
   5 60
   1 85
   0 90
   5 50
   3 70
   4 40
   0 95

Descriptive Statistics

       Mean      SD
   X   2.95    1.731
   Y  70.25   17.583


Pearson r =              -0.804
Degrees of Freedom =    19.000

Data Regression line is: y = 94.32 + -8.16x
```

The scatterplot shows the regression line crossing at 94.32 (intercept), then descending in a negative trend at −8.16 (slope).

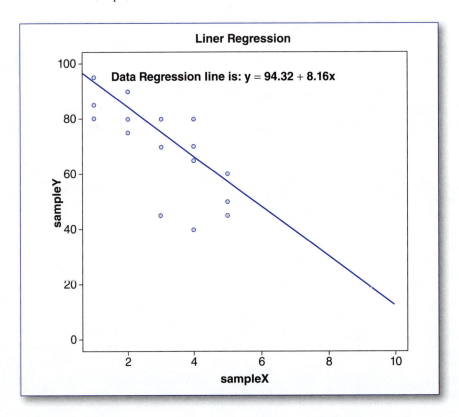

● INTERPRETATION OF LINEAR REGRESSION OUTPUT

The *summary()* function can be used after obtaining results from the *lm()* function to output more diagnostic information. This is done by including the *lm()* function results in the *summary()* function. For example, add these two command lines to the above function in the Output section:

```
> data4 = summary(sampleReg)
> print(data4)
```

The resulting output would be

```
Call:
lm(formula = sampleY ~ sampleX, data = out1)

Residuals:
     Min      1Q  Median      3Q     Max
 -24.842  -3.721   0.417   6.939  18.319
```

```
Coefficients:
              Estimate Std. Error t value Pr(>|t|)
(Intercept)     94.324      4.842  19.479 1.52e-13 ***
sampleX         -8.161      1.425  -5.727 1.98e-05 ***
---
Signif. codes:  0 '***' 0.001 '**' 0.01 '*' 0.05 '.' 0.1 ' ' 1

Residual standard error: 10.75 on 18 degrees of freedom
Multiple R-squared: 0.6457, Adjusted R-squared: 0.626
F-statistic:  32.8 on 1 and 18 DF,  p-value: 1.979e-05
```

The coefficients are in raw score form, which shows the intercept, $a = 94.324$, and regression weight, $b = -8.161$. In addition, the standard error (*SE*) is displayed, which is used to calculate a t test of statistical significance. For the intercept, the t test would be computed as

$$t = \frac{\text{Coefficient}}{\text{Error}} = \frac{b_{\text{int}}}{SE_{b_{\text{int}}}} = \frac{94.324}{4.842} = 19.48.$$

For the regression weight, the t test would be computed as

$$t = \frac{\text{Coefficient}}{\text{Error}} = \frac{b_x}{SE_{b_x}} = \frac{-8.161}{1.425} = -5.727.$$

The intercept and slope are both statistically significant, as indicated by their respective p values, which are given in scientific notation. This was corrected by the command *options(scipen = 999)* in the function. The regression weight, for example, is statistically significant beyond a .05 level of probability at $p = .0000198$—not 1.98e–05 (scientific notation).

The *multiple R-squared* value is .6457. This indicates the amount of variance explained in Y given knowledge of X. In a single-predictor linear regression equation, this would be the same value as squaring the Pearson r coefficient between X and Y—that is,

$$R^2 = r^2$$
$$R^2 = (-.804)^2$$
$$R^2 = .646.$$

We can test the multiple R-squared value from the regression equation for statistical significance by using the F test. The F test was designed to test the ratio of two variances; in this case, it is the ratio of explained variance to unexplained variance in the regression equation. The F test is computed as follows:

$$F = \frac{R^2 / (k)}{1 - R^2 / (N - k - 1)}$$
$$F = \frac{.6457 / (1)}{.3543 / (20 - 1 - 1)}$$
$$F = 32.8.$$

where N = sample size and k = number of predictor variables. The number of predictor variables (k) is the degrees of freedom in the numerator of the F formula; that is, $df_1 = 1$. The expression ($N - k - 1$) is the degrees of freedom in the denominator of the F formula, which is $df_2 = (20 - 1 - 1) = 18$. The numerator and denominator degrees of freedom are used in Table 5 (.05 level of significance) or Table 6 (.01 level of significance) in Appendix A to obtain the respective F value we would expect by chance in the sampling distribution of F values. For the .05 level of probability, $F_{.05;df=1,18} = 4.41$, and for the .01 level of probability, $F_{.01;df=1,18} = 8.29$. The F value from our regression equation ($F = 32.8$) is greater than either F value at the .05 or .01 level of probability, which is reported as $p = .00001978$. The *multiple R-squared* value is therefore statistically significant, which means that the amount of variance in Y predicted by X is statistically significant.

We also know from the *multiple R-squared* value the amount of variance in Y that is *not* explained, that is, $1 - R^2$, or $1 - .646 = .354$, or 35% unexplained variation in Y scores. Recall that the amount of variance explained plus the amount of variance not explained equals the total amount of variance in Y ($S_Y^2 = 309.161$). So 100% of variance = 65% explained + 35% not explained (rounded up). In practical terms, we partition the actual variance in Y scores, as follows:

$$S_r^2 = (17.583)^2 = 309.161$$

$$S_{r\,\text{Explained}}^2 = .65(309.161) = 200.955$$

$$S_{r\,\text{Not explained}}^2 = .35(309.161) = 108.206.$$

A researcher would typically reduce the amount of variance *not* explained (108.206) by including additional predictor variables in the regression equation. We would want any additional predictor variables to be significantly correlated with Y but not have high correlation with the other predictor variables.

The *adjusted R-squared* value is less than the *multiple R-squared* value because it makes an adjustment for both the number of predictors and small sample sizes. The multiple R-squared value can become inflated or spuriously large when the number of predictors is similar to the sample size. The adjusted R-squared value makes an adjustment for the number of predictors in the regression equation, especially with small sample sizes. The formula is as follows:

$$\text{Adj}R^2 = 1 - [(1 - R^2)\left(\frac{N-1}{N-k-1}\right)]$$

$$\text{Adj}R^2 = 1 - [(.3543)(1.055)]$$

$$\text{Adj}R^2 = 1 - [.3737]$$

$$\text{Adj}R^2 = .626.$$

TIP

✓ *Multiple R* is the correlation between the Y scores and the predicted Y scores ($\hat{Y}$) from the regression equation. The square of multiple R is the *multiple R-squared* value (R^2).

Multiple $R = -.804$

Multiple $R^2 = .646$.

✓ The *adjusted R-squared* value makes an adjustment for the number of predictors in the equation, especially with small sample sizes.

Adjusted $R^2 = .626$.

Note: You would have to run the *cor.test()* function to test the statistical significance of the correlation coefficient—and thus a test of the regression weight being statistically significant in linear regression with a single predictor. These R commands would be as follows:

```
> sampleX = c(2,4,3,5,1,2,5,3,2,4,5,1,4,5,1,0,5,3,4,0)
> sampleY = c(90,70,80,60,95,80,50,45,75,65,45,80,80,60,85,90,50,70,40,95)
> cor.test(sampleX, sampleY,alternative = "two.sided", method = "pearson",
conf.level = 0.95)


Pearson's product-moment correlation

data:  sampleX and sampleY
t = -5.7275, df = 18, p-value = 0.00001979

alternative hypothesis: true correlation is not equal to 0

95 percent confidence interval:
 -0.9192124 -0.5602524

sample estimates:
      cor
-0.8035535
```

● HYPOTHESIS TESTING IN LINEAR REGRESSION

We use the same five-step hypothesis-testing approach to outline our test of a null hypothesis in linear regression. An example will illustrate the five-step hypothesis-testing approach.

Step 1. State the research question.
Can I statistically significantly positively predict IQ scores given knowledge of Reading scores?

Step 2. State the null and alternative statistical hypotheses.

$$H_0: \beta_{IQ,READ} = 0$$

$$H_A: \beta_{IQ,READ} \geq .389$$

The *r* value is from the table of critical values at the one-tailed test, alpha = .05 level

IQ	Read
118.00	66.00
99.00	50.00
118.00	73.00
121.00	69.00
123.00	72.00
98.00	54.00
131.00	74.00
121.00	70.00
108.00	65.00
111.00	62.00
118.00	65.00
112.00	63.00
113.00	67.00
111.00	59.00
106.00	60.00
102.00	59.00
113.00	70.00
101.00	57.00

Step 3. State the region of rejection, alpha level, direction of the hypothesis, and sample size.

Sample size = 18, α = .05, one-tailed test, df = 17.

Region of rejection: $\beta_{IQ,READ} \geq .389$.

Step 4. Collect data, and compute the sample coefficient, $\beta_{IQ,Read}$, and summary statistics.

The set of R commands are in the Hypothesis Testing Linear Regression Example script file (chap16c.r), which are as follows:

```
> IQ = c(118,99,118,121,123,98,131,121,1
08,111,118,112,113,111,106,102,113,101)
> Read = c(66,50,73,69,72,54,74,70,65,62
,65,63,67,59,60,59,70,57)
> model = lm(IQ ~ Read)
> mean(IQ);sd(IQ)
> mean(Read);sd(Read)
> summary(model)
> plot(Read, IQ)
> abline(model)
```

The summary statistics, linear regression results, and scatterplot are output as follows:

```
> mean(IQ);sd(IQ)
[1] 112.4444
[1] 9.043829

> mean(Read);sd(Read)
[1] 64.16667
[1] 6.741007

> cor(IQ, Read)
[1] 0.8999127

> summary(model)

Call:
lm(formula = IQ ~ Read)

Residuals:
    Min    1Q   Median    3Q      Max
 -6.487 -2.847  1.031   3.187   6.683
```

```
Coefficients:
                Estimate Std. Error t value Pr(>|t|)
(Intercept)     34.9738      9.4338    3.707  0.00191 **
Read             1.2073      0.1463    8.255  3.68e-07 ***
---
Signif. codes:  0 '***' 0.001 '**' 0.01 '*' 0.05 '.' 0.1 ' ' 1

Residual standard error: 4.065 on 16 degrees of freedom
Multiple R-squared: 0.8098, Adjusted R-squared: 0.798
F-statistic: 68.14 on 1 and 16 DF,  p-value: 3.684e-07
```

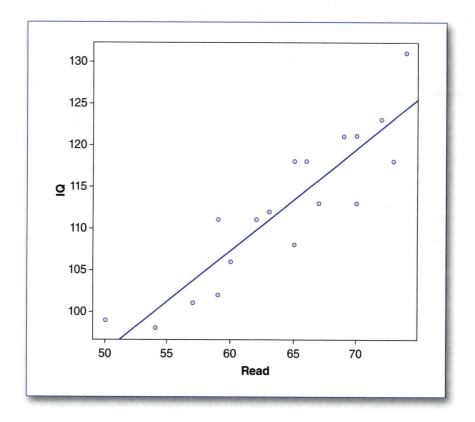

Step 5. State the conclusion, and interpret the results.

The IQ mean = 112.44, *SD* = 9.04; the Read mean = 64.16, *SD* = 6.74. The Pearson $r = \beta_{IQ,Read}$, which is reported as .8999 (rounded to .90). Since our sample β = .90 is greater than the tabled β = .389, we reject the null and accept the alternative hypothesis at the .05 level of significance. The multiple *R*-squared value indicated that .8098 or 81% of the variance in IQ scores is explained or predicted by knowledge of Reading scores. F = 68.14, df = 1, 16 was statistically significant at p = 3.684e–07 = .0000003684. t = (1.2073/0.1463) = 8.255 is greater than the tabled t = 1.74 at the .05 level, one-tailed level of significance, so the b_{Read} parameter (unstandardized estimate) was statistically significant. A scatterplot with the fitted regression line for the equation IQ = 34.9738 + 1.2073 (Reading) is provided by the *plot()* and *abline()* functions. It visually shows that as Reading scores increase, IQ scores increase.

Our summary conclusions are based on comparing the sample regression weight with what is expected by chance given our degrees of freedom and alpha level of significance. We reject the null hypothesis and accept the alternative hypothesis based on this comparison at a specific level of probability. We are also able to test the statistical significance of the unstandardized regression estimate (*b*) using a *t* test. The multiple *R*-squared value is further tested for statistical significance using the *F* test. In addition, we are able to interpret the multiple *R*-squared value as the amount of variance explained in IQ scores given knowledge of Reading scores. Therefore, 81% of (*SD* = 9.04)^2 is explained by knowledge of Reading scores, which is .81(81.7216) = 66.194496, or 66.19. The amount of unexplained variance is (1 − R^2)(81.7216) = 0.19(81.7216) = 15.527104, or 15.51. The total variance in IQ scores, (9.04)^2, is equal to 66.19 (explained variance) + 15.51 (unexplained variance). It may be possible to further explain the variance in IQ scores, and thus reduce the amount of unexplained variance, by hypothesizing another predictor variable. Basically, having more than one predictor variable could yield a better prediction equation, and thus explain more of the variance in the *Y* scores.

We can also report the power for these results, given that R^2 = .8098 is a measure of effect size. The *pwr.f2.test()* function in the *pwr* package provides power calculations for the general linear model. In our example, the R command would be

```
> library(pwr)
> ?pwr.f2.test
pwr.f2.test(u = NULL, v = NULL, f2 = NULL, sig.level = 0.05, power = NULL)
```

Arguments

u	degrees of freedom for numerator
v	degrees of freedom for denominator
f2	effect size
sig.level	Significance level (Type I error probability)
Power	Power of test (1 minus Type II error probability)

```
> pwr.f2.test (u = 1, v = 16, .8098, .05, power = NULL)

Multiple regression power calculation

u = 1
v = 16
f2 = 0.8098
sig.level = 0.05
power = 0.9474134
```

The results indicate sufficient power for the effect size; that is, power = .947 for an effect size of R^2 = .8098.

● LINEAR REGRESSION AND ANALYSIS OF VARIANCE

When the intercept term is removed from the regression equation, it provides a comparison with analysis of variance. The regression formula has the form $y \sim x - 1$ or $y \sim 0 + x$, where y is the dependent variable and x, the independent variable. The tilde (~) sign is used in the regression formula to indicate that y is regressed on x. The 0 or −1 specifies that there is no intercept. We can show the differences and similarity between linear regression and analysis of variance by running the *aov()* and *lm()* functions, with associated output from the *summary()* function.

```
> sampleX = c(2,4,3,5,1,2,5,3,2,4,5,1,4,5,1,0,5,3,4,0)
> sampleY = c(90,70,80,60,95,80,50,45,75,65,45,80,80,60,85,90,50,70,40,95)
> sampleaov = aov(sampleY ~ 0 + sampleX)
> summary(sampleaov)
> samplereg = lm(sampleY ~ sampleX)
> summary(samplereg)
```

Analysis of Variance Output

```
sampleX    1   58625    58625   24.241 9.433e-05 ***
Residuals 19   45950     2418
---
Signif. codes:  0 '***' 0.001 '**' 0.01 '*' 0.05 '.' 0.1 ' ' 1
```

Linear Regression Output

```
Call:
lm(formula = sampleY ~ 0 + sampleX)

Residuals:
   Min    1Q   Median    3Q     Max
-34.65 -19.65  19.24   59.62   95.00

Coefficients:
         Estimate Std. Error t value Pr(>|t|)
sampleX    15.931      3.236   4.924 9.43e-05 ***
---
Signif. codes:  0 '***' 0.001 '**' 0.01 '*' 0.05 '.' 0.1 ' ' 1

Residual standard error: 49.18 on 19 degrees of freedom
Multiple R-squared: 0.5606, Adjusted R-squared: 0.5375
F-statistic: 24.24 on 1 and 19 DF,  p-value: 9.433e-05
```

The multiple R-squared value of .5606 can be computed from the analysis of variance sum of squares value in the summary table. Recall that $SS_T = SS_{Regression} + SS_{Residual}$ (104575 = 58625 + 45950). The multiple R-squared value due to regression is therefore computed as $SS_{Regression}/SS_T = 58625/104575 = .5606$.

The multiple R-squared value is the amount of variance explained due to regressing Y on X. Therefore, $R^2 = 58625/104575 = .5606$. We also know that $1 - R^2 = 45950/104575 = .4394$. Thus, $R^2 + (1 - R^2) = 1$ (100% variance in Y), which is also expressed as $SS_Y = .5606 + .4394$. These two parts are interpreted as the amount of variance explained (R^2) and the amount of variance unexplained ($1 - R^2$), which can be represented in a Venn diagram. Notice that the F test, df, and p values are identical for both types of data analysis. Today, many statistical packages are dropping the separate analysis of variance and multiple regression routines in favor of the general linear model; for example, the IBM SPSS version 21 outputs both results.

SUMMARY

A brief history of multiple regression helps our understanding of this popular statistical method. It expands the early use of analysis of variance, especially analysis of covariance, into what is now called the general linear model. Over the years, researchers have come to learn that multiple regression yields similar results as analysis of variance but also provides many more capabilities in the analysis of data from research designs.

This chapter provided the basic understanding of linear regression. The following concepts were presented:

- The a in the regression equation is the intercept of the least squares line.
- The b coefficient in the regression equation is the slope of the least squares line.
- The intercept in the regression equation is called the y-intercept, the point at which the least squares line crosses the y-axis.
- In the linear regression equation, X is the independent variable and Y is the dependent variable.
- The linear regression equation using z scores for X and Y has a slope equal to the Pearson correlation coefficient.
- The intercept and slope of the linear regression prediction line from sample data are estimates of the population intercept and slope, respectively.
- The purpose of linear regression is to predict Y from knowledge of X using a least squares criterion to select an intercept and slope that will minimize the difference between Y and predicted Y, that is, error of prediction.

This chapter presented the basic linear regression equation for predicting Y from knowledge of X using the *lm()* function, with output provided by the *summary()* function. It is always recommended that a scatterplot of data be viewed to examine the relationship between Y and X using the *plot()* function. The basic algebra indicates that $Y = a + bX + e$, where a is an intercept term or the point where the fitted regression line crosses the y-axis; b is a regression weight determined by minimizing e, the error term; and e is the difference between Y and the predicted Y value. The process of estimating a regression weight (b) that minimizes the error is called the *least squares criterion*. The predicted Y values are computed using the *fitted()* function. A standard error of prediction is used to form confidence intervals around the predicted Y values along the fitted regression line, which indicates the distribution of Y values for each X value. The e values are computed by subtracting the predicted Y values from the Y values. The more X and Y are related or correlated, the better the prediction, and thus the less the error.

We learned that the regression weight should be reported in unstandardized and standardized formats. The *scale()* function creates variables in a standardized format, that is, mean = 0 and standard deviation = 1. A t test for the significance of the regression coefficient is computed using the unstandardized regression weight and associated standard error. The R-squared value is tested for statistical significance using the F test. An adjusted R-squared value was presented, which adjusts R^2 for the number of predictors and small sample sizes.

Hypothesis testing is conducted as with the other statistics. A null and an alternative hypothesis are stated, with the regression weight, R-squared value, or F-test value for a given degree of freedom and sample size. The other remaining hypothesis steps are followed to make a final decision regarding rejection or retention of the null hypothesis. The researcher then interprets the statistical significance of the regression weight, the R-squared value, and the F test to determine whether X predicts Y. The *aov()* and *lm()* functions provide the statistical results for analysis of variance and linear regression, respectively, which permits a comparison and helpful interpretation of the results.

TIP

✓ A list of statistical functions can be obtained by issuing the following command:

```
> library(help = "stats")
```

✓ The following R commands provide the function arguments and online documentation for the linear regression function:

```
> args(lm)
```

```
> help(lm)
```

✓ You can omit missing data that affect Pearson r and regression by using the following R command:

```
> data.new = na.omit(data.old)
```

✓ Right click your mouse on the scatterplot to save the image to the clipboard or print. The selection menu (to the right) will appear in the scatterplot:

✓ You can copy and paste scatterplots into Word documents by using the Alt+PrtScr keyboard keys; then in the Word document, use the Ctrl+V keyboard keys to paste the image. You can resize the image in the Word document by selecting the Format tab, which appears when the image is selected. The Crop tool option will permit easy resizing of the image.

Copy as metafile
Copy as bitmap
Save as metafile...
Save as postscript...
Stay on top
Print...

EXERCISES

1. Briefly explain the regression terms in the equation $Y = a + bX + e$.

2. Given the following summary statistics for Y and X, calculate by hand the intercept and slope, then write out the regression equation. Show the formula and your work with four decimal places.

Variable	Mean	SD	Correlation
Y	6.6	2.702	.948
X	14.8	3.962	

3. Given Y and X below, use the regression equation to compute the predicted Y values and the prediction error values. Show your work with four decimal places. Enter the predicted Y values and their prediction error values in the table.

$$\hat{Y} = -2.9682 + .6465(X).$$

a. Is Y = Predicted Y + Prediction error?

b. Does the sum of the prediction error values equal 0?

Y	X	Predicted Y	Prediction Error
10	20		
8	15		
7	17		
5	12		
3	10		

4. Use the *lm()* and *abline()* functions to compute values, then plot the fitted regression line for the Y and X values in #3 above. Show the R commands and plot (use the Alt+PrtScr keyboard keys to copy and paste the plot).

5. Given the following data vectors for Y and X, use the *lm()* and *summary()* functions to compute the regression equation and descriptive output. Show the R commands and output.

```
y = c(10,8,7,5,3)
x = c(20,15,17,12,10).
```

R commands:

Output:

Interpretation:

a. Is the regression weight for X statistically significant at the $p = .05$ level of probability?

b. Is $F = t^2$?

c. What does the multiple R^2 value imply?

TRUE OR FALSE QUESTIONS

T   F   a.   The Y mean is our best prediction given no knowledge of the X predictor variable.

T   F   b.   The sum of the prediction errors will always equal 0.

T   F   c.   The standard deviation of the Y scores around each predicted Y score is called the standard error of estimate or standard error of prediction.

T   F   d.   The intercept value = 0 when using z scores for Y and X.

T   F   e.   Pearson correlations in a matrix are in a nonstandardized (non–z score) format.

WEB RESOURCES

Chapter R script files are available at http://www.sagepub.com/schumacker

Hypothesis Testing Linear Regression Example R script file: chap16c.r

Linear Regression Example Function R script file: chap16b.r

Linear Regression Function R script file: chap16a.r

## CHAPTER 17

MULTIPLE REGRESSION

● MULTIPLE REGRESSION WITH TWO PREDICTORS

In conducting correlation research, we generally hypothesize a regression equation that has more than a single predictor, hence the term *multiple regression*. The bivariate (two-variable) correlations are not used as estimates of each variable's regression weight in the multiple regression equation. Instead, the bivariate correlation between Y and each X predictor variable computes a beta weight, which uses a standardized part correlation to control for the other variable's influence. The multiple variable relations in multiple regression can take on a different meaning depending on how the researcher views the configuration of the multiple variables. For example, if we had a dependent variable (Y) and two independent predictor variables (X and Z) in the multiple regression equation, six different relations among the variables could occur. The different types of correlated relationships can be illustrated in Venn or Ballentine diagrams.

Venn or Ballentine Diagram

Case 1 shows that no correlation exists between the dependent variable, Y, and the two independent predictor variables, X and Z. Case 2 shows that X and Z correlate, but they have no correlation with Y. We would not hypothesize a regression equation in these situations. Case 3 illustrates that only a single predictor equation using X to predict Y makes sense because Z does not correlate with X or Y. Case 4 is our ideal situation because X and Z are both correlated with Y but do not correlate with each other, so they have unique contributions in explaining the variance in Y. Case 5 illustrates that X correlates with Y, but Z correlates with only X, so it could effect the bivariate correlation of X with Y. Case 6 shows what usually occurs in practice, that is, the independent predictor variables, X and Z, not only are correlated with Y but also correlate with each other.

Part and Partial Correlation

The six bivariate correlation possibilities in the Venn diagrams reveal the importance of theory when estimating regression weights for predictor variables in a multiple regression equation. In

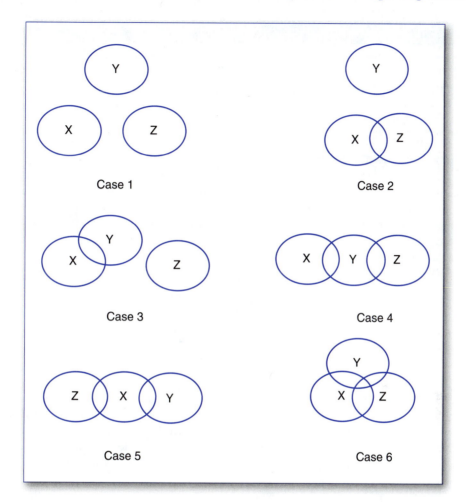

multiple regression, we compute a different type of correlation that will control for the other variables in the equation, thus providing the unique contribution of each (except in Case 4). These different types of correlation coefficients are called part and partial correlations. The *partial correlation coefficient* measures the correlation between two variables while controlling for one or more other predictor variables—for example, the correlation between age and reading comprehension, controlling for reading level. A *part correlation* measures the correlation between age and comprehension with reading level controlled, but only the correlation between comprehension and reading level is removed before age is correlated with comprehension. The part and partial correlations are computed using *Pearson r coefficients*, so an example will demonstrate how to calculate them.

We start with the basic Pearson correlation matrix that shows the bivariate correlation coefficients between reading level and two predictor variables, comprehension and age, for a sample of 100 students. Some basic notation will help us distinguish the types of bivariate correlations in the correlation matrix (1 = *age*, 2 = *comprehension*, 3 = *reading level*).

Correlation Matrix (n = 100)			
Variable	Age	Comprehension	Reading Level
1. Age	1.00		
2. Comprehension	.45	1.00	
3. Reading level	.25	.80	1.00

The partial correlation uses the Pearson r coefficients to remove or control for the effects of the other predictor variables. The partial correlation, $r_{12.3}$, would indicate the unique correlation between age (1) and comprehension (2), controlling for reading level (3). For example, we can compute the *partial* correlation coefficient (the correlation between age and comprehension, controlling for reading level) as follows:

$$r_{12.3} = \frac{r_{12} - (r_{13})(r_{23})}{\sqrt{(1 - r_{13}^2)\ (1 - r_{23}^2)}}$$

$$= \frac{.45 - (.25)\ (.80)}{\sqrt{[1 - (.25)^2]\ [1 - (.80)^2]}}$$

$$= .43.$$

Note: The partial correlation coefficient ($r_{12.3}$ = .43) should be smaller in magnitude than the Pearson bivariate correlation between age and comprehension, which is r_{12} = .45. If the partial correlation coefficient is not smaller than the Pearson correlation coefficient, then a *suppressor variable* may be present. A suppressor variable is a third variable that affects the correlation between the two other variables, which can increase or decrease their bivariate correlation coefficient.

The following is a Venn diagram showing the area of explained variance for the partial correlation coefficient ($r_{12.3}$ = .43):

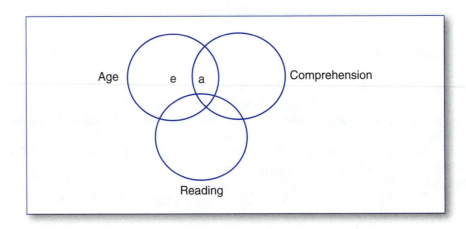

A part correlation, $r_{1(2.3)}$, would indicate the correlation between age (1) and comprehension (2), but reading level (3) is only removed or controlled for in comprehension. The part correlation coefficient, $r_{1(2.3)}$, or the correlation between age and comprehension where reading level is controlled for in comprehension only—hence the parentheses—is computed as

$$r_{1(2.3)} = \frac{r_{12} - (r_{13})(r_{23})}{\sqrt{(1 - r_{23}^2)}}$$

$$= \frac{.45 - (.25)(.80)}{\sqrt{(1 - .80^2)}}$$

$$= .42.$$

Note: The part correlation should be less than the Pearson correlation, otherwise the third variable is affecting the bivariate relationship.

The following is a Venn diagram showing the area of explained variance for the part correlation coefficient, $r_{1(2.3)} = .42$:

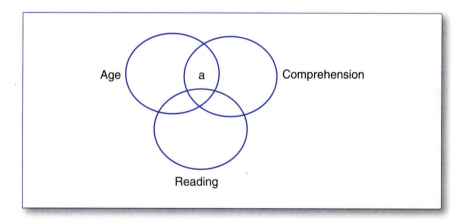

I have only shown one partial correlation and compared it with the corresponding part correlation. It is possible to calculate the other partial correlations, for example, the partial correlation between age and reading controlling for comprehension or the partial correlation between comprehension and reading controlling for age. It is also possible to calculate the other part correlations by simply inserting the corresponding bivariate correlations in the formula. The correlation coefficients, whether bivariate, part, or partial, can be tested for significance, interpreted as variance accounted for by squaring each coefficient, and diagrammed using Venn or Ballentine figures to conceptualize their relations.

Note: We do not need to compute the part or partial correlations in multiple regression, but they are used in calculating the regression coefficients when using two or more predictor variables. Therefore, an understanding of part and partial correlations provides the basis for understanding that the regression coefficients provide a unique weight for each variable in the regression equation controlling for the other variables.

Partial Correlation: pcor() *Function*

The *ppcor* package uses the *pcor()* function to compute partial correlations using either a complete matrix of all variables or individual selection of a single partial correlation. Both methods are shown. We must first install and load the ppcor package:

```
> install.packages ("ppcor")
> library (ppcor)
```

Next, we create three variables and compute their Pearson bivariate correlations:

```
> X = c(1,2,3,4,5,6,8,7,9,10)
> Y = c(3,3,5,4,6,7,4,8,9,7)
> Z = c(1,3,6,4,8,5,8,9,2,10)

> cor.test (X,Y)
```

Pearson's product-moment correlation

```
data:  X and Y
t = 3.1572, df = 8, p-value = 0.01345
alternative hypothesis: true correlation is not equal to 0
95 percent confidence interval:
 0.2169183 0.9356603
sample estimates:
     cor
0.7448191
```

```
> cor.test (X,Z)
```

Pearson's product-moment correlation

```
data:  X and Z
t = 1.9547, df = 8, p-value = 0.08636
alternative hypothesis: true correlation is not equal to 0
95 percent confidence interval:
 -0.09515218   0.88232154
sample estimates:
     cor
0.5685352
```

```
> cor.test (Y,Z)
```

Pearson's product-moment correlation

```
data:  Y and Z
```

```
t = 0.9833, df = 8, p-value = 0.3543
alternative hypothesis: true correlation is not equal to 0
95 percent confidence interval:
 -0.3797817  0.7938616
sample estimates:
    cor
0.328363
```

The Pearson correlation, r_{XY} = .74, was statistically significant (t = 3.1572, df = 8, p = .01345). The other two Pearson correlation coefficients, r_{XZ} = .568 and r_{YZ} = .328, were not statistically significant. It is important to compute the Pearson correlation coefficients and compare them with the partial correlation coefficients. This is an important step because the partial correlation should be less than the Pearson bivariate correlation. *If the partial correlation is greater than the Pearson correlation, we have a suppressor variable effect.* A suppressor variable effect is when a third variable reduces the bivariate correlation between the two variables.

We place our data into a data frame and label the variables for use in the *pcor()* function. This is accomplished by first placing the data vectors (*X, Y, Z*) into a matrix with 10 rows and three columns.

```
> mydata = data.frame(matrix(c(X,Y,Z),10,3))
> names(mydata)=c("X","Y","Z")
```

We are not ready to compute the partial correlations. Our first method outputs all partial correlation combinations of the variables in the data frame by simply entering the data set name into the function

```
> pcor (mydata)
```

The resulting output provides the matrix of partial correlations followed by the matrix of *p* values and *t*-test values. The sample size, number of groups, and type of correlation are also printed. It might be helpful to know that computers use square matrices, while a researcher generally only reports the lower triangle of the correlation matrix.

```
$estimate
            X              Y              Z
X 1.0000000    0.7182776     0.5140106
Y 0.7182776    1.0000000    -0.1732324
Z 0.5140106   -0.1732324     1.0000000

$p.value
            X              Y              Z
X 0.000000000   0.006306744   0.1128718
Y 0.006306744   0.000000000   0.6416696
Z 0.112871844   0.641669562   0.0000000
```

```
$statistic
         X              Y              Z
X 0.000000    2.7313918    1.5854160
Y 2.731392    0.0000000   -0.4653657
Z 1.585416   -0.4653657    0.0000000


$n
[1] 10


$gp
[1] 1


$method
[1] "pearson"
```

The output prints a partial correlation matrix (*$estimate*) of all variables in the data set *mydata*. For example, the partial correlation for $r_{XY.Z}$, that is, the bivariate correlation of X and Y controlling for Z is .7182776, rounded to $r_{XY.Z} = .72$. The Pearson correlation is $r_{XY} = .74$, so the partial correlation is less than the Pearson correlation. The partial correlation for $r_{XZ.Y}$ is .51, which is less than the Pearson correlation $r_{XZ} = .568$. The partial correlation for $r_{YZ.X}$ is −.173, which is less than the Pearson correlation $r_{YZ} = .328$. This does show a suppressor effect because the Pearson bivariate correlation, $r_{YZ} = .328$, has become a negative correlation when controlling for the influence of the variable X.

The output also prints the p values (*$p.value*) for each partial correlation. The partial correlation, $r_{XY.Z}$, was statistically significant ($p = .0063$), indicating that the bivariate correlation was statistically significant when controlling for the influence of the variable X. The t-test values associated with these p values appear in the *$statistic* matrix. The t-test value for $r_{XY.Z}$ was 2.73, with $p = .0063$. The other two partial correlations were not statistically significant, so the t-test and associated p values were greater than $p = .05$. Finally, the output indicates $N = 10$ pairs of scores (complete data pairs are required) with one group and partial correlations based on the Pearson correlation coefficients.

A single partial correlation coefficient with associated t-test and p values can be computed using the *pcor.test()* function. This requires extraction of the built-in variable names in the data set. For example, *mydata$X* refers to the X variable in the data set. The commands are

```
# partial correlation - select variables from larger data set

> pcor.test(mydata$X, mydata$Y, mydata[,c("Z")])

    estimate       p.value    statistic   n   gp   Method
1  0.7182776   0.006306744   2.731392    10   1    pearson
```

The individual partial correlation result, $r_{XY.Z}$, is the same as that obtained when running all of the partial correlations for variables in the data set.

Part Correlation: spcor() *Function*

The ppcor package also contains the *spcor()* function for calculating part (semipartial) correlations. To obtain the part correlations, use either the data file with all variables or individual pairs of variables. To obtain all part correlations of *X* with the other variables in the data set, simply include the data set name in the function:

```
> spcor(mydata)
```

The results are shown once again in matrix form, first the part (semipartial) correlations, then the *t*-test and *p* values. As before, the sample size, number of groups, and type of correlation are also shown.

```
$estimate
          X             Y              Z
X 1.0000000    0.5908975     0.3429820
Y 0.6784503    1.0000000    -0.1155922
Z 0.4855095   -0.1425112     1.0000000


$p.value
          X             Y              Z
X 0.00000000    0.05263944     0.3340224
Y 0.01455092    0.00000000     0.7581645
Z 0.14174233    0.70324977     0.0000000


$statistic
          X             Y              Z
X 0.000000    1.9378671     0.9660435
Y 2.443367    0.0000000    -0.3078920
Z 1.469334   -0.3809373     0.0000000


$n
[1]  10


$gp
[1]  1


$method
[1]  "pearson"
```

The output shows the part correlation matrix, *$estimate*, which indicates the part correlations for *X* with the other variables in the data set. This is followed by a matrix with the statistical significance, *$p.value*, and a matrix with the *t*-test values, *$statistic*. Results indicated that only the part correlation between *X* and *Y*, $r_{X(Y.Z)} = .678$, was statistically significant ($t = 2.44$, $p < .000000001$).

An individual part correlation can be obtained using the built-in variable names with the *spcor()* function; however, *the order of the variables in the function is reversed*. This means that *Z* is removed from X before calculating the correlation of X and Y. The following variable order was required to obtain the same value as output before. This part correlation is obtained by

```
> spcor.test(mydata$Y, mydata$X, mydata[,c("Z")])

    estimate     p.value    statistic   n   gp   Method
1  0.6784503   0.01455092   2.443367   10   1    pearson
```

The part correlation, p value, and t test are the same as in the part correlation matrices above. There are other part correlations, given a three-variable relation as show in the Venn diagrams, but the others were not output because the default specifies part correlations in the order of the variables in the data file. The part correlations in the rest of the matrix are obtained by

```
> spcor.test(mydata$Z, mydata$X, mydata[,c("Y")])

    estimate     p.value    statistic   n   gp   Method
1  0.4855095   0.1417423   1.469334   10   1    pearson
```

```
> spcor.test(mydata$Z, mydata$Y, mydata[,c("X")])

    estimate      p.value     statistic    n   gp   Method
1  -0.1425112   0.7032498   -0.3809373   10   1    pearson
```

I now compared the Pearson, partial, and part correlations. This comparison helps determine if a suppressor variable is present that would affect the regression weights, and thus the significance of the variable. The correlations between the X and Y variables was the only set of correlations found to be statistically significant (Pearson, partial, and part correlations). Results further show that the partial correlation and part correlation are less than the Pearson correlation for the combination of variables. Although the Pearson correlation was nonsignificant, $r_{YZ} = .328$, the partial and part correlations were negative, indicating the presence of a *suppressor* variable.

Pearson Correlation	Partial Correlation	Part Correlation
$r_{XY} = .744$	$r_{XY.Z} = .718$	$r_{Y(X.Z)} = .678$
$r_{XZ} = .568$	$r_{XZ.Y} = .514$	$r_{Z(X.Y)} = .485$
$r_{YZ} = .328$	$r_{YZ.X} = -.173$	$r_{Z.(Y.X)} = -.142$

TIP

✓ Load the R *utils* package.

✓ Use *data()* to list all the available data sets in R.

✓ Use *try(data(package ="ppcor"))* to list all the data sets in the package.

✓ Use *help(mydata)* to get information about a data set.

✓ Use *data(mydata)* to load .r, .rda, .txt, and .csv data file types.

Multiple Regression Example: Unstandardized Solution

Multiple regression results are typically reported in both unstandardized and standardized formats. In R, this requires running the regression analysis separately, then combining the two results. I first ran a set of data and then reported the unstandardized solution.

The following heuristic data display (to the right) Y with two predictor variables, X_1 and X_2:

The *lm()* function does not output unstandardized and standardized (z score: mean = 0; SD = 1) regression coefficients together in the same output. Therefore, two different sets of R commands are needed to obtain the *unstandardized* solution with b and SE_b and the *standardized* solution with β. It is recommended that both the values— (b, SE_b) and β—be provided in the interpretation of the results and in APA-style tables. The multiple R-squared value, F-test value for the multiple R-squared value, and t tests for significance of the regression weights should be the same in both types of analyses (unstandardized and standardized).

The set of R commands in the Multiple Regression Unstandardized Solution script file (chap17a.r) produce the summary statistics and multiple regression *unstandardized* solution:

Y	X_1	X_2
2	1	2
3	2	4
2	2	6
5	3	8
5	4	9
7	5	10
5	6	7
6	8	8
7	9	9
8	10	10

```
# Multiple Regression with two predictor variables - unstandardized
# chap17a.r
# Sample Data


> Y  = c(2,3,2,5,5,7,5,6,7,8)
> X1 = c(1,2,2,3,4,5,6,8,9,10)
> X2 = c(2,4,6,8,9,10,7,8,9,10)


# R commands to compute unstandardized regression coefficients

>  mean(Y);sd(Y)
> mean(X1);sd(X1)
> mean(X2);sd(X2)
> sample = data.frame(matrix(c(Y,X1,X2), nrow = 10, ncol = 3))
> cor(sample)
> model1 = lm(Y ~ X1 + X2)
> summary(model1)
```

The summary statistics for the three variables (mean and standard deviation), the Pearson correlation matrix, and the summary output for the multiple regression equation are

```
> mean(Y);sd(Y)
[1] 5
[1] 2.108185

> mean(X1);sd(X1)
[1] 5
[1] 3.162278

> mean(X2);sd(X2)
[1] 7.3
[1] 2.626785

> sample = data.frame(matrix(c(Y,X1,X2), nrow = 10, ncol = 3))
> cor(sample)

          X1            X2            X3
X1 1.0000000    0.8833333    0.8828296
X2 0.8833333    1.0000000    0.7223151
X3 0.8828296    0.7223151    1.0000000

> model1 = lm(Y ~ X1 + X2)
> summary(model1)

Call:
lm(formula = Y ~ X1 + X2)

Residuals:
     Min          1Q        Median         3Q          Max
-1.43872    -0.29091    0.05539      0.39369      0.89091

Coefficients:
                Estimate    Std. Error    t value    Pr(>|t|)
(Intercept)     0.2892      0.7347        0.394      0.7056
X1              0.3424      0.1120        3.058      0.0184 *
X2              0.4108      0.1348        3.047      0.0187 *
```

```
Signif. codes:   0 '***' 0.001 '**' 0.01 '*' 0.05 '.' 0.1 ' ' 1
```

```
Residual standard error: 0.7346 on 7 degrees of freedom
Multiple R-squared: 0.9056, Adjusted R-squared: 0.8786
F-statistic: 33.56 on 2 and 7 DF, p-value: 0.0002588
```

The means and standard deviations indicate that the variables are not standardized, that is, their variable means are not 0, and their standard deviations are not 1. The t test of significance for X_1 is statistically significant at $p = .0184$. The t test for the significance of X_2 is statistically significant at $p = .0187$. The multiple R^2 value $= .9056$, and $F = 33.56$, $df = 2, 7$, $p = .0002588$, which indicates that X_1 and X_2 explain 91% of the variance in Y. The regression equation with an intercept is $\hat{Y} = .2892 + .3424(X_1) + .4108(X_2)$.

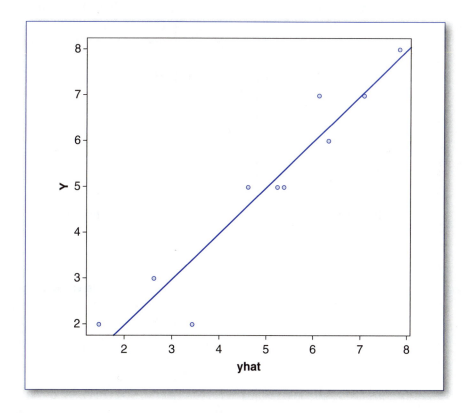

The plot of Y with *yhat* (predicted Y) visually shows that the Y values are close to the fitted regression line, which is drawn using the *yhat* predicted values. Since the R-squared value was close to 1.0, the actual Y values fall close to the regression line. If the R-squared value was much less, then the error of prediction would be greater, and the actual Y values would fall farther from the fitted regression line.

Diagnostic Plots

The script file (chap17a.r) also contains optional commands to output data influence information and draw diagnostic plots in four separate windows or draw four plots in a single window. The *influence()* function returns the predicted *Y* values, individual coefficients for each subject, sigma, and residual error. This information can be used to examine how each set of scores influenced the prediction of *Y*. Removing the # comment markers in the file (diagnostic plots for four plots in a single window) permits a visual inspection of the data influence:

```
# Diagnostic plots - optional 4 plots in a single window
> layout(matrix(c(1,2,3,4),2,2))
> plot(model1)
```

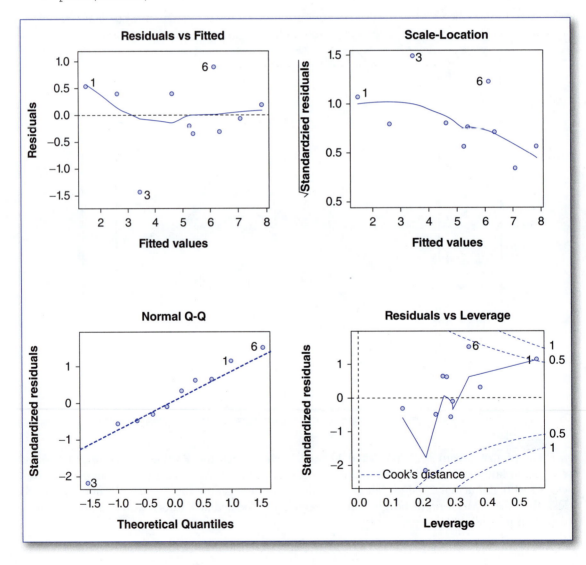

The *fitted values* plot shows how far the errors deviate from 0, for example, pairs of scores for person's 3 and 6 in the data vectors both fall off the zero line. The *leverage* plot is similar, but it reveals the Cooks's distance confidence interval, to show whether the data points fall outside the lines. The *theoretical quantiles* plot indicates any extreme pairs of values, for example, the third pair of numbers in the lower left corner. These plots are important to examine regarding statistical assumptions in multiple regression, that is, independence of errors and presence of outliers that affect estimating regression weights. Fox (2002) provides a very good coverage of diagnosing problems in multiple regression analysis.

Multiple Regression Example: Standardized Solution

The set of R commands in the Multiple Regression Standardized Solution script file (chap17b.r) produces the following summary statistics and multiple regression *standardized* solution:

```
# Multiple Regression with two predictor variables - standardized
# chap17b.r
# Sample Data

> Y   = c(2,3,2,5,5,7,5,6,7,8)
> X1 = c(1,2,2,3,4,5,6,8,9,10)
> X2 = c(2,4,6,8,9,10,7,8,9,10)
> options(scipen = 999)

# R commands to create standardized regression coefficients
# scale function centers variables with mean = 0, sd = 1

>  Y.sc = scale(Y)
> X1.sc = scale(X1)
> X2.sc = scale(X2)
> mean(Y.sc);apply(Y.sc,2,sd)
> mean(X1.sc);apply(X1.sc,2,sd)
> mean(X2.sc);apply(X2.sc,2,sd)

# lm function requires the use of a data.frame not matrix

> standard = data.frame(matrix(c(Y.sc,X1.sc,X2.sc), nrow = 10, ncol = 3))
> cor(standard)
> model2 = lm(Y.sc ~ X1.sc + X2.sc)
> summary(model2)
```

The output indicates that the means and standard deviations have been standardized:

```
> mean(Y.sc); apply(Y.sc,2,sd)
[1] 0.000000000000000111456
[1] 1
```

```
> mean(X1.sc); apply(X1.sc,2,sd)


[1] -0.0000000000000001110223
[1] 1


> mean(X2.sc); apply(X2.sc,2,sd)
[1] 0.00000000000000008184642
[1] 1


> # lm function requires the use of a data.frame not matrix


> standard = data.frame(matrix(c(Y.sc,X1.sc,X2.sc),nrow=10,ncol = 3))
> cor(standard)


          X1           X2           X3
X1 1.0000000    0.8833333    0.8828296
X2 0.8833333    1.0000000    0.7223151
X3 0.8828296    0.7223151    1.0000000


> model2 = lm(Y.sc ~ 0 + X1.sc + X2.sc)
> summary(model2)


Call:
lm(formula = Y.sc ~ 0 + X1.sc + X2.sc)


Residuals:
      Min        1Q       Median        3Q         Max
  -0.68245   -0.13799     0.02627     0.18674     0.42260


Coefficients:
         Estimate    Std. Error    t value    Pr(>|t|)
X1.sc      0.5136        0.1571      3.269      0.0114 *
X2.sc      0.5118        0.1571      3.258      0.0116 *
---
Signif. codes:  0 `***' 0.001 `**' 0.01 `*' 0.05 `.' 0.1 ` ' 1


Residual standard error: 0.3259 on 8 degrees of freedom
Multiple R-squared: 0.9056, Adjusted R-squared: 0.882
F-statistic: 38.36 on 2 and 8 DF, p-value: 0.00007953
```

The *scale()* function created the variables in *z*-score form (standardized with mean = 0 and standard deviation = 1). For example, using *options(scipen = 999)* function to remove scientific notation, the *Y* mean = .00000000000000000111456, which is a very close approximation to 0. The Pearson correlation matrix yields the bivariate correlations in standard score form (*z* score).

The multiple regression solution now provides the β value (standardized beta weights) for the equation. The values for the regression weights are $\beta_{X1} = .5136$ and $\beta_{X2} = .5118$. The multiple R-squared and t-test values are identical to those obtained in the unstandardized multiple regression solution; however, the F test is different because the degrees of freedom for the intercept estimate is dropped. The multiple regression formula in standardized form (intercept = 0) is

$$\hat{Y} = \beta_1 X_1 + \beta_2 X_2$$
$$= .5136(X_1) + .5118(X_2).$$

The standardized beta weights (β) for each predictor variable are computed using the part correlation formula. The beta weights are hand calculated as

$$\beta_1 = \frac{r_{12} - (r_{13}r_{23})}{1 - r_{23}^2} = \frac{.883 - (.882)(.722)}{1 - (.722)^2} = .5136.$$

$$\beta_2 = \frac{r_{13} - (r_{12}r_{23})}{1 - r_{23}^2} = \frac{.882 - (.883)(.722)}{1 - (.722)^2} = .5118.$$

The standard beta weights can be used to calculate the multiple R-squared value. The computations are

$$R_{1.23}^2 = \beta_1 r_{12} + \beta_2 r_{13} = .5136(.883) + .5118(.882) = .9056.$$

The standardized beta weights indicate which variables contribute the most to the prediction of Y. For example, X_1 has a larger standardized beta weight (.5136) than X_2 (.5118). Therefore, X_1 contributes slightly more to the prediction of Y than X_2 in the regression equation. We can see this in a variance accounted for interpretation. X_1 contributes 45.3% (.5136 * .883 = .4535), whereas X_2 contributes 45.1% (.5118 * .882 = .4514). The multiple R-squared value using the standardized beta weights with the Pearson r correlations is the sum of these two variances: .4535 + .4514 = .905.

The *plot()* function is set to have both X and Y axes contain a zero point, using the arguments *ylim* and *xlim*:

```
> plot(yhat, Y.sc, ylim = c(0,2), xlim = c(0,2))
```

The graph now shows the fitted regression line passing through the origin (0, 0) for both X and Y.

We can also compute power given the effect size and degrees of freedom using the *pwr.f2.test()* function in the *pwr* package. The example yielded the following results:

```
Multiple R-squared: 0.9056, Adjusted R-squared: 0.882
F-statistic: 38.36 on 2 and 8 DF, p-value: 0.00007953
```

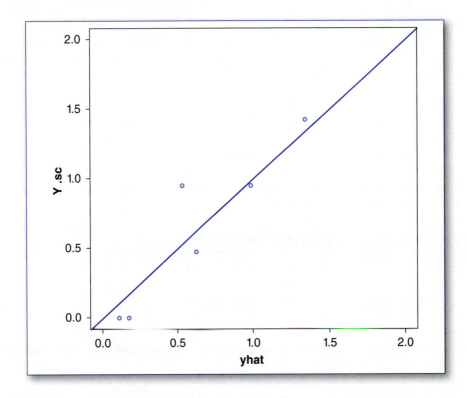

We would load the package and determine the function arguments with the following commands:

```
> library(pwr)
> ?pwr.f2.test
```

```
pwr.f2.test(u = NULL, v = NULL, f2 = NULL, sig.level = 0.05, power = NULL)
```

Arguments

u	Degrees of freedom for numerator
v	Degrees of freedom for denominator
f2	Effect size
sig.level	Significance level (Type I error probability)
Power	Power of test (1 minus Type II error probability)

The R command to obtain power is given as

```
> pwr.f2.test (u = 2, v = 8, .9056, .05, power = NULL)
```

```
Multiple regression power calculation
```

```
u = 2
v = 8
f2 = 0.9056
sig.level = 0.05
power = 0.638259
```

Power = .638 is below the usual level of power = .80, so we are risking a Type II error in falsely rejecting the null hypothesis. Given the small sample size, $n = 10$, it would be prudent to collect more data, thus increasing the sample size, with an accompanying increase in power.

We can compute the partial and semipartial (part) correlations as follows:

```
> library(ppcor)
> Y  = c(2,3,2,5,5,7,5,6,7,8)
> X1 = c(1,2,2,3,4,5,6,8,9,10)
> X2 = c(2,4,6,8,9,10,7,8,9,10)
> mydata= data.frame(matrix(c(Y,X1,X2),10,3))
> names(mydata) = c("Y","X1","X2")
> options(scipen = 999)
> # partial correlation
> pcor(mydata)
> # semi-partial(part) correlation
> spcor(mydata)
```

These commands are in the R script file (chap17b.r) in a separate section. The correlation results are

```
> # partial correlation
> pcor(mydata)
$estimate
            Y            X1            X2
Y   1.0000000    0.7562645    0.7551176
X1  0.7562645    1.0000000   -0.2612462
X2  0.7551176   -0.2612462    1.0000000


$p.value
            Y            X1            X2
Y   0.000000000    0.00222658    0.002308178
X1  0.002226580    0.00000000    0.473954578
X2  0.002308178    0.47395458    0.000000000


$statistic
            Y            X1            X2
Y   0.000000    3.0582174    3.0474162
X1  3.058217    0.0000000   -0.7160596
X2  3.047416   -0.7160596    0.0000000
```

```
$n
[1] 10

$gp
[1] 1

$method
[1] "pearson"

>
> # semi-partial(part) correlation
> spcor(mydata)
$estimate
          Y            X1           X2
Y   1.0000000    0.3552125    0.3539579
X1  0.5230053    1.0000000   -0.1224579
X2  0.5222122   -0.1227056    1.0000000

$p.value
          Y            X1           X2
Y   0.0000000    0.3147195    0.3166780
X1  0.1044862    0.0000000    0.7440838
X2  0.1052115    0.7435767    0.0000000

$statistic
          Y            X1           X2
Y   0.000000     1.0053683    1.0013079
X1  1.623483     0.0000000   -0.3264502
X2  1.620097    -0.3271205    0.0000000

$n
[1] 10

$gp
[1] 1

$method
[1] "pearson"
```

We would compare the partial and semipartial (part) correlations with the Pearson correlation coefficients to determine if any suppressor variable effects are present. We find that the partial correlations, $r_{YX1.X2}$ = .756 and $r_{YX2.X1}$ = .755, are less than the corresponding Pearson correlations, r_{YX1} = .883 and r_{YX2} = .882, respectively. Also, the semipartial (part) correlations, $r_{Y(X1.X2)}$ = .523 and $r_{Y(X2.X1)}$ = .522, are also less than the corresponding Pearson correlation coefficients. We would conclude that there are no suppressor variable effects.

Multiple Regression Summary Table

The unstandardized and standardized results along with the statistical values should be reported in a multiple regression summary table. This permits an examination of all the information required to interpret the statistical significance, the importance of the predictor variables, and power, and a determination of a suppressor variable effect when running multiple regression analyses. A multiple regression summary table would appear as follows:

Multiple Regression Summary Table

| Model | Unstandardized Coefficients | | Standardized | | | | | | | | | |
	b	SE_b	b	t	p	R^2	$F_{2,7}$	p	Power	Pearson Correlation	Partial Correlation	Part Correlation
Intercept	.2892	.7347				.905	33.56	.002	.64			
X_1	.3424	.1120	.5136	3.058	.0184					.883	.756	.523
X_2	.4108	.1348	.5118	3.046	.0187					.882	.755	.522

Placing all of the regression analysis results in a single table aids our interpretation and understanding of the results. We can quickly determine that X_1 and X_2 were statistically significant predictor variables based on the p values for each being less than $p = .05$. We can see that the R-squared value was statistically significant based on the F value (33, 56, $p = .002$). Notice that the reported F value was from the unstandardized regression analysis results. Power = .64 also indicates that the sample size ($n = 10$) is affecting the Type II error. Finally, we can easily compare the Pearson, partial, and part correlations to determine if a suppressor variable effect is present. Many statistical packages will output this type of multiple regression summary table, but in R, you will need to create this table either manually or by writing output code to insert each of the values from the separate analyses into the table format.

TIP

✓ Multiple regression in R uses the *lm()* function to calculate the *a* (intercept) and *b* (regression weights) values. The *plot()* function produces a scatterplot of the data points with the *abline()* function, using the *a* and *b* coefficients from the *lm()* function to draw the fitted regression line on a graph with the data points.

✓ The *ylim* and *xlim* arguments should be used in the plot function when graphing the standardized solution to show the fitted line through the origin of the graph.

✓ The script files show more advanced ways to output diagnostic plots that indicate the influence of data pairs on predicting *Y* and whether outliers exist that deviate far from the fitted regression line.

> **TIP**

> ✓ We use the *unstandardized* solution to compute a *t* test for the significance of the regression weights, that is, *b* divided by SE_b, for each regression coefficient.
>
> ✓ The *standardized solution* is used to compute β, allowing comparison of the regression coefficients and understanding how Pearson *r* is used to compute them.
>
> ✓ The *R*-squared and *t*-test results are the same in both unstandardized and standardized regression solutions.
>
> ✓ The *F* test is different between unstandardized and standardized solutions due to estimation of the intercept in the unstandardized regression equation.
>
> *WARNING:* Do not run both sets of R commands for the different regression solutions together or one after the other, else the computations will be erroneous.
>
> ✓ Create a multiple regression summary table to place all of the separate analyses together for ease of interpretation and understanding.

● NONLINEAR REGRESSION

A common mistake made by researchers in multiple regression analysis is not plotting the bivariate data points in a scatterplot. The reason for displaying the data is to view whether the data are linear or nonlinear (curvilinear). There are many different types of nonlinear data relationships (quadratic, exponential, logistic, etc.), which if not modeled by an appropriate regression equation would yield poor fitting estimates (Bates & Watts, 1988). For example, the linear regression approach would give incorrect estimates if the data were quadratic or cubic (recall that the Pearson *r* value would be 0). We need to modify our approach to multiple regression in the presence of nonlinear data.[1]

The good news is that we can continue to use the *lm()* function to calculate the intercept and regression coefficients in nonlinear regression equations. The nonlinear fitted regression line requires the predicted values from the regression equation, which is obtained by using the *predict()* function. The nonlinear fitted regression line for *Y* and predicted *Y* (*yhat*) is then drawn in the graph using the *lines()* function. We will use the *summary()* function to output results or the *coef()* function to only extract the coefficients. We must use the *lines()* or *curve()* function with the *plot()* function to draw nonlinear fitted regression lines. The *abline()* function is only for drawing a straight line in the scatterplot from a linear regression equation. An example will illustrate the nonlinear regression approach.

Nonlinear Regression Example

Rather than create a data set, we will use an existing data set from the *datasets* package:

```
> library(help = "datasets")
```

We will use the *cars* data set, which is described by issuing the help command.

```
> help(cars)
```

The Internet help window describes the data as being recorded in the 1920s for the speed (in miles per hour, mph) and stopping distance (in feet) of cars. It has 50 observations and two variables (Ezekiel, 1930). We will access these data set by using the *attach()* function and then list the data frame by using the name of the data set.

```
> attach(cars)
> cars
      speed   dist
1        4      2
2        4     10
3        7      4
4        7     22
5        8     16
6        9     10
7       10     18
8       10     26
9       10     34
10      11     17
11      11     28
12      12     14
13      12     20
14      12     24
15      12     28
16      13     26
17      13     34
18      13     34
19      13     46
20      14     26
21      14     36
22      14     60
23      14     80
24      15     20
25      15     26
26      15     54
27      16     32
28      16     40
29      17     32
30      17     40
31      17     50
32      18     42
33      18     56
34      18     76
35      18     84
36      19     36
37      19     46
```

38	19	68
39	20	32
40	20	48
41	20	52
42	20	56
43	20	64
44	22	66
45	23	54
46	24	70
47	24	92
48	24	93
49	24	120
50	25	85

The *help(cars)* function opens an Internet window and gives the R commands for a polynomial regression analysis that includes a test of linear, quadratic, cubic, and quartic trends in the data. A special variable is created, *degree*, which indicates the level of nonlinearity: linear (power of 1), quadratic (power of 2), cubic (power of 3), and quartic (power of 4). I ran the *lm()* function and plotted the results where speed is on the *y*-axis and stopping distance is on the *x*-axis. The R commands are

```
# An example of polynomial regression
> attach(cars)

> fm <- lm(speed ~ poly(dist, degree), data = cars)

> summary(fm)
```

The *poly()* function computes all four types of regression coefficients. The *summary()* function lists the regression coefficients for all four types of regression coefficients (linear, quadratic, cubic, and quartic).

```
Call:
lm(formula = speed ~ poly(dist, degree), data = cars)

Residuals:
      Min        1Q     Median        3Q       Max
  -6.8557   -1.9194    0.2788    2.0023    5.5300
```

Coefficients:

	Estimate	Std. Error	t value	Pr(>|t|)	
(Intercept)	15.40000	0.41248	37.335	<2e-16	***
poly(dist, degree)1	29.86601	2.91669	10.240	2.46e-13	***
poly(dist, degree)2	-8.99505	2.91669	-3.084	0.00348	**
poly(dist, degree)3	3.77928	2.91669	1.296	0.20167	
poly(dist, degree)4	-0.09355	2.91669	-0.032	0.97455	

```
Signif. codes:   0 `***' 0.001 `**' 0.01 `*' 0.05 `.' 0.1 ` ' 1

Residual standard error: 2.917 on 45 degrees of freedom
Multiple R-squared: 0.7206, Adjusted R-squared: 0.6957
F-statistic: 29.01 on 4 and 45 DF, p-value: 5.984e-12
```

The polynomial coefficients are given for the different power or degrees (linear, quadratic, cubic, and quartic), labeled 1, 2, 3, and 4, respectively. Results indicate that a linear or quadratic regression line can be fitted to the data. If we only ran a multiple *linear* regression equation, we would have missed the statistical significance of a quadratic coefficient, which indicates a certain type of nonlinearity.

The power for our data analysis, given these results, would be computed as

```
> pwr.f2.test (u = 4, v = 45, .7206, .05, power = NULL)

Multiple regression power calculation

u = 4
v = 45
f2 = 0.7206
sig.level = 0.05
power = 0.9984877
```

Results indicate that we have sufficient power to detect the polynomial differences for the *R*-squared effect size.

Multiple Linear Regression Only

The R commands for a multiple linear regression equation with the fitted linear regression line in a scatterplot are

```
# An example of linear regression

> attach(cars)

> lnfit = lm(speed ~ dist, data = cars)
> summary(lnfit)

> plot(dist , speed, ylab = "Speed (mph)", xlab = "Stopping distance
(ft)", main = "Linear Regression Line")
> abline(lnfit)
```

The results show the multiple regression output with a statistically significant predictor variable (*dist*). The graph shows the plot of the data values with the fitted regression line.

```
Call:
lm(formula = speed ~ dist, data = cars)

Residuals:
    Min       1Q    Median       3Q      Max
-7.5293  -2.1550   0.3615   2.4377   6.4179

Coefficients:
            Estimate  Std. Error  t value  Pr(>|t|)
(Intercept)  8.28391     0.87438    9.474  1.44e-12 ***
dist         0.16557     0.01749    9.464  1.49e-12 ***

Signif. codes:  0 '***' 0.001 '**' 0.01 '*' 0.05 '.' 0.1 ' ' 1

Residual standard error: 3.156 on 48 degrees of freedom
Multiple R-squared: 0.6511, Adjusted R-squared: 0.6438
F-statistic: 89.57 on 1 and 48 DF, p-value: 1.49e-12
```

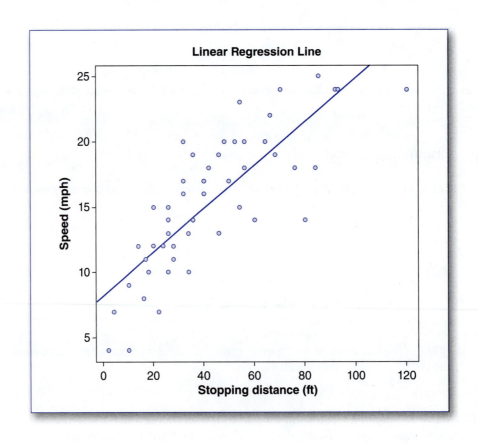

The predictor variable (*dist*) is statistically significant ($t = 9.464$, $p = 1.49\text{e}{-}12$ ***).

The scatterplot shows the linear relationship between the dependent variable, mph (*speed*), and the independent predictor variable, stopping distance (*dist*). We could compute a Pearson correlation using *cor(dist, speed)*. The scientific notation could be removed using the function *options(scipen = 999)*.

Quadratic Regression Only

You can hypothesize a quadratic term in the *lm()* function to estimate the specific type of nonlinear fit. You need to use the identity function, *I()*, to indicate the nonlinear variable in the regression equation. The R commands to compute a *quadratic* nonlinear regression equation are

```
> attach(cars)
> nlfit = lm(speed ~ I(dist^2), data = cars)
> options(scipen = 999)
> summary(nlfit)
> coef(nlfit)
```

The results once again show the multiple regression output, but this time for a *quadratic* predictor indicated by *I(dist^2)*.

```
Call:
lm(formula = speed ~ I(dist^2), data = cars)

Residuals:
    Min       1Q    Median       3Q      Max
-8.2940   -2.4831    0.0584   2.7050   7.0587

Coefficients:
               Estimate   Std. Error   t value          Pr(>|t|)
(Intercept)  12.1644824    0.7203819    16.886  < 0.0000000000000002 ***
I(dist^2)     0.0012952    0.0001909     6.783       0.0000000158  ***

Signif. codes:  0 '***' 0.001 '**' 0.01 '*' 0.05 '.' 0.1 ' ' 1

Residual standard error: 3.817 on 48 degrees of freedom
Multiple R-squared: 0.4894, Adjusted R-squared: 0.4788
F-statistic: 46.01 on 1 and 48 DF, p-value: 0.0000000158

> coef(nlfit)
 (Intercept)       I(dist^2)
12.164482382     0.001295212
```

The *summary()* and *coef()* functions provide the regression results and coefficients for the quadratic regression model. To show a graph of the fitted quadratic regression line, we would use the *predict()*, *plot()*, and *lines()* functions to draw the quadratic curved line based on the nonlinear regression coefficients. *Note: type = "l"* has a lowercase *L*, not a numeric 1.0 value. The R commands are

```
> fitnline = predict(nlfit, data.frame(dist = 0:130))

> plot(dist , speed, ylab = "Speed (mph)", xlab = "Stopping distance(ft)",
main = "Quadratic Regression Line")

> lines(0:130, fitnline, type = "l")
```

The following is a graph of scatterplot data points and the quadratic curved regression line:

poly() Function

The *lm()* function in the *polynomial regression function* script file (chap17c.r) computes the linear and quadratic equations using the *poly()* function. The graph of the *cars* data will visually show the fitted lines for these two regression equations that fit the scatterplot of data points. The goal is to fit the best type of regression line to the data so that our residual values are the smallest. The selection of the regression coefficients that yield the smallest residual error between *Y* and predicted *Y* is called the *least squares criterion.* The *poly()* function yielded the statistical significance of the two types of multiple regression equations, linear and quadratic. The R commands in the script file attach the data set, *cars*, compute the regression equations using the *poly()* function, and then plot the data with the two different fitted regression lines, all of which are embedded in a *for* loop. The *for* loop can be modified to include other polynomial line types (*lty* = 1:4) if they were statistically significant. This permits more than one type of fitted regression line to be drawn in the graph. The *legend()* function provides the list of the line types in the graph. The set of R commands in the script file, which includes a *for{ }* loop, are

```
# Polynomial Regression Lines - chap17c.r
> attach(cars)
> nlfit = lm(speed ~ I(dist^2)+ dist, data = cars)
> summary(nlfit); coef(nlfit)

> plot(dist, speed, xlab = "Stopping
  distance(ft)", ylab = "Speed(mph)", xlim = c(0,120), ylim = c(0,25))

for(degree in 1:2)
{
   fm <- lm(speed ~ poly(dist, degree), data = cars)
   lines(0:120, predict(fm, data.frame(dist = 0:120)), lty = degree)
   legend("topleft", c("linear","quadratic"), bty = "n", title = "Line
Types", lty = 1:2)
}
```

The graph visually shows data that support the multiple regression results, which indicated a quadratic line that fit the data points for *speed* (mph) predicted by *stopping distance* (feet) squared. It shows that increased speed takes more distance to stop, which fits our expectations. However, the quadratic line shows that at 25 mph, the stopping distance tends to level off at 120 feet. *We do not know what the relationship is between speed and stopping distance outside this range of values.* A researcher would need to gather more data beyond 25 mph to determine if a true quadratic relation exists between speed and stopping distance. Logically, it does not make sense that the faster one travels, the less distance it would take to stop (the conclusion of a quadratic relation between speed and distance). Further investigation using different tires, weights of vehicles, types of vehicles, and so on, would provide more information to the tire manufacturer and auto industry. This type of research reveals one of the reasons why companies recommend certain types of tires for your car.

fitted() Function

The *fitted()* function outputs the predicted values for *speed.* So for the quadratic nonlinear regression equation the predicted values would be

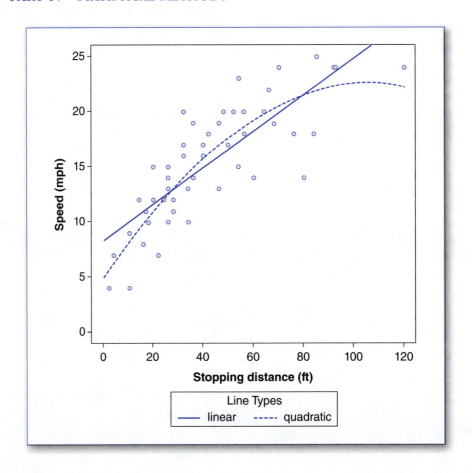

```
> fitted(nlfit)
        1          2          3          4          5          6          7          8
 5.792756   8.265669   6.429325  11.608229   9.991970   8.265669  10.542950  12.624600
        9         10         11         12         13         14         15         16
14.510619  10.268988  13.114445   9.428763  11.081703  12.122528  13.114445  12.624600
       17         18         19         20         21         22         23         24
14.510619  14.510619  16.972840  12.624600  14.951557  19.289106  21.558767  11.081703
       25         26         27         28         29         30         31         32
12.624600  18.369782  14.057455  15.796751  14.057455  15.796751  17.695765  16.201008
       33         34         35         36         37         38         39         40
18.688450  21.202650  21.865976  14.951557  16.972840  20.343693  14.057455  17.340416
       41         42         43         44         45         46         47         48
18.038887  18.688450  19.840853  20.098387  18.369782  20.576773  22.333670  22.378377
       49         50
22.430008  21.935136
```

The following additional command would give the residual error (Y – predicted Y).

```
> error = speed - fitted(nlfit)
> error
```

1	2	3	4	5	6	7
-1.7927564	-4.2656686	0.5706752	-4.6082289	-1.9919700	0.7343314	-0.5429499
8	9	10	11	12	13	14
-2.6246002	-4.5106195	0.7310117	-2.1144454	2.5712369	0.9182971	-0.1225280
15	16	17	18	19	20	21
-1.1144454	0.3753998	-1.5106195	-1.5106195	-3.9728403	1.3753998	-0.9515570
22	23	24	25	26	27	28
-5.2891057	-7.5587666	3.9182971	2.3753998	-3.3697822	1.9425449	0.2032489
29	30	31	32	33	34	35
2.9425449	1.2032489	-0.6957651	1.7989922	-0.6884503	-3.2026499	-3.8659756
36	37	38	39	40	41	42
4.0484430	2.0271597	-1.3436933	5.9425449	2.6595838	1.9611129	1.3115497
43	44	45	46	47	48	49
0.1591466	1.9016132	4.6302178	3.4232271	1.6663298	1.6216232	1.5699925
50						
3.0648640						

Our basic understanding is that $Y = \hat{Y} + \text{error}$. For example, the last car had a stopping distance of 120 feet. Given knowledge of the stopping distance for the car in the quadratic regression equation, it predicted 21.94 mph with 3.06 error, so Y (25 mph) = 21.94 ($\hat{Y}$) + 3.06 (error).

A comparison of the *residual standard error* for each type of regression model helps determine the best-fitting regression equation. We see that the standard error for the linear regression equation is Residual standard error = 3.156 on 48 degrees of freedom, while the standard error for the quadratic regression equation is Residual standard error = 2.907 on 47 degrees of freedom. Therefore, the quadratic fitted regression line has slightly less residual standard error. The multiple R-squared values can also be compared. The multiple R-squared value is higher for the quadratic fitted regression equation than the linear fitted regression equation. Together, the quadratic regression equation yielded a higher multiple R-squared value with a corresponding lower residual standard error than the linear regression equation. We, therefore, suspect that the relationship between the speed of a car and the stopping distance in feet is not exactly linear but displays a quadratic trend in the data beyond a linear relationship. This only holds true for the range of values in Y and X that we have collected. Our instinct and logic tell us that we should collect more data beyond these range of values.

Test of Difference Between Two Multiple R-Squared Values

We can test the difference in the multiple R-squared values between the linear and quadratic regression equations using the F test. This allows us a statistical determination of whether nonlinear regression estimation is statistically significant above and beyond the linear regression estimation. The F test with 1 and 47 degrees of freedom is 9.83 and is calculated as

$$F = \frac{(R^2_{\text{Quadratic}} - R^2_{\text{Linear}}) / (k_{\text{Quadratic}} - k_{\text{Linear}})}{(1 - R^2_{\text{Quadratic}}) / (N - k_{\text{Quadratic}} - 1)}$$

$$= \frac{(.7101 - .6511) / (2 - 1)}{(1 - .7101) / (50 - 2 - 1)}$$

$$= \frac{.059}{(.2899) / 47}$$

$$= \frac{.059}{.006}$$

$$= 9.83.$$

We compare this computed F-test value for differences in the two multiple R-squared values with the tabled F value for the degrees of freedom and alpha level of probability. The tabled F value for $df = 1, 40$ at the .05 level is 4.08, and for $df = 1, 60$, it is 4.00 in Table 5 (Appendix A). The exact tabled F value is not listed, but extrapolation between the F values of 4.0 and 4.08 would be $F = 4.06$ {$[F = (47/60) * (4.08 - 4.00)] + 4.00 = 4.06$}. The computed $F = 9.83$ is greater than the extrapolated $F = 4.06$ with $df = 1, 47$ at the .05 level of significance, so a quadratic fitted regression line does statistically increase the amount of variance explained (multiple R squared) above and beyond the linear regression fitted line. The numerator of the F test indicates the .059 difference (approximately 6%), which is the added variance contribution to prediction by the quadratic regression equation. More data would be necessary to disconfirm a nonlinear relationship between speed and distance and support a linear relationship, which meets our theory and expectations.

Interpretation of Regression Results

The quadratic regression equation indicated a statistically significant multiple R-squared value. In addition, the difference between the linear multiple R-squared and quadratic multiple R-squared values was statistically significant. A quadratic interpretation that the distance to stop decreases as a car goes faster does not make empirical sense. The law of physics suggests that as one drives faster (speed in mph), it would take more time to stop (distance in feet).

My first concern is the range of data values. We should only predict within the range of our data values, that is, 0 to 25 mph for speed. We do not know for certain that it will take less distance if we go faster than 25 mph. Our regression equation was calibrated based on the range of data we used. We should not use other values in the regression equation, only the ones in the data set, otherwise our predictions are suspect.

My second concern is whether we have included all of the relevant predictor variables. If we add one or two more predictor variables, the regression equation should provide a better prediction equation. For example, the type of brakes, disc or drum, and whether all four wheels have disc or drum brakes. My third concern is the control of extraneous variables (covariates) that affect the distance it takes to stop a car at different speeds. For example, the number of persons in the car and/or engine displacement (4 cyl [cylinder], 6 cyl, 8 cyl) could have an effect on the weight of the vehicle, hence the stopping distance. The weight of the vehicle itself makes sense as a predictor variable.

If we collected more data on stopping distances at higher speeds, added additional predictor variables, and controlled for extraneous (covariate) variables, then our prediction equation would be more accurate and the type of fitted regression line (linear, quadratic, cubic, etc.) would be more realistic and provide more realistic prediction estimates. Researchers use multiple regression to predict, but one should not let statistical analysis numb the brain.

TIP

✓ Many generic functions can be embedded in R commands; for example, the *plot()* function contains the regression equation, and the *lines()* function contains the *fitted.values()* function, which makes it easy to plot the fit of the model and add a line to the graph:

```
> plot(speed ~ dist, data = cars)
> lines(dist, fitted.values(lnfit))
```

✓ The *summary()* function can also be used with the *lm()* function to output more diagnostic information.

```
> sampleReg = summary(lm(sampleY ~ sampleX))
> print(sampleReg)
```

✓ *predict()* gives predicted Y values for regression equation.

✓ *influence()* gives influence values: hat values, residual values, and leverage.

✓ This set of R commands output four different diagnostic plots in a single graphic window for a regression equation specified as *model*.

```
> layout(matrix(c(1,2,3,4),2,2))
> plot(model)
```

● MULTIPLE REGRESSION WITH NOMINAL AND CONTINUOUS PREDICTORS

Multiple regression equations can contain nominal as well as continuous predictor variables, thus providing analysis of variance-type results (Wright & London, 2009). Nominal variables are treated as *factors* in R, which require *dummy coding* or *contrast coding* to correctly test mean differences in the levels of the nominal variable. For example, *gender* would have two levels and require dummy coding—0 and 1 for males and females, respectively. Another nominal variable, *occupation*, with three levels (professional, blue collar, white collar) would require contrast codes, 1, 0, and −1, for the occupation levels being compared.

The *contrast()* function provides the required dummy and contrast coding in the regression equation. Our terminology changes when using a *predictor* variable (independent variable) as a contrast-coded variable, which is termed a *regressor* variable (dummy- or contrast-coded variable). A researcher has the option of directly coding the levels of the nominal variable in a data set or using the contrast-coding function. There are three basic types of contrast coding: (1) *contr.treatment*, (2) *contr.sum*, and (3) *contr.helmert*. The default is *contr.treatment*, which creates $(n - 1)$ dummy-coded vectors. An example and explanation of each will provide a better understanding for interpreting the regression coefficients.

Contrast: *contr.treatment*

When a *factor* (nominal variable) is used in a regression model, it automatically produces the correct number of dummy-coded vectors based on the default contrast, *contr.treatment*.

We will use the *PlantGrowth* data set in *library= (help = "datasets")*. The *group* variable in the *PlantGrowth* data set has three levels: (1) *ctrl*, (2) *trt1*, and (3) *trt2*. For the three levels of *group*, two *dummy*-coded vectors, *grouptrt1* and *grouptrt2*, would be created automatically in the *lm()* function. First, attach the data set, and view the data:

```
> attach(PlantGrowth)
> PlantGrowth

      weight    group
1      4.17     ctrl
2      5.58     ctrl
3      5.18     ctrl
4      6.11     ctrl
5      4.50     ctrl
6      4.61     ctrl
7      5.17     ctrl
8      4.53     ctrl
9      5.33     ctrl
10     5.14     ctrl
11     4.81     trt1
12     4.17     trt1
13     4.41     trt1
14     3.59     trt1
15     5.87     trt1
16     3.83     trt1
17     6.03     trt1
18     4.89     trt1
19     4.32     trt1
20     4.69     trt1
21     6.31     trt2
22     5.12     trt2
23     5.54     trt2
24     5.50     trt2
```

25	5.37	trt2
26	5.29	trt2
27	4.92	trt2
28	6.15	trt2
29	5.80	trt2
30	5.26	trt2

Note: R alphabetizes the levels of the regressor variable and defines the dummy coding levels in alphabetical order. The first level alphabetically becomes the baseline level, that is, ctrl.

The data set should be saved as a data frame, *out*. The *lm()* function contains the regression formula, a reference to the data set, and the contrast specification. Output is simplified to only the intercept term and the regression coefficients for the two dummy-coded vectors. Additional output can be obtained by using the *summary()* function. The commands are

```
> out = data.frame(PlantGrowth)
> lm(weight ~ group, data = out, contrasts = "contr.treatment")

Call:
lm(formula = weight ~ group, data = out, contrasts = "contr.treatment")

Coefficients:
(Intercept)        grouptrt1        grouptrt2
      5.032           -0.371            0.494
```

R fits the regression model and automatically creates the two dummy-coded vectors:

$$\text{Weight} = \beta_0 + \beta_1 grouptrt1 + \beta_2 grouptrt2$$
$$= 5.032 + (-.371 grouptrt1) + .494(grouptrt2).$$

The regression equation is predicting the mean weight as a function of the two dummy-coded regressor variables. The dummy-coding results should be interpreted in relation to the baseline group, ctrl, which is the intercept value. The following computations using the regression coefficients would be used to compute the group mean weight values.

$$\mu_{ctrl} = \beta_0$$
$$\mu_{trt1} = \beta_0 + \beta_1$$
$$\mu_{trt2} = \beta_0 + \beta_2.$$

Therefore, the group means are

$$\bar{X}_{ctrl} = 5.032$$
$$\bar{X}_{trt1} = 5.032 + (-.371) = 4.661$$
$$\bar{X}_{trt2} = 5.032 + .494 = 5.526.$$

The *tapply()* function will provide these same group means:

```
> tapply(out$weight, out$group, mean)
```

```
ctrl      trt1        trt2
5.032     4.661       5.526
```

> [!TIP]
> **TIP**
>
> Recall from Chapter 5 that we can install the package *psych*, which has a *describe.by()* function for obtaining summary statistics by group. The R commands after installing the psych package are
>
> ```
> > data(PlantGrowth)
> > describe.by(PlantGrowth, PlantGrowth$group)
> ```
>
> group: ctrl
>
> | | var | n | mean | sd | median | trimmed | mad | min | max | range | skew | kurtosis | se |
> |---|---|---|---|---|---|---|---|---|---|---|---|---|---|
> | weight | 1 | 10 | 5.03 | 0.58 | 5.15 | 5 | 0.72 | 4.17 | 6.11 | 1.94 | 0.23 | -0.23 | 0.18 |
> | group* | 2 | 10 | 1.00 | 0.00 | 1.00 | 1 | 0.00 | 1.00 | 1.00 | 0.00 | NaN | NaN | 0.00 |
>
> --
>
> group: trt1
>
> | | var | n | mean | sd | median | trimmed | mad | min | max | range | skew | kurtosis | se |
> |---|---|---|---|---|---|---|---|---|---|---|---|---|---|
> | weight | 1 | 10 | 4.66 | 0.79 | 4.55 | 4.62 | 0.53 | 3.59 | 6.03 | 2.44 | 0.47 | -0.2 | 0.25 |
> | group* | 2 | 10 | 2.00 | 0.00 | 2.00 | 2.00 | 0.00 | 2.00 | 2.00 | 0.00 | NaN | NaN | 0.00 |
>
> --
>
> group: trt2
>
> | | var | n | mean | sd | median | trimmed | mad | min | max | range | skew | kurtosis | se |
> |---|---|---|---|---|---|---|---|---|---|---|---|---|---|
> | weight | 1 | 10 | 5.53 | 0.44 | 5.44 | 5.5 | 0.36 | 4.92 | 6.31 | 1.39 | 0.48 | -0.32 | 0.14 |
> | group* | 2 | 10 | 3.00 | 0.00 | 3.00 | 3.0 | 0.00 | 3.00 | 3.00 | 0.00 | NaN | NaN | 0.00 |

The *tapply()* function group means are the same as the ones we computed using the regression coefficients. Although the exact values are shown, hand calculations will be off slightly due to rounding error. We can obtain the regression coefficients in the regression equation by subtracting the control group mean from the other group means to obtain β_1 and β_2.

$$\beta_0 = \mu_{ctrl} = 5.032$$
$$\beta_1 = \mu_{trt1} - \mu_{ctrl} = 4.66 - 5.032 = -.371$$
$$\beta_2 = \mu_{trt2} - \mu_{ctrl} = 5.53 - 5.032 = .494.$$

Dummy coding of regressor variables provides the correct solution and indicates that the regression coefficients are measuring the difference in the group means from the baseline group mean. The intercept corresponds to the mean of the baseline group, which is chosen alphabetically. Selection of a baseline group is important when interpreting the differences from other dummy-coded groups.

Contrast: *contr.sum*

Another type of contrast that can be specified in multiple regression for group differences is *contr. sum*. It uses 0 and –1 for contrasting groups with *n* corresponding to the levels of the categorical variable. We first show what the *deviation coding* for our three groups would be:

```
> contr.sum(3)

     [,1]   [,2]
1     1      0
2     0      1
3    -1     -1
```

We assign this deviation coding to our categorical variable and show the results:

```
> contrasts(group)  = contr.sum(3)
           [,1]   [,2]
ctrl        1      0
trt1        0      1
trt2       -1     -1
Levels:  ctrl trt1 trt2
```

Then, we change the *lm()* function and run it as follows:

```
> summary(lm(weight ~ group, contrasts = "contr.sum"))

Call:
lm(formula = weight ~ group, contrasts = "contr.sum")

Coefficients:
(Intercept)          group1              group2
     5.073           -0.041              -0.412
```

R fits the regression model using the same dependent variable, but the regressor variable is coded differently: weight $= \beta_0 + \beta_1 X_1 + \beta_2 X_2$. The deviation coding, therefore, yields different equations for the group means:

$$\mu_{ctrl} = \beta_0 + \beta_1 = 5.073 + (-.041) = 5.03$$
$$\mu_{trt1} = \beta_0 + \beta_2 = 5.073 + (-.412) = 4.66$$
$$\mu_{trt2} = \beta_0 - \beta_1 - \beta_2 = 5.073 - (-.041) - (-.412) = 5.53.$$

The intercept value is calculated in deviation coding as the average of all three group means:

$$\beta_0 = \frac{\beta_0 + \beta_1 + \beta_2}{3} = \frac{\mu_{ctrl} + \mu_{trt1} + \mu_{trt2}}{3} = \frac{(5.03 + 4.66 + 5.53)}{3} = 5.073.$$

Using this new intercept value, $\beta_0 = \mu_{int}$, in the formula above we calculate β_1 and β_2 in the regression equation:

$$\beta_1 = \mu_{ctrl} - \mu_{int} = 5.032 - 5.073 = -.041$$
$$\beta_2 = \mu_{trt1} - \mu_{int} = 4.66 - 5.073 = -.413.$$

Thus, in deviation coding, the coefficients measure the distance between certain individual levels and the mean of all the levels, that is,

β_1 = the difference between the control group mean and the intercept grand mean

β_2 = the difference between the Treatment 1 group mean and the intercept grand mean.

Contrast: *contr.helmert*

Another type of contrast coding is specified by *contr.helmert* as follows:

```
> contrasts(group) = contr.helmert(3)

          [,1]   [,2]
ctrl      -1     -1
trt1       1     -1
trt2       0      2
Levels:  ctrl trt1 trt2
```

We change the *lm()* function to indicate the different contrast method and run it as follows:

```
> lm(weight ~ group, contrasts = "contr.helmert")

Call:
lm(formula = weight ~ group, contrasts = "contr.helmert")

Coefficients:
(Intercept)         group1             group2
     5.0730        -0.1855             0.2265
```

R fits the regression model the same as before, except that the regressor variable has changed due to a different contrast coding, weight = $\beta_0 + \beta_1 X_1 + \beta_2 X_2$. The Helmert coding scheme calculates the group means using the regression coefficients as follows:

$$\mu_{ctrl} = \beta_0 - \beta_1 - \beta_2$$
$$\mu_{trt1} = \beta_0 + \beta_1 - \beta_2$$
$$\mu_{trt2} = \beta_0 + 2\beta_2.$$

Helmert coding, similar to deviation coding, also averages the three group means to compute the intercept term. The β_0 is the intercept that represents the mean of all the groups:

$$\beta_0 = \frac{\beta_0 + \beta_1 + \beta_2}{3} = \frac{\mu_{ctrl} + \mu_{trt1} + \mu_{trt2}}{3} = \frac{(5.03 + 4.66 + 5.53)}{3} = 5.073.$$

The two regressor variable coefficients, however, are calculated differently, where β_1 is the average difference between the Treatment 1 group mean and the control group mean:

$$\beta_1 = \frac{\mu_{trt1} - \mu_{ctrl}}{2} = \frac{4.66 - 5.03}{2} = \frac{-.371}{2} = -.1855.$$

$$\mu_{trt1} - \mu_{ctrl} = 2\beta_1$$
$$\mu_{trt1} - \mu_{ctrl} = 2(-.1855) = -.371.$$

In Helmert contrast coding, if the coefficient β_1 is not statistically significantly different from zero, then the Treatment 1 and control group means are not significantly different, that is, $-.371$ does not indicate a statistically significant mean difference.

We calculate β_2 by averaging the control group and Treatment 1 group means, then subtracting from the Treatment 2 group means, as follows:

$$\beta_2 = \frac{1}{3}\left(\mu_{trt2} - \frac{\mu_{ctrl} + \mu_{trt1}}{2}\right)$$

$$= .33\left(5.53 - \frac{5.03 + 4.66}{2}\right)$$

$$= .33(5.53 - 4.845) = .2265.$$

$$\mu_{trt2} - \frac{\mu_{ctrl} + \mu_{trt1}}{2} = 3\beta_2$$

$$\mu_{trt2} - \frac{\mu_{ctrl} + \mu_{trt1}}{2} = 3(.2265) = .685.$$

In Helmert contrast coding, if β_2 is not statistically significantly different from zero, then the Treatment 2 group mean is not significantly different from the average of the control group and Treatment 1 group means; that is, .685 is not a statistically significant mean difference. Helmert contrast coding compares the mean difference of a group with the average of all other group means; thus, it is appropriate for group mean contrasts that are ordered, because of the sequential group mean comparisons. When testing a trend in the means of groups, for example, in a one-way analysis of variance research design, this type of contrast would be used.

Recall that the *summary()* function will provide a *t* test for the significance of each regressor variable. A researcher would desire to print *t* tests of significance so as to focus on which regressor variable coefficients relate to which group mean comparisons. We would, therefore, include the regression equation and contrast type in the *summary()* function:

```
> summary(lm(weight ~ group, contrasts = "contr.helmert"))

Call:
lm(formula = weight ~ group, contrasts = "contr.helmert")

Residuals:
     Min       1Q    Median       3Q      Max
 -1.0710  -0.4180  -0.0060   0.2627   1.3690

Coefficients:
              Estimate   Std. Error   t value   Pr(>|t|)
(Intercept)    5.07300      0.11381    44.573   < 2e-16 ***
group1        -0.18550      0.13939    -1.331   0.19439
group2         0.22650      0.08048     2.814   0.00901 **
---
Signif. codes:  0 '***' 0.001 '**' 0.01 '*' 0.05 '.' 0.1 ' ' 1

Residual standard error: 0.6234 on 27 degrees of freedom
Multiple R-squared: 0.2641, Adjusted R-squared: 0.2096
F-statistic: 4.846 on 2 and 27 DF, p-value: 0.01591
```

These results, however, have low power to detect the group mean differences. The power is computed as

```
> pwr.f2.test (u = 2, v = 27, .2641, .05, power = NULL)

Multiple regression power calculation

u = 2
v = 27
f2 = 0.2641
sig.level = 0.05
power = 0.6608024
```

Once again, if we increase the three group sample sizes from $n = 10$ to $n = 15$, we would achieve sufficient power to detect group mean differences and protect against a Type II error. The degrees of freedom would now be 2 $(k - 1)$ and 42 $(N - k)$, where $k = $ the number of groups. The R command and power results are

```
> pwr.f2.test (u = 2, v = 42, .2641, .05, power = NULL)

        Multiple regression power calculation

u = 2
v = 42
```

```
f2 = 0.2641
sig.level = 0.05
power = 0.8544457
```

Interpreting Different Contrast Types

The *contr.treatment* contrast coding compares the Treatment 1 and Treatment 2 group means separately with the intercept, which is the baseline group selected alphabetically (control group). This is a common technique used by researchers who form null hypotheses based on treatment and control group comparisons. The *contr.treatment* coding is different from deviation coding in *contr.sum* contrast coding. Deviation coding compares Treatment 1 and Treatment 2 with a grand mean, which is the average of all three group means. Some researchers feel that this is a more fair or unbiased comparison of means. Finally, the *contr.helmert* contrast coding, similar to **Scheffe complex contrasts**, permits a comparison of two or more group average means with a third group mean. For example, the average of the two treatment group means could be compared with the control group mean. Complex contrasts expand the researchers' ability to form different research questions. There are many different types of contrast coding schema possible depending on the research question. The following website for the UCLA Academic Technology Services provides further examples of contrast coding for categorical variables in R: http://www.ats.ucla .edu/stat/r/library/contrast_coding.htm.

Multiple Regression Function

Multiple regression equations with nominal and continuous predictor variables need to be specified correctly; otherwise, the results could be incorrectly interpreted. The following R program example demonstrates the inclusion of a specific contrast in the regression equation, which is tested along with a continuous variable, *Fertamt*, which is the amount of fertilizer used. The control group received 5 ounces of fertilizer, the Treatment 1 group received 10 ounces of fertilizer, and the Treatment 2 group received 15 ounces of fertilizer. The specific contrast tested is whether the plant growth for the control group differs from the average of the two treatment groups, which is denoted by *B*1. The multiple regression function in the script file (chap17d.r) uses the *PlantGrowth* data set and these additional variables as follows:

```
# Multiple Regression with nominal and continuous predictor variables
# chap17d.r

> attach(PlantGrowth)
> B1 = rep(c(1,-.5,-.5), c(10,10,10))
> Fertamt = rep(c(5,10,15), c(10,10,10))
> newdata = data.frame(PlantGrowth, Fertamt, B1)
> newdata
> summary(lm(weight~ Fertamt + B1), data = newdata)
```

The results will list the data set, *newdata*, followed by the results of the multiple regression analysis for the specific contrast.

	weight	group	Fertamt	B1
1	4.17	ctrl	5	1.0
2	5.58	ctrl	5	1.0
3	5.18	ctrl	5	1.0
4	6.11	ctrl	5	1.0
5	4.50	ctrl	5	1.0
6	4.61	ctrl	5	1.0
7	5.17	ctrl	5	1.0
8	4.53	ctrl	5	1.0
9	5.33	ctrl	5	1.0
10	5.14	ctrl	5	1.0
11	4.81	trt1	10	-0.5
12	4.17	trt1	10	-0.5
13	4.41	trt1	10	-0.5
14	3.59	trt1	10	-0.5
15	5.87	trt1	10	-0.5
16	3.83	trt1	10	-0.5
17	6.03	trt1	10	-0.5
18	4.89	trt1	10	-0.5
19	4.32	trt1	10	-0.5
20	4.69	trt1	10	-0.5
21	6.31	trt2	15	-0.5
22	5.12	trt2	15	-0.5
23	5.54	trt2	15	-0.5
24	5.50	trt2	15	-0.5
25	5.37	trt2	15	-0.5
26	5.29	trt2	15	-0.5
27	4.92	trt2	15	-0.5
28	6.15	trt2	15	-0.5
29	5.80	trt2	15	-0.5
30	5.26	trt2	15	-0.5

```
> summary(lm(weight~ Fertamt + B1), data = newdata)

Call:
lm(formula = weight ~ Fertamt + B1)

Residuals:
     Min        1Q     Median        3Q       Max
 -1.0710   -0.4180   -0.0060    0.2627    1.3690
```

```
Coefficients:
                Estimate   Std. Error    t value      Pr(>|t|)
(Intercept)     3.34300     0.56906        5.875       2.95e-06 ***
Fertamt         0.17300     0.05576        3.103       0.00446 **
B1              0.82400     0.32191        2.560       0.01639 *
---
Signif. codes:  0 '***' 0.001 '**' 0.01 '*' 0.05 '.' 0.1 ' ' 1

Residual standard error: 0.6234 on 27 degrees of freedom
Multiple R-squared: 0.2641, Adjusted R-squared: 0.2096
F-statistic: 4.846 on 2 and 27 DF, p-value: 0.01591
```

The results indicate that the amount of fertilizer (*Fertamt*) was statistically significantly related to plant growth (*weight*). In addition, the specific contrast (*B*1) of mean differences was statistically significant. Therefore, the average weight of plants in the two treatment groups was different from the weight in the control group. We can display these group means with the following commands:

```
> tapply(newdata$weight, newdata$group, mean)
  ctrl     trt1     trt2
 5.032    4.661    5.526
A simple hand calculation shows the contrast comparison:
(4.661 + 5.526)/2 versus 5.032
  5.0935 versus 5.032
```

> **TIP**
>
> ✓ Orthogonal contrasts are often preferred and require row and column sums to be equal to zero. Researchers can create their own contrasts and add them to a data frame.
>
> ✓ When dummy coding a categorical variable with n distinct levels, only $(n - 1)$ dummy-coded vectors are needed for the regressor variable. The first level is not reported and is considered the baseline value for comparing the other levels of the regressor variable.

● MULTIPLE REGRESSION WITH REPEATED MEASURES

Research questions can hypothesize change across days, weeks, months, or years. The expected change or growth across time can be in one or more research topics, for example, a person's attitude, achievement, or performance measure. This type of analysis is commonly referred to as longitudinal data analysis. Repeated measures data sets are different from the usual rectangular data set used in other types of statistical analyses. The following rectangular data set can be input as a matrix:

```
> X1 = matrix(c(1,2,3,4,10,12,13,14,25,29,30,36,41,47,42,45), nrow = 4, ncol = 4)
> X1
```

```
         [,1]   [,2]   [,3]   [,4]
[1,]       1     10     25     41
[2,]       2     12     29     47
[3,]       3     13     30     42
[4,]       4     14     36     45
```

The matrix X_1 can also be saved as a data frame with variable names. The data frame Y has the ID variable in the first column, followed by the number of tomatoes grown for each ID from 1990 to 1992.

```
> Y = data.frame(X1)
> names(Y) = c("ID","1990","1991","1992")
> Y

   ID   1990   1991   1992
1   1    10     25     41
2   2    12     29     47
3   3    13     30     42
4   4    14     36     45
```

Creating Repeated Measures Data Set

The first task a researcher should perform to create a longitudinal data set is to *transpose* the rectangular data into the correct format for repeated measures analysis. There are a few functions in R that can create a repeated data file structure, for example, the *make.rm()* function in the *fastR* package, which is available at http://finzi.psych.upenn.edu/R/library/fastR/html/fastR-package .html, or the *wideToLong()* function in the *lsr* package, which is available at http://finzi.psych .upenn.edu/R/library/lsr/html/lsr-package.html.

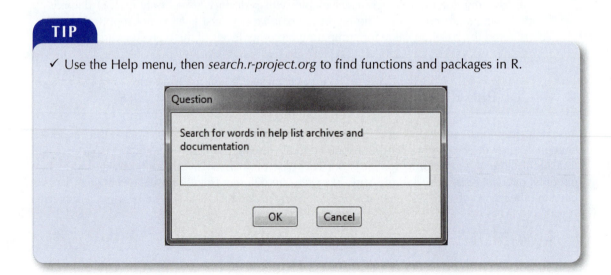

TIP

✓ Use the Help menu, then *search.r-project.org* to find functions and packages in R.

Question

Search for words in help list archives and documentation

OK   Cancel

We will use the *make.rm()* function to create the repeated measures file format. The function is included as a script file (*make.rm.r*) with the other script files for the book. The entire function operations are listed below:

```
make.rm<-function(constant, repeated, data, contrasts) {
  if(!missing(constant) && is.vector(constant)) {
    if(!missing(repeated) && is.vector(repeated)) {
      if(!missing(data)) {
        dd<-dim(data)
        replen<-length(repeated)
        if(missing(contrasts))
          contrasts<-
            ordered(sapply(paste("T", 1:length(repeated), sep = ""),rep, dd[1]))
        else
          contrasts<-matrix(sapply(contrasts, rep, dd[1]), ncol = dim(contrasts)[2])
        if(length(constant) == 1) cons.col<-rep(data[,constant], replen)
        else cons.col<-lapply(data[,constant], rep, replen)
        new.df<-data.frame(cons.col, repdat = as.vector(data.matrix(data[,repeated]))),
contrasts)
        return(new.df)
      }
    }
  }
  cat("Usage: make.rm(constant, repeated, data [, contrasts])\n")
  cat("\tWhere 'constant' is a vector of indices of non-repeated data and\n")
  cat("\t'repeated' is a vector of indices of the repeated measures data.\n")
}
```

You will need to install and load the *fastR* package. The *make.rm()* function will output the matrix data file (X_1), the data frame (Y), and the newly created repeated measures file (Z). I have listed the R commands for you to follow:

```
> install.packages("fastR")
> library(fastR)
> X1 = matrix(c(1,2,3,4,10,12,13,14,25,29,30,36,41,47,42,45), nrow = 4, ncol = 4)
> X1
```

```
      [,1]   [,2]   [,3]   [,4]
[1,]    1     10     25     41
[2,]    2     12     29     47
[3,]    3     13     30     42
[4,]    4     14     36     45
```

```
> Y = data.frame(X1)
> names(Y) = c("ID","1990","1991","1992")
> Y
```

```
     ID   1990   1991   1992
 1   1    10     25     41
 2   2    12     29     47
 3   3    13     30     42
 4   4    14     36     45


 > Z = make.rm(constant = "ID", repeated = c("1990","1991","1992"), data = Y)
 > Z


          cons.col    repdat    contrasts
 1           1          10         T1
 2           2          12         T1
 3           3          13         T1
 4           4          14         T1
 5           1          25         T2
 6           2          29         T2
 7           3          30         T2
 8           4          36         T2
 9           1          41         T3
 10          2          47         T3
 11          3          42         T3
 12          4          45         T3
```

The repeated measures data file (*Z*) will repeat the ID (*cons.col*) in each year with the correspond-ing number of tomatoes (*repdat*). The column labeled *contrasts* is automatically provided such that $T_1 = 1990$, $T_2 = 1991$, and $T_3 = 1993$. This column represents the number of tomatoes in each year, so the average number of tomatoes per year can be contrasted, similar to a one-way analysis of variance.

Multiple Regression Repeated Measures Function

We can also create a repeated measures file structure with just a few simple R commands as fol-lows, where the *rep()* function repeats the values in the data frame *out*:

```
> birth = c(2,5,5,2,7,5,3,2,6,1,2,4)
> id = rep(c(1,2,3,4),c(3,3,3,3))
> year = rep(c("1995","1996","1997"), c(1,1,1))
> out = data.frame(id, year, birth)
> names(out) = c("id","year","birth")
> out
        id    year    birth
 1      1     1995      2
 2      1     1996      5
 3      1     1997      5
 4      2     1995      2
 5      2     1996      7
```

```
 6    2    1997    5
 7    3    1995    3
 8    3    1996    2
 9    3    1997    6
10    4    1995    1
11    4    1996    2
12    4    1997    4
```

The repeated measures file format indicates the number of children (*birth*) in four separate families (id = 1–4) across 3 years (*year*).

The *nlme* package contains the *lme()* function, which stands for linear mixed effects.

The repeated measures data created above are input into a *multiple regression repeated measures function*, which uses the *lme()* function, in a script file (chap17e.r). You need to attach *nlme*, input the data vector, *birth*, and create the factor variables, *id* and *year*, prior to running the function.

```
> library(nlme)
> birth = c(2,5,5,2,7,5,3,2,6,1,2,4)
> id = rep(c(1,2,3,4), c(3,3,3,3))
> year = rep(c("1995","1996","1997"), c(1,1,1))
> chap17e(birth, id, year)
```

The results will first list the data set values, then report the results for the repeated measures analysis of variance.

Program Output

```
birth  year    id
  2    1995    1
  5    1996    1
  5    1997    1
  2    1995    2
  7    1996    2
  5    1997    2
  3    1995    3
  2    1996    3
  6    1997    3
  1    1995    4
  2    1996    4
  4    1997    4
```

Multiple Regression with Repeated Measures

	numDF	denDF	F-value	p-value
(Intercept)	1	6	55.84615	0.0003
year	2	6	4.20000	0.0723

The results indicated that *year* is not statistically significant ($F = 4.2$; $df = 2, 6$; $p = .07$). We interpret this to mean that the number of births did not increase from 1995 to 1997. Repeated measures analyses should not stand alone; rather, you will want to include a scatterplot of the means across the 3 years. Similarly, there are several data issues and assumptions that should be checked prior to running the repeated measures analysis, for example, outliers, distribution of residual error, homogeneity of variance, and sphericity assumption (equal covariance across time).

TIP

✓ Enter the dependent variable first, followed by the year, then the id. Placing data in a different order can cause the *lme()* function to give an error message.

✓ The *reshape* package creates a repeated measures data set from a rectangular data set.

The Reshape Package

Hadley Wickham has created a comprehensive package called *reshape* (http://had.co.nz/reshape/), to alter data structure. An introduction and video are available.

Basically, you alter data so that each row is a unique id-variable combination. Then, you place the data into any structure or shape you want. Here is a very simple example using a rectangular file, *mydata*.

Mydata

id	time	x1	x2
1	1	5	6
1	2	3	5
2	1	6	1
2	2	2	4

```
# example of melt function
> library(reshape)
> newdata <- melt(mydata, id = c("id","time"))
```

Newdata

Id	time	variable	value
1	1	x1	5
1	2	x1	3
2	1	x1	6
2	2	x1	2
1	1	x2	6
1	2	x2	5
2	1	x2	1
2	2	x2	4

> **TIP**
>
> ✓ Repeated measures regression for unbalanced data (unequal sample sizes), binary data (dichotomous), or multilevel equations is beyond the scope of this chapter. Consult specific packages in R or books for these applications. A few examples are given below:
>
> - *lmer* in the *lme4* package is used for fitting generalized linear mixed-effects models. For MCMC (Markov Chain **Monte Carlo**)–generated *p* values, the *languageR* package has the useful *pvals.fnc* function.
>
> - *clmm* in the *ordinal* package does mixed-effects models for ordinal dependent outcomes.
>
> - For binary and Poisson-distributed outcomes, and with a random intercept, *glmmML* (in the *glmmML* package) is recommended as an alternative to lmer.
>
> - Fixed and random effects in hierarchical or multilevel regression equations can be found in the {*arm*} package (Gelman & Hill, 2007; http://www.stat.columbia.edu/~gelman/arm/).
>
> - Contrast coding examples can be found at http://www.ats.ucla.edu/stat/r/library/contrast_coding.htm.

● SELECTING PREDICTOR VARIABLES

Multiple regression focuses on the prediction or explanation of the variability of the dependent variable, Y scores. If Y = test scores and variance is present, this implies individual differences. We are interested in predicting or explaining the variance in Y given knowledge of the predictor variables. On what basis do we decide the predictor variables? First, examine prior research to see what multiple regression analyses have been conducted. Next, develop a theory behind the multiple regression prediction equation. These two steps relate to the multiple regression model validity. Once a set of predictor variables are included in the multiple regression analysis, then a determination of which ones to keep has to be made. A related concern is interpreting which predictor variables are more or less important in predicting or explaining variability in Y scores.

The determination of which predictor variables to keep is based on whether they are statistically significant. However, the statistical significance of a predictor variable may be based on the order of entry (direct, stepwise, forward, backward). A second consideration is the correlation among the predictor variables, which is called multicollinearity given the possibility of different sets of variables that could be used in the multiple regression equation.

Three popular methods are typically used to select the best set of predictor variables (beyond the usual *t* test for regression weights): beta weights, structure coefficients, and commonality analysis. Beta weights are the standardized regression coefficients, thus permitting a comparison based on controlling for other variables in the regression equation. Structure coefficients are computed as the correlation between each predictor variable score and the predicted Y score. Commonality analysis provides all possible subsets where different combinations of predictor variables are included in the multiple regression equation (Nimon, Lewis, Kane, & Haynes, 2008). Each of these is presented below in an applied example.

Applied Multiple Regression Example

The data set used in this multiple regression example is taken from the following website: http://www.amstat.org/publications/jse/v1n1/datasets.lock.html. It contains 93 observations and 26 variables. Car specifications are given for 93 new car models in 1993, which include price, miles per gallon ratings, engine size, body size, and features. The data sources were from *Consumer Reports and PACE New Car & Truck Buying Guide*. The variable column and location in the data set are given as

```
Line 1
Columns
  1 - 14  Manufacturer
 15 - 29  Model
 30 - 36  Type
            Small, Sporty, Compact, Midsize, Large - as defined in the
            _Consumer Reports_ article
 38 - 41  Minimum Price (in $1,000) - Price for basic version of this model
 43 - 46  Midrange Price (in $1,000) - Average of Min and Max prices
 48 - 51  Maximum Price (in $1,000) - Price for a premium version
 53 - 54  City MPG (miles per gallon by EPA rating)
 56 - 57  Highway MPG
 59 - 59  Air Bags standard
            0 = none, 1 = driver only, 2 = driver & passenger
 61 - 61  Drive train type
            0 = rear wheel drive
            1 = front wheel drive
            2 = all wheel drive
 63 - 63  Number of cylinders
 65 - 67  Engine size (liters)
 69 - 71  Horsepower (maximum)
 73 - 76  RPM (revs per minute at maximum horsepower)

Line 2
Columns
  1 -  4  Engine revolutions per mile (in highest gear)
  6 -  6  Manual transmission available
            0 = No, 1 = Yes
  8 - 11  Fuel tank capacity (gallons)
 13 - 13  Passenger capacity (persons)
 15 - 17  Length      (inches)
 19 - 21  Wheelbase (inches)
```

```
23 - 24   Width        (inches)
26 - 27   U-turn space (feet)
29 - 32   Rear seat room (inches)
34 - 35   Luggage capacity (cu. ft.)
37 - 40   Weight (pounds)
42 - 42   Domestic?
                 0 = non-U.S. manufacturer, 1 = U.S. manufacturer
```

Warning

The data set is a tab-delimited ASCII text file, 93cars.dat.txt, which has two lines per manufacturer. The file can be downloaded; however, I had problems reading the tab-delimited data set in R. The problem was caused by the text file not having a single space separating the variable columns; that is, *sep = " "* does not allow for varying spaces between columns of data.

I therefore opened the file in Notepad and created a single line of data for each manufacturer. Next, I opened the file in Excel, saved it, and then read it into SPSS. I then added the variable names and saved the file as Cars93.sav. You must export this SPSS data file with a special file type, Cars93.por, so it can be imported into R. The special argument *use.value.labels* permits the variable labels to be imported. The *Hmisc* package will need to be loaded to use the *spss.get()* function. In *library(foreign)*, the *read.spss()* function also works.

Note: Many of your data input problems can be solved by using a comma-separated file. A comma-separated file (*.csv) will not have different number of spaces between variables. You can create this type of data file by first inputting the text file into Excel, then saving as a comma-separated file.

The R Steps for Conducting Multiple Regression Analysis

Step 1: Preliminary

```
> chooseCRANmirror()
> install.packages("Hmisc")
```

Step 2: Loading libraries

```
> library(Hmisc)
> library(foreign)
```

Step 3: Reading in the SPSS portable file and listing the data set values

```
> mydata <-spss.get("C:/Users/Randy/Desktop/Book Data Sets/Cars93.por",
use.value.labels = TRUE, to.data.frame = TRUE)
# This line of code should be on above line
> mydata
```

Step 4: Conducting multiple regression analyses

I chose to predict highway miles per gallon (HWYMPG) given the following predictor variables: engine size (ENGSIZE), weight of vehicle (WEIGHT), passenger capacity (PASSENGE), engine revolutions (REVOLUTI), and horsepower (HRSEPOWE). These variables made theoretical sense because they all separately and together should affect the miles per gallon of the car on the highway. I used R functions from the *stats* package and loaded the package using *library(stats)*, then created a smaller data frame with just the variables of interest using the *subset()* function *sample*, and finally used the *cor()* function to correlate the variables.

The lm() Function for Unstandardized Multiple Regression Results

```
> library(stats)
> sample = subset(mydata, select = c(HWYMPG,ENGSIZE,WEIGHT,PASSENGE,REVOLUTI,HRSEPOWE))
> cor(sample)
> model1 <- lm(HWYMPG ~ ENGSIZE + WEIGHT + PASSENGE + REVOLUTI + HRSEPOWE, data = mydata)
> summary(model1)
```

CORRELATION OUTPUT

	HWYMPG	ENGSIZE	WEIGHT	PASSENGE	REVOLUTI
HWYMPG	1.0000000	-0.6267946	-0.8106581	-0.466385827	0.5874968
ENGSIZE	-0.6267946	1.0000000	0.8450753	0.372721168	-0.8240086
WEIGHT	-0.8106581	0.8450753	1.0000000	0.553272980	-0.7352642
PASSENGE	-0.4663858	0.3727212	0.5532730	1.000000000	-0.3349756
REVOLUTI	0.5874968	-0.8240086	-0.7352642	-0.334975577	1.0000000
HRSEPOWE	-0.6190437	0.7321197	0.7387975	0.009263668	-0.6003139

	HRSEPOWE
HWYMPG	-0.619043685
ENGSIZE	0.732119730
WEIGHT	0.738797516
PASSENGE	0.009263668
REVOLUTI	-0.600313870
HRSEPOWE	1.000000000

MULTIPLE REGRESSION OUTPUT - UNSTANDARDIZED SOLUTION

Coefficients:

	Estimate	Std. Error	t value	Pr(>|t|)	
(Intercept)	49.427959	4.653941	10.621	< 2e-16	***
ENGSIZE	1.685434	0.731182	2.305	0.0235	*
WEIGHT	-0.007121	0.001578	-4.513	1.99e-05	***
PASSENGE	-0.571081	0.531796	-1.074	0.2858	
REVOLUTI	0.001267	0.001161	1.091	0.2782	
HRSEPOWE	-0.020890	0.013370	-1.562	0.1218	

Signif. codes: 0 '***' 0.001 '**' 0.01 '*' 0.05 '.' 0.1 ' ' 1

Residual standard error: 3.095 on 87 degrees of freedom
Multiple R-squared: 0.6814, Adjusted R-squared: 0.6631
F-statistic: 37.21 on 5 and 87 DF, p-value: < 2.2e-16

Results indicated that engine size (ENGSIZE) and weight (WEIGHT) have the highest correlation with highway mileage (HWYMPG). These variables are also statistically significant predictors of highway mileage (HWYMPG) based on the *t* test for statistical significance.

The scale() Function for Standardized Multiple Regression

The *scale()* function is used to create the standardized variables with mean = 0 and standard deviation = 1. The scaled variables are placed in their own data set. This new data set is used to obtain the standardized multiple regression results. The set of R commands are

```
> attach(sample)

> sHWYMPG <- scale(HWYMPG)
> sENGSIZE <- scale(ENGSIZE)
> sWEIGHT <- scale(WEIGHT)
> sPASSENGE <- scale(PASSENGE)
> sREVOLUTI <- scale (REVOLUTI)
> sHRSEPOWE <- scale(HRSEPOWE)

> sample2 = data.frame(cbind(sHWYMPG,sENGSIZE,sWEIGHT,sPASSENGE,sREVOLUTI,sHRSEPOWE))
> names(sample2) = cbind("sHWYMPG","sENGSIZE","sWEIGHT","sPASSENGE","sREVOLUTI","sHRSEPOWE")
> cor(sample2)

> model2 <- lm(sHWYMPG ~ sENGSIZE + sWEIGHT + sPASSENGE + sREVOLUTI + sHRSEPOWE,
data = sample2)
> summary(model2)
```

CORRELATION OUTPUT

	sHWYMPG	sENGSIZE	sWEIGHT	sPASSENGE
sHWYMPG	1.0000000	-0.6267946	-0.8106581	-0.466385827
sENGSIZE	-0.6267946	1.0000000	0.8450753	0.372721168
sWEIGHT	-0.8106581	0.8450753	1.0000000	0.553272980
sPASSENGE	-0.4663858	0.3727212	0.5532730	1.000000000
sREVOLUTI	0.5874968	-0.8240086	-0.7352642	-0.334975577
sHRSEPOWE	-0.6190437	0.7321197	0.7387975	0.009263668

	sREVOLUTI	sHRSEPOWE
sHWYMPG	0.5874968	-0.619043685
sENGSIZE	-0.8240086	0.732119730
sWEIGHT	-0.7352642	0.738797516
sPASSENGE	-0.3349756	0.009263668
sREVOLUTI	1.0000000	-0.600313870
sHRSEPOWE	-0.6003139	1.000000000

MULTIPLE REGRESSION OUTPUT - STANDARDIZED SOLUTION

```
Coefficients:
               Estimate   Std. Error   t value   Pr(>|t|)
(Intercept)   -1.391e-17   6.019e-02     0.000    1.0000
sENGSIZE       3.279e-01   1.423e-01     2.305    0.0235 *
sWEIGHT       -7.879e-01   1.746e-01    -4.513    1.99e-05 ***
sPASSENGE     -1.113e-01   1.036e-01    -1.074    0.2858
sREVOLUTI      1.179e-01   1.081e-01     1.091    0.2782
sHRSEPOWE     -2.052e-01   1.313e-01    -1.562    0.1218
---
Signif. codes:  0 '***' 0.001 '**' 0.01 '*' 0.05 '.' 0.1 ' ' 1


Residual standard error: 0.5805 on 87 degrees of freedom
Multiple R-squared: 0.6814, Adjusted R-squared: 0.6631
F-statistic: 37.21 on 5 and 87 DF, p-value: < 2.2e-16
```

The Pearson correlation coefficients are the same, which we expect given that they are in standard score form. The predictor variables, sENGSIZE and sWEIGHT, are statistically significant based on the t test for statistical significance. The beta weights can now be used for our additional interpretation, but first we should convert them from scientific notation. Basically, sENGSIZE has a beta weight of .3279, and sWEIGHT has a beta weight of −.7879. A beta weight interpretation would indicate that sWEIGHT is the more important predictor variable, which is also indicated by the t test for statistical significance.

Structure Coefficients

The predicted values are assigned to the variable *yhat* using the *predict()* function. The predicted values are then combined with the other observed variables in a data frame, *newdata*. The *cor()* function then returns the correlation of the scores of the independent variables with the predicted *Y* variable scores.

```
> attach(sample)

> yhat <- predict(lm(HWYMPG ~ ENGSIZE + WEIGHT + PASSENGE + REVOLUTI + HRSEPOWE))

> newdata = cbind(HWYMPG,ENGSIZE,WEIGHT,PASSENGE,REVOLUTI,HRSEPOWE,yhat)

> cor(newdata)
```

	HWYMPG	ENGSIZE	WEIGHT	PASSENGE	REVOLUTI
HWYMPG	1.0000000	-0.6267946	-0.8106581	-0.466385827	0.5874968
ENGSIZE	-0.6267946	1.0000000	0.8450753	0.372721168	-0.8240086
WEIGHT	-0.8106581	0.8450753	1.0000000	0.553272980	-0.7352642
PASSENGE	-0.4663858	0.3727212	0.5532730	1.000000000	-0.3349756
REVOLUTI	0.5874968	-0.8240086	-0.7352642	-0.334975577	1.0000000
HRSEPOWE	-0.6190437	0.7321197	0.7387975	0.009263668	-0.6003139

yhat	0.8254615	-0.7593262	-0.9820664	-0.565000063	0.7117191

	HRSEPOWE	yhat
HWYMPG	-0.619043685	0.8254615
ENGSIZE	0.732119730	-0.7593262
WEIGHT	0.738797516	-0.9820664
PASSENGE	0.009263668	-0.5650001
REVOLUTI	-0.600313870	0.7117191
HRSEPOWE	1.000000000	-0.7499364
yhat	-0.749936428	1.0000000

Structure Coefficients

Predictor	yhat
ENGSIZE	−.759
WEIGHT	−.982
PASSENGE	−.565
REVOLUTI	.711
HRSEPOWE	−.749

The bivariate correlation of the independent variable scores with the predicted Y scores (*yhat*) is shown in the last column of the correlation matrix and listed here:

The WEIGHT structure coefficient is the highest (−.982), followed by ENGSIZE (−.759). This matches both the statistical significance (*t* test) and the beta weight interpretations. Ironically, all of these bivariate correlations are statistically significant at the $p < .0001$ level (tabled $r = .17$, $df = 92$, $p < .05$, one-tailed test). HRSEPOWE might be misinterpreted as important given the closeness of the structure coefficient to ENGSIZE, but the previous results show that this is not the case.

Commonality Analysis

The best way to select the predictors in a multiple regression equation is to run a commonality analysis. The reason is that an all-possible variable combination solution can help identify multicollinearity and suppressor variable effects. The *yhat* package has the *commonalityCoefficients()* function, which computes the all-possible regression equation results. First, you will need to use Install Packages in the main menu, select a CRAN mirror site, select the yhat package from the list, and then install the package. Afterward, the following R commands can be used to conduct this important type of multiple regression analysis:

```
> library(yhat)    # Automatically loads library(MBESS)
> Library(Hmisc)   # Will automatically load library(foreign)


> mydata <-spss.get("C:/Users/Randy/Desktop/Book Data Sets/Cars93.por", use.value.labels =
TRUE, to.data.frame = TRUE)
> attach(mydata)


> model3 <- lm(HWYMPG ~ ENGSIZE + WEIGHT + PASSENGE + REVOLUTI +  HRSEPOWE, data = mydata)
> summary(model3)


> CCout <- commonalityCoefficients(mydata, "HWYMPG", list("ENGSIZE","WEIGHT","PASSENGE",
"REVOLUTI","HRSEPOWE"), "F")
> print(CCout)
```

```
                COMMONALITY ANALYSIS OUTPUT RESULTS

                                                    Coefficient    % Total

Unique to ENGSIZE                                      0.0195        2.86
Unique to WEIGHT                                       0.0746       10.95
Unique to PASSENGE                                     0.0042        0.62
Unique to REVOLUTI                                     0.0044        0.64
Unique to HRSEPOWE                                     0.0089        1.31
Common to ENGSIZE , and WEIGHT                        -0.0158       -2.32
Common to ENGSIZE , and PASSENGE                      -0.0006       -0.09
Common to WEIGHT, and PASSENGE                         0.1383       20.29
Common to ENGSIZE , and REVOLUTI                      -0.0042       -0.61
Common to WEIGHT, and REVOLUTI                         0.0069        1.02
Common to PASSENGE, and REVOLUTI                      -0.0005       -0.08
Common to ENGSIZE , and HRSEPOWE                      -0.0047       -0.70
Common to WEIGHT, and HRSEPOWE                         0.1295       19.00
Common to PASSENGE, and HRSEPOWE                      -0.0042       -0.62
Common to REVOLUTI, and HRSEPOWE                      -0.0010       -0.14
Common to ENGSIZE , WEIGHT, and PASSENGE              0.0052        0.77
Common to ENGSIZE , WEIGHT, and REVOLUTI              0.0006        0.09
Common to ENGSIZE , PASSENGE, and REVOLUTI            0.0006        0.09
Common to WEIGHT, PASSENGE, and REVOLUTI              0.0054        0.79
Common to ENGSIZE , WEIGHT, and HRSEPOWE              0.0425        6.23
Common to ENGSIZE , PASSENGE, and HRSEPOWE            0.0010        0.15
Common to WEIGHT, PASSENGE, and HRSEPOWE             -0.0785      -11.52
Common to ENGSIZE , REVOLUTI, and HRSEPOWE            0.0009        0.13
Common to WEIGHT, REVOLUTI, and HRSEPOWE              0.0023        0.33
Common to PASSENGE, REVOLUTI, and HRSEPOWE            0.0005        0.08
Common to ENGSIZE , WEIGHT, PASSENGE, and REVOLUTI   0.0596        8.75
Common to ENGSIZE , WEIGHT, PASSENGE, and HRSEPOWE   0.0164        2.41
Common to ENGSIZE , WEIGHT, REVOLUTI, and HRSEPOWE   0.1996       29.29
Common to ENGSIZE , PASSENGE, REVOLUTI, and HRSEPOWE -0.0006       -0.08
Common to WEIGHT, PASSENGE, REVOLUTI, and HRSEPOWE   -0.0023       -0.33
Common to ENGSIZE , WEIGHT, PASSENGE, REVOLUTI, and HRSEPOWE  0.0729  10.69
Total                                                 0.6814      100.00


$CCTotalbyVar


          Unique    Common    Total
ENGSIZE   0.0195    0.3734    0.3929
WEIGHT    0.0746    0.5826    0.6572
PASSENGE  0.0042    0.2133    0.2175
REVOLUTI  0.0044    0.3408    0.3452
HRSEPOWE  0.0089    0.3743    0.3832
```

The multiple regression commonality analysis by far gives a better understanding of the unique contribution of each predictor as well as the various combinations of the predictor variables. This provides a much clearer picture of which independent predictor variables should be selected.

In this analysis, WEIGHT provided the highest unique regression coefficient (.0746) and percent variance explained (10.95%), followed by ENGSIZE. This is the same result as the statistical significance (*t* test), beta weights, and structure coefficients; however, commonality analysis provides the added knowledge of how combinations of variables affect prediction of *Y*. This provides insight into suppressor variables and multicollinearity effects.

For example, ENGSIZE, WEIGHT, REVOLUTI, and HRSEPOWE, together in a theoretical explanatory model, account for 29.29% of the variance in HWYMPG. We see in contrast that WEIGHT and PASSENGE account for 20.29%. Examining these different combinations of independent predictor variables provides a better selection of important variables and explanation of their unique and common variance explained.

We also see a suppressor variable effect when examining the relation among WEIGHT, PASSENGE, and HRSEPOWE. For example, all three together show negative common variance (−11.52), yet WEIGHT and PASSENGE are positive (20.29), and WEIGHT and HRSEPOWE are positive (19.00). When introducing PASSENGE and HRSEPOWE (−.62), a negative effect is introduced, thus causing the three variables to have a negative common variance.

```
WEIGHT, PASSENGE, and HRSEPOWE                      -0.0785       -11.52
WEIGHT, and PASSENGE                                 0.1383        20.29
WEIGHT, and HRSEPOWE                                 0.1295        19.00
PASSENGE, and HRSEPOWE                              -0.0042        -0.62
```

Note: We should also be able to see this effect when comparing Pearson, part, and partial correlations.

Interpreting Multiple Regression Through Multiple Lenses

How researchers interpret the results of multiple regression varies depending on training, expertise, and current thought. Nathans, Oswald, and Nimon (2012), as well as others, discuss the different statistical measures (beta weight, structure coefficient, commonality coefficient), which can provide a different answer to the question "What is the best set of predictor variables?" To help researchers interpret multiple regression results through multiple lenses, Nimon and Oswald (in press) introduced an extension to their earlier *yhat* package (Nimon & Roberts, 2012) in R that (a) calculates a comprehensive set of regression results, (b) bootstraps the results, (c) evaluates the bootstrapped results, and (d) plots relevant confidence intervals.

The yhat package with these added features is demonstrated using the Holzinger and Swineford (1937, 1939) data set, available in the MBESS package (Kelley & Lai, 2011), and the regression model reported and interpreted in Nathans et al. (2012), where *deductive mathematical reasoning* was regressed on three measures of mathematical aptitude: *numeric, arithmetic,* and *addition.* Using the code below, the yhat software automatically reports a comprehensive set of predictor results, including a rank order of predictors, paired dominance, and an all-possible-subset, as well as reproducibility and confidence intervals resulting from bootstrap results. The R commands in the Multiple Regression Lenses script file (chap17f.r) are as follows:

```
# Multiple Regression Lenses chap17f.r
# Selecting best set of predictors

# Load necessary libraries
```

```
install.packages("yhat")
install.packages("MBESS")

library(MASS)
library(corpcor)
library(boot)
library(plotrix)
library(miscTools)
library(yhat)

# Set seed to reproduce reported results

set.seed(1234)

# Load Holziner and Swineford dataset

require("MBESS")
data(HS.data)

# Perform Regression

lm.out<-lm(deduct~numeric+arithmet+addition,data=HS.data)

# Calculate yhat metrics

regrOut<-calc.yhat(lm.out)

# Bootstrap Results

boot.out<-boot(HS.data,boot.yhat,1000,lmOut=lm.out,regrout0=regrOut)
result<-booteval.yhat(regrOut,boot.out,bty="perc")

# Print Relevant Results

regrOut
result$tauDS
result$domBoot
plotCI.yhat(regrOut$PredictorMetrics[-nrow(regrOut$PredictorMetrics),],result$upperCIp-
m,result$lowerCIpm,
                pid=which(colnames(regrOut$PredictorMetrics) %in% c("Beta","rs","CD:0","C-
D:1","CD:2", "GenDom","Pratt","RLW") == TRUE),
                nr=3,nc=3)
result$combCIpmDiff[,c("Beta","rs","CD:0","CD:1","CD:2","GenDom","Pratt","RLW")]
plotCI.yhat(regrOut$APSRelatedMetrics[-nrow(regrOut$APSRelatedMetrics),-2],result$upper-
CIaps,result$lowerCIaps,nr=3,nc=2)
result$combCIapsDiff
result$combCIincDiff
```

Figure 17.1 provides the predictor results (*PredictorMetrics*), rank order of predictors (*Ordered-PredictorMetrics*), paired dominance (*PairedDominanceMetrics*), all-possible-subset (*APSRelatedMetrics*), and reproducibility for the predictors (*results$tauDS*) and paired dominance (*results$domBoot*). These results show that while the relative predictor order is fairly consistent across the different approaches, it appears that *addition* is serving as a suppressor variable, suppressing variance in the remaining predictors. It can also be seen that the rank order of the different predictor approaches is fairly stable across bootstrapped samples with the exception of the uniqueness coefficients (*Unique*) and the sum of the common coefficients (*Common*). Results further show that *numeric* generally dominated *arithmetic* across all bootstrapped samples (*Reprod* = 1.00). Figures 17.2 through 17.4 provide the resultant bootstrapped confidence intervals for (a) a select set of predictor approaches, (b) all-possible subset–related approaches, and (c) predictor approach differences, commonality coefficient and R-squared differences, and incremental predictor variance differences.

TIP

```
> regrOut
$PredictorMetrics
          b   Beta     r    rs    rs2 Unique Common  CD:0  CD:1  CD:2 GenDom Pratt   RLW
   num  1.087 0.266 0.397 0.824 0.679  0.054  0.103 0.158 0.078 0.054  0.097 0.106 0.097
   ari  0.395 0.100 0.329 0.683 0.466  0.007  0.101 0.108 0.030 0.007  0.048 0.033 0.047
   add  0.604 0.245 0.381 0.790 0.624  0.047  0.098 0.145 0.069 0.047  0.087 0.093 0.088
 Total    NA    NA    NA    NA 1.769  0.108  0.302 0.411 0.177 0.108  0.232 0.232 0.232

$OrderedPredictorMetrics
      b Beta r rs rs2 Unique Common CD:0 CD:1 CD:2 GenDom Pratt RLW
num 1  1  1  1  1    1      1      1    1    1    1      1     1
ari 3  3  3  3  3    3      2      3    3    3    3      3     3
add 2  2  2  2  2    2      3      2    2    2    2      2     2

$PairedDominanceMetrics
          Comp Cond Gen
num>ari    1    1    1
num>add    1    1    1
ari>add    0    0    0

$APSRelatedMetrics
              Commonality  % Total    R2  num.Inc  ari.Inc  add.Inc
num               0.054    0.233   0.158      NA    0.027    0.067
ari               0.007    0.031   0.108   0.077      NA    0.070
add               0.047    0.204   0.145   0.080    0.033      NA
num,ari           0.026    0.112   0.185      NA      NA    0.047
num,add           0.023    0.097   0.225      NA    0.007      NA
ari,add           0.020    0.087   0.178   0.054      NA      NA
num,ari,add       0.055    0.236   0.232      NA      NA      NA
Total             0.232    1.000      NA      NA      NA      NA

> result$tauDS
          b   Beta     r    rs    rs2 Unique Common  CD:0  CD:1  CD:2 GenDom Pratt   RLW
Mean  0.785 0.678 0.560 0.561 0.560  0.678  0.226 0.562 0.631 0.678  0.629 0.670 0.647
SD    0.369 0.394 0.455 0.455 0.455  0.379  0.560 0.453 0.419 0.379  0.420 0.401 0.406

> result$domBoot
              Dij   Mean    SE    Pij    Pji   Pijno  Reprod
Com_num>ari    1   0.936  0.211  0.904  0.033   0.063  0.904
Com_num>add    1   0.593  0.474  0.560  0.374   0.066  0.560
Com_ari>add    0   0.102  0.236  0.030  0.825   0.145  0.825
Con_num>ari    1   0.936  0.211  0.904  0.033   0.063  0.904
Con_num>add    1   0.593  0.474  0.560  0.374   0.066  0.560
Con_ari>add    0   0.102  0.236  0.030  0.825   0.145  0.825
Gen_num>ari    1   0.938  0.241  0.938  0.062   0.000  0.938
Gen_num>add    1   0.603  0.490  0.603  0.397   0.000  0.603
Gen_ari>add    0   0.097  0.296  0.097  0.903   0.000  0.903
```

Figure 17.1 From `calc.yhat` and Selected Output From `booteval.yhat` for an Illustrative Example

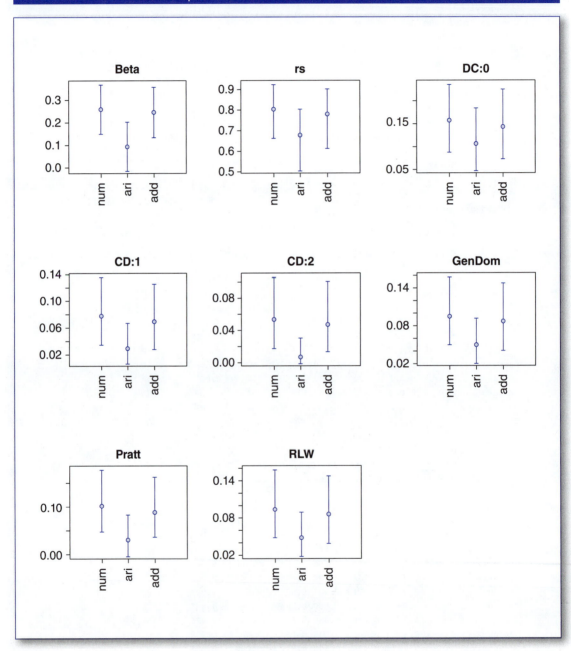

Figure 17.2 Output From `plot.yhat` for a Selected Predictor Approach From an Illustrative Example

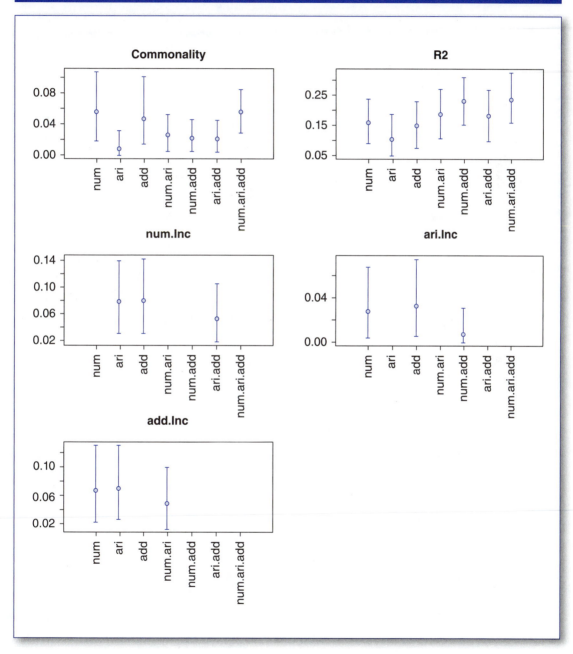

Figure 17.3 Output From `plot.yhat` for All-Possible Subset–Related Approaches From an Illustrative Example

```
> result$combCIpmDiff[,c("Beta","rs","CD:0","CD:1","CD:2","GenDom","Pratt","RLW")]


                  Beta                     rs                 CD:0                 CD:1
    num-ari   0.166(-0.020,0.350)    0.141(-0.071,0.362)    0.050(-0.026,0.128)    0.048
(-0.014,0.109)
    num-add   0.021(-0.162,0.197)    0.034(-0.225,0.294)    0.013(-0.082,0.103)    0.009
(-0.073,0.091)
    ari-add  -0.145(-0.329,0.015)   -0.107(-0.329,0.100)   -0.037(-0.116,0.034)   -0.039
(-0.106,0.015)


                  CD:2                   GenDom                Pratt                 RLW
    num-ari   0.047(-0.003,0.103)    0.049(-0.014,0.109)    0.073(-0.014,0.160)    0.050
(-0.012,0.111)
    num-add   0.007(-0.068,0.078)    0.010(-0.072,0.091)    0.013(-0.089,0.112)    0.009
(-0.072,0.091)
    ari-add  -0.040(-0.097,0.001)   -0.039(-0.106,0.015)   -0.060(-0.148,0.013)   -0.041
(-0.107,0.013)


> result$combCIapsDiff
                    Commonality                  R2
    num-ari         0.047(-0.003,0.103)    0.050(-0.026,0.128)
    num-add         0.007(-0.068,0.078)    0.013(-0.082,0.103)
    ari-add        -0.040(-0.097,0.001)   -0.037(-0.116,0.034)
    num,ari-num,add 0.003(-0.033,0.040)   -0.040(-0.097,0.001)
    num,ari-ari,add 0.006(-0.022,0.035)    0.007(-0.068,0.079)
    num,add-ari,add 0.003(-0.031,0.036)    0.047(-0.003,0.103)


> result$combCIincDiff
          num.Inc-ari.Inc      num.Inc-add.Inc       ari.Inc-add.Inc
    .   0.050(-0.026,0.128)  0.013(-0.082,0.103)   -0.037(-0.116,0.034)
    num          NA                  NA            -0.040(-0.097,0.001)
    ari          NA          0.007(-0.068,0.078)           NA
    add 0.047(-0.003,0.104)          NA                    NA
```

Figure 17.4 Selected Output From booteval.yhat for an Illustrative Example

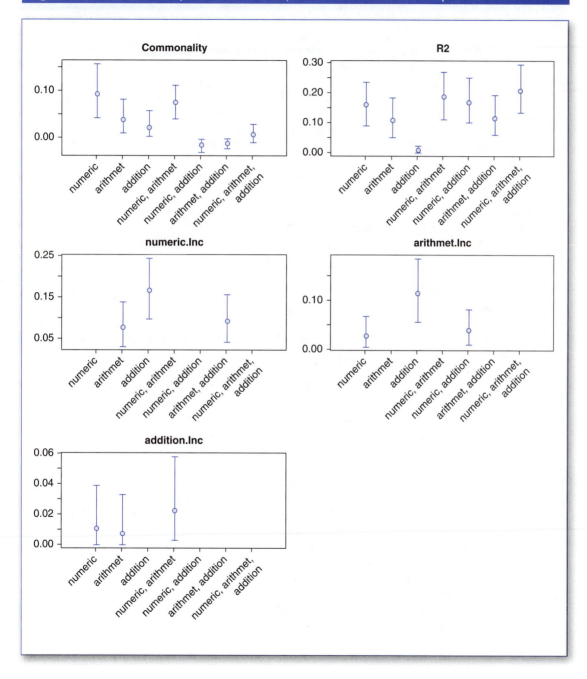

SUMMARY

We have learned that the multiple regression analysis results should be reported in an unstandardized and standardized format along with R^2, F, p, power, and Pearson, partial, and part correlations. The *scale()* function creates variables in a standardized format, that is, mean = 0 and standard deviation = 1. A t test for the significance of each regression coefficient is computed using the unstandardized regression weight and associated standard error. The R-squared value is tested for statistical significance using the F test. The F test is also used when testing the difference between two R-squared values from a full versus restricted regression model. An adjusted R-squared value was presented, which adjusts R^2 for the number of predictors and sample sizes. This could also be reported in the multiple regression summary table if the number of predictor variables and small sample size have an impact on the R-squared value.

Hypothesis testing was illustrated as before with other statistical tests. The null and alternative hypotheses are stated with the regression weight, R-squared value, or F-test value for a given degree of freedom and sample size. The other remaining hypothesis steps are followed to make a final decision regarding rejection or retention of the null hypothesis. A researcher interprets the statistical significance of the regression weight(s), the R-squared value, and the F test to determine a final regression equation for prediction of Y.

This chapter presented the many uses of multiple regression, including two predictor variables, the nominal predictor variable, nonlinear predictor variables, and repeated measures. The *contrast()* function demonstrates various ways in which a nominal regressor variable is coded to test for mean differences in groups. The *poly()* function was used in nonlinear regression to create linear, quadratic, cubic, and quartic variables with corresponding regression coefficients. This permitted a researcher to assess the nature of the fitted regression line. Repeated measures required creating a special data file structure. Finally, the *aov()* and *lm()* functions were run with associated output. This permitted a basic comparison and interpretation of the analysis of variance and multiple regression results, especially their similarity.

The issue of selecting the best set of predictor variables was also presented. A researcher would first examine the individual t tests for each predictor variable, dropping a nonsignificant variable and then re-running the multiple regression equation. After a set of significant predictors are obtained, the researcher should then decide which predictor variables are more important. A researcher's goal is to obtain the best set of predictor variables. The standardized regression solution provides beta weights, which have been used to determine which predictor variables contributed the most variance explained. Structure coefficients, which are the correlation between each independent variable score and the predicted Y score, have also been proposed. Structure coefficients don't appear to add much interpretative value unless multicollinearity is extreme among the predictor variables. Commonality analysis gives a list of all the combinations of variables, thus returning an all-possible subset solution. This is a useful approach to determine the best set of predictors in the presence of multicollinearity among the independent predictor variables or suppressor variables. However, the yhat package now provides a feature that outputs all of these predictor measures (including dominance) with bootstrap and confidence interval results.

TIP

✓ A list of statistical functions can be obtained by issuing the following command:

```
> library(help="stats")
```

✓ The following R commands provide the function arguments and online documentation for the linear regression function:

```
> args(lm)
> help(lm)
```

✓ You can omit missing data that affect Pearson *r* and regression using the following R command:

```
> data.new = na.omit(data.old)
```

✓ Right-click your mouse on the scatterplot to save the image to the clipboard or print. The following selection menu will appear in the scatterplot:

✓ You can copy and paste scatterplots into Word documents by using the Alt+PrtScr keyboard keys, then in the Word document use the Ctrl+V keyboard keys to paste the image. You can resize the image in the Word document by selecting the Format tab, which appears when the image is selected. The Crop tool option will permit easy resizing of the image.

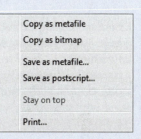

```
Copy as metafile
Copy as bitmap
Save as metafile...
Save as postscript...
Stay on top
Print...
```

EXERCISES

1. Briefly explain the regression terms in the equation $Y = a + b_1X + b_2X^2 + e$.

2. Given the following matrix of Pearson correlation coefficients, calculate the partial and part correlations indicated. Is the Pearson correlation, r_{12}, greater than the partial and part correlations?

	1	*2*	*3*
1	1.0		
2	0.5	1.0	
3	0.7	0.3	1.0

$r_{12.3} =$

$r_{1(2.3)} =$

3. A researcher hypothesized that the number of airports in 20 countries (dependent variable) was related to the number of frequent flyer miles granted and number of pilots (independent variables). Run a regression analysis to determine if the two independent variables predict the dependent variable. Show the results. Interpret your results.

```
> airports = c(130,100,150,110,60,180,100,27,15,460,70,50,130,75,30,20,12,13,18,20)
> miles = c(640,430,220,300,30,150,100,45,13,500,150,75,185,75,140,60,20,40,25,30)
> pilots = c(30,40,90,35,30,25,30,15,5,60,25,40,90,30,40,15,15,10,5,10)

> mydata = data.frame(matrix(c(airports, miles, pilots),20,3))
> names(mydata) = c("airports", "miles", "pilots")
```

4. In #3 above, use the *scale()* function to create all three variables in *z*-score form. Then, run the regression model, and output the standardized regression weights.

```
> zairports = scale(airports)
> zmiles = scale(miles)
> zpilots = scale(pilots)
> options(scipen = 999)
```

5. Use the *lm()* function with special *I()* argument to include a quadratic term for *X* when conducting a nonlinear regression analysis for the following data. Use the *predict()* function to compute predicted values and the *plot()* and *lines()* functions to plot data points, and draw the fitted regression line. Show the R commands, output, and plot. Interpret the results.

```
Y = c(10,20,30,40,50,40,30,20,10)
X = c(1,2,3,4,5,6,7,8,9)
```

6. Conduct a repeated measures analysis for the following longitudinal data, which indicate weight gain from 1995 to 1997 for four individuals. Use the *lme()* function in the *library(nlme)*. Use the *anova()* function to output the analysis of variance table. Show the R commands, data set, and output, and interpret the results.

```
> library(nlme)
> gain = c(2,5,7,5,7,9,3,6,7,1,2,4)
> id = rep(c(1,2,3,4),c(3,3,3,3))
> year = rep(c("1995","1996","1997"), c(1,1,1))
```

TRUE OR FALSE QUESTIONS

T   F   a.   The partial correlation indicates a bivariate correlation controlling for other variables.

T   F   b.   Multiple regression can be used with linear, quadratic, cubic, or quartic data.

T   F   c.   The *spcor()* function computes partial correlations.

T   F   d.   The intercept value = 0 when using *z* scores for *Y* and *X* predictor variables.

T   F   e.   Diagnostic plots visually show which variables are statistically significant.

T   F   f.   Longitudinal analysis of data (repeated measures) requires special formatting of data.

NOTE

1.   Nonlinear regression equations can also be specified using the *nls()* function in R to compute the nonlinear least-squares estimation of regression coefficients. The *nls()* function is located in the R {stats} library: *library(help = "stats")*. The *nls()* function takes formula, data, subset, weights, and related arguments, but the formula argument is treated as a standard algebraic expression rather than as a linear model formula. See the arguments using the *help(nls)* command. The *nls()* function is more difficult to use because *start()* function values need to be specified that contain estimated coefficients for the nonlinear fitted line. Do not use the *nls()* function if your nonlinear data have zero residual data, that is, if the regression equation is a perfect fit to the data. The *lines()* or *curve()* functions are used to draw a fitted nonlinear line in the scatterplot.

WEB RESOURCES

Chapter R script files are available at http://www.sagepub.com/schumacker

Multiple Regression Function R script file: chap17d.r

Multiple Regression Lenses R script file: chap17f.r

Multiple Regression Repeated Measures Function R script file: chap17e.r

Multiple Regression Standardized Solution R script file: chap17b.r

Multiple Regression Unstandardized Solution R script file: chap17a.r

Polynomial Regression Function R script file: chap17c.r

make.rm function (fastR package): http://finzi.psych.upenn.edu/R/library/fastR/html/fastR-package.html

Multiple regression data set: http://www.amstat.org/publications/jse/v1n1/datasets.lock.html

wideToLong function (lsr package): http://finzi.psych.upenn.edu/R/library/lsr/html/lsr-package.html

yhat package: http://cran.r-project.org/web/packages/yhat/index.html

Note: Download and install Window zip files for make.rm, WideToLong, and yhat package.

## CHAPTER 18

LOGISTIC REGRESSION

● INTRODUCTION

The logistic function was invented in the 19th century to describe the growth of populations as well as the course of autocatalytic chemical reactions (Cramer, 2003). In the case of population growth, the model investigated the time and growth rate of populations. Early scholars soon realized that an exponential function used in logistic regression had value but also had certain limitations. Verhulst (1845) formalized his earlier work and coined the name *logistic function*, which today takes the form of the logistic equation. Pearl and Reed (1920) knew of the autocatalytic reaction curves, but not knowing of Verhulst's work, they independently derived the logistic curve function, which they fitted to U.S. census data and that of many other living populations (human and animal).

Logistics regression models are different from the previous ordinary least squares (OLS) multiple regression models (Kleinbaum, 1994). The previous multiple regression models predicted a dependent variable that was measured at the interval or ratio level, and the difference between the predicted value and the actual value yielded an error of prediction. A logistic regression model has a dependent variable that is dichotomous, having only 0 and 1 as coded values. In a logistic regression equation, we predict the probability of Y, for example, between 0 (*not admitted to a program*) and 1 (*admitted to a program*). The probability of a Y value between 0 and 1 for an individual is estimated by knowledge of their values on the independent predictor variables.

In our previous multiple regression models, the estimation method to compute the regression weights was called the *least squares criterion*. The regression weights were computed based on minimizing the sum of squared errors (i.e., the difference between the actual Y and predicted Y values). In logistic regression models, the regression weights are computed based on *maximum likelihood estimation*, which is an iterative estimation process that finds the optimum set of regression weights. There are other differences between the previous OLS regression and logistic regression methods. Logistic regression models have different overall model fit criteria, tests of regression weight significance, odds ratios, and effect sizes. The logistic regression results are therefore different from OLS regression results, yet our goal of prediction and explanation remains the same.

● ASSUMPTIONS

Logistic regression models have a different set of assumptions from OLS regression, the most notable being no assumption of normality. Logistic regression assumptions relate to the following:

1. There is no assumption of linear relationship between the dependent and independent variables.

2. Dependent variable values do not need to be normally distributed.

3. There is no homogeneity of variance assumption among or within categories.

4. Normally distributed error terms are not assumed.

5. Independent variables need not be measured on the interval scale.

6. There are no missing data in the contingency table (nonzero cell counts).

Recall that OLS multiple regression required a normal distribution of the dependent variable, residuals with constant variance and independent of each other, residual errors normally distributed with an average zero value, and independent variables that were not *collinear*—that is, they were highly correlated. However, multicollinearity, linearity, independence of errors, range of X values, and the order of predictor variable entry in the logistic regression equation are important issues to consider, as well as the data conditions a researcher might face when using logistic regression. These are briefly explained.

Multicollinearity is the level of intercorrelation among the independent variables when predicting a dependent variable. It is an important concern in any type of regression model. If the independent variables explain more of their shared variance due to high intercorrelation, then predicting the variation in Y scores is reduced. The ideal regression equation is when all of the independent variables are correlated with Y but are not correlated among themselves. We know this would rarely happen in practice, so detecting its presence in a regression equation is important. The Pearson, part, and partial correlations are one method to explore predictor variable relations; another is to find software that computes a collinearity statistic in logistic regression. Violation of this assumption can lead to unstable predictor variable regression weights and standard errors, or an overall model fit criterion that is significant while the individual regression weights are not.

Linearity is the assumption that the dependent variable has a linear relation with the independent predictor variables. In logistic regression, the dependent variable is binary or dichotomous, so the assumption of linearity is greatly reduced. The predicted value for Y is called a *logit*, so the linearity assumption is between the logit values of the dependent variable and the continuous predictor variables. Hosmer and Lemeshow (2000) suggest ways to detect whether the linearity assumption is violated, for example, by conducting a Box-Tidwell test. The logistic regression model would include the predictor variables and their interaction terms $[X_i * \ln(X_i)]$. Nonlinearity would be indicated by statistically significant interaction terms. Violation of the linearity assumption, which is present with significant interaction terms, can lead to unstable or biased parameter estimates or predicted logit values of Y not increasing across values of X predictor variables.

Independence of errors is the assumption that the errors of prediction are not correlated. Violation of this assumption would lead to inflated tests of regression weights due to underestimated or smaller standard errors. Recall that t = Regression weight/Standard error. Therefore, a smaller standard error would yield larger t-test values, increasing the chance of them being statistically significant, which inflates the Type I error rates.

The *range of X* values is fixed—that is, a logistic regression model is only valid for those X values used in the analysis. The use of X values for predictor variables outside the range of those used to compute the regression weights would provide prediction errors caused by biased predictor variable slopes and intercept. A related data condition that produces biased regression weights and standard errors is when the number of predictor variables and the sample size are equal. For example, a restriction of range occurs with three predictor variables and $N = 3$ subjects because it does not allow for estimation of regression weights.

Missing data in logistic regression are also important to understand. For example, a nominal predictor variable should not have a single coded value, that is, 1 = *college*, which would give a *nonzero cell count* for 0 = *not college*. There should be a reasonable number of 0 = *not college* and 1 = *college* values, otherwise estimation of the regression weight would be incorrect. Basically, logistic regression estimation is affected by a lopsided percent category allocation. Similarly, if the dependent variable is perfectly predicted, the model estimation is suspect due to *nonseparation* of the data.

Outliers affect the maximum likelihood estimation of regression weights (Croux, Flandre, & Haesbroeck, 2002). There are residual plots and diagnostic tests that help identify influential data points when outliers are present in the data. Basically, an influential data point is indicated by standardized residual values >3.0, *DfBeta* values >1, or leverage values >$(m+1)/N$, where m = number of independent variables (close to 0 = *little influence* and close to 1 = *large influence*).

The *sample size* also affects logistic regression because maximum likelihood estimation of the regression weights generally requires larger sample sizes (Long, 1997).

The *order of predictor variable entry* affects the estimation of regression weights (Schumacker, 2005; Schumacker, Anderson, & Ashby, 1999; Schumacker, Mount, & Monahan, 2002). The authors discovered that the various selection criteria (L^2, z, log-odds ratio, R_L^2 model variance, and ΔC^2) for model fit provided different results in the presence of a different order of predictor variable entry. The use of all possible subset selection and ΔC^2 fit criteria was recommended to determine the best set of categorical independent predictor variables in logistic regression.

● LOGISTIC REGRESSION EQUATION

The logistic regression equation is expressed similarly as the OLS multiple regression equation, except that the data values and estimation of the regression weights are different. We are still interested in predicting a Y_i value for each individual given knowledge of the X predictor variables. The equation has an intercept a (the value of Y when all predictor values are 0), regression coefficients b_j, and residual error e_i:

$$Y_i = a + b_1 X_1 + \cdots + b_j X_j + e_i.$$

A heuristic data set with Y (1 = *admit*, 0 = *not admit*), X_1 (1 = *U.S. student*, 0 = *foreign student*), and X_2 (1 = *male*, 0 = *female*) would be coded as seen here, in the left column:

We would run a *binary* logistic regression analysis since the independent predictor variables are dichotomous (binary). We can also run logistic regression analyses when the independent predictor variables are binary and continuous; for example, X_2 now represents the number of support letters for admission. The data with a nominal and a continuous independent predictor variable are as as seen here, in the right column:

In logistic regression analysis, the dependent variable value is predicted as a logit value (natural log of the odds of the dependent variable) using the independent predictor variable regression weights

Y	X_1	X_2
1	1	1
1	1	0
1	0	1
1	0	0
⋮	⋮	⋮
⋮	⋮	⋮
0	1	1
0	1	0
0	0	1
0	0	0

Y	X_1	X_2
1	1	4
1	1	7
1	0	3
1	0	4
⋮	⋮	⋮
⋮	⋮	⋮
0	1	3
0	1	2
0	0	1
0	0	2

estimated by maximum likelihood estimation. The logistic regression equation computes a probability value—the probability that the dependent variable value will occur between the values of 0 and 1. The log odds or risk ratio provides a way to interpret these predicted Y probability values.

● PROBABILITY, ODDS, LOG ODDS, AND LOGIT

Menard (2000a) explains the concepts of probability, logit, and log odds/risk ratio when interpreting the predicted Y values in logistic regression. Each concept is important to understand when interpreting the results from logistic regression, whether one uses nominal or continuous predictor variables. I briefly explain each here and use these terms later in an applied example.

Probability

In logistic regression, the Y variable is scaled 0 and 1, a nominal level of measurement. The logistic regression equation computes a probability value for each individual between 0 and 1, depending on their values for the independent predictor variables. Therefore, $P(1) = 1 - P(0)$ and $P(0) = 1 - P(1)$, so that $P(1) + P(0) = 100\%$. The predicted probability values permit an interpretation of the Y outcome that is not binary (admitted/not admitted); rather, it is a matter of probability of occurrence—for example, "Do U.S. male students have a higher probability of admittance to a program than U.S. female students?"

The logistic regression equation also provides a classification prediction that permits a cross-tabulation with the actual Y binary values. A percent correct classification can be computed, which provides a helpful interpretation of the Y predicted outcome. A chi-square test would determine if the percent classification for actual and predicted values was statistically significant.

Odds and Logits

Odds are the ratio of the two probability outcomes for Y. The odds that the Y outcome is 1 (*admit*) rather than 0 (*not admit*) is the ratio of the odds (probability) that $Y = 1$ to the odds (probability) that Y is not equal to 1—that is, $1 - P(1)$. This can be expressed as

$$\text{Odds}(Y = 1) = \frac{P(1)}{1 - P(1)}.$$

A few *odds* are expressed in the table between 0 and 1 as follows:

P(1)	1 − P(1)	Odds (P(1)/1 − P(1))
.001	.999	0.001
.250	.750	0.333
.500	.500	1.000
.750	.250	3.000
.999	.001	999.000

The *odds* do not provide the property of scale required to make meaningful interpretations. Therefore, the log of the *odds* is taken to create a scale that could range from positive to negative infinity. The *log odds* of Y creates a linear relationship between the probability of Y and the X predictor variables (Pampel, 2000). The log odds are computed by using the *ln* function on a scientific calculator. The log function converts the *odds* into positive and negative values, above and below the center point of 0, which is the value for $.5/.5 = \ln(1.000) = 0$. The tabled values for the *odds* and *log odds*, ln(Odds) are seen here, to the left:

Odds	ln(Odds)
0.001	−6.907
0.333	−1.099
1.000	0
3.000	1.099
999.000	6.907

The logit values for Y are the log odds values—that is, $Y_{\text{logit}} = \ln(\text{Odds})$. The logit values are related to the probabilities; that is, a one-unit change in the logit value equals a change in the probability. The logarithm function creates a linear scale, which permits a regression equation to predict the *log odds*, Y_{logit}:

$$\hat{Y}_{\text{logit}} = a + \beta_1 X_1 + \beta_2 X_2.$$

The logistic regression equation computes a predicted probability value for Y. The residual errors (*e*) are the differences between the actual Y values (0 or 1) and the predicted probability values.

The *log odds*, Y_{logit}, are not by themselves easy to interpret in relationship to the independent predictor variables. Therefore, to interpret each independent variable effect on the dependent variable, the exponent is taken, which converts back to an odds interpretation. The logistic regression equation is now expressed as follows:

$$\hat{e}^{Y_{logit}} = \left(e^a\right)\left(e^{\beta_1 X_1}\right)\left(e^{\beta_2 X_2}\right).$$

The logistic regression equation is now a multiplicative function due to the use of exponential values. On a scientific calculator, the symbol e^x is used for obtaining the exponential value. In the multiplicative equation, a value of $x = 0$ corresponds to $e^0 = 1$, which is a coefficient of 1. *Coefficients greater than 1 increase the odds, and coefficients less than 1 decrease the odds.* The log odds are linked to probabilities by the following equation:

$$P(1) = \frac{e^{a+\beta_1 X_1 + \beta_2 X_2}}{1 + e^{a+\beta_1 X_1 + \beta_2 X_2}}.$$

This linkage shows that the probability values close to 1 indicate more likelihood of the outcome—that is, of being admitted to a program. Probabilities close to 0 would indicate a likelihood of not being admitted to the program. The probability is equal to the constant e or natural log function value, $e = 2.718$, with the exponent being the logistic regression equation. I showed that a probability ratio of .50/.50 = 1 (odds ratio), with ln(Odds) = 0. The logit probability can be converted back, which equals a probability of .50:

$$P(1) = \frac{2.718^0}{1 + 2.718^0} = .50.$$

The logistic regression output provides the log odds value for the independent variables in the regression equation.

Odds Ratio Versus Risk Ratio

The *odds ratio* (OR) is a ratio of the odds of an event, so it is not a probability value.

The *risk ratio* (RR) reflects the probability of an outcome in a group divided by the group's combined probability of success and failure, divided by a second outcome's probability in the group divided by that group's combined probability of success and failure. A risk ratio describes how many more times it is likely for an event to occur given the outcome. For example, RR = 3 for a treatment implies that one is three times more likely to achieve success with the treatment than without it. The following 2 × 2 table shows the cell values to compare the odds ratio and risk ratio computations:

The odds ratio is as follows:

$$OR = \frac{a/b}{c/d}.$$

	Success	*Failure*
Admit	a	b
Not admit	c	d

The risk ratio for admittance to a program is shown in the following formula:

$$RR = \frac{a / (a + b)}{c / (c + d)}.$$

An odds ratio is a measure of the association between a treatment and an outcome. The odds ratio represents the odds that an outcome will occur given the treatment, compared with the odds of the outcome occurring without the treatment. Case–control studies generally report an odds ratio due to predictor variable regression weights in a logistic regression equation. A logistic regression coefficient is estimated and then interpreted as the increase in the log odds of the outcome per unit increase in the value for the treatment group. The exponential function e^b is the odds ratio associated with a one-unit increase in the value for a predictor variable. The binary outcomes, or counts of success versus failure in a number of trials, are interpreted as an odds ratio. The odds ratio can be interpreted as follows:

- OR = 1: The treatment does not affect the odds of the outcome.
- OR > 1: The treatment is associated with higher odds of the outcome.
- OR < 1: The treatment is associated with lower odds of the outcome.

A risk ratio describes how many more times it is likely for an event to occur given the outcome. Randomized control and cohort studies typically report relative risk using Poisson regression methods. The count of events per unit exposure have relative risk interpretations—that is, the estimated effect of a predictor variable is multiplicative on the rate, thus yielding a relative risk (risk ratio). The interpretation of a relative risk between an experimental group and a control group is as follows:

- RR = 1: There is no difference in risk between the two groups.
- RR > 1: The outcome is more likely to occur in the experimental group than in the control group.
- RR < 1: The outcome is less likely to occur in the experimental group than in the control group.

When the 2 × 2 table results have small cell numbers, a and c will be small numbers, so the odds and risk ratios will be similar. It is recommended that an odds ratio be converted to a risk ratio for interpretation, which can be done using the R *orsk* package (Wang, 2013). The risk ratio implies how many more times one is likely to achieve success (outcome) with a treatment than without it.

● MODEL FIT

The model fit criteria are used to determine the overall fit of the predictor variables in predicting Y. For each unit change in the independent variable, the logistic regression coefficient represents the change in the predicted *log odds* value, Y_{logit}. The regression weights can also be tested for the statistical significance of each predictor variable. A final interpretation is possible using classification accuracy from the predicted group membership values. The first two, overall model fit and statistical significance of regression weights, are common when running regression-type analyses. The third, classification accuracy, is unique to logistic regression, and in the binary dependent variable, it affords a chi-square test of independence between the actual and predicted values.

Schumacker et al. (1999) also investigated the various model fit criteria used in logistic regression. Rather than compare R-squared analog values, the authors chose to examine many different selection criteria: L^2, z, log odds ratio, R_L^2, and ΔC^2. They discovered that ΔC^2 was a more robust measure of model fit and that the results differed depending on the order of predictor variable entry. I represent ΔC^2 as $\Delta \chi^2$ in this chapter. Menard (2000b) compared the different R-squared analog coefficients of determination in multiple logistic regression analysis. He recommended R_L^2 over the other R-squared analogs that were compared, based on its conceptual similarity to the OLS coefficient of determination and its relative independence from the base rate. It seems prudent when conducting a logistic regression analysis to examine the overall model fit criteria as well as interpret the statistical significance of the predictor variables. Forward, backward, and stepwise methods for variable selection are not recommended because they lead to erroneous fit statistics, bias standard errors, and ill-determined predictor variable selection. An all-possible subset variable selection method would help determine the best set of predictor variables.

Chi-Square Difference Test

The test of overall model fit in logistic regression can use the likelihood ratio test. A log-likelihood (LL) function provides an index of how much has *not* been explained in the logistic regression equation after the parameters (regression weights) have been estimated. The LL values vary from 0 to negative infinity, with LL values close to 0 indicating a better logistic equation model fit. If we calculate LL for different logistic regression equations, then a test of the difference in LL indicates changes in the overall model fit. For example, calculate LL for a logistic regression equation using the intercept only. Next, calculate LL for a logistic regression equation with the intercept $+B_1 X_1$. A difference in the LL values between these two regression models will indicate whether X_1 is statistically significant above and beyond the intercept-only model. This test is similar to the F test in multiple regression when testing a difference between the full and the restricted model; however, a chi-square difference test is used with the separate logistic regression chi-square values. A chi-square test is possible by multiplying by -2 the difference in the LL functions, with the degrees of freedom equal to the difference in the model degree-of-freedom values. The chi-square difference test is expressed as follows:

$$\Delta \chi^2 = -2\left(\text{LL}_{\text{full model}} - \text{LL}_{\text{restricted model}}\right)$$

and

$$df_{\text{Diff}} = df_{\text{full model}} - df_{\text{restricted model}}.$$

The larger the difference between the full and the restricted model, the better the model fit. Typically, a researcher starts with a baseline model (intercept only) and then sequentially adds predictor variables; each time, the degree-of-freedom difference would be 1. Each variable added in the logistic regression equation is tested for statistical significance given that $\chi^2 = 3.84$, $df = 1$, and $p = .05$. Consequently, any chi-square difference ($\Delta\chi^2$) greater than 3.84 would indicate a statistically significant predictor variable.

Note: The chi-square difference test is based on nested models—that is, adding additional variables from the same data set.

Hosmer-Lemeshow Goodness-of-Fit Test

The *Hosmer-Lemeshow goodness-of-fit* test is based on dividing the individuals into 10 groups (deciles) based on their predicted probabilities. A chi-square is computed for the observed and expected frequencies in the 10 groups. A researcher would desire a nonsignificant chi-square statistic, which indicates that the predicted values are not different from the observed values given the logistic regression equation. The test is considered to lack power to detect the lack of model fit in the presence of nonlinearity of the independent variables. The test also tends to overestimate model fit when the groupings are less than 10 and provides little guidance about predictor variable significance. I mentioned it only because the test is often reported in statistical packages.

R-Squared Analog Tests

The *R*-squared analog tests are considered pseudo *R*-squared values or analogs to the *R*-squared value in OLS regression. As noted before, they have been investigated, with scholars disagreeing on their usefulness. The ones listed here are all variants when using the LL function.

Cox and Snell (1989) proposed the following with sample size = n:

$$R^2_{CS} = 1 - \exp\left(\frac{-2LL_{model} - (-2LL_{baseline})}{n}\right).$$

Nagelkerke (1991) proposed an adjustment to the R^2_{CS} value to achieve a maximum value of 1:

$$R^2_{N} = \frac{R^2_{CS}}{1 - \exp\left(-\frac{-2LL_{baseline}}{n}\right)}.$$

Hosmer and Lemeshow (2000) indicated an *R*-squared value for a ratio of the full model to the restricted model, thus indicating how the model can be improved by adding predictor variables:

$$R^2_{L} = \frac{-2LL_{model}}{-2LL_{baseline}}.$$

Harrell (2001) proposed an adjustment to the Hosmer and Lemeshow *R*-squared value for the number of independent variables (*m*) in the logistic regression equation:

$$R_{LA}^2 = \frac{(-2LL_{model}) - 2m}{-2LL_{baseline}}.$$

The list goes on. The creation of *R*-squared analog tests used the same logic with the *R*-squared and *R*-squared adjusted values for sample size and number of predictor variables in OLS multiple regression. In fact, a researcher can compute an *R*-squared value by squaring the correlation between the observed *Y* values and the predicted *Y* probability values from the logistic regression equation. This would basically be as follows:

```
> Rsq = cor(Y, Yhat)^2
```

I will compute this *R*-squared value in the applied example given later in the chapter.

Predicted Group Membership

A final overall model fit approach can involve using the actual *Y* values (0, 1) with the predicted group membership. For example, if $P \geq .5$, then classify it as group = 1, else group = 0.

A crosstab table will provide the frequency and percentage of cases for the actual versus predicted probabilities for the groups. A correct classification would be for those individuals in the actual *Y* = 1 and predicted *Y* = 1 group and for those individuals in the actual *Y* = 0 and predicted *Y* = 0 group. The other two cell frequencies represent a misclassification. Therefore, the sum of the diagonal percents indicates the percent correctly classified, shown in the table below as percent correctly classified = $\Sigma(a + d)$.

The traditional chi-square test can be conducted using these actual and predicted values.

The Pearson chi-square formula with observed (*O*) and expected (*E*) values and *df* = 1 is

Actual	Predicted	
	Admit	Not Admit
Admit	*a*	*B*
Not admit	*c*	*D*

$$\chi^2 = \Sigma \frac{(O - E)^2}{E}.$$

An alternative form of the chi-square test of classification accuracy given a binomial outcome is as follows:

$$\chi^2 = \frac{[N_i - (np_i)]^2}{np_i},$$

where *N* = total sample size, *n* = number of cases in the cell, and *p* = probability of success. This provides the same Pearson chi-square value as the equation above.

● LOGISTIC REGRESSION COEFFICIENTS

Maximum likelihood estimation is used to determine the logistic regression weights. The iterative estimation method starts with least squares estimates, and then maximizes the LL function for a final set of regression coefficients. The Wald and BIC (Bayesian Information Criterion) statistics are used to test the regression coefficients for statistical significance; standardized coefficients are computed separately, and a confidence interval is generally computed. Each of these is explained next.

Wald Chi-Square Test

The Wald chi-square test is computed as the logistic regression coefficient squared and divided by the square of the standard error (variance). This formula is shown below:

$$W = \frac{\beta_j^2}{(SE_{\beta_j})^2}.$$

When conducting logistic regression, our approach is to first compute a baseline model (intercept only). We then add independent predictor variables, usually one at a time, and check to see if the Wald chi-square value is statistically significant for the regression coefficient.

AIC and BIC Tests

The other tests for the statistical significance of a regression coefficient are the AIC (Akaike Information Criterion) and BIC tests. The difference between the two measures is seen in the added component of either $2 * df$ for AIC, where df is the degrees of freedom associated with the LL function, or $\log(n)$ for BIC, where n is the sample size.

$$AIC = -2 * LL + (2 * df)$$

and

$$BIC = -2 * LL + \log(n).$$

The AIC and BIC values should be positive. The larger the AIC and BIC values, the more likely the added predictor variable is statistically significant; hence, it adds to the prediction in the logistic regression equation.

Standardized Coefficient

The beta regression weights (standardized coefficients) were used in OLS regression to assess which predictor variables were the most important and contributed to the prediction of Y.

In OLS regression, we obtained the standardized coefficients by first scaling the variables using the *scale()* function. This computed the standardized variables, which were then used in the regression function to output standardized beta weights. This is not done in logistic regression; rather, a test of the chi-square difference between a full and a restricted model is computed. In logistic regression, this involves using the $\Delta\chi^2$ test for the difference in models, where one variable is dropped to test whether it contributed significantly to prediction.

Confidence Intervals

A confidence interval (CI) around the logistic regression coefficient b_j provides important information for interpreting the coefficient. The confidence interval is formed using the regression coefficient plus or minus the product of a tabled critical value and standard error. The formula is expressed as follows:

$$CI(b_j) = b_j \pm t_{\alpha/2;n-m-1}(S_{b_j}).$$

If the confidence interval for the regression coefficient contains zero, then the logistic regression coefficient is *not* statistically significant at the specified level of significance (α). We interpret confidence intervals to indicate how much the value might vary on repeated sampling of data.

● EFFECT SIZE MEASURES

The *R*-squared analog coefficients are used as an effect size measure. They indicate the pseudovariance explained in predicted probabilities of *Y* given a set of independent predictor variables. The *odds ratio* is also an effect size measure, similar to the *R*-squared analog coefficients. The odds ratio is computed by the exponent of the regression weight for a predictor variable, e^{b_j}, which is the odds for one group (admit) divided by the odds of the other group (not admit). When OR = 1, there is no relation between the dependent variable and the independent predictor variable. If the independent predictor variable is continuous, the odds ratio is the amount of change for a one-unit increase in the independent variable. If OR > 1, the independent variable increases the odds of the outcome, and when OR < 1, the independent variable decreases the odds of the outcome. The odds ratio can also be converted to a *Cohen's d* effect size:

$$Cohen's\ d = \frac{\ln(OR)}{1.81}.$$

● APPLIED EXAMPLE

The *aod* package is used to obtain the results for a logistic regression model analysis. It provides the functions we need to analyze counts or proportions. The *ggplot* package will be used to graph the predicted probability values. The *Hmisc* package will be used to obtain a data set for the logistic regression analysis. The packages are installed and loaded with the following R commands:

```
> install.packages("aod")
> install.packages("ggplot2")
> install.packages("Hmisc")
> library(aod)
> library(ggplot2)
> library(Hmisc)
```

I found several data sets in the Hmisc package:

```
> getHdata()

 [1] "abm" "acath" "ari" "ari_other"
 [5] "birth.estriol" "boston" "cdystonia" "counties"
 [9] "diabetes" "dmd" "DominicanHTN" "FEV"
[13] "hospital" "kprats" "lead" "nhgh"
[17] "olympics.1996" "pbc" "plasma" "prostate"
[21] "rhc" "sex.age.response" "stressEcho" "support2"
[25] "support" "titanic2" "titanic3" "titanic"
[29] "valung" "vlbw"
```

I chose the data set *diabetes*. The data set appeared in the RGui window, and two separate Internet HTML windows opened with the documentation. The first HTML window indicated that the data set contained 19 variables on 403 of the 1,046 subjects who were interviewed in a study to examine the prevalence of obesity, diabetes, and cardiovascular risk factors for African Americans in central Virginia (Willems, Saunders, Hunt, & Schorling, 1997). The other HTML window provided a codebook for the variables in the data set. The R command was as follows:

Selecting Variables

```
> getHdata(diabetes, "all")
```

I attached the data set and listed the variable names to select the ones I wanted to use in the logistic regression equation.

```
> attach(diabetes)
> names(diabetes)
 [1] "id" "chol" "stab.glu" "hdl" "ratio" "glyhb"
 [7] "location" "age" "gender" "height" "weight" "frame"
[13] "bp.1s" "bp.1d" "bp.2s" "bp.2d" "waist" "hip"
[19] "time.ppn"
```

After examining the list of variable names, I selected *glyhb* (glycosolated hemoglobin), because levels >7.0 is a positive diagnosis of diabetes; *location* (Buckingham, Louisa); *gender* (male, female);

and *frame* (small, medium, large) for my logistic regression analysis. I created a smaller data set, *newdata*, with just these variables in them (*myvars*). I then used the *head()* function to print out the first 6 observations and *dim()* function to indicate the number of observations and number of variables (403 observations and 19 variables) in the data set. The following R commands were used:

```
> myvars = c("glyhb","location","gender","frame")
> newdata = diabetes[myvars]
> head(newdata, n = 6)
  glyhb location  gender frame
1 4.31 Buckingham female medium
2 4.44 Buckingham female large
3 4.64 Buckingham female large
4 4.63 Buckingham   male large
5 7.72 Buckingham   male medium
6 4.81 Buckingham   male large

> dim(diabetes)
[1] 403 19
```

Handling of Missing Data

The first step prior to data analysis is to determine if missing values exist for one or more variables. The variables *glyhb* (n = 390) and *frame* (n = 391) had fewer than the original N = 403 observations. I used the *describe()* function to reveal information about each variable.

```
> describe (newdata)

newdata

4 Variables 403 Observations
---------------------------------------------------------------------
glyhb: Glycosolated Hemoglobin
n missing unique Mean .05 .10 .25 .50 .75 .90
390 13 239 5.59 3.750 4.008 4.380 4.840 5.600 8.846
.95
10.916

lowest: 2.68 2.73 2.85 3.03 3.33, highest: 13.70 14.31 14.94 15.52 16.11
---------------------------------------------------------------------
location
n missing unique
403 0 2

Buckingham (200, 50%), Louisa (203, 50%)
---------------------------------------------------------------------
```

```
gender
n missing unique
403 0 2

male (169, 42%), female (234, 58%)
-----------------------------------------------------------------------------
frame
n missing unique
391 12 3

small (104, 27%), medium (184, 47%), large (103, 26%)
```

We can delete missing values from our statistical analysis using *na.rm = TRUE*, or delete them from the data set prior to conducting statistical analysis. (*Note:* Alternative methods are used to impute missing data, which are beyond the scope of this book.) The data set with listwise deletions resulted in $N = 379$ subjects, a decrease of 24 subjects. The following R commands omitted the 24 subjects and then described the data:

```
> mydata = na.omit(newdata)
> describe(mydata)
mydata

4 Variables 379 Observations
-----------------------------------------------------------------------------
glyhb: Glycosolated Hemoglobin
n missing unique Mean .05 .10 .25 .50 .75 .90
379 0 235 5.601 3.745 4.010 4.380 4.840 5.615 9.172
.95
10.934

lowest: 2.68 2.73 2.85 3.03 3.33, highest: 13.70 14.31 14.94 15.52
16.11
-----------------------------------------------------------------------------
location
n missing unique
379 0 2

Buckingham (182, 48%), Louisa (197, 52%)
-----------------------------------------------------------------------------
gender
n missing unique
379 0 2

male (158, 42%), female (221, 58%)
-----------------------------------------------------------------------------
```

```
frame
n missing unique
379 0 3

small (102, 27%), medium (178, 47%), large (99, 26%)
----------------------------------------------------------------------
> dim(mydata)
[1] 379 4
```

The following command lists the *structure* of the variables in the data set—that is, it shows the class and level of the variables in the data set, *mydata*. The variable *glyhb* is numeric (atomic), while *location* and *gender* are factors with two levels, and *frame* is a factor with three levels.

```
< str(mydata)
'data.frame': 379 obs. of 4 variables:
$ glyhb: Class 'labelled' atomic [1:379] 4.31 4.44 4.64 4.63 7.72 ...
 .. ..- attr(*, "label") = chr "Glycosolated Hemoglobin"

$ location: Factor w/ 2 levels "Buckingham","Louisa": 1 1 1 1 1 1 1 1 1 1 ...

$ gender: Factor w/ 2 levels "male","female": 2 2 2 1 1 1 1 1 1 2 ...

$ frame: Factor w/ 3 levels "small","medium": 2 3 3 3 2 3 2 2 3 1 ...

 - attr(*, "na.action") = Class "omit" Named int [1:24] 44 51 60 64 65 70 109 110 111
117 ...
 .. ..- attr(*, "names") = chr [1:24] "44" "51" "60" "64" ...
```

Coding the Dependent Variable

In the absence of a true dichotomy for a dependent variable, for example, U.S. students versus international students, you will need to create one. I am interested in predicting diabetic condition given knowledge of *location*, *gender*, and *frame* (body size) in a logistic regression equation. I therefore must code *glyhb* into a dichotomous dependent variable (1 = *diabetic*, 0 = *not diabetic*) based on glycosolated hemoglobin levels >7, which would indicate *diabetic*, and values <7, indicating *not diabetic*. To recode *glyhb* into a dichotomous variable, we would use the *ifelse()* function to create two dichotomous values for a variable *depvar* and place them in the data set, *mydata*. The *ifelse()* function codes *depvar* = 1 if *glyhb* > 7, else *depvar* = 0. The R control structure command is as follows:

```
> mydata$depvar = ifelse(mydata$glyhb > 7, c("1"), c("0"))
```
The first few cases are printed again to show that the new variable has been created and
    takes on the intended values.
```
    > head(mydata, n = 6)
```

```
  glyhb location  gender frame depvar
1 4.31 Buckingham female medium  0
2 4.44 Buckingham female large   0
3 4.64 Buckingham female large   0
4 4.63 Buckingham   male  large   0
5 7.72 Buckingham   male  medium  1
6 4.81 Buckingham   male  large   0
```

Checking for Nonzero Cell Counts

A final step prior to running our logistic regression equation is to check the data for nonzero cells in the crosstabs of variables. The *location*, *gender*, and *frame* predictor variables do not have 0 in their crosstab cells with the dependent variable *depvar*. The *xtabs()* function can be used to display the crosstab cell counts for the different variables.

```
> xtabs(~depvar + location, data = mydata)
location
depvar Buckingham Louisa
0  153 168
1  29 29


> xtabs(~depvar + gender, data = mydata)

gender
depvar male female
0       133    188
1        25     33


> xtabs(~depvar + frame, data = mydata)

frame
depvar small medium large
0        93    152    76
1         9     26    23
```

I went step by step through the data input, variable selection, missing data, recoding, and, finally, nonzero cell count processes to show the importance of screening and preparing data for statistical analysis. In the previous chapters, we also took steps and paid attention to some of these activities prior to conducting our statistical analysis. At some point, the phrase "Know your data" will ring true. If you prepare your data prior to statistical analysis and check the required assumptions, fewer problems will occur in the analysis, providing better sample estimates of the population parameters.

Logistic Regression Analysis

My logistic regression analysis can now proceed. First, I must declare categorical variables as *factors*. This requires the following R commands for each:

```
> mydata$location = factor(mydata$location)
> mydata$gender = factor(mydata$gender)
> mydata$frame = factor(mydata$frame)
> mydata$depvar = factor(mydata$depvar)
```

I am now ready to use the *glm()* function to run the logistic regression equation and the *summary()* function to output the results.

```
> mylogit = glm (depvar ~ location + gender + frame, data = mydata,
family = "binomial")
> summary(mylogit)

Call:
glm(formula = depvar ~ location + gender + frame, family = "binomial",
 data = mydata)

Deviance Residuals:
  Min      1Q     Median      3Q      Max
-0.7489 -0.5728 -0.5448 -0.4363 2.2351

Coefficients:
                Estimate Std. Error  z value Pr(>|z|)
(Intercept)    -2.411885 0.440287   -5.478 0.000000043 ***
locationLouisa  0.006289 0.292557    0.021 0.98285
genderfemale    0.107978 0.300643    0.359 0.71948
framemedium     0.573023 0.408740    1.402 0.16094
framelarge      1.169743 0.432837    2.703 0.00688 **
---
Signif. codes: 0 '***' 0.001 '**' 0.01 '*' 0.05 '.' 0.1 ' ' 1

(Dispersion parameter for binomial family taken to be 1)

Null deviance: 324.38 on 378 degrees of freedom
Residual deviance: 316.12 on 374 degrees of freedom
AIC: 326.12

Number of Fisher Scoring iterations: 5
```

The results indicated that *location* and *gender* differences were not statistically significant ($p = .982$ and $p = .719$, respectively). Regarding the *frame* variable, a large person was more indicative of diabetes than a medium or small person ($p = .00688$).

Confidence Intervals

A confidence interval can be computed using the standard error to form the confidence interval around these coefficients. The *confint.default()* function provides the $p = .05$ alpha-level results for a two-tailed percent (2.5% in each tail). The confidence intervals for *location* and *gender* contain the value of zero as expected since they were nonsignificant: Location CI = (−.567, +.579) and gender CI = (−.481, +.697). The medium-frame CI (−.228, +1.374) also contained the value of zero. The large-frame CI (.321, +2.018) did not contain the zero value, and as expected, it was statistically significant.

```
> confint.default(mylogit)

2.5 % 97.5 %
(Intercept) -3.2748312 -1.5489385
locationLouisa -0.5671126 0.5796900
genderfemale -0.4812705 0.6972275
framemedium -0.2280933 1.3741387
framelarge 0.3213982 2.0180873
```

Wald Chi-Square Test of Coefficient Significance

The Wald test in the *aod* package can be used to test the statistical significance of one or more (joint) coefficients, given their variance–covariance matrix. The arguments in the *wald.test()* function are listed as follows:

```
> wald.test(Sigma, b, Terms = NULL, L = NULL, H0 = NULL,
  df = NULL, verbose = FALSE)
```

Sigma	A var-cov matrix, usually extracted from one of the fitting functions (e.g., lm, glm, ...).
b	A vector of coefficients with var-cov matrix Sigma. These coefficients are usually extracted from one of the fitting functions available in **R** (e.g., lm, glm,...).
Terms	An optional integer vector specifying which coefficients should be *jointly* tested, using a Wald *chi-squared* or *F* test. Its elements correspond to the columns or rows of the var-cov matrix given in Sigma. Default is NULL.

These can be printed out individually by the following commands:

```
> b = coef(mylogit)
> b
(Intercept) locationLouisa genderfemale framemedium framelarge
-2.411884853 0.006288706 0.107978490 0.573022739 1.169742731
```

and

```
> Sigma = vcov(mylogit)
> Sigma

            (Intercept) locationLouisa genderfemale framemedium framelarge
(Intercept)  0.19385248  -0.050249138  -0.064462914 -0.123183051 -0.14672993
locationLouisa -0.05024914 0.085589632  0.004409604 -0.001355245 0.01401354
genderfemale -0.06446291  0.004409604  0.090386072  0.002975573 0.02493075
framemedium -0.12318305  -0.001355245  0.002975573  0.167068526 0.12248455
framelarge  -0.14672993   0.014013535  0.024930754  0.122484551 0.18734769
```

To test the statistical significance of any given coefficient using the Wald chi-square test, we would select the row and column values for the *Terms* argument. To test the statistical significance of the *framelarge* variable level, it would be *Terms* = 5:5. This gives the same *p*-value result as in the *summary(mylogit)* function above.

```
> wald.test(b = coef(mylogit), Sigma = vcov(mylogit), Terms = 5:5)

Wald test:
----------


Chi-squared test:
X2 = 7.3, df = 1, P(> X2) = 0.0069
```

Our hand calculation verifies that the chi-square value is correct by using the *b* coefficient and variance term from the Sigma matrix in the formula:

$$\chi^2 = \frac{b^2}{(SE_b)^2} = \frac{(1.169742731)^2}{(.432837)^2} = \frac{1.368298}{0.18734769} = 7.30.$$

We can select different *Terms* for the other coefficients, thus obtaining the Wald chi-square test for each. The *p* values for each coefficient matches that in the *summary(mylogit)* function results above. These are computed below.

Wald Chi-Square Test for the Framemedium Coefficient:

```
> wald.test(b = coef(mylogit), Sigma = vcov(mylogit), Terms = 4:4)

Wald test:
----------


Chi-squared test:
X2 = 2.0, df = 1, P(> X2) = 0.16
```

Wald Chi-Square Test for the Genderfemale Coefficient:

```
> wald.test(b = coef(mylogit), Sigma = vcov(mylogit), Terms = 3:3)

Wald test:
----------

Chi-squared test:
X2 = 0.13, df = 1, P(> X2) = 0.72
```

Wald Chi-Square Test for the Location Coefficient:

```
> wald.test(b = coef(mylogit), Sigma = vcov(mylogit), Terms = 2:2)

Wald test:
----------

Chi-squared test:
X2 = 0.00046, df = 1, P(> X2) = 0.98
```

Wald Chi-Square Test for the Intercept Coefficient:

```
> wald.test(b = coef(mylogit), Sigma = vcov(mylogit), Terms = 1:1)
Chi-squared test:
X2 = 30.0, df = 1, P(> X2) = 0.000000043
```

The Wald chi-square tests are computed using the *b* coefficients divided by the square of their respective standard errors. The *coef()* and *vcov()* functions provide these values. The *Terms* argument specifies which squared standard error term is used for each regression coefficient. Personally, I would like to see these chi-square values in the table created by the *summary()* function.

Model Fit

Since *location* and *gender* were not statistically significant, we would drop them from the analysis and rerun the logistic regression equation. The variable *framelarge* was statistically significant ($p = .00696$), leaving a single predictor variable, *frame*, in the logistic regression equation. We will now continue with other results to provide additional information for interpreting the logistic regression model. The *summary()* function provides the following output:

```
> mylogit = glm (depvar ~ frame, data = mydata, family = "binomial")
> summary(mylogit)

Call:
glm(formula = depvar ~ frame, family = "binomial", data = mydata)
```

```
Deviance Residuals:
    Min      1Q     Median    3Q       Max
-0.7272 -0.5620 -0.5620 -0.4298 2.2035


Coefficients:
               Estimate Std. Error z value Pr(>|z|)
(Intercept)  -2.3354     0.3491     -6.690  0.0000000000223 ***
framemedium   0.5696     0.4085      1.394  0.16325
framelarge    1.1401     0.4225      2.699  0.00696 **
---
Signif. codes: 0 '***' 0.001 '**' 0.01 '*' 0.05 '.' 0.1 ' ' 1


(Dispersion parameter for binomial family taken to be 1)

Null deviance: 324.38 on 378 degrees of freedom
Residual deviance: 316.24 on 376 degrees of freedom

AIC: 322.24

Number of Fisher Scoring iterations: 5
```

Note: The residual deviance value is the −2LL value, which is 316.24.

Odds Ratio

Recall that the odds ratio effect size is computed as e^b, the exponent of each coefficient. This is computed by the R command

```
> exp(coef(mylogit))
(Intercept) framemedium framelarge
0.09677419 1.76754386 3.12719298
```

Confidence intervals can be placed around these odds ratio values as follows:

```
> exp(cbind(OR = coef(mylogit), confint(mylogit)))

Waiting for profiling to be done...

OR 2.5 % 97.5 %
(Intercept) 0.09677419 0.04537424 0.1812271
framemedium 1.76754386 0.82047057 4.1432752
framelarge 3.12719298 1.40744556 7.5042364
```

Many scholars find it hard to correctly interpret an odds ratio, but I continue the tradition of showing how to get the values. As noted earlier, the R *orsk* package will convert the odds ratio to the risk ratio for a probability interpretation. I turn my attention now to the important requirement of using and explaining the LL function.

Log Likelihood (−2LL), AIC and BIC

The LL value is obtained by the following *logLik()* function:

```
> logLik(mylogit)
'log Lik.' -158.1223 (df = 3)
```

You need to multiply the LL value by −2 to obtain the −2LL (residual deviance): −2 * −158.1223 = 316.245. Once we have a final logistic regression model, the −2LL value is used to compute the AIC index (AIC = −2 * LL + 2 * *df*). We can hand calculate this as follows: AIC = −2 * (−158.1223) + (2 * 3) = 322.2447. This is obtained using the R command

```
> AIC(mylogit)
[1] 322.2447
```

The BIC, which is related to the AIC, except for taking the log of the sample size, is computed as follows:

```
> n = nrow(mydata)
> BIC(mylogit)
[1] 334.0573
```

You can quickly see that the *AIC()* function can also obtain the BIC value by simply using the *k* argument to specify the log of the sample size:

```
> AIC(mylogit, k = log(n)) # same as BIC using log of sample size

[1] 334.0573
```

The large positive AIC value indicates that the overall model fit is statistically significant.

Chi-Square Difference Test

The chi-square difference test is yet another way to examine the overall model fit by comparing the null deviance and residual deviance values from the analysis (an intercept-only model vs. a model with one or more regression coefficients). The logistic regression results indicated a null deviance = 324.38 and a residual deviance = 316.24. The chi-square difference test shows the difference of 8.131173 as follows:

```
> with(mylogit, null.deviance - deviance)

[1] 8.131173
```

The degrees of freedom for the difference in the models is given by

```
> with(mylogit, df.null - df.residual)
```

```
[1] 2
```

The *p* value for the chi-square difference test is given by

```
> options(scipen = 999) # removes scientific notation
```

```
> with(mylogit, pchisq(null.deviance-deviance, df.null - df.residual, lower.tail = FALSE))
```

```
[1] 0.01715293
```

The chi-square difference test ($\Delta\chi^2 = 8.13$, $df = 2$, $p = .017$) is statistically significant. This indicates that *frame* is a statistically significant variable that adds variance explained above and beyond an intercept-only baseline (model). In practice, we start with the baseline model, then add variables, each time checking to see if the variable contributes above and beyond the intercept and/or previous variables in the model. This is why the order of the predictor variable entry in the logistic regression equation is important to consider and can lead to different results.

R-*Squared Analog (Pseudovariance* R *Squared)*

I am only reporting the calculations for the Cox and Snell *R*-squared and Nagelkerke *R*-squared values, because these two are the ones most often reported in other statistics packages. Recall that the formulas are as follows:

$$R_{CS}^2 = 1 - \exp\left(\frac{-2LL_{model} - (-2LL_{baseline})}{n}\right)$$

$$= 1 - \exp\left(\frac{324.376 - 316.245}{379}\right) = 1 - \exp\left(\frac{8.131}{379}\right) = .021$$

and

$$R_N^2 = \frac{R_{CS}^2}{1 - \exp\left(-\frac{-2LL_{baseline}}{n}\right)} = \frac{.021}{1 - \exp\left(-\frac{316.245}{379}\right)}$$

$$= \frac{.021}{1 - \exp(-.8344)} = \frac{.021}{.5658} = .037.$$

The reported −2LL model is null deviance = 324.38 with 378 degrees of freedom (intercept-only model). The −2LL baseline is residual deviance = 316.24 with 376 degrees of freedom (intercept plus the *frame* predictor variable). Adding the one predictor variable lowered the −2LL value; the chi-square difference test above indicated a statistically significant change; and the Wald chi-square test indicated that *frame* was a statistically significant predictor variable. Finally, we have an effect size measure in the *R*-squared analog values. We can compute these two *R*-squared values as follows:

```
> Rcs = 1 - exp((mylogit$deviance - mylogit$null.deviance)/379)
> Rcs

[1] 0.02122578
```

and

```
> Rn = Rcs/(1-(exp(-(mylogit$null.deviance/379))))
> Rn

[1] 0.03690875
```

Note: The −2LLfull model (324.376) is the sum of 8.131 (chi-square for the one-predictor model) + 316.245 (−2LL intercept-only model). The *R*-squared values indicate a small effect size (.021–.037).

The power to control for a Type II error can be estimated using the *R*-squared analog values in the *pwr.f2.test()* function in the *pwr* package. We load the package and obtain the arguments as follows:

```
> library(pwr)
> ?pwr.f2.test

pwr.f2.test(u = NULL, v = NULL, f2 = NULL, sig.level = 0.05, power = NULL)
```

Arguments

u	degrees of freedom for numerator
v	degrees of freedomfor denominator
f2	effect size
sig.level	Significance level (Type I error probability)
Power	Power of test (1 minus Type II error probability)

The power for our example would have $df_1 = 2$ ($p − 1$ predictors) and $df_2 = 379$, which is specified and run using the Nagelkerke *R*-squared value as follows:

```
> pwr.f2.test(u = 2, v = 379, f2 = .0369, sig.level = .05, power = NULL)

Multiple regression power calculation

u = 2
v = 379
f2 = 0.0369
sig.level = 0.05
power = 0.9277476
```

So even though this is a small effect size (0.0369), we have sufficient power (.927) to detect the effect size. The determination of a small effect size is based on Cohen's rule of thumb (Cohen, 1988). It is quite possible that in the research literature, this effect size may be considered a moderate or even large effect size. It is best to determine the effect size found in your research area when possible.

Predicted Probabilities

The predicted probabilities are computed using the *predict()* function. I assigned the predicted probabilities to the variable *yhat*.

```
> yhat = predict(mylogit, newdata = mydata, type = "response")
```

Next, I add the predicted probabilities for *yhat* to the data set *mydata* and print out the first six rows of data using the *head()* function. This permitted me to see that the predicted values were included in the data set correctly.

```
> compdata = data.frame(mydata, yhat)
> head(compdata)
glyhb location gender frame depvar yhat
1 4.31 Buckingham female medium 1 0.1460674
2 4.44 Buckingham female large 1 0.2323232
3 4.64 Buckingham female large 1 0.2323232
4 4.63 Buckingham male large 1 0.2323232
5 7.72 Buckingham male medium 2 0.1460674
6 4.81 Buckingham male large 1 0.2323232
```

R-Squared Computation

It is easy to correlate the actual Y values with the predicted Y values using the *cor()* function once the predicted values are added to the data set. The *cor()* function will require the variable names from the *compdata* data set just created. You may recall that the variable names are referenced in a data set by the data set name, $, and the variable name, which is *compdata$depvar* for the actual Y values. We will need to convert the variable *depvar* back to a numeric variable (recall that we declared it as a *factor* variable before). The conversion uses the *as.numeric()* function. The R commands are as follows:

```
> compdata$depvar = as.numeric(compdata$depvar)
> r = cor(compdata$depvar, compdata$yhat)
> r
[1] 0.1468472
```

We now square the correlation to obtain the *R*-squared value for the logistic regression model.

```
> rsq = r^2
> rsq
[1] 0.02156411
```

This value resembles the Cox and Snell R^2_{CS} value; it also indicates a small effect size.

Summary of Logistic Regression R Commands

I have put all of the R commands together in a logical progression to show the steps taken to conduct a logistic regression analysis. You can see that it requires diligence to make sure that all of the right steps are taken in the proper order. I have placed all of these commands in the R Logistic Regression script file (chap18.r), so that you should not have to manually enter them; copy them into your own R script file, add any additional R commands, and save for future use.

```
# Load Hmisc, get data set and attach data set
> library(Hmisc)
> getHdata(diabetes)
> attach(diabetes)

# Select variables from diabetes data set
> myvars = c("glyhb","location","gender","frame")
> newdata = diabetes[myvars]

# Omit missing values
> mydata = na.omit(newdata) # 379 obs 4 variables

# Code dichotomous dependent variable and add to data set
> mydata$depvar = ifelse(mydata$glyhb > 7, c("1"), c("0"))
> mydata # 379 obs 5 variables

# Check for non-zero cells
> xtabs(~depvar + location, data = mydata)
> xtabs(~depvar + gender, data = mydata)
> xtabs(~depvar + frame, data = mydata)

# Designate variables as factors
> mydata$location = factor(mydata$location)
> mydata$gender = factor(mydata$gender)
> mydata$frame = factor(mydata$frame)
> mydata$depvar = factor(mydata$depvar)

# Run logistic regression equation
> mylogit = glm (depvar ~ frame, data = mydata, family = "binomial")
> summary(mylogit)

# Compute R-squared analog values (Cox and Snell and Nagelkerke)
> Rcs = 1 - exp((mylogit$deviance - mylogit$null.deviance)/379)
> Rcs
> Rn = Rcs/(1-(exp(-(mylogit$null.deviance/379))))
> Rn
```

```
# Compute Predicted Probabilities and Add to Data Set
> yhat = predict(mylogit, newdata = mydata, type = "response")
> compdata = data.frame(mydata, yhat)
> head(compdata)

# Convert depvar to numeric, correlate depvar and yhat, square correlation
> compdata$depvar = as.numeric(compdata$depvar)
> r = cor(compdata$depvar, compdata$yhat)
>rsq = r^2
>rsq
```

● JOURNAL ARTICLE

Satcher and Schumacker (2009) published an article using binary logistic regression to predict modern homonegativity among 571 professional counselors. Counselors are ethically bound not to discriminate against persons based on sexual orientation (American Counseling Association, 2005). Sparse research, however, existed on the topic. Modern homonegativity is prejudices against gay men and lesbians based on current issues, such as equality and social justice, measured by the Modern Homonegativity Scale (Morrison & Morrison, 2002). Scores on the instrument were dichotomously coded into 0 = *low* and 1 = *high* modern homonegativity for the dependent variable based on the upper and lower quartiles—yielding 99 counselors with low modern homonegativity scores and 90 counselors with high modern homonegativity scores. Predictor variables that prior research had shown to be related to attitudes toward homosexuality were age, gender, race, political affiliation, education level, religious affiliation, personal contact or friendship, affirming information about homosexuality, and personal view regarding homosexuality having a biological origin.

The logistic regression equation predicted the probability of *Y* occurring for each person given responses on the independent predictor variables. In the logistic regression analysis, the observed and predicted values on *Y* were used to assess the fit of the equation using an LL statistic. The LL statistic indicated just how much unexplained variance was left after the regression model had been fitted—that is, large values indicated poor fitting models, while lower values indicated better fitting models. The first logistic regression model was a baseline model that only included the intercept value, which is based on the frequency of *Y* when *Y* = 1. The improvement in model fit was determined by a chi-square difference test, with 1 degree of freedom between successive models; this involved the subtraction of hypothesized new models with additional predictor variables from the baseline model:

$$\chi^2 = \text{LL (baseline model)} - \text{LL (Model A)}.$$

The individual contribution or statistical significance of independent predictor variables in the logistic regression equation was determined by computing a Wald statistic: Wald = B/SE_B, where B = regression coefficient and SE_B = standard error. The other approach used was to compare successive models, adding unique parameters each time and determining the reduction in −2LL and increase in pseudo *R*-squared and chi-square values, which indicated a better model fit and thus better classification and prediction of the probability of Y. Interpretation of the logistic regression coefficients, or e^B (exp(B)), indicated the change in odds, resulting in a unit change in the predictor variable. For a value greater than 1, the proportion of change in odds indicated that as the predictor variable values increased, the odds of the Y outcome increased. For a value less than 1, the proportion of change in odds indicated that as the predictor increased, the odds of the Y outcome decreased.

The baseline model, which only included the constant, yielded the −2LL statistic = 261.58 and percent classification = 52%. The final logistic regression equation, after adding successive predictor variables, yielded the −2LL statistic = 32.97, percent classification = 85%, Nagelkerke R-squared = .659, and model χ^2 = 128.61.

The final binary logistic regression equation was as follows:

$$P(Y) = \frac{1}{1 + e^{-(-4.54+2.64(\text{attend})+1.77(\text{friend})+2.36(\text{political})+1.17(\text{training})+1.20(\text{age}))}}.$$

The probability of modern homonegativity was now predicted based on the final set of statistically significant predictor variables: attend church, friend, political affiliation, training, and age. For example, a counselor who attends church regularly (*attend* = 1), does not have a gay or lesbian friend (*friend* = 1), is a Republican (*political* = 1), has no training related to gay or lesbian sexual identity (*training* = 1), and is over the age of 48 years (*age* = 1) would have a 99% chance of having high modern homonegativity scores. In contrast, a counselor who does not attend church regularly (*attend* = 0), has a gay or lesbian friend (*friend* = 0), is a Democrat/other (*political* = 0), has training related to gay or lesbian sexual identity (*training* = 0), and is under the age of 48 years (*age* = 0) would have a 1% chance of having high homonegativity scores. The use of individual values that have different combinations of these predictor variables would lead to probability values between the 0 and 1 dependent variable values. The risk ratio was .99 divided by .01, which indicated that counselors are 99 times more likely to have high modern homonegativity scores with the predictor variable characteristics in the logistic regression model. Cohen (2000) clarifies the correct way to interpret odds ratio versus the probability ratio (risk ratio). Basically, an OR of 2:1 is not the same as having twice the probability of an event occurring. The use of the logistic regression equation to predict the probability of Y for any given individual based on the values for the predictor variables is recommended instead.

● CONCLUSIONS

Logistic regression predicts a dichotomous dependent variable, rather than a continuous variable as in OLS regression. The assumptions in logistic regression do not require the dependent variable and the error variances (residuals) to be normally distributed and uncorrelated. There are other assumptions that must be met for logistic regression analyses, with the most severe violation occurring in the presence of nonzero cell counts. The logistic regression equation is also written in a multiplicative form due to exponentiation of the variable values. Finally, the overall model fit, significance of the regression weights, and effect size are computed using different values due to maximum likelihood estimation, rather than the least squares estimation used in OLS regression. For example, a chi-square test is used to indicate how well the logistic regression model fits the data.

The logistic regression analysis example indicated that *location* and *gender* were not statistically significant, but *frame* was at the $p < .05$ level of significance. An easy way to interpret a trend in the levels of this variable is to compute the number at each level who were diagnosed as being diabetic. If we compute the average on Y for those who were diagnosed as diabetic ($Y = 1$), the results will show that as a person's frame (body size) increases, the probability of diabetes incidence too increases. When converting to an e^x value, a probability ratio interpretation is possible. Recall that the percent above a value of 1 indicates an increased probability. Having a large frame (body size) indicates a 26% greater chance of getting Type II diabetes, compared with a 15% chance with a medium frame and only a 9% chance with a small frame.

Frame	Total	Diabetic	Probability	e^x
Small	102	9	.088	1.09
Medium	178	26	.146	1.15
Large	99	23	.232	1.26

If we graph the probability values, a visual depiction shows this increase:

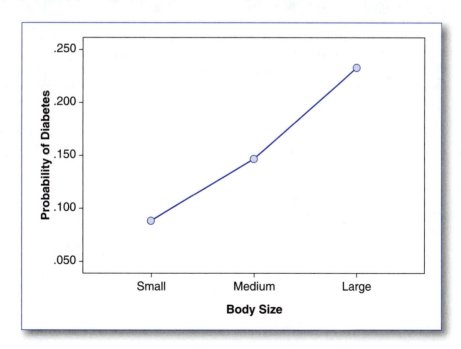

The logistic regression equation provides the computations to determine the significance of a predictor variable in terms of predicting the probability that $Y = 1$, which is referred to as $\hat{p}$. The probability that Y is 0 is $1 - \hat{p}$.

$$\ln\left(\frac{\hat{p}}{1-\hat{p}}\right) = \alpha + \beta_1 X.$$

The *ln* symbol refers to a natural logarithm, and $\alpha + \beta_1 X$ is our familiar equation for the regression line. I showed how the predicted probabilities can be computed from the regression equation using the *predict()* function. So if we know the regression equation, we can calculate the probability that $Y = 1$ for a given value of X:

$$\hat{p} = \frac{\exp(\alpha + \beta_1 X)}{1 + \exp(\alpha + \beta_1 X)} = \frac{e^{\alpha + \beta_1 X}}{1 + e^{\alpha + \beta_1 X}}.$$

The model fit and test of regression coefficient significance is best indicated by a chi-square difference test using $-2LL$ values. We start with a baseline model (intercept-only), then add variables, each time determining if a better model fit occurs. This is similar to a change in the *R*-squared value explained in OLS regression modeling when another variable has been added to the equation. In logistic regression, we expect the $-2LL$ values to decrease when adding variables that improve model fit. The chi-square difference test is not valid unless the two models compared involve one model that is a reduced form of the other model (nested).

SUMMARY

This chapter covered a special type of multiple regression, binary logistic regression, where the dependent variable was measured at the dichotomous level rather than at the continuous level of measurement. I provided the set of special assumptions that affect the use of logistic regression, especially nonzero cell counts. The logistic regression equation and its special multiplicative form and maximum likelihood estimation were then presented. Model fit, tests for regression coefficient statistical significance, confidence interval, and effect size were discussed. These measures were different from the OLS multiple regression presented in the previous chapters. The logic of OLS multiple regression is similar, in that prediction of a dependent variable, determination of significant predictor variables, and model fit are desired, but the statistics used are different based on the binary outcome and maximum likelihood estimation. A binary logistic regression example was provided that took us step by step through the analyses using a set of data. A summary of the R commands used for the logistic regression analysis was provided to show the steps a researcher would take. I did not conduct the analyses in the five-step hypothesis testing approach, leaving that up to you to orchestrate.

The interpretation of logistic regression results from a published research article provided a meaningful end to the chapter. The application, prediction, and interpretation of the findings made it helpful to further understand when and how logistic regression analyses are used. It especially pointed out how different combinations of values for the independent predictor variables would lead to each individual predicted probability value. Beyond interpreting a person's individual probability of occurrence, logistic regression can provide a measure of group membership or classification accuracy. The statistical significance between the actual and predicted group membership can be tested using the chi-square statistic.

This chapter did not cover the many other types of multiple regression equations, for example, Poisson, multinominal, ordinal, probit, longitudinal growth, or mixed models. The treatment of these multiple regression models is beyond the scope of this book. I do, however, cover another special type of multiple regression in the next chapter—that is, log-linear regression models based on frequency counts for the dependent variable.

EXERCISES

1. List four important assumptions in logistic regression.

   a.

   b.

   c.

   d.

2. Given a logistic regression equation with a dependent variable *saver* (0 = *does not save money on a regular basis*, 1 = *saves money on a consistent basis*) and three predictor variables, age (0 = *under 30*, 1 = *over 30*), education (0 = *high school*, 1 = *college*), and income (0 = *less than $50,000*, 1 = *more than $50,000*), the following logistic regression coefficients were reported:

Variable	Coefficient
Intercept	−1.00
Age	1.50
Education	1.15
Income	2.50

   a. State the form of the logistic regression equation using these coefficients.

   b. Predict the probability value for an individual with the following characteristics: over 30, college educated, with income more than $50,000.

   c. Predict the probability value for an individual with the following characteristics: over 30, high school education, with income less than $50,000.

   d. Comparing these two individuals, which one is more likely to be a saver?

   e. Which variable is the determining factor that affects this percent difference the most?

3. Suppose a researcher came to you for help in interpreting her or his logistic regression output. The statistician had run a baseline model with −2LL = 240 and *df* = 4 but then showed another regression model with two predictor variables having −2LL = 340 and *df* = 2. The researcher wanted you to tell whether the two models were statistically significant.

   a. What would you compute?

   b. What are the reported values?

   c. What would you conclude given the results?

TRUE OR FALSE QUESTIONS

T   F   a.   All independent predictor variables in a logistic regression must be continuous.

T   F   b.   A logistic regression equation predicts individual values between 0 and 1.

T   F   c.   The constant term, α, in the logistic regression equation defines the baseline model.

T   F   d. The regression coefficient, β, in the logistic regression equation implies the log odds corresponding to a one-unit change in the variable X_i, controlling for other variables in the equation.

T   F   e. The chi-square difference test should not be used because it leads to erroneous conclusions.

T   F   f. The R-squared analog tests indicate the statistical significance of the regression coefficients.

T   F   g. The logistic regression model involving the predictor variable X binary coded (0,1) is given by $P(Y) = \alpha + \beta X$.

WEB RESOURCES

Chapter R script file is available at http://www.sagepub.com/schumacker

Logistic Regression R script file: chap18.r

orsk package: http://CRAN.R-project.org/package=orsk

## CHAPTER 19

LOG-LINEAR REGRESSION

● INTRODUCTION

Log-linear regression analysis involves using a dependent variable measured by frequency counts with categorical or continuous independent predictor variables. Log-linear regression models extend the researcher's ability to predict frequency counts rather than a continuous or dichotomous dependent variable. Log-linear regression models have also been characterized as conducting multiple chi-square tests for categorical data in a single general linear model. I provide a brief history, review the chi-square test used in log-linear regression, present an understanding of the log-likelihood ratio, and then provide examples of log-linear regression analyses.

The chi-square test, aptly called the Pearson chi-square, was developed in 1900 by Karl Pearson (1857–1936). The motivation for developing the chi-square statistic was based on testing the outcomes from a roulette wheel in Monte Carlo for randomness, that is, statistical independence. In addition, he proposed the idea that the bivariate distribution, based on his Pearson correlation coefficient, was an underlying measure of association for cross-tabulated categorical data. In fact, his term *contingency* was intended to describe a measure of the deviation in the classification outcomes from having independent probability. Today, we know that others have developed measures of association for a 2 × 2 cross-tabulated data table. For example, the tetrachoric correlation is a maximum likelihood estimation of correlation in a normal distribution that assumes an underlying frequency count in the 2 × 2 cells of the cross-tabulated table. The contingency coefficient is a normalization of the chi-square value on the dichotomous (0,1) scale. The history of statistics reveals that controversy ensued, and many prominent names contributed to the development of categorical data analysis.

Brief History

George Yule (1871–1951) developed multiple regression models and partial correlation coefficients, which further extended the work of Francis Galton and Karl Pearson. Yule believed that categorical variables should be treated as *discrete* variables. He therefore treated categorical data as cell counts without any assumption of an underlying normal distribution. He created the *odds ratio* and Yule's *Q* statistic, which is a transformation of the odds ratio to the −1 to + 1 scale. He was heavily chastised by Pearson for his opposite view to Pearson's approach. Today, we accept their different views. In Yule's approach, the categorical classification used nominal variables with no apparent underlying normal distribution, but in Pearson's approach, the categorical classification involved variables that related to an underlying normal distribution. Ironically, Yule's *odds ratio* does characterize general linear models when the data have an approximate underlying normal distribution.

Ronald A. Fisher (1890–1962) also expressed different views from Pearson, resulting in his receiving harsh criticism of his work. Fisher introduced the *degrees of freedom* concept for a 2 × 2 cross-tabulated data table. His *df* index was based on the family of chi-square distributions, where each chi-square distribution had *df* = (row − 1)(column − 1). Pearson, in contrast, argued that *df* = (Number of cells − 1). Fisher argued that he was correct because he was estimating cell probabilities based on row and column probabilities. We know today that Fisher was correct, but anyone who disagreed with Pearson received his wrath. Pearson's prominence in England's statistical circles made it difficult for Fisher and others to get their statistical views published.

Leo Goodman in the 1960s (1968) wrote extensively on log-linear modeling and introduced topics such as partitioning of the chi-square value, model-building procedures, latent class models, and models for ordinal data. Shelby Haberman (1970, 1973), a former student of Dr. Goodman, continued the work on log-linear modeling by introducing analysis of residual values, log-linear models for ordinal data, and discussion of other models (Rasch model) where the number of parameters increased with sample size. Many other statisticians contributed to the growth of log-linear modeling, especially Nelder and Wedderburn (1972), who introduced the concept of generalized linear models for logistic, log-linear, probit, and Poisson models using binomial data.

The field of statistics has a rich history that is documented in several great journal articles and book sources. You are encouraged to read more about the interesting people, the pragmatic problems they addressed, and their conflicting views on statistical topics. I would recommend the following resources to start your reading: Pearson and Kendall (1970), Kendall and Plackett (1977), Joan Fisher Box (1978), Fienberg and Hinkley (1980), and Stigler (1986). You should take the time to learn about the history of statistics, who created the different statistics, when the different statistics were created, why they were created, and who were the prominent people in the field of statistics.

Simpson's Paradox

A unique research problem was discovered and explained by Simpson (1951), called the *Simpson paradox*, which occurred when combining data from several groups. Basically, the correlation value observed between variables in each group is not the same as the correlation between the variables when the data for all the groups are combined. The paradox is that a third variable is influencing the bivariate variable relation. The *Simpson paradox* can occur with any statistical estimate when aggregating data across groups.

The published research by Bickel, Hammel, and O'Connell (1975) on sex bias in graduate admission data is a typical example of the *Simpson paradox*. Cross-tabulated data of men and women by the categories of admitted/not admitted to graduate school indicated that a higher percentage of men were admitted over women (45% men vs. 35% women). The University of California at Berkeley was accused of sex bias in graduate school admissions because more men than women were admitted to graduate school. The aggregate data were misleading, which on further inspection of admissions by departments revealed the opposite—more often women rather than men had a higher frequency of being admitted. Pearl (2009) explained this condition, under which the graduate admissions frequency data from the departments was a proper defense against the sex bias charges by showing that the aggregate data were misleading.

The investigation and solution to the paradox has led to partitioning the overall model chi-square, examining the interaction effects, and knowing how the data were summarized. This leads to checking for other variable influences and not analyzing the aggregate data. For example, males can have a significant chi-square for *age* (young vs. old) by *exercise* (yes vs. no). Females may also have a significant chi-square for *age* by *exercise*. However, when analyzing the aggregate data, *gender* (male/female) by *exercise* (yes/no), no significant chi-square is obtained. In a research study, we need to be cognizant of confounding variables that affect the predictor variables and the outcome.

● CHI-SQUARE DISTRIBUTION

The basic 2 × 2 classification of data is explained first before launching into log-linear regression. Please note that other extended tables of categorical data are possible, but they are beyond the scope of this book (Agresti, 1996; Upton, 1978). The analysis of data in a 2 × 2 table provides row totals, column totals, and cell totals. Chapter 11 provided the chi-square test for categorical data. I review the basic categorical model again, but with a focus on extending it to the log-linear regression model, where the dependent variable is frequency counts.

Assumptions

Independence

The categorical variables must meet the properties of scale for a nominal variable, that is, mutually exclusive categories. The nominal, true dichotomy, or discrete variable, as they are sometimes referred to, has levels of measurement for mutually exclusive groups. A person, object, or event can be in one and only one category. The mutually exclusive category definition meets the assumption of independence. The independence assumption holds that the cell frequencies are mutually exclusive joint probabilities. This further supports the additive nature of the cell frequencies, which must sum to the total. The null hypothesis of independence corresponds to an odds ratio (OR) of $\theta = 1$, where the odds ratio is computed using cell counts in a 2 × 2 cross-tabulation table:

$$\hat{\theta} = \frac{(n_{11}n_{22})}{(n_{12}n_{21})}.$$

The test for a 2 × 2 table was proposed by Fisher and is called the *Fisher exact test*.

Sample Size

The 2 × 2 cross-tabulated table requires a reasonable sample size to permit an accurate chi-square test. When sample sizes are small, as indicated by cells having expected values less than 5, *Fisher's exact test* is the one to calculate. The requirement of sufficient sample size is based on the binomial distribution of frequency counts becoming a normal distribution if the sample size is sufficiently large (central limit theorem). This provides more accurate probability estimates, which meets the large-sample, continuous-distribution assumption of the Pearson chi-square. Basically, larger sample sizes provide better approximation to the chi-square distribution, thus normal distribution.

Yates Continuity Correction

Fisher's approach used small samples where row and column totals, as fixed values, provided the probability estimates as a discrete distribution. Pearson, in contrast, used large samples with probability estimates as a continuous distribution. The approximation to the chi-squared distribution breaks down if expected cell frequencies are too low. The chi-square test is reasonable when no more than 20% of cells have expected frequencies below 5. In a 2 × 2 table with 1 *df*, the approximation is not stable when the expected cell frequencies are below 10. A better approximation can be obtained by reducing the absolute value of each difference between observed (*O*) and expected (*E*) cell frequencies by 0.5 before squaring; this is called the Yates continuity correction (Yates, 1934).

Consequently, when conducting the chi-square test with small samples, the Yates continuity correction was applied to yield a Fisher exact *p* value for chi-square by adjusting the *p* value from the continuous chi-square distribution of the Pearson chi-square value. You may see the Yates continuity correction shown on the computer output of some statistical packages, given the high-speed computers used today, but you should also have the option of computing the Fisher exact *p* value. Usually, the Pearson chi-square is reported; warning messages appear if expected cell sizes are too small, and other types of cross-tabulated statistical tests can be selected.

Chi-Square Test of Independence

The chi-square test of independence determines whether cross-tabulated observations on two variables are independent of each other. In the cross-tabulated table, the researcher is concerned with the observed cell values and expected cell values based on the row and column totals. The row and column totals are often referred to as the marginal or conditional probabilities because they are used to compute the expected cell probabilities. A quick review is helpful.

The following 2 × 2 cross-tabulated table indicates that there were 60 males and 60 females in the sample. When *gender* is cross-classified with *exercise*, 80 subjects exercised and 40 subjects did not exercise. To determine if these two variables are independent (not associated), we compute and sum the difference between the actual and expected probabilities. The expected probabilities are based on the joint distribution of the two variables.

		Exercise		
		Yes	No	Total
Gender	Male	50	10	60
	Female	30	30	60
	Total	80	40	120

The expected cell values are determined by the product of the row and column totals divided by the total sample size. The actual cell frequency and the expected cell frequency both must sum to the total ($N = 120$). For example, the expected counts in the cells would be:

$n_{11} = \dfrac{60 \times 80}{120} = 40$	$n_{12} = \dfrac{60 \times 40}{120} = 20$
$n_{21} = \dfrac{60 \times 80}{120} = 40$	$n_{22} = \dfrac{60 \times 40}{120} = 20$

The chi-square test of independence sums the difference between the observed and expected cell values divided by the expected cell value. The calculation is

$$\chi^2 = \Sigma_{i=1}^{k} \frac{(O_i - E_i)^2}{E_i}$$

$$= \frac{(50 - 40)^2}{40} + \frac{(10 - 20)^2}{20} + \frac{(30 - 40)^2}{40} + \frac{(30 - 20)^2}{20}$$

$$= 2.5 + 5 + 2.5 + 5$$

$$= 15.$$

The degrees of freedom according to Fisher is (row − 1)(column − 1), which in a 2 × 2 table will always be $df = (2 - 1)(2 - 1) = 1$. The tabled chi-square value is $\chi^2 = 3.84$, $df = 1$, $p = .05$. We compare the computed chi-square value, $\chi^2 = 15$, with the tabled chi-square value, $\chi^2 = 3.84$, expected by chance and conclude that *gender* and *exercise* are not statistically independent but, rather, are associated.

Chi-Square Goodness-of-Fit Test

The chi-square goodness-of-fit test is a measure of whether an observed frequency differs from a theoretical distribution. For example, we can test the goodness of fit of a stratified random sample in survey research (observed frequency distribution of sample sizes) to the population distribution (in millions). For example, we surveyed four regions of the country (North, South, East, and West) and wanted to determine if the sample sizes were similar in frequency to the population. Our empirical data are as follows:

Region	North	South	East	West
Survey	100	100	100	100
Population (in millions)	50	100	200	50

The chi-square goodness-of-fit test would be calculated as

$$\chi^2 = \Sigma_{i=1}^{k} \frac{(O_i - E_i)^2}{E_i}$$

$$= \frac{(100 - 50)^2}{50} + \frac{(100 - 100)^2}{100} + \frac{(100 - 200)^2}{200} + \frac{(100 - 50)^2}{50}$$

$$= 50 + 0 + 50 + 50$$

$$= 150.$$

The chi-square results show that the survey sample sizes do not match the population distribution in millions, that is, the ratios of sample size to population size are not similar. The South had a similar sample ratio, the North and West were oversampled, and the East was undersampled. The null hypothesis of no difference is rejected.

Another example tests the hypothesis that a random sample of 200 individuals was drawn from a population with an equal number of men and women. The random sample contained 90 men and 110 women, with the population distribution assumed equal (100 men and 100 women).

The chi-square goodness-of-fit test would be

$$\chi^2 = \frac{(110 - 100)^2}{100} + \frac{(90 - 100)^2}{100}$$

$$= 1 + 1$$

$$= 2.$$

The computed chi-square value is not statistically significant at the $p = .05$ level, therefore the null hypothesis is retained. The number of men and women sampled is not statistically different from that found in the population.

Likelihood Ratio

An alternative to the Pearson chi-square is the likelihood ratio statistic based on the maximum likelihood estimation. In a 2 × 2 table, the degrees of freedom are the same as before, $df = 1$. The likelihood ratio statistic, however, is based on comparing the observed frequency with those pre-dicted (expected) by the model:

$$\log_{\chi^2} = 2\Sigma O_{ij} \ln\left(\frac{O_{ij}}{E_{ij}}\right).$$

We can calculate the likelihood ratio statistic using our previous contingency table observed and expected values for *gender* and *exercise*:

$$
\begin{aligned}
\log_{\chi^2} &= 2\Sigma\left(O_{ij} \ln\left(\frac{O_{ij}}{E_{ij}}\right)\right) \\
&= 2\Sigma\left(50\ln\left(\frac{50}{40}\right) + 10\ln\left(\frac{10}{20}\right) + 30\ln\left(\frac{30}{40}\right) + 30\ln\left(\frac{30}{20}\right)\right) \\
&= 2\Sigma\left(50(0.223) + 10(-0.693) + 30(-0.287) + 30(0.405)\right) \\
&= 2\Sigma\left(11.15 - 6.93 - 8.61 + 12.15\right) \\
&= 2(7.76) \\
&= 15.518.
\end{aligned}
$$

The log-likelihood ratio = 15.52, $df = 1$, which is greater than the tabled chi-square value (3.84, $df = 1$, $p = .05$); therefore, *gender* and *exercise* are related, which is a similar finding to the Pearson chi-square test.

Log-Linear Equation for Chi-Square and Log-Likelihood Statistics

The *gender* and *exercise* data can be combined into a data frame, then run using the *loglm()* function in the *MASS* package to compute the chi-square and log-likelihood statistics. This shows the equivalency of the chi-square and log-likelihood statistics in log-linear regression.

Note: You will be prompted for a CRAN mirror site to download the MASS package.

The set of R commands to install, load, and create the data frame are as follows:

```
> install.packages("MASS")
> library(MASS)
> counts=c(50,10,30,30)
> gender = gl(2,2,4)
> exercise = gl(2,1,4)
> mydata = data.frame(gender, exercise, counts)
> mydata

> mydata
```

```
     gender exercise counts
  1   1          1      50
  2   1          2      10
  3   2          1      30
  4   2          2      30
```

The dependent variable (*counts*) is a frequency count with two categorical independent predictor variables (*gender* and *exercise*). The *loglm()* function inputs the log-linear equation (counts ~ gender + exercise) with results in the file *out*. The *summary()* function returns the values.

```
> options(scipen = 999)
> out = loglm(counts ~ gender + exercise, data = mydata, fit = TRUE)
> summary(out)

Statistics:
X^2 df P(> X^2)
Likelihood Ratio 15.51839 1 0.00008170633
Pearson 15.00000 1 0.00010751118
```

The reported values for the likelihood ratio statistic and the Pearson chi square are identical to the ones previously calculated.

Measures of Association

The chi-square tests provide an indication of whether the pair of variables are independent. If the two variables are not independent, it is possible to have a measure of how much they are related, that is, a measure of association. There are several measures of association that have been created over the years. These single measures of association are often output by statistical packages. The log-linear regression models, however, provide an analysis that doesn't require these measures of association anymore, so I will only discuss two that provide an additional level of understanding regarding a measure of association.

Yule's Q

Yule's Q is calculated as

$$Q = \frac{n_{11}n_{22} - n_{12}n_{21}}{n_{11}n_{22} + n_{12}n_{21}}.$$

The Yule's Q measure of association becomes a normal distribution with larger total sample sizes. When the Q distribution is normal, the variance is

$$S_Q^2 = 1/4(1 - Q^2)^2 \left(\frac{1}{n_{11}} + \frac{1}{n_{12}} + \frac{1}{n_{21}} + \frac{1}{n_{22}} \right).$$

The ability to compute a variance permits an approximate confidence interval around Q. Q has been shown to range from -1 to $+1$, which corresponds to a perfect negative association and perfect positive association, respectively. If $Q = 0$, then no association exists, that is, the two variables are independent.

For the chi-square test between gender and exercise, Q shows the following measure of association:

$$Q = \frac{n_{11}n_{22} - n_{12}n_{21}}{n_{11}n_{22} + n_{12}n_{21}} = \frac{50(30) - 10(30)}{50(30) + 10(30)} = \frac{1200}{1800} = .67.$$

The variance of Q is reported as

$$S_Q^2 = 1/4(1 - Q^2)^2 \left(\frac{1}{n_{11}} + \frac{1}{n_{12}} + \frac{1}{n_{21}} + \frac{1}{n_{22}} \right)$$

$$= .25(1 - .67^2)^2 \left(\frac{1}{50} + \frac{1}{10} + \frac{1}{30} + \frac{1}{30} \right)$$

$$= .25(.4489)^2 (.02 + .10 + .03 + .03)$$

$$= .25(.2015)(.18)$$

$$= .25(.03627)$$

$$= .009.$$

The 95% confidence interval (CI) would be

$$95\% \ CI = .67 \pm 1.96\sqrt{.009}$$

$$= .67 \pm 1.96(.0948)$$

$$= .67 \pm .185$$

$$= (.485, .855).$$

The confidence interval does *not* contain zero, so rejection of the null hypothesis is supported. If the confidence interval contained zero, then the measures would have no association. The confidence interval supports the previous statistically significant chi-square test, which showed that *gender* and *exercise* were related. The confidence interval also provides information about how much the Q value will fluctuate from sample to sample. The narrower the confidence interval, the better the Q sample estimate, that is, the Q value as a measure of association.

Odds Ratio

The *odds ratio* used as a measure of association remains consistent even with an increase in the cell frequency counts. The magnitude of the measure of association is also not affected by the order in which the categories are given. Consequently, a sample odds ratio is given as

$$C = \frac{n_{11}n_{22}}{n_{12}n_{21}}.$$

For our previous *gender* and *exercise* example,

$$C = \frac{50(30)}{10(30)} = \frac{1500}{300} = 5.$$

Yule's Q has the same properties as the odds ratio (not affected by cell frequency size and the order of the categories) and is related to C as follows:

$$Q = \frac{C-1}{C+1} = \frac{5-1}{5+1} = \frac{4}{6} = .67.$$

The odds ratio is seldom reported because it is often misinterpreted and is affected by nonzero cell counts, and the confidence interval is difficult to compute. For practical purposes, Yule's Q is preferred because of easy computation and interpretation and because the confidence interval is easy to compute.

Partitioning the Chi-Square

The chi-square test, whether a test of independence or goodness of fit, provides a test of the null hypothesis. I refer to this as an omnibus chi-square test because overall it indicates whether two variables or a sample distribution compared with a population distribution are independent. Our interpretation of the findings is greatly enhanced by understanding how this omnibus chi-square value can be partitioned into cell effects. Using our previous *gender-by-exercise* example, we can break down the omnibus chi-square value of 15 into its cell components, thus providing a way to interpret which cells contributed significantly to the omnibus chi-square value.

When computing the omnibus chi-square, you may have noticed that you are summing the cell effects. Therefore, examine the chi-square calculations and observe each cell chi-square contribution to the total chi-square value. The males with no exercise (10 observed/20 expected) had a cell $\chi^2 = 5$, and the females with no exercise (30 observed/20 expected) had a cell $\chi^2 = 5$; thus, these two cells contributed the most to the omnibus chi-square. The ratio of the sum of these two cell values to the omnibus chi-square value is $10/15 = 67\%$. The remaining 33% consists of the males and females who responded yes to exercise. (*Note:* If conducting a z test for differences in proportions, the 67% responding no to exercise would likely be statistically different from the 33% who responded yes to exercise.)

$$\chi^2 = \Sigma_{i=1}^{k} \frac{(O_i - E_i)^2}{E_i}$$

$$= \frac{(50-40)^2}{40} + \frac{(10-20)^2}{20} + \frac{(30-40)^2}{40} + \frac{(30-20)^2}{20}$$

$$= 2.5 + 5 + 2.5 + 5$$

$$= 15.$$

Standardized Residuals

Another method used to interpret omnibus chi-square results is to interpret the standardized residuals in each cell. These are computed as

$$\text{Cell residual}_{ij} = \frac{O_{ij} - E_{ij}}{\sqrt{E_{ij}}}.$$

These standardized residuals are z scores, which makes quick interpretation possible. If the cell residual values are greater than ±1.96 ($p < .05$), they are statistically significant. Now that we know how to calculate and interpret standardized residuals, we should request them when possible. The standardized residual values for the four cell counts (frequencies) are

$$\text{Male (yes)} = \frac{50 - 40}{\sqrt{40}} = \frac{10}{6.32} = 1.58$$

$$\text{Male (no)} = \frac{10 - 20}{\sqrt{20}} = \frac{-10}{4.47} = -2.23$$

$$\text{Female (yes)} = \frac{30 - 40}{\sqrt{40}} = \frac{-10}{6.32} = -1.58$$

$$\text{Female (no)} = \frac{30 - 20}{\sqrt{20}} = \frac{10}{4.47} = 2.23.$$

The standardized residual values for male (no exercise) and female (no exercise) are greater than ±1.96, which is interpreted as cells that have statistically significant differences between observed and expected cell frequencies. The percent variance contribution explained earlier when partitioning the omnibus chi-square into cell percent variance contributions supports this conclusion. The standardized residual and the percent variance contribution are both important pieces of information following a statistically significant omnibus Pearson chi-square statistic.

Note: In log-linear regression models with categorical variables having more than a 2 × 2 cross-tabulation, subtables are formed based on the levels of one variable. The rule to follow is that if there are T degrees of freedom in the original table, then there can be no more than T subtables. The observed cell frequencies can only appear in one of the subtables. Each table's row or column margin value should also appear as a frequency in another subtable. The important point is that the chi-square cell values are additive and thus able to provide a percent variance explained.

● LOG-LINEAR MODELS

Several functions in R can be used to fit log-linear models. They include *loglin()* and *glm()* in the *stats* package (loaded by default) or the *loglm()* function in the MASS package. I chose the *loglm()*

and *glm()* functions for the examples in the chapter, which can input either the original data file with coded categorical variables (data frame) or a contingency table.

Data Frame or Contingency Table

The log-linear analysis can use either a data frame or a contingency table (cross-tabulation–style table). We previously used the data frame as our data file with two categorical variables. It is also possible to create a contingency table by using either the *table()* function or the *xtabs()* functions. I will demonstrate how to input the contingency table to provide a comparison between the two types of data sets. Returning to our *gender* and *exercise* data, we coded this into a data frame, *mydata*.

```
> mydata

  gender exercise  counts
1   1        1        50
2   1        2        10
3   2        1        30
4   2        2        30
```

A contingency table can be created using the variables in the data frame *mydata* with the *xtabs()* function:

```
> ctTable = xtabs(counts ~ gender + exercise, data = mydata)
> ctTable

       exercise
gender  1    2
    1   50   10
    2   30   30
```

This contingency table can now be used as data for the log-linear equation. However, no dependent variable is specified in the function because the cell frequencies become the log values. In the log-linear equation, "~" indicates the default dependent variable. The R command would be

```
> loglm(~ gender + exercise, data = ctTable)
```

Log-Linear Equation

Log-linear models describe the association and interaction among a set of two or more categorical variables. Since we are using categorical variables, we take the log values to create a linear model. The dependent variable data can be cell percents or frequency counts. Returning to our *gender* and *exercise* data, I will designate *gender* as an *A* effect and *exercise* as a *B* effect, with the cells indicating the percent (frequency count). The log-linear equation is additive when taking the log of both sides for the 2 × 2 table, which is expressed as

$$\log O_{ij} = \lambda + \lambda_i^A + \lambda_j^B.$$

The log-linear equation indicates that log O_{ij} depends on an intercept term, λ, which is based on sample size; an A effect (gender), which is based on the probability in row i; and a B effect (exercise), which is based on the probability in column j. The null hypothesis of independence between the two categorical variables assumes that this log-linear equation is true. The chi-square test is a goodness-of-fit test of this log-linear model. This is considered the independence model because the AB interaction effect is set to zero.

Saturated Model

The saturated log-linear model has the main effects for A and B as well as the interaction effect, AB. If the A and B variables are dependently related, then the full model should indicate a significant interaction effect. The log-linear equation becomes

$$\log O_{ij} = \lambda + \lambda_i^A + \lambda_j^B + \lambda_{ij}^{AB}.$$

The AB interaction indicates the degree of deviation from independence of A and B. If the interaction parameter is statistically significant, then the effect of one variable on the expected cell percent (count) depends on the level of the other variable.

The AB interaction also defines the log odds ratio. When the AB parameter equals 0, the log odds is 0, so OR = 1, suggesting that A and B are independent.

$$\log \theta = \lambda_{11}^{AB} + \lambda_{22}^{AB} - \lambda_{12}^{AB} - \lambda_{21}^{AB}.$$

Estimating these parameters and doing the calculations will achieve the same value as the odds ratio. The odds ratio was calculated by cross-multiplying the counts in the 2 × 2 table:

$$\text{OR} = \frac{50(30)}{10(30)} = \frac{1500}{300} = 5.$$

The $\ln(\text{OR}) = \ln(5) = 1.609$. This is the parameter estimate for the AB interaction effect reported in the *glm()* function of the saturated log-linear model shown in the next section.

Estimating Parameters

The approach taken in running log-linear (LL) models is to begin with a saturated model, then systematically remove higher-level effects until the model becomes significant—that is, there is a significant difference in the −2LL model values. When the model is significant, we go back to the previous effect that was dropped and interpret it. So given an *A*, *B*, and *C* main effects model, we would have several parameters (models) to estimate:

A = main effect

B = main effect

C = main effect

AB = two-way interaction

AC = two-way interaction

BC = two-way interaction

ABC = three-way interaction

We would begin by estimating the log-linear model with all main effects and two-way and the three-way interaction effects first, which would be a saturated model because it contains all of the parameters. We would expect the chi-square and log-likelihood statistics to be zero in a saturated model.

In our data set we have *A*, *B*, and *AB* effects for *gender* and *exercise*. We first install and attach the MASS package prior to running the log-linear regression analysis. The R commands are

```
> install.packages("MASS")
> library(MASS)
```

We can now run a saturated model using the *loglm()* function, which contains the main effects for *gender* and *exercise* as well as the interaction of *gender* by *exercise*. The R commands would be

```
> options(scipen = 999)
> results = loglm(~gender + exercise + gender:exercise, data = ctTable)
> summary(results)

Statistics:
  X^2 df P(> X^2)
Likelihood Ratio 0 0 1
Pearson 0 0 1
```

The results for the saturated model yield both a likelihood ratio and Pearson chi-square statistics of zero, which is expected. If we drop the interaction effect and run a main effects–only model, the R commands and output would be

```
> results = loglm(~gender + exercise, data = ctTable)
> summary(results)

Statistics:
  X^2 df P(> X^2)
```

```
Likelihood Ratio 15.51839 1 0.00008170633
Pearson 15.00000 1 0.00010751118
```

The results match those we computed earlier when comparing the log-linear model with these two statistical tests. In our log-linear approach, we interpret this as a significant *AB* interaction. A chi-square difference test between the saturated model (full) and restricted model (main effects only) would be $15.518 - 0 = 15.518$, which is greater than the tabled chi-square statistic at the .05 level (tabled $\chi^2 = 3.84$, $df = 1$, $p = .05$).

Some researchers like to use the *glm()* function because it gives estimates of parameters and the log-likelihood values usually seen when running other regression models. The researcher must select the right family of distributions, however; otherwise, the estimation of parameters will be faulty. Since we are using counts, the Poisson distribution is correct. For the *A* and *B* main effects–only log-linear model, this would be computed as

```
> options(scipen = 999)
> myglm = glm(counts ~ gender + exercise, family = poisson, data = mydata)
> summary(myglm)

Call:
glm(formula = counts ~ gender + exercise, family = poisson, data = mydata)

Deviance Residuals:
   1      2      3      4
 1.521  -2.477  -1.655   2.080

Coefficients:
                  Estimate              Std. Error         z value
(Intercept)  3.6888794542326      0.1443366680588         25.557
gender2     -0.0000000002022      0.1825725825582          0.000
exercise2   -0.6931471793147      0.1936459001519         -3.579
Pr(>|z|)
(Intercept) < 0.0000000000000002 ***
gender2 1.000000
exercise2 0.000344 ***
---
Signif. codes: 0 '***' 0.001 '**' 0.01 '*' 0.05 '.' 0.1 ' ' 1

(Dispersion parameter for poisson family taken to be 1)

Null deviance: 29.110 on 3 degrees of freedom
Residual deviance: 15.518 on 1 degree of freedom
AIC: 41.918

Number of Fisher Scoring iterations: 4
```

The deviance residuals indicate which cells are statistically significant (2: −2.477 and 4: 2.080). We need the contingency table data labeled to effectively know that *males* (no exercise) and *females* (no exercise) had the significant deviance residual values, −2.477 and 2.08, respectively (boldfaced values). The parameter estimates indicated a statistically significant difference for *exercise* (λ_2 = −.693, z = −3.579, p < .000344). We interpret this to mean that *exercise* (yes) versus *exercise* (no) was a statistically different main effect, while *gender* differences were not. The residual deviance = 15.518, which is the log-likelihood statistic.

A saturated model would yield the following log-linear model output:

```
> options(scipen = 999)
> myglm = glm(counts ~ gender + exercise + gender:exercise, family
= poisson, data = mydata)
> summary(myglm)

Call:
glm(formula = counts ~ gender + exercise + gender:exercise, family
= poisson,
  data = mydata)

Deviance Residuals:
[1] 0 0 0 0

Coefficients:
                  Estimate   Std. Error     z value
(Intercept)        3.9120       0.1414      27.662
gender2           -0.5108       0.2309      -2.212
exercise2         -1.6094       0.3464      -4.646
gender2:exercise  2 1.6094      0.4320       3.725
Pr(>|z|)
(Intercept) < 0.0000000000000002 ***
gender2 0.026971 *
exercise2 0.00000338 ***
gender2:exercise2 0.000195 ***
---
Signif. codes: 0 `***' 0.001 `**' 0.01 `*' 0.05 `.' 0.1 ` ' 1

(Dispersion parameter for poisson family taken to be 1)

Null deviance: 29.1103166032368747551 on 3 degrees of freedom
Residual deviance: -0.0000000000000035527 on 0 degrees of freedom
AIC: 28.4

Number of Fisher Scoring iterations: 3
```

The log-linear saturated model using the *glm()* function gives the added benefit of showing a test of the *AB* interaction effect. The *gender-by-exercise* interaction effect was statistically significant (λ_3 = 1.6094, z = 3.725, p < .001). The parameter estimate is exactly the same as the ln(OR) = ln(5) = 1.609 that was computed earlier. In the presence of a statistically significant interaction effect, we do not interpret the main effects, and we conclude that the *A* and *B* effects are statistically significantly related.

Model Fit

We have examined the approach used in log-linear regression models, that is, starting with the saturated model, then dropping higher effects until a significant fit is obtained. This follows the chi-square difference test approach between the −2LL full model and subsequent restricted models. In our basic example, there is only one restricted model, that is, a dropping of the *AB* interaction effect.

The chi-square difference test for the log-linear model gives the following results:

$$\text{Full model: } -2\text{LL} = 29.11, \text{ } df = 3 \text{ (Equation: } A + B + AB\text{)}$$

$$\text{Restricted model: } -2\text{LL} = 15.518, \text{ } df = 2 \text{ (Equation: } A + B\text{)}$$

$$\Delta X^2 = 29.11 - 15.518 = 13.592$$

$$\Delta df = 3 - 1 = 2.$$

$\Delta\chi^2 = 13.592$, $\Delta df = 2$ is statistically significant beyond the .05 level of significance (tabled $\chi^2 = 5.99$, $df = 2$, $p = .05$). The chi-square difference test indicates that the full model with the *AB* interaction is statistically significant. We can compute the −2LL difference, degrees of freedom, and p value using the following R commands:

```
> chidiff = myglm$null.deviance - myglm$deviance
> chidiff

[1] 13.59192

> chidf = myglm$df.null - myglm$df.residual
> chidf

[1] 2

> chisq.prob = 1 - pchisq(chidiff, chidf)
> chisq.prob

[1] 0.001118282
```

We can examine the *power* of this test by using the *pwr.chisq.test()* function in the *pwr* package. The R commands to load the package and obtain the arguments are

```
> library(pwr)
> ?pwr.chisq.test

pwr.chisq.test(w = NULL, N = NULL, df = NULL, sig.level = 0.05, power = NULL)
```

Arguments

W	Effect size
N	Total number of observations
df	degree of freedom (depends on the chosen test)
sig.level	Significance level (Type I error probability)
power	Power of test (1 minus Type II error probability)

The power for the test to control for a Type II error is obtained by

```
> pwr.chisq.test(w = 13.59192, N = 120, df = 2, sig.level = .001, power = NULL)

Chi squared power calculation

w = 13.59192
N = 120
df = 2
sig.level = 0.001
power = 1
```

Note: N is the number of observations.

The results indicate that the chi-square difference test had sufficient power to detect a difference controlling for a Type II error.

Standardized residuals from our log-linear results provide an interpretation of which cells contribute to the statistical significance of the omnibus chi-square test. The deviance residuals will appear in all models except a saturated model. Our deviance residuals indicated that the male (no exercise) and female (no exercise) cells in the contingency table were statistically significant, that is, values were greater than ±1.96.

Confidence intervals are also possible given the output from the *glm()* function, which reports the parameter estimates, standard error, and z value for each parameter. This permits the interpretation of confidence intervals around the parameter estimates. For example, the *AB* interaction parameter estimate was 1.6094 with a standard error of 0.4320. The 95% confidence interval is

$$95\% \text{ CI} = 1.6094 \pm 1.96(0.4320)$$

$$95\% \text{ CI} = (0.763, 2.456).$$

The 95% confidence interval does not contain the zero value, which further supports the finding that the parameter estimate was statistically significant. More important, it points out how much the parameter estimate might change from sample to sample of data.

A *measure of association* provides another quick check on model fit. Earlier we calculated Yule's $Q = .67$ with a confidence interval (.485, 855), which indicated that *gender* and *exercise* were dependently related.

Effect size is a final point to consider when interpreting model fit. This is best done by examining the log of the odds ratio as shown before. OR = 5. The parameter estimate is log(OR) = ln(5) = 1.609, and we have already learned that $e^B = e^{1.6094} = 5$. We interpret the odds ratio in terms of the change in odds. When the value is greater than 1.0, it indicates that as the predictor increases, the odds of the outcome occurring increases. In this example, we can say that the odds of a male exercising is five times higher than that of a female exercising. We can obtain these odd ratios for the coefficients in the saturated model by

```
> exp(myglm$coefficients)
(Intercept) gender2 exercise2 gender2:exercise2
50.0 0.6 0.2 5.0
```

Schumacker (2005) indicated that researchers using general linear models for categorical data analysis typically only report the chi-square or likelihood ratio test and associated p value for model fit to the sample data. The author suggested that power, effect size (log odds ratio), and confidence interval should also be reported to further explain the outcome, so that the $p < .05$ criteria are not the sole criteria for significance testing.

Summary of Log-Linear Regression R Commands

I have put all of the R commands together in a logical progression to show the steps taken to conduct the data analysis. You can see that it requires diligence to make sure that all of the right steps are taken in the proper order. I have placed all of these commands in the Loglinear Regression R script file (chap19.r), so you should not have to reenter them.

```
> install.packages("MASS")
> library(MASS)

# Create Data Frame
Counts = c(50,10,30,30)
gender = gl(2,2,4)
exercise = gl(2,1,4)
mydata = data.frame(gender, exercise, counts)
mydata

# Use Data Frame in Log Linear Model
options(scipen = 999)
results = loglm(counts ~ gender + exercise, data = mydata, fit = TRUE)
summary(results)

# Create Contingency Table
ctTable = xtabs(counts ~ gender + exercise, data = mydata)
ctTable
```

```
# Use Contingency Table in Saturated Log Linear Model
options(scipen = 999)
results = loglm(~gender + exercise + gender:exercise, data = ctTable)
summary(results)


# Use Contingency Table in Restricted Log Linear Model
results = loglm(~gender + exercise, data = ctTable)
summary(results)


# Use glm() function to provide parameter estimates using Data Frame
options(scipen = 999)
myglm = glm(counts ~ gender + exercise + gender:exercise, family = poisson,
 data = mydata)
summary(myglm)


# Chi-square difference test, df, and p-value
chidiff = myglm$null. deviance - myglm$deviance
chidiff
chidf = myglm$df.null - myglm$df.residual
chidf
chisq.prob = 1-pchisq(chidiff, chidf)
chisq.prob


# Odd ratio of parameter estimates in saturated model

exp(myglm$coefficients)
```

● APPLIED LOG-LINEAR EXAMPLE

I am conducting a log-linear analysis using the frequency counts of surviving passengers on the *Titanic* from a well-published data set (British Board of Trade, 1990). The data set, *Titanic*, is available in the *datasets* package. The data set is acquired by

```
> data(Titanic)
```

Titanic Data Set Description

A description of the data set is available online by issuing the R command in the RGui window:

```
> ?Titanic
```

Survival of passengers on the Titanic

Description

This data set provides information on the fate of passengers on the fatal maiden voyage of the ocean liner "Titanic," summarized according to economic status (class), sex, age, and survival.

Usage

Titanic

Format

A 4-dimensional array resulting from cross-tabulating 2201 observations on 4 variables. The variables and their levels are as follows:

No	Name	Levels
1	Class	1st, 2nd, 3rd, Crew
2	Sex	Male, Female
3	Age	Child, Adult
4	Survived	No, Yes

The variables and the categorical levels are displayed by

```
> dimnames(Titanic)

$Class
[1] "1st" "2nd" "3rd" "Crew"

$Sex
[1] "Male" "Female"

$Age
[1] "Child" "Adult"

$Survived
[1] "No" "Yes"
```

A break down by levels with sample size is given by

```
> Titanic

, , Age = Child, Survived = No
```

```
Sex
Class Male Female
  1st   0      0
  2nd   0      0
  3rd   35     17
  Crew 0 0

 , , Age = Adult, Survived = No

Sex
Class    Male   Female
  1st     118      4
  2nd     154     13
  3rd     387     89
  Crew    670      3

 , , Age = Child, Survived = Yes

Sex
Class Male Female
  1st    5     1
  2nd   11    13
  3rd   13    14
  Crew  0     0

 , , Age = Adult, Survived = Yes

Sex
Class    Male   Female
  1st     57     140
  2nd     14      80
  3rd     75      76
  Crew   192      20
```

The *mosaicplot()* function provides a visual display of the amount of data in each cross-classified category in the *Titanic* contingency table. For example, you can visually see that more males were in the Crew class ($N = 192$). The R commands are

```
> require(graphics)
> mosaicplot(Titanic, main = "Survival on the Titanic")
```

We would think that there would be higher survival rates with women and children. Is this thinking correct? The breakdown of the data indicated that 28 female and 29 male children survived, compared with 35 male and 17 female children who did not survive. This shows that 57 children survived, compared with 52 children who did not survive, almost a 1:1 ratio. There

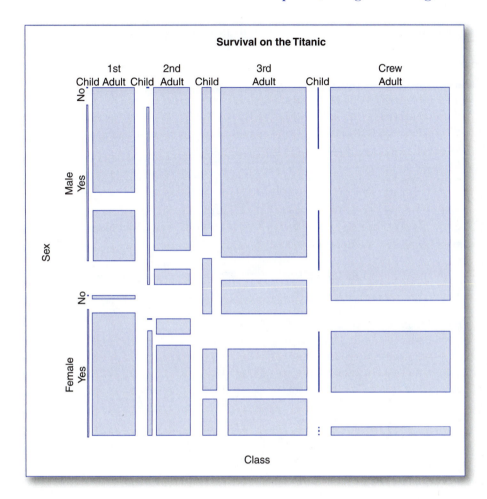

were 316 women who survived, compared with 109 women who did not survive. The difference in survival rates in children is not remarkable, but the difference for women is around a 3:1 ratio. I also wonder if *class* had an impact on these differences? Let's analyze the data and find out.

Log-Linear Analysis

I am now ready to proceed with a log-linear regression analysis given the categorical predictor variables (*Class*, *Sex*, *Age*, and *Survived*). The *Titanic* data set is in a contingency table format, so if I do not convert it to a data frame, I will need to conduct numerous −2LL chi-square difference tests and place the results in a table to interpret. I prefer to see my data and especially have parameter estimates printed for the model or models I am estimating. So I will convert the *Titanic* contingency table into a data frame, *Titanic.glm*:

```
> Titanic.glm = as.data.frame(Titanic)
```

I can then print the data to look at the variable names and the values.

```
> Titanic.glm

   Class  Sex     Age    Survived  Freq
1  1st    Male    Child  No        0
2  2nd    Male    Child  No        0
3  3rd    Male    Child  No        35
4  Crew   Male    Child  No        0
5  1st    Female  Child  No        0
6  2nd    Female  Child  No        0
7  3rd    Female  Child  No        17
8  Crew   Female  Child  No        0
9  1st    Male    Adult  No        118
10 2nd    Male    Adult  No        154
11 3rd    Male    Adult  No        387
12 Crew   Male    Adult  No        670
13 1st    Female  Adult  No        4
14 2nd    Female  Adult  No        13
15 3rd    Female  Adult  No        89
16 Crew   Female  Adult  No        3
17 1st    Male    Child  Yes       5
18 2nd    Male    Child  Yes       11
19 3rd    Male    Child  Yes       13
20 Crew   Male    Child  Yes       0
21 1st    Female  Child  Yes       1
22 2nd    Female  Child  Yes       13
23 3rd    Female  Child  Yes       14
24 Crew   Female  Child  Yes       0
25 1st    Male    Adult  Yes       57
26 2nd    Male    Adult  Yes       14
27 3rd    Male    Adult  Yes       75
28 Crew   Male    Adult  Yes       192
29 1st    Female  Adult  Yes       140
30 2nd    Female  Adult  Yes       80
31 3rd    Female  Adult  Yes       76
32 Crew   Female  Adult  Yes       20
```

If the data frame were larger, I would use the option $n = 15$ to print only 15 lines of data:

```
> head(Titanic.glm, n = 15)
```

I now proceed by running the saturated model for the log-linear regression analysis.

```
> glm.model = glm(Freq ~ Class * Age * Sex * Survived, data =
Titanic.glm, family = poisson)
```

The *summary()* function shows what we should expect, that is, nonsignificant estimates across the full model.

```
> summary(glm.model)

Call:
glm(formula = Freq ~ Class * Age * Sex * Survived, family = poisson, data = Titanic.
glm)

Deviance Residuals:
 [1] 0 0 0 0 0 0 0 0 0 0 0 0 0 0 0 0 0 0 0 0 0 0 0 0 0 0 0 0 0
[30] 0 0 0

Coefficients:
```

	Estimate	Std. Error	z value	Pr(>|z|)
(Intercept)	-2.430e+01	1.148e+05	0	1
Class2nd	2.142e-08	1.624e+05	0	1
Class3rd	2.786e+01	1.148e+05	0	1
ClassCrew	1.834e-08	1.624e+05	0	1
AgeAdult	2.907e+01	1.148e+05	0	1
SexFemale	2.498e-08	1.624e+05	0	1
SurvivedYes	2.591e+01	1.148e+05	0	1
Class2nd:AgeAdult	2.663e-01	1.624e+05	0	1
Class3rd:AgeAdult	-2.667e+01	1.148e+05	0	1
ClassCrew:AgeAdult	1.737e+00	1.624e+05	0	1
Class2nd:SexFemale	-2.653e-08	2.297e+05	0	1
Class3rd:SexFemale	-7.221e-01	1.624e+05	0	1
ClassCrew:SexFemale	-2.230e-08	2.297e+05	0	1
AgeAdult:SexFemale	-3.384e+00	1.624e+05	0	1
Class2nd:SurvivedYes	7.885e-01	1.624e+05	0	1
Class3rd:SurvivedYes	-2.690e+01	1.148e+05	0	1
ClassCrew:SurvivedYes	-2.591e+01	1.989e+05	0	1
AgeAdult:SurvivedYes	-2.664e+01	1.148e+05	0	1
SexFemale:SurvivedYes	-1.609e+00	1.624e+05	0	1
Class2nd:AgeAdult:SexFemale	9.124e-01	2.297e+05	0	1
Class3rd:AgeAdult:SexFemale	2.637e+00	1.624e+05	0	1
ClassCrew:AgeAdult:SexFemale	-2.024e+00	2.297e+05	0	1
Class2nd:AgeAdult:SurvivedYes	-2.459e+00	1.624e+05	0	1
Class3rd:AgeAdult:SurvivedYes	2.599e+01	1.148e+05	0	1
ClassCrew:AgeAdult:SurvivedYes	2.539e+01	1.989e+05	0	1
Class2nd:SexFemale:SurvivedYes	1.776e+00	2.297e+05	0	1
Class3rd:SexFemale:SurvivedYes	2.406e+00	1.624e+05	0	1
ClassCrew:SexFemale:SurvivedYes	1.609e+00	2.813e+05	0	1
AgeAdult:SexFemale:SurvivedYes	5.892e+00	1.624e+05	0	1
Class2nd:AgeAdult:SexFemale:SurvivedYes	-1.845e+00	2.297e+05	0	1

```
Class3rd:AgeAdult:SexFemale:SurvivedYes     -5.206e+00  1.624e+05  0      1
ClassCrew:AgeAdult:SexFemale:SurvivedYes    -2.746e+00  2.813e+05  0      1


(Dispersion parameter for poisson family taken to be 1)


Null deviance: 4.9531e+03 on 31 degrees of freedom
Residual deviance: 4.4622e-10 on 0 degrees of freedom
AIC: 191.4


Number of Fisher Scoring iterations: 22
```

The *anova()* function provides the −2LL deviance values for the different effects in the model. This keeps our efforts using the *loglm()* function to compute chi-square difference tests to a minimum. The R commands are

```
> options(scipen = 999)
> anova(glm.model, test = "Chisq")


Analysis of Deviance Table

Model: poisson, link: log

Response: Freq

Terms added sequentially (first to last)
```

	Df	Deviance	Resid.Df	Resid.Dev	Pr(>Chi)	
NULL			31	4953.1		
Class	3	475.81	28	4477.3	< 0.00000000000000022	***
Age	1	2183.56	27	2293.8	< 0.00000000000000022	***
Sex	1	768.32	26	1525.4	< 0.00000000000000022	***
Survived	1	281.78	25	1243.7	< 0.00000000000000022	***
Class:Age	3	148.33	22	1095.3	< 0.00000000000000022	***
Class:Sex	3	412.60	19	682.7	< 0.00000000000000022	***
Age:Sex	1	6.09	18	676.6	0.01363	*
Class:Survived	3	180.90	15	495.7	< 0.00000000000000022	***
Age:Survived	1	25.58	14	470.2	0.0000004237462045370	***
Sex:Survived	1	353.58	13	116.6	< 0.00000000000000022	***
Class:Age:Sex	3	4.02	10	112.6	0.25916	
Class:Age:Survived	3	35.66	7	76.9	0.0000000882518926162	***
Class:Sex:Survived	3	75.22	4	1.7	0.0000000000000003253	***
Age:Sex:Survived	1	1.69	3	0.0	0.19421	
Class:Age:Sex:Survived	3	0.00	0	0.0	1.00000	

```
---
Signif. codes: 0 '***' 0.001 '**' 0.01 '*' 0.05 '.' 0.1 ' ' 1
```

The likelihood ratio statistic is in the column labeled *Deviance*. The NULL model is listed first. The NULL model with *Resid.Df* = 3 is the independence model where all variables are not related, thus *Resid.Dev* = 4953.1, which is the total amount that can be explained by the predictor variables. When adding in predictor variable effects, the subsequent terms can have reductions in *Deviance*. The amount being reduced at each step is placed in the *Resid.Dev* column. Therefore, class *Deviance* = 475.81, with *Resid.Dev* = 4477.3, which together total the NULL *Resid.Dev* = 4953.1. The age *Deviance* = 2183.56 with *Resid.Dev* = 2293.8, which together total the class *Resid.Dev* = 4477.3. So each successive reduction for the predictor variable is equal to the previous variable's *Resid.Dev* value.

The *p* value in the last column is based on the change in *Deviance* and the change in *Df* when that term is added into the log-linear model. Our interpretation is based on the *significant reduction in deviance*, which indicates whether the new variable added increases the ability to predict the cell frequencies. The results indicate that we should drop the four-way interaction and the *Age* by *Sex* by *Survived* three-way interaction because of nonsignificant *p* values. I am hesitant to add the *Class* by *Age* by *Sex* three-way interaction, although it is nonsignificant, because I have learned that the order of variable entry can have an effect on the results. In addition, I like a univariate approach, that is, dropping one variable at a time, rather than a multivariate approach, where several variables are dropped together. Since the four-way interaction had no effect, replacing it with the *Age* by *Sex* by *Survived* is essentially dropping only one predictor effect.

Revised Log-Linear Analysis

The new log-linear model can be run using the *update()* function. This permits subtraction of effects from the full model, which makes it easier than writing out the entire set of predictor effects. The function can be embedded in the *anova()* function. The R command is now

```
> anova(update(glm.model,.~.-(Class:Age:Sex:Survived + Age:Sex:Survived)),test = "Chisq")

Analysis of Deviance Table

Model: poisson, link: log

Response: Freq

Terms added sequentially (first to last)
```

	Df	Deviance	Resid.Df	Resid.Dev	Pr(>Chi)	
NULL			31	4953.1		
Class	3	475.81	28	4477.3	< 0.00000000000000022	***
Age	1	2183.56	27	2293.8	< 0.00000000000000022	***
Sex	1	768.32	26	1525.4	< 0.00000000000000022	***
Survived	1	281.78	25	1243.7	< 0.00000000000000022	***
Class:Age	3	148.33	22	1095.3	< 0.00000000000000022	***

```
Class:Sex              3    412.60    19     682.7  < 0.00000000000000022 ***
Age:Sex                1      6.09    18     676.6    0.01363 *
Class:Survived         3    180.90    15     495.7  < 0.00000000000000022 ***
Age:Survived           1     25.58    14     470.2    0.0000004237462045370 ***
Sex:Survived           1    353.58    13     116.6  < 0.00000000000000022 ***
Class:Age:Sex          3      4.02    10     112.6    0.25916
Class:Age:Survived     3     35.66     7      76.9    0.0000000882518926162 ***
Class:Sex:Survived     3     75.22     4       1.7    0.0000000000000003253 ***
---
Signif. codes:  0 '***' 0.001 '**' 0.01 '*' 0.05 '.' 0.1 ' ' 1
```

The results do show that the *Class* by *Age* by *Sex* three-way interaction is not statistically significant. However, the log-linear model with these predictor effects indicated very little *Resid.Dev* amount left to explain, that is, *Resid.Dev* = 1.7 (almost zero). A quick check to determine if the log-linear model with this chi-square value is nonsignificant can be done with the following R command:

```
> > 1-pchisq(1.7, df = 4)
[1] 0.7907176
```

This log-linear model had a residual deviance of 1.7 with 4 degrees of freedom. The chi-square test indicated a nonsignificant p value = .79. Consequently, this log-linear model with its set of predictor variables significantly predicts the cell frequencies.

Interpretation of Log-Linear Model

Once we have determined the number and type of predictor variable effects, a more detailed analysis is required. When a three-way interaction effect is present, this involves analyzing sub-tables, which ultimately results in chi-square tables for categorical variables by a third variable. For example, the log-linear model indicated that *Class* by *Age* by *Survived* and *Class* by *Sex* by *Survived* were statistically significant. A reasonable subtable analysis would be to conduct a separate *Age*-by-*Survived* chi-square analysis for each level of *Class*. Second, we could conduct a *Sex*-by-*Survived* chi-square analysis for each level of *Class*. The rationale is that these two variables would yield different frequency outcomes depending on for what class level a passenger had paid a ticket. In a two-way interaction, no subtables are required, so the chi-square and/or log-likelihood statistics are interpreted.

We first access the *Titanic* contingency table data, create the *Titanic.glm* data frame, attach the data frame, then list the names in the file. We see next how the *subset()* function is used to conduct the subtable analyses.

```
> data(Titanic)
> Titanic.glm = as.data.frame(Titanic)
> attach(Titanic.glm)
> names(Titanic.glm)

[1] "Class" "Sex" "Age" "Survived" "Freq"
```

Age-by-Survived Simple Effect in Class

The *subset()* function can be used to extract only the *Age*-by-*Survived* subtables for each level of *Class*:

```
> class1 = subset(Titanic.glm, Class == "1st", select =
c(Class,Age,Survived,Freq))
> class1
```

```
   Class  Age   Survived  Freq
1   1st  Child    No        0
5   1st  Child    No        0
9   1st  Adult    No      118
13 1st  Adult    No        4
17 1st  Child   Yes        5
21 1st  Child   Yes        1
25 1st  Adult   Yes       57
29 1st  Adult   Yes      140
```

The log-linear model is then run for just the two-way interaction effect *Age by Survived* as follows:

```
> glm1 = glm(Freq ~ Age:Survived, data = class1)
```

The *anova()* function reports the same *Deviance, Df*, and *Resid.Dev* from the full model:

```
> anova(glm1)
Analysis of Deviance Table

Model: gaussian, link: identity

Response: Freq

Terms added sequentially (first to last)
```

	Df	Deviance	Resid.Df	Resid.Dev
NULL			7	23611.9
Age:Survived	3	13661	4	9950.5

The *summary()* function provides the parameter estimates for each of the cells in the two-way interaction effect. None of the cell frequency parameters are statistically significant.

```
> summary(glm1)
Call:
glm(formula = Freq ~ Age:Survived, data = class1)
```

```
Deviance Residuals:
 1  5  9  13  17  21  25  29
 0.0  0.0  57.0  -57.0  2.0  -2.0  -41.5  41.5
```

```
Coefficients: (1 not defined because of singularities)
                      Estimate Std. Error t value Pr(>|t|)
(Intercept)             98.50    35.27      2.793   0.0492 *
AgeChild:SurvivedNo    -98.50    49.88     -1.975   0.1195
AgeAdult:SurvivedNo    -37.50    49.88     -0.752   0.4940
AgeChild:SurvivedYes   -95.50    49.88     -1.915   0.1280
AgeAdult:SurvivedYes      NA       NA         NA       NA
---
Signif. codes:  0 `***' 0.001 `**' 0.01 `*' 0.05 `.' 0.1 ` ' 1
```

```
(Dispersion parameter for gaussian family taken to be 2487.625)

    Null deviance: 23611.9  on 7  degrees of freedom
Residual deviance: 9950.5  on 4  degrees of freedom
AIC: 89.711
```

```
Number of Fisher Scoring iterations: 2
```

Since we are actually conducting a chi-square test for a 2 × 2 table, it is easy to check these results by first converting the data frame into a cross-tabulated data file (contingency table) using the *xtabs()* function, printing out the new contingency table to inspect the cell frequencies, and then running a chi-square test. The R commands are

```
> ct1 = xtabs(Freq ~ Age + Survived, data = class1)
> ct1
```

```
     Survived
Age      No   Yes
Child     0     6
Adult   122   197
```

The chi-square test is given by the **chisq.test()** function:

```
> chisq.test(ct1)
```

```
Pearson's Chi-squared test with Yates' continuity correction
```

```
data: ct1
X-squared = 2.2237, df = 1, p-value = 0.1359
```

```
Warning message:
In chisq.test(ct1) : Chi-squared approximation may be incorrect
```

The inspection of our 2 × 2 contingency table quickly points out that we have a problem. The cell *Child* by *No* has zero frequencies, which does not meet the assumption of cell size required for running a chi-square analysis. The warning message clues us into this problem.

We next extract and examine *Age* by *Survived* for *Class* Level 2 frequencies.

```
> class2 = subset(Titanic.glm, Class == "2nd", select =
c(Class,Age,Survived, Freq))
> class2
```

	Class	Age	Survived	Freq
2	2nd	Child	No	0
6	2nd	Child	No	0
10	2nd	Adult	No	154
14	2nd	Adult	No	13
18	2nd	Child	Yes	11
22	2nd	Child	Yes	13
26	2nd	Adult	Yes	14
30	2nd	Adult	Yes	80

Before proceeding any further with our analysis, the data clearly show a missing cell frequency if we cross-tabulate the data, that is, the Child (No) cell. We know that a chi-square test does not meet our assumption of nonzero cells. We show this as follows:

```
> ct2 = xtabs(Freq ~ Age + Survived, data = class2)
> ct2
```

```
       Survived
Age     No   Yes
Child    0    24
Adult  167    94
```

We continue our subtable breakdown for *Class* Level 3.

```
> class3 = subset(Titanic.glm, Class == "3rd", select = c(Class,Age,Survived,
Freq))
> class3
```

	Class	Age	Survived	Freq
3	3rd	Child	No	35
7	3rd	Child	No	17
11	3rd	Adult	No	387
15	3rd	Adult	No	89
19	3rd	Child	Yes	13
23	3rd	Child	Yes	14

```
27 3rd   Adult   Yes      75
31 3rd   Adult   Yes      76
```

Since we do not have zero cell frequencies in this subtable, we can create the contingency table and run a chi-square test.

```
> ct3 = xtabs(Freq ~ Age + Survived, data = class3)
> ct3

  Survived
Age     No   Yes
Child   52   27
Adult  476  151


> chisq.test(ct3)

    Pearson's Chi-squared test with Yates' continuity correction

data: ct3
X-squared = 3.2749, df = 1, p-value = 0.07035
```

The nonsignificant chi-square results indicated that a null hypothesis of no association would be retained, that is, the two variables are independent.

A final subtable involves the *Class* crew level. We repeat the steps for this analysis, being careful to first check the contingency table cell frequencies. We quickly notice that the contingency table has zero cell frequencies, and we stop any further analysis.

```
> class4 = subset(Titanic.glm, Class == "Crew", select =
c(Class,Age,Survived,Freq))
> class4

      Class   Age   Survived Freq
4     Crew    Child   No        0
8     Crew    Child   No        0
12 Crew    Adult   No      670
16 Crew    Adult   No        3
20 Crew    Child   Yes       0
24 Crew    Child   Yes       0
28 Crew    Adult   Yes     192
32 Crew    Adult   Yes      20
```

Sex-by-Survived Simple Effect in Class

To facilitate a quick check on the data structure, we will first create and examine the data for each *Class* level. For Level 1, the chi-square assumption is not met:

```
> class1 = subset(Titanic.glm, Class == "1st", select =
c(Class,Sex,Survived,Freq))
> class1

    Class  Sex   Survived  Freq
1   1st   Male     No        0
5   1st   Female   No        0
9   1st   Male     No      118
13  1st   Female   No        4
17  1st   Male     Yes       5
21  1st   Female   Yes       1
25  1st   Male     Yes      57
29  1st   Female   Yes     140
```

For Level 2, the chi-square assumption is not met:

```
> class2 = subset(Titanic.glm, Class == "2nd", select =
c(Class,Sex,Survived,Freq))

> class2

    Class  Sex   Survived  Freq
2   2nd   Male     No        0
6   2nd   Female   No        0
10  2nd   Male     No      154
14  2nd   Female   No       13
18  2nd   Male     Yes      11
22  2nd   Female   Yes      13
26  2nd   Male     Yes      14
30  2nd   Female   Yes      80
```

For Level 3, the chi-square assumption is met, so a chi-square test is possible:

```
> class3 = subset(Titanic.glm, Class == "3rd", select =
c(Class,Sex,Survived,Freq))

> class3
    Class  Sex Survived Freq
3   3rd   Male     No     35
7   3rd   Female   No     17
11  3rd   Male     No    387
15  3rd   Female   No     89
19  3rd   Male     Yes    13
23  3rd   Female   Yes    14
27  3rd   Male     Yes    75
31  3rd   Female   Yes    76
```

For Level 4, the chi-square assumption is not met:

```
> class4 = subset(Titanic.glm, Class == "Crew", select =
c(Class,Sex,Survived,Freq))

> class4

   Class  Sex     Survived Freq
4  Crew   Male    No         0
8  Crew   Female  No         0
12 Crew   Male    No       670
16 Crew   Female  No         3
20 Crew   Male    Yes        0
24 Crew   Female  Yes        0
28 Crew   Male    Yes      192
32 Crew   Female  Yes       20
```

After examining the subtables for each *Class* level, only the third Class level has complete data. Our analysis indicated that we have found where the three-way interaction effect is statistically significant. It is for *Sex* by *Survived* at *Class* Level 3.

```
> ct3 = xtabs(Freq ~ Sex + Survived, data = class3)
> ct3
       Survived
Sex      No  Yes
  Male   422   88
Female   106   90

> options(scipen = 999)
> chisq.test(ct3)

        Pearson's Chi-squared test with Yates' continuity correction

data: ct3
X-squared = 60.182, df = 1, p-value = 0.000000000000008648
```

We can now continue to conduct chi-square tests to provide interpretation of the various 2 × 2 subtables.

Two-Way Interaction Effects

The two-way interaction effects with a contingency table and the *chisq.test()* function will report statistical significance for the various subtables. After obtaining the omnibus chi-square statistics, standardized residuals should be examined to determine which cells are contributing statistical significance to the omnibus chi-square. This provides the simple effect interpretation we seek. Here is a list of results for the 6 two-way interaction effects, where I begin by turning off the scientific notation using the following R command:

```
> options (scipen = 999)
```

Class by Age

```
> ctCLAge = xtabs(Freq ~ Class + Age, data = Titanic.glm)
> ctCLAge

       Age
Class  Child Adult
  1st      6   319
  2nd     24   261
  3rd     79   627
  Crew     0   885

> results1 = chisq.test(ctCLAge)
> results1

	Pearson's Chi-squared test

data: ctCLAge
X-squared = 118.4133, df = 3, p-value < 0.00000000000000022

> results1$stdres

       Age
Class       Child      Adult
  1st   -2.795647   2.795647
  2nd    2.892908  -2.892908
  3rd    9.268913  -9.268913
  Crew  -8.781852   8.781852
```

Class by Sex

```
> ctCLSex = xtabs(Freq ~ Class + Sex, data = Titanic.glm)
> ctCLSex

       Sex
Class  Male  Female
  1st   180     145
  2nd   179     106
  3rd   510     196
  Crew  862      23
```

```
> results2 = chisq.test(ctCLSex)
> results2

    Pearson's Chi-squared test

data: ctCLSex
X-squared = 349.9145, df = 3, p-value < 0.00000000000000022

> results2$stdres

      Sex
Class     Male        Female
  1st  -11.083954    11.083954
  2nd   -6.993369     6.993369
  3rd   -5.041320     5.041320
  Crew  17.607380   -17.607380
```

Class by Survived

```
> ctCLSur = xtabs(Freq ~ Class + Survived, data = Titanic.glm)
> ctCLSur

      Survived
Class  No    Yes
  1st  122   203
  2nd  167   118
  3rd  528   178
  Crew 673   212

> results3 = chisq.test(ctCLSur)
> results3

    Pearson's Chi-squared test

data: ctCLSur
X-squared = 190.4011, df = 3, p-value < 0.00000000000000022

> results3$stdres

      Survived
Class       No          Yes
  1st  -12.593038    12.593038
  2nd   -3.521022     3.521022
  3rd    4.888701    -4.888701
  Crew   6.868541    -6.868541
```

Age by Sex

```
> ctAgeSex = xtabs(Freq~ Age + Sex, data = Titanic.glm)
> ctAgeSex

      Sex
Age    Male Female
Child    64     45
Adult  1667    425

> results4 = chisq.test(ctAgeSex)
> results4

        Pearson's Chi-squared test with Yates' continuity correction

data: ctAgeSex
X-squared = 25.8905, df = 1, p-value = 0.0000003613

> results4$stdres

      Sex
Age        Male     Female
Child  -5.20814    5.20814
Adult   5.20814   -5.20814
```

Age by Survived

```
> ctAgeSur = xtabs(Freq~ Age + Survived, data = Titanic.glm)
> ctAgeSur

      Survived
Age     No  Yes
Child   52   57
Adult 1438  654

> results5 = chisq.test(ctAgeSur)
> results5

        Pearson's Chi-squared test with Yates' continuity correction

data: ctAgeSur
X-squared = 20.0048, df = 1, p-value = 0.000007725

> results5$stdres

      Survived
Age         No         Yes
Child -4.577718    4.577718
Adult  4.577718   -4.577718
```

Sex by Survived

```
> ctSexSur = xtabs(Freq~ Sex + Survived, data = Titanic.glm)
> ctSexSur

  Survived
 Sex      No    Yes
  Male   1364   367
Female    126   344

> results6 = chisq.test(ctSexSur)
> results6

 Pearson's Chi-squared test with Yates' continuity correction

data: ctSexSur
X-squared = 454.4998, df = 1, p-value < 0.00000000000000022

> results6$stdres

  Survived
 Sex         No         Yes
  Male    21.37461  -21.37461
Female   -21.37461   21.37461
```

The six different chi-square tests are all statistically significant as expected. We are therefore interested in interpreting the standardized residuals for each cell after the omnibus chi-square test. We find that in most cases the standardized residual values are greater than ±1.96, indicating that they all contributed, more or less, to the omnibus chi-square value.

The log-linear analysis with the subtable breakdown provides a clearer interpretation of where the frequency counts differ by the predictor variable effects. In the log-linear model, we are not interested in prediction because obviously the Titanic has sunk, but we see that the general linear model approach can be used for explanation. Here, the log-linear regression model, as a special case of the general linear model, provides us an explanation of how frequency counts differ. The follow-up analysis of the data provides a clearer picture of who survived this catastrophic event.

TIP

✓ Use *data.frame()* to create a data set with frequency count and predictor variables.

✓ Use *as.data.frame()* to convert contingency table formatted data.

✓ Use *glm()* to provide parameter estimates and standard errors.

✓ Use *anova()* to extract the deviance values for the *glm()* function.

✓ Use *update()* to subtract the predictor effects from the log-linear model.

✓ Use the *chisq.test()* function for two-way tables and to output standardized residuals.

✓ Report the −2LL null model, chi-square, confidence interval, and effect size for the log-linear model.

SUMMARY

Log-linear regression models provide a framework for using frequency counts as a dependent variable. The independent predictors can include categorical or continuous measured variables. The examples in the chapter used categorical variables and explored how log-linear models use chi-square and likelihood ratio statistics.

A brief history was provided to illustrate the development of ideas regarding how to analyze categorical data. This included the development of multiple regression models and the controversy over whether to treat categorical variables as discrete (Yule) or continuous (Pearson). Yule's Q also introduced the concept of the odds ratio for interpretation of results from categorical data analysis. Leo Goodman in the 1960s made extensive contributions to log-linear modeling, which are being practiced today.

The *Simpson paradox* was presented to provide an understanding that in log-linear models, subtables are generally required to explain the categorical predictor effects. It is possible that the aggregate cross-tabulated data mislead the interpretation of the outcome, when in fact levels of a third variable more clearly show the true outcome. In the *Titanic* example, we see some of this subtable partitioning better explaining the survival frequencies.

The chi-square statistic is affected by sample size, where the *Yates* correction was introduced to make an adjustment for small sample sizes. However, this is not required anymore because one can use the Fisher exact test. The chi-square test of independence, chi-square goodness-of-fit test, and log-likelihood ratio tests were presented because they are used in categorical data analysis. An example showed how the log-linear regression equation yields these statistics. This was followed by an understanding of how to interpret measures of association, specifically *Yule's Q* and the corresponding odds ratio. The partitioning of the omnibus chi-square was also presented to help explain which cells contributed to the overall statistical significance of the chi-square value. In addition to the percent variance explained, the standardized residual was presented because it provides an interpretation of whether each cell statistically significantly contributed to the overall chi-square value.

The log-linear model example demonstrated how data in a data frame format can be used with the *glm()* function to provide a useful interpretation of the results. This was especially true when using the *anova()* function to extract the log-linear model results. The resulting deviance values and associated p values provided an easier interpretation of the predictor variable effects, that is, main and interaction effects. The log-linear model analysis, therefore, included a description of the chi-square difference test, standardized residuals, confidence intervals, measures of association, and effect size. The *Titanic* log-linear model analysis showed the necessity of using subtables to further explore and explain the true outcome effects for the frequency of survivors.

EXERCISES

1. Given the following data frame (*input*), run a log-linear regression analysis using the *glm()* and *summary()* or *anova()* function for the saturated model, and assign it to a file, *results*.

```
> install.packages("MASS")
> library(MASS)
> counts = c(25,10,5,40)
> pass = gl(2,2,4)
> gender = gl(2,1,4)
> input = data.frame(gender, pass, counts)
> input
  gender pass counts
1   1     1     25
2   2     1     10
3   1     2      5
4   2     2     40
```

2. Given the data frame (*input*), convert it to a contingency table, *ctinput*, using the *xtabs()* function.

3. Using the contingency table, *ctinput*, conduct and interpret the chi-square analysis. Place the output in a file, *results2*. Are *gender* and *pass* dependently related?

4. For the chi-square test, report and interpret the cell standardized residuals from the file *results2*.

TRUE OR FALSE QUESTIONS

T   F   a.   The log-linear regression model predicts frequency counts.

T   F   b.   The log-linear model can have categorical and/or continuous predictor variables.

T   F   c.   A chi-square test should never be conducted when running a log-linear analysis.

T   F   d.   Yule created the odds ratio and the *Q* statistic.

T   F   e.   The Simpson paradox indicates that aggregate data are better to analyze.

T   F   f.   The chi-square difference test indicates significance of a predictor when comparing nested models.

T   F   g.   A contingency table or data frame file structure can be used in log-linear analysis.

T   F   h.   The Fisher exact test can be used with small sample sizes.

T   F   i.   The nonzero cell frequency assumption is important when conducting log-linear regression models.

T   F   j.   The interaction effect in log-linear analysis is how we test the independence between predictor variables.

T   F   k.   The likelihood ratio, chi-square, effect size, and confidence interval should all be reported in log-linear regression results.

WEB RESOURCES

Chapter R script file is available at http://www.sagepub.com/schumacker

Loglinear Regression R script file: chap19.r

MASS function guide: http://cran.r-project.org/web/packages/MASS/MASS.pdf

MASS package: http://cran.r-project.org/web/packages/MASS

PART V

REPLICATION AND VALIDATION OF RESEARCH FINDINGS

CHAPTER 20

REPLICATION OF STATISTICAL TESTS

This chapter presents the cross-validation, jackknife, and bootstrap methods. These methods are not typically covered in a statistics course. However, I think computers and procedures have advanced in the past few decades to permit these techniques to be applied to one's data analysis. R software makes it easy to conduct these methods for replication (validation) of research findings. The three methods are used when a researcher is not able to replicate his or her study due to limited time and resources. The results are useful and provide an indication of the replicability of one's research findings.

● CROSS-VALIDATION

A researcher asks important research questions, which are translated into a statistical hypothesis that can be tested. The research questions are generally formed after a careful review of the research literature on the topic of interest. To test the statistical hypothesis and answer the research question, the researcher gathers information or data. The importance of taking a random sample of sufficient size cannot be understated, because this is the basis for making an inference from the sample statistic to the population parameter. Also, different sampling distributions of a statistic are used to determine if the sample statistic is statistically significant beyond a chance level.

Once the researcher has postulated a statistical hypothesis, taken a random sample, computed the sample statistic, and determined whether it is statistically significant, then the research question is answered and conclusions are drawn. The remaining question we could ask is whether the results are valid. Would we find the same results if we conducted the study a second time? A third time? The confidence interval indicates how much a sample statistic would vary on repeated sampling, and cross-validation is one way in which the confidence interval can be checked to determine the replicability of the study results.

For study results to be replicated, the methods and procedures used in the original research need to be documented. Published research typically describes the participants, instrumentation, design, methods, and procedures. This permits another person to replicate the study and report his or her findings. If the original research findings were valid, then others should report similar findings to the original research. Unfortunately, not many research studies are replicated. This is due primarily to lack of the time, money, and resources needed to replicate research studies, although some research topics do receive extensive research funding (e.g., cancer, smoking, obesity, etc.). The cross-validation method was developed to provide replication of research findings without having to formally repeat the original research.

The cross-validation approach takes the original sample data and randomly splits them into two equal halves or sample data sets. A sample statistic is computed using one half of the sample data and then compared with the sample statistic from the other half of the sample data. If the sample statistics for the two randomly split data halves are similar, we assume that the research findings could be replicated. Otherwise, the findings are deemed not consistent and probably not capable of being replicated, which does not rule out further research. A large random sample is generally needed to provide two randomly split data halves that are of sufficient sample size so that Type I and Type II errors are controlled. For example, a sample of size $N = 1,000$ randomly drawn from a population would be randomly split into equal halves; each cross-validation sample size would be $N = 500$.

The cross-validation method can be accomplished using a few different approaches. The first approach involves a random split of the data, where a sample statistic on the first set of sample data is compared with the sample statistic from the second set of sample data. A second approach is to compute sample statistics on one half of the original sample, then apply them to the second sample, as in a regression prediction equation. A third approach is to randomly sample from the original data set and replicate the cross-validation results. These three different approaches to cross-validation are presented in this chapter. It should be noted that if the original sample statistic is not a good estimator of the population parameter, the cross-validation results would not improve the estimation of the population parameter.

Note: Cross-validation is not the same as comparing sample means from two random samples of data drawn from different populations and testing whether the means are similar or dissimilar (independent *t* test for mean differences). We are not testing two sample proportions to determine if they are similar or dissimilar (*z* test for differences in proportions). We are not comparing a sample mean with a population mean (one-sample *t* test).

Two Separate Random Samples

The first cross-validation approach is based on a random split of the original data into two separate sample data sets. A linear regression analysis is conducted separately on each sample data set. The R function is in the Random Split Cross Validation script file (chap20a1.r), which randomly splits a sample of data, then calculates separate regression equations on each of the sample data sets. The regression equation and *R*-squared values for Sample A are printed along with the regression equation and *R*-squared values for Sample B. The R function will return different values for the regression equation each time because *set.seed()* is not specified.

```
> Size = 500
> Xs = rnorm(Size,10,20)
```

```
> Ys = 5 + (.5 * Xs) + rnorm(length(Xs),25,10)
> chap20a1(Size, Xs, Ys)
```

PROGRAM OUTPUT

```
 First Regression Equation

 Y = 30.526 + 0.499 X
 R-squared = 0.474


 Second Regression Equation

 Y = 29.457 + 0.48 X
 R-squared = 0.464
```

This approach to cross-validation indicates how the multiple regression parameters (intercept, slope, and R-squared value) can change due to random sampling. Although, a large random sample was split in half, creating two smaller random samples, the results seem to indicate stability of the regression coefficients. We might be tricked into thinking that an F test could be computed for the difference in the R-squared values, but they are not computed from the usual full versus restricted models, thus it is not possible. In practice, the confidence interval around the regression coefficient from a single sample would indicate how much they varied from sample to sample.

Sample A Estimates Applied in Sample B

This second approach to cross-validation splits the original sample data into two data sets but takes sample estimates computed from the first and applies them to the second data set. The regression equation estimates from Sample A are used to obtain estimates using Sample B. The R function is in the Cross Validation Sample A to Sample B script file (chap20a2.r), which returns the intercept (α), regression weight (β), and R-squared value for Sample A along with the R-squared value from Sample B. The least squares criterion demonstrates that the regression coefficients selected in Sample A minimize the sums of squares error, so when using Sample A regression coefficients in Sample B, we would expect our prediction of Y to be less than optimum. The amount of R-squared difference between Sample A and Sample B is called *R-squared shrinkage*. The function will return different results each time because a *set.seed()* value is not used.

```
> Size = 500
> Xs = rnorm(Size,10,20)
> Ys = 5 + (.5 * Xs) + rnorm(length(Xs),25,10)
> chap20a2(Size, Xs, Ys)
```

PROGRAM OUTPUT

```
 Original Regression Equation
```

```
Y = 30.526 + 0.499 X
R-squared = 0.474


Cross Validation
R-squared = 0.489
```

A smaller *R*-squared value for cross-validation in Sample B is expected because we are using the regression coefficients from Sample A to predict *Y* values in Sample B. The *R*-squared shrinkage, however, may not always occur when randomly splitting the original data set into two sample data sets because randomly splitting the original data set may create two sample data sets that are identical or one that yields a better regression equation. Therefore, we can expect the cross-validation *R*-squared value to sometimes be lower and at other times higher when applying the sample estimates from Sample A to the Sample B data. In this program run, the cross-validation R^2 (.489) was higher than the original regression equation R^2 (.474), which is not what usually occurs.

Replication by Sampling

A third approach to cross-validation can be thought of as taking a random sample from the original data set. If a random sample was taken a few times, it should show some fluctuation in the sample estimates. We would expect the sample statistic to fall within the confidence interval, say, 95% of the time. When we replicate the original findings using this third cross-validation approach, we will find that sometimes the *R*-squared value is higher and sometimes lower due to random sampling. The R function is in the Replication by Sampling script file (chap20a3.r), which demonstrates this third approach. Once again, no *set.seed()* value is used, so results will be different each time the function is run.

```
> bTrue = .25
> aTrue = 3
> Size = 1000
> numReps = 5
> chap20a3(bTrue, aTrue, Size, numReps)

PROGRAM OUTPUT

 Original Regression Equation

 Y = 2.971 + 0.25 X

 R-squared = 0.27
```

	a intercept	b weight	R^2 A	R^2 B
Replication 1	3.029	0.236	0.244	0.236
Replication 2	2.936	0.252	0.270	0.280
Replication 3	2.905	0.256	0.272	0.297
Replication 4	3.068	0.237	0.248	0.237
Replication 5	3.044	0.231	0.231	0.231

The intercept and regression weights for each replication can be compared with the original regression equation, which would indicate differences due to random sampling variation. Of interest is the difference between the R-squared value in Sample A and the R-squared value in Sample B. We see from the replications, that sometimes R^2 A is less than R^2 B, and other times R^2 A is greater than R^2 B; we even see that R^2 A = R^2 B in Replication 5. We expect these to be different but want them to be close, which would indicate a degree of replication in our findings using our original regression equation.

● R FUNCTIONS FOR CROSS-VALIDATION

R provides functions for the k-fold cross-validation approach, where k represents the number of samples. In k-fold cross-validation, the data are first partitioned into k equally (or nearly equally) sized samples or folds. Subsequent k iterations of training and validation are performed such that within each iteration a different sample of the data is held out for validation, while the remaining $k - 1$ samples are used for training. The concept of training is to use the $k - 1$ sample coefficients to better estimate the final regression coefficients used in the validation sample.

Cross-validation results provide the residual sums of squares (SSR), sample size of the group (N), and mean square error (MSE) for interpretation of which sample the regression equation fits the best. The cross-validation MSE is computed as SSR divided by the sample size (N). A smaller cross-validation MSE for a sample implies a better fit of the regression equation to the data.

CVlm() Function

The *CVlm()* function in the *DAAG* package easily performs this k-fold cross-validation method. We must first install and load the DAAG package. Next, the arguments for the *CVlm()* function with m = number of samples are given:

```
> install.packages("DAAG")
> library(DAAG)
> help(CVlm)
> CVlm(df = houseprices, form.lm = formula(sale.price ~ area), m =
3, dots = FALSE, seed = 29, plotit = TRUE, printit = TRUE)
```

The *k-fold cross-validation function* in the R script file (chap20b1.r) uses a sample size of n = 30 for the original analysis of variance. However, for $k = 3$ folds, the sample size is divided by 3, yielding 10 unique numbers out of the 30 original numbers for each analysis of variance. The 10 unique numbers that are used in the separate analysis of variance calculations are listed in the output. The R commands are

```
> Size = 30
> Xs = rnorm(Size,10,20)
> Ys = 5 + (.5 * Xs) + rnorm(length(Xs),25,10)
> options(scipen = 999)
```

```
> chap20b1 = function(Size, Xs, Ys)

Analysis of Variance Table

Response: Y
      Df Sum Sq Mean Sq F value Pr(>F)
X      1   1923    1923    30.3  7e-06 ***
Residuals 28       1776      63
---
Signif. codes: 0 `***' 0.001 `**' 0.01 `*' 0.05 `.' 0.1 ` ' 1

fold 1
Observations in test set: 1 3 4 8 13 18 22 25 27 29
  X1 X3 X4 X8 X13 X18 X22 X25 X27 X29
x = X 3.16 9.61 38.33 -18.97 10.1 10.73 -3.68 -38.68 29.13 45.2
Predicted 31.93 34.50 45.95 23.11 34.7 34.95 29.21 15.25 42.29 48.7
Y 36.38 28.43 48.79 32.53 22.1 27.84 25.11 5.24 33.78 35.8
Residual 4.45 -6.08 2.83 9.42 -12.6 -7.11 -4.10 -10.01 -8.51 -12.9

Sum of squares = 720 Mean square = 72 n = 10

fold 2
Observations in test set: 2 5 6 9 15 16 17 20 23 30
  X2 X5 X6 X9 X15 X16 X17 X20 X23 X30
x = X -18.84 1.07 15.65 45.00 13.09 5.74 13.0 6.0 -28.82 -18.52
Predicted 24.41 30.70 35.31 44.59 34.50 32.18 34.5 32.3 21.25 24.51
Y 21.32 37.71 27.50 49.52 38.64 30.28 46.9 18.2 14.78 14.77
Residual -3.09 7.00 -7.81 4.92 4.14 -1.90 12.4 -14.0 -6.47 -9.74

Sum of squares = 650 Mean square = 65 n = 10

fold 3
Observations in test set: 7 10 11 12 14 19 21 24 26 28
  X7 X10 X11 X12 X14 X19 X21 X24 X26 X28
x = X 53.97 15.06 8.12 -6.73 10.84 10.66 -13.7 35.31 18.4 1.68
Predicted 48.61 33.36 30.64 24.82 31.71 31.64 22.1 41.30 34.7 28.12
Y 51.22 38.73 34.70 23.31 40.68 36.48 36.5 31.47 50.2 37.10
Residual 2.61 5.36 4.06 -1.51 8.97 4.84 14.4 -9.82 15.6 8.98

Sum of squares = 790 Mean square = 79 n = 10
Overall ms
 71.9
```

The threefold results indicate that three separate data sets of $n = 10$ were created, each having a unique set of numbers. It is best to have an even number of data points in each randomly created sample; that is, if $m = 3$ with $n = 300$, then each data set would have 100 unique data points. A comparison table shows that *MSE* is calculated as SSR divided by *N*. Fold 2 (Sample 2) had the smallest *MSE*, hence the best fit.

Sample	SSR	N	MSE
Fold 1	720	10	72
Fold 2	650	10	65
Fold 3	790	10	79

A plot of the three regression lines visually shows each regression equation's fit to the data. The Fold 2 regression line displays the best fit because of the smaller *MSE*. Increasing the number of *k* folds would generate more random samples, hence more *MSE* values and corresponding regression lines. The graph is generated automatically with symbols and colored lines in three line styles (line, dash, dot).

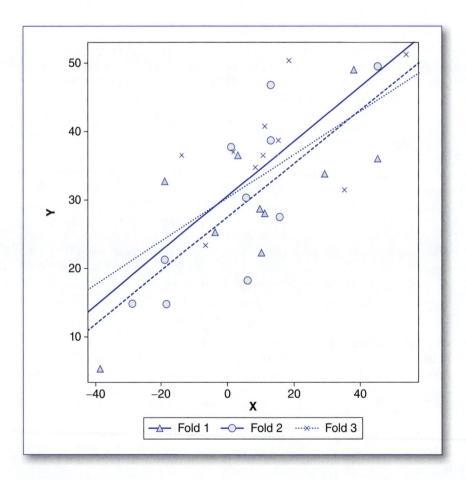

R *crossval()* Function

The *R*-squared shrinkage via *k*-fold cross-validation can be calculated using the *crossval()* function in the *bootstrap* package. You will need to install and load the bootstrap package. First, select

Package from the main menu, and click on *Set CRAN Mirror* to select a download site. The following command line should appear in your R Console window:

```
> chooseCRANmirror()
```

The window to the right should open:

After you have selected a CRAN download site, the Install Packages item on the main menu will open a window for you to select the bootstrap package (see screenshot on page 532).

R^2 Shrinkage Function

After installing and loading the bootstrap package, the *crossval()* function will be available to compute the *R*-squared shrinkage. Another approach to installing R packages is to use the *install.packages()* function; it will still prompt for a CRAN mirror site near you for the download. The *library()* function then loads the package.

```
> install.packages("bootstrap")
> library(bootstrap)
```

The *R² shrinkage function* is in the script file (chap20b2.r), which is set for two groups with 30 numbers, where *X* is randomly drawn and *Y* is based on values of *X*. The *X* and *Y* values do not have to be randomly sampled; rather, data vectors can be input and used in the function. The required input values are

```
> k = 2 # Number of groups
> Size = 30
> X = rnorm(Size,10,20)
> Y = 5 + (.5 * X) + rnorm(length(X),25,10)
> chap20b2(k, Size, X, Y)
```

WARNING

✓ The bootstrap package was built under R version 2.13.2 and will not run on earlier versions. It is not uncommon to see functions that run under later or newer versions of R.

The *R*-squared shrinkage output indicates two unique groups of data, based on the *k* value specified in the function (*k* = number of groups). The first data set is used to compute the regression coefficients (intercept, regression weight), which are then used to obtain predicted *Y* values in the second data set. The *R*-squared shrinkage is apparent when the *cross-validation R-squared* value is less than the *original R-squared* value.

```
PROGRAM OUTPUT

 Unique Data for 2 Groups

[[1]]
 [1]  7 13 30 28 27  2 24 12 18 29  8 14 22 25  5

[[2]]
 [1]  6 11 21 15  3 23  1 19 20 17 26  4  9 10 16

 Original R-Squared = 0.484

 Cross Validation R-Squared = 0.459
```

Summary

Three cross-validation approaches were presented. The first example discussed taking an original random sample and then randomly dividing it into two data sets. A regression equation was run separately on the two samples of data and the *R*-squared values visually compared. The second approach created two random data sets from the original, where the regression coefficients from Sample A were applied in the second data set, Sample B. This demonstrated the concept of *R*-squared shrinkage. A third approach expanded our understanding of the role random sampling plays, because replications of random samples from an original data set indicated that sometimes the *R*-squared value was higher, lower, or the same.

R software has many packages and functions that conduct cross-validation. Therefore, only the *CVlm()* function in the DAAG package and the *crossval()* function in the bootstrap package were discussed. The *k*-fold cross-validation output listed the unique data sets where the first *n* – 1 data sets were used to *train* the regression equation. Training involves determining a stable set of regression coefficients to be used in the last data set, called a *test* data set. *R*-squared shrinkage was also demonstrated using the *crossval()* function with two groups.

Although a researcher seldom has the time or resources to replicate his or her research study, cross-validation provides a way to investigate how results are affected. A large random sample is usually required because sample size can affect the precision in the cross-validation results. The three cross-validation approaches presented in the chapter illustrate a few different conceptual approaches to replication of the study findings. The cross-validation approach is not the same as other statistical tests, which randomly sample from a population and test sample estimates of the population parameter. The cross-validation approach does not improve the sample statistic as an estimate of the population parameter. A comparison of two regression equations from two equal halves of randomly split sample data should, however, indicate the stability of the intercept and regression weight, thus affording a measure of replicability of findings.

> ### TIP
>
> You can select a CRAN mirror site, then use Install Package from the main menu to install these and other popular packages used in cross-validation:
>
> ✓ *library(leaps)*, for selection of all possible variable subsets (Lumley, 2006)
>
> ✓ *library(lars)*, for the *cv.lars()* cross-validation function (Hastie & Efron, 2007)

● JACKKNIFE

The jackknife procedure involves the use of a single random sample of data drawn from a population of data (Shao & Tu, 1995). Quenouille (1949) and Tukey (1958) provided early discussions of the use of the jackknife procedure. The jackknife procedure is concerned with whether the sample statistic as an estimate of the population parameter is affected by any single data value. Recall that the sample statistic is an estimate of the population parameter.

The sample statistic as an estimate of a population parameter is influenced by several factors. For example, we know that the sample mean is affected by extreme data values or outliers, which is indicated by an inflated mean and the standard deviation of the sample data. The plotting of data can indicate the influential data points or outliers, especially when computing r as an estimate of p (population bivariate correlation). The sample statistic as an estimate of the population parameter also depends on the sample size, with larger sample sizes providing a better estimate. Jackknife procedures, therefore, help validate sample estimates of population parameters, assess the stability of the sample statistic as an estimator of the population parameter, and establish the accuracy of confidence intervals around the sample statistic estimate.

The jackknife approach uses a single sample of data, computes the original sample statistic (mean, r, etc.), and then computes the sample statistic for each sample of size $n - 1$. The jackknife approach uses a *leave one out* approach when calculating the $n - 1$ sample statistic. The jackknife approach uses *sampling without replacement*. Basically, each sample mean, except the original sample mean, would be computed based on the omission of one data point, that is, a different data point in each calculation of the sample statistic.

The jackknife approach is, therefore, useful in determining whether an influential data point (outlier) exists that dramatically changes the sample statistic. The jackknife method can be applied to any sample statistic based on a random sample drawn from a population. For example, the jackknife method can compute a *jackknife mean* based on the exclusion of a different data point each time from the calculation of the sample mean. The number of jackknife replications, therefore, equals the original sample size (n), so that the influence of each data point on the sample statistic can be determined.

Jackknife Example Without Outlier

The following example uses the jackknife method where the data do not have an outlier. A random sample of 15 numbers is drawn from a population. The numbers are 2, 4, 9, 12, 8, 7, 15, 11, 3, 14, 10, 15, 20, 25, 22. The sum of the numbers is 177. The sample mean is calculated as 177 divided by 15, which equals 11.8. This sample mean is an estimate of the population mean. The jackknife procedure calculates 15 additional sample means using $n = 14$ data values, but each time with a different data value omitted. To compute each jackknife mean, the data value omitted is subtracted from the sum of 177, and this new sum is divided by $n = 14$ to yield the jackknife mean. The jackknife results for these data values are obtained from the R Jackknife No Extreme Data script file (chap20c1.r). The R commands are

```
> library(bootstrap)
> # First jackknife function - no extreme values
> data = c(2,4,9,12,8,7,15,11,3,14,10,15,20,25,22)
> chap20c1(data)


Original mean= 11.8 Original standard deviation= 6.84

Sample Size Jackknife Mean Values Used Value Omitted

14  12.5   4,9,12,8,7,15,11,3,14,10,15,20,25,22  2
14  12.36  2,9,12,8,7,15,11,3,14,10,15,20,25,22  4
14  12     2,4,12,8,7,15,11,3,14,10,15,20,25,22  9
14  11.79  2,4,9,8,7,15,11,3,14,10,15,20,25,22  12
14  12.07  2,4,9,12,7,15,11,3,14,10,15,20,25,22  8
14  12.14  2,4,9,12,8,15,11,3,14,10,15,20,25,22  7
14  11.57  2,4,9,12,8,7,11,3,14,10,15,20,25,22  15
14  11.86  2,4,9,12,8,7,15,3,14,10,15,20,25,22  11
14  12.43  2,4,9,12,8,7,15,11,14,10,15,20,25,22  3
14  11.64  2,4,9,12,8,7,15,11,3,10,15,20,25,22  14
14  11.93  2,4,9,12,8,7,15,11,3,14,15,20,25,22  10
14  11.57  2,4,9,12,8,7,15,11,3,14,10,20,25,22  15
14  11.21  2,4,9,12,8,7,15,11,3,14,10,15,25,22  20
14  10.86  2,4,9,12,8,7,15,11,3,14,10,15,20,22  25
14  11.07  2,4,9,12,8,7,15,11,3,14,10,15,20,25  22
```

The jackknife sample means ranged from 10.86 to 12.5. The omission of a low data value would inflate (increase) the average jackknife mean as an estimate of the population mean; that is, omitting a value of 2 inflated the jackknife mean to 12.5. The omission of a high data value would deflate (lower) the average jackknife mean as an estimate of the population mean; that is, omitting a value of 25 deflated (decreased) the jackknife mean to 10.86. Both of these outcomes are possible and help us understand how extreme data values (*outliers)* affect the sample statistic as an estimate of a population parameter.

The jackknife means are essentially a sampling distribution of means around the original sample mean. We, therefore, expect the average of the jackknife means to equal the original sample mean of the data. However, if the jackknife means are unduly influenced by an extreme value, the standard deviation of the jackknife means would increase. The 95% confidence interval would also become larger as the standard deviation of the jackknife means increased.

A few simple R commands will provide the sample mean and standard deviation, the average jackknife mean and standard deviation, and the 95% confidence interval for the jackknife means around the original sample mean. We need to enter the jackknife means into a second data vector, then run the *jack()* function in the R script file (chap20c1.r) to show the results of the jackknife method with no extreme data values:

```
> # Second jackknife function - no extreme value
> x = c(2,4,9,12,8,7,15,11,3,14,10,15,20,25,22)
> jackmeans = c(12.5,12.36,12,11.79,12.07,12.14,11.57,11.86,12.43,1
1.64,11.93,11.57,11.21,10.86,11.07)
> jack(x,jackmeans)

PROGRAM OUTPUT

  Sample Mean = 11.8
  Sample SD = 6.836875

  Average Jackknife Mean = 11.8
  Jackknife SD = 0.488847

  95% Confidence Interval
  ( 10.84 to 12.76 )
```

The results provide the sample mean (11.8) and sample standard deviation (6.836875), the average jackknife mean (11.8) and jackknife standard deviation (.488847), and the 95% confidence interval for the jackknife means around the sample mean (10.84, 12.76). The average jackknife mean is the same as the original sample mean, that is, 11.8, which we would expect from a sampling distribution of a statistic (see Chapter 6: "Sampling Distributions"). The jackknife standard deviation is small, which indicates little difference in the jackknife means; that is, *Jackknife SD =* 0.48, which indicates little variability or difference in the jackknife means. The 95% confidence interval for the jackknife means around the sample mean is narrow, indicating little influence of an extreme data point on any jackknife mean.

Jackknife Example With Outlier

Another example of the jackknife method will show the detection of an influential data value (outlier); that is, a data value of 75 replaces the first data value of 2 in the original data vector for the R function in the Jackknife Outlier script file (chap20c2.r). The results are summarized below. The jackknife means ranged from 12.5 to 17.64 with an original sample mean of 16.67. Notice that the sample mean of 12.5 occurs when omitting the influential data value, 75. This demonstrates how the removal of an extreme data value can affect the sample statistic value.

```
Data Values = 75 4 9 12 8 7 15 11 3 14 10 15 20 25 22

Original mean= 16.67 Original standard deviation= 17.32

Sample Size Jackknife Mean Values Used Value Omitted

14 12.5  4,9,12,8,7,15,11,3,14,10,15,20,25,22 75
14 17.57 75,9,12,8,7,15,11,3,14,10,15,20,25,22 4
14 17.21 75,4,12,8,7,15,11,3,14,10,15,20,25,22 9
14 17   75,4,9,8,7,15,11,3,14,10,15,20,25,22 12
14 17.29 75,4,9,12,7,15,11,3,14,10,15,20,25,22 8
14 17.36 75,4,9,12,8,15,11,3,14,10,15,20,25,22 7
14 16.79 75,4,9,12,8,7,11,3,14,10,15,20,25,22 15
14 17.07 75,4,9,12,8,7,15,3,14,10,15,20,25,22 11
14 17.64 75,4,9,12,8,7,15,11,14,10,15,20,25,22 3
14 16.86 75,4,9,12,8,7,15,11,3,10,15,20,25,22 14
14 17.14 75,4,9,12,8,7,15,11,3,14,15,20,25,22 10
14 16.79 75,4,9,12,8,7,15,11,3,14,10,20,25,22 15
14 16.43 75,4,9,12,8,7,15,11,3,14,10,15,25,22 20
14 16.07 75,4,9,12,8,7,15,11,3,14,10,15,20,22 25
14 16.29 75,4,9,12,8,7,15,11,3,14,10,15,20,25 22
```

Once again, we can use the *jack() function* in the R script file (chap20c2.r) to help with our understanding and interpretation of the jackknife mean results. The data vector, *x*, and another data vector, *jackmeans*, are entered for analysis. The R commands are at the bottom of the R script file:

```
# Second jackknife function - extreme value 75

> x = c(75,4,9,12,8,7,15,11,3,14,10,15,20,25,22)
> jackmeans = c(12.5,17.57,17.21,17,17.29,17.36,16.79,17.07,17.64,1
6.86,17.14,16.79,16.43,16.07,16.29)
> jack(x,jackmeans)

PROGRAM OUTPUT

 Sample Mean = 16.66667
 Sample SD = 17.31501

 Average Jackknife Mean = 16.66733
 Jackknife SD = 1.236599

 95% Confidence Interval
 ( 14.24 to 19.09 )
```

The results show that the *Average Jackknife Mean* (16.67) is similar to the *Sample Mean* (16.67), which is expected. The standard deviation of the jackknife means (*Jackknife SD* = 1.236599), however, indicates more variability or difference in the jackknife means than in the previous analysis, which did not have the extreme value. The 95% confidence interval for the jackknife means around the sample mean (14.24, 19.09) is, therefore, greater than before. The jackknife mean of 12.5, where the extreme value was omitted, falls outside this 95% confidence interval, which indicates the impact of omitting an extreme value on the calculation of the jackknife mean.

Comparison of Two Jackknife Examples

An important comparison can be made between the first and second examples. In the first example, the standard deviation of the jackknife means was small, indicating little difference. In the second example, the standard deviation of the jackknife means was greater, indicating more difference in the jackknife means. Here we see that the inclusion of the extreme value, 75, in the other jackknife mean calculations inflated the sample mean estimate. The jackknife mean in the first example was 11.8, and the jackknife mean was 12.5 in the second example, where the jackknife mean with the extreme value omitted fell outside the 95% confidence interval. With the extreme value omitted, the jackknife mean was a more reasonable sample estimate (sample mean) of the population parameter (population mean). Basically, the first jackknife mean (11.8) was closer to the second jackknife mean (12.5) when the extreme value was omitted. A researcher would decide to omit this extreme value after investigating the reason for the extreme data value (coding error, response anomaly).

The descriptive information can be used to compare the dispersion of the jackknife means around the sample mean in the two examples. Notice that the jackknife means are close to the original sample means, 11.8 and 16.67, which we would expect. The standard deviation or variance in the second example is higher, indicating more variability or greater difference in the jackknife means (*Jackknife SD* = 0.48 vs. 1.24). The 95% confidence interval is also wider in the second example, indicating less precision in estimating the sample mean, and the jackknife mean with the extreme value omitted, fell outside the confidence interval. All of these results are summarized to make these comparisons between the two examples.

Descriptive Information	First Example	Second Example
Sample Size	N = 15	N = 15
Range	10.86 to 12.5	12.5 to 17.64
Sample Mean	11.8	16.67
Jackknife Mean	11.8	16.67
Jackknife SD	.48	1.24
Variance	.23	1.54
95% Confidence Interval	(10.84, 12.76)	(14.24, 19.09)

TIP

✓ The standard error of a sampling distribution of means is called the *standard error of the mean* and indicates the precision of the sampling mean in estimating the population mean. A smaller *standard error of the mean* would provide a narrower confidence interval, indicating better precision in the sample mean as an estimate of the population mean. In Chapter 6, we learned that the *standard error of the mean* was

$$S_{\bar{X}} = \frac{S}{\sqrt{n}},$$

which indicates that sample size influences our *standard error of the mean* estimate.

✓ We would generally form a 95% confidence interval as

$$95\% \ CI = \bar{X} \pm t_{\alpha/2, n-1}\left(\frac{S}{\sqrt{n}}\right),$$

where $t = 1.96$, for a two-tailed test with $df = n - 1$.

● R *JACKKNIFE()* FUNCTION

A *jackknife()* function is available in the bootstrap package installed from a downloaded zip file (http://cran.r-project.org/web/packages/bootstrap/index.html). The *jackknife()* function is very simple to run, *jackknife(data vector, sample statistic)*. In the following example, a data vector, *x*, is created with numbers 1 to 10. I included the computation of the standard error of the jackknife means, *jack.se*, to show that the output in the function is the same as the standard error of the mean computed from the standard formula (Fox, 1997, p. 512). The R command lines are

```
> x = (1:10)
> jack.se = sd(x)/sqrt(length(x))
> jack.se

[1] 0.9574271
> jackknife(x, mean)
$jack.se
[1] 0.9574271
$jack.bias
[1] 0
$jack.values
  [1] 6.000000 5.888889 5.777778 5.666667 5.555556 5.444444 5.333333 5.222222
  [9] 5.111111 5.000000
$call
jackknife(x = x, theta = mean)
```

A *jackknife function* (chap20c3.r) was created to list the jackknife *n*, the jackknife mean, the data values, and the single data point omitted in each calculation of the jackknife mean. You need to install the *boot* function and create the data vector, *data*, then run the function.

```
> library(boot)
> data = c(2,4,9,12,8,7,15,11,3,14,10,15,20,25,22)
> chap20c3(data)
```

The function will output the original sample mean and standard deviation, followed by a list of the $n - 1$ jackknife means, the data values used each time, and the data value omitted. The jackknife *n*, range, mean, standard deviation, variance, standard error, and confidence interval are also reported.

```
PROGRAM OUTPUT

Sample Mean = 11.8
 Sample SD = 6.84


Sample Size Jackknife Mean Values Used Value Omitted

14 12.5  4,9,12,8,7,15,11,3,14,10,15,20,25,22 2
14 12.36 2,9,12,8,7,15,11,3,14,10,15,20,25,22 4
14 12  2,4,12,8,7,15,11,3,14,10,15,20,25,22 9
14 11.79 2,4,9,8,7,15,11,3,14,10,15,20,25,22 12
14 12.07 2,4,9,12,7,15,11,3,14,10,15,20,25,22 8
14 12.14 2,4,9,12,8,15,11,3,14,10,15,20,25,22 7
14 11.57 2,4,9,12,8,7,11,3,14,10,15,20,25,22 15
14 11.86 2,4,9,12,8,7,15,3,14,10,15,20,25,22 11
14 12.43 2,4,9,12,8,7,15,11,14,10,15,20,25,22 3
14 11.64 2,4,9,12,8,7,15,11,3,10,15,20,25,22 14
14 11.93 2,4,9,12,8,7,15,11,3,14,15,20,25,22 10
14 11.57 2,4,9,12,8,7,15,11,3,14,10,20,25,22 15
14 11.21 2,4,9,12,8,7,15,11,3,14,10,15,25,22 20
14 10.86 2,4,9,12,8,7,15,11,3,14,10,15,20,22 25
14 11.07 2,4,9,12,8,7,15,11,3,14,10,15,20,25 22


Jackknife N = 15
Jackknife Range = 10.86 12.5
Jackknife Mean = 11.8
Jackknife SD = 0.488847
Jackknife Variance = 0.2389714
Jackknife SE = 1.765273
95% Confidence Interval
( 8.34 to 15.26 )
```

We can run the *jackknife()* function to compare some of the output from my jackknife function above, which only yields the jackknife standard error of the mean and the jackknife means. You should see that these values match my output from the R function.

```
> data = c(2,4,9,12,8,7,15,11,3,14,10,15,20,25,22)
> jackknife(data, mean)

$jack.se
[1]  1.765273

$jack.bias
[1]  0

$jack.values
 [1]  12.50000 12.35714 12.00000 11.78571 12.07143 12.14286 11.57143 11.85714
 [9]  12.42857 11.64286 11.92857 11.57143 11.21429 10.85714 11.07143

$call
jackknife(x = data, theta = mean)
```

$jack.se = 1.765, which is the same as my jackknife *SE* (standard error) value. *$jack.bias* = 0 because there was no difference between the original sample mean (11.8) and the bootstrap mean (11.8). The *$jack.values* in the data vector are the same as in my table.

TIP

✓ Sometimes R packages listed in a CRAN mirror site and downloaded do not work. In those cases, it is best to download and install the package from a zip file, which can be obtained by searching the Internet using a browser, *Explorer*, *Firefox*, or *Safari*.

✓ The *jackknife()* function is available in the bootstrap package in a CRAN mirror site, but it is recommended that it be installed from a downloaded zip file (http://cran.r-project.org/web/packages/bootstrap/index.html).

Summary

The jackknife method uses the original random sample drawn from a population to estimate additional sample means (or other sample statistics) based on $n - 1$ sample data points. The jackknife approach uses sampling without replacement. The jackknife method is useful for identifying influential, extreme, or outlier data values in a random sample of data. The jackknife method can be used with any sample statistic that is computed from a random sample of data drawn from a well-defined population, that is, percent, mean, *r*, and so on. The jackknife approach helps validate whether a sample of data provides a good estimate of the population parameter. It specifically reveals whether an influential data value has affected the estimate of the sample statistic. Our interpretation of the confidence interval around a set of jackknife means is important in determining if the sample statistic falls within or outside the interval. A narrower confidence interval indicates less variability or difference between the jackknife means.

● BOOTSTRAP

Simon (1969) provided an early discussion of the bootstrap concept, but Efron (Diaconis & Efron, 1983; Efron, 1979a, 1979b, 1982; Efron & Gong, 1983) is credited with inventing the bootstrap methodology. The bootstrap procedure calculates the bootstrap estimate, the standard error of the bootstrap estimate, and the confidence interval around the bootstrap estimate (Davison & Hinkley, 1997). The bootstrap estimate is used to determine whether the sample statistic is a good estimate of the population parameter. The bootstrap method differs from the jackknife approach because it uses *sampling with replacement* to create the sampling distribution of the statistic. The bootstrap method, therefore, doesn't take a random sample from a population; rather, the initial random sample serves as a *pseudopopulation*. This implies that all data values sampled are put back into the *pseudopopulation* and can be drawn again and again for each bootstrap sample. This permits a distribution of bootstrap sample values for a statistic, with the mean of the sampling distribution being compared with the pseudopopulation mean. The difference between the sampling distribution mean and the pseudopopulation mean is referred to as bias in the sample. The bootstrap method is useful for reproducing the sampling distribution of any statistic, for example, mean, correlation, or regression weight.

There are *nonparametric bootstrap* (which only describe sample characteristics) and *parametric bootstrap* (which infer the population parameter) procedures. The bootstrap procedures in R are available in the *boot()* function or the *bootstrap()* function. The nonparametric bootstrap provides bootstrap estimates for the median, Spearman rank correlation, and logistic regression. The parametric bootstrap provides bootstrap estimates for means, Pearson correlation, and least squares regression. Both nonparametric and parametric bootstrap approaches are presented. The basic bootstrap concept is that conclusions are made about a population parameter from sample estimates derived by repeated sampling with replacement from the pseudopopulation. The *bootstrap estimate* is the average of all the sample statistics derived from the repeated sampling. A confidence interval around the bootstrap estimate indicates how much the bootstrap estimate varies. We infer the population parameter from this bootstrap estimate.

Bootstrap Procedures

The bootstrap procedure uses a random sample of data as a substitute for the population data, hence the term *pseudopopulation*. The bootstrap resampling technique takes random samples from the pseudopopulation with replacement. Using the pseudopopulation, we know the population parameters, so we can compare the average of the sampled statistics (sampling distribution) with the mean of this population (pseudopopulation).

In the bootstrap procedure, each randomly selected data value is returned to the pseudopopulation before taking the next random data value. It is possible to have the same data value selected more than once in a random sample. The sample statistic, for example, sample mean, may be calculated using the same data value twice.

The probability discussed in Chapter 4 was based on *random sampling without replacement*, where each individual, object, or event has an equally likely chance of being selected. The bootstrap method uses probability based on *random sampling with replacement*, where each individual, object, or event has an equally likely chance of being selected every time a data value is randomly drawn.

The bootstrap procedure involves the following steps:

Step 1: A random sample of data for a given sample size N is drawn from the population with mean μ and standard deviation σ.

Step 2: The random sample of data size N acts as a *pseudopopulation* with mean μ^* and standard deviation σ^*.

Step 3: The bootstrap method takes n bootstrap samples of sample size N from the pseudopopulation, each time replacing the randomly sampled data point. For each sample of size N, a sample statistic is computed.

Step 4: A frequency distribution of the n bootstrap sample statistics is graphed, which represents the sampling distribution of the statistic. The mean of this sampling distribution is the bootstrap estimate, θ^*, which has a standard error of estimate, SE_{θ^*}, computed as

$$SE_\theta = \sqrt{\frac{\sum(\theta_i^* - \theta^*)^2}{n-1}}.$$

Step 5: The amount of bias in the pseudopopulation estimate of the population parameter is calculated by subtracting the bootstrap mean from the pseudopopulation estimate: $\mu^* - \theta^*$. If the bootstrap estimate is similar to the pseudopopulation parameter, then no bias is present. A small difference would still indicate that the pseudopopulation parameter is a good estimate of the population parameter.

Step 6: Calculate a confidence interval around the bootstrap estimate using the standard error of the bootstrap estimate and the level of significance, Z. The confidence interval is computed by

$$CI_\theta = \theta^* \pm Z(SE_{\theta^*}).$$

The bootstrap method can be based on samples of size N that equal the original sample size or sample sizes that are larger, because it involves sampling data points with replacement. Most bootstrap applications resample using sample sizes equal to the size of the pseudopopulation.

The original random sample data should be representative of the population, else the sampling distribution of the data and the resulting bootstrap estimate would not be good estimates of the population parameter.

Note: The bootstrap method is only useful for determining the amount of bias in the sample statistic when the original sample is randomly drawn and representative of the population.

Basic Bootstrap Example

The bootstrap method is used to determine the amount of sample statistic bias in the original sample, called a pseudopopulation, which we infer as an estimate of the population parameter. We can see the bootstrap method in operation by first using a small set of data. Recall that bootstrap takes random samples with replacement of the data values each time, therefore data values can appear more than once in a data set. For example, data for each bootstrap sample are given below, which shows that some data values were resampled.

Run	Sample Size	Bootstrap Data	Bootstrap Mean	Bootstrap Standard Deviation
1	10	1, 3, 5, 4, 5, 8, 9, 7, 2, 6	5.0	2.58
2	10	5, 2, 7, 4, 5, 5, 9, 7, 3, 6	5.3	2.06
3	10	8, 5, 3, 2, 4, 6, 7, 8, 9, 5	5.7	2.31
4	10	2, 3, 4, 5, 5, 6, 1, 7, 8, 9	5.0	2.58
5	10	5, 5, 2, 4, 6, 7, 3, 8, 7, 3	5.0	2.00

The bootstrap estimate, based on the average of the five bootstrap means ([5.0 + 5.3 + 5.7 + 5.0 + 5.0]/5), is $\theta^* = 5.2$. The standard error of the bootstrap estimate, based on the square root of the sum of squares difference between each bootstrap mean and the bootstrap estimate, divided by the number of bootstrap samples minus 1 is $SE_{\theta^*} = .137$. To establish a 95% confidence interval, a Z value of 1.96 under the normal distribution is used. The 95% confidence interval is therefore computed as 95% $CI_{\theta} = \theta^* \pm Z(SE_{\theta^*})$. This is shown as

$$95\% \ CI_{\theta} = 5.2 \pm 1.96(.137)$$
$$95\% \ CI_{\theta} = 5.2 \pm .268$$
$$95\% \ CI_{\theta} = (4.93, 5.478).$$

The amount of bias is indicated by $\mu^* - \theta^*$, which is $5.0 - 5.2 = -.2$. On average, the bootstrap means were 0.2 units higher than the pseudopopulation mean. The sign of the *bootstrap estimate* will be either positive or negative depending on whether the bootstrap estimate is lower or higher than the pseudopopulation parameter, respectively. Since the *bootstrap confidence interval* captures the pseudopopulation mean, we would conclude that the pseudopopulation mean (the original sample mean) is a good estimate of the population mean.

A bootstrap procedure is readily available in R to demonstrate the simulation of population data, resampling of the data, and computation of the statistic of interest. You first must load the *boot* package:

```
> library(boot)
```

Now create a random sample of 1,000 data points drawn from a population with mean = 50 and standard deviation = 10 with random error. This random sample now becomes a pseudopopulation. The *rnorm()* function is used to obtain the random sample of $n = 1,000$.

```
> mydata = 50 + 10*rnorm(1000)
```

The pseudopopulation has a mean, $\mu^* = 50.26$, and standard deviation, $\sigma^* = 10.04$. The bootstrap procedure randomly samples data points with replacement from this pseudopopulation. The boot function requires the input of a statistics function, which is the statistic to be calculated for each bootstrap estimate. I created the *mn()* function to compute the variable *avg*, which is the mean of each random sample in the data vector *mydata*.

```
> mn = function(mndata,i)
  {
  avg = mean(mydata[i])
  return(avg)
  }
```

The bootstrap sample means are returned to the file *results*. The number of bootstrap samples are specified in the function as $R = 100$.

```
> results = boot(data = mydata, statistic = mn, R = 100)
> results
ORDINARY NONPARAMETRIC BOOTSTRAP


Call:
boot(data = mydata, statistic = mn, R = 100)


Bootstrap Statistics:
  original bias std. error
t1* 50.26235 -0.01614291 0.3497858
```

The result for the difference between the original sample mean (50.262) and the bootstrap mean is indicated as bias (−0.016). Therefore, we can conclude that no bias is present in the sample. If the original sample data used as a pseudopopulation are not a good representation of the actual population, then any bootstrap estimator would be misleading.

Nonparametric Bootstrap

The nonparametric bootstrap uses the *boot()* function with the following arguments:

```
> ?boot
boot(data, statistic, R, sim = "ordinary", stype = c("i","f","w"),
  strata = rep(1,n), L = NULL, m = 0, weights = NULL,
  ran.gen = function(d, p) d, mle = NULL, simple = FALSE, ...,
  parallel = c("no","multicore","snow"),
  ncpus = getOption("boot.ncpus", 1L), cl = NULL)
```

An R nonparametric bootstrap approach can use the *boot()* function to obtain bootstrap estimates of the median, ranks, or Spearman correlation.

Nonparametric Bootstrap Function

The *nonparametric bootstrap function* in the script file (chap20d1.r) uses the *boot()* function to calculate the Spearman rank correlation coefficient bootstrap estimates using data from the file *CO2* for the ordinal variables concentration (*conc*) and carbon dioxide uptake in grass plants (*uptake*). You will need to load the *boot* function and attach the *CO2* data frame, then run the function.

```
> library(boot)
> attach(CO2)
> chap20d1(CO2)
```

The output shows the bootstrap statistic, bias, and standard error followed by a list of the Spearman correlation values for each bootstrap sample. The mean of these bootstrap samples is then given along with a confidence interval. A histogram is printed to visually show the distribution of the Spearman correlation coefficients from each bootstrap sample.

```
PROGRAM OUTPUT

ORDINARY NONPARAMETRIC BOOTSTRAP

Call:
boot(data = CO2, statistic = rho, R = 100)

Bootstrap Statistics :
 original bias std. error
t1* 0.5800041 -0.01364339 0.08752838

List of Bootstrap Spearman rho Values

  [,1]
 [1,]  0.6025860
```

```
[2,]    0.5143930
[3,]    0.6455845
[4,]    0.5343986
[5,]    0.4516223
[6,]    0.5652166
[7,]    0.6161799
[8,]    0.5819224
[9,]    0.7001874
[10,]   0.5556114
[11,]   0.6259707
[12,]   0.5176491
[13,]   0.5133402
[14,]   0.5527761
[15,]   0.4984064
[16,]   0.4769941
[17,]   0.6468171
[18,]   0.6404062
[19,]   0.6099558
[20,]   0.4604224
[21,]   0.4222864
[22,]   0.4855306
[23,]   0.7149573
[24,]   0.4469315
[25,]   0.5251580
[26,]   0.6112545
[27,]   0.5574898
[28,]   0.6387964
[29,]   0.4361817
[30,]   0.6491071
[31,]   0.6014702
[32,]   0.7167399
[33,]   0.5212154
[34,]   0.4312964
[35,]   0.6408715
[36,]   0.5886607
[37,]   0.5081214
[38,]   0.4630683
[39,]   0.5189283
[40,]   0.5589862
[41,]   0.4199974
[42,]   0.5508522
[43,]   0.4627600
[44,]   0.4591656
[45,]   0.6042090
[46,]   0.4072293
[47,]   0.6468516
[48,]   0.6860552
[49,]   0.7142293
[50,]   0.5965465
[51,]   0.5925645
```

```
 [52,]  0.3804237
 [53,]  0.5618575
 [54,]  0.5705611
 [55,]  0.5308861
 [56,]  0.4817435
 [57,]  0.7231590
 [58,]  0.6611242
 [59,]  0.6175093
 [60,]  0.5947874
 [61,]  0.6792549
 [62,]  0.5998792
 [63,]  0.5464071
 [64,]  0.4291724
 [65,]  0.6073417
 [66,]  0.5010919
 [67,]  0.6986545
 [68,]  0.7265491
 [69,]  0.5130233
 [70,]  0.5352131
 [71,]  0.5325058
 [72,]  0.5163078
 [73,]  0.5712785
 [74,]  0.6891038
 [75,]  0.5608466
 [76,]  0.6601758
 [77,]  0.4826565
 [78,]  0.4969635
 [79,]  0.6545556
 [80,]  0.4669880
 [81,]  0.6122793
 [82,]  0.7100196
 [83,]  0.5938552
 [84,]  0.5788439
 [85,]  0.5610962
 [86,]  0.5958029
 [87,]  0.5125317
 [88,]  0.4278312
 [89,]  0.5132354
 [90,]  0.5221245
 [91,]  0.5990298
 [92,]  0.5510410
 [93,]  0.7485509
 [94,]  0.4895588
 [95,]  0.3918123
 [96,]  0.7275622
 [97,]  0.6606874
 [98,]  0.5185009
 [99,]  0.6186103
[100,]  0.6251205
```

```
Mean Bootstrap Estimate
[1] 0.5663607

BOOTSTRAP CONFIDENCE INTERVAL CALCULATIONS
Based on 100 bootstrap replicates

CALL :
boot.ci(boot.out = results, conf = 0.95, type = "bca")

Intervals :
Level BCa
95% (0.4201, 0.7355)
Calculations and Intervals on Original Scale
Some BCa intervals may be unstable
```

The list of 100 bootstrap estimates of the Spearman correlation coefficient shows that it varies from sample to sample. The original Spearman rank correlation was .5800041. The mean of the 100 bootstrap estimates was .5663607. The difference or amount of bias is .5663607 − .5800041 = −.01364339, which indicates that the mean of the bootstrap estimates slightly underestimates the original Spearman rank correlation (ρ = .58 vs. bootstrap ρ = .57). The standard error was .0875, which is used to calculate a confidence interval. The unadjusted 95% confidence interval would be 0.42 to 0.76 (.5889 ± 1.96(.0875)). However, the bootstrap bias–corrected and accelerated (BCa) bootstrap adjusts for both bias and skewness in the bootstrap distribution (Efron, 1987); the BCa-adjusted confidence intervals are reported, which are 0.4201 to 0.7355. A histogram displays a graph of the 100 bootstrap estimates, with the .4 to .7 range of bootstrap estimates indicated on the x-axis.

Note: Each time you run the function, different results will be obtained because no *set.seed()* value was used.

TIP

✓ The number of bootstrap estimates should be equal to or greater than the sample size. For CO_2 data, N = 84, so $R ≥ 84$. In the example, R = 100 bootstrap estimates.

✓ The *boot()* function requires a user-defined function that computes the statistic to be bootstrapped; the argument is statistic = rho. In the example, *rho()* is the user-defined function to compute the Spearman correlation statistic.

Parametric Bootstrap

The parametric bootstrap method is used to obtain bootstrap estimates of statistics that a researcher infers as the population parameter, for example, mean, Pearson correlation, and least squares regression. The *bootstrap()* function is downloaded and installed from a zip file (http://cran.r-project

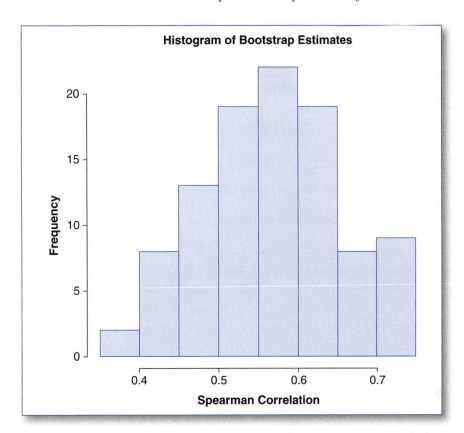

Histogram of Bootstrap Estimates

Frequency (y-axis: 0, 5, 10, 15, 20)

Spearman Correlation (x-axis: 0.4, 0.5, 0.6, 0.7)

.org/web/packages/bootstrap/index.html). Click on Packages, then select the option for installing a package from local zip files:

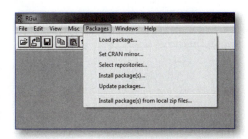

Next, click on Packages again and select Load package for bootstrap:

Efron and Tibshirani (1993) created the *bootstrap()* function. The arguments are obtained by the following commands:

```
> ?bootstrap

bootstrap(x, nboot, theta,..., func = NULL)

where,
x = vector of data
nboot = number of bootstrap samples
theta = function to be bootstrapped
func = distribution type of bootstrap estimates
```

If you are bootstrapping the *mean*, the *bootstrap()* function with the data vector *x* is simply

```
> x = rnorm(20)
> mean(x)
> bootstrap(x, 100, mean)
or alternatively with a function specified:
> theta = function(x) { mean(x) }
> results = bootstrap(x, 100, theta)
> print(results)
```

For more complicated functions, the user-defined function is expanded:

```
# To bootstrap Pearson correlation coefficient for N = 15

> xdata = matrix(rnorm(30), ncol = 2)
> n = 15
> cor(xdata)
> theta = function(x, xdata){cor(xdata[x,1], xdata[x,2])}
> results = bootstrap(1:n, 20, theta, xdata)
> print(results)
> mean(results$thetastar)
```

The results of these calculations are

```
> $thetastar

 [1]  0.163253499  0.059865024 -0.020104042 -0.002404075  0.245275100
 [6] -0.222805104 -0.011648811  0.042516113 -0.160438775  0.061712965
[11]  0.217662937  0.106166399 -0.131377831  0.152198722 -0.047393781
[16] -0.035173351  0.168007033  0.032098282  0.119522818  0.094863064


> cor(xdata)

          [,1]        [,2]
[1,] 1.000000    0.015025
[2,] 0.015025    1.000000


> mean(results$thetastar)

[1]  0.04158981
```

Notice that I have calculated the original correlation, *cor(xdata)*, to compare with the 20 bootstrap correlation estimates *($thetastar)* and included the mean of the bootstrap estimates, *mean(results$thetastar)*. Bias is indicated as the difference between the original correlation coefficient and the mean of the bootstrap estimates. Bias = .04 − .015 = .025, therefore the mean of the correlation bootstrap estimates overestimated the pseudopopulation correlation by .025.

Note: Results will differ each time these R commands are run because no *set.seed()* value was used.

Parametric Bootstrap Function

The *parametric bootstrap function* in the script file (chap20d2.r) uses the *bootstrap()* function from the bootstrap package. The original Pearson correlation, which corresponds to the mean of the pseudopopulation, is compared with the mean bootstrap Pearson correlation. The amount of bias is the difference between the original Pearson correlation and the mean bootstrap Pearson correlation. The confidence intervals around the bootstrap correlation coefficient estimates are reported for the 5% and 95% confidence levels. A histogram of the bootstrap Pearson correlation estimates is also displayed. No *set.seed()* values are used, so different results will occur each time the function is run. The *parametric bootstrap function* only requires the *bootstrap()* function to be loaded and the *cars* data attached prior to running the function.

```
> library(bootstrap)
> attach(cars)
> chap20d2(cars)
```

The output shows the original Pearson correlation, the mean bootstrap correlation, and the bias or difference between these two correlation values. The 95% confidence interval is reported along with the output of the bootstrap correlation values. A histogram shows the distribution of the bootstrap Pearson correlation coefficients.

```
PROGRAM OUTPUT
Original Pearson Correlation = 0.8068949

Mean Bootstrap Correlation = 0.8018283

Bias = 0.005066569

95% Bootstrap Confidence Interval

 ( 0.7250803 ; 0.8660198 )

 Correlation Bootstrap Estimates

$thetastar

  [1] 0.7362747 0.8658256 0.8058323 0.8269390 0.8440785 0.8055524 0.8453018
  [8] 0.6771340 0.8551635 0.7985795 0.8411589 0.8399676 0.8505008 0.7831521
 [15] 0.7686242 0.7845418 0.8179727 0.7837413 0.8082072 0.8100191 0.8897477
 [22] 0.7727495 0.7584939 0.7818703 0.8067213 0.8582375 0.8036984 0.8069562
 [29] 0.8225566 0.7687466 0.8147866 0.7921036 0.7656930 0.7628458 0.8639429
 [36] 0.7888144 0.7257335 0.8538558 0.7853790 0.8264141 0.7956964 0.8201997
 [43] 0.8619834 0.8149768 0.8425771 0.8162029 0.7376582 0.7495528 0.8304359
```

```
[50]  0.8888415 0.8403078 0.7791948 0.8519203 0.8584956 0.7856542 0.7549796
[57]  0.7927030 0.7834472 0.7887921 0.8158885 0.7569404 0.7810584 0.8099779
[64]  0.7125417 0.6731037 0.8600233 0.8164287 0.7974268 0.7827076 0.8290451
[71]  0.7541184 0.7732904 0.7830807 0.8634902 0.8012987 0.7887822 0.6805997
[78]  0.8180592 0.8129127 0.8193146 0.7734219 0.7536768 0.7675014 0.8584698
[85]  0.8156478 0.8697108 0.8225179 0.7472813 0.8705309 0.8461523 0.8531075
[92]  0.7453751 0.7405588 0.8187815 0.7728930 0.8547987 0.8086391 0.8726785
[99]  0.7567990 0.7126691

$func.thetastar
NULL

$jack.boot.val
NULL

$jack.boot.se
NULL

$call
bootstrap(x = 1:N, nboot = 100, theta = theta, cars)
```

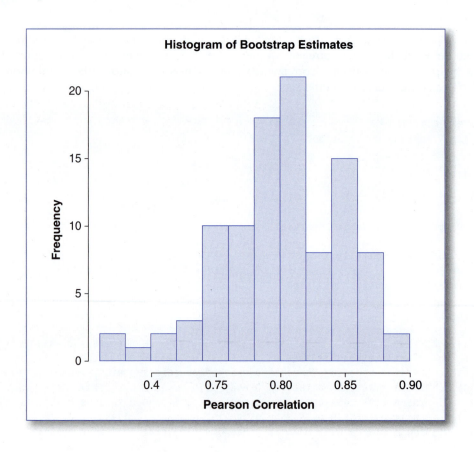

The original Pearson correlation = .8068949, and the mean bootstrap correlation = .8018283, with the bias = .005. Basically, the pseudopopulation correlation value of .806 and the mean of the 100 bootstrap estimates, .801, only had a bias of .005, so essentially there was no difference. This is interpreted to imply that the sample data yield an accurate sample correlation estimate of the population correlation. The 95% bootstrap confidence interval was from 0.7250803 to 0.8660198, which includes the bootstrap correlation estimate. The histogram displays the distribution of bootstrap correlation estimates.

Summary

The bootstrap methods use a random sample of data, which serves as a pseudopopulation parameter. The bootstrap procedure resamples the pseudopopulation with replacement. The bootstrap samples of data can contain the same data points more than once because of sampling with replacement. The bootstrap estimate is the average of the number of bootstrap sample statistics estimated. These bootstrap estimates form a sampling distribution of the sample statistic. The bootstrap standard deviation is based on the dispersion of the bootstrap estimates. The bootstrap confidence interval should capture the pseudopopulation parameter when the original sample statistic is a good estimate of the population parameter. The bootstrap method is used to determine the amount of bias between the pseudopopulation parameter and the average of the bootstrap estimates.

The bootstrap method can be used with any sample statistic to help determine if the sample statistic is a good estimate of the population parameter. The nonparametric bootstrap method is used when the random sample of data and the associated statistic (median, Spearman correlation, etc.) are not considered representative of the population data. The parametric bootstrap method, in contrast, is used when the random sample of data and the associated statistic (mean, Pearson correlation, etc.) are inferred to be a sample estimate of the population parameter.

TIP

The bootstrap package listed in the Install Package window for the R 2.13.2 and 2.14.1 versions did not work. So a later R version may work, or use the URL cited to download the zip file. I searched the Internet for "CRAN R bootstrap" and found the following URL: http://cran.r-project.org/web/packages/bootstrap/index.html; this provided a Windows zip file for download: Windows binary, bootstrap_1.0-22.zip. After downloading the zip file, I clicked on the Packages icon on the main menu and selected Install Package(s) from local zip files. Then, I clicked again on the Packages icon and again selected Install Packages, then chose the bootstrap package listed.

NOTE: The *bootstrap()* function (bootstrap, cross-validation, jackknife) was designed for use with examples in the book by Efron and Tibshirani (1993).

CROSS-VALIDATION EXERCISES

1. A researcher has collected data on a number of extracurricular activities by high school students (Y) and a wellness score (X). Report the Pearson correlation between X and Y. Plot X and Y. Show the R commands and output, and interpret the results.

   R Commands:

   ```
   Y = c(0,0,1,1,2,2,3,3,4,4)
   X = c(2,5,6,5,8,5,11,12,13,15)
   ```

   Output:
   Plot:
   Interpretation:

2. The researcher is interested in predicting the number of extracurricular activities given a student wellness score. The researcher is unable to replicate the study but would like to determine the stability of the regression equation solution. She splits the data and runs two separate regression equations. Using the original data in #1, use the *lm()* and *summary()* functions to compare the original results with each individual sample result. Place the results in the table below. What would you conclude?

   R Commands:

   ```
   Y1 = c(0,0,1,3,4)
   X1 = c(2,5,5,12,13)
   and

   Y2 = c(1,2,2,3,4)
   X2 = c(6,8,5,11,15)
   ```

   Output:
   Interpretation:

Regression Coefficient	Original	Sample 1	Sample 2
Intercept			
X			
F			
R^2			

3. Use the *CVlm()* function in the *library(DAAG)* to conduct a cross-validation of the regression equation with a second sample. *Hint:* Set the CRAN mirror site, and install the DAAG package. Show the R commands and output. Compute the *MSE* for each fold. Which fold provides a better-fitted regression line?

R Commands:

```
library(DAAG)
Y = c(0,0,1,1,2,2,3,3,4,4)
X = c(2,5,6,5,8,5,11,12,13,15)
```

Output:
Plot:
Interpretation:

4. Run the R^2 *shrinkage function* (chap20b2.r) using the data from #1 and *set.seed (157911)*. Report the results, and interpret them. *Hint:* Add *set.seed()*, replace the Y and X data vectors, and change the size to 10.

R Commands:

```
> install.packages("bootstrap")
> library(bootstrap)
> set.seed(157911)
> k = 2 # Number of groups
> Size = 10 # Number of values
> Y = c(0,0,1,1,2,2,3,3,4,4)
> X = c(2,5,6,5,8,5,11,12,13,15)
```

Output:
Interpretation:

TRUE OR FALSE QUESTIONS (CROSS-VALIDATION)

T   F   a.   Cross-validation involves randomly splitting the data where one sample of data computes the sample statistic (calibration), which is applied in a second sample of data for validation.

T   F   b.   *R*-squared shrinkage occurs when the correlation coefficient is affected by outliers.

T   F   c.   A smaller cross-validation *MSE* for a sample implies a better fit of the regression equation to the data.

T   F   d.   The *CVlm()* function in the *library(DAAG)* performs cross-validation by using *m* = number of samples.

T   F   e.   The *crossval()* function in the *library(bootstrap)* reports *R*-squared shrinkage from *k*-fold cross-validation.

T   F   f.   A researcher should replicate his or her study when possible, but cross-validation provides evidence of the replicability of research findings.

JACKKNIFE EXERCISES

1. Load the *library(bootstrap)*. Use the *jackknife()* function and *jack.se* command with the following data for the sample statistic, mean. Show the R commands and output, and interpret the results.

   R Commands:

   ```
   library(bootstrap)
   Q = c(50,60,50,70,90,105,150,125,85,1000)
   ```

   Output:
   Interpretation:

2. Load the *library(bootstrap)*. Use the *jackknife()* function and *jack.se* command with the following corrected data for the sample statistic, mean. Show the R commands and output, and interpret the results.

   R Commands:

   ```
   library(bootstrap)
   Q = c(50,60,50,70,90,105,150,125,85,100)
   ```

   Output:
   Interpretation:

TRUE OR FALSE QUESTIONS (JACKKNIFE)

T   F   a.   The jackknife procedure is concerned with whether the sample statistic as an estimate of the population parameter is affected by any single data value.

T   F   b.   The jackknife approach uses sampling with replacement.

T   F   c.   The number of replications in the jackknife method equals the original sample size.

T   F   d.   The jackknife means are essentially a sampling distribution of means around the original sample mean.

T   F   e.   The jackknife approach helps validate whether a sample of data provides a good estimate of the population parameter.

T   F   f.   A smaller jackknife standard error indicates a wider confidence interval with more variability or difference between the jackknife means.

BOOTSTRAP EXERCISES

1. Install the *library(boot)*. Run key parts of the R *nonparametric bootstrap* (chap20d1.r) *rho function*, the *results* and *avg* command lines, for the ordinal data in *mydata*. Bootstrap 20 times the

Spearman correlation coefficient between *J* and *Z*. Show the R commands and output. Interpret the Spearman correlation for bias, and interpret the standard error of the bootstrap estimate.

R Commands:

```
> library(boot)
> J = c(1,2,4,5,3,7,6)
> Z = c(2,2,3,4,5,6,7)
> mydata= matrix(c(J,Z),7,2)
```

Output:
Interpretation:

2. Install the *library(bootstrap)*. Use *set.seed(37911)*. Run 20 parametric bootstraps of the mean for the data in the file *data = rnorm(100)*. Show the R commands and output, and interpret the results.

R Commands:

```
> library(boot)
> set.seed(37911)
> data = rnorm(100)
```

Output:
Interpretation:

TRUE OR FALSE QUESTIONS (BOOTSTRAP)

T F a. The bootstrap estimate is used to determine whether the sample statistic is a good estimate of the population parameter.

T F b. The bootstrap method uses sampling with replacement.

T F c. The bootstrap estimate is the average of all the sample statistics derived from the repeated sampling.

T F d. The bootstrap procedure uses a random sample of data as a substitute for the population data, hence the term *pseudopopulation*.

T F e. The *bootstrap()* function yields bootstrap estimates for parametric statistics.

T F f. The number of bootstrap estimates should be equal to or greater than the sample size.

WEB RESOURCES

Chapter R script files are available at http://www.sagepub.com/schumacker

Cross Validation Sample A to Sample B R script file: chap20a2.r

Jackknife Function R script file: chap20c3.r

Jackknife No Extreme Data R script file: chap20c1.r

Jackknife Outlier R script file: chap20c2.r

k-Fold Cross Validation R script file: chap20b1.r

Non-Parametric Bootstrap R script file: chap20d1.r

Parametric Bootstrap R script file: chap20d2.r

R^2 Shrinkage R script file: chap20b2.r

Random Split Cross Validation R script file: chap20a1.r

Replication by Sampling R script file: chap20a3.r

DAAG authors website: http://www.stats.uwo.ca/DAAG/

DAAG function guide: http://cran.r-project.org/web/packages/DAAG/DAAG.pdf

DAAG package: http://cran.r-project.org/web/packages/DAAG/

Jackknife and bootstrap function guide: http://cran.r-project.org/web/packages/bootstrap/bootstrap.pdf

Jackknife and bootstrap functions (*bootstrap* package): http://cran.r-project.org/web/packages/bootstrap/index.html

## CHAPTER 21

SYNTHESIS OF RESEARCH FINDINGS

● META-ANALYSIS
_____

Science attempts to discover underlying patterns, trends, and principles, which can result from an accumulation of knowledge gained from several research studies on a topic of interest. Most research studies conducted in education, psychology, business, and other disciplines, however, have only involved single experiments or studies that rarely provide definitive answers to research questions. We learned from Chapter 20 that researchers seldom replicate their research studies and instead use cross-validation, jackknife, or bootstrap methods to determine the stability or accuracy of the sample statistic as an estimate of the population parameter. Another approach is to quantitatively summarize findings in several research studies on the same topic, which is called **meta-analysis**.

A review of the research literature is invaluable in summarizing and understanding the current state of knowledge about a topic. Rather than rely on subjective judgments or interpretations of the research literature, meta-analysis techniques provide a quantitative objective assessment of the study results. The earliest approach to synthesizing research on a topic used p values to combine the research studies. The concept of an effect size, however, went beyond the statistical significance of studies—that is, p values—to include r and d effect size estimates. The use of r and d effect size estimates required converting various statistics (χ^2, t, F, r) to a common metric. Once the different statistical values found in research studies were converted to a common scale, the meta-analysis procedure combined the results to yield an r or d effect size estimate. Current meta-analysis procedures also weight studies by sample size when combining effect size measures because rarely do different studies have the same sample sizes.

Meta-analysis is the application of statistical procedures to the empirical findings in research studies for the purpose of summarizing and concluding whether the findings in the studies were significant overall. The meta-analytic approach, therefore, provides a method to synthesize research findings from several individual studies. It makes sense that if several hundred studies had researched socioeconomic status and achievement in school, then a summarization of the findings in these individual studies would aid our understanding of this relationship. From a scholarly point of view, we might ask, "After 20 years of studying the efficacy of psychotherapy, what have we learned?" At some point in time, it becomes frugal to assess what we have learned from the research that was conducted. Further research in an area may be unproductive or unscientific or may take a wrong direction if we don't stop from time to time and assess what we have learned. If we view science as an objective activity, then it becomes critical to establish an objective method to integrate and synthesize similar research studies. Meta-analysis is therefore an objective analysis of the statistical results from several individual studies for the purpose of integrating and summarizing the findings.

Sir Ronald A. Fisher (1932) and Karl Pearson (1933) both addressed the issue of statistically summarizing the results of research studies. Mordecai H. Gordon, Edward H. Loveland, and Edward E. Cureton (1952) produced a chi-square table for use in combining the probability values from independent research studies. Jacob Cohen (1965, 1977) provided measures of effect size for many common statistical tests. Gene Glass (1976, 1977), however, is credited with first using the term *meta-analysis* to describe the statistical analysis of a collection of results from several individual studies. He provided guidelines for converting various statistics into a common metric, so that comparisons could be made on the same reference scale. Given a common metric (scale), the effect size measure is interpreted as an index of the degree of departure from the null hypothesis in standard units. Examples of these various approaches to combining results from several research studies are presented in this chapter.

Comparison of the Fisher and Chi-Square Approaches

The Fisher approach to combining p values from several independent research studies was accomplished by using a natural logarithmic transformation of the p value, that is, $\log_e p$. The natural log or log base e is equal to 2.7182818. Gordon et al. (1952) computed chi-square values based on $-2 *$ $\log_e p$, for example, $-2(-2.9957) = 5.9915$. They created tabled chi-square values based on $\chi^2 = -2\Sigma(\log_e p)$, with degrees of freedom equal to $2n$, where $n =$ the number of studies. The Gordon et al. (1952) total chi-square result can be obtained by summing the Fisher values, which would be as follows: $-2 * (-10.8198) = 21.6396$ (i.e., -2 times the sum of the natural log values). Table 21.1 helps illustrate Fisher's and Gordon et al.'s (1952) approaches, with $\chi^2 = 21.64$, $df = 6$, $p = 0.0015$.

Table 21.1 Comparison of the Fisher and Gordon et al. Approaches to Combining p Values

Study	P	Fisher (ln p)	Gordon et al. (χ^2)
1	.05	−2.9957	5.9915
2	.01	−4.6052	9.2103
3	.04	−3.2189	6.4378
Total		−10.8198	21.6396

NOTE: In 1953, Lyle V. Jones and Donald W. Fiske further demonstrated Fisher's approach of taking a natural logarithm of a p value to calculate a summary chi-square value. They used log base 10 (log p + 10), which yielded $\chi_2 = -2(\log_e 10)(\Sigma(\log p + 10) - 10n)$, with degrees of freedom equal to $2n$, where $n =$ the number of studies.

A basic approach in conducting a meta-analysis across several related research studies is to combine the results and determine if there was an *overall* significant effect. The use of p values from research studies readily lends itself to a summary chi-square value. If a study has several p values, a simple average of the p values can represent the study result. The chi-square value further indicates the significance of the combined research study results. The meta-analysis formula for combining the p values from individual studies is $\chi^2 = -2\Sigma(\log_e p)$. The combined chi-square value reported in Table 21.1 was 21.6396. This chi-square value is tested for significance using $2n$ degrees of freedom ($df = 6$) to determine the overall effect across the different research studies. The tabled chi-square value at $p = .01$ for 6 degrees of freedom is 16.812. The combined chi-square of 21.6396 exceeds the tabled value and therefore indicates an overall significant effect across the three research studies. Gordon et al. (1952) produced a chi-square table with the chi-square values for various p values, thus making this task easier.

Fisher Meta-Analysis Function

The *Fisher meta-analysis function* in the script file (chap21a.r) inputs the p values for the example and prints out the results. It reports the total *chi-square*, *df*, and p value. We would conclude from these meta-analysis results that the three combined studies overall were statistically significant. You can combine more p values from other studies in the function by simply entering their p values in the *pvals* data vector and then running the function.

```
> pvals = c(.05,.01,.04)
> chap21a(pvals)
```

The function results will list the p values for each study along with the Fisher ln p and Gordon et al. chi-square values. This is followed by the overall chi-square, *df*, and p value.

```
PROGRAM OUTPUT

Study    p      Fisher ln(p)  Gordon et al
  1     0.05    -2.996          5.991
  2     0.01    -4.605          9.210
  3     0.04    -3.219          6.438

Chi-square = 21.64 df = 6 p = 0.00141
```

TIP

✓ Use the R command *options(scripen = 999)* to stop the scientific notation from printing, that is, for $p = 1.5e{-}3$, it now prints $p = .0015$.

NOTE: R will print scientific notation sometimes even when specifying options(scripen = 999) or round(x, digits = 5). The options and digit settings are suggestions that are often overridden when printing output in R.

● CONVERTING VARIOUS STATISTICS TO A COMMON METRIC

Glass (1976) reported that various test statistics reported in the research literature could be converted to the Pearson product moment correlation coefficient (r)—for example, χ^2, t, and F. This provided a common metric to compare the various statistical values reported in research studies. The formula for transforming r to each statistic is presented below.

$$\chi^2 : r = \sqrt{\frac{\chi^2}{n}}.$$

$$t : r = \sqrt{\frac{t^2}{t^2 + df}}.$$

$$F : r = \sqrt{\frac{F}{F + df_{\text{error}}}}.$$

● CONVERTING VARIOUS STATISTICS TO EFFECT SIZE MEASURES

Cohen (1977) expanded Glass's idea to include a formula that would use an effect size measure (d) in the computation of the correlation statistic. The effect size formula is as follows:

$$r = \frac{d}{\sqrt{d^2 + 4}}.$$

Effect Size

The formula for transformation to a d effect size measure for each statistic is presented below.

$$t : d = \frac{2t}{\sqrt{df}}.$$

$$F : d = \frac{2\sqrt{F}}{\sqrt{df_{\text{error}}}}.$$

$$r : d = \frac{2r}{\sqrt{1 - r^2}}.$$

● COMPARISON AND INTERPRETATION OF
  EFFECT SIZE MEASURES

The concept behind an effect size measure, d, was to determine the amount of departure from the null hypothesis in standard units. Consequently, an effect size measure in an experimental versus control group study was determined by the following formula:

$$d = \frac{\bar{Y}_{\text{EXP}} - \bar{Y}_{\text{CTRL}}}{S_{\text{CTRL}}}.$$

If $d = .50$, then the experimental group scored $\frac{1}{2}$ standard deviation higher than the control group on the dependent variable. If the population standard deviation is known, it would be used instead of the control group sample standard deviation estimate. Another alternative was to use the pooled estimate of the standard deviation from both the experimental and the control groups in the denominator. Recall that pooling is the average of the sum of squared deviations from the two groups (see Chapter 14 on analysis of variance).

Not all research studies, however, used an experimental versus control group design, so the development of other effect size formulas was very important when comparing results in those studies. A comparison of the r and d effect size measures for a set of studies will help us better understand how the two methods are computed and interpreted. A comparison of r and d is listed below for four studies, each with a different statistic reported.

Study	Statistic	N	Df	p (One-Tailed)	Effect Size Measures	
					R	d
1	$t = 2.00$	62	60	.025	.25	.516
2	$F = 4.21$	30	1, 27[a,b]	.05	.367	.789
3	$\chi^2 = 9.488$	100	4	.05	.308	.647
4	$r = .295$	61	60	.01	.295	.617

a. In the meta-analysis program, only the F degree-of-freedom error is input.

b. This is the second degree of freedom listed for the F value.

The calculations are straightforward, using the formula for the r and d effect size measures. For example, given that $t = 2.00$, the r effect size is computed as follows:

$$r = \sqrt{\frac{t^2}{t^2 + df}} = \sqrt{\frac{(2.0)^2}{(2.0)^2 + 60}} = \sqrt{\frac{4}{64}} = \sqrt{.0625} = .25.$$

The d effect size for $t = 2.00$ is computed as follows:

$$d = \frac{2t}{\sqrt{df}} = \frac{2(2)}{\sqrt{60}} = \frac{4}{7.7459} = .516.$$

The r and d effect size measures for a chi-square value can also be computed. The calculation of the r effect size measure for the chi-square value is as follows:

$$r = \sqrt{\frac{\chi^2}{n}} = \sqrt{\frac{9.488}{100}} = .308.$$

This r effect size value for chi-square should be used in the formula for computing the corresponding d effect size measure for the chi-square value as follows:

$$d = \frac{2r}{\sqrt{1-r^2}} = \frac{2(.308)}{\sqrt{1-(.308)^2}} = .647.$$

Given $\chi^2 = 9.488$ with a sample size of 100, the r effect size measure is .308. This r effect size value is used in the d effect size formula to obtain the value of $d = .647$.

Statistical results from various studies can be compared since the various statistics from the different research studies can be converted to a common metric (scale). Study 2 had the highest r effect size measure, followed by Studies 3, 4, and 1. The corresponding d effect size measures also indicate the same order and help our interpretation by indicating how much the dependent variable (Y) changed for a unit change in the independent variable (X). Notice that this interpretation is directly related to the use of the correlation coefficient as an effect size measure. If we had used the experimental versus control group d effect size measure, our interpretation would be how much the experimental group increased on average over the control group with regard to the dependent variable.

The null hypothesis always implies that the effect size is zero. If the alternative hypothesis is accepted, then the effect size departs from zero and leads to a standardized interpretation. Jacob Cohen (1977) offered basic guidelines for interpreting the magnitude of the d and r effect size measures: $d = .2$ (small), $d = .5$ (medium), and $d = .8$ (large); $r = .10$ (small), $r = .30$ (medium), and $r = .50$ (large); however, any interpretation of an effect size measure is relative. Knowledge of the professional discipline and the distribution of effect size measures in similar research studies should provide reference points for interpretation in that field of research.

Sometimes, no effect size estimates are reported in research studies, so no standard reference point is available. In this instance, the computation of effect size estimates in several hundred studies can provide the necessary distribution and reference point. Summary statistics printed in a stem-and-leaf plot will facilitate the interpretation of the distribution of d and r effect size measures. Given the standard deviation unit interpretation, it is important to determine whether a $\frac{1}{2}, \frac{1}{3}$, or, $\frac{1}{4}$ standard deviation improvement is due to some type of intervention that implies a meaningful effect size for the interpretation of the research study outcome.

In the case of using an r effect size measure, the correlation coefficients reported for the different research studies can be averaged using the following formula:

$$\bar{r} = \frac{\sum r}{n}.$$

For example, given the following r effect size measures, the overall r effect is as follows:

$$\bar{r} = \frac{\sum r}{n} = \frac{(.25 + .367 + .308 + .295)}{4} = \frac{1.22}{4} = .305.$$

In the case of using a d effect size measure, the individual values are also averaged:

$$\bar{d} = \frac{\sum d}{n} = \frac{(.516 + .789 + .647 + .617)}{4} = \frac{2.569}{4} = .642.$$

● SAMPLE SIZE CONSIDERATIONS IN META-ANALYSIS

An important concern in combining studies using meta-analytic techniques is the influence that different sample sizes may have on the overall interpretation. Some studies may be based on small sample sizes whereas others may be based on larger sample sizes. Since the correlation coefficient is not a function of sample size, procedures were developed to take into account the different sample sizes from the research studies when averaging the d effect size estimates. Hedges and Olkin (1985) as well as Rosenthal (1984) and Rosenthal and Rubin (1986) separately developed a formula for calculating an *unbiased estimate* of the average d effect size. The formula was

$$\bar{d} = \frac{\sum wd}{\sum w},$$

with w calculated as (N = total sample size).

$$w = \frac{2N}{8 + d^2}.$$

The results of applying this unbiased weighted approach to the previous example are listed below.

Study	N	d	w
1	62	.516	15.001
2	30	.789	6.959
3	100	.647	23.757
4	61	.617	14.557

The calculation of the unbiased, weighted average effect estimate is as follows:

$$\bar{d} = \frac{\sum wd}{\sum w} = \frac{(15.001)(.516) + (6.959)(.789) + (23.757)(.647) + (14.557)(.617)}{15.001 + 6.959 + 23.757 + 14.557}$$

$$= \frac{37.58}{60.27} = .624.$$

The *unbiased* weighted average d effect size measure of .624 is then compared with the *biased* weighted average d effect size measure of .642 reported earlier. The amount of bias, or the value .642 − .624 = .018, is due to the research studies having very different sample sizes. In practice, we would report the unbiased, weighted d effect size—in this case the d = .624 value.

● META-ANALYSIS FUNCTION

The *meta-analysis function* in the script file (chap21b.r) inputs the various statistical values and the corresponding N, df, and p values, then converts them to the common metric; plus it computes and reports the r and d effect size measures. The average effect size for r, the average effect size for d, the unbiased d effect size measure, and the amount of sample size bias are also given. You need to input the various statistical values, then the data vectors for the corresponding sample size (N), degrees of freedom, and probability values (pvals) prior to running the function. These values would be input as follows:

```
> t = 2.00
> F = 4.21
> C = 9.488
> r = .295
> N = c(62,30,100,61)
> df = c(60,27,4,60)
> pvals = c(.025,.05,.05,.01)
> chap21b(t, F, C, r, N, df, pvals)
```

The function will list the types of statistics, their statistical values, and the corresponding N, df, and p values. Additionally, the r, d, and w (weighted) effect size measures are listed. The overall effect size measures for r and d are then printed, which are followed by the unbiased effect size (weighted value) and the amount of sample size bias. This is considered a fixed effects meta-analysis.

```
PROGRAM OUTPUT
```

Type	Statistic	N	df	p	r	d	w
t	2	62	60	0.025	0.25	0.516	15.001
F	4.21	30	27	0.05	0.367	0.789	6.959
Chisq	9.488	100	4	0.05	0.308	0.647	23.757
r	0.295	61	60	0.01	0.295	0.617	14.557

```
Effect size(r) = 0.305 Effect size(d) = 0.642

Unbiased effect size(d) = 0.624

Sample Size bias = 0.018
```

The unbiased effect size (*d*) would be reported to indicate that an experimental group performed .624 standard deviations better than the control group. We could also convert the *p* values to chi-square values, then sum the chi-square values. A comparison of the total chi-square value with the tabled chi-square value, given the degrees of freedom, would indicate whether the combined study effects were statistically significant overall.

R Functions for Meta-Analysis

There are several *MA** packages in R that conduct meta-analysis. You can learn more about them at the following website: http://rwiki.sciviews.org/doku.php?id=packages:cran:ma_meta-analysis. There are currently five related packages for conducting a meta-analysis in R:

1. *compute.es* (converts different statistics to a common metric)

2. *MAc* (meta-analysis with correlations)

3. MAc GUI (graphic user interface for MAc)

4. *MAd* (meta-analysis with mean differences)

5. MAd GUI (graphic user interface for MAd)

For example, you can install and load the MAd package as follows:

```
> install.packages('MAd') # install the MAd package

> library(MAd) # load the MAd package
```

The MAc and MAd packages include fixed, random, and mixed meta-analysis functions for correlation and mean difference, respectively.

compute.es() Package

The *compute.es* package is the most useful because it contains several functions for calculating and converting various statistics, such as a *t* test or *p* value and sample size, to effect size estimates of *d* (mean difference), *g* (unbiased estimate of *d*), *r* (correlation coefficient), *z* (Fisher's *z*), and the log odds ratio. The variances of these estimates are also computed. The calculations and conversion functions are a particularly useful resource during the preliminary stages of a meta-analytic project when deriving effect sizes from research studies.

To install the compute.es package, first select "Set CRAN mirror site" from the main menu, then Install Packages, and finally select the package, compute.es.

An R command will provide information on the compute.es package:

```
> library(help = "compute.es")
```

The index of functions is listed as follows:

```
Index:

a.fes ANCOVA F-statistic to Effect Size
a.mes Mean Values from ANCOVA F-statistic to Effect Size
a.mes2 Mean Values from ANCOVA F-statistic with Pooled SD to
Effect
 Size
a.pes One or Two-tailed p-value from ANCOVA to Effect Size
a.tes t-test Value from ANCOVA to Effect Size
chies Chi-Squared Statistic to Effect Size
compute.es-package Compute Effect Sizes
des Mean Difference (d) to Effect size
failes Failure groups to Effect Size
fes F-test to Effect Size
lores Log Odds Ratio to Standardized Mean Difference (d)
mes Means to Effect Size
mes2 Means with Pooled SD to Effect Size
pes p-value to Effect Size
propes Proportions to Effect Size
res Correlation coefficient (r) to Effect Size
tes t-test Value to Effect Size
```

A complete reference (February 14, 2012) is provided with discussion and examples in the following PDF document: http://cran.r-project.org/web/packages/compute.es/compute.es.pdf.

pes() *Function*

For converting *p* values to an effect size *d*, the *pes()* function would be used. It yields one- or two-tailed *p* values for independent groups to an effect size *d* (mean difference). Values for *g* (unbiased estimate of *d*), *r* (correlation coefficient), *z* (Fisher's *z*), and the log odds ratio, and the variances of these estimates are also output. The function with arguments is given as follows:

```
pes(p, n.1, n.2, tail = "two")

where:
p = p-value
n.1 = sample size for treatment group
n.2 = sample size for comparison group
tail = one or two-tailed p = value; default is two
```

Results are easily obtained for any function after loading the compute.es package:

```
> library(compute.es)
> pes(.01, 30, 30, tail = "two")
```

```
$MeanDifference
```

```
         d          var.d           g          var.g
0.68765773 0.07060728 0.67872711 0.06878523
```

```
$Correlation
```

```
         r         var.r
0.32514647 0.01262437
```

```
$Log_Odds
```

```
log_odds   var.log_odds
1.2472732    0.2322886
```

```
$Fishers_z
```

```
         z         var.z
0.33739130 0.01754386
```

```
$TotalSample
```

```
n
60
```

tes() *Function*

For converting a *t*-test value to effect size *d* with similar output, the *tes()* function is used:

```
tes(t, n.1, n.2)
where:
```

```
t = t-test value reported in study.
n.1 = Sample size of treatment group.
n.2 = Sample size of comparison group.
```

For example,

```
> library(compute.es)
> tes(2.38, 30, 30)

$MeanDifference

      d        var.d         g        var.g
0.61451336 0.06981356 0.60653266 0.06801199


$Correlation

     r       var.r
0.2982831  0.0140673


$Log_Odds

log_odds    var.log_odds
1.1146039    0.2296774


$Fishers_z

     z           var.z
0.30763395  0.01754386


$TotalSample

n
60
```

Researchers could use the different functions in the compute.es package to easily create their own user-defined function.

● STATISTICAL SIGNIFICANCE VERSUS PRACTICAL INTERPRETATION

Statistical significance testing has been criticized because the researcher controls the criteria that can determine whether a research study's outcome is statistically significant or not. For example, by simply changing the alpha level ($p = .01$ to $p = .05$), the findings could become statistically significant. Also, when changing from a one-tailed to a two-tailed hypothesis, the statistical significance test changes. Basically, sample size, alpha level, whether it is a one- or two-tailed test, power, and effect size are all under the control of the researcher. How then do we make sense of our research findings?

Journals and other outlets for published research today often require the reporting of confidence intervals along with the statistical significance test. The confidence interval provides additional information about the sample statistic as an estimate of the population parameter. In addition, effect sizes are now often reported, which helps to establish a practical or meaningful way to extend knowledge on a research topic. This becomes important since most research studies are not replicated but rather report cross-validation, jackknife, or bootstrap results to explain the results in a single study. Statistical significance testing, based on probability, only provides part of our understanding of the research findings. The effect size gives us a practical understanding of the importance of our research results.

In previous chapters, statistical tests of null hypotheses for different types of data were presented. The statistical tests were the chi-square test, z test, t test, analysis of variance, correlation, and linear regression and multiple regression models. The outcomes of the statistical tests were to either retain the null hypothesis or reject the null hypothesis in favor of an alternative hypothesis based on the significance of the statistic computed. Type I and Type II errors were illustrated to better understand the nature of falsely rejecting the null hypothesis or falsely retaining the null hypothesis at a given level of significance for the sample statistic. The level of significance (p value) that we choose, that is, .05 or .01, to test our null hypothesis has come under scrutiny due to the nature of statistical significance testing.

Researchers have criticized significance testing because it can be manipulated to achieve the desired outcome, namely, a significant finding. This can be illustrated by presenting different research outcomes based on only changing the p value selected for the research study. The research study involves fifth-grade boys and girls who took the Texas Assessment of Academic Skills (TAAS) test. The researcher was interested in testing whether fifth-grade boys on average scored statistically significantly higher than girls on the TAAS test (a directional or one-tailed test of the null hypothesis). The researcher took a random sample of 31 fifth-grade boys and 31 fifth-grade girls and gave them the TAAS test under standard administration conditions. An independent t test was selected to test for mean differences between the groups in the population at the .01 level of significance with 60 degrees of freedom ($df = N - 2$). The study results are reported as follows:

Group	N	Mean	Standard Deviation	t
Boys	31	85	10	1.968
Girls	31	80	10	

The researcher computed the t value as follows:

$$t = \frac{85 - 80}{\sqrt{\dfrac{30(100) + 30(100)}{31 + 31 - 2}\left(\dfrac{1}{31} + \dfrac{1}{31}\right)}} = \frac{5}{2.54} = 1.968.$$

The tabled t value that was selected for determining the research study outcome (based on a directional, one-tailed test, with 60 degrees of freedom at the .01 level of significance) was $t = 2.39$. Since the computed $t = 1.968$ was not greater than the tabled t value of 2.66 at the .01 level of significance, the researcher would *retain* the null hypothesis. However, if the researcher had selected a .05 level of significance, the tabled t value would equal 1.67, and the researcher would *reject* the null hypothesis in favor of the alternative hypothesis. The two possible outcomes in the research study are solely based on the different levels of significance a researcher could choose for the statistical test. This points out why significance testing has been criticized, namely, the researcher can have statistically significant research findings by simply changing the p value.

Researchers could also manipulate whether statistically significant results are obtained from a research study by using a *one-tailed test* rather than a *two-tailed test*. In the previous example, a two-tailed test of significance would have resulted in a tabled $t = 2.66$ at the .01 level of significance or a tabled $t = 2.00$ at the .05 level of significance. If the researcher had chosen a two-tailed test rather than a one-tailed test, the null hypothesis would have been rejected at either level of significance or p value. This illustrates how changing the directional nature of the hypothesis (one-tailed vs. two-tailed test) can result in finding or not finding a statistically significant result.

Researchers can also increase the *sample size*, hence degrees of freedom, and achieve statistically significant research results. If we increase our sample sizes to 100 boys and 100 girls, we enter the t table with infinite degrees of freedom. The resultant tabled t values, given a one-tailed test, would be 1.645 at the .05 level of significance or 2.326 at the .01 level of significance. An examination of the t table further indicates that the tabled t values are larger for smaller degrees of freedom (smaller sample sizes). The bottom row indicates tabled t values that are the same as corresponding z values in the normal distribution, given larger sample sizes. This illustrates how increasing the sample size (greater than 120 degrees of freedom greater) can yield a lower tabled t value for making comparisons with the computed t value in determining whether the results are statistically significant.

When significance testing, the researcher obtains a sample statistic or point estimate of the population parameter. The researcher could compute *confidence intervals* around the sample statistic, thereby providing an additional interpretation of the statistical results. The confidence interval width provides valuable information about capturing the population parameter beyond the statistical significance of a point estimate of the population value. If the 95% confidence interval for a sample mean ranged from 2.50 to 3.00, then we would conclude with 95% confidence that the interval contained the population mean. Each time we took a random sample of data, the confidence interval would change. If we took all possible samples and computed their confidence intervals, then 95% of the intervals would contain the population mean and 5% would not; therefore, one should not report that the probability is 95% that the interval contains the population mean. Unfortunately, many researchers either do not report confidence intervals or misreport them.

Previous chapters also highlighted additional methods a researcher could use to present research findings and address the practical importance of the research study findings. The most meaningful technique would be to *replicate* the study. This provides the best evidence of research findings or outcomes. Researchers, however, often choose to conduct *cross-validation, jackknife,* or *bootstrap* methods to assess the stability of their findings. In some cases, a researcher might synthesize several findings from research studies by conducting a *meta-analysis*. Most researchers, however, do not take the time to replicate their study, whether by cross-validation, jackknife, boot-strap, or meta-analysis. These methods are well-known but are not available in most commercial statistical packages and, therefore, not readily available to researchers. The R software package is the solution to having these tools readily available.

Another important consideration above and beyond the significance of a statistical test is the *effect size* or magnitude of the difference reported. The interpretation of the effect size can directly indicate whether the statistically significant results have any practical importance. An example will better illustrate the practical importance of research findings based on an effect size. The previous research study reported a 5-point average difference between boys and girls in the population on the TAAS test. Is this average 5-point difference of practical importance? If we retain the null hypothesis of no difference in the population based on our statistical test of significance, then we conclude that the fifth-grade boys and girls achieved about the same on the TAAS test. Alternatively, if we reject the null hypothesis in favor of an alternative hypothesis based on our statistical test of significance, then we conclude that the fifth-grade boys scored statistically significantly higher on average than the girls at a given level of significance.

What are the consequences of our decisions based on a statistical test of significance? If we retain the null hypothesis when it is really false, we make the error of not spending additional money for programs to better educate fifth-grade girls. If we reject the null hypothesis when it is really true, we make the error of spending additional money on programs that are not needed to better educate fifth-grade girls. The effect size helps our practical understanding of the magnitude of the difference detected in a research study. The average 5-point difference between the boys and girls, in practical terms, was based on a test score difference of 2 to 3 points. The effect size becomes more meaningful when interpreted based on a synthesis of findings in several other related studies. This comparison provides a frame of reference for interpreting whether the effect size value is small, medium, or large.

The overall recommendation is to report all this information so that the research findings can be better interpreted and the results can be used when synthesizing results with other studies. The important information to report is summarized in Table 21.2. For example, when conducting an independent t test of mean difference between Group 1 ($n = 30$, mean = 48.82, standard deviation = 9.52) and Group 2 ($n = 30$, mean = 47.65, standard deviation = 8.24), the recommended tabled results would be as given in Table 21.2.

Table 21.2   Independent t Test Summary Table

Group	N	Mean	SD	t	df	p
Experimental	30	48.82	9.52	.51	58	.614
Control	30	47.65	8.24			

NOTE: 95% CI (−3.439, 5.769); r effect = .066; d effect = .131.

The *tes()* function in the compute.es package easily computes the r and d effect sizes for the summary table.

```
> tes(.51,30,30)

$MeanDifference

        d         var.d          g          var.g
0.13168143  0.06681117  0.12997129  0.06508708


$Correlation

        r         var.r
0.06681663  0.01679815


$Log_Odds

log_odds    var.log_odds
0.2388437      0.2197999


$Fishers_z

        z         var.z
0.06691633  0.01754386


$TotalSample

n
60
```

Early scholars who developed the statistical formula we use today investigated the phenomena of their time. Their purpose was to understand individual differences, whether in the field of heredity or general intelligence. It became evident that analyzing the variability of individuals (analysis of variance) was the key to determining individual differences. The average weight for a group of people gave a basic description, but the standard deviation provided a measure of how much people varied above or below the average. If everyone weighed the same, then no variability in weight and no individual difference existed; that is, everyone weighed the same.

The analysis of variance by Fisher was an effort to understand why crop production varied based on water levels, soil, and fertilizer. Pearson investigated individual differences based on variability in hereditary variables. His correlation coefficient measured the association between variables, but when squared, it indicated the amount of variance in Y explained by knowledge of X. To understand statistics, we need to understand that our hypotheses and analysis of data encompass the notion of predicting or explaining variability.

Prediction and explanation are the cornerstone of our interpretation of findings from research designs and the use of statistical formulas. Prediction of Y values is affected by the statistical significance of the predictor variables. Statistical significance is based on the probability of obtaining a statistic at a specified alpha level given the sampling distribution of the statistic. Probability, therefore, plays a role in determining whether the statistic we compute from our sample data occurs beyond a chance level. Explanation is based on how much of the variability in Y is accounted for by knowledge of other variables. If all we knew was the mean and standard deviation of Y (test scores), we could describe the average test score and how much the scores vary or deviate around the mean, but we would not know *why* they vary, implying individual differences. Given knowledge of the amount of time spent studying (X_1), some of the variability in the test scores could be explained, but not all. We would hypothesize other variables as being important in further explaining the variability in the test scores. So our analysis efforts are geared toward finding a few variables that explain the individual differences in the test scores.

In statistics, we have the determination of statistical significance, which is influenced by the directional nature of our hypothesis, alpha, sample size, effect size, and power considerations. These criteria help determine the probability of obtaining a statistic (chi-square, t, F, r, or R) beyond chance. A practical consideration would take into account how much of the variability in Y is being explained. The standard deviation of Y (test scores) would be squared, yielding the variance. How much of this variance we can explain based on independent variables provides a practical interpretation. Moreover, an effect size provides a meaningful practical interpretation. We could compute a sample statistic that is statistically significant; for example, boys and girls differ on average test scores (t test) beyond a .05 level of probability, yet the effect size indicates that they differ on average by 1 point (boys' mean = 50; girls' mean = 51). So, practically speaking, is a 1-point difference, although statistically significant, of any real practical importance? Would we change the school curriculum based on these findings? I would hope not.

A few final words of wisdom can be given when faced with significance testing and issues related to the practical importance of research findings. In conducting basic applied research, one asks a question, analyzes data, and answers the research question. Beyond this task, we need to be reminded of several concerns. How do our research findings relate to the research findings in other related research studies? What is the educational importance of our findings? What implications do our research findings have on practice? What recommendations can we make that might affect or modify the underlying theory? What recommendations can we make that might enhance future research efforts?

SUMMARY

Meta-analysis is an objective quantitative method for combining the results of several independent research studies. The easiest approach is to combine research findings using the log of the p values found in a set of studies. If several p values are included in a study, then the average p value could be used for the study in the Fisher Meta-Analysis Function R script file. The overall significance of the combined studies effect using p values is indicated by a total chi-square value, which is the sum of the individual study chi-square values.

The d effect size measure was introduced because of the importance of determining an experimental versus control group effect size estimate, which is determined by subtracting the two group means and dividing by the standard deviation of the control group. The d effect size indicates the departure from the null hypothesis in standard units. The r effect size was introduced based on statistics that were correlation based. Both these approaches to combining research findings, the r and d effect size estimates, involve the transformation of different statistics to a common metric or scale. The overall significant effect from several studies, using the transformed statistics, is obtained by averaging either the r or the d effect size measures. The overall *d* effect size measure can be weighted by sample size to compute an unbiased, average *d* effect size measure.

Meta-analysis compares the relative importance of findings in several research studies by interpreting the effect size measures. R contains several packages that assist in conducting meta-analysis. MAc is used with correlations and has a corresponding graphical user interface. MAd is used with mean differences and has a corresponding graphical user interface. I only covered the compute.es package because it has functions that convert different statistics to effect sizes. The many functions can be used to customize your own user-defined function.

EXERCISES

1. Use the *Fisher Meta-Analysis Program* to determine if the following set of *p* values from four independent research studies have an overall significant effect. Show the R function and the output, and interpret the results.

   R Commands:

   ```
   > pvals = c(.025,.01,.046,.09)
   ```

   Output:

   Interpretation:

2. Install the *MAd* package. Load the package *library(Mad)*. Install the compute.es package.

   Use the *pes()* function to convert the following *p* values from the studies. Enter the results in the table. Compute the average *r* and *d* effect sizes. Using Cohen's interpretation, what is the overall combined effect size interpretation for the four studies?

   R Commands:

   ```
   > library(compute.es)
   > pes(p, n1, n2, tail) # Enter values individually for each study
   ```

   Output:

   Interpretation:

Study	p	n1	n2	Tail	r	d
A	.025	30	30	Two		
B	.010	40	50	One		
C	.046	25	30	Two		
D	.090	50	50	One		

3. Install the *MAd* package. Load the package *library(Mad)*. Install the compute.es package.

Use the *tes()* function to convert the following *t* values from the studies. Enter your results in the table. Compute the average *r* and *d* effect sizes. Using Cohen's interpretation, what is the overall combined effect size interpretation for the four studies?

R Commands:

```
library(compute.es)
tes(t, n1, n2)  # Enter t and sample sizes for each study
```

Output:

Interpretation:

Study	t	n1	n2	r	d
A	1.94	30	30		
B	2.78	40	50		
C	4.15	25	30		
D	3.00	50	50		

TRUE OR FALSE QUESTIONS

T   F   a.   Meta-analysis quantitatively summarizes the findings in several research studies on the same topic.

T   F   b.   The use of *p* values from independent research studies readily lends itself to a summary chi-square value to measure the overall significant effect.

T   F   c.   An *r* effect size can be computed for chi-square, *t*, and *F* values in research studies.

T   F   d.   The *d* effect size measure reports the amount of departure from the null hypothesis of no difference in means in standard units.

T   F   e.   The null hypothesis always implies that the effect size is zero.

T   F   f.   Cohen's *r* and *d* effect size measures are guidelines for interpretation of the overall combined effect.

WEB RESOURCES

Chapter R script files are available at http://www.sagepub.com/schumacker

Fisher Meta-Analysis Function R script file: chap21a.r

Meta-Analysis Function R script file: chap21b.r

Meta-analysis software: http://rwiki.sciviews.org/doku.php?id=packages:cran:ma_meta-analysis

compute.es function: http://cran.r-project.org/web/packages/compute.es/compute.es.pdf

GLOSSARY OF TERMS

Alpha level: The level of statistical significance selected prior to a test for incorrectly rejecting a true null hypothesis, for example, the .05 alpha level of significance (See **Type I error**).

Alternative hypothesis: A statistical hypothesis that indicates a difference in population parameters (e.g., "The means of two populations are different")—that is, it indicates possible outcomes not stated in the null hypothesis.

Analysis of covariance: The statistical adjustment of the dependent variable group means using extraneous variables not controlled in the study design.

Analysis of variance: A technique that tests whether the dependent variable means of three or more mutually exclusive groups are statistically significantly different at a specified level of significance. The F test is the ratio of mean square between groups to mean square within groups.

Bell-shaped curve: Describes a normal or symmetrical distribution of data in which the intervals around the mean are known.

Box-whisker plot: Displays the distribution of scores on a variable where the middle of the data distribution is indicated. A box is placed around this middle value to indicate the upper and lower range of values where 50% of the scores are distributed. Extending out the top and bottom of the box are two lines referred to as whiskers, hence its name.

Bimodal: A frequency distribution of data that has two modes, that is, two scores that occur most frequently in a set of data.

Binomial distribution: A probability distribution based on objects, events, or individuals belonging to one of only two groups. For example, if you tossed an unbiased coin 1,000 times, it should land approximately 500 heads and 500 tails.

Binomial probability distribution: A probability distribution generated by taking $(a + b)$ to the nth power. It is used in a binomial test to determine whether the probability of two outcomes exceeds the chance level of occurrence.

Bootstrap: An approach that samples with replacement to generate a sampling distribution of a statistic that serves as the population distribution. The mean of the bootstrap sampling distribution or bootstrap estimate is used to determine the amount of bias in a random sample.

Central limit theorem: A theorem that provides a mathematical basis for using a normal distribution, such as a sampling distribution of a statistic for a given sample size, to test a statistical hypothesis. For example, the theorem states that (a) a sampling distribution of means for a given sample size is normally distributed,

(b) the sampling distribution mean is equal to the population mean, and (c) the sampling distribution variance is equal to the variance divided by the sample size.

Central tendency: A concept that implies that most scores fall in the middle of a symmetrical distribution, with the scores spreading out evenly toward both tails of the distribution.

Chi-square distribution: A probability distribution or family of curves generated by the difference between observed and expected frequencies. The sampling distribution of chi-square values is used in both parametric and nonparametric tests of significance.

Chi-square statistic: A nonparametric test that measures the difference between the observed frequencies and expected frequencies in two or more groups.

Combinations: The different ways in which different subsets of events or numbers can be selected.

Conditional probability: The probability of Event B based on the occurrence or nonoccurrence of Event A.

Confidence interval: A high and a low value that form an interval around the sample statistic that should contain the population parameter. The interval will be different depending on the percentage used, that is, 68%, 95%, or 99%.

Confidence level: A percentage that indicates how certain we are that the interval around the sample statistic contains the population parameter (see **Alpha level**).

Contrasts: A post hoc procedure that compares the mean differences between groups. The group comparisons can be coded in different ways, for example, dummy coded or effect coded.

Correlation: A statistic that indicates the strength and direction of the association between two sets of scores. The strength is indicated by a correlation value closer to 1.0, and the direction is indicated by a ± sign. A positive correlation indicates that both variables increase in value across the range of scores, while a negative correlation indicates that one set of scores increases as the other set of scores decreases.

Cross-validation: An original sample of data is randomly split into two equal samples, then a sample statistic is computed using one sample of data and applied to the other sample of data.

Cumulative frequency distribution: A frequency distribution of raw scores that indicates successive addition of the number of events, individuals, or objects up to the total number, or 100%.

Degrees of freedom (*df*): The number of observations or groups minus the restrictions placed on them. For example, if four out of five sample means are known, the one remaining unknown sample mean can be determined; hence, $df = 5 - 1 = 4$.

Dependent *t* test: A statistical test of whether two sample means from the same subjects or group are significantly different. It is also called a paired *t* test or correlated *t* test.

Dependent variable: The variable we measure or the outcome variation we attempt to explain by knowledge of independent variables. For example, test score variation is explained by knowledge of hours spent studying.

Dichotomous population: A population of data that can be divided into two mutually exclusive categories.

Directional hypothesis: A hypothesis that states that one population parameter is greater than the other. The direction can be stated in a positive or a negative direction, for example, boys' verbal scores will be lower on average than girls' verbal scores. It is a one-tailed test because the region of rejection is only in one tail of the sampling distribution.

Effect size: Conveys the magnitude of difference in standard units between the mean of the experimental group and the mean of the control group. It is used in conjunction with the sample size, alpha level, and direction of the statistical hypothesis to select a value for power.

Equally likely events: Events, individuals, or objects that have the same chance of being selected.

Experiment-wide error rate: The probability of making a Type I error increases based on the number of post hoc multiple comparison tests conducted.

Experimental design: A study design that involves a random assignment of subjects to a treatment group compared with a random assignment of subjects to a control group.

Exponential function: A relationship between two sets of data points that does not have a constant rate of change for a random variable X, that is, $Y = 2^X$.

Extraneous variables: Variables not controlled in a quasi-experimental design that are used to statistically control for influence on the variation of the dependent variable.

F curve: A positively skewed frequency distribution of F values for specific degrees of freedom.

F distribution: A probability distribution or family of curves that requires 2 degrees of freedom. The normal, t, and chi-square distributions are special cases of the F distribution.

F test: In analysis of variance, the test to determine if sample means are different beyond a chance expectation. The F test is the ratio of mean square between groups to mean square within groups.

Factor: A categorical independent variable where group membership explains the variation in the dependent variable.

Factorial notation: Indicated as $n!$, for example, $3! = 3 \times 2 \times 1 = 6$.

Factoring: A product of sequential numbers that indicates the total number of choices possible (see **Factorial notation**).

Finite population: A population of data where the number of individuals, objects, or events is known, hence exact probabilities of occurrence can be computed.

Fixed factor: An independent variable for which specific levels are specified in the study design, for example, gender (male and female).

Frequency distribution: A tabulation of data that indicates the number of times a score or value occurs.

Hartley F_{max} test: A test of whether three or more sample variances are statistically different. The largest sample variance is divided by the smallest sample variance to form an F ratio with degrees of freedom from the two sample sizes.

Heterogeneity: Refers to a grouping of dissimilar individuals, objects, or events.

Histogram: A bar chart that indicates the frequency of numbers on the y-axis and the mutually exclusive groups or categories on the x-axis (see **Pie chart**).

Homoscedasticity of variance: The assumption that the distribution of Y scores around each predicted Y value is normal.

Homogeneity: Refers to a grouping of similar individuals, objects, or events.

Independent *t* test: A statistical test of whether two independent sample means are significantly different, implying that the two population means are different.

Independent variable: The variable we manipulate or define that explains the variation in the dependent variable. For example, hours spent studying explains the variation in test scores.

Infinite population: A population of data where the individuals, objects, or events are too numerous to count, hence exact probabilities of occurrence cannot be computed.

Interaction effect: The joint effect of two or more independent variables that defines cell means on the dependent variable in analysis of variance. For example, gender by ethnicity would define cell means on test scores, the dependent variable.

Intercept: The point in a linear equation where the line of best fit crosses the y-axis. The intercept is the predicted value of Y when the X variable equals zero, that is, the value a in the linear regression equation $Y = a + bX + e$.

Interquartile range: A score that represents the distance between the first and third quartiles. It indicates the range of scores in the middle 50% of a frequency distribution. Gives values using the summary() function.

Jackknife: An approach that uses a single sample of data and computes sample statistics based on different $n - 1$ sample sizes.

Joint probability: The probability of two events occurring that is determined by multiplying the independent probabilities of the two events.

Kurtosis: A measure that indicates the flatness or peakedness of the frequency distribution of scores. Leptokurtic implies a peaked distribution, mesokurtic a bell-shaped normal distribution, and platykurtic a flattened distribution of scores.

Law of complements: Given the probability of Event A, $P(A)$, the complement is $1 - P(A)$, or the remaining probability, since $P(A) + [1 - P(A)] = 1$.

Leaves: The numbers to the right of the vertical line in a stem-and-leaf plot.

Level of significance: The probability of making a Type I error (see **Alpha level**).

Line of best fit: In linear regression, the line formed by the predicted Y values that passes through the scatterplot of X and Y values. The line indicates the best prediction that minimizes the sum of squared errors of prediction.

Linear function: An angled straight line of data points that indicates a constant rate of change for a random variable X, that is, $Y = bX$.

Linear regression: A statistical technique designed to predict values of Y (dependent variable) from one or more X variables (independent predictor variables). The regression equation is $Y = a + bX + e$.

Main effects: The individual independent variables that are tested in an analysis of variance.

Mean: The arithmetic mean, computed as the sum of a set of scores divided by the number of scores. It is typically referred to as a measure of central tendency.

Mean square: A variance estimate computed by dividing the sum of squares by the degrees of freedom.

Mean square between groups: The sum of the squared deviations of group means around the grand mean weighted (multiplied) by the sample size of each group and divided by the number of groups minus 1. It indicates whether the group means are similar or different based on how much they vary.

Mean square within groups: The sum of squared deviations of individual scores around each group mean divided by the number of scores in each group minus the number of groups. It indicates how much the scores vary within each group.

Median: The middle score in a distribution of odd-numbered scores or the midpoint in an even-numbered set of scores. It is typically referred to as a measure of central tendency.

Meta-analysis: A statistical procedure that averages the effect sizes across several studies to determine the overall significance of a large number of research studies on the same topic.

Mode: The most frequently occurring score in a set of scores. It is possible to have a single modal score (unimodal), two scores that occur the most (bimodal), or even three or more scores that occur the most. It is typically referred to as a measure of central tendency.

Monte Carlo: An approach that describes a statistical technique that simulates data and approximates the probability density functions of population distributions to study the robustness and properties of statistical tests.

Multiplication law: The independent probabilities of two events can be multiplied to obtain their probability of joint occurrence, that is, $P(J) = P(A) * P(B)$.

Nondirectional hypothesis: A hypothesis that states that two population parameters are different, rather than stating that one population parameter is greater than the other. It is a two-tailed test because the region of rejection is in both tails of the sampling distribution.

Normal curve: A symmetric distribution of data based on a mathematical equation formulated by Abraham de Moivre in 1733 and further developed by Carl Fredrick Gauss.

Normal distribution: A frequency distribution of scores that when graphed produces a symmetrical, bell-shaped distribution with skewness and kurtosis of zero. It is sometimes referred to as a mesokurtic distribution.

Null hypothesis: A statistical hypothesis that indicates no difference in population parameters (e.g., "The means of two populations are equal"). The null hypothesis is either retained or rejected in favor of an alternative hypothesis.

Ogive: A graph of the cumulative frequency distribution of data that has a characteristic S-shaped curve.

One-sample *t* test: A statistical test of whether a sample mean is significantly different from a population mean.

One-way analysis of variance: A statistical test that is an extension of the independent *t* test to test whether three or more independent sample means are statistically different, implying that the population means are different.

Outlier: An extreme or influential score or data value that affects the sample statistic, for example, the sample mean.

Parameters: Population values or characteristics that are estimated by sample statistics, for example, the population mean or population correlation.

Parametric statistics: Inferential statistics, based on the researcher being able to randomly draw a sample from a well-defined population, estimate the sample statistic, and make an inference about the population parameter. For example, the sample mean is an estimate of the population mean.

Pearson correlation: A measure of the association between two linear continuous variables.

Permutations: A technique used to determine the different ways individuals, objects, or events can be ordered.

Pie chart: A circle with portions of the circle indicated for each mutually exclusive group or category (see **Histogram**).

Population: A set of individuals or scores that are well-defined and share some characteristic in common. Typically, population data are randomly sampled and sample statistics computed to estimate the population values because the population is typically too large to measure all the data (see **Parametric statistics**).

Power: The probability of rejecting the null hypothesis when it is false. The expression $1 - \beta$ is used to indicate the level of power. The value of .80 is typically selected for power; power is a function of the sample size, alpha level, effect size, and directional nature of the statistical hypothesis (one-tailed or two-tailed test).

Probability: The ratio of the number of favorable outcomes to the total possible number of outcomes.

Properties of estimators: Important characteristics we want sample statistics to possess as estimates of population parameters, that is, they should be unbiased, consistent, efficient, and sufficient.

Pseudorandom numbers: Numerical values typically generated by a random number generator on a computer but not truly independent or unbiased because they will eventually correlate and repeat.

Quartile: A score that divides a set of data into four equal parts, that is, the first quartile is a score that separates the bottom 25% of the data in a frequency distribution from the other data values.

Quasi-experimental design: A study design that uses a treatment group and a comparison group. Typically, it does not involve a random assignment of subjects to groups but rather works with intact or existing groups of subjects.

Random assignment: The process of assigning individuals, objects, or events randomly to experimental and control groups.

Random number generator: A mathematical algorithm in a software program that is run on a computer to generate pseudorandom numbers.

Random numbers: Independent, unbiased numerical values that have an equally likely chance of being selected.

Random sample: A sample of data from a well-defined population where every individual, object, or event has an equally likely chance of being selected.

Random sampling: The process of selecting individuals, objects, or events from a well-defined population in which all members have an equal and independent chance of being selected. It is not the same as random assignment.

Random sampling with replacement: Each randomly sampled data point is returned to the population before another data point is randomly sampled; therefore, it is possible for a data point to be selected more than once.

Random sampling without replacement: Each randomly sampled data point is not returned to the population before another data point is randomly sampled, therefore each data point is uniquely drawn and cannot be selected again.

Range: A score that indicates the distance between the highest and lowest data values in a set of data.

Region of rejection: The area under a sampling distribution where sample statistics fall that are highly improbable if the null hypothesis is true.

Regression weight: In regression analysis, the regression coefficient or the slope of the line of best fit that passes through the predicted Y values, that is, the value b in the linear regression equation $Y = a + bX + e$. It is a weight computed by the least squares method of minimizing the sum of squared errors of prediction.

Repeated measures analysis of variance: A statistical procedure in which subjects are measured two or more times and the total variation of scores is partitioned into three components: (1) variation among subjects, (2) variation among occasions (time), and (3) residual variation.

Sample: A random selection of individuals, objects, or events from a well-defined population of data.

Sample error: The difference between a sample statistic and the population parameter.

Sample statistic: A sample value that estimates a population parameter.

Sampling distribution: A probability frequency distribution of a sample statistic formed for all possible random samples of a given sample size. Examples of sampling distributions include (a) sampling distribution of means, (b) t distribution, (c) chi-square distribution, and (d) F distribution.

Sampling error: The error in using a sample statistic as an estimate of a population parameter.

Scatterplot: Displays pairs of numbers for y and x variables, which are called coordinate points.

Scheffe complex contrasts: A type of post hoc "t test" for conducting multiple comparisons of group mean differences after an analysis of variance F test.

Skewness: A measure of deviation from symmetry in a frequency distribution of scores. Negative skew indicates a distribution with more scores above the mean. Positive skew indicates a distribution with more scores below the mean.

Slope: The amount of change in Y that corresponds to a change of one unit in X (see **Regression weight**).

Standard deviation: The square root of the average squared deviations of scores around the mean. It is a measure of how much individual scores deviate from the mean.

Standard error of prediction: The standard deviation of Y scores around each predicted Y value for a given X value.

Standard error of statistic: The standard deviation of the sampling distribution of the statistic that indicates the amount of error in estimating the population parameter.

Standard score: A score computed by dividing the deviation of the raw score from the group mean by the group standard deviation. It is also called a z score.

Statistical control: The variation in the dependent variable is statistically adjusted based on the influence of extraneous or covariate variables. It is generally done in a quasi-experimental design.

Stem: The numbers in the ones position (e.g., 1, 2, and 3) in a stem-and-leaf plot.

Stem-and-leaf plot: A graphical display that illustrates the shape of a distribution of scores.

Sum of squared deviations: The deviations of each score from the group mean squared and then summed for all scores.

Symmetric distribution: A sampling distribution or frequency distribution of scores that is the same on either side of the median value. The normal distribution is an example of a symmetric distribution.

t **distribution:** A probability distribution or family of *t* curves for different degrees of freedom that is used to determine whether an obtained *t* value between two sample means is statistically significant at a specified alpha level.

Trimmed mean: A sample mean with the extreme values omitted at the tails of a sample distribution of data.

Type I error: The rejection of the null hypothesis of no difference in population parameters when it is true, that is, the probability that a null hypothesis would be rejected in favor of an alternative hypothesis. The probability is set by selection of an alpha level (see **Alpha level**). If the alpha level is set at .05, then 5% of the time a true null hypothesis would be incorrectly rejected in favor of the alternative hypothesis. The symbol α is used to refer to this type of error.

Type II error: The retention of a null hypothesis of no difference in population parameters when it is false, that is, the probability that we failed to reject the null hypothesis in favor of an alternative hypothesis. The symbol β is used to refer to this type of error.

Uniform distribution: A rectangular distribution of scores that are evenly distributed in the range of possible values.

Unimodal distribution: A symmetrical distribution with a single mode.

Variance: A positive value that measures how scores vary around a group mean. If all scores are the same, then the variance is 0. It is calculated as the sum of squared deviations around the group mean divided by the number of scores.

z **score:** A frequency distribution of raw scores that have been standardized to a mean of 0 and a standard deviation of 1. Sometimes called a standard score, a *z* score indicates the direction and degree to which a score deviates from the mean of a distribution of scores.

z **test:** A statistical test for the significant difference in independent or dependent population proportions.

GLOSSARY OF R PACKAGES, FUNCTIONS, AND COMMANDS USED IN THE BOOK

`=`	Assigns objects
`?`	Helps with R function when known
`#`	Used to insert comments in R programs
`$`	Used to extract a value from function results
`+, - , *, /`	Basic math operations of add, subtract, multiply, and divide
`^`	Basic math operation to designate exponential power
`~`	Tilde used in regression equations
`X1*X2`	Designates interaction and all effects in a regression equation
`/n`	Inserts line break when printing output
`1 - pchisq`	Function returns p value for the chi-square statistic
`abline`	Adds a straight line in plots for two variables in a linear regression
`AIC`	Function for Akaike Information Criteria and Bayesian Information Criteria
`anova`	Outputs the ANOVA (analysis of variance) table; compares ANOVA models
`aod`	Package for logistic regression
`aov`	Analysis of variance to compare mean differences
`as.data.frame`	Function to convert contingency table format to data frame
`as.numeric`	Function to convert variables to numeric format
`attach`	Activates a data set in the workspace environment
`barplot`	Graphs data values in vertical bars
`biserial.cor`	Function to compute the point-biserial/biserial correlation
`boot`	Package for nonparametric bootstrap estimates
`boot.ci`	Function for computing bootstrap confidence intervals
`bootstrap`	Package for parametric bootstrap estimates

C	Symbol to combine or concatenate variables, labels, etc.
cbind	Combines columns of data or text
chisq.test	Computes the chi-square statistic
coef	Regression function that returns regression coefficients
compute.es	Meta-analysis package; other packages are in library(MAd)
confint	Function for confidence intervals
contr.helmert	Contrast coding for Scheffe-type complex contrasts
contr.sum	Contrast coding groups using 0, 1, −1
contr.treatment	Contrast coding using dummy-coded vectors
contrast	Function for dummy and contrast coding in regression
cor	Correlation/covariance matrix of several variables
cor.test	Correlation test between pairs of variables
crossval	Cross-validation function; in library(bootstrap)
curve	Draws a curved line in a plot
cv.lars	Function for cross-validation; in library(lars)
Cvlm	Cross-validation function; in library(DAAG)
data	Function to acquire a data set in R
data.entry	To view data in spreadsheet format
data.frame	Combines data vectors into a data set with variable names
dbinom	Probability density function of binomial distribution; in library(Normal)
dchisq	Probability density function of chi-square; in library(Chisquare)
describe	Summary statistics for a sample of data; uses library(psych)
describe.by	Summary statistics by group; uses library(psych)
detach	Removes the data set from the active work environment
dexp	Probability density function of exponential distribution
df	Probability density function of F values; in library(Fdist)
digits	Controls the number of digits to display
dim	Number of rows and columns in a matrix or data frame
dimnames	Adds variable names to rows and columns in a matrix
dnorm	Probability density function of normal distribution
dotchart	Graph with dots for data values
dt	Probability density function of t values; in library(TDist)
dunif	Probability density function of uniform distribution
edit	To view data in R Data Editor
factor	Function that defines groups in analysis of variance
FALSE	Argument that omits value in a function
file.choose	Function that opens a search window to locate data files

fitted	Regression function that outputs predicted *Y* values
fitted.values	Plots the predicted *Y* values in a plot
fix	Shows the R source code of a function
for	Repeats the sequence of commands; loop operations
foreign	Package that allows data to be read and written to other statistical packages
function	Set of commands and arguments defined as a function
getHdata	Codebook from URL for a data set; library(Hmisc)
getwd	Function to indicate a working directory on a computer to locate a data file
ggplot	Graphics package
glm	Function for running a logistic regression
head	Function to print out the first few lines of data (default = six observations)
help	Describes a function when the function name is known
help.start	Manuals, references, and materials in R
hist	Histogram graph for a variable
Hmisc	Data sets available in R
I()	Identity function for quadratic terms in a regression
ifelse	Function for selecting or recoding variable values or selecting subjects
influence	Regression function that shows residual values, leverage, etc.
install.package	Loads packages from the web, CRAN onto a computer
is.na	Indicates if a data vector has missing values
jack	Function to compute jackknife estimates from jackknife means
jackknife	Jackknife function for single-observation influence; in library(boot)
leaps	Library for all possible variable subset selection in multiple regression
legend	Function to list line types in a graph
length	Number of values in a variable
library	Set of packages that can be loaded into an active environment
lines	Draws linear and curved lines in a plot; more flexible than *abline* function
list	Lists values in a data vector or matrix
lm	Linear regression model
lme	Linear mixed regression model; in library(nlme)
lmer	Linear generalized mixed model
logLik	Function for computing a log-likelihood value in logistic regression
loglm	Function for log-linear regression; computes chi-square and log-likelihood statistics; MASS package
ls	Lists all active variables in the work environment
ltm	Package for point-biserial/biserial correlation and other correlation types
lty	Changes line type in a plot

lwd	Change line width in a plot
main	Title of a plot or figure
MAc	Package for meta-analysis with correlations
MAd	Package for meta-analysis with mean differences
make.rm	Transposes data for repeated measures; in library(fastR)
matrix	Function to put data in rows and columns
max	Maximum value in a data vector
mean	Arithmetic average of scores
median	Middle score in a set of scores
melt	Creates repeated measures data; in library(reshape)
min	Minimum value in a data vector
mosaic.plot	Graph of data frequency in cross-tabulated categories
na.rm	Removes missing values from a data set
names	Provides names to values in a data frame
nlfit	Nonlinear regression
options	Changes R environment parameters; stops scientific notation
orsk	Function to convert odds ratio to relative risk (risk ratio)
par	Function for formatting a graphic window
paste	Combines text
pbinom	Central density function of binominal distribution
pchisq	Central density function of chi-square
pcor	Partial correlation function
pcor.test	Partial correlation statistical test of significance
pes	Function to convert p values to effect size d values
pexp	Central density function of exponential distribution
pf	Central density function of F
plot	Draws a figure with y- and x-axes
pnorm	Central density function of normal distribution
poly	Computes orthogonal contrasts in regression (linear, quadratic, cubic)
polygon	Function that colors in area under graph
ppcor	Package for partial and semipartial (part) correlations
predict	Calculates predicted values from a regression model
print	Outputs results: variables, matrix, data frame
prop.test	Difference in proportions; reports the chi-square statistic
pt	Central density function for t
punif	Central density function of uniform distribution
qbinom	Quantile distribution of binomial distribution

`qchisq`	Quantile distribution of chi-square
`qf`	Quantile distribution of *F*
`qnorm`	Quantile distribution of normal distribution
`qt`	Quantile distribution of *t*
`qunif`	Quantile distribution of uniform distribution
`rbind`	Combines rows of data or text
`rbinom`	Creates binomially distributed random variables
`rchisq`	Random sample of chi-square values
`read.csv`	Reads comma-separated data files
`read.dta`	Function to read STAT data files; in library(foreign)
`read.spss`	Function to read SPSS data files; in library(foreign)
`read.systat`	Function to read SYSTAT data files; in library(foreign)
`read.table`	Reads data in text format from a computer or the web
`rep`	Repeats a value or set of values a specific number of times
`rexp`	Random samples from exponential distribution
`rf`	Random sample of *F* values
`rho`	Function to compute Spearman correlation
`rm`	Removes variables from the work environment
`rnorm`	Random samples from normal distribution
`round`	Rounds up a data value to a certain number of decimal places
`rt`	Random sample of *t* values
`runif`	Random samples from uniform distribution
`sasxport.get`	Function to read SAS transport data files; in library(Hmisc)
`scale`	Creates standardized variables (mean = 0; standard deviation = 1)
`sd`	Standard deviation for a set of scores
`sep`	Option in *paste* command to designate what separates text
`set.seed`	Seed number for random number generation and to obtain the same results
`setwd`	Changes working directory to a new path
`sort`	Sorts variables in a data set, in ascending or descending order
`source`	Loads functions from a website
`spcor`	Part or semipartial correlation function
`split`	Randomly splits data for cross-validation
`spss.get`	Function to read SPSS data sets; in library(Hmisc)
`stat.desc`	Summary of data; uses library(pastecs)
`stats::(name)`	Shows the R source code of a function (name)
`stem`	Creates a stem-and-leaf plot of data values

`sqrt`	Square root in statistical expression
`str`	Function that reveals the structure of a data frame
`subset`	Function to extract subtables in cross-tabulated contingency tables
`sum`	Sum of numbers in a data set
`summary`	Reports summary output from statistical functions
`t.test`	Computes the *t*-test mean difference between two groups (independent, dependent)
`table`	Creates a contingency table with cell counts or frequency values
`tapply`	Calculate statistics for variables in different groups
`tes`	Function to convert *t*-test value to effect size *d* value
`TRUE`	Argument that includes value in a function
`TukeyHSD`	Function that performs multiple comparisons of mean differences
`update`	Function to subtract predictor variables in a log-linear equation
`utils`	Package of utility functions
`vcov`	Function for variance–covariance matrix
`wald.test`	Function for statistical significance of regression coefficients; library(aod)
`which.max`	Returns mode in a data set with frequency of value
`wideToLong`	Function to transpose data sets
`write.dta`	Writes out data to a STATA file format
`write.foreign`	Writes out data to a file in another statistics package
`write.table`	Writes data to a file
`xlab`	Label for *x*-axis
`xtabs`	Creates a contingency table with cell counts or frequency values
`yhat`	Package for structure coefficient, commonality analysis, and all possible subset and related multiple regression predictor variable selection criteria
`ylab`	Label for *y*-axis

SOURCE: The R functions for running many of these analyses can be found in the book chapters and are available at the following website: http://www.sage.com/schumacker.

APPENDIX A: STATISTICAL TABLES

Table 1. Areas Under the Normal Curve (z Scores)

z	.00	.01	.02	.03	.04	.05	.06	.07	.08	.09
					Second Decimal Place in z					
.0	.0000	.0040	.0080	.0120	.0160	.0199	.0239	.0279	.0319	.0359
.1	.0398	.0438	.0478	.0517	.0557	.0596	.0636	.0675	.0714	.0753
.2	.0793	.0832	.0871	.0910	.0948	.0987	.1026	.1064	.1103	.1141
.3	.1179	.1217	.1255	.1293	.1331	.1368	.1406	.1443	.1480	.1517
.4	.1554	.1591	.1628	.1664	.1700	.1736	.1772	.1808	.1844	.1879
.5	.1915	.1950	.1985	.2019	.2054	.2088	.2123	.2157	.2190	.2224
.6	.2257	.2291	.2324	.2357	.2389	.2422	.2454	.2486	.2517	.2549
.7	.2580	.2611	.2642	.2673	.2704	.2734	.2764	.2794	.2823	.2852
.8	.2881	.2910	.2939	.2967	.2995	.3023	.3051	.3078	.3106	.3133
.9	.3159	.3186	.3212	.3238	.3264	.3289	.3315	.3340	.3365	.3389
1.0	.3413	.3438	.3461	.3485	.3508	.3531	.3554	.3577	.3599	.3621
1.1	.3643	.3665	.3686	.3708	.3729	.3749	.3770	.3790	.3810	.3830
1.2	.3849	.3869	.3888	.3907	.3925	.3944	.3962	.3980	.3997	.4015
1.3	.4032	.4049	.4066	.4082	.4099	.4115	.4131	.4147	.4162	.4177
1.4	.4192	.4207	.4222	.4236	.4251	.4265	.4279	.4292	.4306	.4319
1.5	.4332	.4345	.4357	.4370	.4382	.4394	.4406	.4418	.4429	.4441
1.6	.4452	.4463	.4474	.4484	.4495	.4505	.4515	.4525	.4535	.4545
1.7	.4554	.4564	.4573	.4582	.4591	.4599	.4608	.4616	.4625	.4633
1.8	.4641	.4649	.4656	.4664	.4671	.4678	.4686	.4693	.4699	.4706
1.9	.4713	.4719	.4726	.4732	.4738	.4744	.4750	.4756	.4761	.4767
2.0	.4772	.4778	.4783	.4788	.4793	.4798	.4803	.4808	.4812	.4817
2.1	.4821	.4826	.4830	.4834	.4838	.4842	.4846	.4850	.4854	.4857
2.2	.4861	.4864	.4868	.4871	.4875	.4878	.4881	.4884	.4887	.4890
2.3	.4893	.4896	.4898	.4901	.4904	.4906	.4909	.4911	.4913	.4916
2.4	.4918	.4920	.4922	.4925	.4927	.4929	.4931	.4932	.4934	.4936
2.5	.4938	.4940	.4941	.4943	.4945	.4946	.4948	.4949	.4951	.4952
2.6	.4953	.4955	.4956	.4957	.4959	.4960	.4961	.4962	.4963	.4964
2.7	.4965	.4966	.4967	.4968	.4969	.4970	.4971	.4972	.4973	.4974
2.8	.4974	.4975	.4976	.4977	.4977	.4978	.4979	.4979	.4980	.4981
2.9	.4981	.4982	.4982	.4983	.4984	.4984	.4985	.4985	.4986	.4986
3.0	.4987	.4987	.4987	.4988	.4988	.4989	.4989	.4989	.4990	.4990
3.1	.4990	.4991	.4991	.4991	.4992	.4992	.4992	.4992	.4993	.4993
3.2	.4993	.4993	.4994	.4994	.4994	.4994	.4994	.4995	.4995	.4995
3.3	.4995	.4995	.4995	.4996	.4996	.4996	.4996	.4996	.4996	.4997
3.4	.4997	.4997	.4997	.4997	.4997	.4997	.4997	.4997	.4997	.4998
3.5	.4998									
4.0	.49997									
4.5	.499997									
5.0	.4999997									

Table 2.   Distribution of *t* for Given Probability Levels

df	Level of significance for one-tailed test					
	.10	.05	.025	.01	.005	.0005
	Level of significance for two-tailed test					
	.20	.10	.05	.02	.01	.001
1	3.078	6.314	12.706	31.821	63.657	636.619
2	1.886	2.920	4.303	6.965	9.925	31.598
3	1.638	2.353	3.182	4.541	5.841	12.941
4	1.533	2.132	2.776	3.747	4.604	8.610
5	1.476	2.015	2.571	3.365	4.032	6.859
6	1.440	1.943	2.447	3.143	3.707	5.959
7	1.415	1.895	2.365	2.998	3.499	5.405
8	1.397	1.860	2.306	2.896	3.355	5.041
9	1.383	1.833	2.262	2.821	3.250	4.781
10	1.372	1.812	2.228	2.764	3.169	4.587
11	1.363	1.796	2.201	2.718	3.106	4.437
12	1.356	1.782	2.179	2.681	3.055	4.318
13	1.350	1.771	2.160	2.650	3.012	4.221
14	1.345	1.761	2.145	2.624	2.977	4.140
15	1.341	1.753	2.131	2.602	2.947	4.073
16	1.337	1.746	2.120	2.583	2.921	4.015
17	1.333	1.740	2.110	2.567	2.898	3.965
18	1.330	1.734	2.101	2.552	2.878	3.992
19	1.328	1.729	2.093	2.539	2.861	3.883
20	1.325	1.725	2.086	2.528	2.845	3.850
21	1.323	1.721	2.080	2.518	2.831	3.819
22	1.321	1.717	2.074	2.508	2.819	3.792
23	1.319	1.714	2.069	2.500	2.807	3.767
24	1.318	1.711	2.064	2.492	2.797	3.745
25	1.316	1.708	2.060	2.485	2.787	3.725
26	1.315	1.706	2.056	2.479	2.779	3.707
27	1.314	1.703	2.052	2.473	2.771	3.690
28	1.313	1.701	2.048	2.467	2.763	3.674
29	1.311	1.699	2.045	2.462	2.756	3.659
30	1.310	1.697	2.042	2.457	2.750	3.646
40	1.303	1.684	2.021	2.423	2.704	3.551
60	1.296	1.671	2.000	2.390	2.660	3.460
120	1.289	1.658	1.980	2.358	2.617	3.373
∞	1.282	1.645	1.960	2.326	2.576	3.291

Table 3. Distribution of *r* for Given Probability Levels

	Level of significance for one-tailed test			
	.05	.025	.01	.005
	Level of significance for two-tailed test			
df	.10	.05	.02	.01
1	.988	.997	.9995	.9999
2	.900	.950	.980	.990
3	.805	.878	.934	.959
4	.729	.811	.882	.917
5	.669	.754	.833	.874
6	.622	.707	.789	.834
7	.582	.666	.750	.798
8	.540	.632	.716	.765
9	.521	.602	.685	.735
10	.497	.576	.658	.708
11	.576	.553	.634	.684
12	.458	.532	.612	.661
13	.441	.514	.592	.641
14	.426	.497	.574	.623
15	.412	.482	.558	.606
16	.400	.468	.542	.590
17	.389	.456	.528	.575
18	.378	.444	.516	.561
19	.369	.433	.503	.549
20	.360	.423	.492	.537
21	.352	.413	.482	.526
22	.344	.404	.472	.515
23	.337	.396	.462	.505
24	.330	.388	.453	.496
25	.323	.381	.445	.487
26	.317	.374	.437	.479
27	.311	.367	.430	.471
28	.306	.361	.423	.463
29	.301	.355	.416	.486
30	.296	.349	.409	.449
35	.275	.325	.381	.418
40	.257	.304	.358	.393
45	.243	.288	.338	.372
50	.231	.273	.322	.354
60	.211	.250	.295	.325
70	.195	.232	.274	.303
80	.183	.217	.256	.283
90	.173	.205	.242	.267
100	.164	.195	.230	.254

Table 4. Distribution of Chi-Square for Given Probability Levels

df	Probability													
	.99	.98	.95	.90	.80	.70	.50	.30	.20	.10	.05	.02	.01	.001
1	0.00016	0.00663	0.00393	0.0158	0.0642	0.148	0.455	1.074	1.642	2.706	3.841	5.412	6.635	10.827
2	0.0201	0.0404	0.103	0.211	0.446	0.713	1.386	2.408	3.219	4.605	5.991	7.824	9.210	13.815
3	0.115	0.185	0.352	0.584	1.005	1.424	2.366	3.665	4.642	6.251	7.815	9.837	11.345	16.266
4	0.297	0.429	0.711	1.064	1.649	2.195	3.357	4.878	5.989	7.779	9.488	11.668	13.277	18.467
5	0.554	0.752	1.145	1.610	2.343	3.000	4.351	6.064	7.289	9.236	11.070	13.388	15.086	20.515
6	0.872	1.134	1.635	2.204	3.070	3.828	5.348	7.231	8.558	10.645	12.592	15.033	16.812	22.457
7	1.239	1.564	2.167	2.833	3.822	4.671	6.346	8.383	9.803	12.017	14.067	16.622	18.475	24.322
8	1.646	2.032	2.733	3.490	4.594	5.527	7.344	9.524	11.030	13.362	15.507	18.168	20.090	26.125
9	2.088	2.532	3.325	4.168	5.380	6.393	8.343	10.656	12.242	14.684	16.919	19.679	21.666	27.877
10	2.558	3.059	3.940	4.865	6.179	7.267	9.342	11.781	13.442	15.987	18.307	21.161	23.209	29.588
11	3.053	3.609	4.575	5.578	6.989	8.148	10.341	12.899	14.631	17.275	19.675	22.618	24.725	31.264
12	3.571	4.178	5.226	6.304	7.807	9.034	11.340	14.011	15.812	18.549	21.026	24.054	26.217	32.909
13	4.107	4.765	5.892	7.042	8.634	9.926	12.340	15.119	16.985	19.812	22.362	25.472	27.688	34.528
14	4.660	5.368	6.571	7.790	9.467	10.821	13.339	16.222	18.151	21.064	23.685	26.873	29.141	36.123
15	5.229	5.985	7.261	8.547	10.307	11.721	14.339	17.322	19.311	22.307	24.996	28.259	30.578	37.697
16	5.812	6.614	7.962	9.312	11.152	12.624	15.338	18.418	20.465	23.542	26.296	29.633	32.000	39.252
17	6.408	7.255	8.672	10.085	12.002	13.531	16.338	19.511	21.615	24.769	27.587	30.995	33.409	40.790
18	7.015	7.906	9.390	10.865	12.857	14.440	17.338	20.601	22.760	25.989	28.869	32.346	34.805	42.312
19	7.633	8.567	10.117	11.651	13.716	15.352	18.338	21.689	23.900	27.204	30.144	33.687	36.191	43.820
20	8.260	9.237	10.851	12.443	14.578	16.266	19.337	22.775	25.038	28.412	31.410	35.020	37.566	45.315
21	8.897	9.915	11.591	13.240	15.445	17.182	20.337	23.858	26.171	29.615	32.671	36.343	38.932	46.797
22	9.542	10.600	12.338	14.041	16.314	18.101	21.337	24.939	27.301	30.813	33.924	37.659	40.289	48.268

(Continued)

Table 4. Distribution of Chi-Square for Given Probability Levels (Continued)

	Probability													
df	.99	.98	.95	.90	.80	.70	.50	.30	.20	.10	.05	.02	.01	.001
23	10.196	11.293	13.091	14.848	17.187	19.021	22.337	26.018	28.429	32.007	35.172	38.968	41.638	49.728
24	10.856	11.992	13.848	15.659	18.062	19.943	23.337	27.096	29.553	33.196	36.415	40.270	42.980	51.179
25	11.524	12.697	14.611	16.473	18.940	20.867	24.337	28.172	30.675	34.382	37.652	41.566	44.314	52.620
26	12.198	13.409	15.379	17.292	19.820	21.792	25.336	29.246	31.795	35.563	38.885	42.856	45.642	54.052
27	12.879	14.125	16.151	18.114	20.703	22.719	26.336	30.319	32.912	36.741	40.113	44.140	46.963	55.476
28	13.565	14.847	16.928	18.939	21.588	23.647	27.336	31.391	34.027	37.916	41.337	45.419	48.278	56.893
29	14.256	15.574	17.708	19.768	22.475	24.577	28.336	32.461	35.139	39.087	42.557	46.693	49.588	58.302
30	14.953	16.306	18.493	20.599	23.364	25.508	29.336	33.530	36.250	40.256	43.773	47.962	50.892	59.703
32	16.362	17.783	20.072	22.271	25.148	27.373	31.336	35.665	38.466	42.585	46.194	50.487	53.486	62.487
34	17.789	19.275	21.664	23.952	26.938	29.242	33.336	37.795	40.676	44.903	48.602	52.995	56.061	65.247
36	19.233	20.783	23.269	25.643	28.735	31.115	35.336	39.922	42.879	47.212	50.999	55.489	58.619	67.985
38	20.691	22.304	24.884	27.343	30.537	32.992	37.335	42.045	45.076	49.513	53.384	57.969	61.162	70.703
40	22.164	23.838	26.509	29.051	32.345	34.872	39.335	44.165	47.269	51.805	55.759	60.436	63.691	73.402
42	23.650	25.383	28.144	30.765	34.147	36.755	41.335	46.282	49.456	54.090	58.124	62.892	66.206	76.084
44	25.148	26.939	29.787	32.487	35.974	38.641	43.335	48.396	51.639	56.369	60.481	65.337	68.710	78.750
46	26.657	28.504	31.439	34.215	37.795	40.529	45.335	50.507	53.818	58.641	62.830	67.771	71.201	81.400
48	28.177	30.080	33.098	35.949	39.621	42.420	47.335	52.616	55.993	60.907	65.171	70.197	73.683	84.037
50	29.707	31.664	34.764	37.689	41.449	44.313	49.335	54.723	58.164	63.167	67.505	72.613	76.154	86.661
52	31.246	33.256	36.437	39.433	43.281	46.209	51.335	56.827	60.332	65.422	69.832	75.021	78.616	89.272
54	32.793	34.856	38.116	41.183	45.117	48.106	53.335	58.930	62.496	67.673	72.153	77.422	81.069	91.872
56	34.350	36.464	39.801	42.937	46.955	50.005	55.335	61.031	64.658	69.919	74.468	79.815	83.513	94.461
58	35.913	38.078	41.492	44.696	48.797	51.906	57.335	63.129	66.816	72.160	76.778	82.201	85.950	97.039
60	37.485	39.699	43.188	46.459	50.641	53.809	59.335	65.227	68.972	74.397	79.082	84.580	88.379	99.607
62	39.063	41.327	44.889	48.226	52.487	55.714	61.335	67.322	71.125	76.630	81.381	86.953	90.802	102.166
64	40.649	42.960	46.595	49.996	54.336	57.620	63.335	69.416	73.276	78.860	83.675	89.320	93.217	104.716
66	42.240	44.599	48.305	51.770	56.188	59.527	65.335	71.508	75.424	81.085	85.965	91.681	95.626	107.258
68	43.838	46.244	50.020	53.548	58.042	61.436	67.335	73.600	77.571	83.308	88.250	94.037	98.028	109.791
70	45.442	47.893	51.739	55.329	59.898	63.346	69.335	75.689	79.715	85.527	90.531	96.388	100.425	112.317

NOTE: For larger values of *df*, the expression $\sqrt{(\chi^2)^2} - \sqrt{2df} - 1$ may be used as a normal deviate with unit variance, remembering that the probability for chi-square corresponds with that of a single tail of the normal curve.

Table 5. Distribution of F for a Given Probability Level (.05)

df_2	\multicolumn{19}{c}{df_1}
	1	2	3	4	5	6	7	8	9	10	12	15	20	24	30	40	60	120	∞
1	161.4	199.5	215.7	224.6	230.2	234.0	236.8	238.9	240.5	241.9	243.9	245.9	248.0	249.1	250.1	251.1	252.2	253.3	254.3
2	18.51	19.00	19.16	19.25	19.30	19.33	19.35	19.37	19.38	19.41	19.41	19.43	19.45	19.45	19.46	19.47	19.48	19.49	19.50
3	10.13	9.55	9.28	9.12	9.01	8.94	8.89	8.85	8.81	8.79	8.74	8.70	8.66	8.64	8.62	8.59	8.57	8.55	8.53
4	7.71	6.94	6.59	6.39	6.26	6.15	6.09	6.04	6.00	5.96	5.91	5.86	5.80	5.77	5.75	5.72	5.69	5.66	5.63
5	6.61	5.79	5.41	5.19	5.05	4.95	4.88	4.82	4.77	4.74	4.68	4.62	4.56	4.53	4.50	4.46	4.43	4.40	4.36
6	5.99	5.14	4.76	4.53	4.39	4.28	4.21	4.15	4.10	4.06	4.00	3.94	3.87	3.84	3.81	3.77	3.74	3.70	3.67
7	5.59	4.74	4.35	4.12	3.97	3.87	3.79	3.73	3.68	3.64	3.57	3.51	3.44	3.41	3.38	3.34	3.30	3.27	3.23
8	5.32	4.46	4.07	3.84	3.69	3.58	3.50	3.44	3.39	3.35	3.28	3.22	3.15	3.12	3.08	3.04	3.01	2.97	2.93
9	5.12	4.26	3.86	3.63	3.48	3.37	3.29	3.23	3.18	3.14	3.07	3.01	2.94	2.90	2.86	2.83	2.79	2.75	2.71
10	4.96	4.10	3.71	3.48	3.33	3.22	3.14	3.07	3.02	2.98	2.91	2.85	2.77	2.74	2.70	2.66	2.62	2.58	2.54
11	4.84	3.98	3.59	3.36	3.20	3.09	3.01	2.95	2.90	2.85	2.79	2.72	2.65	2.61	2.57	2.53	2.49	2.45	2.40
12	4.75	3.89	3.49	3.26	3.11	3.00	2.91	2.85	2.80	2.75	2.69	2.62	2.54	2.51	2.47	2.43	2.38	2.34	2.30
13	4.67	3.81	3.41	3.18	3.03	2.92	2.83	2.77	2.71	2.67	2.60	2.53	2.46	2.42	2.38	2.34	2.30	2.25	2.21
14	4.60	3.74	3.34	3.11	2.96	2.85	2.76	2.70	2.65	2.60	2.53	2.46	2.39	2.35	2.31	2.27	2.22	2.18	2.13
15	4.54	3.68	3.29	3.06	2.90	2.79	2.71	2.64	2.59	2.54	2.48	2.40	2.33	2.29	2.25	2.20	2.16	2.11	2.07
16	4.49	3.63	3.24	3.01	2.85	2.74	2.66	2.59	2.54	2.49	2.42	2.35	2.28	2.24	2.19	2.15	2.11	2.06	2.01
17	4.45	3.59	3.20	2.96	2.81	2.70	2.61	2.55	2.49	2.45	2.38	2.31	2.23	2.19	2.15	2.10	2.06	2.01	1.96
18	4.41	3.55	3.16	2.93	2.77	2.66	2.58	2.51	2.46	2.41	2.34	2.27	2.19	2.15	2.11	2.06	2.02	1.97	1.92
19	4.38	3.52	3.13	2.90	2.74	2.63	2.54	2.48	2.42	2.38	2.31	2.23	2.16	2.11	2.07	2.03	1.98	1.93	1.88
20	4.35	3.49	3.10	2.87	2.71	2.60	2.51	2.45	2.39	2.35	2.28	2.20	2.12	2.08	2.04	1.99	1.95	1.90	1.84
21	4.32	3.47	3.07	2.84	2.68	2.57	2.49	2.42	2.37	2.32	2.25	2.18	2.10	2.05	2.01	1.96	1.92	1.87	1.81
22	4.30	3.44	3.05	2.82	2.66	2.55	2.46	2.40	2.34	2.30	2.23	2.15	2.07	2.03	1.98	1.94	1.89	1.84	1.78
23	4.28	3.42	3.03	2.80	2.64	2.53	2.44	2.37	2.32	2.27	2.20	2.13	2.05	2.01	1.96	1.91	1.86	1.81	1.76
24	4.26	3.40	3.01	2.78	2.62	2.51	2.42	2.36	2.30	2.25	2.18	2.11	2.03	1.98	1.94	1.89	1.84	1.79	1.73
25	4.24	3.39	2.99	2.76	2.60	2.49	2.40	2.34	2.28	2.24	2.16	2.09	2.01	1.96	1.92	1.87	1.82	1.77	1.71
26	4.23	3.37	2.98	2.74	2.59	2.47	2.39	2.32	2.27	2.22	2.15	2.07	1.99	1.95	1.90	1.85	1.80	1.75	1.69
27	4.21	3.35	2.96	2.73	2.57	2.46	2.37	2.31	2.25	2.20	2.13	2.06	1.97	1.93	1.88	1.84	1.79	1.73	1.67
28	4.20	3.34	2.95	2.71	2.56	2.45	2.36	2.29	2.24	2.19	2.12	2.04	1.96	1.91	1.87	1.82	1.77	1.71	1.65
29	4.18	3.33	2.93	2.70	2.55	2.43	2.35	2.28	2.22	2.18	2.10	2.03	1.94	1.90	1.85	1.81	1.75	1.70	1.64
30	4.17	3.32	2.92	2.69	2.53	2.42	2.33	2.27	2.21	2.16	2.09	2.01	1.93	1.89	1.84	1.79	1.74	1.68	1.62
40	4.08	3.23	2.84	2.61	2.45	2.34	2.25	2.18	2.12	2.08	2.00	1.92	1.84	1.79	1.74	1.69	1.64	1.58	1.51
60	4.00	3.15	2.76	2.53	2.37	2.25	2.17	2.10	2.04	1.99	1.92	1.84	1.75	1.70	1.65	1.59	1.53	1.47	1.39
120	3.92	3.07	2.68	2.45	2.29	2.17	2.09	2.02	1.96	1.91	1.83	1.75	1.66	1.61	1.55	1.50	1.43	1.35	1.25
∞	3.84	3.00	2.60	2.37	2.21	2.10	2.01	1.94	1.88	1.83	1.75	1.67	1.57	1.52	1.46	1.39	1.32	1.22	1.00

Table 6. Distribution of *F* for a Given Probability Level (.01)

df_2 \ df_1	1	2	3	4	5	6	7	8	9	10	12	15	20	24	30	40	60	120	∞
1	4052	4999.5	5403	5625	5764	5859	5928	5982	6022	6056	6106	6157	6209	6235	6261	6287	6313	6339	6366
2	98.5	99.00	99.17	99.25	99.30	99.33	99.36	99.37	99.39	99.40	99.42	99.43	99.45	99.46	99.47	99.47	99.48	99.49	99.50
3	34.12	30.82	29.46	28.71	28.24	27.91	27.67	27.49	27.25	27.23	27.05	26.87	26.69	26.60	26.50	26.41	26.32	26.22	26.13
4	21.20	18.00	16.69	15.98	15.52	15.21	14.98	14.80	14.66	14.55	14.37	14.20	14.02	13.93	13.84	13.75	13.65	13.56	13.46
5	16.26	13.27	12.06	11.39	10.97	10.67	10.46	10.29	10.16	10.05	9.89	9.72	9.55	9.47	9.38	9.29	9.20	9.11	9.02
6	13.75	10.92	9.78	9.15	8.75	8.47	8.26	8.10	7.98	7.87	7.72	7.56	7.40	7.31	7.23	7.14	7.06	6.97	6.88
7	12.25	9.55	8.45	7.85	7.46	7.19	6.99	6.84	6.72	6.62	6.47	6.31	6.16	6.07	5.99	5.91	5.82	5.74	5.65
8	11.26	8.65	7.59	7.01	6.63	6.37	6.18	6.03	5.91	5.81	5.67	5.52	5.36	5.28	5.20	5.12	5.03	4.95	4.86
9	10.56	8.02	6.99	6.42	6.06	5.80	5.61	5.47	5.35	5.26	5.11	4.96	4.81	4.73	4.65	4.57	4.48	4.40	4.31
10	10.04	7.56	6.55	5.99	5.64	5.39	5.20	5.06	4.94	4.85	4.71	4.56	4.41	4.33	4.25	4.17	4.08	4.00	3.91
11	9.65	7.21	6.22	5.67	5.32	5.07	4.89	4.74	4.63	4.54	4.40	4.25	4.10	4.02	3.94	3.86	3.78	3.69	3.60
12	9.33	6.93	5.95	5.41	5.06	4.82	4.64	4.50	4.39	4.30	4.16	4.01	3.86	3.78	3.70	3.62	3.54	3.45	3.36
13	9.07	6.70	5.74	5.21	4.86	4.62	4.44	4.30	4.19	4.10	3.96	3.82	3.66	3.59	3.51	3.43	3.34	3.25	3.17
14	8.86	6.51	5.56	5.04	4.69	4.46	4.28	4.14	4.03	3.94	3.80	3.66	3.51	3.43	3.35	3.27	3.18	3.09	3.00
15	8.68	6.36	5.42	4.89	4.56	4.32	4.14	4.00	3.89	3.80	3.67	3.52	3.37	3.29	3.21	3.13	3.05	2.96	2.87
16	8.53	6.23	5.29	4.77	4.44	4.20	4.03	3.89	3.78	3.69	3.55	3.41	3.26	3.18	3.10	3.02	2.93	2.84	2.75
17	8.40	6.11	5.18	4.67	4.34	4.10	3.93	3.79	3.68	3.59	3.46	3.31	3.16	3.08	3.00	2.92	2.83	2.75	2.65
18	8.29	6.01	5.09	4.58	4.25	4.01	3.84	3.71	3.60	3.51	3.37	3.23	3.08	3.00	2.92	2.84	2.75	2.66	2.57
19	8.18	5.93	5.01	4.50	4.17	3.94	3.77	3.63	3.52	3.43	3.30	3.15	3.00	2.92	2.84	2.76	2.67	2.58	2.49
20	8.10	5.85	4.94	4.43	4.10	3.87	3.70	3.56	3.46	3.37	3.23	3.09	2.94	2.86	2.78	2.69	2.61	2.52	2.42
21	8.02	5.78	4.87	4.37	4.04	3.81	3.64	3.51	3.40	3.31	3.17	3.03	2.88	2.80	2.72	2.64	2.55	2.46	2.36
22	7.95	5.72	4.82	4.31	3.9	3.76	3.59	3.45	3.35	3.26	3.12	2.98	2.83	2.75	2.67	2.58	2.50	2.40	2.31
23	7.88	5.66	4.76	4.26	3.94	3.71	3.54	3.41	3.30	3.21	3.07	2.93	2.78	2.70	2.62	2.54	2.45	2.35	2.26
24	7.82	5.61	4.72	4.22	3.90	3.67	3.50	3.36	3.26	3.17	3.03	2.89	2.74	2.66	2.58	2.49	2.40	2.31	2.21
25	7.77	5.57	4.68	4.18	3.85	3.63	3.46	3.32	3.22	3.13	2.99	2.85	2.70	2.62	2.54	2.45	2.36	2.27	2.17
26	7.72	5.53	4.64	4.14	3.82	3.59	3.42	3.29	3.18	3.09	2.96	2.81	2.66	2.58	2.50	2.42	2.33	2.23	2.13
27	7.68	5.49	4.60	4.11	3.78	3.56	3.39	3.26	3.15	3.06	2.93	2.78	2.63	2.55	2.47	2.38	2.29	2.20	2.10
28	7.64	5.45	4.57	4.07	3.75	3.53	3.36	3.23	3.12	3.03	2.90	2.75	2.60	2.52	2.44	2.35	2.26	2.17	2.06
29	7.60	5.42	4.54	4.04	3.73	3.50	3.33	3.20	3.09	3.00	2.87	2.73	2.57	2.49	2.41	2.33	2.23	2.14	2.03
30	7.56	5.39	4.51	4.02	3.70	3.47	3.30	3.17	3.07	2.98	2.84	2.70	2.55	2.47	2.39	2.30	2.21	2.11	2.01
40	7.31	5.18	4.31	3.83	3.51	3.29	3.12	2.99	2.89	2.80	2.66	2.52	2.37	2.29	2.20	2.11	2.02	1.92	1.80
60	7.08	4.98	4.13	36.5	3.34	3.12	2.95	2.82	2.72	2.63	2.50	2.35	2.20	2.12	2.03	1.94	1.84	1.73	1.60
120	6.85	4.79	3.95	3.48	3.17	2.96	2.79	2.66	2.56	2.47	2.34	2.19	2.03	1.95	1.86	1.76	1.66	1.53	1.38
∞	6.63	4.61	3.78	3.32	3.02	2.80	2.64	2.51	2.41	2.32	2.18	2.04	1.88	1.79	1.70	1.59	1.47	1.32	1.00

Table 7. Distribution of Hartley's *F* for Given Probability Levels

df = n − 1	a	2	3	4	5	6	7	8	9	10	11	12
							k = Number of Variances					
4	.05	9.60	15.5	20.6	25.2	29.5	33.6	37.5	41.4	44.6	48.0	51.4
	.01	23.2	37.0	49.0	59.0	69.0	79.0	89.0	97.0	106.0	113.0	120.0
5	.05	7.15	10.8	13.7	16.3	18.7	20.8	22.9	24.7	26.5	28.2	29.9
	.01	14.9	22.0	28.0	33.0	38.0	42.0	46.0	50.0	54.0	57.0	60.0
6	.05	5.82	8.38	10.4	12.1	13.7	15.	16.3	17.5	18.6	19.7	20.7
	.01	11.1	15.5	19.1	22.0	25.0	27.0	30.0	32.0	34.0	36.0	37.0
7	.05	4.99	6.94	8.44	9.70	10.8	11.8	12.7	13.5	14.3	12.2	15.8
	.01	8.89	12.1	14.5	16.5	18.4	20.0	22.0	23.0	24.0	19.8	27.0
8	.05	4.43	6.00	7.18	8.12	9.03	9.78	10.5	11.1	11.7	10.3	12.7
	.01	7.50	9.9	11.7	13.2	14.5	15.8	16.9	17.9	18.9	16.0	21.
9	.05	4.03	5.34	6.31	7.11	7.80	8.41	8.95	9.45	9.91	9.01	10.7
	.01	6.54	8.5	9.9	11.1	12.1	13.1	13.9	14.7	15.3	13.4	16.6
10	.05	3.72	4.85	5.67	6.34	6.92	7.42	7.87	8.28	8.66	9.01	9.34
	.01	5.85	7.4	8.6	9.6	10.4	11.1	11.8	12.4	12.9	13.4	13.9
12	.05	3.28	4.16	4.79	5.30	5.72	6.09	6.42	6.72	7.00	7.25	7.48
	.01	4.91	6.1	6.9	7.6	8.2	8.7	9.1	9.5	9.9	10.2	10.6
15	.05	2.86	3.54	4.01	4.37	4.68	4.95	5.19	5.40	5.59	5.77	5.93
	.01	4.07	4.9	5.5	6.0	6.4	6.7	7.1	7.3	7.5	7.8	8.0
20	.05	2.46	2.95	3.29	3.54	3.76	3.94	4.10	4.24	4.37	4.49	4.59
	.01	3.32	3.8	4.3	4.6	4.9	5.1	5.3	5.5	5.6	5.8	5.9
30	.05	2.07	2.40	2.61	2.78	2.91	3.02	3.12	3.21	3.29	3.36	3.39
	.01	2.63	3.0	3.3	3.4	3.6	3.7	3.8	3.9	4.0	4.1	4.2
60	.05	1.67	1.85	1.96	2.04	2.11	2.17	2.22	2.26	2.30	2.33	2.36
	.01	1.96	2.2	2.3	2.4	2.4	2.5	2.5	2.6	2.6	2.7	2.7
∞	.05	1.00	1.00	1.00	1.00	1.00	1.00	1.00	1.00	1.00	1.00	1.00
∞	.01	1.00	1.00	1.00	1.00	1.00	1.00	1.00	1.00	1.00	1.00	1.00

APPENDIX B:
GUIDE FOR SELECTING
A STATISTICAL TEST

A statistic is selected by a researcher based on the level of measurement of the dependent variable and the independent variables. A list of the statistics presented in the book are given in the table, where the terms *continuous, categorical, percentage,* and *frequency* relate to the type of data required. The term *continuous* indicates interval/ratio data, while the term *categorical* indicates nominal/ordinal data. The dependent variable is what is measured (test scores, weight gain, etc.), while the independent variable represents group membership variables (gender, year in school, region, etc.). The *DecisionKit* App (iPhone, iPad, iPod) provides more help in measurement, statistics, and research design selection.

Statistic	Dependent Variable	Independent Variable
Chi-square	Categorical	Categorical
z Test		
Single sample	Percentage	
Independent groups	Percentage	Categorical
Dependent (paired groups)	Percentage	Categorical
t Test		
Single sample	Continuous	
Independent groups	Continuous	Categorical
Dependent (paired groups)	Continuous	Categorical

Statistic	Dependent Variable	Independent Variable
Analysis of variance		
One way	Continuous	Categorical
Analysis of covariance	Continuous	Categorical
Fixed factor	Continuous	Categorical
Repeated measures	Continuous	Categorical—time periods
Correlation		
Phi	Categorical—nominal	Categorical—nominal
Point biserial/biserial	Categorical—nominal	Continuous
Kendall tau	Categorical—ordinal	Categorical—ordinal
Spearman	Categorical—ordinal	Categorical—ordinal
Pearson	Continuous	Continuous
Multiple regression		
Ordinary least squares	Continuous	Continuous, categorical
Logistic	Categorical	Continuous, categorical
Log-linear	Frequency	Continuous, categorical

REFERENCES

Agresti, A. (1996). *An introduction to categorical data analysis.* New York, NY: Wiley.

Agresti, A. (2007). *An introduction to categorical data analysis* (2nd ed., p. 38.). New York, NY: Wiley.

Ahrens, J. H., & Dieter, U. (1972). Computer methods for sampling from the exponential and normal distributions. *Communications of the ACM, 15,* 873–882.

American Counseling Association. (2005). *Code of ethics.* Retrieved from http://www.counseling.org/Resources/aca-code-of-ethics.pdf

Bang, J. W., Schumacker, R. E., & Schlieve, P. (1998). Random number generator validity in simulation studies: An investigation of normality. *Educational and Psychological Measurement, 58*(3), 430–450.

Bartlett, M. S. (1937). Properties of sufficiency and statistical tests. *Proceedings of the Royal Society, 160*(901), 268–282.

Bashaw, W. L., & Findley, W. G. (1967, June 29–July 1). *Symposium on general linear model approach to the analysis of experimental data in educational research,* Athens, GA (ERIC: ED026737). Washington, DC: Department of Health, Education, and Welfare, Office of Education, Bureau of Research.

Bates, D. M., & Watts, D. G. (1988). *Nonlinear regression analysis and its applications.* New York, NY: Wiley.

Bickel, P. J., Hammel, E. A, & O'Connell, J. W. (1975). Sex bias in graduate admissions: Data from Berkeley. *Science, 187*(4175), 398–404.

Boneau, A. C. (1960). The effects of violations of assumptions underlying the *t* test. *Psychological Bulletin, 57,* 49–64.

Box, J. F. (1978). *R. A. Fisher: The life of a scientist.* New York, NY: Wiley.

Box, G. P., & Cox, D. R. (1964). An analysis of transformations. *Journal of the Royal Statistical Society, Series B, 26*(2), 211–252.

British Board of Trade. (1990). *Report on the loss of the "Titanic" (S.S.)* (Inquiry Report, reprint). Gloucester, England: Allan Sutton.

Camilli, G., & Hopkins, K. D. (1978). Applicability of chi-square to 2×2 contingency tables with small expected frequencies. *Psychological Bulletin, 85,* 163–167.

Campbell, D. T., & Stanley, J. C. (1963). Experimental and quasi-experimental designs for research on teaching. In N. L. Gage (Ed.), *Handbook of research on teaching* (pp. 171–246). Chicago, IL: Rand McNally.

Campbell, D. T., & Stanley, J. C. (1966). *Experimental and quasi-experimental designs for research.* Boston, MA: Houghton Mifflin Company.

Cochran, W. G. (1941). The distribution of the largest of a set of estimated variances as a fraction of their total. *Annals of Human Genetics, 11*(1), 47–52.

Cochran, W. G. (1954). Some methods for strengthening the common χ^2 tests. *Biometrics, 10,* 417–451.

Cohen, J. (1965). Some statistical issues in psychological research. In B. B. Wolman (Ed.), *Handbook of clinical psychology* (pp. 95–121). New York, NY: McGraw-Hill.

Cohen, J. (1977). *Statistical power analysis for the behavioral sciences.* New York, NY: Academic Press.

Cohen, J. (1988). *Statistical power analysis for the behavioral sciences* (2nd ed.). Hillsdale, NJ: Lawrence Erlbaum.

Cohen, M. P. (2000). Note on the odds ratio and the probability ratio. *Journal of Educational and Behavioral Statistics, 25,* 249–252.

Cramer, J. S. (2003). *Logit models from economics and other fields*. Cambridge, England: Cambridge University Press.

Croux, C., Flandre, C., & Haesbroeck, G. (2002). The breakdown behavior of the maximum likelihood estimator in the logistic regression model. *Statistics & Probability Letters, 60,* 377–386.

Davey, A., & Savla, J. (2010). *Statistical power analysis with missing data*. New York, NY: Routledge Taylor & Francis.

Davison, A. C., & Hinkley, D. V. (1997). *Bootstrap methods and their application*. Cambridge, England: Cambridge University Press.

Derenzo, S. E. (1977). Approximations for hand calculators using small integer coefficients. *Mathematics of Computation, 31,* 214–225.

Diaconis, P., & Efron, B. (1983). Computer intensive methods in statistics. *Scientific American, 248*(5), 116–130.

Draper, N. R., & Smith, H. (1966). *Applied regression analysis*. New York, NY: Wiley.

Efron, B. (1979a). Bootstrap methods: Another look at the jackknife. *Annals of Statistics, 7*(1), 1–26.

Efron, B. (1979b). Computers and the theory of statistics: Thinking the unthinkable. *Siam Review, 21,* 460–480.

Efron, B. (1982). *The jackknife, the bootstrap, and other resampling plans* (CBMS 38, SIAM-NSF) [Monograph]. Montpelier, VT: Capital City Press.

Efron, B. (1987). Better bootstrap confidence intervals. *Journal of the American Statistical Association, 82*(397), 171–185.

Efron, B., & Gong, G. (1983). A leisurely look at the bootstrap, the jackknife, and cross-validation. *American Statistician, 37,* 36–48.

Efron, B., & Tibshirani, R. (1993). *An introduction to the bootstrap*. New York, NY: Chapman & Hall.

Enders, C. K. (2010). *Applied missing data analysis*. New York, NY: Guilford Press.

Ezekiel, M. (1930). *Methods of correlation analysis*. New York, NY: Wiley.

Faul, F., Erdfelder, E., Buchner, A., & Lang, A.-G. (2009). Statistical power analyses using G*Power 3.1: Tests for correlation and regression analyses. *Behavior Research Methods, 41,* 1149–1160.

Faul, F., Erdfelder, E., Lang, A.-G., & Buchner, A. (2007). G*Power 3: A flexible statistical power analysis program for the social, behavioral, and biomedical sciences. *Behavior Research Methods, 39,* 175–191.

Ferguson, A., Myers, C., Bartlett, R., Banister, H., Bartlett, F., Brown, W., . . . Tucker, W. (1940). Final report of the committee appointed to consider and report upon the possibility of quantitative estimates of sensory events. *Report of the British Association for the Advancement of Science, 2,* 331–349.

Fienberg, S. E., & Hinkley, D. V. (1980). *R. A. Fisher: An appreciation*. Berlin, Germany: Springer-Verlag.

Fischer, H. (2010). *A history of the central limit theorem: From classical to modern probability theory*. New York, NY: Springer.

Fisher, R. A. (1922). On the mathematical foundations of theoretical statistics. *Philosophical Transactions of the Royal Society of London, Series A, 22,* 594–604.

Fisher, R. A. (1925). *Statistical methods for research workers*. Edinburgh, Scotland: Oliver & Boyd.

Fisher, R. A. (1932). *Statistical methods for research workers* (4th ed.). London, England: Oliver & Boyd.

Fox, J. (1997). *Applied regression analysis, linear models, and related methods* (p. 512). Thousand Oaks, CA: Sage.

Fox, J. (2002). *An R and S-plus companion to applied regression*. Thousand Oaks, CA: Sage.

Galton, F. (1889). *Natural inheritance*. London, England: Macmillan.

Galton, F. (1892). *Finger prints*. London, England: Macmillan.

Galton, F. (1895). *Fingerprint directories*. London, England: Macmillan.

Gelman, A., & Hill, J. (2007). *Data analysis using regression and multilevel/hierarchical models*. New York, NY: Cambridge University Press.

Glass, G. (1976). Primary, secondary and meta-analysis of research. *Educational Researcher, 5,* 3–8.

Glass, G. (1977). Integrating findings: The meta-analysis of research. *Review of Research in Education, 5,* 351–379.

Goodman, L. A. (1968). The analysis of cross-classified data: Independence, quasi-independence, and interactions in contingency tables with or without missing entries. *Journal of American Statistical Association, 63,* 1091–1131.

Gordon, M. H., Loveland, E. H., & Cureton, E. F. (1952). An extended table of chi-square for two degrees of freedom, for use in combining probabilities from independent samples. *Psychometrika, 17*(3), 311–316.

Graybill, F. A. (1961). *An introduction to linear statistical models.* New York, NY: McGraw-Hill.

Haberman, S. J. (1970). *The general log-linear model* (Doctoral dissertation). Chicago, IL: University of Chicago, Department of Statistics.

Haberman, S. J. (1973). Log-linear models for frequency data: Sufficient statistics and likelihood equations. *Annals of Statistics, 1*(4), 617–632.

Hartley, H. O. (1940). Testing the homogeneity of a set of variances. *Biometrika, 31,* 249–255.

Hartley, H. O. (1950). The use of range in analysis of variance. *Biometrika, 37,* 271–280.

Hastie, T., & Efron, B. (2007). *lars: Least angle regression, lasso and forward stagewise* (R Package Version 0.9-7). Retrieved from http://cran.r-project.org/web/packages/lars/index.html

Hedges, L. V., & Olkin, I. (1985). *Statistical methods for meta-analysis.* New York, NY: Academic Press.

Hinkle, D. E., Wiersma, W., & Jurs, S. G. (2003). *Applied statistics for the behavioral sciences* (5th ed.). New York, NY: Houghton Mifflin.

Holzinger, K. J., & Swineford, F. A. (1937). The bi-factor method. *Psychometrika, 2,* 41–54.

Holzinger, K. J., & Swineford, F. A. (1939). *A study in factor analysis: The stability of a bi-factor solution* (Supplementary Education Monographs, No. 48, pp. 81–91). Chicago, IL: University of Chicago Press.

Hosmer, D. W., & Lemeshow, S. (2000). *Applied logistic regression* (2nd ed.). New York, NY: Wiley.

Hsu, J. (1996). *Multiple comparisons: Theory and methods.* Boca Raton, FL: Chapman & Hall/CRC Press.

Jones, L. V., & Fiske, D. W. (1953). Models for testing the significance of combined results. *Psychological Bulletin, 50*(5), 375–382.

Kabacoff, R. I. (2011). *Quick-R.* Retrieved from http://www.statmethods.net/

Kabacoff, R. I. (2012). *Quick-R.* Retrieved from http://www.statmethods.net/stats/power.html

Kelley, K., & Lai, K. (2011). *MBESS* (R Package Version 3.2.1). Retrieved from http://cran.r-project.org/package=MBESS

Kendall, M. G., & Plackett, R. L. (Eds). (1977). *Studies in the history of probability and statistics* (Vol. 2). London, England: Griffin.

Kleinbaum, D. G. (1994). *Logistic regression: A self-learning text.* New York, NY: Springer Verlag.

Levene, H. (1960). Robust tests for equality of variances. In I. Olkin (Ed.), *Contributions to probability and statistics: Essays in honor of Harold Hotelling* (pp. 278–292). Palo Alto, CA: Stanford University Press.

Linacre, M. (2013). *Winsteps: A Rasch computer program.* Retrieved from www.winsteps.com

Long, J. S. (1997). *Regression models for categorical and limited dependent variables.* Thousand Oaks, CA: Sage.

Lumley, T. (2006). *leaps: Regression subset selection* (R Package Version 2.7, using Fortran code by Alan Miller). Retrieved from http://cran.r-project.org/web/packages/leaps/leaps.pdf

McNeil, K., Newman, I., & Fraas, J. W. (2012). *Designing general linear models to test research hypotheses.* Lanham, MD: University Press of America.

Menard, S. (2000a). *Applied logistic regression analysis* (2nd ed.). Thousand Oaks, CA: Sage.

Menard, S. (2000b). Coefficients of determination for multiple logistic regression analysis. *The American Statistician, 54*(1), 17–24.

de Moivre, A. (1756). *Doctrine of chances: Or, a method of calculating the probabilities of events in play* (3rd ed.). London, England: Pearson.

Morrison, M. A., & Morrison, T. G. (2002). Development and validation of a scale measuring modern prejudice toward gay men and lesbian women. *Journal of Homosexuality, 43,* 15–37.

Nathans, L. L., Oswald, F. L., & Nimon, K. (2012). Interpreting multiple linear regression: A guidebook of variable importance. *Practical Assessment, Research & Evaluation, 17*(9), 1–19.

Nelder, J., & Wedderburn, R. W. M. (1972). Generalized linear models (2nd ed.). *Journal of the Royal Statistical Society, Series A, 135,* 370–384.

Nimon, K., Lewis, M., Kane, R., & Haynes, R. M. (2008). An R package to compute commonality coefficients in the multiple regression case: An introduction to the package and a practical example. *Behavior Research Methods, 40*(2), 457–466.

Nimon, K., & Oswald, F. L. (in press). Understanding the results of multiple linear regression: Beyond standardized regression coefficients. *Organizational Research Methods.*

Nimon, K., & Roberts, J. K. (2012). *yhat: Interpreting regression effects* (R Package Version 1.0-4). Retrieved from http://cran.r-project.org/web/packages/yhat/index.html

Pampel, F. C. (2000). *Logistic regression: A primer.* Thousand Oaks, CA: Sage.

Pearl, J. (2009). *Causality: Models, reasoning, and inference* (2nd ed.). Cambridge, England: Cambridge University Press.

Pearl, R., & Reed, L. J. (1920). On the rate of growth of the population of the United States and its mathematical representation. *Proceedings of the National Academy of Sciences, 6,* 275–288.

Pearson, E. S. (1938). *Karl Pearson: An appreciation of some aspects of his life and work.* Cambridge, England: Cambridge University Press.

Pearson, E. S. (1939). William Sealy Gosset 1876–1937: "Student" as statistician. *Biometrika, 30,* 210–250.

Pearson, E. S. (1990). *Student: A statistical biography of William Sealy Gosset.* Oxford, England: Oxford University Press.

Pearson, E. S., & Kendall, M. G. (Eds) (1970). *Studies in the history of probability and statistics* (Vol. 1). London, England: Griffin.

Pearson, K. (1924). Historical note on the origin of the normal curve of errors. *Biometrika, 16,* 402–404.

Pearson, K. (1933). On a method of determining whether a sample of size *n* supposed to have been drawn from a parent population having a known probability integral has probably been drawn at random. *Biometrika, 25,* 379–410.

Quenouille, M. (1949). Approximate tests of correlation in time series. *Journal of the Royal Statistical Society, Series B*(11), 18–84.

Roscoe, J. T. (1975). *Fundamental research statistics for the behavioral sciences* (2nd ed.). New York, NY: Holt, Rinehart, & Winston.

Roell, K. (2012). *Average national SAT Scores for 2012.* Retrieved from http://testprep.about.com/od/SAT_Scores/a/2012_Average_SAT.htm

Rosenthal, R. (1984). *Meta-analytic procedures for social research.* Beverly Hills, CA: Sage.

Rosenthal, R., & Rubin, D. (1986). Meta-analytic procedures for combining studies with multiple effect sizes. *Psychological Bulletin, 99,* 400–406.

Satcher, J. F., & Schumacker, R. (2009). Predictors of modern homonegativity among professional counselors. *Journal of LGBT Issues in Counseling, 3*(1), 21–36.

Scheffé, H. (1953). A method for judging all contrasts in the analysis of variance. *Biometrika, 40,* 87–104.

Schumacker, R. E. (2005). Effect size and confidence intervals in general linear models for categorical data analysis. *Multiple Linear Regression Viewpoints, 31*(1), 19–22.

Schumacker, R. E., Anderson, C., & Ashby, J. (1999). Logit regression: Best model selection. *Multiple Linear Regression Viewpoints, 25*(2), 22–27.

Schumacker, R. E., Mount, R. E., & Monahan, M. P. (2002). Factors affecting multiple regression and discriminant analysis with a dichotomous dependent variable: Prediction, explanation, and classification. *Multiple Linear Regression Viewpoints, 28*(2), 32–39.

Schumacker, R. E., & Tomek, S. (2013). *Understanding statistics using R.* New York, NY: Springer-Verlag.

Shadish, W. R., Cook, T. D., & Campbell, D. T. (2001). *Experimental and quasi-experimental designs for generalized causal inference* (2nd ed.). Independence, KY: Cengage Learning.

Shao, J., & Tu, D. (1995). *The jackknife and bootstrap*. New York, NY: Springer-Verlag.

Simon, J. (1969). *Basic research methods in social science* (pp. 424–426). New York, NY: Random House.

Simpson, E. H. (1951). The interpretation of interaction in contingency tables. *Journal of the Royal Statistical Society, Series B (Methodological), 13*(2), pp. 238–241.

Stevens, S. S. (1946). On the theory of scales of measurement. *Science, 103*(2684), 677–680.

Stevens, S. S. (1951). *Mathematics, measurement, and psychophysics*. In S. S. Stevens (Ed.), *Handbook of experimental psychology* (pp. 1–49). New York, NY: Wiley.

Stevens, S. S., & Hallowell, D. (1938). *Hearing: Its psychology and physiology*. New York, NY: Wiley.

Stigler, S. (1986). *The history of statistics: The measurement of uncertainty before 1900*. Cambridge, MA: Harvard University Press.

Thurstone, L. L. (1927). A law of comparative judgment. *Psychological Review, 34,* 273–286.

Trochim, M. K. (2006). *Research methods knowledge base*. Retrieved from http://www.socialresearchmethods.net/kb/

Tukey, J. W. (1949). Comparing individual means in the analysis of variance. *Biometrics, 5,* 99–114.

Tukey, J. (1958). Bias and confidence in not quite large samples (abstract). *Annals of Mathematic Statistics, 29,* 614.

Upton, G. J. G. (1978). *The analysis of cross-tabulated data*. New York, NY: John Wiley.

Urbaniak, G. C., & Plous, S. (2013). *Research randomizer*. Retrieved from http://www.randomizer.org/

Verhulst, P.-F. (1845). Recherches mathematiques sur la loi d'accroissement de la population [Mathematical research on the law of population growth]. *Nouveaux Memoires de l'Academie Royale des Sciences, des Lettres et des Beaux-Arts de Belgique, 20,* 1–32.

Viklund, A. (2008). *The standard normal distribution in R*. Retrieved from http://msenux.redwoods.edu/math/R/StandardNormal.php

Wang, Z. (2013). *orsk: Converting odds ratio to relative risk in cohort studies with partial data information* (R package Version 0.1-6). Retrieved from http://CRAN.R-project.org/package=orsk

Wickham, H. (2009). *ggplot2: Elegant graphics for data analysis*. New York, NY: Springer-Verlag.

Wikipedia. *Central limit theorem.* Retrieved from http://en.wikipedia.org/wiki/Central_limit_theorem

Willems, J. P., Saunders, J. T., Hunt, D. E., & Schorling, J. B. (1997). Prevalence of coronary heart disease risk factors among rural Blacks: A community-based study. *Southern Medical Journal, 90,* 814–820.

Wright, D. B., & London, K. (2009). *Modern regression techniques using R: A practical guide for students and researchers*. Thousand Oaks, CA: Sage.

Yates, F. (1934). Contingency tables involving small numbers and the chi-square test. *Journal of the Royal Statistical Society Supplement, 1,* 217–235.

AUTHOR INDEX

SUBJECT INDEX

Note: Page numbers in *italics* indicate figures and tables.

⑤SAGE researchmethods

The essential online tool for researchers from the world's leading methods publisher

Find exactly what you are looking for, from basic explanations to advanced discussion

More content and new features added this year!

"I have never really seen anything like this product before, and I think it is really valuable."

John Creswell, University of Nebraska–Lincoln

Discover **Methods Lists**— methods readings suggested by other users

Watch video interviews with leading methodologists

Explore the **Methods Map** to discover links between methods

Search a custom-designed taxonomy with more than 1,400 qualitative, quantitative, and mixed methods terms

Uncover more than 120,000 pages of book, journal, and reference content to support your learning

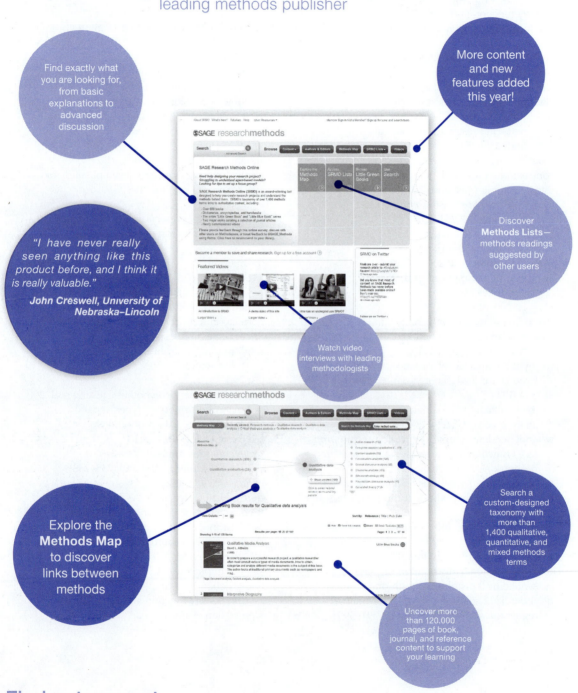

Find out more at
www.sageresearchmethods.com